QuarkXPress® 5 Bible

Galen Gruman and Barbara Assadi with Kelly K. Anton

Hungry Minds™

Best-Selling Books • Digital Downloads • e-Books • Answer Networks • e-Newsletters • Branded Web Sites • e-Learning

New York, NY✦ Cleveland, OH ✦ Indianapolis, IN

QuarkXPress® 5 Bible

Published by
Hungry Minds, Inc.
909 Third Avenue
New York, NY 10022
www.hungryminds.com

Library of Congress Catalog Control Number: 2001099733

ISBN: 0-7645-3416-5

Printed in the United States of America

10 9 8 7 6 5 4 3 2 1

1B/RT/QS/QS/IN

Distributed in the United States by Hungry Minds, Inc.

Distributed by CDG Books Canada Inc. for Canada; by Transworld Publishers Limited in the United Kingdom; by IDG Norge Books for Norway; by IDG Sweden Books for Sweden; by IDG Books Australia Publishing Corporation Pty. Ltd. for Australia and New Zealand; by TransQuest Publishers Pte Ltd. for Singapore, Malaysia, Thailand, Indonesia, and Hong Kong; by Gotop Information Inc. for Taiwan; by ICG Muse, Inc. for Japan; by Intersoft for South Africa; by Eyrolles for France; by International Thomson Publishing for Germany, Austria, and Switzerland; by Distribuidora Cuspide for Argentina; by LR International for Brazil; by Galileo Libros for Chile; by Ediciones ZETA S.C.R. Ltda. for Peru; by WS Computer Publishing Corporation, Inc., for the Philippines; by Contemporanea de Ediciones for Venezuela; by Express Computer Distributors for the Caribbean and West Indies; by Micronesia Media Distributor, Inc. for Micronesia; by Chips Computadoras S.A. de C.V. for Mexico; by Editorial Norma de Panama S.A. for Panama; by American Bookshops for Finland.

For general information on Hungry Minds' products and services please contact our Customer Care department within the U.S. at 800-762-2974, outside the U.S. at 317-572-3993 or fax 317-572-4002.

For sales inquiries and reseller information, including discounts, premium and bulk quantity sales, and foreign-language translations, please contact our Customer Care department at 800-434-3422, fax 317-572-4002 or write to Hungry Minds, Inc., Attn: Customer Care Department, 10475 Crosspoint Boulevard, Indianapolis, IN 46256.

For information on licensing foreign or domestic rights, please contact our Sub-Rights Customer Care department at 212-884-5000.

For information on using Hungry Minds' products and services in the classroom or for ordering examination copies, please contact our Educational Sales department at 800-434-2086 or fax 317-572-4005.

For press review copies, author interviews, or other publicity information, please contact our Public Relations department at 317-572-3168 or fax 317-572-4168.

For authorization to photocopy items for corporate, personal, or educational use, please contact Copyright Clearance Center, 222 Rosewood Drive, Danvers, MA 01923, or fax 978-750-4470.

Library of Congress Cataloging-in-Publication Data

Hungry Minds™ is a trademark of Hungry Minds, Inc.

Credits

Acquisitions Editor
Michael Roney

Project Editor
Elizabeth Kuball

Technical Editors
Steve Arany and Debbie Gates

Editorial Manager
Rev Mengle

Senior Vice President, Technical Publishing
Richard Swadley

Vice President and Publisher
Mary Bednarek

Project Coordinators
Bill Ramsey and Ryan Steffen

Graphics and Production Specialists
Sean Decker, Brian Drumm,
Joyce Haughey, LeAndra Johnson,
Barry Offringa, Laurie Petrone,
Jill Piscitelli, Heather Pope,
Betty Schulte, Jeremey Unger,
Mary J. Virgin

Quality Control Technician
Laura Albert, David Faust,
John Greenough, Andy Hollandbeck,
Carl Pierce, Linda Quigley

Permissions Editor
Carmen Krikorian

Media Development Specialist
Angela Denny

Media Development Coordinator
Marisa Pearman

Proofreading and Indexing
TECHBOOKS Production Services

About the Authors

Galen Gruman is editor of *M-Business* magazine, where he manages the monthly publication's editorial content and its Web site. He has also been editor of *Macworld,* executive editor of *Upside,* West Coast bureau chief of *Computerworld,* and vice president of content for ThirdAge.com. He is coauthor of 12 other books on desktop publishing. In 1986, Gruman led one of the first successful conversions of a national magazine to desktop publishing and has covered publishing technology since then for several publications, including the trade weekly *InfoWorld,* for which he began writing in 1986, and *Macworld,* whose staff he joined in 1991. He continues to write for *Macworld.* Originally a newspaper reporter in Los Angeles, Gruman got caught by the production-technology bug in 1979 and hasn't recovered.

Barbara Assadi is a principal at Bay Creative, a San Francisco–based advertising agency that produces custom publishing, marketing, and advertising collateral and services for print and online media. Prior to cofounding that company, she was creative programs manager at Oracle Corporation, where she managed the creation, design, and production of the company's annual report and product marketing collateral. Assadi previously held similar positions at Quark, Inc., and Pacific Mutual Life Insurance, and also served as manager of *Macworld*'s online and syndicated content. She was an early pioneer in desktop publishing technology, especially as applied to corporate communications, and began evaluating publishing tools for the trade weekly *InfoWorld* in 1988. Assadi has cowritten eight other books on QuarkXPress. She plans eventually to write a novel.

Kelly K. Anton develops documentation, training, and marketing materials for high-end publishing products. She also writes and copyedits for Denver-area magazines, book publishers, and associations. A veteran of Quark, Inc., she started on the QuarkXPress 3.2 team and eventually led the development of the QuarkXPress 4.0 documentation. She has developed training for Quark, provided technical review for several QuarkXPress books, and is coauthor of the *Adobe InDesign Bible* and *Using QuarkXPress.* Her main interest is her family, including her husband, John, and her five-year-old son, Robert.

From Galen Gruman: To Ingall Bull, who's put up with book projects and crazy magazine schedules gracefully for far too long.

From Barbara Assadi: To Khossrow Assadi, who stays with me through thick and thin.

From Kelly K. Anton: To John Anton, for his everlasting support.

Foreword

It is hard to imagine the impact that personal computers, laser printers, PostScript, and layout software had upon us in the 1980s. Today, the mere act of using a computer to build a magazine, a comic book, or a Web site has become mundane, but back then, publishing was an "old school" industry. The computers that were used for typesetting cost tens of thousands of dollars, and the software they ran to build rudimentary pages cost nearly as much, if not more — and often did a bad job at it.

Pundits often point to the combination of the Macintosh, the LaserWriter, and Aldus PageMaker as the combination that broke the code, but I think it was the second generation — the Mac II, the Linotronic imagesetter, and, most important, QuarkXPress — that really opened up publishing.

I can recall my first encounter with QuarkXPress, in late 1986, at the first Seybold Seminar on Desktop Publishing in San Francisco (it was the same conference where Steve Jobs called Hewlett-Packard "brain-damaged" for not adopting Adobe PostScript in its laser printers, as Apple had done). By this time, Aldus had revolutionized the publishing world with PageMaker, and most conference attendees dismissed QuarkXPress as a confused imitation of the market leader — if they even took notice. I remember Quark CEO Fred Ebrahimi, standing alone in the company's small booth, which was decorated solely with a pedestal, upon which a copy of the QuarkXPress box sat. There wasn't even a demo of the program available on the show floor, although it was shown to a few VIPs and members of the press. The booth was never crowded, and I remember remarking to a colleague about how forlorn it seemed.

But what I also remember was the confidence. QuarkXPress *would* prevail. It didn't matter that it was feature-anemic and somewhat buggy. It didn't matter that PageMaker was the darling of the publishing set (despite being feature-anemic and buggy as well — go figure). QuarkXPress *would* be the better product, and everyone would use it. Both Fred and QuarkXPress's primary visionary Tim Gill said so.

Time has served QuarkXPress well. PageMaker's simple digital analog of the traditional paste-up artist's workspace got designers and publishers to understand that personal computers could produce magazines, newsletters, and even daily newspapers. What Aldus failed to do was to add the industrial-strength features that those people needed to get their products out on time — Aldus (and subsequently Adobe Systems, which bought the company) insisted on extending the simple pasteboard interface until it collapsed under its own weight. Quark understood what customers wanted, and capitalized on it over and over again in the next decade, to the point where it is a rarity to find a professional magazine or newspaper that doesn't use QuarkXPress. The pretender to the throne has become the king.

Despite repeated attempts to unseat it in the ensuing years, QuarkXPress has remained strong, and now, with version 5 of XPress, the company is looking to continue its dominance of the publishing industry. QuarkXPress 5 is the first major revision to the program since 1997, and it boasts more new and improved features than any version I can recall: expanded table support, a true layers feature, full design and layout support for HTML and XML Web standards, complete integration with Adobe's Portable Document Format (PDF), more comprehensive printing and color management support, and lots more.

Whether you're new to QuarkXPress or moving up from an earlier version, I can think of no better guides to the world of QuarkXPress 5 than the three authors who have produced this book. Galen Gruman, Barbara Assadi, and Kelly Anton have years of experience on all sides of the publishing trenches, as journalists, authors, designers, and production consultants.

Galen has a long and distinguished career in magazine publishing, holding executive editorial positions at *Macworld, Computerworld,* and *Upside,* and is currently the Editor of *M-Business* magazine. He also has coauthored a dozen books on desktop publishing and is one of those rare journalists who can truly claim to be an expert in the fields he covers.

Barbara is the co-owner of Bay Creative, a San Francisco–based ad/creative agency with an extensive list of high-profile clients in the print, multimedia, and Web worlds. Barbara also worked as Editorial Director at Quark, so she understands XPress from the inside — valuable insight that shows in these pages. She has also coauthored, with Galen, several books on desktop publishing.

Another former Quark insider, Kelly led the teams that produced the documentation for various versions of QuarkXPress, writes documentation and marketing materials for many software companies that specialize in publishing technologies, and works for various magazine and book publishers in Denver. Kelly is well qualified to show you the hidden tips and tricks of XPress 5, but she also makes sure that you understand the foundation upon which XPress is built.

Kelly, Barbara, and Galen have turned their expertise into *QuarkXPress 5 Bible,* creating a valuable tool that will help both newcomers and longstanding QuarkXPress users navigate the complex shoals of Quark's important contribution to the world of publishing.

Rick LePage
Editor-in-Chief
Macworld

Preface

Welcome to the *QuarkXPress 5 Bible* — your personal guide to a powerful, full-featured publishing program that offers precise control over all aspects of page design. Our goal is to guide you each step of the way through the publishing process, showing you as we go how to make QuarkXPress work for you. You'll also learn tips and tricks about publishing and design that you can use in any document, whether it was created in QuarkXPress or not.

QuarkXPress does more than offer a wide range of desktop publishing capabilities to sophisticated designers who develop magazines, books, ads, and product brochures. It also gives the power of the press to individuals and groups who use the program's impressive set of publishing tools to communicate their thoughts, dreams, and philosophies.

The market for QuarkXPress knows no limits in terms of publishing applications. It also knows no national boundaries. The program is sold throughout the world in many languages, and its founders take pride in enabling people to communicate.

Simply put, the philosophy of the people who gave us QuarkXPress is to provide the best publishing tools to those who strive to educate, inform, and document the world in which we live. Join us in learning how to use those tools.

Why You Need This Book

When QuarkXPress comes with good documentation that is chock-full of examples, why do you need this book? In a phrase, "to see the bigger picture." Publishing design involves much more than understanding a particular program's tools — it involves knowing when, how, and, most important, *why* to use them. In this book, we help you realize the potential of QuarkXPress by applying its tools to real-world publishing design needs.

Desktop publishers in general, and QuarkXPress users in particular, are an interesting bunch of people. Some have years of high-end creative, design-intensive experience. Others are just getting started in publishing, perhaps by producing simple newsletters or flyers to advertise a community event. Not a few are working in the brave new world of Web publishing.

Desktop publishers fall into several classes:

◆ Experienced designers new to desktop technologies

◆ Novice designers new to desktop technologies

◆ Designers new to QuarkXPress but familiar with other desktop technologies

◆ Designers familiar with print publishing but new to the Web

No matter which class you're in, you'll find that this book addresses your needs. The book is aimed at meeting the needs of those who design publications with QuarkXPress. That doesn't mean a degree in design or ten years' experience producing national ad campaigns — it means anyone responsible for developing and implementing the look of documents, whether a four-page company newsletter or a four-color billboard ad. The basic techniques and issues are the same for both ends of the spectrum. And we, of course, cover in detail the specialized needs — such as table creation, image control, color output, and Web and interactive publishing — of specialty designers. (For those just learning such advanced techniques, be sure to read the sidebars that explain the underlying issues.)

Regardless of your level of familiarity with desktop publishing, this book will help you use QuarkXPress. It's written with plenty of detail for experienced designers, while still including enough step-by-step introductory material for the newest user.

How to Read This Book

If you're a novice publisher or designer, we suggest you read the book in order, from beginning to end. We've organized the book so that each basic area is grouped — so all information on working with graphics, for example, is in Part V: "Graphics," while the Web-related information is all in Part X: "Interactive and Web Publishing." This way you'll get a solid understanding of each facet of QuarkXPress, all in one place.

If you're experienced, read the book in any order you want — pick those chapters or sections that cover the design issues you want to know more about, either as basic design issues or as QuarkXPress implementation issues. You should find the exhaustive index a real aid in locating what you're looking for.

Whether you're reading the book sequentially or nonsequentially, you'll find the many cross-references helpful. Publication design is ultimately successful because the result is more than the sum of its parts — and the tools used to create and implement your designs cannot be used in isolation. Because this is true, it's impossible to have one "right" order or grouping of content; the cross-references let you know where to get additional information when what you're seeking to understand or learn doesn't fit into the way we've organized this book.

How This Book Is Organized

The previous version of this book was organized according to level of difficulty, feeding you a little bit of each topic over the course of the book. The beginning got you started, the middle gave you a little more power, and the final sections brought you to the level of a publishing professional. This version of the book is organized more by topic, giving you everything you need to know about one topic before continuing on to the next — for example, everything you need to know about graphics or everything you need to know about boxes. Because of that, the book is chock-full of cross-references to help you pull together all the knowledge you gain and create interesting and effective design work — work that outputs the way you want it to.

The book is divided into parts, which are described in the following sections.

QuarkXPress QuickStart

This section serves as a tutorial so users new to QuarkXPress can jump in and make something right away. It teaches you how to make the fundamental components of a page — boxes — and how to fill them with pictures and text. Then it takes you into adding formatting and color.

Part I: Welcome to QuarkXPress

The five chapters that make up this part take you through the fundamental structure of QuarkXPress to the computing environment in which you operate. Along the way, you'll learn how to navigate the software, set preferences, and perform basic file-management tasks.

Part II: Layout for Print

In the five chapters here, you first learn the principles of good design — because no matter how good you are at QuarkXPress, your design skills dictate whether your publication can communicate effectively. With that foundation, you can go on to learn how to set up new documents and how to add and manipulate items on the pages. After you master the page, you learn about handling multiple pages and layers of items within pages.

Part III: Text

Here, in three chapters, you get a look at the basic text-handling capabilities of QuarkXPress. This is where you learn how to prepare text files in a word processor, how to import them, and how to flow the text through a document. In addition, you're exposed to the process of editing text, from using the spell checker and the search and replace functions to creating your own auxiliary dictionaries.

Part IV: Typography

This part shows where QuarkXPress excels—not in the handling of text files but in the beautifying of the text itself. Typography is an art form, and first you'll learn about its basic rules. Then you can start putting the rules into action by learning all the options for formatting paragraphs and characters, including how to fine-tune the spacing. High-end typographic techniques are covered here, along with the process of combining your skills to produce tables.

Part V: Graphics

The process of adding a graphic to QuarkXPress is simple, but as the four chapters in this part show, the way you prepare and manipulate the graphic file has a significant impact on how graphics output. You'll learn about graphic file formats and when to use them and about how to manipulate graphics in QuarkXPress, including using higher-end features such as clipping paths. You'll also discover how to effectively combine type with graphics.

Part VI: Illustrations

Although QuarkXPress is not an illustration tool, the three chapters here show you how to get the most out of the software's many drawing features. The many graphics in this section show you how to do everything from draw freehand to combine simple shapes into complex illustrations.

Part VII: Color

A must-read part for novice publishers, this section describes the basics of viewing and printing in color. You'll then learn how to create and apply colors in QuarkXPress, and for the professional, how to create color traps to prevent problems on-press.

Part VIII: Managing Projects

Sometimes, having QuarkXPress skills is not enough—you need to learn how to pull all those skills together in a workgroup to manage a large project. Here, we cover everything from communication (both verbal and electronic) to the use of style sheets, templates, and libraries for enforcing consistent formatting. Longer publications can also benefit from the lists (for tables of contents), books (for combining multiple documents), and indexing features.

Part IX: Output

There is no use in designing if your work is stuck in QuarkXPress. Throughout this book, we help you tailor your typographic and image use toward successful printing. Here, we talk about setting up printers on both Mac and Windows, setting the myriad print options, and communicating effectively with a service bureau or printer.

Part X: Interactive and Web Publishing

This part introduces many of the new features in QuarkXPress 5, including Web authoring tools, XML conversion tools, and PDF export. Your success with these features will depend first on your mastery of QuarkXPress itself — if you can build lean, well-designed pages, you'll have better luck transferring those pages to another format. You'll learn about the strengths of each format and how QuarkXPress helps you get there.

Part XI: Going Beyond the Program

The beauty of QuarkXPress is that it can be more than the sum of its parts because you can add all the parts you want, customizing it through third-party add-ons called XTensions. Often, you can find an XTension to fill any feature gaps encountered in your day-to-day work — from HTML conversion to automatic drop-shadow creation. For Mac users, you can automate the software and add features through AppleScript or other Apple-events scripting languages.

Part XII: Appendixes

Typically. you think of appendixes as the place to bury dry information. But in this book, the appendixes are a valuable resource. Look here to learn how to install or upgrade QuarkXPress and how to use the CD that comes with this book. You'll also find a list of keyboard shortcuts to make your work easier, learn to use XPress Tags for formatting text, and explore cross-platform issues you may face in a mixed Mac and PC environment.

What This Book Offers

What distinguishes this book from other books is that it doesn't attempt to replace the documentation that accompanies QuarkXPress. Instead, it guides you through the process of publishing a document — whether you're creating four-page company newsletters, four-color billboard ads, or interactive Web sites. It provides plenty of detail for experienced designers — such as image control, color output, and Web publishing—while including enough step-by-step introductory material (in distinctive boxes) for the newest user. For a deeper look at QuarkXPress features, many informative sidebars explain the underlying issues. And there are also these added features:

✦ **A 16-page, 4-color insert:** Not just another collection of pretty pictures, this four-color insert offers a comprehensive overview of how QuarkXPress handles color, with comparative examples and text.

✦ **A bonus CD:** The CD that accompanies this book contains a wealth of software—some free, some demo, and some shareware. All are meant to make QuarkXPress work even better. Some are XTensions that enhance QuarkXPress directly, while others are stand-alone utilities that you'll use before or after QuarkXPress. Appendix E tells you everything you need to know to install, road-test, and enjoy what's on the CD.

What's New in This Edition

Obviously, this edition covers the latest version of QuarkXPress—version 5. And we've reorganized much of the content for added clarity. But this edition covers more than that:

✦ **Web-specific issues:** QuarkXPress 5 integrates Web and interactive functions from several other Quark programs, such as QuarkImmedia and Avenue.Quark, so we explain how these new components work in one area devoted to nonprint publications.

✦ **Windows-specific issues:** QuarkXPress 5 is practically identical on the Mac and on Windows, but because the great majority of QuarkXPress users use the Mac, we've used the Mac as our primary platform. However, if you use QuarkXPress for Windows—and an increasing number of people do—you'll appreciate that a quarter of the chapters use Windows-based screen shots and that we also note any issues between the various versions of Windows. For cross-platform users, we note any differences or issues that could get in your way as you move documents back and forth.

✦ **Time-saving features:** In the appendixes, you'll see a chapter on essential keyboard shortcuts and context menus—both are real time-savers.

Conventions Used In This Book

Before we begin showing you the ins and outs of QuarkXPress, we need to spend a few minutes reviewing the terms and conventions used in this book.

QuarkXPress commands

The QuarkXPress commands that you select by using the program menus appear in this book in normal typeface. When you choose some menu commands, a related pull-down menu or a pop-up menu appears. If we describe a situation in which you need to select one menu and then choose a command from a secondary menu or list box, we use an arrow symbol. For example, *Choose View ⇨ Thumbnails to display the pages in thumbnail (reduced) view* means that you should choose the Thumbnails command from the View menu.

QuarkXPress 5 uses tabbed panes extensively, even more so than in version 4. Tabbed panes are a method of stuffing several dialog boxes into one dialog box. You see tabs, like those in file folders, and by clicking a tab, the pane of options for that tab come to the front of the dialog box. This book tells you to select the tab (where the name of the pane is) to display the pane.

Mouse conventions

Because you use a mouse to perform many functions in QuarkXPress, you need to be familiar with the following terms and instructions. And, yes, by *mouse,* we include other pointing devices, such as trackballs and pen tablets.

✦ **Pointer:** The small graphic icon that moves on the screen as you move your mouse is a *pointer* (also called a *cursor*). The pointer takes on different shapes depending on the tool you select, the current location of the mouse, and the function you're performing.

✦ **Click:** Quickly press and release the mouse button once. On most Mac mice, there is only one button, but on some there are two or more, and on all PC mice there are at least two buttons — if you have a multibutton mouse, click the leftmost button when we say to click the mouse.

✦ **Double-click:** Quickly press and release the mouse button twice. On some multibutton mice, one of the buttons can function as a double-click (you click it once, the mouse clicks twice) — if your mouse has this feature, use it, because it saves strain on your hand.

✦ **Right-click:** A Windows feature, this means click the right-hand mouse button. On a Mac's one-button mouse, hold the Control key when clicking the mouse button. On multibutton Mac mice, assign one of the buttons to the Control+ click combination.

✦ **Drag:** Dragging is used for moving and sizing items in a QuarkXPress document. To drag an item, position the mouse pointer on it. Press *and hold down* the mouse button, and then slide the mouse across a flat surface to "drag" the item.

Keyboard conventions

We use the standard Mac keyboard conventions throughout the book:

◆ The Command key (shown at left) is the most-used shortcut key. Its Windows equivalent is Ctrl.

◆ Shift is the same on the Mac and Windows. In many programs' menus, you'll see Shift represented as the symbol to the left.

◆ The Option key on the Mac is the same as the Alt key on Windows. In many programs' menus, you'll see Option represented as the symbol to the left.

◆ The Control key (shown as at left in menus) on the Mac has no Windows equivalent.

If you're supposed to press several keys together, we indicate that by placing plus signs (+) between them. Thus Shift+⌘+A means press and hold the Shift and ⌘ keys, then press A. After you've pressed the A key, let go of the other keys. (The last letter in the sequence doesn't need to be held down.)

We also use the plus sign to join keys to mouse movements. For example, Option+drag means to hold the Option key while dragging the mouse.

Icons

You will notice special graphic symbols, or *icons,* used throughout this book. We use these icons to call your attention to points that are particularly important or worth noting:

The New Feature icon indicates a feature that was added to or significantly changed in version 5 of QuarkXPress.

The Tip icon indicates a technique or action in QuarkXPress that will save you time or effort.

The Note icon indicates information that you should remember for future use — something that may seem minor or inconsequential but will, in reality, resurface.

 The Caution icon indicates something that could cause a serious problem — such as data loss, major unplanned rework, or unacceptable results — if not understood in advance.

 The Platform Difference icon indicates information about differences in using QuarkXPress in Windows and on the Macintosh.

 The Cross-Reference icon indicates that related information is available in another chapter.

The Next Step

Publishing is an exciting field, and desktop publishing has brought that excitement to the masses, revolutionizing communications and giving deeper meaning to the words *freedom of the press*. We've been excited about desktop publishing since the early days (18 years ago!), and we hope that you share that enthusiasm — or that we infect you with it!

Desktop publishing is an ever-changing field. QuarkXPress has evolved significantly since its first version, even though its chief competitor and the original publishing icon, Adobe PageMaker, has remained essentially unchanged since 1997. Today, PageMaker is being replaced by Adobe InDesign, which we hope will continue to evolve and keep Quark from becoming complacent. Despite this evolution, the principles of publishing remain the same, so we hope you'll find this book's advice valuable over the years, even when you're using QuarkXPress 6.

Acknowledgments

Steve Gray contributed to Part VI: "Illustrations."

The original photos in many of the example publications featured in this book's screenshots were taken by Lisa Assadi, Ingall W. Bull III, Galen Gruman, and Leah Walthert, and used with permission. Other images are royalty-free images.

The book also displays the layouts of several talented designers in its examples: Peter Tucker of CMP Media's *M-Business,* Tom Visocchi of *Buzz in the 'Burbs,* Kristina Owlett-Smith of *5280 Magazine,* and Tim Giesen of *Building Systems Magazine.* All are used by permission and are copyrighted by their respective publishing companies.

Contents at a Glance

Contents

Part III: Text   245

Part V: Graphics   435

Chapter 20: Working with Graphic Files 437

Chapter 21: Modifying Graphics 461

Part VI: Illustrations   525

Chapter 24: Drawing Tools and Terms 527

Chapter 25: Creating Illustrations 539

Chapter 26: Creating Composite Illustrations 549

Part XII: Appendixes   855

QuarkXPress 5 QuickStart

Although QuarkXPress is a complex program that lets you do everything from designing a fashion magazine to indexing a book to generating separation plates for professional printing, you can get started building documents with just a few simple skills. If you're in a hurry to get started on a project — or you have a job interview tomorrow based on your "proficiency" in QuarkXPress — work through the steps in this section. Here you'll learn the basic building blocks of documents (text boxes, picture boxes, and lines) and the two primary tools (Item and Content).

By all means, do not assume that these steps provide all you need to know about QuarkXPress. From here, head to related sections of the book and explore the full functionality of the program. If you're not sure where to start, figure out what you'll be doing the most. For example, if you'll be flowing text into a newsletter template, head to Parts III and IV.

To create the sample project shown in Figure QS-1, you'll need

- ✦ QuarkXPress
- ✦ A text file from a program such as Microsoft Word
- ✦ A graphic file, such as a JPEG
- ✦ A laser or inkjet printer

You can follow the steps exactly (substituting your own text, graphic, and fonts), or you can vary the design as much as you want.

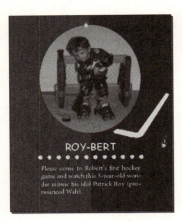

Figure QS-1: Combining formatted text and a graphic with a few simple boxes and lines produces a completely designed card.

Creating a New Document

When you create a new document in QuarkXPress, you're actually specifying the final size and setup of the pages. To create a new document, follow these steps:

1. Start QuarkXPress.

2. Choose File ⇨ New ⇨ Document, or press ⌘+N or Ctrl+N. The New Document dialog box displays.

3. In the Page area, type **4"** in the Width field and **5"** in the Height field.

4. Uncheck Facing Pages and Automatic Text Box, as shown in Figure QS-2. The column and margin settings do not matter to this exercise.

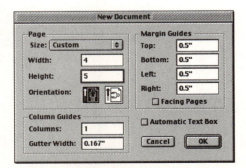

Figure QS-2: Set up the page size for your project in the New Document dialog box.

5. Click OK to create the new document. QuarkXPress creates one 4-x-5-inch page.

6. Choose File ⇨ Save As, or press ⌘+Option+S or Ctrl+Alt+S.

7. In the Save Current Document As field, type **sample.qxd**, as shown in Figure QS-3.

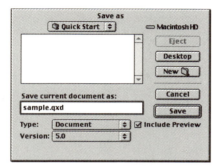

Figure QS-3: Use the Save As dialog box to name a new document.

8. Choose a location for the file, and then click Save.

Cross-Reference For more information about creating a new document, see Chapter 7.

Working with Boxes

To create a colored background for this card, you'll create two rectangular picture boxes. To create two rectangular picture boxes, follow these steps:

1. Select the Rectangle Picture Box tool. (To see the names of the tools, point your mouse at them until a Tool Tip displays.)

2. Click and drag to create a box that is approximately 2 inches wide and 5 inches tall, as shown in Figure QS-4. (You will fine-tune the size and placement in the next steps.) The new box is selected, as indicated by the black handles. If the box becomes deselected in the following steps, click on it to select it.

3. Highlight the X field in the Measurements palette, which specifies the item's *origin across* (its placement from the left edge of the page). Type **0** in this field.

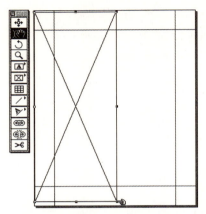

Figure QS-4: Use any of the box
tools to create background shapes
to which you will later apply color.

4. Tab to the Y field, which specifies the item's *origin down* (its placement from
   the top of the page). Type **0** in this field.

5. Tab to the W field, which specifies the item's width. Type **2"** in this field.

6. Tab to the H field, which specifies the item's height. Type **5"** in this field.

7. Press Return to reposition and resize the box according to the values shown
   in Figure QS-5.

X: 0"	W: 2"	◿ 0°	➡ X%: 100%	✛ X+: 0"	◿ 0°
Y: 0"	H: 5"	◿ 0"	➡ Y%: 100%	✛ Y+: 0"	◿ 0°

Figure QS-5: The Measurements palette lets you
precisely size items.

8. Choose Item ➪ Duplicate, or press ⌘+D or Ctrl+D. If necessary, first click on
   the new box to select it.

9. Highlight the X field in the Measurements palette, then type **2"**. Tab to the
   Y field, then type **0**. Press Return to reposition the second box as shown in
   Figure QS-6. Later, you will add color to these boxes.

**Cross-
Reference**   For more information about working with boxes, see Chapter 8.

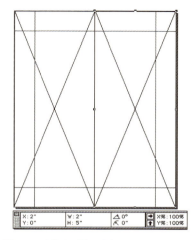

Figure QS-6: The Measurements palette lets you precisely position items.

Working with Text

In QuarkXPress, text goes inside a text box. You can type text into the box or import a text file in various formats. After text is inside the box, you can change the font, size, color, and many more options. To enter text into a box, follow these steps:

1. Select the Rectangle Text Box tool.

2. Click and drag to create a box that is approximately 3 inches wide and 2 inches tall, as shown in Figure QS-7. The new box is selected, as indicated by the black handles. If the box becomes deselected in the following steps, click on it to select it.

3. To size and place the box precisely, type the following values in the Measurements palette:

   - X: **0.75"**
   - Y: **3.25"**
   - W: **2.5"**
   - H: **1.5"**

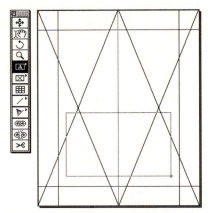

Figure QS-7: Use the Rectangle Text
Box tool to create a container for text.

4. Select the Content tool (the hand), and then click in the new text box.

5. Type a person's name in the text box, and then press Return.

6. Click and drag to highlight the entire name.

7. Click the All Caps icon on the lower-right side of the Measurements palette.
   (To see the names of the icons, point at them with your mouse until a Tool Tip
   displays.)

8. Choose a different font from the Font menu (we selected ComicSansMS).
   Choose 18 pt from the Size menu, as shown in Figure QS-8.

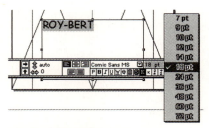

Figure QS-8: When text is
highlighted, you can format it using
controls on the left side of the
Measurements palette.

9. Choose Style ⇨ Formats, or press ⌘+Shift+F or Ctrl+Shift+F.

10. Type **0.25"** in the Space After field. Choose Centered from the Alignment
    menu, and then click OK.

11. Click in the next line below the name. (If you didn't click Return after the name before, do so now.)

12. To import text at this point, choose File ⇨ Get Text, or press ⌘+E or Ctrl+E.

13. Locate a text file in a format such as Microsoft Word (preferably one containing only a single sentence). Click on the file to select it, and then check Include Style Sheets.

14. Click Open (see Figure QS-9). If the MS-Word Filter dialog box displays, click Use New.

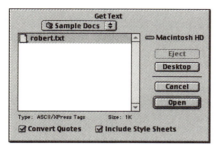

Figure QS-9: Use the Get Text command to import text from a word processor.

If the text file you import does not fit in the box, a red square in the lower-right corner indicates that text is overflowing. You don't need to worry about that for these purposes. If you do not have a text file, simply type another sentence in the box.

15. Click in the new sentence four times to highlight it.

16. Choose a different font from the Font menu (we selected Minion). In the Size field, type **12**. If necessary, click the All Caps icon to remove the All Caps type style.

17. Click the Justified icon, as shown in Figure QS-10.

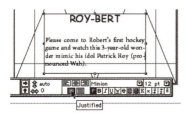

Figure QS-10: After you click Justify, your project should look something like this.

18. Choose File ⇨ Save, or press ⌘+S or Ctrl+S to save your work.

Cross-Reference

For more information about entering, importing, and formatting text, see Parts III and IV.

Working with Pictures

In QuarkXPress, any image that you import into a document — whether it's a digital photograph, a chart, or a line drawing — is referred to as a *picture*. Pictures go inside picture boxes. After a picture is inside a box, you can change its size and placement. To create a picture box, follow these steps:

1. Click and hold on the Rectangle Picture Box tool to display additional tools. Drag your mouse to the right to select the fourth tool, the Oval Picture Box tool.

2. Position the pointer on the page, and then click and drag to create an oval picture box of any shape, as shown in Figure QS-11. The new box is selected, as indicated by the black handles. If the box becomes deselected in the following steps, click on it to select it.

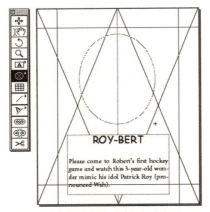

ROY-BERT

Please come to Robert's first hockey game and watch this 3-year-old wonder mimic his idol Patrick Roy (pronounced Wah).

Figure QS-11: Use the Oval Picture Box tool (or any other picture box tool) to create a container for graphics.

3. To size and place the box precisely, type the following values in the Measurements palette:

   - X: **0.75"**
   - Y: **0.25"**
   - W: **2.5"**
   - H: **2.75"**

4. To import a picture, choose File ⇨ Get Picture, or press ⌘+E or Ctrl+E.

5. Locate a graphic file such as a TIFF, JPEG, GIF, or EPS, as shown in Figure QS-12. Select the file and click Open.

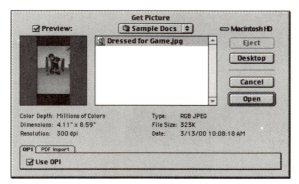

Figure QS-12: The Get Picture command lets you import graphics into picture boxes.

6. Highlight the X% (Scale Across) field in the Measurements palette. Type a new scale, such as 80%. Tab to the Y% (Scale Down) field and type the same value. Press Return to resize the picture.

7. If necessary, select the Content tool. Click inside the picture box (as shown in Figure QS-13), and drag the picture around as necessary to position it in the box. The X+ and Y+ fields in the Measurements palette reflect the new position.

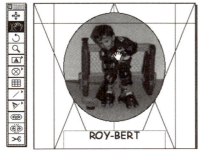

Figure QS-13: Select the Content tool to drag a picture around within its box.

Cross-Reference

For more information about working with pictures, see Chapter 20.

Working with Lines

You can create lines of any shape and size, then change the style, width, and color. To create lines, follow these steps:

1. Select the Line tool.

2. Position the mouse under the name you entered. Click and drag to create a line, as shown in Figure QS-14. (Press the Shift key while you drag to constrain the tool to drawing a horizontal or vertical line.) The new line is selected, as indicated by the black handles. If the line becomes deselected in the following steps, click on it to select it.

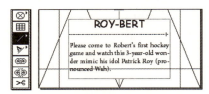

Figure QS-14: Use the Line tool to create lines at any angle.

3. Select the Item tool (the top tool on the Tool palette). Drag the line under the name to separate it from the body text. Drag either end of the line to resize it as necessary. Our line ended up with the following values in the Measurements palette: X1: 0.75", Y1: 3.625", X2: 3.25", Y2: 3.625".

4. Click the menu next to the W field on the Measurements palette, and then select 8 pt.

5. Click the Style menu on the Measurements palette, and then select All Dots, as shown in Figure QS-15.

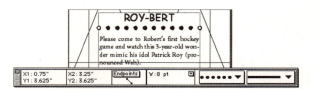

Figure QS-15: Select options from the left side of the Measurements palette to format lines.

6. Choose File ⇨ Save, or press ⌘+S or Ctrl+S to save your work.

Cross-Reference

For more information about working with lines, see Chapter 8.

Drawing a Shape

In addition to creating rectangular and oval picture boxes, you can create irregular shapes and lines with the drawing tools. Depending on the tool you select, the shapes can contain text, pictures, or simply color, and the lines can have text flowing along them. To draw a shape, follow these steps:

1. Scroll to the pasteboard at the right side of the document so you have a little work space.

2. Click and hold on the Oval Picture Box tool to display additional tools. Drag your mouse to the right to select the fifth tool, the Bézier Picture Box tool.

3. Using the shape and numbered points shown in Figure QS-16 as a guide, draw the hockey stick. First, position your pointer where our point 1 is, then click.

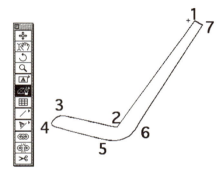

Figure QS-16: Follow the points on this image to draw an approximation of a hockey stick for your project.

4. Click at point 2.

5. Click at point 3, but without releasing the mouse button, drag toward point 4. Release the mouse button when the curve somewhat resembles ours.

6. Click at point 4.

7. Click at point 5, but without releasing the mouse button, drag toward point 6. Release the mouse button when the curve somewhat resembles ours.

8. Click at point 6, and then click at point 7.

9. Position the pointer over point 1 to see a Close Shape icon (a circle), then click to close the shape.

10. Select the Item tool, then drag the hockey stick onto the card as shown in Figure QS-17.

11. Choose View ➪ Hide Guides, or press F7.

Cross-Reference   For more information about drawing shapes, see Chapter 25.

ROY-BERT

Please come to Robert's first hockey
game and watch this 3-year-old wonder mimic his idol Patrick Roy (pronounced Wah).

Figure QS-17: The finished project consists of
items (a text box, picture boxes in various shapes,
and a line) and contents (text and pictures).

Creating Colors

To apply the color you want to an item or text, first you need to mix that color. By
default, QuarkXPress provides a few colors: cyan, magenta, yellow, black, red, blue,
green, white, and registration. In most cases, you'll be creating additional colors to
suit your projects. To create colors, follow these steps:

1. Choose Edit ⇨ Colors, or press Shift+F12.

2. Click New to open the Edit Color dialog box.

3. From the Model menu, choose PANTONE(r) Process. This will create a color
   based on premixed Pantone inks that designers often use to guarantee a
   consistent color for a corporate identity.

4. In the PANTONE S field, type **2-3**. (You can also select a color swatch in the
   upper-right corner.) This automatically selects the color and names it as
   shown in Figure QS-18.

5. Click OK to create the color and return to the Edit Color dialog box.

6. Click New again. This time, choose CMYK from the Model menu.

7. Type **Avalanche Red** in the Name field.

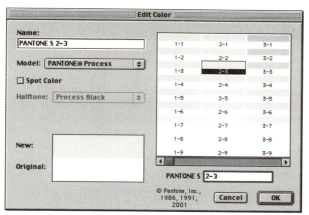

Figure QS-18: Create a Pantone color by entering a name or selecting a color swatch.

8. On the color wheel on the right, click in a red area that you like. To fine-tune the color, type the following values in the fields:

- C: **15**
- M: **80**
- Y: **55**
- K: **20**

This sets a value of 15 percent for cyan, 80 percent for magenta, 55 percent for yellow, and 20 percent for black—the four basic colors used in most color printing to make all other colors (see Figure QS-19).

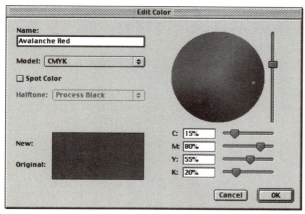

Figure QS-19: Create a CMYK color by clicking in the color wheel or entering values in the fields.

9. Click OK to create the color. Click New again.

10. Type **Avalanche Blue** in the Name field.

11. If necessary, choose CMYK from the Model menu, and then type the following values in the fields:
    - C: **90**
    - M: **70**
    - Y: **0**
    - K: **0**

12. Click OK to return to the Colors dialog box, shown in Figure QS-20. Click Save to add the colors to the document.

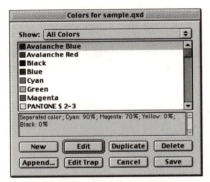

Figure QS-20: The Colors dialog box lists all the colors you create for a document.

 Cross-Reference For more information about creating colors, see Chapter 28.

Applying Colors

QuarkXPress provides a Colors palette that makes experimenting with different colors easy. You can apply colors to box backgrounds, lines, and text. To apply colors, follow these steps:

1. Choose View ➪ Show Colors, or press F12 to open the Colors palette.

2. Click on the background picture box on the left.

3. If necessary, click the Background Color icon on the Colors palette (the third icon from the left). This tells QuarkXPress what you want to color.

4. Click the name Avalanche Red in the lower half of the Colors palette, as shown in Figure QS-21. If necessary, use the scroll bar on the right to locate the color.

Figure QS-21: Click a color to apply it to the background of a box.

5. Click on the background picture box on the right.

6. Click the small color swatch next to Avalanche Blue, and then drag it over the white picture box, as shown in Figure QS-22. Release the mouse button to apply the color. (If you'd rather select another color, drag the color back.)

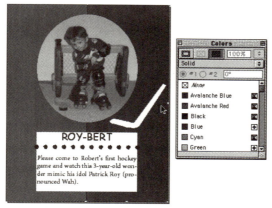

Figure QS-22: To experiment with colors, you can drag swatches over items.

7. Click on the text box at the bottom of the page to select it, and then click None at the top of the Colors palette. (Make sure the Background Color icon is still selected.)

8. Click on the line to select it, and then click PANTONE S 2-3. Click on the hockey stick to select it, and then click PANTONE S 2-3 again.

9. Select the Content tool, and then click and drag to highlight all the text in the text box.

10. Click the Text Color icon at the top of the Colors palette. Click White, as shown in Figure QS-23.

Figure QS-23: Click the Text Color icon to apply a color to highlighted text.

11. Click the close box on the Colors palette.

For more information about applying colors, see Chapter 28.

Printing a Composite

Whether you're designing a document for black-and-white photocopying, color printing, professional printing, or even for a PDF, you'll need to review drafts. By default, QuarkXPress is set up to print a grayscale composite to a laser printer with just a few clicks. To print a composite, follow these steps:

1. Choose File ⇨ Print, or press ⌘+P or Ctrl+P.

If you press Return/Enter as soon as the Print dialog box displays, chances are that QuarkXPress will print a usable draft on your laser printer. However, if you've selected a different page size, orientation, or other option, you may want to confirm the other settings first.

2. Click the Setup tab. The Printer Description is usually set to Generic B&W by default. You can leave this setting or locate and select the printer you're actually using. Selecting your actual printer is better.

3. Click the Output tab, and make sure the Print Colors menu is set to Grayscale.

4. Click the Preview tab, and make sure the page (indicated by the blue outline) fits within the printer paper (indicated by the dotted line), as shown in Figure QS-24.

5. Click Print.

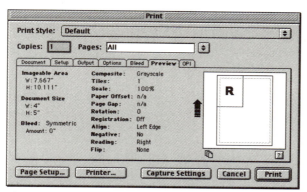

Figure QS-24: The Preview tab lets you confirm that your project fits on the paper in the selected printer.

For more information about printing, see Chapter 35.

✦   ✦   ✦

Welcome to QuarkXPress

No one is born a desktop-publishing expert. People who are familiar with traditional layout and production techniques and those who are skilled using computers often have much to learn. The marriage between the two areas requires a strong foundation in both. And these days, with desktop publishing having replaced nearly all traditional manual layout, the fundamentals behind layout and production are harder to come by.

In this part, we cover the fundamentals of publishing, Macintosh and Windows computers, and, of course, QuarkXPress itself. If you're an experienced user in any of these areas, feel free to skip over parts of the text that cover subjects you've mastered. (But do skim — there may be a tidbit here and there you don't yet know.) If you're new to desktop publishing, or if you're just beginning to use QuarkXPress, start here. No matter how experienced you are, you can look back to this part of the book when you're not quite sure what we're talking about.

QuarkXPress has many features, but it's not difficult to learn. The trick is to take it one step at a time. Some words of advice: Use QuarkXPress any chance you get so that you get plenty of practice. The more you use QuarkXPress, the better you'll be at using it and the more features you'll know how to use. These features give you the power to do increasingly creative work. And isn't that what desktop publishing is all about?

Introducing QuarkXPress

QuarkXPress 5 is a powerful and complex program, and whether you're new to the subject or an old hand, it's best to begin at the beginning. This chapter details the wide range of uses QuarkXPress is being put to around the globe, points out the ways in which QuarkXPress can be of use to you, illuminates some of the new features of version 5, and describes the basic metaphor on which the program is based. You'll also find a comprehensive list of the terms — clearly and concisely defined — that we use throughout the book. So whether you're an expert or novice, read on — and prepare yourself for a great adventure.

Looking At What QuarkXPress Can Do

QuarkXPress is used by a long and impressive list of people. Nearly three-quarters of all American magazines — including *Rolling Stone, Us, Macworld,* and *Readers Digest* — are produced with QuarkXPress, as are many newspapers around the world. It's also the best-selling page-layout program among professional design firms. QuarkXPress is the leading publishing program in Europe, and the international version of QuarkXPress — QuarkXPress Passport — supports most Western and Eastern European languages.

What does this information mean for you? It means that QuarkXPress can handle sophisticated tasks such as magazine and newspaper page layout, as shown in Figure 1-1, while its simple approach to publishing also makes it a good choice for smaller projects, such as fliers and newsletters.

Figure 1-1: The publisher of *5280: Denver's Mile-High Magazine* originally came to Denver to work at Quark, which is based there. He now produces this sophisticated, glossy magazine in QuarkXPress.

QuarkXPress can also be a good choice for corporate publishing tasks such as proposals and annual reports, often distributed via print, PDF (Adobe Acrobat Portable Document Format), and the Web. Long-document features make it a viable tool for books and other lengthy publications. Using QuarkXPress puts you in good company.

Discovering the QuarkXPress Approach

QuarkXPress is considered to be a page-layout program. But what does that mean? What can you do with it and how? Well, you can do everything from writing letters and printing them on your laser printer to designing high-end glossy magazines that you send out for color separations and four-color printing. And, in QuarkXPress 5, you can go beyond print to designing Web pages, PDF documents, and XML (Extensible Markup Language) content. (XML content is media-independent and can be output in a number of ways.) But due to the paste-up method that lies behind designing in QuarkXPress, it's better suited for some projects than it is for others.

The paste-up method

You build pages in QuarkXPress by using the paste-up method — so it literally feels as if you're creating little blocks of text and graphic elements, placing them on a page, then resizing and scooting them around until you're satisfied. First, you set up the basic framework of the document, including the page size and orientation, margins, number of columns, and so on. You then fill that framework with boxes that contain text, boxes that contain pictures, and lines, as shown in Figure 1-2.

Figure 1-2: This simple ad consists of a picture imported into a picture box (the globe), text imported into an oval text box with a black frame, and a dotted line.

Because of the emphasis on boxes, QuarkXPress is considered to be a box-based program. Although the idea of text boxes, picture boxes, and lines sounds simple and straightforward, in the right hands it can generate truly impressive results. These page elements are explained further in the "Speaking the Language" section of this chapter.

The right — and wrong — projects for QuarkXPress

Like other programs, QuarkXPress has its strengths and weaknesses. For example, it's great for producing a brochure that requires color separations and trapping. On its own, it's not so great for a textbook that requires scientific equations and footnotes. You can, however, meet special needs such as these by adding features with *XTensions,* which are plug-in modules for QuarkXPress (covered in more detail in Chapter 41).

Although you can adapt QuarkXPress to almost any publishing need, its roots in layout and print can cause problems. With the paste-up method and the emphasis on boxes, the items you place on pages in QuarkXPress can end up being tied to the pages. So changing or multipurposing the content has been difficult in the past (although the XML support may help change that). In addition, QuarkXPress has a lot of features and may be too much to learn for simpler projects.

In general, the following projects are ideal for QuarkXPress:

✦ Anything printed in four colors or more

✦ Books with a high level of design, such as coffee-table books

✦ Magazines and newsletters

✦ Corporate identity pieces, such as letterheads, envelopes, and business cards

✦ Brochures and fliers

✦ Advertisements and posters

✦ Novelty items and packaging

✦ Content that may need to be output in many different forms (print, PDF, Web, and so on)

The following projects may not fare as well, at least without XTensions:

✦ Books with footnotes and more complex indexes

✦ Books with headers and footers that change with the page content

✦ Text that includes scientific equations

✦ Text that relies on automatic numbering, such as an outline or many numbered steps that change often

✦ Letters or articles that need to be distributed to many people for customization (stick with Microsoft Word for this type of thing)

✦ Publications with a low level of design but a high level of editorial demands (such as tracking changes)

When deciding whether to use QuarkXPress, remember the old saying, "Use the simplest tool for the job." Writing letters to friends in QuarkXPress is surely overkill, but forcing Microsoft Word to lay out brochures is painful. And keep in mind that just because QuarkXPress can do something doesn't mean it will do it exactly the way you want it or need it. Be prepared to experiment, adjust your workflow, and add XTensions before solving your unique publishing situations.

The Publishing Workflow

Obviously, your publishing workflow will depend largely on where you work and what you're creating. A one-person newsletter operation will have a significantly different workflow than a national newsmagazine. And a graphic designer creating ads will work differently than a textbook publisher. But, in general, most workflows reflect the need to play to a program's strengths. This means you let each program in your publishing environment do what it does best. So you:

✦ **Write in a word processor.** Even if you're working alone, you'll benefit from writing and editing text in a word processor. You can take advantage of the superior spell checker, multiple undos, and revision tracking in a program such as Microsoft Word — while concentrating on the words rather than the layout. Then import the text into QuarkXPress for formatting.

✦ **Draw in an illustration program.** Yes, you can make curvy items in QuarkXPress and combine text and graphics in dramatic ways. But for the ultimate flexibility, use an illustration program such as Adobe Illustrator for your line art. You can then use the picture file in as many places as you want.

✦ **Prepare pictures in an image-editing program.** Whether you're starting with scans, images from Photo CDs, files from digital cameras, or images you've grabbed from the Internet, you'll generally need to save the picture in an image-editing program. Again, QuarkXPress does give you some cropping, resizing, and retouching tools. But most images will benefit from the professional tools in a program such as Adobe Photoshop.

✦ **Pull it all together in QuarkXPress.** QuarkXPress is the place to design your layout — the way your text and graphics interact with each other and with other elements on the page. After you get the structure of your pages in place, you can start collecting the text and graphics files (from yourself or from others), importing them into the QuarkXPress document, and formatting them as you like.

✦ **Print proofs, make revisions, and perform final output from QuarkXPress.** Whether your project will be printed on your laser printer or color separated onto film by a service bureau, this is one of the reasons you're using QuarkXPress — for reliable output.

In a workgroup, many of the steps in the publishing process are happening at the same time. Writers are writing, artists are creating graphs and illustrations, photographers are submitting pictures. Meanwhile, a graphic designer is producing the shell of a publication. When the contents are ready, the graphic designer pops them into place and makes them look good. Figure 1-3 shows the various components that make up a QuarkXPress document.

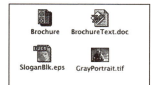

Figure 1-3: A QuarkXPress document and the imported Word, EPS, and TIFF files used in it.

But the beauty of QuarkXPress is that you don't have to work this way. You *can* do everything in QuarkXPress. If you're a one-person, one-program shop, you can still get a lot done. You can write in QuarkXPress, edit in QuarkXPress, import pictures from a Photo CD directly into QuarkXPress, and be done.

Speaking the Language

To understand the way you put pages together in QuarkXPress, it helps to know exactly what makes up a page. And if you call the items on the page the same thing that we call them — and the same thing that Quark calls them — it's easier to communicate with other users and to look things up when you're confused. QuarkXPress documents for print consist primarily of pages, items, and contents. To make these things look good, you use item attributes and styles. We'll take a quick look at each.

See Chapter 38 for information about the basic components of Web documents.

Pages and layers

Each document in QuarkXPress is made up of pages, which are outlined on your screen in black. Depending on how you've set up the document, the pages may be side by side in spreads, and they may have margins and columns indicated by blue lines. Generally, each page in a document will end up being a page in a printed piece. But sometimes you'll have multiple "pages" on a page, such as with a trifold brochure on an 8½-x-11-inch page or a page of business cards.

You can create *layers* for pages, which function like clear overlays that you can show, hide, and print as necessary. When you create a layer, it applies to all the pages in a document. Layers are handy for storing two different versions of text or graphics in the same document. They're also good for isolating items so you can work on them without being distracted by other items on a page. A page consisting of several layers is shown in Figure 1-4.

Items and contents

To really understand QuarkXPress is to understand the distinction it makes between items and contents. *Items* are things you draw on a page — such as squares, circles, lines, and wavy shapes — and then fill with color, *stroke* (frame), rotate, and so on. You can also import text and graphics — *contents* — into items. The primary items in QuarkXPress are picture boxes and text boxes, but there are also lines, text paths, and tables.

Contents, as mentioned, are text and pictures. (QuarkXPress calls any imported graphic a *picture,* whether it's a logotype, a chart, a line drawing, or a photograph.) Contents are always placed within an item — so you can have items without contents, but you cannot have contents without items. Figure 1-5 shows a picture (content) moving around within its box (an item).

Figure 1-4: This page consists of one layer for the background picture and one layer for the text and logo.

Figure 1-5: A box is an item, and the picture you import into it is its content.

You need to understand the distinction between items and contents because QuarkXPress provides different tools and menus for handling them. The two primary tools at the top of the Tool palette — the Item tool and the Content tool — are designed to work with their respective page elements (although as QuarkXPress has evolved, the tools have become increasingly flexible and their functions now overlap quite a bit). Generally, you select and manipulate items such as boxes with the Item tool. And you select and modify text and pictures with the Content tool. QuarkXPress also provides the Style menu for modifying the look of contents and the Item menu for modifying the look of items.

Item types

The broad category of items in QuarkXPress consists primarily of boxes and lines. You can create, format, and manipulate boxes and lines in basically the same ways — the primary difference among the different types is what you can put inside them. Figure 1-6 shows each type of item in QuarkXPress.

Figure 1-6: Top row, from left to right: a text box, a picture box, and a no-content box filled with a diamond blend. Bottom row, from left to right: a line with a dotted-line style, a text path, and a table.

Here are the different item types available in QuarkXPress:

✦ **Text boxes:** A text box is a container for text. You need to create one to type, paste, or import text.

✦ **Picture boxes:** A picture box is a container for any graphic that originated outside QuarkXPress (in Photoshop, for example).

✦ **No-content boxes:** A no-content box is a box that cannot contain text or pictures; they are primarily used for colored backgrounds and shapes.

✦ **Lines:** A line is just what it sounds like — a straight, diagonal, curvy, or irregular line that you draw on the page as decoration.

✦ **Text paths:** A text path is like a line in shape, but you can flow text along it.

✦ **Tables:** A table is really a series of grouped and linked text boxes, which you can use to format or import data.

If all this sounds incredibly structured, you'll be happy to know that the items are flexible. You can convert the type of any boxes, so if you start out with a no-content box, you can convert it to a text box. If you draw a nice curved line, then decide to flow text on it, you can convert it to a text path. And if you draw an exquisite closed shape with a line tool, you can convert it to any type of box so it can have contents.

Attributes and styles

By themselves, items and contents don't look like much. It's the attributes you apply to the items, and the styles you apply to the contents, that bring your documents to life.

Item attributes

Aside from adding content, you can do two basic things to items: Add color and stroke them. For boxes, you add a background color. To stroke boxes, you actually specify a frame, including its width, line style, and colors. For lines and text paths, you simply pick a color, width, and style. Of course, you can do a lot of other things to items themselves, including rotating and skewing them. The Item menu, and in particular the Modify command, provides the controls you need for applying attributes to items.

For frame and line styles (or strokes), QuarkXPress provides various styles such as double lines and dots, and it lets you create your own patterns with its Dashes & Stripes command (in the Edit menu).

 Tip   Most publishing and graphics arts programs use the term *stroke* to mean adding a border to an item, whether it's a box or a line. QuarkXPress never uses that term, preferring *frame* for strokes on boxes and *width* for strokes on lines and text paths. To make matters more confusing, other programs use the term *frame* for what QuarkXPress calls a *box.* When it comes to QuarkXPress, remember that a shape is a box and the border around it is a frame.

Text and picture styles

QuarkXPress provides all kinds of styles for formatting text and manipulating pictures. You can select and apply options such as fonts, sizes, underlines, justification, and much more to text. And you can resize, distort, and flip pictures at will. When text is selected, the Style menu for text (shown in Figure 1-7) provides all the options. (You can even save most of the formats you apply to text in Style Sheets through the Edit menu.) When a picture is selected, the Style menu for pictures (shown in Figure 1-8) provides options specific to that type of picture.

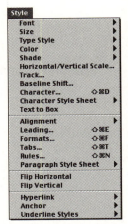

Figure 1-7: The Style menu for text.

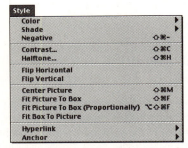

Figure 1-8: The Style menu for pictures.

What's New in Version 5

The most significant change from QuarkXPress 4 to QuarkXPress 5 is the built-in tools for publishing on the Web. For the print publisher, things haven't changed too dramatically — you'll find a few new features and some interface changes, but nothing that will trip you up. If you're making the transition from version 4 to version 5, skim through this list to familiarize yourself with QuarkXPress 5.

Application-level changes

Power users may notice a few changes to the overall application: Required Components, a new Preferences dialog box, and a streamlined Tool palette.

Required Components

Version 5 of QuarkXPress includes one significant change to the application itself — the addition of Required Components. These small software modules add features such as tables, HTML export, and GIF import to QuarkXPress. Unlike XTensions (optional add-ons for QuarkXPress), Required Components must be present for QuarkXPress to run. Many of Quark's old XTensions, such as Cool Blends, now exist as Required Components. The idea is that Quark can update and distribute these small modules without updating the entire program. Plus, Quark no longer has to test the software in all the different configurations with and without XTensions. Required Components are stored in a folder called Required Components inside your QuarkXPress folder, which is where you should leave them.

Preferences consolidated

One other across-the-board change is the Preferences dialog box, shown in Figure 1-9. QuarkXPress used to have two preferences dialog boxes — Application and Document — along with assorted preferences for the various XTensions you were using. Now the application has one big Preferences dialog box for Application Preferences, Document Preferences, and the new Default Web Document Preferences. Plus, you'll still get assorted preferences dialog boxes for XTensions.

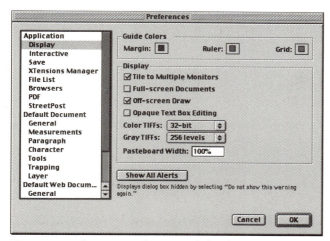

Figure 1-9: The new Preferences dialog box in version 5.

Even though the preferences are all in one dialog box, accessed through the redundant command of Edit ⇨ Preferences ⇨ Preferences (⌘+Y or Ctrl+Y), they still work the same:

> ✦ Application Preferences apply to the QuarkXPress application, not to individual documents.

✦ Document Preferences apply to the active QuarkXPress document. If no documents are open, they become program defaults.

✦ The new Web Document Preferences work the same as Document Preferences — they apply to the active Web document or, if no Web documents are open, they become program defaults.

Tools streamlined

When you first launch QuarkXPress 5, you'll also notice a streamlined Tool palette, as shown in Figure 1-10. Quark has combined all the various types of picture boxes into a single pop-out for picture box tools, and combined the two line tools into a pop-out as well. This should have happened in version 4, when QuarkXPress grew from fewer than 15 tools to more than 30. But engineers were afraid to scare people off, so they kept it looking as much like QuarkXPress 3.3 as possible. The new, tidy Tool palette showcases one of each type of tool while still providing customization.

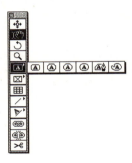

Figure 1-10: The tidier Tool palette in version 5.

You'll also spot the new Table tool, and, if you never upgraded to QuarkXPress 4.1, the Scissors tool looks new. If you create a Web document, you'll get an additional Tool palette for creating items such as image maps.

New features

When you start to dig into the QuarkXPress 5 menus, you'll stumble across many of the new features. The primary features are listed here, but you'll find that many of your favorite features are now slightly enhanced — for example, for those of us who like to index, you can now change the width of the Index palette. (Not a huge deal, until you start trying to decipher the index entries at their default width.) Look for:

✦ **Web Documents:** Create documents specifically for Web publishing, set up with the measurements and tools you prefer.

✦ **Interactivity:** Add interactivity to Web documents with rollovers, image maps, and hyperlinks. Incorporate tables and meta tags as well.

✦ **XLM Content:** Use the XML features of the included Avenue.Quark XTension to create media-independent content.

✦ **PDF:** Add hyperlinks to exported PDF pages.

✦ **Tables:** Create tables that contain linked text cells and graphics.

✦ **Layers:** Use layers to organize components of a design or versions of content (such as multiple versions of a similar ad).

✦ **Underline Styles:** Create custom underline styles — including color, shade, width, and offset — and apply them to text.

✦ **Line Check:** Search for text-flow issues such as widows, orphans, and text overflow.

Summary

QuarkXPress is the most popular publishing application in the world — and with good reason. With its paste-up method of working and its flexibility, QuarkXPress is ideal for projects running the gamut from black-and-white garage-sale fliers to newspapers to glossy coffee-table books.

To understand QuarkXPress, you need to understand the concept of items (boxes and lines) and contents (text and pictures). To work, you'll need to know how to use these different elements, and to communicate, you'll need to know what to call them. If you're already familiar with QuarkXPress, you'll appreciate the new features for layers, tables, and Web publishing.

✦　　✦　　✦

Taking a Tour of QuarkXPress

If you use other Macintosh and Windows programs, you're already familiar with such standard user-interface components as file folders, document icons, and the set of menus at the top of the document window. This chapter explains the interface components specific to QuarkXPress. We look at how the document window, menus, and dialog boxes operate. And we explore some of QuarkXPress's handy keyboard shortcuts and the look and feel of the program's various mouse pointers. A major portion of this chapter is devoted to palettes — a powerful feature of QuarkXPress that can increase your performance considerably. The differences between active and selected items are also explained.

Cross-Reference For important information on hardware and software recommendations, as well as upgrading and first-time installation — for both Mac and Windows users — see Appendix A.

Exploring the Program Files

QuarkXPress includes several programs in addition to the main QuarkXPress program. Including extra programs is fairly common today, because it lets software developers create modules for new and updated features without changing the basic program. In the QuarkXPress folder, you'll see these various components. You don't really need to worry much about them, except if something critical is missing (it's accidentally deleted or somehow gets corrupt on your hard drive) or if you want to add or update functionality.

Application files

The QuarkXPress folder has several items in it that you should generally leave untouched:

✦ **QuarkXPress,** the actual application.

✦ **Dictionaries,** which provide correct spelling and hyphenation for the languages you selected during installation. Typically, this will be Dict U.S. English, but if you installed International English or bought the multilingual Passport edition of QuarkXPress, you'll see other dictionaries as well for languages you installed.

✦ **Preferences folder,** which contains the application and XTension preferences, or preferred settings based on how you configure the Preferences dialog box in Quark and any XTension-specific preferences. The Preferences folder also contains the PPD folder, which stores PostScript printer description files that tell QuarkXPress what specific functions a printer has.

✦ **Color folder,** which includes the color definitions that come with QuarkXPress and are used in the Color palette and the Edit Colors dialog box.

✦ **Help folder,** which contains the files displayed when you activate QuarkXPress's help function.

✦ **Registration folder,** which contains the online registration components for QuarkXPress.

✦ **Scripts folder,** which contains any *scripts* (miniature programs to automate QuarkXPress) that you or someone else writes.

 Chapter 42 covers scripts in more detail.

Required Components

 QuarkXPress 5 adds a new feature called Required Components. These are plug-ins to the program, like the familiar XTensions. But in version 5, Quark has decided to make several plug-ins required for the program to operate, and it has created this folder for them. You should not remove these components.

You can tell a required component from a standard XTension by the icon and, in Windows, the file-name extension. Figure 2-1 shows the different icons. The Windows extension for a required component is .qrc, while the extension for an XTension is .xnt.

 **Figure 2-1:** The icon for a required component (left), for an XTension (middle), and for an XTension support component (far right is the Windows icon, the other is the Mac icon).

The former XTensions that are now required components are Cool Blends, GIF Filter, and JPEG Filter. Quark has also moved the spell-checking function from the main program into a required component, and it has used required components to implement the new Web publishing, tables, and layers features.

XTensions

Quark pioneered a marvelous idea that it calls XTensions, which are plug-in features. QuarkXPress comes with many such added features, and several companies create and sell plug-ins of their own. XTensions allow you to add features you need without Quark having to develop every component every user may need. It also lets you remove functionality you don't need to keep the program as simple as possible.

Most of the new XTensions in version 5 are previously available features from other Quark products or from the Quark Web site:

✦ **Avenue.Quark,** a formerly separate product that lets Web-page creators extract the content of QuarkXPress files into Extensible Markup Language (XML), a format commonly used for Web-content management systems.

✦ **ImageMap,** which lets you create *image maps* (graphical areas that include hyperlinks) in documents intended for the Web. This function was brought over from the QuarkImmedia product to create dynamic Web pages.

✦ **Item Sequence,** which lets you control the sequence of display for items on Web documents. This function was brought over from the QuarkImmedia product to create dynamic Web pages.

✦ **OPI,** which lets Quark support the Open Prepress Interface (OPI), in which high-resolution files are stored on a separate server and designers use a lower-resolution version in their QuarkXPress file. During printing, the OPI feature replaces the document's lower-resolution images with the high-resolution ones. This XTension adds an OPI tabbed pane or option to many dialog boxes involving images. QuarkXPress has supported OPI in previous versions, and this XTension includes those previous functions plus several enhancements.

✦ **PNG Import,** which lets QuarkXPress import the Web-oriented PNG graphic format.

✦ **RTF Import,** which lets QuarkXPress import the Rich Text Format developed by Microsoft as a platform-neutral standard for text that supports formatting such as boldface and font changes.

✦ **Script,** a Mac-only XTension that adds a Script menu to the right of the Utilities menu. The Script menu provides easy access to Apple-events scripts stored in the Scripts folder inside the QuarkXPress folder.

✦ **Street Post,** a feature that aids in the creation of XML-based forms.

Several other included XTensions are free XTensions Quark has long had on its Web site, including:

✦ **Jabberwocky,** which puts random "dummy text" in a text box.

✦ **Super Step and Repeat,** which lets you tell QuarkXPress how many copies to make of an item and where to place the copies.

✦ **Type Tricks,** which adds fraction- and price-formatting functions.

There are also several XTensions that came with the version 4.04 and 4.1 updates that Quark distributed free via the Web, including Dejavu (which adds a list of recently opened documents to the File menu and lets you set default folders from which to open files), QuarkLink (which launches your browser for easy access to various www.quark.com pages), and Scissors (which lets you cut apart curves and boxes).

Caution   Quark has changed the standard for XTensions, so QuarkXPress 5 is unlikely to run ones from previous versions (some may work, but don't count on it). That means you'll have to replace any older XTensions and may lose some functionality if the developer doesn't have a version 5–compatible version of your XTension ready yet. (Or you may delay installing version 5 until those XTensions are available, depending on how critical they are to your production operations.)

Note   Quark has also dropped some of its own XTensions, including Font Creator (which created multiple master variations for Adobe Multiple Master fonts), POCE (a color-management system that duplicated much of Quark's own CMS XTension), and several import filters (PCX Import, MacWrite, and MS Works on the Mac, and MS Write on Windows). Also missing are CPSI Fixer and TransparentEPS, which are now integrated into the main application.

With all these XTensions, it can quickly get confusing. So you'll likely want to turn off many of the ones that come with QuarkXPress. (Chapter 41 covers this in detail.) We recommend that, unless you are producing Web pages, you turn off the Web- and XML-related XTensions, including Avenue.Quark, ImageMap, Item Sequence, Street Post, and XML Import. Unless you're using OPI, also turn off the OPI XTension. Many users won't need QuarkLink, because they don't often go to Quark's site and can simply launch their browser manually when they need to. We recommend you leave all the file import filters on, because you never know when you may receive a file in a supported format.

Other components

You'll also see these folders in your QuarkXPress folder:

✦ **Documents folder,** which contains addenda to the print manual and other such information from Quark.

✦ **Tech Support folder,** which contains information on how to get support from Quark.

✦ **Templates folder,** which you can use to store any *templates* (documents that you use as a consistent starting point for new documents, such as the shell of a magazine layout whose look is the same each time but whose content changes, such as a monthly opinion column).

Finding Your Way Around the Document Window

When you open a document in QuarkXPress, the program displays a document window. The following items are specific to QuarkXPress documents:

✦ **Ruler origin box:** This lets you reset and reposition the *ruler origin,* which is the point at which the side and top rulers are zero.

✦ **Vertical and horizontal rulers:** These items, on the left and top of the window, reflect the measurement system currently in use.

✦ **Pasteboard:** This is a work area around the document page. You can temporarily store text boxes, picture boxes, or lines on the pasteboard. Items that reside completely on the pasteboard do not print. (QuarkXPress displays a shadow effect around the document page. The shadow indicates where the pasteboard begins.)

✦ **View percent field:** This shows the magnification level of the currently displayed page. To change the magnification level, enter a value between 10 and 800 percent in the field, and then press the Return key or click elsewhere on the screen.

✦ **Palettes:** Various palettes can be displayed depending on what you set in the View menu.

The following list describes the elements of the document window common to any program:

✦ **Title bar:** The name of the open document appears on the title bar, located at the top of the document window. You can move the document window around in the screen display area by clicking and dragging the title bar.

✦ **Scroll bar, buttons, and arrows:** Use the scroll bars, buttons, and arrows to shift the document page around within the document window. If you hold down the Option key while you drag the scroll box, the view of the document is refreshed as it moves.

✦ **Close box:** Use the close box to close a window. If the file is unsaved, you'll be asked whether you want to save it before closing it.

Note   To close multiple windows at once on the Mac, use Option+⌘+W or Option+click the close box on any open document.

A few window elements differ depending on whether you're using a Mac or a PC. Figures 2-2 and 2-3 show the differences.

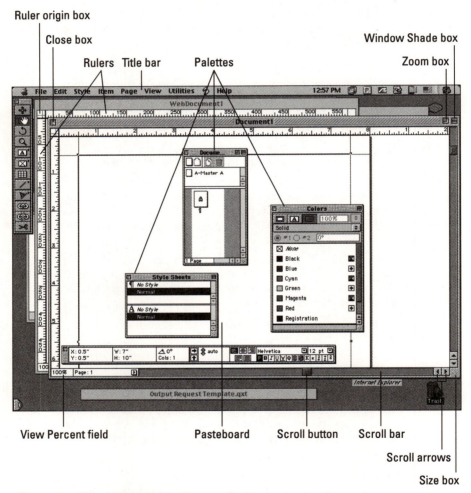

Figure 2-2: The document window on the Mac.

Ruler origin box   Rulers   Title bar   Palettes   Minimize box   Maximize box   Close box

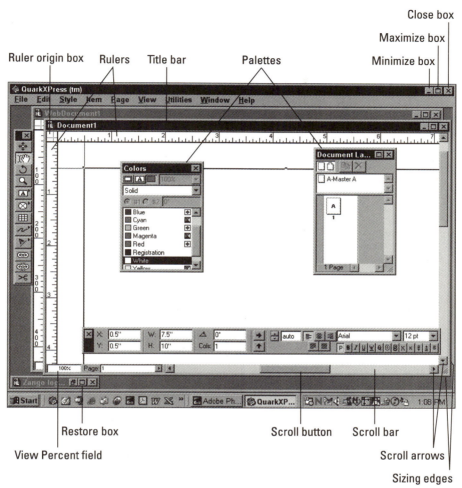

Restore box   Scroll button   Scroll bar

View Percent field   Scroll arrows

Sizing edges

Figure 2-3: The document window in Windows.

On the Mac, you'll find:

✦ **Zoom box:** If you have reduced or enlarged the document window, clicking the zoom box at the top-right corner of the document window returns it to its previous size.

✦ **Size box:** Clicking and dragging the size box resizes the document window as you move the mouse.

✦ **Window Shade box:** Clicking the Window Shade box collapses the document window so that just its title bar appears. Clicking it again opens the window.

In Windows, you'll find:

✦ **Minimize box:** Clicking the minimize box collapses the document window so that just its title bar appears. Clicking it again opens the window.

✦ **Maximize box:** Clicking the maximize box makes the document window fit the entire screen within the confines of the application's window. Double-clicking the title bar will maximize a document window as well.

✦ **Restore box:** Clicking the restore box will return the document window to its normal size. Double-clicking the title bar of a maximized document will restore its size as well.

✦ **Sizing edges:** You can click and drag any side or corner of a document window to resize it. These settings are retained, and clicking the restore box on a minimized or maximized window will bring you back to the last sizing settings.

Beyond these sizing and window-management commands, QuarkXPress has several options to manage multiple document windows. A few window-management options are different on Mac and Windows. On the Mac, the View menu has a Windows menu option, which in turn has three sets of options:

✦ **Stack Documents,** which arranges windows on top of each other so that each title bar is visible.

✦ **Tile Documents,** which arranges documents so that all are on-screen in their own area. Each document gets a horizontal slice of the available space.

✦ **The Windows menu,** which lists all open documents so you can select the ones you want whether or not they're visible on-screen.

In Windows, a separate Window menu has several document-management options:

✦ **Cascade,** which arranges windows on top of each other so that each title bar is visible. It also moves each window to the right a bit, so no matter what window you select, there is at least a corner of every other window available to be clicked.

✦ **Tile Horizontally,** which arranges documents so that all are on-screen in their own area. Each document gets a horizontal slice of the available space.

✦ **Tile Vertically,** which is like Tile Horizontally but arranges the slices vertically.

✦ **Arrange Icons,** which moves all minimized document windows to the bottom of the screen.

✦ **Close All,** which closes all open document windows.

✦ **The Window menu,** which lists all open documents so you can select the ones you want, whether or not they're visible on-screen.

Navigating the Documents

If you observe QuarkXPress users, you'll find that some work very quickly, their hands flying over the keyboard and different pages flying across the screen. These are people who know how to navigate through a document. And the more you know about navigation, the faster you'll be at the mundane task of finding the part of a document you want to work on. First, we explain why each page in a document is surrounded by white space — called the *pasteboard* — then we explain the many ways to get from page to page.

Working with the pasteboard

In the old days of publishing, people who composed document pages often worked at a large table (or pasteboard) that held not only the documents on which they were working, but also the odds and ends associated with its layout. They might have put a headline, a picture, a caption, or a section of text on the pasteboard until they were ready to place the element on the page. Even though QuarkXPress has automated the page-composition process, it includes a tremendously useful pasteboard (refer to Figures 2-2 and 2-3) that surrounds each document *spread* (one or more pages that are side by side). You can maneuver around the spread and the pasteboard by using the scroll controls.

The maximum width and height of the combined pasteboard and document spread is 48 inches. QuarkXPress reduces the pasteboard size, if necessary, in order to keep the pasteboard and spread at or below the 48-inch maximum width.

Usually, the default *pasteboard size* (the width of the document page) is sufficient, but you can modify it if you need more or less room on-screen. Choose Edit ➪ Preferences ➪ Preferences, or Option+Shift+⌘+Y or Ctrl+Alt+Shift+C, and then select the Display pane. Enter a percentage value in the Pasteboard Width field (toward the bottom of the pane). A value of 100 percent means that the pasteboard width is equal to — or 100 percent of the size of — the width of the document page. When the pasteboard width is to your liking, click OK to save the change.

This may not be a factor for most users, but keep in mind that the larger the pasteboard, the more memory is required. If you're not short on computer memory, use the default pasteboard width. If you are running short on computer memory, consider reducing the size of the pasteboard to something less than 100 percent.

Scrolling around

Although you can use ⌘+0 (zero) or Ctrl+0 (zero) to make a page or spread fit on-screen, you'll often want to zoom in so you can see more detail. That typically means some of your page will be off-screen, and you'll have to scroll to those other parts when you want to work on them. There are two basic ways to do this: the scroll bars or the page grabber hand.

As we showed earlier in this chapter, the document window includes scroll bars. Those scroll bars have arrows you can click and hold to scroll the window in the chosen direction as well as scroll buttons along the right and bottom sides of your windows that you can drag to scroll the document. This is standard Mac and Windows functionality.

But, like other layout and art programs, QuarkXPress uses a technique called the *grabber hand* so you don't have to use the scroll bars. Just hold Option or Alt and your Item or Content tool turns into the Page Grabber icon. As long as you hold Option or Alt, moving your mouse will scroll you through the document in the direction you move your mouse. Using the page grabber hand can be faster than using the scroll bars, because you can go diagonally rather than just horizontally or vertically.

Turning pages

Of course, most QuarkXPress documents are composed of multiple pages, so scrolling is not enough to navigate. There are several ways to change pages in QuarkXPress:

✦ Next to the view percentage box you'll find an arrow, which pops up a list of pages, as shown in Figure 2-4. Just click the page you want to go to. The lettered pages are master pages (page templates are described in more detail in Chapter 9).

✦ Use Page ➪ Go To, or ⌘+J or Ctrl+J, to get the Go to Page dialog box, where you specify the page you want to go to. The Page menu also has options to go to the first, previous, next, and last page in the document.

✦ Use the Document Layout palette (View ➪ Document Layout, or F10) to see the pages in your document arranged as they are meant to be printed. You then double-click the page you want to go to. Figure 2-5 shows this palette and the Page menu.

Figure 2-4: The page pop-up list lets you move to a new page.

Specifying a page number

Because the page number that displays and prints on the document page doesn't have to match the position of the page in the document—for example, the third page might be labeled *iii*—there are two methods for entering the page number you want to jump to: relative page numbers and absolute page numbers.

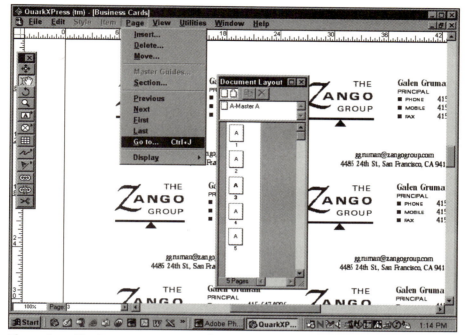

Figure 2-5: The Document Layout palette and the Page menu are two ways to move from one page to another.

Relative page numbers

A *relative page number* matches the page number. So if the document is set to start on page 2, the eighth page from the beginning would be page 9. You would enter 9 in QuarkXPress dialog boxes to get to that page.

Absolute page numbers

An *absolute page number* indicates a page's position in the document, such as 1 for the first page, 2 for the second page, and so on. To specify an absolute page number, you enter a plus sign before the number that represents the page's position. For example, the first page in the document is always +1, the second page is always +2, and so on.

Working with section pages

A section page number, specified through the Section dialog box (Page ➪ Section) is a customized page number. You would use section numbers if your document needs to start on a page other than 1 — for example, if you're working on a magazine and each article is saved in a different document, or a book in which the introduction pages use roman numerals. You can also split a single document into separate sections of page numbers (for example, sections 1–, 2–, and so on, or sections A–, B–, and so on), and use section page numbers to change the format of numbers to roman numerals, letters, and so on. Figure 2-6 shows the Section dialog box.

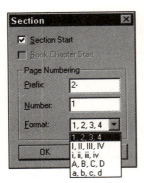

Figure 2-6: The Section dialog box lets you create sections within a document that can have their own set of numbers.

To jump to or print a page with a section page number, you might think to indicate which section it is and what page number is displayed on the page. For example, if you want to go to page 5 in section 2, you would specify 2-5 as the page number in the Go to Page dialog box. After all, you'll see 2-5 as the page number in the page pop-up and in the Document Layout palette. But that won't work. QuarkXPress requires you to enter an absolute number in this case. If you enter just 5, QuarkXPress will go to page 5 in the first section that has a page 5.

Changing views

The other navigation you'll do frequently in QuarkXPress is changing your view magnification. QuarkXPress provides several options to do this.

The Zoom tools are great for making small adjustments or for selecting a specific area you want to zoom into. The simplest way is by selecting the Zoom tool then clicking in your document. Each click zooms in another 25 percent (a setting you can change in the Tools pane in the Preferences dialog box; click the Zoom tool in that pane, then the Modify button). If you hold Option or Alt when clicking, you zoom out instead.

You can also use the View menu to choose from preselected zooms: Fit in Window, 50%, 75%, Actual Size, 200%, and Thumbnails (shown in Figure 2-7). Several of these have keyboard shortcuts: ⌘+0 (zero) or Ctrl+0 (zero) for Fit in Window, ⌘+1 or Ctrl+1 for Actual Size, and Shift+F6 for Thumbnails.

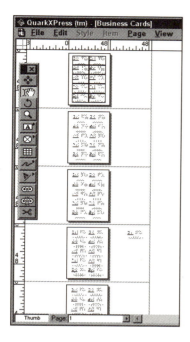

Figure 2-7: The Thumbnails view lets you see multiple pages and spreads at once.

The lower-left corner of the document window contains a field/pop-up menu that lets you change the document's view percent. The view scale can be as small as 10 percent and as large as 800 percent, and you can modify it in 0.1-percent increments. (You can enter T to go to thumbnail views.) You have two options for using the view percentage box:

✦ To change the view to a specific value, highlight the value in the field, enter a new value, and press Return or Enter.

✦ To jump into the field quickly and enter a specific value, press Control+V or Ctrl+Alt+V, enter a new value, and press Return or Enter. This method lets you change the view without taking your hands off the keyboard.

Working with Guides

QuarkXPress has several tools to ensure items are placed precisely, using guide lines. Guides and rulers are important tools for a layout artist because they help to position the elements correctly. In the Display pane of the Preferences dialog box (Edit ➪ Preferences ➪ Preferences, or Option+Shift+⌘+Y or Ctrl+Alt+Shift+Y), QuarkXPress provides the following types of guides to help you align items:

✦ **Margin (normally blue):** The margin guides show you the default column and gutter positions for text boxes.

✦ **Ruler (normally green):** The ruler guides are lines you drag from the horizontal and vertical rulers so that you can tell whether a box lines up to a desired point.

✦ **Grid (normally magenta):** The baseline grid shows the position of text baselines (the invisible line on which characters rest).

The color of these guides can be important in helping you distinguish them from other lines and boxes in your layout. It's not at all uncommon to have all three guides visible at the same time.

More often than not, you use margin guides routinely and ruler guides occasionally, particularly when you want to align something within a box to a ruler point. It's easier to use the box coordinates (their X and Y positions in the Measurements palette) to make sure that boxes or their margins are placed exactly where you want them. The baseline grid, however, can help you estimate column depth and see if odd text such as a headline causes vertical alignment problems.

Changing guide colors

You can change the colors of these guides to any color available by using the computer's color picker.

 The color-definition process varies slightly between Mac and Windows.

On the Mac, just click the color square for the guide whose color you want to change to bring up the color-selection options. The left side of the dialog box lists the various color-selection models you can use. The color in the New field shows the new color; the color in the Original field shows the original color. When using the color wheel, as we did in Figure 2-8, select a point in the wheel for the hue you want and use the fields at the right of the dialog box to control the hue angle, saturation, and lightness.

In Windows, just click the color square for the guide whose color you want to change to bring up the color-selection options. You'll get a list of default colors, as well as a Define Custom Colors >> button so you can create your own. The Custom Colors dialog box is shown in Figure 2-9. Select a point in the color map for the hue you want and use the fields at the bottom of the dialog box to control the hue angle, saturation, and lightness, or to specify red, green, and blue values. Click Add to Custom Colors to make your new color available (you can have 16 custom colors).

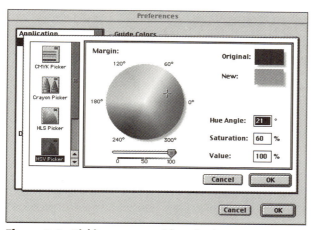

Figure 2-8: Picking a new guide color in Mac QuarkXPress.

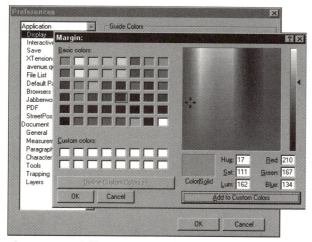

Figure 2-9: Picking a new guide color in Windows QuarkXPress.

Turning guide colors on and off

Although you set colors for guides in the Display pane of the Preferences dialog box, use the View menu to display the guides. Select View ➪ Show Guides (or press F7) to display margin and ruler guides, and choose View ➪ Hide Guides to hide margin and ruler guides. (This is a feature that you toggle on and off, so the shortcut F7 also hides them.) Likewise, select Show Baseline Grid and Hide Baseline Grid (Option+F7 on the Mac; Ctrl+F7 in Windows) to turn baseline grids on and off.

Working with ruler guides

To obtain a ruler guide, simply use the mouse to position the cursor within the vertical or horizontal ruler, and then hold down the mouse button as you pull the ruler guide into place. Ruler guides display whether or not you activate Show Rulers or Hide Rulers. To get rid of a ruler guide, select it and drag it back to the ruler. If the ruler is not displayed, drag it off the page past where the ruler would be. (For information on how to set rulers, turn to "Setting measurement preferences," later in this chapter.)

Placing guides in front of or behind boxes

Use the Guides option in the General pane of the Preferences dialog box to specify whether guides appear in front of boxes (the default setting) or behind them. When guides are behind boxes, it can be easier to see what is in the boxes but harder to tell if elements within the boxes line up with margins, gutters, or baselines. Figure 2-10 shows guides turned on and set at Behind.

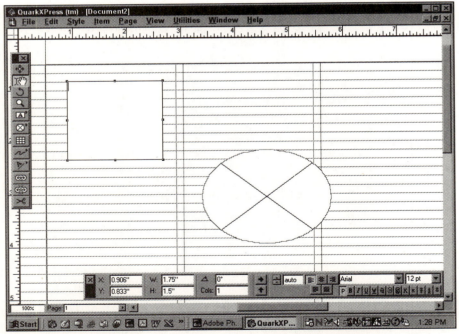

Figure 2-10: Guides set to display behind boxes. The picture box obscures the guides because it has a solid white background, and the smaller text box knocks out because it is currently selected with the Content tool.

Boxes will "knock out" of guides — obscure the guide lines — if they have a background color or, for text boxes, if they are selected with the Content tool *and* you've selected Opaque Text Box Editing in the Preferences dialog box's Display pane.

 New Feature The Opaque Text Box Editing option is new in QuarkXPress 5. It's a neat addition that gives a text box with no background color a temporary background color of white while you're editing text. This not only helps make text readable with guides turned on but also makes text readable in boxes that overprint other items.

Notice in Figure 2-10 that the grid lines appear inside the main text box but not in the pull-quotes' text boxes. To do this, we have given the pull-quotes' text boxes a background of White (accessed by choosing Item ⇨ Modify, or ⌘+M or Ctrl+M). The other text boxes have a background of None, which lets the guides show through. (We have guides set to Behind. If they were set to In Front, they'd appear over the pull-quotes' boxes, too.)

Using the Snap to Guides feature

Another handy feature for lining up elements on a page is the Snap to Guides feature, which you access through the View menu (the keyboard shortcut Shift+F7 also accesses it). When you select this feature, guides have an almost magnetic pull on objects you place on the page, making them "snap" into alignment with the closest guide. You'll appreciate this feature for some layout tasks, but you'll want to disable it for others.

So when do you want the Snap to Guides feature enabled? Imagine that you're creating a structured document containing illustrations framed with a 0.5-point line and aligned with the leftmost margin. In this case, select Snap to Guides so that the illustrations snap into position on the margin. If, on the other hand, you have a document containing design elements that are placed in a variety of locations on the page, you may want to position them visually or by means of the Measurements palette instead of having them automatically snap to the nearest guide line.

You can control the distance within which an item snaps to guides by entering a value in the Snap Distance field in the General pane in the Preferences dialog box. Snap distance is specified in pixels, and the range is 1 to 100. If the snap distance is set to 6 pixels (the default), any element within 6 or fewer pixels of a guide snaps to that guide.

Using the Guide Manager

Beyond the margin, ruler, and baseline guides, QuarkXPress lets you add more guide lines with the new Guide Manager feature added in version 4.1 You access this tool via Utilities ⇨ Guide Manager; Figure 2-11 shows the dialog box.

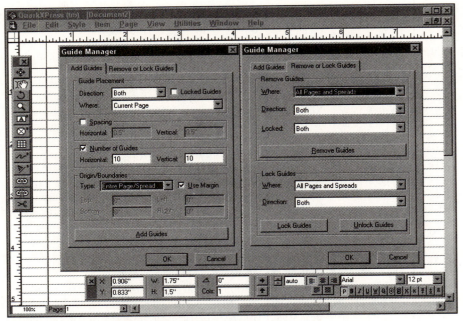

Figure 2-11: The Guide Manager's two panes.

The Guide Manager is essentially an automated version of ruler guides, so it's no surprise that any guides you create with it are the same color as ruler guides. The dialog box and its two panes at first look complicated, but they're not that hard. Here are some tips to keep in mind:

✦ In the Add Guides pane, start with the Guide Placement section. Here, you specify whether you want horizontal or vertical guides, or both, and whether you want those guide lines locked (so they can't be dragged to new positions). You also specify whether you want them on the current page only, current spread only, all pages, or all spreads.

✦ The next two sections are related: Spacing and Number of Guides. You can use either or both. If Spacing is checked, you can tell QuarkXPress how far apart you want the guide lines. If Number of Guides is checked, you can tell QuarkXPress how many guide lines you want. If *only* Spacing is checked, QuarkXPress will create as many guide lines as needed for the page or spread. If *only* Number of Guides is checked, QuarkXPress will space out that number of guide lines across your page or spread. If *both* are checked, QuarkXPress will create the exact number of guides specified at the exact distances specified.

✦ The Origin/Boundaries section lets you specify where the guide lines begin. Inset moves in by the specified amounts, using the Top, Left, Bottom, and Right settings as the boundaries. So, entering 3" in Bottom means to set the bottom boundary 3 inches from the bottom. Absolute Position makes you specify the dimensions exactly, so entering 3" in Bottom means that 3 inches down from the top of the file is the bottom boundary for the guide lines. Entire Page/Spread tells QuarkXPress to run the guidelines across the whole page or spread (no boundaries). Finally, if you check Use Margins, all calculations are done from the upper-left page margin rather than from the default upper left of the page.

Click Add Guides when the settings are to your liking. If what then displays on-screen doesn't match your expectations, just click Cancel to undo the guide lines. Click OK to accept them.

After you create guide lines, you can use the Remove or Lock Guides pane to adjust them:

✦ The options in the Remove Guides section delete any guides. You specify whether you want them deleted from all spreads and pages, all spreads, all pages, the current spread, or the current page. You can also specify if you want horizontal, vertical, or both types of guides deleted, and whether you want locked, unlocked, or both types of guides deleted. Click Remove Guides when your settings are to your liking. *Remember:* You can click Cancel to undo them if you don't like the results. Click OK to accept the changes.

✦ Lock Guide works like Remove Guides and has the same options to pick the pages to lock or unlock guides on and to choose whether to unlock horizontal, vertical, or both types of guides. Use Lock Guides to lock the guides specified or Unlock Guides to unlock them. *Remember:* You can click Cancel to undo them if you don't like the results. Click OK to accept the changes.

Introducing Tools

The Tool palette is one palette you'll often use when you build a document in QuarkXPress. After all, QuarkXPress is highly dependent on tools to make its feature accessible. When you first open the program, the Tool palette appears along the left edge of the document window. If it's not there, you can get it to appear by selecting Show Tools from the View menu (or by pressing F8). This palette contains tools that you use to create, change, link, view, and rotate text boxes, picture boxes, and lines.

To use a tool on the palette, you first need to activate it. To do this, use the mouse to place the pointer on the tool icon that you want to use, and click the mouse button. Some tools have variations (which have an arrow on the right-hand side) that display if you hold the mouse down when you select the tool. Depending on the tool you select, the pointer takes on a different look, reflecting the function the tool performs. When you click the Linking tool and then click a text box, for example, the pointer changes to look like links in a chain.

In the remaining chapters in this book, we explain in greater detail many of the functions you can perform with the Tool palette. The following sections in this chapter provide brief descriptions of each tool. Figure 2-12 shows the standard tools.

Note   The Web Tool palette displays only if you create a new Web page or open an existing Web page. If it is open, the View menu changes so that the Tools option has a submenu, one to control the display of the Tool palette and one to control the display of the Web Tool palette.

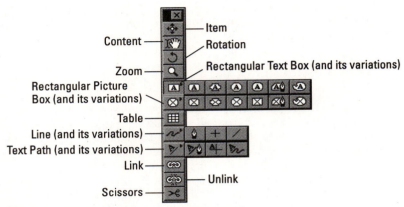

Figure 2-12: The standard QuarkXPress tools.

New Feature   QuarkXPress 4.x let you customize the Tool palette, moving, for example, picture box tools onto the main palette from the pop-up menu or back. In version 5, Quark has eliminated that feature, though the last tool you select from a pop-up tool menu does still become the tool shown by default on the Tool palette until you select another variation.

Manipulation tools

The first five tools in the Tool palette let you do things to existing page items. The two most important tools in all of QuarkXPress are the Item tool and the Content tool.

Item tool

The Item tool, the topmost tool in the Tool palette, handles the *external* aspects of an item on a page — for example, its location. (If you want to change something *within* an item on the page, you use the Content tool, described in the following section.) The Item tool controls the size and positioning of items. When you want to change the shape, location, or presence of a text box, picture box, or line, use the

Item tool. The Item tool enables you to select, move, group, ungroup, cut, copy, and paste text boxes, picture boxes, lines, and groups. When you click the Item tool on a box, the box becomes *active,* meaning that you can change or move it. Sizing handles appear on the sides of an active box or line; you can click and drag these handles to make the box or line a different size.

Content tool

Although the Item tool controls the external aspects of an item on a page, the Content tool (the second tool from the top in the Tool palette) controls its internal aspects. Functions you can perform with the Content tool include *importing* (putting text into a text box or putting a picture into a picture box), cutting, copying, pasting, and editing text. To edit text in a text box, first select the Content tool. Then select the areas of text that you want to edit by clicking and dragging the Content tool to highlight the text or by using different numbers of mouse button clicks.

In a picture box, the Content tool cursor changes to a hand shape. You can use this tool in a picture box to move (or crop) the contents of the box. You can also use it to manipulate the picture's contents, such as applying shades, colors, or printing effects.

Rotation tool

By clicking and dragging with the Rotation tool (the third tool from the top in the Tool palette), you can rotate items on a page. Using the Rotation tool, you can click a text box, picture box, or line and rotate it by dragging it to the angle that you want. You can also rotate items on a page using the Measurements palette or the Modify command in the Item menu (⌘+M or Ctrl+M).

Zoom tool

As you're working on a document in QuarkXPress, you may want to change the magnification of the page on-screen. For example, you may be making edits on text that is set in 8-point type; increasing the displayed size of the text makes it easier to see what you're doing as you edit. The Zoom tool, the fourth tool from the top in the Tool palette, lets you reduce or enlarge the view that you see in the document window. When you select the Zoom tool, the cursor looks like a small magnifying glass. When you hold the cursor over the document window and click the mouse button, QuarkXPress magnifies that section in increments of 25 percent. Pressing Option or Alt, and clicking the Zoom tool *reduces* the magnification by 25 percent instead.

Scissors tool

Introduced in QuarkXPress 4.1, the Scissors tool (the bottommost in the Tools palette) lets you cut a line, path, or box. You would use this feature to create unusual box shapes or to edit illustrations created in QuarkXPress.

Item-creation tools

The second section of tools in the Tool palette lets you actually create items on your document pages. Without items — primarily text boxes and picture boxes — you cannot have contents — text and pictures.

Text Box tools

QuarkXPress is box-based. Although you can import text from a word processor file or enter text directly onto a document page using the word-processing features built into QuarkXPress, you need a text box to hold the text. You can instruct QuarkXPress to create rectangular text boxes on each page of the document automatically. You can also create a text box manually using one of the Text Box tools (refer to Figure 2-12): rectangular, rounded-corner, concave corner, beveled corner, oval, Bézier, or freehand Bézier. The Text Box tools are the fifth from the top in the Tool palette. QuarkXPress remembers the text box tool you last used and makes that the default tool for the next time you create a text box.

Picture Box tools

Picture boxes are containers you create to hold graphics that you import from graphics programs. QuarkXPress offers seven Picture Box tools, occupying the sixth position in the Tool palette. Using these tools, you can draw the same shapes as available for text boxes.

Table tool

The Table tool lets you create tables in QuarkXPress, a new feature. Tables are essentially a series of linked text and picture boxes, so you have most of the same controls over table cells as you would for a text or picture box.

 The ability to create tables is new to QuarkXPress 5.

Line tools

The Line tools, in the eighth position in the Tool palette, let you draw lines, or *rules*. After you draw a line, you can change its thickness *(weight)* or line style (dotted line, double line, and so on). There are tool variations for different kinds of straight and curved lines.

Text Path tools

Similar to the Line tools, the Text Path tools let you create paths along which text runs. You use these tools to have text follow curves, circles, or other such shapes.

Text-box linking tools

Near the bottom of the Tool palette are the Linking and Unlinking tools.

The Linking tool lets you link text boxes together so that text flows from one text box into another.

You use the Unlinking tool to break the link between text boxes.

Linking is particularly useful when you want to *jump* text — for example, when a story starts on page 1 and jumps to (continues on) page 4.

Cross-Reference   Chapter 12 covers linking in more detail.

Web tools

The Web tools, shown in Figure 2-13, let you create items specific to Web pages such as image maps (pictures containing links) and forms (for users to fill in). To display the Web tools, choose View ➪ Tools ➪ Web Tools.

 New Feature   The Web tools are all new to QuarkXPress 5.

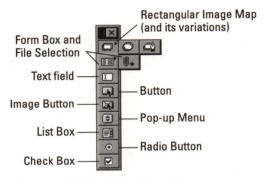

Figure 2-13: The Web-oriented QuarkXPress tools.

Image Map

The Image Map tool has three versions, for different shapes of image maps. An image map is a graphic that, when clicked on the Web, has a hyperlink to bring the user to a new Web page.

Form Box and File Selection

These two tools let you create two kinds of forms for Web pages. The Form Box tool creates a standard fill-in-the-blank form for Web users to fill in information, such as subscription information. The File Selection tool creates a dialog box that lets users select a file for downloading.

Text Field

The Text Field tool is essentially a one-line version of the Form Box tool.

Button and Image Button

These tools let the Web page designer create buttons the user can click to perform an action. The Button tool creates a button, while the Image Button tool creates a picture box that acts as a button.

Pop-Up Menu

The Pop-Up Menu tool creates a pop-up menu for the Web user to be able to make a selection from.

List Box

The List Box tool creates a box in which a user can enter a list of items, such as for filling in a database over the Web.

Radio Button and Check Box

These tools let users select options on a Web page. The Radio Button tool makes the user choose just one option in a list, while the Check Box tool lets the user select multiple items from the list.

Introducing Palettes

One of the most innovative features of the QuarkXPress interface is its *palettes.* Now copied by many programs, palettes let you perform a wide range of functions on an open document without having to access menus. They are the biggest time-saving feature of the QuarkXPress interface, and using them really speeds up the process of creating documents. You will undoubtedly find yourself using a couple of the palettes — the Tool palette and the Measurements palette — all the time.

Using palettes

QuarkXPress provides a variety of interactive palettes that provide quick access to commonly used features. You can perform almost every action available in every palette using a menu command and dialog box, but you'll often find that palettes are more convenient — especially because you can see your changes as you make them.

Opening and closing

To open a palette or pane, choose its menu command (such as View ⇨ Show Colors). Some have keyboard shortcuts, as indicated in the menu. To close a palette, click its Close box in the upper-left corner (Macintosh) or upper-right corner (Windows). You can also choose its menu command (such as View ⇨ Hide Colors).

Resizing palettes

To shrink a palette down to its title bar, click its Zoom box (Macintosh) or Minimize box (Windows). On the Mac, to collapse a palette down to its title bar, which doesn't actually contain a title, click the Window Shade box (or double-click the title bar if the Mac OS Appearances control panel is set up to allow that option). To move a palette, drag its title bar.

A few palettes contain arrows in the lower-right corner that you can drag to resize the palette.

Entering information in palettes

Palettes provide a variety of controls for entering information, including menus, fields, and arrows that you click. The controls work the same, regardless of which palette you're using.

- ✦ **Menus:** Click on a menu to display the list of options. Select an option, and the change takes effect immediately.

- ✦ **Fields:** Highlight a value in a field to enter a new value. (Note that fields accept values in all different measurement systems.) To implement the new value, press Shift+Return or Shift+Enter, press Tab to jump to the next field, press Shift+Tab to jump to the previous field, or simply click elsewhere in the palette or document. To get out of a field you've modified, leaving the object unscathed, hit Escape.

- ✦ **Arrows:** Some fields include up and down arrows that you can click to increase or decrease the value in the field.

- ✦ **Icons:** Click an icon, such as the B for bold in the Measurements palette, to instantly implement a change.

The Measurements palette

The Measurements palette, shown in Figure 2-14, was first developed by Quark and has since been widely imitated by other software programs. This palette is certainly one of the most significant innovations to take place in the evolution of desktop publishing. You will use it all the time. The Measurements palette gives you precise information about the position and attributes of any selected page element, and it lets you enter values to change those specifications. If you want to see the Measurements palette, you need to have a document open as you choose View ➪ Show Measurements (or press F9).

Figure 2-14: The Measurements palette when text is selected.

Note You can highlight the next field in the Measurements palette by pressing the Tab key, and you can highlight the previous field by pressing Shift+Tab. If you enter an invalid value in a field and get an error message, you can revert to the previous value by pressing ⌘+Z or Ctrl+Z.

How it works with text

The information displayed on the Measurements palette depends on the element currently selected. When you select a text box, the Measurements palette displays the text box position coordinates (X and Y), size (W and H), amount of rotation, and number of columns (Cols). The two buttons with arrows on them let you flip the text in the box horizontally or vertically.

Using the up– and down-pointing outlined arrows on the palette, you can modify the leading of the selected text (or you can simply type in a value in the space next to the outlined arrows); use the right- and left-pointing arrows to adjust kerning or tracking for selected text. You can specify text alignment — left, center, right, justified, or force-justified — by using the alignment icons. In the type section of the palette, you can control the font, size, and type style of selected text.

How it works with pictures

If you select a picture box, the Measurements palette displays a different set of information (see Figure 2-15). It shows the position of the box (X and Y), its size (W and H), the amount it is rotated, and its corner radius.

Figure 2-15: The Measurements palette when a picture is selected.

The items to the right of the heavy vertical bar in the middle refer to the image in the picture box. The two buttons with arrows on them let you flip the picture horizontally or vertically. The fields to the right of these buttons let you assign the following: a reduction or an enlargement percentage (X percent and Y percent), repositioning coordinates (X+ and Y+), the amount of picture rotation within the box, and the amount of slant.

How it works with lines

When you select a line, the left side of the Measurements palette displays information about the line's position and length. (It can do this in a variety of ways, depending on which option is selected from the pop-up menu.) The right side of the palette displays the line width, line style, and *endcap* (line ending) style (see Figure 2-16). The line-style list box lets you select the style for the line.

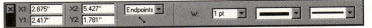

Figure 2-16: The Measurements palette when a line is selected.

The Document Layout palette

The Document Layout palette lets you create, name, delete, move, and apply master pages. You can also add, delete, and move document pages. To display the Document Layout palette, shown in Figure 2-17, choose View ➪ Show Document Layout (or press F10 on the Mac or F4 in Windows).

At the top of the palette are *master pages* — templates on which you can have new pages created or that you can apply to existing pages — while at the bottom are document pages.

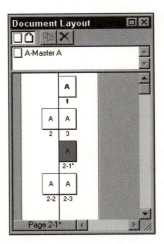

Figure 2-17: The Document Layout palette.

The Style Sheets palette

The Style Sheets palette, shown in Figure 2-18, displays the names of the paragraph style tags applied to selected paragraphs and the character style tags applied to selected characters. The Style Sheets palette also lets you apply style sheets to paragraphs and characters. To display the Style Sheets palette, choose View ➪ Show Style Sheets (or press F11).

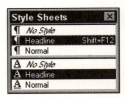

Figure 2-18: The Style Sheets palette.

A paragraph style is a set of attributes applied to an entire paragraph, such as font, alignment, indentation, and leading. A character style is a set of attributes applied to a selection of text, such as type style (italics or boldface), size, and font. Style sheets let you define these settings once and have them applied properly to all text that should have specific attributes.

The Colors palette

The Colors palette, shown in Figure 2-19, lets you designate the color and shade (percentage of color) that you want to apply to text, pictures, and backgrounds of text and picture boxes. You also can produce color blends, using one or two colors, to apply to box backgrounds. To display the Colors palette, choose Show Colors from the View menu (or press F12).

Figure 2-19: The Colors palette.

Special-purpose palettes

In addition to providing palettes for expediting common tasks, QuarkXPress provides additional palettes that are the only method for completing a task. Depending on the type of work you do, you may never encounter these palettes. For example, the Lists palette is useful for creating a table of contents, but if you only work on single-page ads, you may never need it. The special-purpose palettes in QuarkXPress are described in the following sections.

Library palettes

QuarkXPress lets you store layout elements (text boxes or picture boxes, lines, or groups) in a Library palette. To use this feature, you select the element from the document or the pasteboard and drag it into an open Library palette. You then can use items stored in the library in other documents. To open a Library palette such as the one shown in Figure 2-20, choose File ⇨ Open ⇨ Library.

Chapter 33 covers libraries in detail.

Figure 2-20: A Library palette.

Trap Information palette

Trapping controls how one color in a document prints next to another color. In the Trap Information palette (shown in Figure 2-21) you can set or change trapping specifications for selected items: the range is –36 to 36 points. To display the Trap Information palette, choose View ⇨ Show Trap Information (or press Option+F12 on the Mac or Ctrl+F12 in Windows).

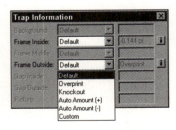

Figure 2-21: The Trap Information palette.

Chapter 30 provides more information about trapping.

Don't use the Trap Information palette unless you know what you're doing. Trapping is considered an expert feature, and you may produce uneven results when you print your document if you aren't sure how to use it.

Profile Information palette

The Profile Information palette, shown in Figure 2-22, shows information related to color management for a selected image.

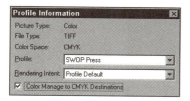

Figure 2-22: The Profile Information palette.

Lists palette

A *list* is a group of paragraph style sheets that lets you list the text of this style at a different location. For example, if you're building a long document, you can specify a "chapter" and a "section" style sheet as a list, and then use the Update button on the Lists palette (see Figure 2-23) to cause QuarkXPress to automatically create the table of contents for the document. The Lists palette displays all the text associated with the style sheets in the document's list configuration. To display the Lists palette, choose View ➪ Lists (or press Option+F11 on the Mac or Ctrl+F11 in Windows).

Cross-Reference For more information on these innovative and powerful tools, see Chapter 16.

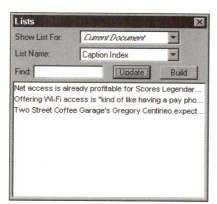

Figure 2-23: The Lists palette.

Layers palette

The new Layers palette, shown in Figure 2-24, lets you separate your document's components into layers. You could, for example, put annotations or instructions on a layer then hide that layer for final output, or in a multilingual document have each language's text on its own layer so you can selectively output one language at a time while reusing the graphics and basic layout. However you use it, the Layers palette is a great way to organize your document's components.

Figure 2-24: The Layers palette.

Index palette

QuarkXPress lets you insert markers on certain words in a document as you're creating it or reading it. The Index palette, shown in Figure 2-25, then copies the marked text and generates an alphabetized, hierarchical index. When you're satisfied that the Index palette has all the entries, you build the index by choosing Utilities ➪ Build Index. To display the Index palette, choose View ➪ Index (or press Option+⌘+I or Ctrl+Alt+I).

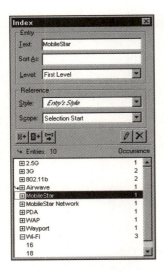

Figure 2-25: The Index palette.

Web-oriented palettes

All the Web palettes are new to QuarkXPress 5.

Placeholders palette

The Placeholders palette, shown in Figure 2-26, is used in creating XML files, a database language used to produce structured Web content. It shows the records defined in a particular XML file.

Chapter 39 covers XML in more detail.

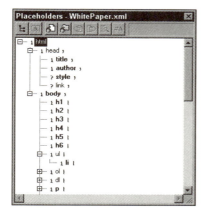

Figure 2-26: The Placeholders palette.

Sequences palette

The Sequences palette, shown in Figure 2-27, builds a list of objects to be displayed or linked to in a Web page. The sequence created in this palette is essentially a mini-program to display certain items in a certain order.

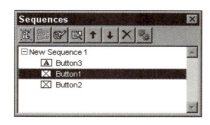

Figure 2-27: The Sequences palette.

Hyperlinks palette

The Hyperlinks palette, shown in Figure 2-28, contains a list of hyperlinks to Web pages and to document pages used in the current QuarkXPress Web document.

Figure 2-28: The Hyperlinks palette.

Introducing Menus

The menu bar appears across the top of the screen. To display, or *pull down,* a menu, click the menu title and hold down the mouse button. From the menu, you can select any of the active menu commands; other commands that aren't available to you (that is, commands whose functions don't apply to whatever you happen to be doing at a given moment in the program) cannot be selected. QuarkXPress displays inactive menu commands with *dimmed* (grayed-out) letters.

To select one of the active menu commands, you simply continue to hold down the mouse button as you slide through the menu selections. As you gain familiarity with the program, you can avoid using menus by using the keyboard equivalents for menu selections. Keyboard equivalents are displayed to the right of the command name. If an arrow appears to the right of a menu command, QuarkXPress displays a second, associated menu when you choose that command. This secondary menu appears automatically when you highlight the first menu command.

✦ **File menu:** This contains the basic commands to open, save, print, and otherwise work with files.

✦ **Edit menu:** This contains the menu items to change program and document settings and to create basic components, such as style tags and color definitions.

✦ **Style menu for text:** This contains the options to format text and create hyperlinks in Web pages.

✦ **Style menu for pictures:** This contains the options to manage the appearance of images as well as to create hyperlinks within Web pages.

✦ **Style menu for lines:** This contains the options to manage the appearance of lines.

✦ **Item menu:** This contains the options to manage attributes of items, from modifying size and shape to setting text that wraps around them to determining basic interactive functionality for the Web.

✦ **Page menu:** This provides controls for creating and managing pages, as well as navigating among them.

✦ **View menu:** This lets you change how documents display on-screen, as well as control which QuarkXPress palettes are displayed. Windows has a separate Window menu that manages the document-window display; on the Mac, this is part of the View menu.

✦ **Utilities menu:** This provides access to various mini-programs within QuarkXPress, such as spell checking, tracking definitions, and font and image usage.

✦ **Scripts menu:** When the Scripts XTension is running, you can launch Apple-events scripts from this menu — provided that those scripts are stored in the Scripts folder inside your QuarkXPress folder. (This menu is available only on the Mac.)

✦ **Help menu:** This menu provides access to Quark's online help files.

Using Measurement Systems

QuarkXPress lets you select a measurement system for both the horizontal and vertical rulers you use to lay out a document. (Rulers and guides are covered earlier in this chapter.) You select a measurement system by choosing Edit ➪ Preferences ➪ Preferences (or by pressing Option+Shift+⌘+Y or Ctrl+Alt+Shift), and then selecting the Measurements pane, as shown in Figure 2-29. In the figure, the options for Vertical Measure are shown; the same options are available for Horizontal Measure. Many publishers use picas for horizontal measurements but inches for vertical (as in the phrase *column inch*).

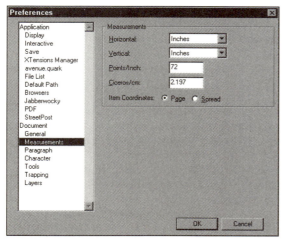

Figure 2-29: The Measurements pane in the Preferences dialog box.

Setting measurement preferences

Whichever system of measurement you use, you can control how the coordinates for layout elements are calculated. Select Item Coordinates in the Measurements pane of the Preferences dialog box to tell QuarkXPress whether to base your ruler and box coordinates on a page or on a spread. If you treat each page as a separate element, keep the option set to Page, which is the default setting (refer to Figure 2-29). If you work on a spread as a single unit, change the setting to Spread. If you choose Spread, the coordinate system is continuous from the left edge of the leftmost page to the right edge of the rightmost page. If you choose Page, the rightmost horizontal coordinate of the right page is the same as the rightmost horizontal coordinate of the left page (0, unless you've moved the ruler origin).

Entering values

No matter what you choose, you can use any measurement in any dialog box or palette; just enter the code (shown in parentheses in the following list) that tells QuarkXPress what the system is. The measurement system options, which can be different for the horizontal and vertical rulers, are as follows:

✦ **Inches:** Inches (") are displayed on the ruler divided into eighths, in typical inch format (¼-inch, ½-inch, and so on).

✦ **Inches decimal:** Inches (") are displayed on the ruler in decimal format, divided into tenths.

✦ **Picas:** One pica (p) is about 0.166 inches. There are 6 picas in an inch.

✦ **Points:** One point (pt) is approximately ½₂ (0.01388) of an inch, or 0.351 millimeter.

✦ **Millimeters:** A metric measurement unit — 25.4 millimeters (mm) equals 1 inch; 1 mm equals 0.03937 inch.

✦ **Centimeters:** A metric measurement unit — 2.54 centimeters (cm) is an inch; 1 cm equals 0.3937 inch.

✦ **Ciceros:** This measurement unit is used in most of Europe; 1 cicero (c) is approximately 0.1792 inch. This is close in size to a pica, which is 0.167 inch.

✦ **Agates:** One agate (ag) is 0.071 inch.

Performing math

In addition to entering values in fields, you can enter calculations. You can add, subtract, multiply, and divide values in fields using the following operators +, −, * (multiply), and / (divide). For example, to reduce the width of a frame by half, you might type **/2** next to the current value of 4.5 in. in the Width field. Or, to increase the length of a line by 6 points, you can type **+6** next to the current value in the Length field.

The two-sided cicero

There are two accepted measurements for a cicero. A cicero, used in France and most of continental Europe, is based on 12 Didot points. But a Didot point has a different measurement in the United States and Britain than it does elsewhere.

The QuarkXPress default of 2.1967 ciceros per centimeter matches the standard European cicero size. If you use the American-British cicero, the number should be 2.3723. Most people don't have problems using the default values, but it can make a difference in large documents, such as banners, where registration and tiling of multiple pieces is important.

In the Measurements pane of the Preferences dialog box (Option+Shift+⌘+Y or Ctrl+ Alt+Shift+Y), you can set the number of points per inch and the number of ciceros per centimeter through the Points/Inch and Ciceros/cm options, respectively. QuarkXPress uses a default setting of 72 points per inch and 2.1967 ciceros per centimeter. The reason you may want to change these is because the actual number of points per inch is 72.271742, although most people now round that off to 72. (QuarkXPress requires you to round it to 72.271 if you use the actual value.)

Caution   Because of this automatic calculation system, you must be careful how you enter fractional values. Entering $^7/_8$ is fine to get the fraction $^7/_8$ or the decimal 0.875, but entering 7 $^7/_8$ will be read by QuarkXPress as 7$^7/_8$, or 9.625. To enter the equivalent of 7$^7/_8$, you must enter 7+$^7/_8$.

Summary

The more you understand about the QuarkXPress environment you're working in, the easier it is to use. That's why it's important to understand the files that make up the program — including the Required Components (which must be present) and XTensions (which are optional).

After you get the program running and get inside a document, you'll see that Quark has made every effort to create a standard working environment. The document window should operate similar to document windows in your other programs, as should elements of the interface such as menus, dialog boxes, and palettes. Other parts of QuarkXPress are tailored to a design environment — for example, on-screen guides, the pasteboard, and item-creation tools make you feel like you're pasting up a document on a table. QuarkXPress also provides a variety of measurement systems so you can work in the one you're most comfortable with.

✦   ✦   ✦

Setting Preferences and Defaults

Because publishers produce many different types of documents — not to mention PDF files, Web pages, and XML content — you can set up QuarkXPress in almost infinite ways. QuarkXPress 5 expands on an already bewildering array of preference and default settings, providing more than 100 controls over the standard behavior of everything from item-creation tools to hyperlinks. Despite the plethora of controls, you can actually get away with changing little to no preferences and default settings. But if you don't change anything, you're likely to be making the same changes in documents and performing the same workarounds over and over again.

To set up QuarkXPress and your files the way you want them, delving into preference and default settings is definitely worthwhile. Skim through this chapter to pinpoint areas that will ease your daily work. Then look into related chapters for more information as necessary. We discuss most preferences in context of their related features — for example, preferences regarding leading are discussed in the chapter that covers leading. This chapter, therefore, often points you to another chapter.

Understanding Global and Local Controls

Global settings affect everything you do — every document you create, every item you make, and so on. They govern how the software behaves when you perform certain actions. Local changes, on the other hand, affect only selected objects, such as highlighted text or an active page or item. Almost all the preference settings are found in the Preferences dialog box (Edit ➪ Preferences ➪ Preferences, or Option+Shift+⌘+Y or Ctrl+Alt+Shift+Y), which is divided into two main areas: Application and Document/Web Document. Default settings are spread throughout the software but mostly exist in Edit menu commands such as Colors and Style Sheets. In QuarkXPress, global and local changes work as follows:

✦ **Application Preferences are exclusively global.** They define how various features in your copy of QuarkXPress work with any type of file open. In general, Application Preferences don't affect how documents print.

✦ **Document and Web Document Preferences can be global or local.** If you change them with no documents open, they change the behavior of QuarkXPress features for all future documents. If you change them with a document open, they affect only the active document.

✦ **Default settings are changes you make to the list of available colors, H&J sets, style sheets, print styles, and so on.** Some of these lists, such as print styles, are always global. Other lists, such as style sheets, become program defaults when no documents are open, but they apply only to the active document when documents are open.

Sticky settings

In addition to preference and default settings, QuarkXPress has dialog boxes that remember their settings from one use to the next — primarily, New Document and Get Text. The settings are called *sticky* because they don't have defaults; they simply retain your settings until you change them.

In the New Document dialog box (File ➪ New ➪ Document, or ⌘+N or Ctrl+N), this means that the document size, orientation, margins, columns, and so on, that you set up for one document are still there when you set up the next new document. In the Get Text dialog box (File ➪ Get Text, or ⌘+E or Ctrl+E), your settings for Convert Quotes (changing double hyphens to em dashes and straight quotes to curly quotes) and Include Style Sheets (importing style sheets from a word processor), retain their settings until you change them.

Another thing you might consider sticky is which palettes and libraries are open. Every time you launch QuarkXPress, the palettes and libraries you were using last time will open again, in the same position. The tool you're using is also sticky — so if you're working with the Content tool in one document, then switch to another document, you're still using the Content tool.

As we cover the various types of preferences and defaults, we reiterate whether you are making a global or local change.

Changing Default Settings

Default settings, such as the list of colors available, are settings you can make with no documents open. The settings then become part of all new documents you create. Some of the default settings that you change globally can be modified for individual documents. Other settings remain application-wide defaults. The default settings you can change are in the Edit menu and the Utilities menu.

Edit menu defaults

The Edit menu has two types of defaults: Some you can change globally and edit locally, while others you can only change globally. The ones you can edit locally are located between Find/Change and Dashes & Stripes. The ones that cannot be saved with individual documents are located below the line separating Dashes & Stripes and Print Styles, as shown Figure 3-1.

Figure 3-1: When no documents are open, commands for default settings remain active in the Edit menu.

You can change these settings for all new documents, but then change them for an individual document that is active:

✦ **Style Sheets:** You can modify the Normal style sheets (changing the default font, for example) and add your own commonly used style sheets.

✦ **Colors:** You can delete colors you never use — such as the default Red, Green, and Blue, and then add commonly used colors such as the Pantone color in your company logo.

✦ **H&J sets:** You can modify the Standard hyphenation and justification set to suit your editorial style, then add other H&J sets you use often (although H&J sets often need to be modified within documents depending on fonts, column width, and so on).

✦ **Lists:** If you're generating automatic tables of contents (from paragraph style sheets), you can create default lists to be included in all new documents.

✦ **Dashes & Stripes:** You can customize the dash and stripe patterns for lines and frames and include your patterns with all new documents.

Tip

Rather than create style sheets, colors, H&J sets, lists, and dash/stripe patterns when no documents are open, you can use the Append feature to import definitions from existing documents. You can either use the Append button in each dialog box (Style Sheets, Colors, and so on) or the global Append command (File ➪ Append, or Option+⌘+A or Ctrl+Alt+A).

The commands at the bottom of the Edit menu, separated by a line from the other commands, are global. The settings are saved with your copy of QuarkXPress and never with individual documents. These include:

✦ **Print Styles:** You can import and export these print settings to share them with other users since they're not saved with documents.

✦ **Jabberwocky Sets:** These are sets of words that make up "dummy" text for use in preliminary designs; as with print styles, you can import and export jabberwocky text.

✦ **Meta Tags and Menus:** If you create your own meta tags and menus for interactive documents, they are also saved with QuarkXPress.

Utilities menu defaults

When no documents are open, changes you make to any options in the Utilities menu affect all new documents. These include Hyphenation Exceptions, Auxiliary Dictionaries, Tracking Edit, and Kerning Edit. You can also make changes in the XTensions Manager, which will control which XTensions load with QuarkXPress but has no effect on individual documents.

Setting Application Preferences

Application preferences are saved in the XPress Preferences file and not with each document. These preferences control how QuarkXPress works with all files — print documents, Web documents, libraries, and so on — so any changes you make in Application Preferences apply to all files you create or edit using your copy of QuarkXPress.

To open Application Preferences, choose Edit ⇨ Preferences ⇨ Preferences, or press Option+Shift+⌘+Y or Ctrl+Alt+Shift+Y at any time. Click a pane under the Application heading to change any settings.

New Feature

In previous versions of QuarkXPress, Application Preferences were stored tidily in their own dialog box, so it was clear that they were a different type of setting. Now, with the scroll list in the comprehensive Preferences dialog box, you'll just have to pay attention to the fact that you're in the Application area.

Cross-Reference

If it's important that all members of your workgroup use the same Application Preferences, see Chapter 31 for information about copying and distributing XPress Preferences files.

Display pane

Options in the Display pane, shown in Figure 3-2, control the way QuarkXPress displays guides, documents, picture previews, and more. The way you set these will vary depending on your personal preferences and your system.

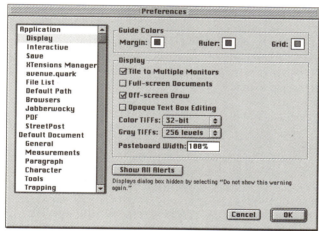

Figure 3-2: The Display pane of Application Preferences.

Guide Colors area

You can change the color of Margin, Ruler, and Grid guides used for positioning items and text. These colors also correspond to guides that display when you're editing clipping and runaround paths. The Margin color displays on the item, the Ruler color displays on the clipping path, and the Grid color displays on the text runaround path.

See Chapter 2 for information about changing Guide Colors.

Monitor display options

Three options in the Display pane of Application Preferences control how QuarkXPress documents relate to the monitor's screen area. The default view, which appears each time you start up the application or open a new document, is Actual Size (100 percent). The following list describes each option in detail:

✦ **Tile to Multiple Monitors:** If you have multiple monitors attached to your Mac, this tells QuarkXPress to automatically put some document windows on your secondary monitor(s) when you choose Tile Documents. Use the Monitors control panel that comes with your system disks to set up multiple monitors.

Although Windows does support multiple monitors, QuarkXPress for Windows does not support the Tile to Multiple Monitors option.

✦ **Full-Screen Documents:** If you check this box, the document window will appear at the screen's far left, under the default position for the Tool palette. Unless you move the Tool palette down, you'll find that having this option enabled obscures the document window's close box. Therefore, we recommend that you not routinely use this option. There *is* one advantage to using it, however: It can give your document window enough width to fully display a document. When you use it, just make sure that you move your Tool palette so that you can click the close box.

The Full-Screen Documents option is not available in QuarkXPress for Windows.

✦ **Off-screen Draw:** This option controls how QuarkXPress displays elements on your screen as you scroll through a document. If checked, it redraws each element displayed in order of display. If unchecked, it draws them in memory first and then displays them all simultaneously. This is a legacy feature that Quark continues to hold onto from previous versions — both options take the same amount of time to redraw the screen, so there is no advantage to either setting. Note that with the Speed Scroll option selected in the Interactive pane, the Off-screen Draw option has no noticeable effect.

Opaque Text Box Editing

This addition, which was introduced in QuarkXPress 4.1, controls whether the background of the active text box is opaque. Why do you care? Because when the background is opaque, it's often easier to see the text and edit it. But when it's not, you can see any background illustrations or graphics and edit text in relation to them. Set this according to how design-intensive your documents are — if interplay between text and graphics is imperative, leave it unchecked.

Image-display options

The Color TIFFs and Gray TIFFs settings control the accuracy of the colors and shades in the on-screen previews generated for imported TIFF images. Lower bit depths can result in considerably smaller document files because of the low bit depth of the resulting TIFF image previews. If you're trying to match colors on-screen, and you have a higher-end system, you can set the bit depths higher.

Tip

The image-display controls are designed primarily to let you control the balance between speed and fidelity. Typically, layout artists don't need to see a superior-quality image of the things they're placing. They just need to see what the image looks like and what its dimensions are. QuarkXPress lets you determine the trade-off between speed and fidelity through the Color TIFFs and Gray TIFFs settings.

QuarkXPress for Windows has a unique option called Display DPI Value. This should remain at 96 dpi. Using a larger number permanently zooms the monitor view, while a smaller number zooms out the view.

Pasteboard size

The pasteboard, a nonprinting area at the sides of each page or spread, serves as an electronic scratchpad for creating page elements. If you don't use the pasteboard, you may want to reduce its size. Even if empty, the pasteboard takes up space on your screen that affects scrolling because the scroll width includes the pasteboard area. At 100 percent, the pasteboard is equal to one page. If you do reduce your pasteboard, items may extend beyond it and appear to be cut off; they actually remain intact.

Cross-Reference

See Chapter 2 for information about changing the pasteboard size.

Show All Alerts button

New Feature

The Show All Alerts button is a new feature in QuarkXPress 5.

This new feature is kind of a "reset" button for the many alerts in QuarkXPress that give you the option of turning them off. For example, when you append style sheets to another document, QuarkXPress warns you that the style sheet is bringing any necessary colors, H&J sets, and so on with it. Because this is expected (and good) behavior, you can turn off this alert by checking Do Not Show This Warning Again. Sometimes, you regret turning off alerts, or perhaps a novice user is now working with a copy of QuarkXPress that has the alerts turned off and, thus, doesn't realize what is happening in the background. If you want to reenable the alerts, just click Show All Alerts to reset your copy of QuarkXPress.

Interactive pane

The Interactive pane of Application Preferences, shown in Figure 3-3, would more accurately be called the Miscellaneous pane. (You could make a case, we suppose, that the controls over scrolling, smart quotes, dragging, and so on affect how you interact with QuarkXPress.)

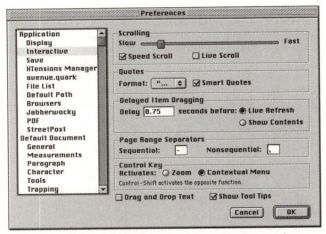

Figure 3-3: The Interactive pane of Application Preferences.

Scrolling

Use the Scrolling slider to control how fast the page scrolls when you click the arrows in the scroll bars. If you set the slider closer to Slow, QuarkXPress moves more slowly across your document, which is helpful if you want to pay close attention to your document while scrolling. If you set the slider closer to Fast, QuarkXPress zips across the document, which may cause you to move past a desired element.

Most people prefer a Scrolling setting somewhere in the middle range. You may have to adjust the setting a few times until it feels right to you. Generally, it should be slightly closer to Fast than to Slow.

The two other options in the scrolling section of the dialog box work as follows:

✦ **Speed Scroll:** This option speeds up scrolling in graphics-intensive documents by masking out the graphics and blends as you scroll. After you stop scrolling, the graphics and blends are redrawn. Generally, you should check this option.

✦ **Live Scroll:** If you check this option, QuarkXPress redraws pages while you're dragging the box in the scroll bar. Generally, you should check this option, unless you're working on a slower computer.

Smart Quotes

In the Quotes area, the Smart Quotes check box controls whether straight quotes are converted to typographer's quotation marks as you type. The style of quotes you select from the menu is used when you check Convert Quotes in the Get Text dialog box (File ➪ Get Text, or ⌘+E or Ctrl+E).

Cross-Reference

See Chapter 11 for more information about setting the Quotes options.

Delayed Item Dragging

The options in the Delayed Item Dragging area control how items display when you drag them with the Item tool. If you simply select an item and drag it immediately, these controls are ignored (all you see is the outline of the item until you finish moving it, then the text reflows as necessary and the item displays again). However, if you click and hold for a certain time, then drag the item, you have the option of either seeing the text wrap change or simply seeing the contents of the item.

✦ The value you enter in the Delay Seconds field controls the time (in seconds ranging between 0.1 and 5) that you must press and hold the mouse button before Show Contents or Live Refresh is activated.

✦ If Live Refresh is selected when you press and hold the mouse button as you begin dragging an item, the contents of the item are visible as you drag it, and the screen also refreshes to show item layers and text flow.

✦ If Show Contents is selected and you press and hold the mouse button as you begin dragging an item, the contents of the item are visible as you drag it (but the text flow doesn't update until you finish moving the item).

If you're working with design-intensive text wraps, we recommend that you check Live Refresh.

Page Range Separators

The Page Range Separators option may look like an addition to QuarkXPress, but it isn't. This refugee from the QuarkXPress 4 Print dialog box defines the characters used to define a range of pages that you're printing. But it's only necessary if you're using the Section feature — and then only if you're using a hyphen or a comma within your section page numbers. By default, you use a hyphen in a sequential range of pages and a comma between nonsequential pages, but with the Section feature you might actually use a hyphen within a page number (page A-1, A-2, and so on). And, conceivably, you could use a comma in page numbers, however unlikely a scenario that is. If you do end up using one of the default page range separators within your page numbers, you can change them here.

Control Key

This Mac-only feature lets you decide whether pressing the Control key lets you zoom in or access one of the context menus (Control+Option will still let you zoom out). The default setting, Contextual Menu, means that when you Control+click a page or item, a menu of editing options displays. You will need to press Control+Shift to zoom. If you change the setting to Zoom, then the Control key lets you zoom in while Control+Shift displays context menus.

Experienced QuarkXPress for Mac users may wish to change the Control Key setting to Zoom so the software continues to work as it has for the last decade. QuarkXPress used to use the Control key as a quick way to activate the Zoom tool, but when Apple introduced context menus in Mac OS 8, QuarkXPress conflicted with a standard Mac OS function. But for those users who don't want to change their behavior, QuarkXPress 5 has this option to let them still use just Control for zooming.

Because Windows has no Control key, there is no Control Key option in Windows QuarkXPress. You simply right-click to get context menus in Windows QuarkXPress.

Drag and Drop Text

When Drag and Drop Text is checked, you can highlight text and drag it to a new location rather than using cut and paste. If you hold down the Shift key, a copy of the highlighted text is moved to the new location instead of the original.

On the Mac, you can enable drag-and-drop editing even when the Drag and Drop Text option is not enabled by pressing Ô+Control (to move text) or Shift+Ô+ Control (to copy text).

See Chapter 13 for more information about using drag-and-drop editing.

Show Tool Tips

This helpful option shows you the official name of each tool and icon on the many palettes that make up QuarkXPress. Simply point at something, and if it has a Tool Tip, a little box shows up. Knowing the official name makes it much easier to look up information in the help file, the manuals provided by Quark, and books such as this. (It is, after all, difficult to look up "the little hand tool.") This is checked by default, and since it does no harm, you may as well leave it that way.

Save pane

The Save pane contains several preferences related to how QuarkXPress files are saved. You can choose to automatically save files, create automatic backups of files, automatically save libraries, and save the position of documents on-screen. These options are found in the Save pane of Application Preferences, shown in Figure 3-4.

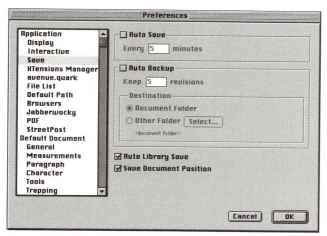

Figure 3-4: The Save pane of Application Preferences.

Auto Save

Checking Auto Save prompts QuarkXPress to save all open documents at regular intervals. You determine that interval through the value you enter in the Every Minutes field. Auto Save is off by default, because it has an annoying tendency to interrupt your work—and because many people are already in the habit of constantly saving their work. We recommend that you check it, but then experiment with the interval to find something that works for you. You may be reluctant to lose even 5 minutes of work, and therefore you may be willing to put up with the disruptive saves. Or you may be willing to work for up to 15 minutes without a save. (After all, you can still save manually in between automatic saves.)

When an auto save occurs, QuarkXPress does not actually save your document to its regular document file; instead, it creates an autosave document (with a file name that ends in .AutoSave on the Mac and .asv in Windows). If your computer crashes, you can revert your file to its last auto-saved condition by opening the autosave document.

Tip   QuarkXPress provides an interesting option for you to revert a document to its last auto-saved version. Because the software doesn't really announce when it's performing an auto save (aside from interrupting your work if you're doing anything during an auto save), it's difficult to see when the need for this would arise. Nonetheless, you can do it by pressing Option or Alt while you choose Revert to Saved from the File menu.

Auto Backup

You can also have QuarkXPress retain backup copies of your document by checking the Auto Backup box. When this option is checked, QuarkXPress creates a backup copy of your document every time you manually save it—that means that every time you choose File ➪ Save (or press ⌘+S or Ctrl+S), QuarkXPress creates an entire additional copy of your document and stores it on your computer.

✦ You decide how many versions to keep by entering a value up to 100 in the Keep Revisions field. (Keep in mind the size of your documents when setting this option — retaining a large number of revisions can quickly eat up hard drive space.) When the maximum number of revisions has been saved, QuarkXPress starts deleting the oldest revision to make room for the newest.

✦ You determine where backups are stored by choosing one of the two destination buttons. The default location is in the same folder as the current document, but we highly recommend that you change it because it's very easy to then open the wrong version of a file. Click Other Folder, then use the Select button to select or create a backups folder. If you need to access a backup, navigate to this folder.

Tip   Auto Backup is off by default. If you're in the habit of constantly saving documents manually, you may as well leave it off because your automatic backups will each represent only a few more minutes of work. To have Auto Backup function as a true revisions feature — for example, to show the work you did on a document each time you open it — let the Auto Save feature save your documents, then let Auto Backup create one revision when you close the file.

Auto Library Save

When Auto Library Save is checked, as it is by default, any changes you make to libraries are instantly saved. Otherwise, QuarkXPress saves changes to libraries when you close them or quit QuarkXPress. There is little reason to ever uncheck this, although some contend that it makes adding a multitude of library items a tiny bit slower.

Save Document Position

When Save Document Position is checked, QuarkXPress saves the size and position of the document window along with the document itself. If you're sharing documents among users with monitors of different sizes, or you often rearrange document windows to drag items among documents, you may want to uncheck this. After all, the previous user's size and position may not make sense in your workflow.

XTensions Manager pane

The XTensions Manager pane of Application Preferences, shown in Figure 3-5, controls if and when the XTensions Manager dialog box displays when you launch QuarkXPress. In a service bureau, for example, you might want to see the XTensions Manager at every launch.

Cross-Reference   See Chapter 41 for complete information about setting these options.

Avenue.Quark pane

The Avenue.Quark pane of Application Preferences, shown in Figure 3-6, lets you establish some tagging standards for XML files.

Cross-Reference   See Chapter 39 for information about setting these options.

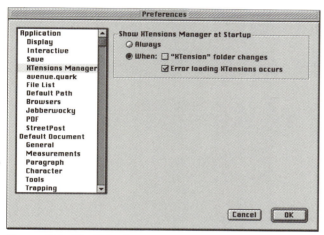

Figure 3-5: The XTensions Manager pane of Application Preferences.

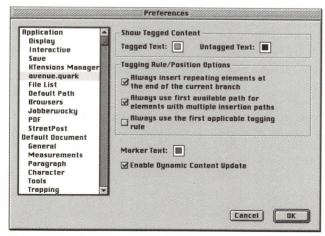

Figure 3-6: The Avenue.Quark pane of Application Preferences.

File List pane

The File List pane of Application Preferences, shown in Figure 3-7, is a product of an XTension bundled with QuarkXPress since version 4.1 called Dejavu. This XTension adds a list of recently opened files to the File menu or to the File ➪ Open submenu, as you prefer, for easier access — you simply select the file name and QuarkXPress goes out, finds it, and opens it for you. But you'll need to tweak the settings to appreciate this feature's value.

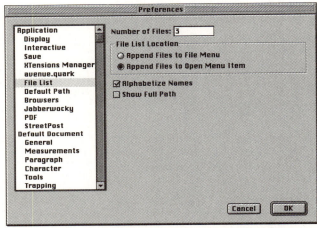

Figure 3-7: The File List pane of Application Preferences.

Number of Files

The Number of Files field controls how many recently opened files are listed. The default setting, three, is fairly small. Five might be better, or even ten for a service bureau environment.

Listing recently opened files

The File List Location area controls where recently opened files are shown in the File menu. The default setting, Append Files to Open Menu Item, adds a submenu to the Open command in the File menu. Although this keeps the File menu nice and short, it makes the Open command inaccessible except through the submenu. We prefer Append Files to File Menu. Two check boxes control how the files are listed in the location you specify:

✦ **Alphabetize Names** gives you an alphabetical rather than chronological list of recently opened files. Most users, however, expect a chronological list that shows the most-recently opened file first (since this is usually the one you end up needing to reopen); the default setting of Alphabetical Names is therefore disconcerting, so we recommend you uncheck it.

✦ **Show Full Path** precedes each file name with its location (truncated if necessary). The full paths can certainly consume screen real estate, but they may be useful if you need to find a file to send it elsewhere, or if you have multiple versions of a file in different locations. Most users can stick with the default setting of unchecked for Show Full Path.

Default Path pane

Another product of the bundled Dejavu XTension, the Default Path pane, shown in Figure 3-8, lets you point QuarkXPress in the right direction when you're opening files, saving files, or importing text and pictures. To do this, you tell QuarkXPress where you commonly store these items. Then when you open their respective dialog boxes, you're in the right location. For example, if you always store text files in one folder, you can have that folder automatically open every time you choose File ⇨ Get Text (or ⌘+E or Ctrl+E). Obviously, this is only helpful if you keep all your documents in one location, your graphics files in another location, and so on, instead of grouping files by project or client.

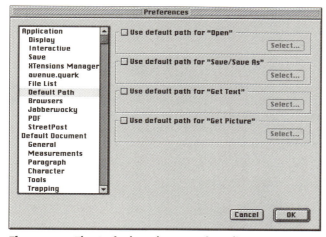

Figure 3-8: The Default Path pane of Application Preferences.

You can set a default path for the following File menu options: Open, Save/Save As, Get Text, and Get Picture. Simply check its box and use the Select button to specify the default folder for that dialog box.

Browsers pane

The Browsers pane of Application Preferences, shown in Figure 3-9, lets you specify the Web browsers that you want to use for previewing Web documents. Most Web designers preview documents in at least the latest versions of Internet Explorer and Netscape Navigator.

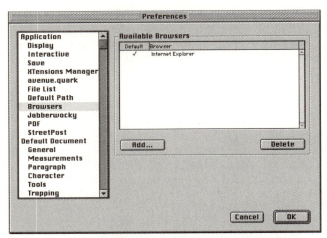

Figure 3-9: The Browsers pane of Application Preferences.

Cross-Reference   For more information about this preference, see Chapter 38.

Jabberwocky pane

Jabberwocky is a popular XTension from Quark that lets you generate customized dummy text for preliminary designs. It's been around as a freebie for years but wasn't actually bundled with QuarkXPress until version 4.1. The Jabberwocky pane of Application Preferences, shown in Figure 3-10, lets you specify the default word set used for dummy text and its format.

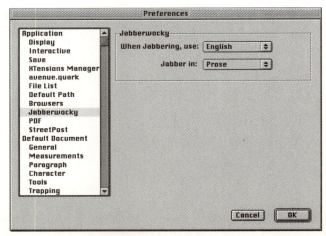

Figure 3-10: The Jabberwocky pane of Application Preferences.

See Chapter 12 for complete information about using Jabberwocky and setting these preferences.

PDF pane

If you're using the PDF Filter XTension included with QuarkXPress 5 to create PDF files, the PDF pane of Application Preferences (shown in Figure 3-11) lets you specify when the files are distilled. The Options button lets you specify how hyperlinks are translated, override some Distiller options, and change output settings.

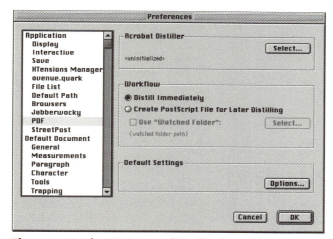

Figure 3-11: The PDF pane of Application Preferences.

See Chapter 40 for complete information about using the PDF Filter XTension and setting these preferences.

StreetPost pane

The StreetPost pane of Application Preferences, shown in Figure 3-12, comes into play when you're working with Avenue.Quark and XML.

See Chapter 39 for more information.

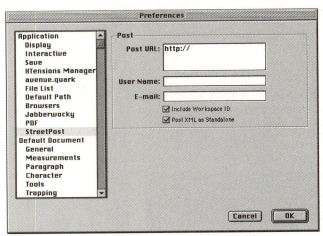

Figure 3-12: The StreetPost pane of Application Preferences.

Setting Document and Web Document Preferences

When no documents are open, Document Preferences — and Web Document Preferences, which offer essentially the same options — are saved in the XPress Preferences file and affect all future documents. When documents are open, changes to Document Preferences and Web Document Preferences affect only the active document.

Note   The Web Document Preferences panes are available only when a Web document is open or no documents are open.

To open Document Preferences, choose Edit ➪ Preferences ➪ Preferences, or press ⌘+Y or Ctrl+Y at any time. Click a pane under the Document or Web Document heading to change any settings.

Tip   You can use the simple shortcut ⌘+Y or Ctrl+Y to go straight to the General pane of the Document preferences. The more cumbersome Option+Shift+⌘+Y or Ctrl+Alt+Shift+Y shortcut, which is the standard shortcut for accessing the Preferences dialog box, goes to the last-opened Preferences pane.

New Feature   Over the last few versions of QuarkXPress, document-based preferences have morphed from their own dialog boxes (Measurements, Typographic, and so on) in version 3.x, to the multi-paned Document Preferences dialog box in version 4.x, and finally to the comprehensive Preferences dialog box in version 5. When you're working in the Preferences dialog box, be sure to pay attention to where you're at — under Application or Document — to know how the changes will affect your work.

General pane

The General pane of Document Preferences, shown in Figure 3-13, contains a cornucopia of controls, ranging from whether graphics display to how boxes are framed.

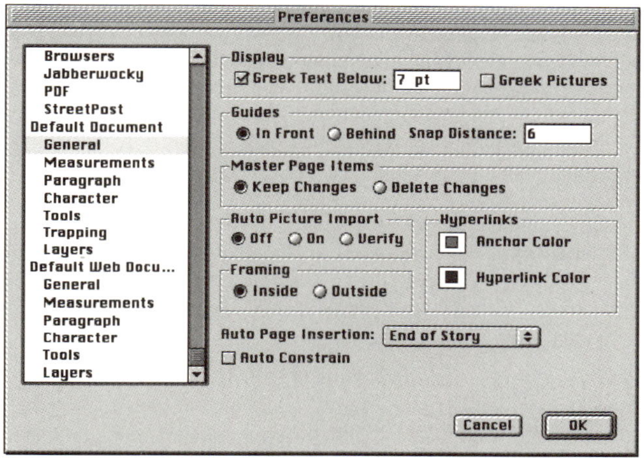

Figure 3-13: The General pane of Document Preferences.

With the exception of the Display options, these controls are discussed in other chapters, so we'll point you in the right direction:

- ✦ **Guides:** See Chapter 2.
- ✦ **Master Page Items:** See Chapter 9.
- ✦ **Auto Picture Import:** See Chapter 20.
- ✦ **Hyperlinks:** See Chapter 38.
- ✦ **Framing:** See Chapter 8.
- ✦ **Auto Page Insertion:** See Chapter 12.
- ✦ **Auto Constrain:** See Chapter 8.

Display options

When you use greeking, QuarkXPress displays a gray area to represent text or pictures on the page. Turning on greeking speeds up the display of your QuarkXPress document because QuarkXPress doesn't have to draw every tiny bit of text and every graphic. In fact, greeking—particularly when used for pictures—is one of the best ways to save screen redraw time. When you print, images are unaffected by greeking.

✦ **Greek Text Below:** This option tells QuarkXPress to greek the text display when text is below a certain point size. The default value is 7 points, but you can enter any value from 2 to 720 points. To disable greeking, uncheck the Greek Below box. Note that this feature is affected by view scale, so if you're viewing a document at 200 percent, only text below 3.5 points is greeked; if you're viewing a document at 50 percent, text below 14 points is greeked.

✦ **Greek Pictures:** This option tells QuarkXPress to display all unselected graphics as gray shapes, which speeds up the display considerably. This feature is useful after you position and size your images and no longer need to see them on your layout. You can still view a greeked picture by clicking it.

Measurements pane

In the Measurements pane of Document Preferences, shown in Figure 3-14, you can set the default measurement system displayed in most fields (although some options, such as type size, are always expressed in points). Although you set up Web documents in pixels (equal to points on-screen), the measurement systems work the same for both print and Web documents.

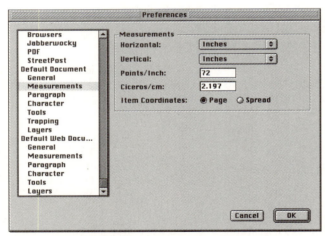

Figure 3-14: The Measurements pane of Document Preferences.

Cross-Reference   For information about setting these preferences, see Chapter 2.

Paragraph pane

The Paragraph pane of Document Preferences, shown in Figure 3-15, offers options for horizontal and vertical spacing: leading, baseline grid, and hyphenation. These features are all discussed in detail in Part IV. The hyphenation setting is only there to keep QuarkXPress compatible with previous versions, but the leading and baseline grid options have a significant impact on spacing in documents. The Paragraph pane has its own keyboard shortcut: Option+⌘+Y or Ctrl+Alt+Y.

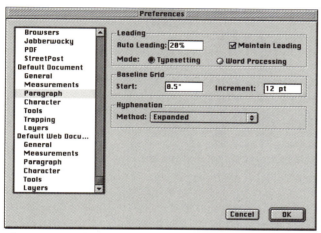

Figure 3-15: The Paragraph pane of Document Preferences.

 For information about leading, see Chapter 16. The baseline grid and hyphenation preferences are discussed in Chapter 17.

Character pane

You can customize character attributes such as type styles in the Character pane of Document Preferences, shown in Figure 3-15. For the most part, you'll make these decisions only once, as they are appropriate for most documents. Some, however, are related to your designs and workflow — for example, if you work in a cross-platform environment, you may want to turn off Ligatures, because they aren't supported on Windows. Or, if a particular design uses Small Caps frequently, you might tweak its settings in one document.

 The features in the Character pane are all covered in Part IV. See Chapter 15 for information about Superscript, Subscript, Small Caps, Superior, and Auto Kern Above. See Chapter 17 for information about Flex Space Width and Standard Em Space. Chapter 18 covers Ligatures and Accents for All Caps.

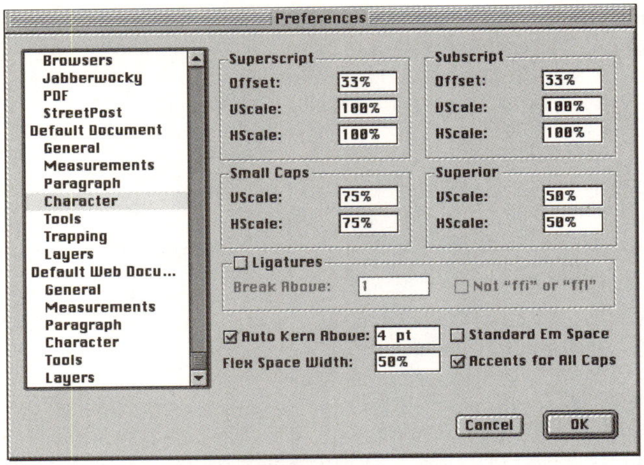

Figure 3-16: The Character pane of Document Preferences.

Tools pane

QuarkXPress lets you customize how its basic tools — in particular the item-creation tools and the Zoom tool — work by changing settings in the Tools pane of Document Preferences (see Figure 3-17). The ability to customize certain settings comes in handy. You can, for example, give oval picture boxes an offset of 1 pica, or set text boxes to have a 3-point frame and a transparent background. To open the Tools pane, you can double-click any tool that can be modified.

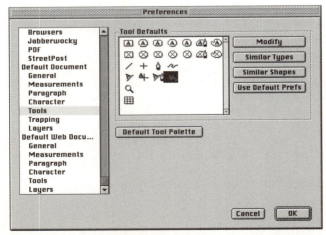

Figure 3-17: The Tools pane of Document Preferences.

Selecting tools to customize

After the Tools pane is open, you first need to select the tools you want to modify:

✦ To select one tool, simply click on it.

✦ To select noncontiguous tools, ⌘+click or Ctrl+click them.

✦ To select a range of continuous tools, Shift+click them.

✦ To select all the item-creation tools of one type (text box, picture box, line, or text path), select one and then click Similar Types.

✦ To select all the tools that create items of the same shape (for example, all oval boxes), select one and then click Similar Shapes.

When the tools are selected, you can click Modify to access the customizable options that the tools have in common. If you select all the text-box creation tools, for example, you'll be able to specify a default number of columns for all text boxes. Commands that don't make sense as defaults — such as size and placement — are not included.

Tools you can customize

The tools you can customize fall into the following groups:

✦ **Zoom tool:** You can change the minimum and maximum zoom views to any value between 10 and 800 percent. You also can specify how much QuarkXPress zooms into your document each time you click the document with the Zoom tool active. To do this, enter any value from 10 to 800 percent, in increments of 1 percent, into the Increment field.

✦ **Box tools:** You can set the item settings for all the Text Box and Picture Box tools. You can establish settings for options normally available for the individual boxes via the Item menu's Modify, Frame, and Runaround options. If you select one of these box tools from the Tool pane and click Modify, a dialog box containing three tabbed panes — corresponding to those item menu options — appears, and you can set these options just as you do if you select a box on a document page. The difference is that you're setting them as defaults.

Tip

One change we recommend making: Get rid of the default 1-point text inset for all text-box creation tools (unless you frame every box). You can change this in the Text Inset area of the Text pane that displays when you modify text-box tools.

✦ **Drawing tools:** You can establish defaults for new lines that you draw with the Line and Text Path tools. You can set most regular-line options that are normally available through the Item menu. You can also set other line-specification and runaround options, such as line color and weight.

✦ **Tables tool:** You can modify some default characteristics of tables — for example, the number of rows and columns in a table and the table borders.

Tip

When changing preferences for the item-creation tools, pay attention to whether any documents are open. If no documents are open, the changes affect all new documents and should therefore be largely appropriate for all your designs. Changes you make to the behavior of the Zoom tool are likely to be appropriate for all your documents, so you might want to be sure no documents are open.

Reverting to default tools

If you find that modifications made to tools are not appropriate to a document (or any document), you can revert the changes made in the Tools pane. Simply select the tools you want to revert, and then click Use Default Prefs.

If your Tool palette has been added to and reorganized beyond recognition, you can also revert the palette to its default state by clicking Default Tool Palette. This moves all the tools back into their pop-outs, leaving you with one of each tool.

Trapping pane

Trap options define how QuarkXPress prints overlapping colors when you print separations to PostScript printers. The Trapping pane has its own shortcut: Option+Shift+F12 or Ctrl+Shift+F12.

Cross-Reference

The options in the Trapping pane of Document Preferences, shown in Figure 3-18, are covered in full in Chapter 30.

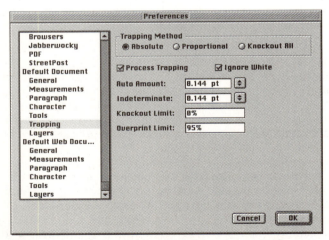

Figure 3-18: The Trapping pane of Document Preferences.

Layers pane

Layers are slices of a document, similar to overhead transparencies or the rubyliths of manual paste-up days, that are stacked on top of each other. Layers, which are actually document-wide rather than page-specific, help you organize content and store multiple versions of the same publication in a single document file.

Cross-Reference For information about options in the Layers pane of Document Preferences, shown in Figure 3-19, see Chapter 10.

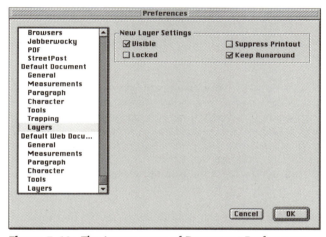

Figure 3-19: The Layers pane of Document Preferences.

Setting Special-Purpose Preferences

Outside of the comprehensive Preferences dialog box, you'll find several other options in the Preferences submenu of the Edit menu — depending on which XTensions you're running. If the default set of XTensions that ship with QuarkXPress are loaded, you'll see the Color Management, Index, and Fraction/Price options.

✦ Color Management Preferences, covered in Chapter 29, are saved in the XPress Preferences file, not with individual documents. You can change many of the options while importing graphics into and printing from individual documents. (If the Quark CMS XTension is not running, you will not have Color Management Preferences available.)

✦ Index Preferences, covered in Chapter 34, are saved with the active document. If no documents are open, the preferences become program defaults. The preferences relate mostly to punctuation within an index, so if you create standard indexes for all publications, you'll want to set program defaults. (If the Index XTension is not running, you won't have Index Preferences available.)

✦ Fraction/Price Preferences, covered in Chapter 18, are saved only in the XPress Preferences file. This is unfortunate, because the settings may vary according to the actual type sizes and fonts in use. If you change these settings for specific designs, jot them down. (If the Type Tricks XTension is not running, you won't have Fraction/Price Preferences available.)

Summary

Most users jump into QuarkXPress and work away — for years — without ever touching preference or default settings. This is unfortunate because it leads to duplication of effort and workarounds. Every time you find yourself repeating the same actions, from creating the same color over and over to changing the same attributes of every picture box, look into preference and default settings. Chances are, you'll be able to make documents include options that you want, and you'll be able to have tools behave your way. A few things to remember about default settings and preferences:

✦ You modify default settings, such as the default list of colors included with documents, when no documents are open. These changes affect all new documents.

✦ You modify default Document Preferences when no documents are open. These changes affect all new documents. You can also modify Document Preferences exclusively for the active document.

✦ Application Preferences affect all documents and always function as program-wide default settings.

✦ Preferences implemented through XTensions are sometimes saved with the active document, but often are application-wide defaults. Look into each XTension's preferences carefully to determine the case.

✦   ✦   ✦

Managing Files

QuarkXPress creates six types of files — print documents, print templates, Web documents, Web templates, libraries, and books — which you open, save, and close using File menu options. QuarkXPress also provides a variety of keyboard shortcuts for speeding up these processes and preferences for automating them. As you become comfortable with QuarkXPress, you'll discover the options that you prefer.

The QuarkXPress file types fill different publishing needs, including creating documents for professional printing, creating HTML files for Web sites, and managing multiple documents that make up a publication. The file types are as follows:

+ **Print document:** The standard file type used to create original documents, such as brochures and magazines that will be printed.

+ **Print template:** A preformatted print document used as a starting point for new documents that will have similar designs. Templates generally contain the "shell" of a document, such as the standing nameplate, headers, footers, and graphics.

+ **Web document:** A document set up specifically for easy conversion to HTML.

+ **Web template:** A preformatted Web document used as a starting point for new Web documents.

+ **Library:** A floating palette used to store commonly used QuarkXPress items, such as logos and graphics. Libraries provide easy drag-and-drop access to items.

+ **Book:** A floating palette used to track the files used in a publication made up of multiple QuarkXPress documents.

Cross-Reference
QuarkXPress also lets you create XML files, which are discussed in Chapter 39.

In general, handling a file in QuarkXPress is the same as handling a file in any other program on your operating system. For example, the Open dialog box that lets you locate files works the same as any other Open dialog box on Macintosh or in Windows. The navigation features that allow you to find a file or select a place to save it conform to your operating system's standards. However, because you may have different file-saving needs or be working with documents from different versions of QuarkXPress, you need to know how QuarkXPress handles files.

Opening Files

QuarkXPress lets you open up to 25 files at once. Basically, there are three methods for opening files: locating the file using the Open dialog box in QuarkXPress, double-clicking a file icon on the desktop, or choosing a recently opened file from the File menu. In general, using the Open dialog box provides more information about files, but double-clicking or choosing a recently opened file can be faster. Use the method that works best for you.

If you move a Windows file to Macintosh or a Macintosh file to Windows, you may not be able to double-click those files and have QuarkXPress launch to open them. If that happens, open QuarkXPress first, then use File⇨Open, or ⌘+O or Ctrl+O, to open the file. If the transferred file doesn't display in the file list, choose Files of All Type in the Files of Type pop-up menu.

If you have more than one version of QuarkXPress on your machine, it's a good idea to get out of the habit of double-clicking files to open them. When you double-click files to open them, you don't know for sure which version of QuarkXPress will launch (usually it's the latest version) and whether the version is appropriate for that file. For example, if you accidentally open and save a library from version 4 in version 5, you will not be able to use that library with version 4 again.

Book and library files are not cross-platform. You cannot open a Macintosh library or book on a Windows PC, and you cannot open a Windows library or book on a Macintosh computer.

Using the Open dialog box

When you open a file through the Open dialog box, you get precise information about the file, such as its type and the version of QuarkXPress last used to save it. If you're receiving files from various clients who may be using different versions of QuarkXPress, this is important information. Version 5 lets you open documents saved in QuarkXPress version 3.1 and greater.

STEPS: Opening a file

1. Choose File ➪ Open, or press ⌘+O or Ctrl+O.

2. Use the standard Macintosh or Windows navigation tools to locate the document, template, library, or book that you want to open.

Tip　On Windows, you can choose to display Display All Files, All QuarkXPress Files, or only Document by choosing an option from the File of Type menu. If you're having trouble locating a file, choose Display All Files.

3. Click on the file to select it, as shown in Figure 4-1. On a Macintosh, you'll see the file type, version, date it was last saved, and file size along the bottom of the dialog box. If a document or template was saved with a preview, you can view the first page of the document by checking Preview. On Windows, you'll see the file type and version in the lower-left corner.

Figure 4-1: The Open dialog box provides information such as the file size about the file you want to open.

4. Use the information in the Open dialog box to determine if this is the file you want to open. If it is, double-click the file name or click Open.

Double-clicking files to open

If you prefer to open files from the desktop, you can do that, too. If QuarkXPress is not running, your operating system will launch it. (If you have more than one copy of QuarkXPress on your computer, the latest version is *supposed to* launch. Actual results are inconsistent.) Figure 4-2 shows the icons for QuarkXPress files.

Choosing a recently opened file

If the Dejavu XTension is running, the Open command in the File menu includes a submenu of recently opened files. You can choose one of these files to open it.

Figure 4-2: Top, from left to right: print document, print template, book. Bottom, from left to right: library, Web document, Web template.

The Dejavu XTension is provided with QuarkXPress and installed by default. You can move the list of recently opened files to the bottom of the File menu using the File List pane of the Preferences dialog box (Edit ➪ Preferences ➪ Preferences, or Option+Shift+⌘+Y or Ctrl+Alt+Shift+Y). You can also specify how many files are listed and the order in which they're listed. See Chapter 3 for more information.

Macintosh

From the Macintosh desktop, locate any QuarkXPress file icon. Double-click the icon to open the file, launching QuarkXPress if necessary. If the file was created with Windows, sometimes the icon or file type information is missing and the Macintosh reports that it can't find the application that created the file. In this case, open the file through the QuarkXPress Open dialog box.

Windows

From the Windows desktop, locate any QuarkXPress file icon. Double-click the left mouse button to open it. If you double-click a QuarkXPress document that has an unrecognized file name extension (or no file name extension at all), it may give you a message that the file could not be opened because the application that created it is missing. (This often happens with files that originate on Macintosh.) In this case, open the file through the QuarkXPress Open dialog box. For more information about file name extensions, see the "Saving Files" section later in this chapter.

Notes on open files

The way a file opens differs according to file type. For example, when you open a document, nobody else can open it. But when you open a template, a new document is created based on the template. When QuarkXPress opens a file, it scans the file contents and often displays alerts.

Print and Web documents

Only one person at a time can open and work on a document. Documents stay open until you close them or you quit QuarkXPress. When you open documents, a couple of alerts often display: Nonmatching Preferences and Missing Fonts.

Nonmatching Preferences

The Nonmatching Preferences dialog box, shown in Figure 4-3, seems to open almost every time you open a document. Although the dialog box looks threatening, you can always safely ignore it by clicking Keep Document Settings (the default option). This ensures that nothing in your document changes. (The Nonmatching Preferences dialog box indicates that settings saved in your XPress Preferences file, including hyphenation exceptions and kerning/tracking tables, are different from those saved in the document.)

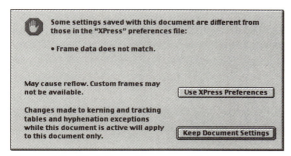

Figure 4-3: Click Keep Document Settings to bypass the Nonmatching Preferences dialog box.

Missing Fonts

If the document uses any fonts that are not active (or open) on your system, a warning displays. The warning gives you the option to Continue and open the document without worrying about the missing fonts. Or you can click List Fonts, which displays the Missing Fonts dialog box, shown in Figure 4-4. At this point, you can jot down the font names, and then activate them through your operating system or a font manager such as Font Reserve, Suitcase, or ATM Deluxe. If you do not have the fonts and cannot acquire them — and you don't care if the text reflows — you can use the Missing Fonts dialog box to select replacement fonts for missing fonts.

Figure 4-4: Use the Missing Fonts dialog box to determine which fonts you need to activate or to replace missing fonts.

Templates

When you open a template, QuarkXPress creates a new, unsaved copy of the template. You need to give the file a name and save it. Because the template isn't really open, multiple users can access templates.

As with documents, when you open a template, the Nonmatching Preferences and/or Missing Fonts dialog boxes may display. Handle these alerts the same way you would for a document.

Libraries and books

Libraries and books, shown in Figures 4-5 and 4-6, respectively, stay open until you close them. They even reopen automatically when you restart QuarkXPress. Libraries and books are often stored on a server so multiple users can open the same ones.

Figure 4-5: A QuarkXPress library contains a collection of items ready to drag-and-drop into documents.

Figure 4-6: A QuarkXPress book helps you keep track of the multiple documents that make up a larger publication.

Tip   If you store a library or book on a server, make sure you're logged on to that server before you launch QuarkXPress. Otherwise, QuarkXPress will not be able to automatically reopen libraries and books.

Saving Files

When you create a new document or open a template, the new document is unsaved. You need to choose a location for the file and name it. Libraries and books, on the other hand, receive a name and location when you create them. When you name and save files, QuarkXPress for Windows adds the appropriate file name extension automatically. On a Macintosh, which does not use file extensions, you should add them if there's a chance that someone using Windows will need the file. (***Remember:*** Libraries cannot be opened across platforms.) The QuarkXPress file extensions are:

✦ **.qxd:** document

✦ **.qxt:** template

✦ **.qwd:** Web document

✦ **.qwt:** Web template

✦ **.qxl:** library

✦ **.qxb:** book

Tip

On Windows, you can easily rename a file with the correct file name extension. The easiest way to do this is to right-click the file icon and select Rename from the pop-up menu. If you're deft with a mouse, you can single-click the icon's file name and wait a second for the text to be highlighted, letting you rename it or edit its name.

Saving new documents

When you create a new document by using File ➪ New, pressing ⌘+N or Ctrl+N, or opening a template, you need to name and save the file. If QuarkXPress or your machine crashes with an unnamed document open, you will lose all your work. Saving documents is the same for print documents, print templates, Web documents, and Web templates.

STEPS: Saving a file

1. Choose File ➪ Save As, or press ⌘+Option+S or Ctrl+Alt+S.

2. Use the standard Macintosh or Windows navigation tools to choose a location for the new file.

Tip

If you're starting a new project, create a new folder for the document in which you can store the library and graphic files as well.

3. Type a descriptive name for the file in the Save Current Document As field (Macintosh), as shown in Figure 4-7, or the File Name field (Windows). Windows adds the appropriate file extension to the name; on Macintosh, add the .qxd file extension if you want.

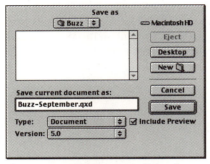

Figure 4-7: The Save As dialog box.

4. To save the file as a print or Web document in version 5, leave the Type menu (Macintosh) or Save As Type menu (Windows) set to Document and the Version menu set to 5.0.

5. On Macintosh, if you want a thumbnail of the first page of the document to display in the Open dialog box, check Preview.

The Windows version of QuarkXPress does not offer this preview feature.

6. Click Save to name and save the new document.

If you're designing a document to be used as a *template* (a preformatted starting place for new documents), save the file as a document while you're designing it. When you're finished with the page design, resave the document as a template by choosing Template from the Type menu (Macintosh) or Save As Type menu (Windows) in the Save As dialog box. The file extension for print templates is .qxt, and the file extension for Web templates is .qxw.

Saving copies of documents

To create a copy of a document while you're in QuarkXPress, you simply save it with a new name. If you've been working on the document and you want to save the changes with the original document, choose File ➪ Save, or press ⌘+S or Ctrl+S, before creating the copy. If you don't want the changes to affect the original document, go ahead and choose File ➪ Save As. In the Save As dialog box, specify a different name and/or location for the new copy of the document.

Tip

Many designers use previous documents as the starting place for new documents. For example, if they're starting the November issue of a newsletter, they open the October issue, delete the text and graphics, then save the document with a new name. Although this method works, starting projects from a template is preferable. When you start with a completed project, you're including all the colors specific to that job, any extra style sheets specific to that text, and any problems that exist in that file.

Downsaving to a previous version

If you need to open a print document in a previous version of QuarkXPress, you can *downsave* the document to an earlier version. Generally, each version of a software program has its own file format, and you cannot open documents from a later version using a previous version. For example, you can't open QuarkXPress 5 documents in QuarkXPress 4. To get around this, you can downsave documents from version 5 in version 4 format.

The Version menu in the Save As dialog box (File ➪ Save As, or Option+⌘+S or Ctrl+Alt+S) lets you save QuarkXPress 5 print documents back to version 4. Be forewarned that you will lose any document attributes specific to the later version of QuarkXPress — for example, all layers are flattened and table cells are converted to individual text boxes. Because of this, saving a copy of the document in a previous version is best. To easily identify the downsaved file, you may want to include the version in the file name, such as "Dining Guide 4.qxd."

Saving your work

QuarkXPress provides a variety of strategies for saving your work. On a daily basis, saving documents as you work is very important. But for long-term projects, making sure changes are saved to libraries is also important.

Note

Any changes you make in a book are automatically saved with the book file.

Saving documents

QuarkXPress provides two methods for saving your work in print and Web documents: manual and automatic. Manual saves occur whenever you choose File ➪ Save, or press ⌘+S or Ctrl+S. You should save a document manually after completing a significant amount of work (that you're happy with), before completing an action such as moving pages that cannot be undone, and any time you pause in your work.

If you're accustomed to relying on automatic saves in other applications, you can use Auto Save in QuarkXPress. Even if you're in the habit of saving often, Auto Save can give you an extra level of protection. The downside is that Auto Save can interrupt your work for a few seconds (depending on the file size) to save your work. In addition to automatically saving your work, you can automatically retain revisions of documents by using the Auto Backup feature.

Auto Save and Auto Backup are off by default. For instructions on how to turn them on, see Chapter 3.

Saving templates

Attempting to manually save changes to a template triggers the Save As dialog box. This is because templates, intended as the starting place for new documents, are protected from overwriting. To save changes to a template file, use the exact same file name and location to save over the existing template.

Saving libraries

When you close a library or you quit QuarkXPress, all the changes you've made are saved with the file. Libraries offer an extra level of protection: Auto Library Save. This feature is on by default, and it ensures that each change you make to a library is saved the moment you make it. The only reason to uncheck Auto Library Save is if you're adding several items to a library and the constant saving is slowing down your work.

 For more information about Auto Library Save, see Chapter 3.

Reverting to a previous version

Whenever you're working on a print or Web document, you have the option of reverting to the last saved version. This option is particularly helpful when you perform a complicated operation that cannot be undone. For example, moving pages cannot be undone — yet the move of pages doesn't always turn out the way you expect. To revert to the last manually saved version of a document, choose File ➪ Revert to Saved. If you're using Auto Save, you can revert to the last auto-saved version (although you may not know when the last auto save actually occurred). To do this, press the Option or Alt key as you choose File ➪ Revert to Saved.

Closing Files

Although you can keep up to 25 files open, when you're finished using a file you may as well save the changes and close it. Keeping open files you're not using leaves them vulnerable to corruption if QuarkXPress or your machine should crash.

Closing documents

To close the active document (the document in the frontmost window), choose File ➪ Close, or press ⌘+W or Ctrl+F4. You can also close a document by clicking the close box on the document window. Quitting QuarkXPress will close all open documents. When you close a document with unsaved changes, an alert gives you the opportunity to save the document or cancel closing it.

On the Macintosh, you can press Ô+Option+W or Option+click the close box to close all open documents.

Closing libraries and books

The only way to close a library or book is to click its close box. Quitting QuarkXPress only closes these files temporarily. When you launch QuarkXPress again, previously open libraries and books reopen. Closing a library or book automatically saves all changes with the file.

Summary

The process of managing QuarkXPress files is intentionally consistent with other Macintosh and Windows programs. The basic commands are in the File menu — Open, Save, and Close — and the keyboard commands are consistent with your operating system's standards. Depending on the file type, though, QuarkXPress files do behave differently. Only one user at a time can open and work on a print or Web document, whereas multiple users can open templates, libraries, and books.

✦   ✦   ✦

The Publishing Environment

Q uarkXPress by itself doesn't do anything. You need
to work with it in the context of a computer, add-on
hardware, other software, and of course the operating system
of your Mac or PC. And after you have the equipment and
platform that's right for you, you need to learn to make the
most of it. This chapter gives you the basic information you
need to get the right equipment and to get started on your
platform of choice. However, we do recommend that you pick
up more-detailed books on Mac OS or Windows; the publisher
of this book, Hungry Minds, has several good books for
beginners (in the *For Dummies* series) and for more
experienced users (in the *Bible* series).

Choosing the Right Hardware

You don't need the fastest computer available to use
QuarkXPress, but factors such as processor (CPU) speed, RAM,
hard disks, removable media, connectivity, and input/output
devices can make a difference. The following sections take you
on a tour of what works best in a full spectrum of publishing
situations.

The computer

Quark provides system requirements, but the system
requirements are just the bare minimum you need to run the
software. They don't take into consideration whether you can
run QuarkXPress and Photoshop at the same time or whether
your font manager will run on the operating system it supports.
But because you need to be concerned about your entire
publishing system — not just QuarkXPress — in this section we
provide a realistic minimum system for Mac OS and Windows.
Then we give you a wish list for the ideal publishing system.

Minimum system

For Quark's official system requirements, see Appendix A. But for best results, we recommend the following minimum publishing system:

✦ **Mac OS:** Any G3 or higher Macintosh computer running Mac OS 9.1 with a minimum of 128MB of RAM and a 10GB hard drive. Note that QuarkXPress 5 does not run natively in Mac OS X, although Quark says it will make a Mac OS X version at some point. In the meantime, the initial version of QuarkXPress 5 will run under Mac OS X in compatibility mode, which will slow it down a bit.

✦ **Windows:** An Intel Pentium II, AMD K6-II, or newer processor running at least at 266 MHz (no Celeron processors at this level), and running Windows 2000, Windows XP, or Windows NT 4.0 (not Windows 98 or Windows Me), with 128MB of RAM and a 10GB hard drive. We recommend you use an NT-based version (2000, XP, or NT 4.0) of Windows because it is faster and more stable than the 9x series.

Ideal system

In any kind of graphic arts environment, you typically need to run at least QuarkXPress, Adobe Photoshop, and Adobe Illustrator — not to mention an e-mail program and a Web browser — at the same time. Adobe Photoshop, in particular, runs faster and more reliably with plenty of RAM. Plus, images, EPS files, and the like eat up disk space quickly. As a rule, buy as much RAM and the largest hard disk you can afford. If you're just getting started, or you've just come into some money, set yourself up right with the following system:

✦ **Mac OS:** A Macintosh G4 computer running Mac OS 9.1 with anywhere from 256MB to 512MB of RAM, a 30GB hard drive, a Zip removable storage drive, and a CD-RW (read/write) drive.

✦ **Windows:** A Pentium III or AMD Athlon computer running Windows 2000 or XP with 256MB of RAM, a 30GB hard drive, a Zip removable storage drive, and a CD-RW (read/write) drive. Windows typically requires less operational overhead than Mac OS; however, the RAM requirements for applications are the same. Windows 2000 and XP provide better memory management for high-end applications, but they aren't an absolute requirement.

Memory and storage capacity

Today, the newer computers usually come with plenty of RAM (memory) and storage capacity (hard drive space). But if you have an older computer or you're taxing your current system, upgrading RAM and storage capacity can speed up your work significantly. When evaluating your publishing system, consider the following hardware suggestions:

✦ **RAM:** Adding RAM lets the computer work more efficiently. You'll want 64MB of RAM as a bare minimum, which you can get by with if you work with just one program at a time. Better for publishers is 128MB to 256MB, and even more than that if you're doing complex work on large files in Adobe Photoshop as well (256MB is typical for such users).

✦ **Hard disks:** Programs and files eat through disk space. So these days, a 10GB to 20GB hard drive (which holds about 10 to 20 billion characters) is considered small. Look for 10GB to 40GB or higher. And remember that you can add hard drives to your Mac or PC—you don't have to replace your existing one in most cases.

✦ **CD-RW or DVD R/W:** Using a read/write CD drive (also called a *CD burner*) as part of your storage solution is your best choice for long-term archiving. CDs also work well for delivering large projects—that include documents, graphics, and fonts—to service bureaus and printers. CD-RW drives are relatively cheap ($250 to $600) depending on the speed, and the CD-R discs themselves are very inexpensive. (You can also use the more expensive CD-RW discs, which let you erase and modify the CD's contents, but for delivering, say, an issue of a magazine to a printer, there's no reason to use a rewritable disc, because you're not expecting the CD back. CD-RWs are great, though, for storing templates that may be adapted over time and as a backup device.) Each CD can hold 650MB of data, and they're easy to store, permanent, and universal. DVD R/W drives and their discs are newer and more expensive, but they can hold twice the data.

✦ **Zip drives:** If your computer didn't come with a Zip drive, and you don't have a CD-RW drive, you may need to invest in an external Iomega Zip drive. This $150 device uses 100MB or 250MB cartridges that cost about $10 to $30 each. Zip cartridges can be handy for backup and for delivering files to service bureaus or for sharing them with other users who aren't on your network. CD-R and CD-RW discs are starting to make Zips less frequently used, but they remain common in service bureaus and within larger publishing organizations because, for years, they were the only way to transport lots of data in a convenient mechanism.

✦ **Tape drives:** If you don't have a CD-RW drive and don't work on a network that automatically backs up files to a server, you can use a tape drive for backups. Prices range from $100 to $1,000 depending on the capacity, with the majority under $400. These drives back up your system on inexpensive tapes, saving your work in case your hard drive gets damaged. If you're making a living from your computer, don't put that living at risk. Macintosh users will find a much more limited selection of tape drives than Windows users, though the newer external USB and FireWire drives are increasingly available in Mac versions.

Connectivity

Another essential component in workgroup environments is a network. At the very least, you want peer-to-peer networks, in which your Macs and PCs are connected to one another so they can share files. Both the Mac OS and Windows have this capability built in.

The Mac/PC connection

The following list describes programs that Macs and PCs use to connect to each other and read each other's disks:

✦ Miramar Systems's PC MacLAN lets PCs join Mac-based networks. It costs about $200 per person but only needs to be installed on PCs (Macs have AppleTalk networking, the protocol used by PC MacLAN, built in.) It also supports the faster IP protocol for connections to Mac OS 9.x computers.

✦ DataViz's MacOpener and Media4's MacDrive let PCs read Mac disks (floppies, CDs, Zips, SyQuests, external hard drives, and so on). They cost about $50 per person.

✦ DataViz's MacLinkPlus let Macs read PC disks. It costs about $75 per person. There's also a version that offers file translation, which most people don't need because most programs now use the same file format on Mac and Windows. But if you tend to use older or specialty programs, MacLinkPlus/ Translator is a necessity. Apple's Mac OS 7.6 and later support PC disks natively as well, although with less control than MacLinkPlus allows.

The network connection

Ethernet has become the standard networking topology. *Ethernet* is a fairly fast yet inexpensive kind of wiring that lots of different transmission protocols, like TCP/IP or AppleTalk, can run. All new Macs have Ethernet connectors built in, and so do most PCs. For those that don't, the cost is $50 to $100 per computer for the needed card or adapter box.

Older Macs have both AppleTalk and Ethernet, so you need to tell the Mac which you want to use, and you can switch back and forth. We recommend you stick with Ethernet, using AppleTalk only if you have a printer that isn't Ethernet-compatible (such as a color inkjet printer). Similarly, on a PC, getting an Ethernet version of your printers is better than relying on the slow, single-user parallel port or USB connection. Of course, if you're a one-person design firm, that's not a big issue.

The Internet connection

Even if you're working on print projects, you'll need to be on the Internet. You need to be able to send and receive files (from e-mail to text files to entire QuarkXPress documents and graphics), download program updates, and use your computer as a fax. Basically, you should get the fastest Internet connection available to you. Unfortunately, the availability is often limited by the phone lines and other factors in your area.

If you can get a cable, ISDN, or DSL connection from your cable or phone company, that's ideal. DSL is quickly becoming the connection of choice based or cost, availability, and ease of use. It lets you access and download data at 384 kilobits per second (Kbps) or higher. Most often, the provider will send you the equipment you need or tell you what to buy. Make sure you carefully research all the types of DSL available in your area. Price, speed, and flexibility vary a lot from company to company. The best service is one that isn't shared — where that 384 Kbps is always yours only. Some companies offer shared DSL, while *all* cable modems are shared with other users in your neighborhood. (Not only can sharing slow performance, it also means your computers could be accessed by someone else on the connection unless you have security software or hardware installed.)

If you're stuck with a dial-up account — because DSL or other services aren't available where you live — you need some type of modem. Most newer computers, such as iMacs or any PC, have an internal 56 Kbps modem, so all you do is plug a phone line into the computer. If you need an external modem, be sure to buy one that supports speeds of 56 Kbps.

Input and output devices

The following sections cover some of the things you'll need to consider in the input/output realm: printers, scanners, digital cameras, CD-ROM drives, multibutton mice, trackballs, and pen-based tablets.

Printers

Invest in a good printer. You'll want a black-and-white laser printer that is capable of 600 dots per inch (dpi) output or better. Older printers support 300-dpi output, which is acceptable but not as sharp when it comes to printing text and images.

Fast network printers

If you work in an office and need only black-and-white or grayscale output, you can buy one or two fast network printers (16 to 25 pages per minute [ppm] or faster) and share them. Such printers — such as the Hewlett-Packard 1200n, 2200dn, or 4100tn series — cost between $800 and $2,500 each. They typically have PostScript, the printing language standard for desktop publishing, already installed and can hold lots of paper, often in several sizes.

Personal laser printers

If you work alone and need only black-and-white or grayscale output, you can consider an affordable laser printer such as the HP 1200 or 3200 series. Look for one that prints between 9 and 15 ppm. Consider getting a refurbished printer, especially if it has Ethernet built in (Ethernet is an expensive option for personal laser printers). A better choice for personal printing is one of the newer color inkjets.

PostScript printers

If you're producing final output, as opposed to proofs, you'll want a PostScript-capable printer, because that's the language that all professional output devices, such as imagesetters, use. Printers aimed at Mac owners almost always have PostScript, whereas printers aimed at PC owners usually do not. Mac-oriented printers almost always work with PCs, so PC owners will find it easier to get PostScript by looking at Mac-oriented printers than by looking at PC-oriented printers. In fact, most work with both at the same time. You can have Macs and PCs plugged into them and using them simultaneously.

Note
Be sure to go to Adobe's Web site (www.adobe.com) and download its free PostScript printer driver rather than use the one that comes with Windows — the Windows PostScript driver is less capable and can result in output errors. On a Mac, the Apple PostScript driver that comes with the OS is fine, although Adobe also offers its own version.

Color inkjet printers

For graphic arts applications, the inexpensive color inkjet printers, such as an Epson Color Stylus or Canon S series, are a great choice. These printers are essential if you're doing color work and want to get color proofs occasionally. And for low-volume color printing, they're a great deal and very convenient.

Color inkjets cost between $250 and $500. Although they're slower than most laser printers, they provide glorious color and grayscale output. Most color inkjets do not support PostScript, but you can purchase a PostScript Software RIP, such as Adobe's PressReady and Strydent Software's PowerPrint, for most models for about $200. Just be sure it works with your inkjet printer. (Epson offers a few models for about $1,000 to $3,000 that include PostScript.)

Color scanners

One device that has recently become very affordable is a color scanner. Umax Technologies, Agfa, and Canon are all excellent and are inexpensive ($200 to $500) yet have color quality that approaches that of a professional scanner costing several thousand dollars. They work with both Macs and PCs, feature USB connectivity, and at these low prices and great quality it's almost a requirement to own. They also can double as copy machines or fax machines. You scan in a paper document and then print it to your printer or fax it from your Internet connection.

Digital cameras

Digital cameras are becoming popular, and their image quality is presentable; however, you'll need to spend $600 or more for the 2- to 3-megapixel versions. This resolution is adequate for print publishing if your final output is under 5 x 7 inches (sometimes up to 8 x 10 inches) and you're doing super-high-quality printing. The biggest problem with using a digital camera for print publishing is that most of the cameras use JPEG image compression, so you're not necessarily dealing with optimum quality, no matter how high the resolution of the camera is. The best solution is to experiment — some image subjects work better than others. For Web publishing, however, digital cameras are fine, and using them is more convenient than having your 35mm film processed and scanned.

CD-ROM drives

Every computer now comes with a CD-ROM drive, which is great, because it makes software installation a snap (no more floppy shuffle!). If your computer doesn't have a CD-ROM drive, invest $100 or so in one. You probably don't need anything faster than 4x speed. These days, CD-RWs, which let you read and write CDs, are also inexpensive and ubiquitous, so opt for one of those rather than a standard CD-ROM drive.

Caution

Beware the new DVD-ROM drives. This CD-ROM replacement works with CDs (although not necessarily with CD-RWs or CD-Rs), but there are several versions of DVD-ROM that are not completely compatible with each other. If you want to have it all, consider the Richo combo DVD/CD-RW drive, which costs about $400 and supports almost every CD format in existence. The only thing you can't do with it is write a DVD disc; drives to do that still cost at least $1,000 and are in limited supply.

Mice, trackballs, and tablets

Also consider getting a multibutton mouse. The extra buttons can save you strain on your hands and arms by being used for common operations such as dragging and double-clicking. And now that Mac OS 8 and above adds contextual pop-up menus via the Control+click shortcut (similar to the Windows right-click), Mac owners will benefit from at least a two-button mouse. However, we advise both Mac and Windows users to get a three- or four-button mouse (or trackball, if that's your fancy); Kensington Microware and Logitech both offer good models for both platforms. A pen-based tablet makes sense if you're also doing illustration work, but consider that a secondary input device, not a primary one. However many buttons you get on your mouse, we strongly recommend the new optical mice, which don't require a mouse pad, don't get gunk in their gears that can interfere with scrolling, and generally are easier to operate.

Getting the Essential Software

A flurry of utility programs, specialized software, fonts, and XTensions can help you complete your specific publishing environment. The following items detail some of the more outstanding ones (see Chapter 41 and the CD that comes with this book for comprehensive coverage of XTensions):

✦ **An image editor:** Almost all publishers need an image editor, and the standard is really Adobe Photoshop for both Macintosh and Windows. Even if you're more of an editor, you'll be surprised at how often you'll need to open a graphic file in Photoshop to simply crop or edit a photograph. For professional work, get the full version. If you really just need to resize and crop photos and other images, you can get by with the much cheaper LE version.

✦ **An illustration program:** If you draw, or you need to edit EPS files, you need an illustration program such as CorelDraw, Adobe Illustrator, or Macromedia FreeHand. They're all good cross-platform programs, so try them out first to see what feels best to you. All three companies let you download demo versions from their Web sites.

✦ **A word processor:** A word processing program is a must. Microsoft Word is the standard, but many still use WordPerfect — it's up to you.

✦ **A font manager, such as ATM Light, and a font menu manager:** See the next section, "Working with Fonts," for more information.

✦ **A compression utility:** Files are always too big, so compression utilities are a must. On the Mac, there's no substitute for StuffIt Deluxe, a $50 utility package that reads both Mac StuffIt files and PC Zip files, as well as several Internet compression formats. On Windows, the equivalent program to StuffIt Deluxe is the $30 shareware program WinZip, from Niko Mac Computing.

A demo version of WinZip is on the book's CD.

✦ **XTensions:** You'll probably want add-on programs, known as *XTensions,* for QuarkXPress, which extend its capabilities. Chapter 25 and the chapters in Part VI of this book cover XTensions in more detail.

To keep your Mac OS and Windows software up to date, check out www. techtracker.com for updates, or try the TechTracker Desktop application on the CD. The application automatically matches the most current software versions and patches from their database to the software on your computer and notifies you when software on your machine needs updating. The free Windows version is full featured and the Mac version is a 30-day demo.

Working with Fonts

Fonts, traditionally known as *typefaces,* are a collection of characters that share a similar look. Fonts, such as Times and Garamond, usually include several variations such as **bold** and *italic.* The electronic files that make up fonts are managed by your operating system or other utilities, not by QuarkXPress. QuarkXPress doesn't come with fonts, and it doesn't manage fonts. So when you're talking about fonts, you're talking about *foundries* (companies that design and distribute fonts), Mac OS and Windows features, and third-party utilities and applications that manage fonts.

Procuring fonts

No matter what type of design or publishing you're doing, you'll need — or you'll eventually acquire — lots of fonts. You can never have enough fonts, and there are so many interesting yet useful ones. You can get fonts in three ways: free with applications, through colleagues, or by purchasing them.

Fonts versus typefaces

Desktop publishing has changed the meaning of some fundamental typographic terms, which can lead to confusion. When you see the word *font* in the context of a computer, it means what a traditional typographer would call a *face* — one basic variant of a typeface. (In traditional typography, a *font* means a face at a particular point size, a context that digital typesetting has all but eliminated.) Thus, you'll see the word *font* used to mean, for example, Times Roman or Times Italic. A typographer would call these variants *faces*.

Many people use the word *font* informally to mean *typeface*, which is a collection of related faces. Thus, your service bureau would understand the phrase, "I'm using the News Gothic font in my brochure," to mean that you are using the News Gothic typeface, and that the bureau needs to ensure it downloads the whole family to the imagesetter when printing your job.

✦ **Free fonts:** More and more programs come with free fonts (all the image-editing and illustration programs mentioned earlier in this chapter do, for example). In addition, you can download free fonts from many Web sites. Just type "free fonts" into a search engine such as Google (www.google.com) and it's a free-for-all. Although this is an inexpensive way to build a font collection, it may not provide all the fonts you need. The quality can vary, and service bureaus may balk at using some of these fonts, because they don't come from a source they know.

✦ **Acquired fonts:** Often, people will e-mail fonts with a file they want you to edit. And most people will send you fonts upon request, because the files are small and easily portable. In most cases, this is in violation of the font's license agreement, so this isn't a good way to build a font library. Providing fonts to a service bureau for one-time output is usually okay, but "acquiring" fonts is generally a poor — even illegal — way to build a font collection.

✦ **Purchased fonts:** Although you can go into a computer store and purchase font CDs, the most convenient method is to buy them online. You can do everything from purchasing base collections of fonts to get you started to buying a single font you need to work on a client's document. Good sites include www.adobe.com, www.fontsite.com, and www.myfonts.com (shown in Figure 5-1). All three sites are worth visiting if you want to learn about and explore typography.

Tip A book such as the *Adobe Type Library Reference Book*, available from www.adobe.com, shows printed samples of hundreds of typefaces. You can use this type of book to select a typeface for a specific job. Then you can purchase the font. This can save you hours in sifting through your fonts and poring over Web pages to find the typeface you want to use.

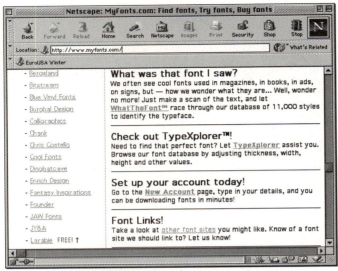

Figure 5-1: Font sites allow you to preview, purchase, and download fonts for immediate use. This site, `www.myfonts.com`, even lets you upload a scanned image of a font to find out its name.

PostScript, TrueType, or OpenType?

The most basic question about fonts is usually what kind to use. The answer depends on the work you do. If you produce newsletters, magazines, ads, or brochures that you output on a typesetter or imagesetter, use PostScript, because that is the standard format on these devices. If your final output is to a laser or inkjet printer, TrueType or OpenType is probably the better bet because they print faster in most cases, especially if you print to a non-PostScript printer. However, you don't have to use one font format exclusively.

Here are the basic types of fonts you have to choose from:

✦ **PostScript Type 1:** This is the publishing industry's standard for fonts. Anyone outputting to an imagesetter or other prepress device must use these fonts. On the Mac OS 8.x and 9.x, basic PostScript Type 1 font support is built into the operating system via the inclusion of Adobe Type Manager Light. It is native to Mac OS X, although until Quark releases a version of QuarkXPress that runs in Mac OS X native mode, you'll have to use ATM or other font manager since Mac OS X's Classic Mode is simply Mac OS 9.1. Windows does not support PostScript natively and so requires a font-management utility such as Adobe Type Manager Deluxe, DiamondSoft Font Reserve, or Extensis Suitcase to work with PostScript fonts.

✦ **TrueType:** Codeveloped by Microsoft and Apple Computer, this is the standard font format in Windows, and it also is supported natively on the Mac OS. However, TrueType fonts are not supported by most imagesetters and prepress devices, and their use in your layouts can cause output problems. Don't use them in any professionally published document. **Note:** If you're outputting to the Acrobat portable document format (PDF), either for prepress or electronic distribution, avoid using TrueType fonts. You cannot embed TrueType fonts in PDF files.

✦ **OpenType:** This new version of PostScript, codeveloped by Adobe and Microsoft, combines some TrueType technology and is meant to eventually replace both Type 1 and TrueType. Windows 2000 supports it natively, but for any other version of Windows and for any version of the Mac OS, you'll need to add support for OpenType to your computer via a font-management utility, and you'll need to make sure that your imagesetter or other prepress device can handle them—most cannot. At press time, only Font Reserve for Windows and Adobe Type Manager (Light and Deluxe) 4.6 (Mac) and 4.1 (Windows) support OpenType. Plus, Adobe Systems has decided not to make future versions of this product, so we recommend you avoid OpenType fonts until the remaining font managers—Suitcase and Font Reserve for Mac—support the format or until support is built into Windows and the Mac OS natively.

Because OpenType is fairly new, most of the time you're simply considering whether to use TrueType or PostScript fonts. Consider the following:

✦ **If you see a TrueType typeface that you want to use in your typeset document, use it.** The Mac and Windows operating systems automatically convert TrueType fonts into PostScript format when printing to a PostScript device (or to a file designated for use by a PostScript device). The drawback is that this conversion process may make your files larger, because the computer must download the converted TrueType font file into your document.

✦ **Conversely, if you have PostScript typefaces, there's no reason to give them up if you switch to TrueType.** On a PostScript printer, you can use both formats. On other printers, all you need is a program such as Adobe Type Manager Light to make the outlines of the letters appear smooth when they print.

✦ **Don't base decisions about whether to use TrueType or PostScript fonts on assumptions about quality.** Both technologies provide excellent results, so any quality differences are due to the font manufacturer's standards. If you purchase typefaces from recognized companies, you don't need to worry. (Many smaller companies produce high-quality fonts as well.)

Installing fonts through the operating system

After you get a font on your computer, you need to install it so applications such as QuarkXPress can recognize it — and let you use it. The procedures are different depending on your operating system and whether you're using a font manager.

Macintosh fonts

To install fonts through the Mac OS, drag the files into the Fonts folder inside your System Folder. Better yet, use a font manager, which enables most programs to recognize new fonts right away.

> **Note**
>
> When you install Mac fonts, make sure you install both the screen fonts and the printer fonts for each PostScript font. You may have a font suitcase — a special font file — with several screen fonts for your PostScript font, or you may have separate files for each screen font, depending on which option the company decided to use. TrueType fonts don't come in several files — all variants are in one suitcase.

Windows fonts

You can add TrueType fonts to Windows through the Fonts control panel. PostScript fonts, however, require a font manager such as Font Reserve, ATM Deluxe, or Suitcase.

STEPS: Adding TrueType fonts to Windows

1. Go to Start ➪ Settings ➪ Control Panel, and then double-click the Fonts folder.

2. Go to File ➪ Install New Font to get the Add Fonts dialog box.

3. Navigate the dialog box using the Folders and Drives scroll lists to get to the folder or disk that has the TrueType fonts you want to install. A list of fonts will appear in the dialog box.

4. Select the fonts to install, and click OK.

Using a font manager and font utilities

Although you can manage fonts to a certain extent through the operating system, we highly recommend that you use a font manager. With a font manager, you can control precisely which fonts are active at any one time. This is important because many different versions and kinds (PostScript, TrueType, OpenType, and so on) of fonts exist with the same name — and simply using any font with the same name is not okay. For example, if you use TrueType Helvetica instead of PostScript Helvetica, the text in the document may reflow, altering the design and even cutting off text. In addition to a font manager, most users will need ATM Light for viewing PostScript fonts on-screen, and most Mac users will want a font menu manager.

Using font managers

With a font manager such as DiamondSoft Font Reserve, Extensis Suitcase (formerly Symantec Suitcase), or Adobe ATM Deluxe, you can see more information about fonts and activate fonts on-the-fly without restarting programs. Our favorite, in terms of compatibility and features, is Font Reserve. On the Mac, the drag-and-drop interface makes installing and exporting fonts easy; in Windows, you can easily create a library of all the TrueType, PostScript, and OpenType fonts on your system. On both platforms, Font Reserve provides features such as on-screen previews, sample printing, character maps, and sets for grouping fonts for projects (see Figure 5-2).

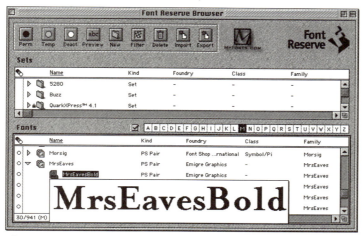

Figure 5-2: Font Reserve provides an intuitive interface for installing fonts, activating fonts on-the-fly, previewing fonts, and creating font sets.

Font Reserve Light, a full-functioning version of Font Reserve that is limited to managing 100 font files, is on the book's CD.

Because Extensis Suitcase (formerly Symantec Suitcase) was the first popular font manager, many Mac OS and Windows users are accustomed to using it and prefer to stick with it (you can find it at www.extensis.com). Although continuing to use Suitcase is fine, we recommend that you shy away from Adobe's ATM Deluxe on the Mac. It tends to be more unstable, and it provides less information about your fonts. In fact, Adobe will not develop ATM Deluxe for Mac OS X. Adobe has also not kept its Windows version up to date.

Using ATM Light

A potentially confusing issue with font managers is that a necessary control panel — ATM Light — often masquerades as the font manager ATM Deluxe. You need the ATM Light control panel to render PostScript fonts on-screen for both Mac OS (prior to OS X) and Windows. ATM Light comes with many programs and is available from www.adobe.com.

Although ATM Deluxe provides the capabilities of ATM Light, you don't need it — and in fact, you can't use it — if you're using another font manager or installing fonts through the operating system. If you're using Suitcase or Font Reserve, you can't simply disable the Deluxe features of ATM Deluxe. To prevent conflicts, you need to remove ATM Deluxe and replace it with ATM Light.

Note   Mac OS X renders PostScript fonts on-screen by itself. However, the initial release of QuarkXPress 5 will only run in Classic Mode (the compatibility mode) on OS X. This means it will actually be running on Mac OS 9, which requires ATM Light to render fonts on-screen.

Using a font menu manager

On the Mac, you can purchase utilities that streamline font menus by combining typeface families (collapsing all variations of a font such as regular, bold, and italic, into a submenu, for example). Many utilities also provide previews of the fonts in the actual menus. Font menu managers include:

✦ Adobe Type Reunion Deluxe (www.adobe.com)

✦ TypeTamer (www.typetamer.com)

✦ Action WYSIWYG (www.poweronsoftware.com), shown in Figure 5-3

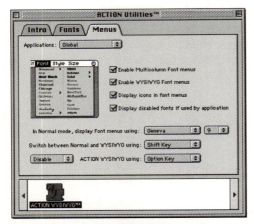

Figure 5-3: Action WYSIWYG provides options for customizing font menus, including customizing the font list per application, rearranging fonts, combining fonts into typeface families, and displaying previews.

Although useful, especially for novices who like to choose fonts based on previews, these utilities can be buggy. Adobe Type Reunion, in particular, tends to conflict with QuarkXPress and even Adobe applications. Plus, it can hog your system memory. These utilities also can slow down menu redraw, because every font in the menu must be rendered.

Summary

Your success in QuarkXPress will largely be determined by its operating environment. Run it on an old, slow computer with little RAM, and it can be slow and frustrating. Limit yourself to one or two applications, system fonts, and little connectivity, and your creativity may be stifled. Skip add-ons such as CD burners and Zip drives, and your creations may be trapped on your computer.

But if you invest in solid software and hardware, QuarkXPress will provide optimum speed and performance. With all the typefaces, graphics, and access to information you need, your publishing system will be capable of truly professional publications.

✦   ✦   ✦

Layout for Print

A ppearance counts — for a lot — which is why the layout of a document is so critical to its success. An attractive, engaging design draws the readers to your documents, so they actually read your pearls of wisdom. Even before you perceive what a document is all about, assimilate the contents of a graphic, or scan the text, you form an impression of the document based on its construction — particularly the arrangement of text and graphics on each page.

Skill with layout takes time, training, and an eye for good design. QuarkXPress can give you the tools but not the talent. By taking the time to think through the design process, you'll continue to develop your skills at designing layouts that invite the readers to read your content. And with the process thought through, you'll be able to take advantage of QuarkXPress's tools.

This part brings you through the process of creating effective layouts — first with the setup tasks that lay a strong foundation for your document, next with the basic elements used to create the layout, then with special techniques that add layout oomph, and finally with the labor-saving techniques that will reduce your work on the next similar document.

Layout Theory

Many QuarkXPress users are not trained graphic designers—they're administrators, hobbyists, entrepreneurs, or volunteers who have something to say. Armed with the best layout and typography tool in the world, they sometimes forget that they're not, in fact, armed with the training (and sometimes the talent) that producing clear, interesting publications requires. That's okay. A quick review of standard layout terminology and design rules helps any user get started in the right direction. Then, by dissecting other people's designs and messages, you can learn to plan and create publications that clarify and reinforce your message. Armed with this background in layout and design, you can step into the world of QuarkXPress and have at it.

Understanding Layout Terms

Document layout—the placement of text, images, and other items on a page—involves many elements. To communicate effectively with your peers and service providers, it helps to understand layout terminology, much of which is rooted in printing and production history. A brief primer on layout terms follows.

Layout tools

When a graphic designer creates a layout, she uses the following tools—either on paper or through software such as QuarkXPress.

- ✦ **Grid:** The basic layout design of a publication. It includes standard positions of folios, text, graphics, bylines, and headlines, as shown in Figure 6-1. A layout artist modifies the grid when necessary. Grids also are called *templates*.

- ✦ **Dummy:** A rough sketch of the layout of a particular story.

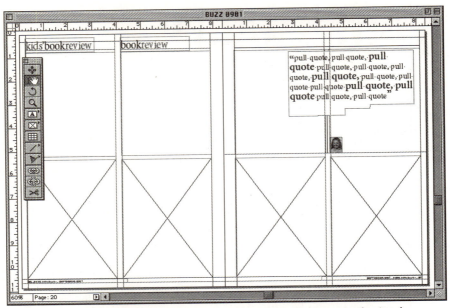

Figure 6-1: This template for this local newsletter, called *Buzz in the 'Burbs*, contains picture boxes at the bottom of each page for ads. The ads are generally imported in PDF form.

✦ **Guidelines:** Lines that show the standard placement of columns and margins in the grid. In most layout programs, guidelines are nonprinting lines that you can use to ensure that elements align.

✦ **Overlay:** A piece of transparent paper or film laid over a layout board. On the overlay, the artist can indicate screens in a different color or overprinted material such as text or graphics. QuarkXPress has the electronic equivalents of overlays: layers (View ⇨ Layers).

✦ **Knockout:** When one element cuts out the part of another element that it overlaps. A designer would say that one element *knocks out* the other or that one element is *knocked out of* the other. In either phrasing, it means the first element covers up the part of the other element under it. This differs from overlaying the other element, because in an overlay, both elements are visible (as in a superimposed image).

✦ **Galleys:** Single columns of type that are not laid out in any sort of printed-page format. In the past, publishers used galleys to check for proper hyphenation and to proof for errors. Galleys also were sent to authors for proofreading so that corrections could be made before the text was laid out. Galleys have all but disappeared from publishing, as most people now proofread on the first draft of page layouts, rather than make the intermediate step to proofread on galleys.

Design elements

Most publications, regardless of size and style, consist of the same basic design elements: columns, margins, frames, and so on. Take a look at what you'll be dealing with:

✦ **Column:** A block of text.

✦ **Gutter:** The space between columns that are placed side by side. (In newspapers and magazines, gutter space is usually 1 or 2 picas.)

✦ **Margin:** The space between the edge of a page and the nearest standard block of text. Some designers allow text or graphics to intrude into the margin for visual effect.

✦ **Bleed:** A graphic element or block of color that extends to the trimmed edge of the page.

✦ **Wrap:** When text follows the contours of an obstructing element such as a graphic or other text. The column margins are altered so that the column text wraps around the intruding graphic or text instead of being overprinted by the intruding element. Depending on what the text wraps around and the capabilities of the layout program, a wrap can be rectangular, polygonal, curved, and irregular. QuarkXPress can wrap text around any shape, including a picture's clipping path, as shown in Figure 6-2.

Figure 6-2: QuarkXPress lets you easily wrap text around the contours of images.

✦ **Folio:** The page number and identifying material (such as the publication name or month) that appears at the bottom or top of every page.

✦ **White space:** The part of the page left empty to create contrast to the text and graphics. White space provides visual relief and emphasizes the text and graphics.

✦ **Boxes:** The frames that hold layout elements (text, graphics, and blocks of color) on a page. Using a mouse, you can delete, copy, resize, reshape, or otherwise manipulate boxes in your layout.

✦ **Frames:** The ruling lines around boxes that hold layout elements. In QuarkXPress, these lines are called *frames,* but in other programs they're called *strokes.*

✦ **Template:** By filling a document with empty boxes and defining style tags in advance, you can use the resulting template repeatedly to create documents that use the same boxes and styles.

Image manipulation

Page-layout programs make it easy for you to decide which parts of an image to display and at what size. Although QuarkXPress doesn't provide the power of a dedicated illustration program such as Adobe Photoshop, you can perform some special effects as well:

✦ **Cropping:** Selecting a part of an image for use on the page.

✦ **Sizing (scaling):** Determining how much to reduce or enlarge the image (or part of the image). With layout programs, you often can distort an image by sizing it differently horizontally and vertically, which creates special effects such as compressing or stretching an image.

✦ **Reversing:** Also called *inverting* in some programs, reversing exchanges the black and white portions of an image. This effect is similar to creating a photographic negative.

✦ **Special effects:** *Flipping* (mirroring) and *skewing* (slanting) are other popular design effects. QuarkXPress even lets you apply color to some types of grayscale images.

Knowing the Seven Basic Rules of Good Design

Think about it: Many documents are off-putting. What makes them that way, and how do you build a layout that's inviting? Figure 6-3 shows two pages that contain the same information but use different layouts. The page on the left has body text set close to the headline. The leading is tight, and, except for a spot around the illustration, the white space is in short supply. Notice how the page on the right has a lighter, more vibrant look. Also note the variety of sizes, the use of generous margins, and a few strategic elements that don't quite align with the others (providing something for the eye to follow). Which page are you more inclined to read?

Figure 6-3: The page on the left is clean but dull — even the image adds little visual interest. The page on the right uses different typefaces, alignment, color, and text wraps to create interest and reinforce the subject matter without getting too busy.

If you're a trained graphic designer, you already know the basics. You can immediately put QuarkXPress to use, creating effective layouts. But if you're new to the field of graphic design, try keeping the following seven basic rules in mind as you begin learning about layout.

Rule 1: Keep an idea file

As you read magazines, books, newspapers, annual reports, ads, and brochures, save page layouts you like and dislike. Keep these layouts — good and bad — in a file, along with notes to yourself about which aspects of the layout work well and which work poorly. As you build your layout file, you educate yourself about layout basics.

Rule 2: Plan your document

It sounds corny, but it's true: Laying out a document is a lot like taking a journey. If you know where you're headed, it's much easier to find your way. Because QuarkXPress makes it easy to experiment as you design a document, it's also easy to end up with a messy conglomeration of text and images. You can avoid this pitfall by knowing ahead of time what you're trying to accomplish with the document's layout.

Rule 3: Keep it simple

When it comes to page layout, simple is better. Even the most experienced, trained graphic designers can tell you that this rule applies at least 99 percent of the time. If you're just beginning to learn how to lay out pages, you'll make far fewer design mistakes if you follow this rule. Regardless of the application, simple layouts are appealing in their crispness, their readability, and their straightforward, no-gimmicks approach.

Rule 4: Leave some white space

Pages that are crammed full of text and pictures tend to be unappealing—meaning that the average, busy reader is likely to skip them. Keep some space between text columns and headlines and between page edges and layout elements. This white space is refreshing and encourages the reader to spend some time on the page. Regardless of the particular document type, readers always appreciate having a place on every page to rest their eyes, a place that offers an oasis in a sea of ink.

Rule 5: Don't use every bell and whistle

QuarkXPress is powerful, yes, but that doesn't mean that it's necessarily a good idea to push the program to its limits at all times. You can, for example, lay out a page with 30 columns of text—but would you want to try reading such a page? With QuarkXPress, you can achieve an amazing number of special effects:

- ✦ Stretch, condense, and scale type
- ✦ Create boxes of almost any shape, and then fill and frame them
- ✦ Add graphics and lines (with custom dash or stripe patterns)
- ✦ Bleed photos and artwork off the edge of the page
- ✦ Flow text along a path, wrap text around all sides of any shape
- ✦ Add colors and create a variety of vignettes (called *blends*)
- ✦ Rotate and skew text and graphics

Using all these effects at once, however, can overwhelm readers and cause them to miss any message you're trying to convey. A good rule: Use no more than three special typographic or design effects per two-page spread.

Rule 6: Make it look like what it is

Lay out the document so that someone looking at it can get an idea of what it is. This sounds like a common-sense rule, but you'd be surprised at how often this rule is broken. If you're laying out an ad for a product, make sure the layout *looks* like an ad, not like a technical brochure. See Figure 6-4 for a sidebar that ended up looking like an ad.

Figure 6-4: There's nothing wrong with this design — except that it's supposed to be a sidebar, not an ad. Placed on a crowded page, its intent was lost on readers.

Rule 7: Don't break Rule 6

Creativity is okay — and QuarkXPress helps you express your layout ideas creatively — but unless you know what you're doing, don't get carried away. If you *are* laying out a technical brochure, for example, don't make it look like a display ad unless you understand that this may confuse readers, and you're doing it for a compelling reason.

Variations on a theme

After you come up with a design, expect it to evolve over time. Styles change, and so does your content. So don't be afraid to try different techniques over the months and years — just make sure that you're not making changes willy-nilly, for change's sake. Figure 6-5 shows the cover of a suburban publication as it grew from a neighborhood family newsletter to a more sophisticated parenting magazine.

Figure 6-5: The newsletter's initial nameplate, from February 1999, reflected the fun, kid focus of the broadsheet newsletter. The middle version, which maintained the basic size and look, debuted in 2000 when the publication became more focused on parents and less focused on kids. In September 2001, as the publication's content matured and it picked up higher-end advertisers, the newsletter became a glossy, standard-size magazine.

Getting Started

The key to a successful layout is planning, a rule that matches the QuarkXPress approach to design. You don't just start doing a layout in QuarkXPress. Instead, you start building the foundation of your document—the page size and columns, the paragraph and character styles, the standard elements such as page numbers and logos—to serve as a receptacle for the content. The idea is that most content you create is a variation on a theme. For example, if you produce a magazine, each issue is different, but the basic design structure is the same from month to month. Rather than start each month from scratch, you start with a template and modify it each month as necessary. The same approach works for newspapers, catalogs, brochures, newsletters, and books.

Visualizing your layout

Even before you build your basic structure, you need a mental image of what your document will be. Have no fear—nothing is cast in stone. If you change your mind as you work on your first document, you can modify your structure. It helps immensely, however, to have an initial structure in mind before starting.

Sketching your layout on paper

How do you start to develop a layout plan? If you're still thinking about what the pages should look like, you can develop some more-specific ideas by spending a few minutes sketching out the layout before you sit down to produce the document on the computer.

Using the dummy approach

Let's say you want to create an eight-page newsletter that has standard, 8½-x-11-inch pages. One way to do this is to create a dummy document, a valuable layout-planning aid. Figure 6-6 shows a sample dummy—the cover and the first two pages.

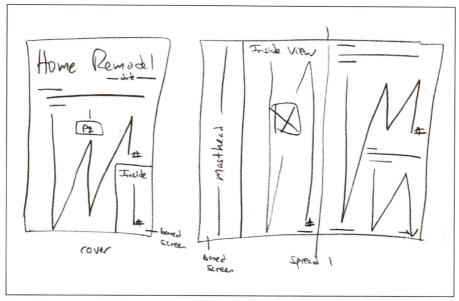

Figure 6-6: A pencil-sketch dummy lets you think through the basic structure quickly and easily.

STEPS: Creating a dummy

1. Take two sheets of blank, 8½-x-11-inch paper, aligning one on top of the other, and folding them in half across the width of the paper. This technique gives you a miniature version of your eight-page newsletter.

2. Next, use a pencil to sketch the dummy's masthead, the cover art and/or stories, and the running headers or footers for each page.

3. Form an idea about how wide you want the top, side, and bottom margins to be, and mark them on the pages.

4. Now indicate which pictures and stories go on each page. Of course, because you will be using QuarkXPress to format the document, you can make changes right up to the point when you produce camera-ready pages.

Here are some conventions to remember as you make your sketches:

✦ A down arrow means the story continues on another page, while a # symbol means the story ends.

✦ Horizontal lines usually indicate titles, bylines, and other such specific text elements, while vertical lines indicate a column of text.

✦ A box with an *X* through it indicates a picture or photo.

✦ The abbreviation *pq* means a pull-quote—text that is taken from the article and put in a box or other shape to draw attention, similar to a photo.

✦ A *screen* is a background of color or gray ink.

You can see from Figure 6-6 that the basic layout structure is three columns, with a self-contained front page that has a small table of contents and interior pages that put the *masthead* (the list of staff) and a viewpoint column on the second page. The third page has two stories, which of course may not start exactly where indicated on the sketch. The point is, merely, that multiple stories can appear on a page.

Taking the next step

You should find all this planning—which actually doesn't take that much time in relation to the other publishing tasks involved—to be time well spent. The process of sketching out the layout helps clarify your thoughts about the basic layout of your document. You can make preliminary decisions about such things as where to put each illustration and section of text on a page, how many columns of text to use, and whether to use any repeating elements (such as headers and footers).

Sketching your layout in QuarkXPress

If you're already comfortable using QuarkXPress, you may decide to forgo the paper-and-pencil sketching of a new document and use QuarkXPress to do the rough design instead. The obvious advantages to this approach are as follows:

✦ **Experimenting with different approaches:** When a document has a set number of text and graphic elements, you can use QuarkXPress to make a series of sketches of the document. If you like, you can save each sketch as a separate file with a distinct file name. In each sketch, you can use different element positioning, type styles, masthead placement, and so on. Then you can print a copy of each file and use the copies to assist you in finalizing the look of the layout.

✦ **Printing thumbnail views:** If you're considering many different layout possibilities, you can develop them quickly in QuarkXPress and then print the series in *thumbnail* (miniature) size (select File ➪ Print, and then check the Thumbnails box in the Document pane, as shown in Figure 6-7). Seeing the pages in thumbnail view makes it easier to evaluate the overall balance between page elements, because you aren't distracted by the text or the graphics in such a reduced view.

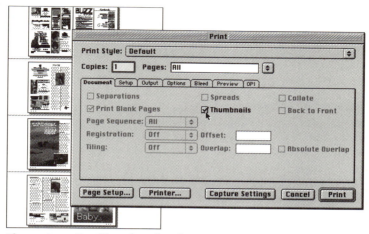

Figure 6-7: Checking Thumbnails in the Document pane of the Print dialog box lets you print miniature versions of your pages.

✦ **Getting your client's approval:** Printed QuarkXPress copies of rough sketches have a cleaner look, which is especially helpful if you're designing a layout for a client. The advantage to presenting rough sketches that look more "final" is that it tends to make the client approval process go more smoothly, and it can make it easier for you to sell the client on your design. At the same time, slick-looking rough drafts do have a disadvantage: They make it more difficult for clients to understand that what they're seeing is just a rough draft and not a final copy.

Imitating and Creating Good Designs

Imitation is the sincerest form of flattery, and as long as you don't cross the line into blatant copying, go ahead and flatter as many people as you can. Go to the newsstand and thumb through a bunch of magazines. (But buy just the ones you really like.) Get a couple of colleagues — or just consult the other coffee lovers in line with you — and look through designs together. Talk about what you like, what you don't like, and — most important — why you react the way you do.

You can call this flower-power consciousness-raising. Or you can call it being a copycat. The point is, it's the best way to learn good design. As with any good design ideas, the ones here are based on years of experience and, of course, honest-to-goodness pilfering of other people's good work.

Avoiding formulas

Although we say to steal ideas and follow the rules, we don't mean for you to flat-out copy other designs, making yours look exactly like someone else's. Your designs should elucidate *your* message—not somebody else's.

Stealing from great artists

A couple more clichés to drive home the point: Good writers read good writers. (We're sure someone has said "Good designers look at good designers," but this hasn't gotten enough buzz to become a cliché yet.) Good artists imitate; great artists steal.

Avoiding design recipes

Don't confuse examples of good design with recipes. We don't pretend to be Picasso or even Haring. Our designs (and our colleagues' designs) might make no sense for your documents. After all, you need to make sure the designs you produce meet several needs:

- ✦ Your sense of aesthetics.
- ✦ The requirements of the content being presented.
- ✦ The image you or your organization wants to convey.
- ✦ The financial limitations you're working under. (We'd all love to do everything in full, glorious color, but until money comes out of printers without resulting in jail terms, we do have some concerns about costs.)

The design of the ad in Figure 6-8 works well for the company, Center Stage, because the simple black-and-white graphic communicates a 3-D stage. Plus, the company can rotate out the center text each month to sell whatever is hot that month. But when a new drugstore came to town and asked a designer to adapt the design of this ad for its grand opening, the designer had to refuse—it was just the wrong approach for a grand opening.

Learning to improvise

Use design samples as starting points, and don't confuse the techniques and fundamental principles they illustrate with the implementation we happened to choose for the particular example. You could use those same techniques and fundamental principles and come up with completely different designs for your projects. Great artists may steal, but they also improvise.

Laying out ads and circulars

The elements of ads, *circulars* (fliers), and other such sales– and marketing-oriented materials are a critical type of publication, because they must work the first time. You may be willing to put up with a design you don't care for in a newsletter that contains information you find valuable. But an ad has the burden of needing to attract your attention, holding you long enough to deliver its message, and letting you go with a favorable impression. In the following sections, we look at three ads to see the techniques they use to accomplish these goals. ***Remember:*** Whether it's an ad, a report cover, a prospectus, a pamphlet, or other such publication, these techniques apply.

Figure 6-8: The design of this ad works well for its original content, but it isn't likely to adapt well to another type of business.

An airline ad mockup

Figure 6-9 shows an ad mockup for a fictitious airline. Notice the following about its design:

✦ **The large type:** This is kerned so that the spacing between each pair of characters is the same—just at the point of touching.

✦ **The small type:** This forces the eye to take a look, because of the contrast with the big type above and all the space on either side. This use of contrast is a good way to get attention. Never underestimate the power of type. It's as important as graphics in garnering attention and conveying both the substance and the nuances of the message.

✦ **The airline logo:** This uses reverse-video and shadow effects on a fairly common font (Bauhaus). Notice the sun symbol to the logo's left: That's a symbol in the Zapf Dingbats font. The use of symbols really helps establish a logo as a logo, rather than just a bunch of letters. Also notice the use of a catch-phrase (also called a *tag line*) in the same font as the logo. You would do this for a catch-phrase that you plan to use in several places. It becomes an extension of the logo. (The desert tableau is a color image, and in color the text is very striking against the colors; in black-and-white, it loses a little of that zing.)

✦ **White space:** Blank areas provide a visually calm port in a storm of images and text. Be sure to provide these resting spots in all your work.

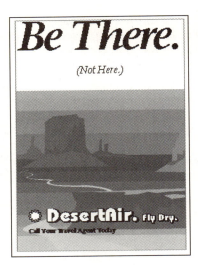

Figure 6-9: A simple ad with a simple message deserves a simple treatment to attract attention. But notice that simple does not mean simplistic — every element has a character of its own.

A restaurant ad mockup

The ad mockup in Figure 6-10, for a seafood restaurant, shows a tighter interplay of text and graphics. It also shows, although not at first glance, the power of QuarkXPress's graphics manipulation tools. Here's what to look for:

✦ **The schools of fish:** They're in glorious color, although you can't see that in black-and-white, and there are really only three fish in the ad. We used the copy function in QuarkXPress to create the schools. And to make sure that they didn't look like clones, we used the rotate and skew tools to make each cloned fish slightly different from the others.

We used only a very slight skew (less than 5 percent); the rotation accounts for most of the difference in the fishes' appearance. The lesson: Don't forget to use basic tools such as rotation and copying.

✦ **The descriptive text:** The text describing all the sumptuous seafood options ("Atlantic cod. Alaska salmon.") is wrapped around the pictures of fish, using QuarkXPress's Bézier picture box to hold the pictures, combined with the ability to have text wrap around both sides of an image.

✦ **The headlines:** Can you tell what this ad is selling? Why, fresh fish, of course! The repetitive use of the text reinforces the message. Placing the repeating text in different positions among the fish makes sure it doesn't look repetitive. (Predictability is a major reason that repetition is boring, so this design finds a way to repeat without being boring.)

✦ **The tag line:** This added repetition of "Fresh Fish" reinforces the primary message. In the case of this ad, there's no large text identifying the restaurant (it's in the body text), but this tag line is one the restaurant uses a lot, so the ad can get away with the low-key treatment of the restaurant's name — just as if an ad said only "Have it your way," you'd probably think of Burger King, while "Just do it!" would evoke Nike.

✦ **Italics:** All the text here, except the list of locations at the bottom, is in italics, which is unusual. But the fluidity of italics works well with the fish theme (underwater, get it?), and by making the text large enough and the layout uncluttered, it works.

✦ **Going beyond the margins:** The fish swim past the margins on the page, which makes the page feel less boxed-in. It's often a good idea to overstep margins to provide a feeling of flexibility and give the eye something unusual to notice.

Figure 6-10: The interplay between the text and graphics in this ad reinforces the message.

A public service announcement

Let's take a look at one more ad. This one is not a full page. It's the kind of ad you'd probably run in an in-house publication: what magazines call a PSA (public service announcement). It's the type of thing you can easily put together using clip art and basic typefaces when you have a hole to fill or need to make an announcement or advertisement for your organization (see Figure 6-11). Look at the following:

✦ **The simple graphic:** This simple graphic works well in black-and-white. Photos can be very effective in catching attention, because they scream, "Real!" The simple composition is also pleasing. You'll find many such images in clip-art libraries.

✦ **The message:** Simple text with a simple message that ties into the image — that's the ticket.

✦ **The headline:** A loud, bold title would have competed with the photo. This one's easy to read, but it doesn't fight for attention. If you see the photo and stop, you'll see the headline, and that's all that's required. The centering makes sure that it's clear the headline goes with the text below. It also follows the centered shape of the chair.

✦ **The alignment:** The more ways things line up, the more distracting a layout can be, so try to use only one or two alignments. A left alignment might have worked here, but then the symmetry of the chair would not have been picked up in the rest of the ad — and such reuse of basic visual themes is a hallmark of pleasing design. People just get all warm and fuzzy with such continuity.

✦ **The justified text:** The text is short, readable, and justified. Although having justified text may seem to violate the minimal-alignment rule above, the fact is that centered text is rarely easy to read if there's more than a few lines of it. Having the text justified keeps the symmetry of the centered text, because the right and left margins in justified text are symmetrical.

✦ **The dashed lines:** We all know what a dashed line means. The ad fairly screams, "Cut me out!" To get a dashed box, just use one of QuarkXPress's box tools and change the frame style to a dashed one. To reinforce the "Cut me out!" message, you could add a pair of scissors (from a symbols font or from clip art) along a top corner of the dashed box.

✦ **The coupon:** In the box is the coupon you're hoping people will fill out. The font here is different (a condensed sans serif, compared to the text's normal serif). The font reinforces that it's a separate element. You want the readers to think of the coupon as separate, so they know that it's okay to remove it from the rest of the ad. The use of a condensed font also gives you more room for the information you want people to fill in. The underlines are right-aligned tabs using an underline leader. That's the simplest way to create fill-in-the-blank lines.

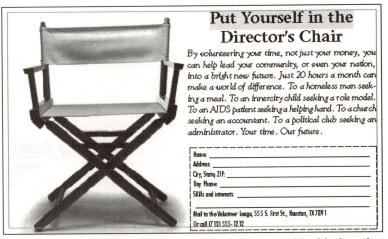

Figure 6-11: A public service announcement designed for black-and-white reproduction.

Creating newsletters

Quintessentially, publishing newsletters and magazines represents the focus of page-layout programs, even though QuarkXPress is also great for a whole range of documents, including ads, reports, and catalogs. But when you think publishing, you think newsletters and magazines. So we'll spend a little time going over ways of making top-notch newsletters and magazines, without hiring a huge crew of designers.

Designing a neighborhood newsletter

Figure 6-12 shows the table of contents page and an inside article from what started as a neighborhood newsletter and has since undergone several redesigns. The pages are from three different issues, one from 1999, one from June 2001, and one from a major redesign in September 2001. Take a look. They use different fonts and embellishments, yet they all share a familiar look.

Getting a new look

Newsletters and magazines generally redesign themselves every couple years. The redesign might be subtle, or it might be extreme — but it happens. Why? Because the new art director or publisher wants to put his imprint on the publication, you might say.

Well, that's partially true, but the real reason is more basic: If you don't revisit your look every once in a while, you look stale, and people will think you're lazy or don't care about them. People do it for their personal appearance, too. (Want proof? Take a look at a snapshot of yourself from five years ago.) Note how this design evolved (refer to Figure 6-12):

✦ **A two-column TOC:** The original table of contents, at top left, broke the content into features and departments. Although simple and fun, it did little to encourage readers to flip to a story. The more professional table of contents in the middle maintained the distinction between features and departments, but it provided for graphics and tag lines to entice readers. Unfortunately, it became too crowded. The most recent table of contents, at top right, streamlined the information while still providing visual interest.

✦ **A two-column format:** All the designs are based on a two-column format, although the designer sometimes experimented with four columns. Because the first two designs were printed on broadsheet, the two columns were actually too wide to be read comfortably. When the smaller size debuted in September 2001, the two columns were just the right size.

✦ **The same basic elements:** All use the same basic elements: a department name, a headline, a kicker under the headline, a byline, a pull quote, and an author bio. For the most part, the designers stuck with a serif font for body text and a sans serif font for headlines and subheads.

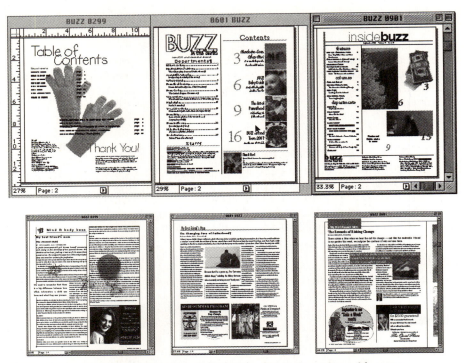

Figure 6-12: As this newsletter evolved into a glossy magazine with more sophisticated content, its design evolved as well.

Yet they differ significantly in the following areas:

✦ **The original design:** In this design from the late 1990s, the emphasis was on making the newsletter fun and friendly. The designer used a different dingbat from a font such as MiniPicsArtJam next to each department name in each issue. In addition, she screened a fun but relevant image behind the story. The department name, in 22-point Rotis Semi Serif Bold, is clean and bold, and the headline for the story is clear in 16-point Future Extra Bold. The byline, in 8-point All Caps Futura Extra Bold, probably gained a little more attention than it deserved — although at this time the publication could not pay its writers, so flattery was important. The lead paragraph is in 13-point Garamond Italic with a generous 18 points of leading. For the column width, the body text is a fairly small 10-point Garamond Book, but the 15 points of leading helped the readability somewhat. A pull quote in 15-point Rotis Semi Serif with 25 points of leading reflects the typeface of the department head and conveyed the thesis of the monthly column. On these 11-x-13-inch pages, the columns were actually almost 4.75 inches wide and the body text was justified — two factors that made it somewhat hard to read and detracted from the friendliness. At this point, the publication was very kid-focused, even including a list of birthday party ideas and a kids' page.

✦ **The midway point:** Around 2000 (shown here is the June 2001 issue), the design started to become less whimsical and more professional. The designer changed the body text to flush left—a significant improvement to the readability—and experimented with three– and four-column layouts. In another significant change, a new designer changed the body text from Garamond Book to Minion, which has smaller serifs and is a little easier to read. To retain the fun feel, the department name is in a tall, thin sans serif font called OptiJake at 32 points. The headline remained in Futura, this time in 16-point Futura Bold. The byline, remaining at 8 point, lost its All Caps setting and dropped back to Futura Light, losing emphasis (but the writers started to receive payment!). The lead paragraph, here, is in 14-point Minion Italic with 18 points of leading, and the body text remained at 10 points with 15 points of leading, something that helped retain continuity with the previous design. The pull quote, at 18 points with 30 points of leading, picks up the headline look with the use of Futura Condensed Light. During this time, the content and advertisements became a little more sophisticated and well-rounded.

✦ **The final design:** In September 2001, the publishers of *Buzz in the 'Burbs,* Sheryl Perri and Lisa Zimmermann, decided a magazine size would look more upscale and be more convenient for readers to carry and save. As the size changed from 11 x 13 inches to 8¼ x 11 inches, a new budget allowed for more color and glossy paper as well. At this time, graphic designer Tom Visocchi dropped many remaining elements from the original design—while still retaining a friendly look. Just about the only thing to survive the transition was the left-aligned 10-point Minion for the body text, although the leading dropped down to a more standard 13 points. Visocchi dropped the multitude of fonts, using only variations of Helvetica for contrast—its cleaner lines looking more modern than the overused Futura. The department heads are in 18-point Helvetica Condensed Bold, the headlines in 21-point Minion SemiBold, the byline in 8-point Helvetica Light, and the lead paragraph in 16-point Helvetica Condensed Light with 19 points of leading. The pull quote, now reversed out in a color block, is in 18-point Minion Condensed with 23 points of leading. The new template also incorporated a photo of the columnist into the bio. At this point, the publication was carrying ads from high-end restaurants, salons, cosmetic surgeons, and money managers along with its standard content of cooking, parenting, style, and health articles.

Dealing with change

As you can see from the example in Figure 6-12, each design had a set of goals in mind. The goals changed over time, even as the basic content did not. The opposite can also happen: The content changes over time but the design and "image" goals do not. When the content changes but the image goals don't, the situation is a little trickier, because you need to update the design to accommodate the new content (such as increased use of profiles, short stories, gossip and rumors, question-and-answer interviews, and so on) while still reflecting the feel of the old design.

For examples of what we mean, take a look at current issues of *The New York Times, The Wall Street Journal, Business Week, Time,* or *Newsweek.* Then compare them with issues from five years ago. You'll find a different look and mix of content, but the same overall feel.

Understanding newsletter basics

A newsletter's main goal is to provide information. So the focus should be on text: how to make it readable, how to call attention to it, and how to make sure the reader knows where all relevant content is. Take a look at the newsletter in Figure 6-13. It's the same newsletter as in Figure 6-12, but the page chosen is a typical feature with a sidebar. It shows the basic components of the newsletter, around which you can add embellishments (such as graphics).

Figure 6-13: The most basic elements of a newsletter — columns and sidebars.

Here are some basic newsletter design issues to consider:

✦ **Column width:** Most newsletters are two or three columns wide. A three-column format gives you more flexibility, because you can have graphics of three different sizes (one, two, and three columns wide), plus you can add sidebars and separate stories fairly easily to a page, because again there are multiple sizes to choose from. A two-column format is more straightforward, but it gives you fewer options. It's best for newsletters that are essentially sequential — without multiple stories and sidebars on a page or spread.

✦ **Page numbers and folios:** As always, make sure you add page numbers and an identifier of the publication (called a *folio*). Some include a corporate symbol after the page number, to add visual interest and reinforce the identity.

✦ **Body text:** The body text uses a very readable, straightforward font: Minion Regular. It's a typical size for newsletters and magazines: 10 points with 13 points leading. Generally speaking, point size should range from 9 to 10 points (you can use half-point sizes), and leading from 10.5 to 13 points, with the most typical being 2 points more than the font size. Justified text is often used for an authorative look and left-aligned text for a friendlier look.

✦ **Drop caps:** Using a drop cap is an effective way to alert the reader to the beginning of a new story — you can also use it for the beginning of the conclusion — as well as to provide a visual contrast on the page. Often, drop caps are in a different typeface (sometimes picking up the headline font) and color from the body text. Generally, you should boldface the drop cap, to make it more readable. (Otherwise, the drop cap looks wimpy, which isn't what you want for such a big element.)

✦ **Headlines, kickers, and bylines:** The headline, the *kicker* (the type above it, also called a *slug line* for reasons that have nothing to do with gardening), and the byline are usually related. For example, the headline may reflect the body text (Minion Condensed Bold and Minion, respectively) and the kicker and byline may be from the same typeface (Helvetica Condensed Medium and Helvetica Light, respectively). Using related typefaces provides consistency while still producing a subtle difference from the rest of the text.

Caution

Be careful when combining multiple fonts. If they don't work together, it can be a disaster. A rule of thumb is to restrict the number of fonts (not including variants such as boldface and small caps) to two per page. You can break this rule occasionally by using a font that has similarities to one of the other two.

✦ **Dingbats:** A nice touch is to end a story with a *dingbat* (publishing speak for a symbol). The dingbat might be as simple as a single character or the corporate logo — anything that reinforces the identity. Making a dingbat is easy: Just add the symbol after the last paragraph, either by putting a tab before it (and defining the tab in your text style to be flush right against the right margin, or using Option+Tab on the Mac or Shift+Tab on Windows to create a right-aligned tab) or an em space (which is two nonbreaking en spaces, or two uses of the keyboard shortcut Option+⌘+spacebar on the Mac or Ctrl+Alt+Shift+6 in Windows). Either way is fine for justified text. Pick one based on your preferences. But use only the em space if your text isn't justified.

✦ **Sidebars:** You can make a sidebar or separate, minor story distinct by putting a shaded background behind it. Make sure you have a margin between the edge of the background and the text. You can also box a sidebar, with or without the background, using frames. Or you could just put a line above and below the background, as done in Figure 6-13. We chose the line approach to pick up the lines at the top and bottom of each page. Notice, too, that the text is two columns wide here, so it really looks different from the surrounding text.

✦ **Pull quotes:** A pull quote is a great way to call out some interesting material in a story to attract readers' attention. Often, the style reflects the sidebars, including a shaded background or lines above and below. Any embellishments, such as dingbats, should help the text stand out while still providing continuity with the overall design.

Working with magazines

Magazines are very similar to newsletters, except that they generally have color images, more graphics, a cover that has no stories on it, and a full-page (or larger) table of contents.

Creating tables of contents

Let's look first at a sample contents page from a magazine. Note, though, that magazines usually are highly designed, which means they often look very different from one another (see Figures 6-14 and 6-15). So take the following techniques as starting points:

✦ **The logo:** This should be distinct and readable. In Figure 6-14, the "5280" is large and clear, and the designer applied the same color to it as the color in the shaded sidebar.

✦ **The banner:** The issue date and number is called a *banner*. There's a generous amount of space and an en bullet between the months and year, the volume number, and the issue number. (An en bullet and the space around it is typically the width of the letter *n* in the respective font. This [•] is the type of bullet you see most often.)

Tip   When you use a banner, make sure the text is bold; otherwise, it's hard to read.

✦ **Feature and column entries:** Magazines generally have *features* (longer articles that appear only once), along with *columns* (regular, short articles that appear in each issue, usually covering a certain topic). Label the content accordingly (in Figure 6-14, the columns are called *Departments*). The Univers Light Ultra Condensed on the "Departments" head is used in the folios and in the magazine's department heads. The "Contents" head is in Bauer Bodoni as are the blurbs describing each feature.

✦ **Page numbers:** The use of large page numbers for the features reinforces that this is a table of contents. In Figure 6-14, the page numbers are in Bauer Bodoni, and they're 24 points. For the departments, the page numbers remain in Univers Extra Black, but they're set off from the text with two spaces.

✦ **Photo and graphic listings:** Putting a page number near any photo or graphic you have in your contents page is a good idea. If people are interested in the photo, they should be able to know where to find the associated article.

Figure 6-14: A one-page table of contents for a magazine.

Formatting feature articles

An eye-catching design is critical to enticing readers to sample a publication's contents. Most publications use a variety of tools — for example, QuarkXPress, Adobe Illustrator, Macromedia FreeHand, and Adobe Photoshop, among others — to create visually rich pages. Feature articles showcase a magazine's many design approaches, because articles of that length give the designers the opportunity to use multiple techniques within the overall design framework.

Working with flexible grids

The magazine's design offers a flexible grid that allows different numbers of columns and column widths from feature to feature (see Figure 6-16). By having a standard grid, the magazine's design director can be assured that the entire package will be cohesive. By allowing individual designers options within that structure, appropriate creative flexibility is available to keep the reader engaged. Every standard element — body text, sidebars, screen images, diagrams, tables, and captions — must take up an integral number of columns, but the number per element is up to the designer.

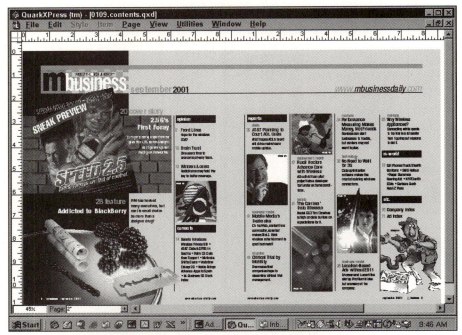

Figure 6-15: A two-page table of contents for a magazine.

Knowing how multiple grids work

You can see the use of the multiple grids in the layout in Figure 6-17. For the first page of this feature, the designer placed the headline and introductory paragraph in boxes that span four columns in the grid. The columns for body text, on the right side of the first page and on the second page, are placed in the standard position. The many options for placing columns and sidebars give the designer flexibility for handling all the illustrations, photographs, and sidebars that make up this active story.

Mixing grids on a page

You can also mix grids on a page, as shown in Figure 6-18. The main text follows a two-column grid. But the sidebar on the left-facing page spans all the columns in the grid, allowing for wider columns. A small box in the first column on the right-facing page spans one column in the grid. Staying within the geometry of the grid, the designer can easily connect sidebars and graphics to related text while creating enough visual distinction. That's the beauty of having multiple grids to use in a layout.

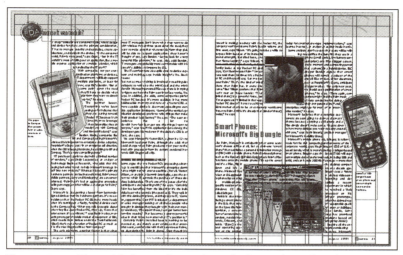

Figure 6-16: The grid shows the options designers have for placement of standard elements.

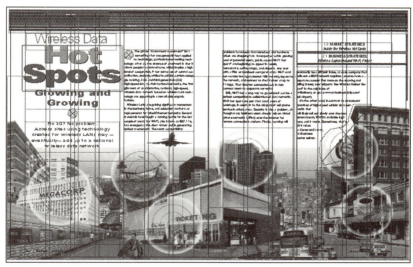

Figure 6-17: A grid gives designers the opportunity to vary the layout as necessary.

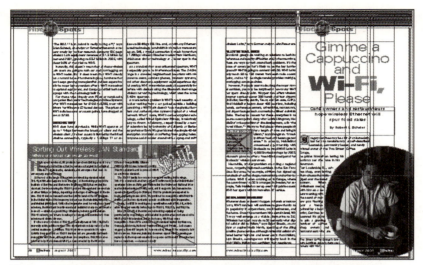

Figure 6-18: By mixing two-, three-, and four-column grids, the designer easily separates unlike elements and keeps like elements together.

Working with gatefolds

Every once in a while, you see a magazine that has an article with a fold-out page. Called a *gatefold,* this kind of page requires some special work in your layout. Figure 6-19 shows a gatefold that was actually an extension of the magazine cover — *5280* used the gatefold to call attention to its first "Top Singles" story.

To create a gatefold, you just add a page to the right of an existing right-hand page, making sure to add an extra page to the left of the next spread's existing left-hand page. (To do this, use the Document Layout palette, available in the View menu.) That's the easy part. But there are three possible hazards:

✦ **Although it appears on-screen as if the three pages are one long sheet of paper, in the actual magazine, the far-left page is a separate sheet of paper, while the two right pages are indeed one sheet of paper (folded where the line numbers are).**

Tip

Be sure to leave sufficient space between the two sheets so text and images don't get swallowed up in the gutter. In this layout, notice how the "single in the city" headline has a little more space after *single* to compensate for the gutter.

✦ **The folded-over page in a gatefold needs to be a bit narrower than the other pages.** That's so when it's folded, it doesn't actually get so far into the gutter that it's bound shut into the magazine. Typically, you want to keep an extra pica (⅙ inch) on the outside edge of a gatefold's folded page.

✦ **A gatefold must be at the beginning or end of a *form* (the sequence of pages printed and bound at one time on a printing press).** That's because the extra-wide sheet must be the first or last sheet in the stack. (Magazines are composed of multiple forms, usually of 8, 16, 24, or 32 pages in length.)

Tip

Check with your printer before using a gatefold. Also, tell your service bureau you're outputting a gatefold, so the staff can ensure that the extra width doesn't inadvertently get cut off during output to film.

Figure 6-19: A gatefold calls attention to content.

Doing other cool stuff

By combining various techniques, you can create some cool-looking stuff, for any of a variety of documents. Figure 6-20 shows some examples, which are described as follows:

✦ **Embossed text:** You can create various embossed-text effects by duplicating a text box and making one slightly overlap the other. Then make the one on top white (or the paper color).

✦ **Textual graphics:** By duplicating a text box several times and rotating each copy at a different angle, then applying different shades of gray to each, you can create a textual graphic. Here, each subsequent copy of the word *shade* is rotated 10 degrees more than the previous and is 10 percent darker.

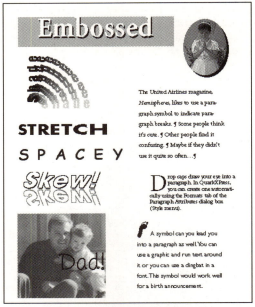

Figure 6-20: Various special effects (from top to bottom, left to right).

✦ **Stretched text:** Each letter in the word *Stretch* is set 10 percent wider than the previous letter, which gives it the effect of being stretched.

✦ **Spaced-out text:** By increasing the space between letters, you can space out text — an effect lots of designers use. You could put spaces (whether regular spaces, en spaces, or em spaces) between the letters, but by using the inter-character spacing controls (tracking), you ensure that the text is treated as one word and you make it easy to change your spacing settings. (It's easier to adjust the tracking than, say, to replace em spaces with en spaces between every character.)

✦ **Combining skew and shadow:** By combining the skew feature with the shadow feature for text, you can alter how a font looks to create logos. Here, with the word *skew,* we went a step further and mirrored the text block and changed its color to a shade of gray (by defining a tint of 40 percent black).

✦ **Tinting grayscale images:** For grayscale images, you can apply a color or tint to make them ghostly or subtle. It's a great way to mute a photo enough so that you can place text over it, like we did with the photo of a father and child.

✦ **Cameo effects:** By using an oval or Bézier picture box (with a very thick frame), you can create a cameo effect. This is a way to create a different type of shape or frame.

✦ **Altered opening-page text:** In some publications, the text on the opening page has a radically different style from the rest of the pages. Often, there is little text on the opening page, because the title and graphics usually take up much of the space. The text that's on the page is also treated graphically. One method is to have no paragraph breaks but to instead use a symbol to indicate paragraph breaks (like you see in the United Airlines paragraph).

✦ **Embedded graphics:** Although drop caps are popular, you can also use an embedded graphic to accomplish the same purpose. Or, if you want the graphic to be dropped down into the text, you can place the graphic at the appropriate location and turn on text wrap.

✦ **Graphical drop caps:** You can use a graphic or a symbol character from a pi font as a drop cap, as shown in the paragraph beginning with the footprint symbol. If you use a graphic, we suggest you use the anchor feature (covered in Chapter 23) to ensure that the graphic stays with the text as it reflows in your document.

Distinctive article openers

Figures 6-21 and 6-22 show two approaches to distinctive article openers. Figure 6-21 shows an introductory paragraph set off through the use of a different typeface, larger size, and increased leading. The typeface and spacing have a clean, no-nonsense look — like the characters you see in a Big Red tablet — to complement the topic of going back to school. The designer used Photoshop to blur the edges of "Wise Words" to make it look like chalk on a blackboard, to reemphasize the theme.

Figure 6-21: For that public-school feel, the graphic designer used clean typeface and generous spacing for this article's lead paragraph. The background of the story picks up the yellow from the school bus and the boy's backpack in the image.

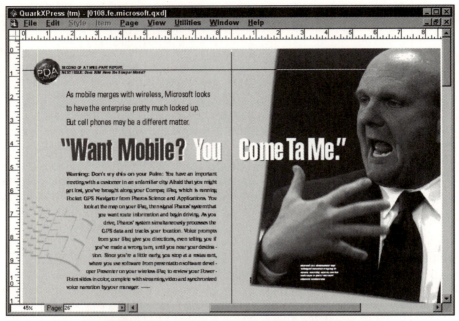

Figure 6-22: A very bold photo deserves very bold text, yet the designer also introduced a few soft elements to act as a visual counterweight.

Figure 6-22 also shows the use of different type sizes and typefaces, and combines them with a very direct photo. The interplay between the bold text and the bold photo is enhanced by the otherwise spare design — there is a lot of white space, which just showcases the bold elements more. However, the designer didn't confuse direct with rigid — he used QuarkXPress's text-wrap feature to give a bit of motion to the text and images, to provide a more relaxed counterweight to the overall boldness.

Defining visual treatments

Another cool effect is to recognize a defining visual treatment in part of your layout and use it throughout the layout. In Figure 6-23, notice how the designer picked up the hot spots in the illustration and used the QuarkXPress gradient-fill feature to add similar elements in the opener's typography.

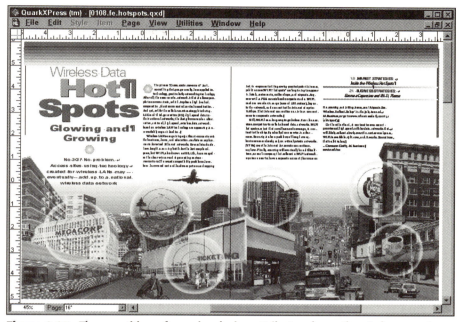

Figure 6-23: The repetition of a major design attribute—here, the circle or spot—adds whimsy and style to a layout. With such a strong visual, take advantage of it.

Looking at common threads

Creative design means taking some risks: trying out new ideas. Because it's easy to use QuarkXPress to try out ideas—and to abandon those that just don't cut it—you should set aside some time in every project to play around with your design. Save a copy of your original, of course, and then see if you can discover some new approach that adds that special edge. While you're doing that, keep the following principles in mind:

✦ **Look intentional.** A former boss gave one of us some advice we'll never forget: Make sure you look intentional. Everything in your design should look like you wanted it to be there. If something looks odd, it should look as if it were meant to look odd. If it looks intentional—whether or not it actually was!—the reader will think you put a lot of care and attention into your work, which enhances your credibility.

✦ **Have enough white space.** People need a visual resting place as they thumb through a publication. Give it to them. If you don't, they'll start to fall asleep, and they'll stop reading. If it's too *gray* (where everything looks like everything else) or too *busy* (where there are so many things to look at that you don't know where to start), people will stop making the effort.

✦ **Make the text readable.** Remember that the basic point of publishing is to convey information. So don't make it hard for the reader to get the information you're providing. Make sure the text is readable. Captions and headlines should be both informative and interesting. Make sure people can tell where a story continues and which stories are related to each other.

✦ **Use type creatively.** Fonts are neat and fun. Invest in several fonts, and use them creatively by applying effects such as small caps, colors, banner backgrounds, rotation, skewing, and mixed sizes (but not all at once, of course).

✦ **Use graphics effectively.** They should be fairly large—lots of small images are hard to look at—and should complement the rest of the layout.

✦ **Use visual themes.** Use a core set of fonts. If you use lines in one place, they may be effective in another. If you use boxes to separate some elements, don't use colored backgrounds to separate others. Instead, pick one approach and stick with it. There can be variances within the approaches, but by picking up variations of the same core approach, you keep your reader from getting distracted by visual chaos, yet you can still be creative.

✦ **Use color judiciously.** Color is expensive and can overwhelm the content. Used well, grays can provide as much visual interest as color. In fact, in something laden with color, a gray image will stand out as distinct and gain more attention than the surrounding color images.

Summary

As much as you might love the hands-on approach—getting in the software and creating those neat-looking columns and boldface type—you need to do your homework first. You need to understand the terminology and the tenets of good design, then you need to think through a project before you jump in and start laying it out. The more you know about design, the more quickly you can produce designs with QuarkXPress.

Sketches or rough proofs produced in QuarkXPress help designers get buy-in on their approach. Whether you're showing ideas to a client, a board of directors, or a supervisor—or even reviewing them yourself—getting your different ideas on paper helps you decide on a direction. Then, when you get into QuarkXPress, you can focus on perfecting the final look that speaks to *your* content—not someone else's.

✦   ✦   ✦

Creating a New Document

When you're starting off a traditional publication such as a magazine or brochure in QuarkXPress, the most important thing you need to know is the finished page size. QuarkXPress is actually quite unforgiving on this topic. If you kick off a document at the wrong size and place several items on the pages, there's almost no way out. Although you can resize a document and make global adjustments on master pages, you may end up adjusting the size and placement of every item on every page. In addition to knowing the page size, it helps to have something in mind for the margins and the number of columns — but these are fairly easy to change.

In some cases, page size will not matter as much (for example, if you're experimenting with logo designs, creating artwork for a T-shirt, designing a quarter-page ad, or producing a sheet of mailing labels or business cards). In these cases, you'll need to know how the document will be output. For example, the QuarkXPress elements for an ad may be pulled out of your document and into a completed newsletter document. Or, if you're printing on forms for mailing labels or business cards, you'll need to know the page size and the size and placement of each printable area on the form.

Starting a New Document

First, open a new document by selecting File ⇨ New ⇨ Document, or use ⌘+N or Ctrl+N. This displays the New Document dialog box, shown in Figure 7-1.

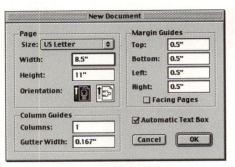

Figure 7-1: The New Document dialog box lets you specify the page size, columns, and margins for a new document.

When using the File ⇨ New menu sequence, QuarkXPress provides a submenu that lets you decide on the type of file you want to create: a document, a library, a book, an XML publication, or a Web document. Most of the time, you simply want to create a new document. To get past the submenu and quickly create a new document, use the keyboard shortcuts ⌘+N or Ctrl+N.

On the Macintosh, you can also choose File ⇨ New very quickly, and QuarkXPress will assume that you want to create a document. On Windows, selecting File ⇨ New always shows a submenu for specific file types. To quickly create a new QuarkXPress document in Windows, you must use the shortcut Ctrl+N.

Selecting the page size

In the New Document dialog box, the first thing you need to do is select the size of your final pages from the menu. (The size you choose, by the way, need not necessarily be exactly the same size as the paper your printer can hold. We cover this more fully in Chapter 35.) QuarkXPress offers five standard page size selections in the dialog box and also gives you the opportunity to specify a custom page size. The standard page sizes are as follows:

- ✦ **US Letter:** Width 8.5 inches, height 11 inches
- ✦ **US Legal:** Width 8.5 inches, height 14 inches
- ✦ **A4 Letter:** Width 8.268 inches, height 11.693 inches
- ✦ **B5 Letter:** Width 6.929 inches, height 9.843 inches
- ✦ **Tabloid:** Width 11 inches, height 17 inches

QuarkXPress also lets you create custom page sizes. In this case, don't worry about which page size is selected in the Size list. Instead, simply enter the desired page dimensions in the Width and Height fields, ranging from 0.111 inch by 0.111 inch to 48 inches by 48 inches. Figure 7-2 shows the starting page size for a magazine that is actually trimmed to 8.25 x 10.75 inches.

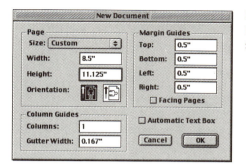

Figure 7-2: The Page area in the New Document dialog box lets you specify a Custom page size.

If you're outputting your document directly to negatives and you want crop marks to be automatically printed at the page margins for a trimmed page (such as the 7⅞-x-10½-inch page size used by many magazines), enter those page dimensions in the Height and Width fields. For fractional dimensions, don't pull out your calculator—QuarkXPress can do the math for you. For example, if you want a page width of 7⅞ inches, enter 7+7/8 rather than 7.875. Note the + sign: It's essential. Entering 7 7/8 is read as 7⅞, or 9.625.

Knowing how QuarkXPress displays measurements

In the New Document dialog box, QuarkXPress always displays page width and height in inches, even if you select a different measurement unit in the General tab of the Document Preferences dialog box (which you access when a document is open by selecting Edit ➪ Preferences ➪ Document, or by using ⌘+Y or Ctrl+Y). You can specify page dimensions to 0.001 of any measurement unit, and QuarkXPress automatically makes the conversion to inches in the Width and Height fields.

Determining the best page size

How do you know which page size is best? The answer to that question is really up to you, but it's useful to note which page sizes are typically used. Many newsletters use letter size, which is a convenient size for mailing. Magazines tend to use a size slightly smaller than letter size. (As paper costs have increased, publishers have trimmed away from the old letter-size standard, reducing both the amount of paper and the total weight, which in turn reduces mailing costs.) Newspapers and larger-format magazines frequently use tabloid size.

Working with facing pages

Although we need to jump slightly out of order in the New Document dialog box, you really need to decide whether your document will have facing pages before you specify the margins. Check the Facing Pages box if the document pages are to be printed on both sides, with the right and left pages facing each other when the document is open. If you check it, you can set Inside and Outside margins rather than Left and Right margins, as shown in Figure 7-3. QuarkXPress will then create right and left pages that mirror each other in terms of right and left margins.

If you select Facing Pages, see the "Tips for margin mavens" sidebar.

Figure 7-3: The Margin Guides area contains the Facing Pages check box, which lets you control whether pages are placed side by side and whether you set Inside and Outside margins rather than Left and Right margins.

Setting the margins

After you've decided on the Facing Pages setting, use the Margin Guides area of the New Document dialog box to enter measurement values (to 0.001 of any unit of measurement) for the top, left, bottom, and right margins of the document's basic text box (or if you're using facing pages, the inside and outside margins rather than the left and right margins). If you're using ragged-right text in the document — text that aligns to the left margin but not the right margin — you can set right margins a bit smaller than you need for justified text. (To create ragged-right text, you actually set the text to be left-aligned.)

Margin guides appear as colored lines on-screen, but the lines don't print. If you opt for an automatic text box, it will contain the number of columns you specify. You can turn off the display of guides via View ➪ Hide Guides (F7 or Shift+F7).

Determining the number of columns

In the Columns field (in the Column Guides area of the New Document dialog box), enter the number of text columns you want to use on most pages, as shown in Figure 7-4. (The reason we say "most" pages is because you can, for example, select three columns in this dialog box and then, within the document, use a different number of columns on a particular page.) You can specify as many as 30 columns per page, although you won't often need that many, particularly on a standard 8½-x-11-inch paper. As with margins, column guides appear as colored lines on-screen, but the lines do not print.

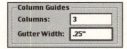

Figure 7-4: Use the Columns field to specify how many columns of text will appear on most pages.

Tips for margin mavens

When you're working in a word processor, typing a letter for example, margins are a snap. Usually, you just add half an inch or an inch around all edges of the page. But in professional publishing, especially when you're working with facing pages and bound documents, margins can become more confusing. Here are a few things to know about margins:

✦ **Margin measurements determine how far from the outside edges of the paper you expect to place the document's text boxes and picture boxes.** The margins are for the whole document, but they are by no means set in concrete. For example, you can place individual text boxes or picture boxes anywhere on the page, even within the preset margin spaces, as shown in the figure. One situation in which a page element may cross over into the margin is when you create a *bleed,* an illustration that extends past the edge of the physical page.

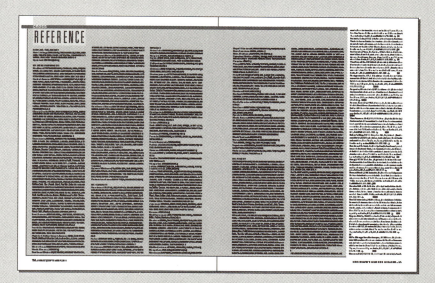

✦ **In facing-page documents, you may want to consider having one margin larger than the margins on the other three sides of a page.** For example, if you plan to saddle-stitch or three-hole punch a document, make the inside margin wider so that it can accommodate the staples or holes. (You may need to discuss this with a printer instead of guessing how much space to leave.)

✦ **Be careful not to make margins too large, because doing so can give the text and pictures on the page an appearance of insignificance.** By the same token, don't make margins too small, because it can produce an equally unappealing look that results from having too much information on a page.

Continued

Continued

✦ **After you set up the document specifications in the New Document dialog box, QuarkXPress lets you redefine the margins by changing the margins for the corresponding master page.** Choose Page ⇨ Display ⇨ [master page name], and then choose Page ⇨ Master Guides to change the margins.

Tip

Just because you plan to have a certain number of text columns in a document doesn't necessarily mean you should enter that exact number in the Columns field of the New Document dialog box. Suppose your publication has three columns, plus pull-quotes that are set out of alignment with the text margins. You may want to try using an eight-column grid, and use some of the column grid lines to align the pull quotes. Of course, if you use this design tip, you don't want text to flow through all columns, so you need to disable (uncheck) Automatic Text Box in the New Document dialog box.

Figure 7-5 shows a QuarkXPress document that was set up in the New Document dialog box to have eight columns. We did not select Automatic Text Box; doing so would have flowed the text across all eight columns, when all we want is to see the columns for visual alignment of various boxes. Instead, we used the Text Box tool to create each of the text boxes that would actually contain text, and the Picture Box tool to create the picture box containing the photo. Note how we used the column markers as alignment guides in setting up a variety of column treatments, which include pull-quote boxes and columns that vary in width from the top part of the page to the bottom.

Choosing a column gutter

In the Column Guides area of the dialog box, enter a measurement in the Gutter Width field to specify the amount of space between columns of text. Gutters can be as small as 3 points (0.042 inch) or as large as 288 points (4 inches). We recommend keeping columns to a reasonable width — generally no wider than 21 picas. Otherwise, the columns may strain the reader's eyes. (**Remember:** If you're using inches for the measurement system, you can still enter values in points or picas by including, respectively, the abbreviation *pt* or *p* with the value.)

Tip

Don't make gutters too narrow. This causes the columns of text to appear to run together and makes the document difficult to read. A good guideline to keep in mind is that the wider the columns, the wider the margins need to be to give the reader a clear visual clue that it's time to move to the next line.

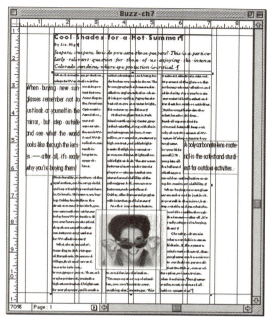

Figure 7-5: You can use column markers as alignment guides, not just for column boundaries.

Activating the automatic text box

In QuarkXPress, you need a text box to start typing text or to import it using the File ➪ Get Text command, or ⌘+E or Ctrl+E. If you want a text box on the master page that automatically flows text to other pages as they're inserted into the document, check the Automatic Text Box option. If you don't select Automatic Text Box, you must use one of the Text Box tools to draw text boxes. Make this decision based on how much continuous text you have to import into the document — for example, if you're laying out a book, you will almost certainly use the automatic text box, but if you're laying out an advertisement, you probably won't.

After you finish making selections in the New Document dialog box, as shown in Figure 7-6, click OK to create the new document. The new document has one page, showing the margin and column guides you specified, and is surrounded by a pasteboard.

Figure 7-6: After you've considered all the options in the New Document dialog box, you can click OK to create the new document.

Changing a Document's Size

It's always possible that, after you create a document, the parameters of the project may change and you may need to modify the size, number of columns, or other features of the layout. As with most things, the farther along you are in the process, the more painful these changes will be. To change a document's size, orientation, and facing-pages status, use the Document Setup dialog box (File ➪ Document Setup, or Option+Shift+⌘+P or Ctrl+Alt+Shift+P). To change the margin and column guides, use the Master Guides dialog box (Page ➪ Master Guides) while a master page is displayed.

Adjusting the layout

When you've determined that a document's page size needs to change, the first thing to do is review the current item placement and see how the change will affect the items. Making a document larger is rarely a problem, because all the items will still fit on the pages. Making a document smaller, on the other hand, can be very problematic. If items won't fit on the pages, QuarkXPress simply won't let you make the pages smaller. The same thing happens if you try to change the orientation (for example, turn a page sideways) — if items will no longer fit, you can't do it. To force items to fit, you can either move them or scale them. To ensure that the items end up within the new page boundaries, make sure the rulers and guides are showing (choose View ➪ Show Rulers and View ➪ Show Guides to be sure).

Tip Depending on how far along you are in the design process, you may want to consider starting a new document if several changes are necessary. You can always copy and paste items and text from the original document into the new document. Or store items in a library (File ➪ New ➪ Library) to use in the new document. The more radical the size change you're making, the more practical it may be to start a new document.

Folding and other page-size factors

Because starting with the correct page size, margins, and columns set up is fairly important, you need all the information you can get about how to make these decisions. If the document will be folded, issues become even more complicated. You may need to discuss these issues with a printer first. When you're deciding on page size, especially in folded documents, consider the following factors:

✦ **Gutter space:** Choose a page size that allows adequate gutter space. Gutters should be wide enough that folds don't occur in the middle of text or pictures.

✦ **Page creep:** *Creeping* is the apparent movement of text toward the gutter on outside pages because of the fact that these outside pages have to fold around the inside ones, so that some of the gutter space is lost where the sheet of paper wraps around inside sheets. Set an outside margin that is big enough to accommodate any creeping of pages, which can occur in multipage documents that are saddle-stitched (stapled along the fold). *Note:* If you're using imposition software, it may compensate for creep for you.

✦ **Column widths:** If you are creating a trifold brochure — for example, one that is printed on 9-x-12-inch paper and folded into a 4-x-9-inch brochure — setting up the page into even columns with even gutters doesn't work, because the space you need to accommodate the folds uses up gutter space. The same is true for any brochure or document that's folded more than two times. If possible, work with your commercial printer to find out what page and column size to use to accommodate the folds. If you are designing a multifold brochure that will not be commercially printed, allow time to experiment with column widths, margins, and folding.

✦ **Paper choice:** The paper on which a folded brochure is printed is a major factor in determining the success of the document. Your paper choice also plays a large role in how you need to set up the document during layout. Obviously, thick paper reacts differently to folding than thin paper, and thick paper also has a different effect in terms of the amount of page creeping that results in a multipage document. Depending on the weight and texture of the paper, a $1/4$-inch outside margin set on the first page of a 36-page, saddle-stitched document could be gradually reduced on each page, shrinking to $1/16$ of an inch by the centerfold. Talk with your printer ahead of time if your document has multiple folds or if you're planning a document with 24 or more folded pages and saddle stitching.

✦ **Guides on pages:** Guides on pages are useful if you want to align an element with another element within a box — such as a part of a picture — and the location is not identified in the Measurements palette (the Measurements palette shows the box's values, not those of its internal elements). You should, however, rely on the numeric values shown in the Measurements palette rather than the pull-out ruler guides when you're concerned about placing boxes and lines precisely on a page.

A good commercial printer should be experienced in handling the issues related to paper weight and can give you some important guidelines about how to lay out a folded document. If your document will be folded, take the time to talk with your printer before you get too far into the layout process.

Moving items to fit

One option for making sure items fit on a page is to move them all. First, go to each master page and move all the items so they're within the new page boundaries (you can also place items on the pasteboard or in a library). Then go to each document page and make sure all the page items are within the new page boundaries.

To move items, use the Item tool and click and drag the items as shown in Figure 7-7. To multiple-select items, Shift+click them. To judge the item placement, make sure the guides (View ➪ Show Guides, or F7) and rulers (View ➪ Show Rulers, or ⌘+R or Ctrl+R) are showing. You can also use the X and Y fields in the Measurements palette to judge item placement.

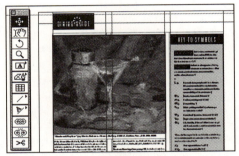

Figure 7-7: Use the Item tool to select page items and move them within new page boundaries.

Scaling items to fit

Another option for placing items within new page boundaries is to scale them simultaneously. To do this, select the Item tool, then choose Edit ➪ Select All (⌘+A or Ctrl+A) to select all the items on a page. Then choose Item ➪ Group (⌘+G or Ctrl+G) to group all the items. Now that the items are grouped, you can scale them simultaneously (as shown in Figure 7-8) by dragging a handle and pressing a keyboard command. Start by scaling items on master pages, then check each document page.

To scale all the items together, simply drag a handle. To scale all the items proportionally, press Option+Shift+⌘ or Ctrl+Alt+Shift while you drag. To constrain the bounding box of the group to a square while you drag, press Shift+⌘ or Ctrl+Shift.

Note   Although scaling a group is a convenient method for forcing a design into a new page size, keep in mind that the text is scaled in addition to the items and images. When we scaled the group shown in Figure 7-8 down to accommodate a 1-inch reduction in page size, the text was reduced from 7 points to 5.899 points, which is no longer readable.

Figure 7-8: You can scale all the items in a group simultaneously.

Changing Document Setup

When you're sure that the items on pages will fit within new page boundaries, you can change the page size using the Document Setup dialog box.

STEPS: Using the Document Setup dialog box

1. Choose File ➪ Document Setup, or press Option+Shift+⌘+P or Ctrl+Alt+Shift+P.

2. If you're moving toward a standard page size, choose an option from the Size menu. The options are the same as those in the Size menu of the New Document dialog box.

3. If you need a nonstandard page size, enter values between 0.111 inch and 48 inches in the Width and Height fields.

4. To quickly reverse the values in the Width and Height fields, click the Orientation buttons as shown in Figure 7-9.

Figure 7-9: The Document Setup dialog box lets you make adjustments to the page size and orientation of an existing document.

5. If you decide you need facing pages after starting a document, you can check this option. However, if you start out with facing pages and decide you don't need them, it can be difficult to change. If you've placed items on both sides of the master page spread, you won't be able to uncheck Facing Pages. (In this case, you should flow the text and paste the items into a new document.)

6. When you're finished making changes, click OK. If you weren't diligent about moving or scaling items, don't be surprised if an alert tells you that the changes can't be made. (Fortunately, the alert explains why.)

Changing Master Guides

Although changing page size can be a challenge, you can change the margin and column guides just about any time. Of course, these are just guides anyway — they don't really control where you place items. You're free to place text outside the columns and items outside or overlapping the margins any time. However, if you're making a global change to a document — such as increasing the margins from 0.5 inch to 0.75 inch — you'll want to adjust the guides so you can easily see where items should go. To make a global change, you'll need to adjust the margin and column guides on each master page that you're using in a document.

STEPS: Using the Master Guides dialog box

1. Choose Page ➭ Display ➭ A-Master A (or another master page).

2. When the master page is displayed, choose Page ➭ Master Guides to display the Master Guides dialog box, shown in Figure 7-10.

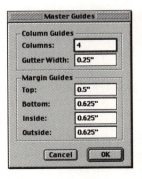

Figure 7-10: The Master Guides dialog box lets you change the margins and number of columns in an existing document.

3. To change column guides on the page, change the values in the Columns and Gutter Width fields. If you're using the automatic text box, these changes will affect the columns in it.

4. To change the page margins, change the values in the Top and Bottom fields and the Left and Right fields (or Inside and Outside fields for facing-pages documents). If you're using the automatic text box, these changes affect its placement on the page.

5. To implement the changes, click OK.

6. If necessary, move items on the master page to fit within the new margins.

7. Choose Page ➪ Display ➪ Document to return to the document.

8. If necessary, move items on the document pages to fit within the new margins.

Summary

When you create a new document, you need to specify the page size, margins, and number of columns. Although it's okay to kick off a document and start experimenting without having final decisions on these matters, the more you know at the beginning of the process, the less time you'll spend making adjustments. In addition to knowing the size, you may need to know how the document will be printed and folded to make decisions about the margins and columns. If you start with a dummy, as discussed in Chapter 6, you'll have an easier time creating new documents that meet all your layout and production needs.

✦   ✦   ✦

Working with Items

Items — boxes, lines, and text paths — are the basic elements of your QuarkXPress pages. In fact, without items, you'd have nothing but blank white pages. Everything you see on a printed page is an item that the graphic designer created and modified with a certain effect in mind. That bright blue background on the advertising postcard you received? It's probably a picture box filled with a color. The border around the coupon? It's probably a dashed frame on a text box.

QuarkXPress supplies a variety of tools for creating items of any shape, size, and type. After you have items, you can easily manipulate them with the Item tool and commands in the Item menu. The basics of item manipulation are similar, whether you're working with an oval text box, a polygon picture box, or a curved text path. You can generally change an item's size and shape at will, fill it with color, stroke its edges, group it with other items, and lock it in place on a page. This chapter covers the basic item-creation tools. The Bézier tools for illustration are covered in Part VI.

Identifying the Different Types of Items

QuarkXPress offers a variety of items to meet all your design needs: text boxes, picture boxes, no-content boxes, lines, and text paths. The items have a great deal in common, especially in the way you create, move, resize, and modify them. What's different about the items is what you can do inside them — flow text, import a graphic, add a background color, and so on. Fortunately, if you create the wrong type of item for what you need to do, you can easily convert it. Chapter 1 covers item types in detail, but here's a quick review:

✦ **Text boxes contain the bulk of the text you see in QuarkXPress.** As discussed in Chapter 12, you can link text boxes together or let QuarkXPress create an automatic text box for you.

✦ **Picture boxes contain all imported or pasted graphic files.** They're also commonly used for blocks of color and frames (without graphics).

✦ **No-content boxes cannot contain text or pictures — they're exclusively for backgrounds and frames.** To create a no-content box, you have to convert an existing text box or picture box. Because the feature is relatively new (introduced in version 4) and is not convenient to use, most people use picture boxes in place of no-content boxes.

✦ **Lines are drawn on the page as a design element, and they can have different widths and patterns applied to them.** QuarkXPress uses the term *rules,* which is usually interchangeable with *lines,* to indicate a paragraph attribute that automatically places lines above and below paragraphs.

✦ **Text paths are lines that text flows along.** Usually, these lines are invisible, used only as a guide for the text. Text paths are usually curved because using a straight text path is no different from using a rectangular text box.

You can create all these items at any size that fits on your pages and in almost any conceivable shape. Don't let the term *box* fool you — text boxes and picture boxes don't need to be rectangular. QuarkXPress provides a variety of tools for common shapes and lets you draw your own shapes. You can create anything from a rectangular text box to a polygonal picture box to a wavy text path.

QuarkXPress 5 introduces a new type of item: the table. A table is essentially a collection of grouped text boxes and picture boxes. Tables are covered in Chapter 19.

Creating Items

Creating an item is simple: Select a tool, then click and drag with it. When you release the mouse button — voilà — you have an item! That's the basics, but of course there's more to it. You have to decide from the bevy of item-creation tools — 23 in all — that QuarkXPress provides, and you have to work a little to create items with any precision. But because most people want to get started creating right away, we'll give you the steps for creating an item first, then explain the tools in more detail later in this chapter.

Part VI covers using the Freehand and Bézier tools, which are quite different from the standard tools.

STEPS: Creating an item

1. Make sure the Tool palette is showing (View ➪ Show Tools, or F8).

2. Click one of the item-creation tools showing on the Tool palette to select it. Or click and hold one of the tools to display its pop-out tools; drag to the right and release the mouse button to select one of the pop-out tools. Figure 8-1 shows the Tool palette with the item-creation tools highlighted.

Tip   A quick way to select the next tool down in the Tool palette is to press Option+⌘+Tab or Ctrl+Alt+Tab. If you press it repeatedly, you can scroll through all the tools until you hit the one you want. If you add in the Shift key, you can select the previous tool.

Figure 8-1: The item-creation tools are grouped together in the center of the Tool palette.

3. The pointer changes to a cross or a plus (+) icon. Click the crosshair on the page where you want to start creating the item.

4. Hold down the mouse button and drag toward the opposite corner.

5. When you've reached the opposite corner, let go of the mouse button, and your box, line, or text path appears.

6. If your box is not exactly the right size or in exactly the right location, you can change it, as discussed later in this chapter.

Tip   After you create an item, QuarkXPress automatically reselects the Item tool or the Content tool — whichever you were using last — because the program assumes you want to modify the item right away. If this isn't the case, and you'd rather create a variety of the same type of item, Option+click or Alt+click a tool to select it. This keeps the tool selected until you select another.

Fine-tuning items during creation

While you're creating an item, you can use the X and Y fields in the Measurements palette, the rulers on the document window, and any guides you've created to judge the item's size and placement. Use the Show Measurements (F9), Show Rulers (⌘+R or Ctrl+R), and Show Guides (F7) commands in the View menu as necessary. Figure 8-2 shows a 2-inch square text box created at 1.5 inches from the top and sides of the page.

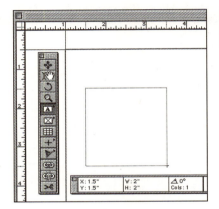

Figure 8-2: Use the layout tools (rulers, guides, Measurements palette) in QuarkXPress to judge item size and placement.

When you create standard-shape items, you can also gain more control by pressing the Shift key to constrain the item shape. This has the following effect:

✦ Rectangles are constrained to squares (this includes beveled-corner and concave-corner boxes).

✦ Ovals are constrained to circles.

✦ Lines are straight and angled in 45-degree increments, primarily horizontal and vertical.

What this means is that if you select the Rectangle Picture Box tool, then you press the Shift key while you create the picture box, you can only create a square. Or, if you select the Line Text-Path tool, you can only create horizontal or vertical lines.

Reviewing the tools

By default, the Tool palette shows a limited selection of item-creation tools. But, as discussed in the sidebar "Changing the Tool palette's lineup," you can change that. Each item-creation tool that is showing (except for the Table tool) has a little arrow on it that indicates a pop-out containing more tools, as shown in Figure 8-3. Click and hold to see all the tools in a pop-out.

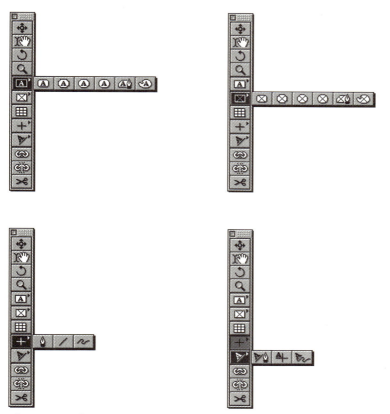

Figure 8-3: The pop-outs containing item-creation tools.

New Feature

Note that the default Tool palette has changed from version 4, which showed one of each item-creation tool along with a few picture box tools that used to display in version 3. This was to ease the transition from version 3 to 4, but it has been dropped in favor of a streamlined palette for version 5.

Text box and picture box tools

QuarkXPress provides the same set of tools for creating text boxes and picture boxes. The only difference is that text box tools have an "A" inside them and picture box tools have an "X" through them. From left to right (in the default order), the box tools include the following:

✦ The Rectangle Box tools are the default tools showing in the palette, and they produce standard rectangular boxes to fill with text and pictures.

✦ The Rounded-Rectangle Box tools produce boxes with customizable rounded corners.

- ✦ The Oval Box tools produce elliptical boxes.

- ✦ The Concave-Corner Box tools produce boxes with customizable notched corners.

- ✦ The Beveled-Corner Box tools produce boxes with corners cut off by a diagonal line.

- ✦ The Bézier Box tools produce polygons — shapes composed of a series of flat sides and/or curves.

- ✦ The Freehand Box tools produce curved shapes — shapes composed of a series of curves.

Line and text-path tools

QuarkXPress also provides the same set of tools for creating lines and text paths. The text-path tools are distinguished by the "A" on them. From left to right (in the default order), the line/text-path tools include the following:

- ✦ The Line tools produce lines or text paths of any angle.

- ✦ The Bézier tools produce straight or curved line segments to make up a line or text path.

- ✦ The Orthogonal tools produce horizontal or vertical lines only (except when you press the Shift key — then you can constrain its lines to 45-degree increments).

- ✦ The Freehand tools produce curved lines and text paths.

Selecting and Deselecting Items

To work with an item, you have to select it. This tells QuarkXPress which items you want to change. You can select a single item at a time or you can select multiple items so you can modify, move, or resize them all at once. When an item is selected, it's considered to be *active,* as indicated by the selection handles (the little boxes) at the corners and edges of the item.

Most of the time that you're working with items, you'll need to select the Item tool. However, the beauty of QuarkXPress is that the two primary tools are flexible, so you can perform all the selection functions using the Item tool or the Content tool. Figure 8-4 shows an active picture box, selected with the Item tool. The pointer finger indicates that you can pull on this handle to resize or reshape the box.

Changing the Tool palette's lineup

By default, the Tool palette shows you one of each kind of item-creation tool. The tools that are showing each contain a pop-out menu of additional tools for you to choose from. You have a few options for modifying the tools that are showing:

✦ You can replace the default tool by simply selecting another tool from a pop-out.

✦ You can add a tool to the palette by pressing the Control or Ctrl key while you select it from a pop-out.

✦ You can stuff a tool back into its pop-out by Control+clicking or Ctrl+clicking on it.

✦ In Windows, you can make the Tool palette horizontal by Ctrl+clicking its title bar.

Take a look at the Tool palette here, modified for a designer who uses a lot of circles and Bézier items.

Don't worry about making too many changes to the Tool palette — you can always change back to the default setup. Just double-click any item-creation tool to open the Tools pane of the Preferences dialog box, then click the Default Tool Palette button.

Figure 8-4: You can tell which items are selected by the selection handles on the corners and edges of the items.

Selecting items

No matter what type of item or items you need to select, the process works the same way:

✦ To select one item, click anywhere inside it.

✦ To select multiple items, Shift+click each item. You can also click and drag to marquee various continuous items.

✦ To select all the items on a page, choose Edit ➪ Select All (or ⌘+A or Ctrl+A) when the Item tool is selected.

✦ To select an item that is entirely behind other items, press Option+Shift+⌘ or Ctrl+Alt+Shift to click through the items in the front and reach the items behind.

✦ To select a single item within a group, use the Content tool to click on it. Grouping items is covered later in this chapter.

Tip   If you're having trouble seeing where one item begins and another ends, choose View ➪ Show Guides (F7) to display the edges of items.

Deselecting items

When you're finished working with selected items, you need to deselect them so you can move on to something else:

✦ To deselect an item, select another item or click on a blank area of the page or pasteboard.

✦ To deselect all items, you can also press the Tab key if the Item tool is selected.

✦ To deselect one item while keeping other items selected, Shift+click that item.

Modifying Items

As soon as you've created some items, you're likely to start changing them. You may want to simply adjust them — move them, resize them, change their shape — or you may even want to change what they contain. In addition to your mouse and keyboard, QuarkXPress supplies the following tools to do all these things and more:

✦ **Modify dialog box:** This multipaned dialog box provides many controls for how items look and behave. To open the Modify dialog box, choose Item ➪ Modify, press ⌘+M or Ctrl+M, or double-click an item with the Item tool. Additional keyboard shortcuts open specific panes of the Modify dialog box.

✦ **The Measurements palette:** Open most of the time, the left side of the Measurements palette provides item-based controls — size, position, rotation, and so on. The right side contains style controls such as graphic size, font, and so on. To open the Measurements palette, choose View ➪ Show Measurements or press F9.

✦ **Item menu:** This entire menu is devoted to the manipulation of the selected item or items.

Not all options described in this section for these panes and palettes are displayed for all items. In some cases, an option simply doesn't make any sense for a specific type of item — such as the corner radius option for a circular picture box — so QuarkXPress simply omits those options. Similarly, if you have multiple items selected, QuarkXPress omits options that aren't relevant to all selected items.

Note   The measurement units displayed in the Modify dialog box and Measurements palette fields are whatever unit you select in the General pane of the Preferences dialog box (Edit ➪ Preferences ➪ Preferences, or ⌘+Y or Ctrl+Y).

What follows is a summary of the item controls for basic layout creation and adjustment. The Modify dialog box, Measurements palette, and Item menu have many other controls useful in layout, but they're aimed at positioning text, enhancing graphics, illustrating, and creating special effects — not basic layout creation.

A tour of the Modify dialog box

Depending on the item you select, the Modify dialog box displays different panes. Some panes, such as the Box pane, are repeated for different types of items. The basic types of items display the following panes in the Modify dialog box:

✦ **Text boxes:** Box, Text, Frame, and Runaround panes

✦ **Picture box:** Box, Picture, Frame, and Runaround panes

✦ **Line:** Line and Runaround panes

✦ **Text path:** Line, Text Path, and Runaround panes

After you get in the panes, you'll see similar controls for different types of items along with controls tailored to the needs of each item. You'll be spending a lot of time in the Modify dialog box, so getting to know it is definitely worthwhile.

Box pane

The fundamental pane of the Modify dialog box is the Box pane, and it's available for text boxes, picture boxes, and no-content boxes (discussed later in this chapter). This pane controls the fundamental size and placement of the box itself — not its content. The Box pane, shown in Figure 8-5, lets you:

✦ Change a box's position with the Origin Across and Origin Down fields and change its size with the Width and Height fields.

✦ Rotate a box with the Angle field and slant a box with the Skew field.

✦ Apply a background color with the Color and Shade menus in the Box section, and specify a background blend using the Style, Angle, Color, and Shade menus in the Blend section.

✦ Prevent a box's content from printing by checking the Suppress Printout option. Any frames applied will still print, which is handy for creating keylines for for-position-only (FPO) boxes, in which images are manually added to the negatives later. This suppression feature is also handy for adding items that you don't want printed but you do want visible on-screen, such as notes to a designer.

✦ Change the Corner Radius for rounded-, concave-, and beveled-corner boxes.

Tip   This is the place to make a box's background transparent. Simply select None from the Color menu in the Box section. When a box has a background of None, you can layer it on top of other boxes and see what's inside them.

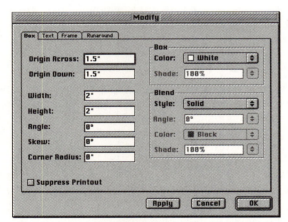

Figure 8-5: The Box pane of the Modify dialog box.

Runaround pane

Another fundamental pane of the Modify dialog box, the Runaround pane (shown in Figure 8-6) is available for all item types—boxes, lines, and text paths. Because Runaround is accessed frequently, it has its own menu command and keyboard shortcut: Item➪Runaround, or ⌘+T or Ctrl+T. The Runaround pane controls whether and how text wraps around the selected item.

The options in the Runaround pane are discussed in detail in Chapter 23.

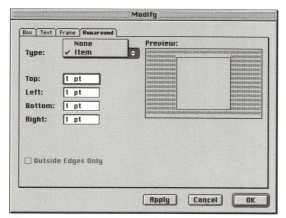

Figure 8-6: The Runaround pane of the Modify dialog box.

Frame pane

You can stroke the edges of any type of box—frame it, in QuarkXPress lingo— using the Frame pane. Another popular option, the Frame pane has its own Item menu command and keyboard shortcut: Item ➪ Frame, or ⌘+B or Ctrl+B. The Preview area gives you an idea how the frame settings you specify will look. As shown in Figure 8-7, you have the following frame controls:

✦ **Width:** You can enter a value in the field or choose an option from the menu. To remove a frame from a box, simply give it a width of zero.

✦ **Style:** This menu lists all the default frame styles included with QuarkXPress plus any that you created in the Dashes & Stripes dialog box (Edit ➪ Dashes & Stripes).

 Previous versions of QuarkXPress for Mac shipped with a utility called Frame Editor for designing and customizing bitmap frames. Although the utility no longer ships with QuarkXPress, its default frames are included with QuarkXPress for both Mac and Windows—Yearbook, Certificate, Coupon, and so on—and they display at the bottom of the Style menu. These options are available only for rectangular boxes.

✦ **Color and Shade:** The Frame area lets you select a Color and Shade (hue) for the lines or dashes that make up the frame.

✦ **Gap Color and Shade:** If you pick a frame style that includes white space (as in a striped or dashed style), you can select a Color and Shade for the white space in the Gap area.

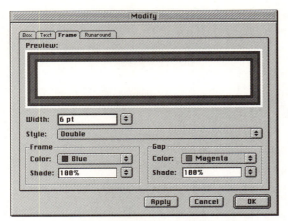

Figure 8-7: The Frame pane of the Modify dialog box.

Text pane

The Text pane of the Modify dialog box, shown in Figure 8-8, is available only for text boxes. This pane controls how all the text in a box is positioned within it. In the Text pane, you can assign:

✦ The number of columns and the space between them (in the Columns and Gutter Width fields).

✦ The margin between the edge of the box and the text (in the Text Inset field). This is handy to keep the text from running into the box's frame.

✦ The rotation and slant for the text, separately from the slant and rotation of the box itself (use the Text Angle and Text Skew fields).

✦ Mirroring (with the Flip Horizontal and Flip Vertical check boxes).

✦ The baseline start position.

✦ The vertical alignment of text within the box.

✦ Whether text runs around all sides of this box, if another box is placed wholly within this text box.

Cross-Reference   The options in the Text pane are discussed in Chapter 12, with the exception of Run Text Around All Sides, which is covered in Chapter 23.

Picture pane

The Picture pane of the Modify dialog box, shown in Figure 8-9, is available only for picture boxes. This pane lets you assign:

✦ The position of the picture within the box, for cropping (in the Offset Across and Offset Down fields)

✦ The size of the picture within the box (in Scale Across and Scale Down)

✦ The rotation and slant of the picture in the box, separately from the slant and rotation of the box itself (use the Picture Angle and Picture Skew fields)

✦ Mirroring (with Flip Horizontal and Flip Vertical)

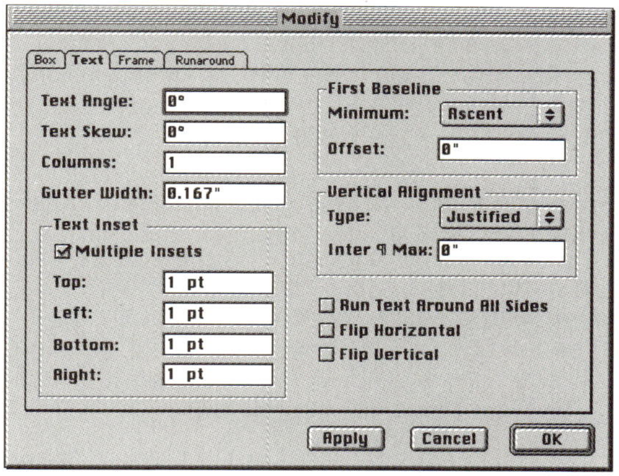

Figure 8-8: The Text pane of the Modify dialog box.

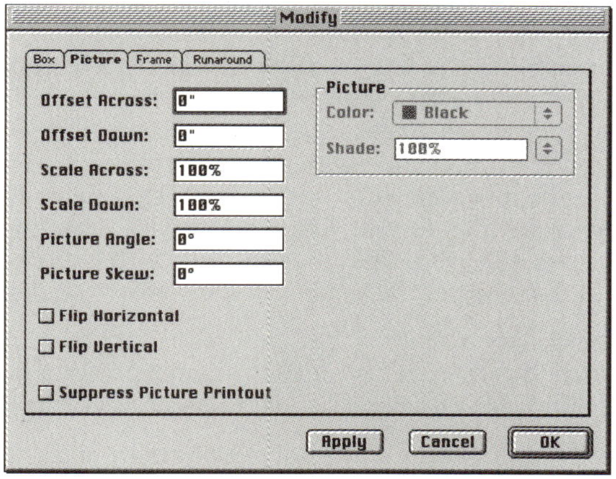

Figure 8-9: The Picture pane of the Modify dialog box.

You can also prevent the picture from printing (with Suppress Picture Printout). This is handy when you're printing drafts and don't want to spend time waiting for the printer to render images. Note that any frame and background shade will still print if this option is selected. Additionally, you can choose the background color and shade for the area around the picture (and, for black-and-white and grayscale TIFF, BMP, PCX, PICT, and Scitex CT images, the background color and shade of the picture itself).

Cross-Reference The Picture pane's controls are covered in detail in Chapter 21.

Line pane

The Line pane of the Modify dialog box, shown in Figure 8-10, is available for both lines and text paths. This pane controls the size, position, and formatting of regular lines and the lines underlying text paths. Line pane options include:

✦ **Style:** This menu lists all the default line styles included with QuarkXPress plus any that you created in the Dashes & Stripes dialog box (Edit ➪ Dashes & Stripes).

✦ **Line Width:** You can enter a value in the field or choose an option from the menu. (If you don't want to see the line under a text path, enter 0 for the width.) The default line width, Hairline, is actually 0.25 point wide — but it prints wider as necessary on laser and dot matrix printers.

✦ **Mode:** This menu controls how you specify the position of the line. If you want to position it according to the starting point and the ending point, choose Endpoints. If you want to position it according to the left endpoint or the right endpoint, choose Left Point or Right Point, respectively. If you want to position a line according to its midpoint (the center of the line), choose Midpoint.

Depending on the Mode you choose, you'll have different controls for positioning the line. If you stick with the default, Endpoint, you'll have four fields for positioning the line's endpoints: Left Across, Left Down, Right Across, and Right Down. In this case, the line's angle and length are determined by the location of its endpoints. If you choose another option, you'll get fields for positioning that point on the line (for example, if you choose Midpoint, you'll get Midpoint Across and Midpoint Down fields). In addition, with Left Point, Midpoint, or Right Point, you can specify an Angle and Length for the line.

✦ **Suppress Printout:** If you're printing a draft of text, you may want to suppress the printout of lines (especially if they're very wide) for faster printing and to save toner or ink. Checking Suppress Printout prevents lines from printing.

✦ **Arrowheads:** This menu lets you pick from a default set of arrowheads and/or tailfeathers for your lines. (QuarkXPress doesn't let you customize these — if you need a special effect, you can draw your own arrowheads or tailfeathers, then group them with lines.)

✦ **Color and Shade:** The Line area lets you select a Color and Shade (hue) for the line.

✦ **Gap Color and Shade:** If you pick a line style that includes white space (as in a striped or dashed style), you can select a Color and Shade for the white space in the Gap area.

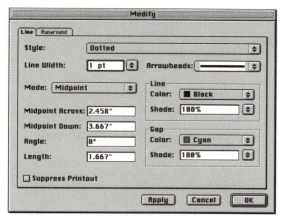

Figure 8-10: The Line pane of the Modify
dialog box.

 Tip

When a line is selected, the Line Style, Arrowheads, Width, Color, and Shade
commands in the Modify dialog box are also available through submenus of the
Style menu. This is one of the few occasions at which you can modify an item
through the Style menu rather than the Item menu.

Text Path pane

When a text path is selected, the Modify dialog box includes the Text Path pane,
which is shown in Figure 8-11. The options in this pane control how text is positioned
in relation to the line (whether the line is visible or not).

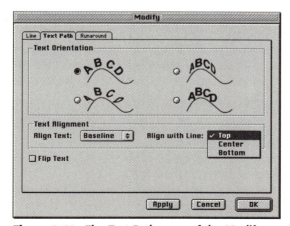

Figure 8-11: The Text Path pane of the Modify
dialog box.

Cross-Reference   The options in the Text Path pane are discussed in detail in Chapter 23.

Special-purpose panes

If you're working with a group of items, the Modify dialog box will include a Group pane. The Group pane will provide all the controls common to the items in the group (at the very least, you'll be able to position the group). For picture boxes that contain graphics, the Clipping pane appears; it's discussed in Chapter 22. Depending on the type of graphic, you may also see an OPI pane, discussed in Chapter 35.

A tour of the Measurements palette

The Measurements palette offers quick access to the most commonly changed attributes of items — size, position, angle, and more. For the most part, the attributes that apply to items (rather than their contents) are relegated to the left side of the Measurements palette. So we'll take a look at the options on the left for boxes, lines, and text paths.

Measurements palette for boxes

Whether you have a text box or a picture box selected, the controls on the left side of the Measurements palette are similar, as shown in Figure 8-12.

✦ **X and Y coordinates:** These display, respectively, the horizontal and vertical coordinates of the box location (these are the same as the Origin Across and Origin Down fields in the Modify dialog box).

✦ **W and H dimensions:** These are the same as the Width and Height fields in the Modify dialog box and show the size of the box.

✦ **Angle field:** This lets you rotate the box itself. This is the same as the Angle field in the Box pane of the Modify dialog box.

✦ **Cols field:** For text boxes only, the Cols field lets you specify the number of columns. This is the same as the Columns field in the Text pane of the Modify dialog box.

✦ **Corner-Radius field:** For picture boxes only, this field lets you change the corner radius of a box, which controls the amount of beveling in a beveled-corner box, the rounding in a rounded-rectangle box, and the notching in a concave-corner box. A bigger number increases the bevel depth, rounding, or notching. If you change the corner radius on a regular rectangular box, it becomes a rounded-rectangle box.

Measurements palette for lines and text paths

Whether you have a line or a text path selected, the controls on the left side of the Measurements palette are similar, as shown in Figure 8-13. When a line or text path is selected with the Item tool, the right side offers controls for formatting it. But, when a text path is selected with the Content tool, you'll see controls for formatting the text.

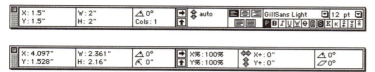

Figure 8-12: The Measurements palette for text boxes (top) and picture boxes (bottom).

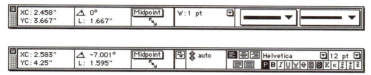

Figure 8-13: The Measurements palette for lines (top) and text paths (bottom).

As with the Line pane of the Modify dialog box, discussed previously, the fields available on the right side of the Measurements palette hinge on the line's mode: Endpoints, Left Point, Midpoint, or Right Point. When you choose an option from the menu on the Measurements palette, a helpful icon shows you which mode you're in. You'll then have fields for either positioning both endpoints or for positioning the selected endpoint plus an Angle and Length field. For both lines and text paths, the Width field lets you change the thickness of the line.

Mouse and keyboard modifications

Instead of using fields to specify exact sizes and locations, you can use the tools and keyboard to fine-tune your items:

✦ When an item is selected with the Item tool, you can drag it to a new location or move it slightly using the keyboard's arrow keys. For even finer adjustments, add the Option or Alt key while you click the arrow keys.

✦ When an item is selected with the Content tool, you can press ⌘ or Ctrl for temporary access to the Item tool. This will let you drag the item to a new position.

✦ Any time an item is active, whether it's selected with the Item tool or the Content tool, you can drag one of the handles (the little black boxes) on it and drag them to resize and reshape the item.

✦ When a line or text path is selected, you can use keyboard shortcuts to change its width. To increase by 1 point, press Option+Shift+⌘+> or Ctrl+Alt+Shift+>. To decrease by 1 point, use the same modifiers, but replace the greater-than symbol (>) with the less-than symbol (<): Press Option+Shift+⌘+< or Ctrl+Alt+Shift+<. You can also increase or decrease line width within the preset increments of 0 (for hairline), 2, 4, 6, 8, 12. To increase within this range, press Shift+⌘+> or Ctrl+Shift+>; to decrease within this range, press Shift+⌘+< or Ctrl+Shift+<.

Tips and tricks for resizing and reshaping

When it comes to resizing and reshaping, you can combine keyboard commands and other techniques you've learned to make these tasks easy and to achieve special effects.

✦ When resizing with the mouse, hold Option+Shift or Alt+Shift when dragging a control handle to keep the resized item proportional to its original dimensions. Add the ⌘ or Ctrl key and you'll resize any contents (graphics or text) as well.

✦ To reshape a box, the mouse is the best tool. Use the control handles on the box to resize. Selecting a corner with the mouse resizes both width and height in whatever direction you move the mouse, while selecting a side's control handle stretches or contracts the box in one dimension only. Note that on a nonrectangular box, the control handles may not actually be on the box's outline.

✦ If you hold the ⌘ or Ctrl key while resizing a box, the text or graphic inside is resized as well. For text boxes, this is particularly handy if you're working with ads, brochures, and other documents in which the text size is not predetermined based on a standard style (unlike magazines and newsletters). Instead of highlighting the text and trying different sizes, this resize-with-the-box feature lets you quickly make text fit the appropriate space, as shown in the figure. Use Option+Shift+⌘ or Ctrl+Alt+Shift to resize the box — and its contents — proportionally to their original dimensions.

✦ If you hold the Shift key when resizing a box, it will become as wide as it is high — a perfect square for rectangular boxes and a perfect circle for oval boxes. Holding Shift while resizing a line constrains diagonal lines to 45-degree increments.

✦ Using the mouse is the simplest way to move an item. That's great for gross movement, but you need a keen eye and a steady hand to place the item exactly where you want it. For exact positioning, use the keyboard's arrow keys to nudge the item where you want it, or use the Measurements palette's positioning fields to enter the specific coordinates for the item. You can use the Modify dialog box, but unless you're using other controls in it, you save time by just using the keyboard or Measurements palette.

✦ In addition to entering a specific size for an item, you can make an item proportionally bigger by having QuarkXPress perform math for you. For example, in the Width and Height fields in the Measurements palette or Modify dialog box, you can multiply the box's current size by a certain amount. Say you have a box that's 1.14 inches wide and want to double its size. To do this, add *2 to the end of the current W value (it will thus appear as 1.14"*2) and then QuarkXPress will automatically change the W field's value to the new size, 2.28", when you press Return or click a different field. To reduce a dimension, such as to 35 percent, you'd add *0.35 to the current value—this multiplies the current value by 35 percent. When you're changing both the Width and Height values, it's easier to let QuarkXPress do the math for you. Just be careful when working with fractions: +8 7/8, for example, will be interpreted by QuarkXPress as +8$\frac{7}{8}$, not as +8$\frac{7}{8}$.

Automatically Spacing and Aligning Items

It's not at all uncommon to have a set of two or more layout elements that you want to line up to a certain X or Y coordinate. You may also want to line up these elements with a certain amount of space between them. QuarkXPress lets you align items according to their left, right, top, or bottom edges, or to their centers. You can also control the amount of space between multiple items, and you can specify whether these items are evenly spread across the page or staggered horizontally or vertically.

The Space/Align Items dialog box is a powerful feature that lets you control the spacing and alignment of elements in your layout. How does Space/Align work? Showing an example is the best way to illustrate it. Say you have four picture boxes on a page, and you want the boxes to be precisely aligned by their left edges with 0.5 inch of vertical space between the boxes. Figure 8-14 shows the settings that you specify in the Space/Align Items dialog box to accomplish this layout. To establish a layout like the one shown in the example, use the following steps.

STEPS: Aligning multiple elements

1. With the Item tool selected, hold down the Shift key and click each of the four boxes to select them.

2. Choose Item ⇨ Space Align or press ⌘+comma or Ctrl+comma to display the Space/Align Items dialog box.

3. Check the Vertical box to select it.

4. Choose Space (which is below the Vertical box) and enter 0.25" in the Space field.

5. Select Items from the Between list box.

6. Check the Horizontal box to select it. Choose Space (which is below the Horizontal box) and enter 0.25" in the Space field.

7. Select Apply to see what the settings will result in (to make sure that you've entered the right settings), and then choose OK to implement the changes.

If you're new to QuarkXPress and want to increase your layout expertise, do some experimenting. Draw a few text boxes and apply different X and Y coordinates to them in the Measurements palette. Also, try using different settings in the Space/Align Items dialog box. This is a great way to learn how these features work.

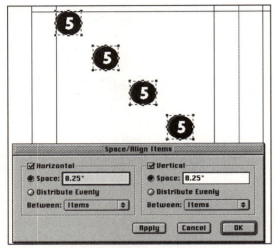

Figure 8-14: The Space/Align Items dialog box with the settings used to align the four grouped circular boxes on the page.

Automatically Reproducing and Spacing Items

Whenever you can, it's a good idea to let the computer do the work for you—and QuarkXPress makes it easy for the computer to do extra work. As an example, the program has the ability to create multiple copies of selected elements and to space them horizontally or vertically at regular intervals. This powerful feature is called Step and Repeat.

In addition to the standard Step and Repeat feature, QuarkXPress includes a free XTension called Super Step and Repeat (first introduced in version 4.1). This XTension adds the Super Step and Repeat command toward the bottom of the Item menu. With this feature, you can make changes to items as you replicate them—for example, changing the scale, angle, and shade. This lets you create special effects such as a box getting smaller as it fades into the background.

Using Step and Repeat

The standard Step and Repeat that QuarkXPress has always offered is great for automatically copying and positioning items and groups on a page. For example, you may have a page with graphics and captions running down the side of the page. All you need to do is create one picture box and one text box, group them, and then use Step and Repeat. To use Step and Repeat, first select the items or groups you want to copy. Then choose Item ⇨ Step and Repeat (or Option+⌘+D or Ctrl+Alt+D) to open the dialog box shown in Figure 8-15.

✦ **Repeat Count:** In this field, enter the number of copies of the selected items or groups that you want QuarkXPress to create.

✦ **Horizontal Offset:** Here, you need to specify how far to the right or left to place the repeated items. (A positive value places repeated elements to the right of the original; a negative value places them to the left.) Note that the offset is measured from the left edge of the previous item, so if you want to leave space between all the repeated items, the offset value should be the sum of the width of the item and the space you want between them. (For example, if you want to place 0.5 inch between 1-inch wide boxes, you'll need to enter 1.5" in the Horizontal Offset field.) Enter 0 to create a vertical column of items.

✦ **Vertical Offset:** Similar to the Horizontal Offset, the value you enter in this field specifies how far up or down to place the repeated items. (A positive value places repeated elements below the original element; a negative value places it above.) To leave space between items, be sure to use the sum of the height of the item and the space you want between them. Use 0 to distribute items horizontally only.

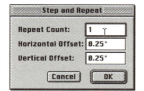

Figure 8-15: The Step and Repeat dialog box lets you specify how many copies of selected items to create, and where to place them.

Figure 8-16 shows a design element produced with Step and Repeat.

Tip

When you use the Step and Repeat feature, QuarkXPress remembers the offsets you use. If you subsequently use the Duplicate feature (Item ⇨ Duplicate, or ⌘+D or Ctrl+D), QuarkXPress uses those offsets there, too. If you want to clone items (create copies of items in the same positions as the originals), first do a Step and Repeat with horizontal and vertical offsets of 0". From then on until you quit the program, every time you use the Duplicate feature, the duplicate appears in the same position as the original. This is preferable to using Copy and Paste because pasting always places the copy in the center of the current page.

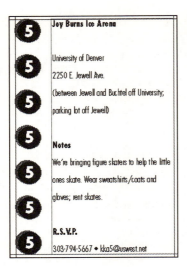

Figure 8-16: We used the Step and Repeat function to copy and align the 5s in circles along the left side of the page.

Using Super Step and Repeat

When the Super Step and Repeat XTension is running, which you can confirm in the XTensions Manager dialog box (Utilities ➪ XTensions Manager), you have more control over replicated items. To see this XTension in action, select an item and choose Item ➪ Super Step and Repeat. (Note that you cannot use Super Step and Repeat with groups — only with a single item.) The Repeat Count, Horizontal Offset, and Vertical Offset controls work the same as the standard Step and Repeat controls. The remaining controls let you make incremental changes to each repeated item, such as making the frame wider and making the box wider. Figure 8-17 shows the settings used to create this fading graphic of a hockey puck.

When you use Step and Repeat or Super Step and Repeat, QuarkXPress places each replicated item in front of the previous item (although you won't notice this if you leave space between each item). To create some special effects, you may need to change the stacking order of the items, as explained in the "Stacking Items" section later in this chapter.

Designing Frame and Line Styles

Although QuarkXPress does have 11 predefined styles for lines and frames, artistically inclined users will want even more styles available to them. The Dashes & Stripes feature lets you create your own styles, which you can use for box frames, for independent lines and text paths, and for rules placed above and below paragraphs (through Style ➪ Rules). A dash style is made up of line segments as you would see in a coupon border, while a stripe style is made up of multiple lines as you would see in a 3-D border.

To create and edit these styles, choose Edit ⇨ Dashes & Stripes to open the dialog box shown in Figure 8-18. Similar to the Style Sheets, Colors, and H&Js dialog boxes, here you can create new styles, edit styles, and *append* (import) styles from other documents. If you work with Dashes & Stripes when a document is active, the styles are saved with that document only. If no documents are open, your style changes are applied to all new documents. The process of creating dashes and stripes is somewhat different, so we'll supply steps for both.

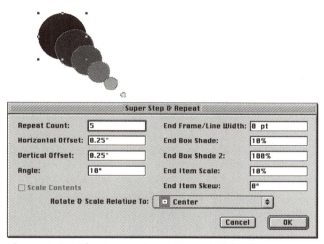

Figure 8-17: The Super Step & Repeat dialog box.

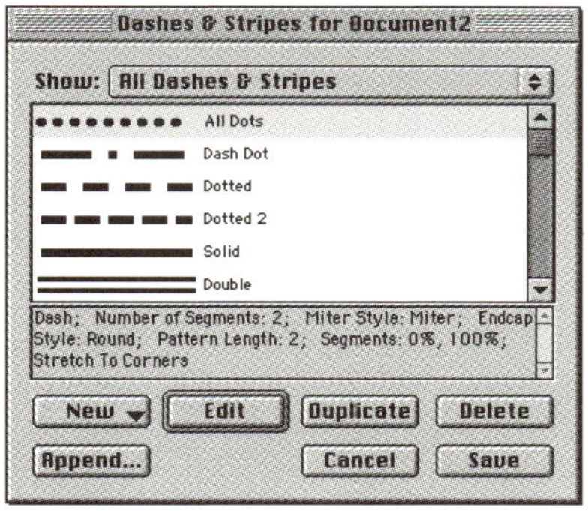

Figure 8-18: The Dashes & Stripes dialog box.

STEPS: Creating a dash pattern

1. Choose Edit ➪ Dashes & Stripes.

2. Click the New button, then choose Dash to open the Edit Dash dialog box.

3. Enter a meaningful name for your dash pattern in the Name field. Generally, you'll want the name to indicate that this is a custom pattern rather than one of the defaults. The most useful names are those that indicate how the style is to be used — for example, *Coupon Borders*.

4. To specify how often your pattern repeats over the length of a line or frame, use the Repeats Every area. The default setting is Times Width, which makes the pattern repeat in increments of the line width. Thus, the thicker the line, the longer the segments, and the smaller the number you enter, the finer the dash elements. (The Preview slider helps you see the effects of your choice at different line and frame widths.) The other option, Points, lets you enter a point value for the dash pattern to fit within. This means the dashes will always have the same width and spacing, regardless of how thick the line or frame is.

5. To create the actual dashes, move your mouse to the top section of the dialog box that has the ruler. The default is a solid line. To change that, click to where you want the first segment to end. The rest of the dash will become empty.

6. You add the next segment by clicking the mouse on the ruler (like adding a tab). If you hold down the mouse button when adding a segment, you can drag the segment to the desired width. (You can also enter the ruler location in the Position field and click the Add button.)

7. You resize an existing segment by clicking and holding the mouse on one side of the segment boundaries on the ruler and dragging to expand or contract the segment.

8. You can move a segment by dragging it to the left or to the right within the window, as shown in Figure 8-19 (the mouse should be on the segment itself, not on the ruler).

9. Check Stretch to Corners to ensure that no corner of your box has a segment only in one direction.

10. Set the miter type. A miter is the connection method for lines at a corner, and your choices are for the corner to be a right angle (the default), curved, or beveled. For fine lines (2 points and narrower), all three options look the same, so you may as well leave the option set to a right angle for such lines.

11. Choose the *endcap*, which is the shape of the dash segment at the beginning and end. The default puts the endpoint of the dash segment where the dash ends. But you can also set a rounded endcap, which adds a curve at the end of the dash segment — extending slightly past the dash's endpoint. Another option is a squared-off endcap, which adds a rectangle at the end of the dash segment — again, extending slightly past the dash segment's endpoint. (You can delete a dash by clicking the dash (not the ruler) and dragging it out of the dialog box.)

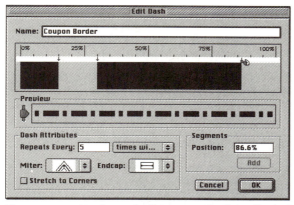

Figure 8-19: Moving a dash segment in the Edit Dash dialog box.

12. If you want to start over again with a solid line, Option+click or Alt+Click anywhere on the line or ruler while in the Edit Dash dialog box. When you finally decide on a pattern, click OK. Then click Save in the Dashes & Stripes dialog box to save all your changes.

STEPS: Creating a stripe pattern

1. Choose Edit ⇨ Dashes & Stripes.

2. Click the New button, then choose Stripe to open the Edit Stripe dialog box.

3. Enter a meaningful name for your stripe pattern in the Name field. You might use a name such as *Head Shot Frame* if you're creating a pattern used for framing pictures of a newsletter's columnists.

4. To create the actual stripes, move your mouse to the top section of the dialog box that has the ruler. The default is a solid stripe. To change that, click where you want the first segment to end. The rest of the stripe will become empty.

Creating true dots

You can create true dots with the Dashes & Stripes feature. Typically, your "dots" will simply be squares. But if you choose a rounded endcap, your square becomes a circle.

You can also edit the dotted line that comes with QuarkXPress. Possible modifications include changing the spacing by changing the Repeats Every value and changing the dots into rounded dashes by adding a dash segment. We recommend you duplicate the All Dots line style and work with that duplicate rather than editing the original style, so you don't lose the default settings.

5. You add the next segment by clicking the mouse on the ruler (like adding a tab). If you hold down the mouse button when adding a segment, you can drag the segment to the desired width. (You can also enter the ruler location in the Position field and click the Add button.)

6. You resize an existing segment by clicking and holding the mouse on one side of the segment boundaries on the ruler and dragging to expand or contract the segment, as shown in Figure 8-20.

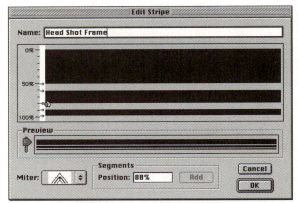

Figure 8-20: Adjusting a stripe segment in the Edit Stripe dialog box.

7. Finally, you can move a segment by dragging it up or down within the windows. The mouse should be on the segment itself, not on the ruler. You can delete a stripe by clicking the stripe (not the ruler) and dragging it out of the dialog box.

8. If you want to start over again with a solid line, Option+click or Alt+click anywhere on the line or ruler while in the Edit Stripe dialog box. When you finally decide on a pattern, click OK. Then click Save in the Dashes & Stripes dialog box to save all your changes.

Changing Item Types

When you create any item in QuarkXPress, the tool you use determines its type: text box, picture box, line, or text path. If you happen to create an item of the wrong type—for example, if you decide to flow text on a line or import a picture into a text box—you can easily convert an item's type. This is particularly handy if the item is already carefully sized, placed, and integrated into a layout.

To change an item's type, select it, and then choose an option from the Item ⇨ Content submenu, as shown in Figure 8-21:

✦ Text, which converts boxes to text boxes and lines to text paths

✦ Picture, which converts text boxes to picture boxes

✦ None, which converts text boxes and picture boxes to no-content boxes, and converts text paths to lines

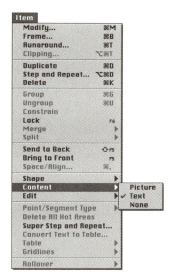

Figure 8-21: The Content submenu of the Item menu.

The None option is intended for boxes that will contain only colored backgrounds, blends, and/or frames. But using empty picture boxes and text boxes for this purpose is fine. The only advantage to a no-content box over an empty picture box is that, when guides are showing, no-content boxes don't display a large X. In a workgroup environment, using no-content boxes may help designers keep track of which boxes still need pictures imported (empty picture boxes) versus those intended only to be used as a graphic element (no-content boxes) — but most people use picture boxes for both purposes.

 Caution When you convert an item's type, its current contents will be deleted.

Stacking Items

When you add items to pages, QuarkXPress arranges them in a stacking order, from back to front. The first item you create is at the bottom of the stacking order, and the last item you create is at the top of the stacking order. Often, you can't see the stacking order because the items aren't overlapping. But if you draw two text boxes side-by-side, then drag one over the other, the first one you created will end up behind the second one you created, as shown in Figure 8-22. While you create items, you have no control over the stacking order — it just happens.

Figure 8-22: The box on the right was created after the box on the left; therefore, when the items overlap, it will be placed on top.

You don't necessarily think from back to front while you're creating items, but changing their stacking order is easy. For example, if you decide to add a colored background behind an entire page, you can draw a box the size of the page, move it all the way to the back, and fill it with color.

Cross-Reference

In addition to the stacking order occupied by each item on each page, QuarkXPress also offers document-wide layers for overlapping content. Each layer in QuarkXPress has its own stacking order, and items on the top layers are in front of items on the back layers. For more information about layers, see Chapter 10.

Changing the stacking order

To change an item's position within the stacking order, first select it. Then choose one of the following commands from the Item menu:

✦ **Send to Back (Shift+F5):** Moves the selected item to the very back of the stacking order.

✦ **Bring to Front (F5):** Moves the selected item to the very front of the stacking order.

✦ **Send Backward (Option+Shift+F5 or Ctrl+Shift+F5):** Moves the selected item one position back in the stacking order. On the Mac, hold the Option key while selecting the Item menu to have this command appear.

✦ **Bring Forward (Option+F5 or Ctrl+F5):** Moves the selected item one position forward (up) in the stacking order. On the Mac, hold the Option key while selecting the Item menu to have this command appear.

Note that in the Windows version of QuarkXPress, the Send Backward and Bring Forward commands are always in the Item menu — no special keystroke is required as it is on the Mac.

How stacking order works

Figure 8-23 shows how stacking order works. In the top example, the black box is at the back, the white box is in the middle, and the gray box is at the front of the stacking order. In the lower example, the white box has been moved to the front of the stacking order. As you can see, the ability to overlap items can be a powerful layout tool. You can overlap a filled box with another box of text, for example, creating a shadowed or multidimensional effect.

Figure 8-23: By changing the stacking order, you can achieve dramatically different layout effects and design elements.

Note

Items retain their stacking order, even when you move them to other pages or when you cut, copy, and paste them.

Grouping Items

To mimic a feature common to drawing programs, QuarkXPress lets you select two or more items and group them. When items are grouped, QuarkXPress treats them as a single item when you're moving, resizing, and editing them. (You can, however, still edit individual items within a group.) Grouping the items prevents you from accidentally moving one of the items out of place and allows you to move the items as a single unit.

Caution

QuarkXPress lets you create *nested groups,* which are groups within groups. For example, you can select two groups, then group them. Or you can select a group, select another item, then group that item to the group. This can get confusing, so you may want to avoid it. If you need to modify the contents of a group, it's often best to ungroup all the items, reselect all the items you want in the group, then group them.

Creating a group

To group multiple items, first select them using the Item tool or the Content tool (drag to marquee the items or Shift+click them). Then choose Item ➪ Group, or use ⌘+G or Ctrl+G. When a group is selected, the group is bounded by a dotted line (see Figure 8-24). To ungroup previously grouped items, select the group and choose Item ➪ Ungroup, or use ⌘+U or Ctrl+U.

Figure 8-24: A dotted line surrounds the outer boundaries of a selected group.

Working with groups

When you select a group to move, resize, modify, cut, copy, or paste it, be sure to use the Item tool. This lets QuarkXPress know that you want to work with the entire group. While a group is selected, you'll notice that many controls in the Measurements palette and the Modify dialog box are limited to controls that apply to the entire group. In fact, the Box or Line pane of the Modify dialog box will be replaced with a Group pane that lets you perform functions on the entire group (namely, change its position, size, and rotation).

Tip   As with other items, you can resize all the items in a group at the same time. To do this, select the group with the Item tool and drag one of its handles. Use the keyboard shortcuts discussed in the "Tips and tricks for resizing and reshaping" sidebar earlier in this chapter to control the resizing. For example, press Option+Shift+⌘ or Ctrl+Alt+Shift while you drag to keep all the items and contents proportional.

When you want to modify an individual item within the group, select that item with the Content tool. You can even move a single item within a group by selecting it with the Content tool, then pressing ⌘ or Ctrl while you drag the item, as shown in Figure 8-25.

Locking and Constraining Items

The ability to move items freely about the page gives you the ultimate design flexibility in QuarkXPress. Unfortunately, you can have too *much* flexibility, leaving the items in your designs vulnerable to accidental moving or misplacement. QuarkXPress provides two features to help limit layout flexibility—to keep your designs looking the way you intended them to.

Figure 8-25: To work with an individual item within a group, select it with the Content tool. To move the item, press ⌘ or Ctrl while you drag it.

Locking items in place

Suppose you've been working on a page layout for some time, and you've positioned an item — for example, the masthead — exactly where you want it to be. Knowing that you still have several items to place on the page, how can you prevent yourself from accidentally moving or resizing the masthead with an errant mouse click? The answer: Lock the item into position.

To lock an item, select it and choose Item ➪ Lock or use the F6 key. Figure 8-26 shows a locked item. You can tell if an item is locked because the Item tool's pointer changes to a lock icon when you position it over a locked item. To unlock a locked item, select the item and choose Item ➪ Unlock, or use F6.

Figure 8-26: When you try to move a locked item with the Item tool, the lock icon displays.

You can still move and resize a locked item, but you must do so using the Measurements palette or options in the Item menu. Essentially, what locking buys you is protection from accidental changes. Just because an object is locked, however, doesn't mean you can't edit it. For example, although you can't move or resize a locked box with the mouse, you can move it with the arrow keys and move or resize it with the Measurements palette.

Tip

When you're completing a template for use in a workgroup, locking all standing page elements in place is a good idea. This helps keep documents consistent by preventing accidental changes. Plus, if a designer does make a change, the fact that the item is locked prompts the person to carefully consider whether the change is appropriate.

Cross-Reference If you're working with the layers feature, you can lock all the items on an entire layer so they can't be edited with the mouse. If a layer is locked, all items are locked, regardless of whether you use the Item ⇨ Lock command. See Chapter 10 for more information.

Constraining boxes

Unique to QuarkXPress is the ability to constrain a box: You can specify that any new box placed over an existing box cannot be sized or moved beyond the limits of the existing box. Constraining boxes can be considered a subset of grouping, but the two processes actually differ. Constrained boxes behave more like a parent-and-child relationship: The child box is unable to leave the confines of the parent box. It also means the parent can't get smaller than the child. In a hierarchy of boxes, the constraining box parent is the rearmost box in the hierarchy. It must be large enough to hold all the child boxes you want to constrain within it (see Figure 8-27).

Figure 8-27: Here, the constraining box has a dashed border. You cannot move the smaller picture box or text box outside the larger box.

When to constrain

Documents that can take advantage of constraining usually are highly structured. One such document is a product catalog. You may set up a large text box that holds descriptive text to constrain a smaller picture box that holds a product illustration. If you develop such a document and you know ahead of time that you need constrained boxes, you can specify that a particular box is to be constrained or that all boxes in a document are to be constrained.

How to constrain

To constrain all the boxes in a document, check Auto Constrain in the General pane of the Preferences dialog box (Edit ⇨ Preferences ⇨ Preferences, or ⌘+Y or Ctrl+Y). To constrain a particular box, first make sure that the parent box is larger than the boxes within it and that all the child boxes are wholly within the parent box. Then select all the boxes, including the parent box, and choose Item ➪ Constrain to constrain them to the parent.

After a set of boxes is constrained, you can move and resize individual items within the constrained group using the Content tool as long as the child items still fit within the parent box. If you move a constrained box, all items constrained within it also move.

Summary

QuarkXPress pages are made up of items — primarily text boxes, picture boxes, lines, and text paths. The process of creating items is similar, regardless of the item type. You select a tool, then click and drag to create the item. When it comes to modifying items, you have various options:

✦ The Modify dialog box (Item ➪ Modify, or ⌘+M or Ctrl+M) gives you control over the size and placement of the item, its color, the placement of its contents, and how text wraps around it. Many of these commands are replicated in the Measurements palette.

✦ You can use the mouse and keyboard, along with keyboard commands, to visually resize and scale items and contents to fit your layout.

✦ The Item menu provides additional controls for modifying selected items, including the Send/Bring commands (for changing stacking order), the Content submenu (for changing item types), the Group/Ungroup commands (for grouping items so they can be treated as a single unit), the Lock command (for preventing accidental changes with the mouse), and the Constrain command (for limiting an item's movement).

✦ For automatically distributing items on a page, the Item menu provides the Space/Align command, and for creating and distributing copies of items, it provides Step and Repeat along with Super Step and Repeat.

✦ When you're working with lines and frames, you can create your own dash patterns and stripe patterns.

✦   ✦   ✦

Working with Pages

CHAPTER

9

As you know, most documents consist of more than one page. Chapter 12 covers the process of automatically inserting pages as you import lengthy text files. But in many projects, you'll be adding pages manually, and often you'll be moving and deleting pages as a publication's content comes into focus. For example, if you're working on a newsletter, you may start at 16 pages but then have it grow to 20 when the salespeople pick up more ads (or, in a slower economy, the opposite happens and you have to cut from 20 back to 16).

The pages you add can be single pages, facing-page spreads, or multipage spreads. And the pages can be blank, or they can be based on a *master page* — a preformatted page used as the basis for new pages. To help users navigate your documents, you can add page numbers, break a document into sections of page numbers, and produce "continued on" and "continued from" lines that update automatically.

Adding, Deleting, and Moving Pages

QuarkXPress documents can contain up to 1,999 pages, although if you need that many pages for a publication, you'll generally break it into multiple (and more manageable) documents. You also can delete and move pages at will, making QuarkXPress documents very adaptable to change. You have the option to work with pages visually, using the Document Layout palette or thumbnails, or numerically using commands in the Page menu.

When a page is not a page

Some documents *appear* to consist of several pages but really don't. For example, a trifold brochure usually consists of columns that strategically divide a single page into three "pages." That way you can print a single page on both sides and then fold it to delineate the pages. When you're working with business forms (for business cards or labels, for example), multiple "pages" print on the same actual page. Again, in this case, you'll need to strategically divide the page into areas that mimic the size and placement of the forms. You do much of this in the New Document dialog box (File ⇨ New ⇨ Document, or ⌘+N or Ctrl+N) and with on-screen guides, as shown in the illustration. In the trifold mailer shown here, the three horizontal pages are contained within one letter-size page.

Adding pages

Using the automatic text box makes sense only when you're importing long text files — a 5-page article or a 20-page chapter of a book, for example. The rest of the time, you'll be adding a page, then adding the content. Or you'll add all the pages you'll need, then add the content on a page-by-page basis.

Cross-Reference

If you work with the same layouts over and over again, you can add all the necessary pages to a document, then save the document as a template. A template serves as the empty shell of a document — a great starting place for the next issue of a publication. See Chapter 33 for more information.

Before you add pages, take a look at the document and determine where the pages need to go — between existing pages, at the end of the document, at the beginning, and so on. Also, consider what type of pages you want to add: a single page, two-page spreads, pages based on master pages. When you're ready to add pages, you have two options: using the Document Layout palette or using the Insert Pages dialog box.

Note   If you include a prefix in the document page numbers (an example of a prefix is the *20-* in page 20-1), be sure to include the prefix when you specify pages to insert, delete, or move. You can also specify absolute page numbers by using a plus sign (+) before the absolute page number. For example, if the page you want to move is numbered 20-1, but it's actually the 30th page in the document, you can use either 20-1 or +30.

Using the Document Layout palette

The Document Layout palette works best for adding just a few pages, especially when you prefer to see exactly where they're going. The icons are also handy when document pages are based on many different master pages. You cannot undo actions performed in the Document Layout palette, so you may want to save the document first, giving you the option to Revert to Saved if something goes awry.

STEPS: Adding pages with the Document Layout palette

1. Choose View ➪ Show Document Layout, or press F10 on the Mac or F4 in Windows.

2. In the Document Layout palette, indicate what type of page you want to add by clicking a page icon at the top of the palette.

   - In the top section, you'll see a blank single-sided page icon and a blank facing-page icon (in a document set up with Facing Pages in the New Document dialog box).

   - In the middle section, you'll see a scroll list of all the master pages in the document (A-Master A is the default master page).

3. After you've clicked an icon, drag it into the pages area at the bottom of the Document Layout palette, as shown in Figure 9-1. When the icon is on top of or between existing pages, arrows indicate where the new page or spread will go. Or you can simply drop the page in a blank area at the end of the document.

4. Release the mouse button to insert the pages.

Tip   To add multiple pages from the Document Layout palette, you can press the Option or Alt key while you drag in a new page. This opens the Insert Pages dialog box so you can specify how many pages to add and where.

The facing-page shuffle

When you insert or move pages in a document, QuarkXPress automatically moves all affected pages as necessary, even updating automatic page numbering. In facing-page documents, if you insert a page into the middle of a two-page spread, all the other pages are adjusted accordingly, with right-facing pages becoming left-facing pages and vice versa. This process is called *shuffling*.

When the left-hand page and the right-hand page have slightly different designs, as they usually do, shuffling can have undesirable effects. Namely, with shuffling you end up with items from both the left-facing and right-facing master page on the document pages. (Granted, this only happens if you've made local changes to master page items on the page—but you almost always do.) Because of this, it's important that you add or move pages as entire two-page spreads when working in facing-page documents.

Some graphic designers get around the perils of the facing-page shuffle by not using the Facing Pages feature. In a single-sided document, they simply create a left-facing master page and a right-facing master page, then place the pages side-by-side in the document using the Document Layout palette. When you move single-sided pages, shuffling doesn't occur. Of course, you'll still need to be sure you have the left-facing master page on left-facing pages and the right-facing master page on right-facing pages. This process, however, makes it much easier to switch the order of two right-facing pages without altering the formatting of the entire document.

In the document shown here, the designer faked facing pages by placing pages side-by-side. The pages based on A-Master A are formatted as left-facing pages, and the pages based on B-Master B are formatted as right-facing pages. Setting up the document this way gives the graphic designer the ability to switch pages around easily, without the hassles of shuffling.

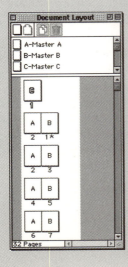

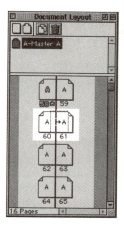

Figure 9-1: Inserting a page based on A-Master A between pages 60 and 61.

Adding pages with the Insert Pages dialog box

The Insert Pages dialog box works great for adding pages in bulk, especially when those pages are based on the same master page. For example, to create a 24-page newsletter, you may use the Insert Pages dialog box to add the 23 pages that follow page 1. This is much more efficient than dragging icons in the Document Layout palette. To use the Insert Pages dialog box, choose Page ⇨ Insert.

✦ Enter the number of pages to add in the Insert field. Then click the buttons shown in Figure 9-2 to specify where the pages are added. ***Remember:*** It's best to add facing pages in pairs.

✦ If you're inserting pages into the middle of an automatic text chain, and you're adding pages that contain an automatic text box, you can check Link to Current Text Chain. This will keep the text flowing through the pages you insert.

✦ The Master Page menu lists all the master pages you've created so you can choose a format for the pages you're adding.

When you click OK in the Insert Pages dialog box, QuarkXPress automatically numbers the inserted pages and renumbers those that follow.

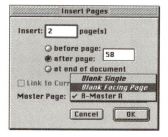

Figure 9-2: The Insert Pages dialog box lets you specify where to add pages and what master page to base those pages on.

Starting on a left-facing page

In a facing-page document, QuarkXPress will not let you start the document on a left-facing page. Therefore, if you add a page before page 1, it will replace the existing page 1 and shuffle all the following pages. There is one workaround, and it involves using section page numbers to give the first page in the document an even page number. See the section "Numbering Pages and Sections" in this chapter for the steps.

Deleting pages

When you delete pages, QuarkXPress deletes all their contents with one exception: Text in a chain of linked boxes simply flows into remaining boxes in the chain. After the deletion, QuarkXPress automatically renumbers the pages. You cannot undo page deletions, so you may want to save your document first so you have the option to revert it. Your two options for deleting pages are:

✦ Use the Document Layout palette (View ➪ Show Document Layout, or F10 on the Mac or F4 in Windows). Select the icons for the pages you want to delete, and then click the Delete button on the palette. To select multiple pages, ⌘+click or Ctrl+click them; to select a continuous range, Shift+click the first and last page in the range.

✦ Use the Delete Pages dialog box (Page ➪ Delete), shown in Figure 9-3. Enter the pages you want to delete, then click OK.

Figure 9-3: The Delete Pages dialog box.

You can delete all but the first page in the document. To prevent shuffling in a facing-page document, try to delete entire facing-page spreads.

Moving pages

As with adding and deleting pages, be sure to carefully consider which pages to move, where to move them, and what effect that will have on remaining pages in the document (especially in a facing-pages document). You have three options for moving pages: moving icons in the Document Layout palette, moving thumbnails of pages, and using the Move Pages command.

Save first, because you cannot undo page moves.

Using the Document Layout palette

The Document Layout palette (View ➪ Show Document Layout, or F10 on the Mac or F4 in Windows) is helpful for moving a few pages because you can see how other pages will move in the document. First, click on the icons of the pages you want to move (⌘+click or Ctrl+click to select multiple pages; to select a continuous range, Shift+click the first and last page in the range). Then drag the pages to a new location, as shown in Figure 9-4. Arrows indicate how the remaining pages will move.

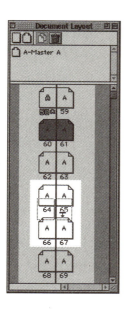

Figure 9-4: Moving pages by dragging icons in the Document Layout palette. In this example, pages 60 and 61 will be placed after pages 64 and 65.

Moving thumbnails of pages

QuarkXPress provides a view called Thumbnails, which displays pages at about 10 percent of their original size. (You can go to Thumbnails via the menu sequence View ➪ Thumbnails, via the keyboard shortcut Shift+F6, or by entering T in the View Percentage field.) In Thumbnails view, you can drag pages around the same way you move page icons in the Document Layout palette. But the advantage to thumbnails is you can see the page contents, as shown in Figure 9-5, in addition to the effect the move has on the document.

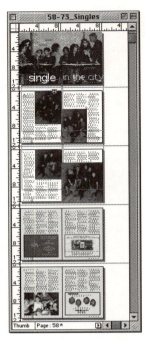

Figure 9-5: You can move a page by dragging it into position while the document is in Thumbnails view.

To move thumbnails, first choose View ➪ Thumbnails (or Shift+F6). Select the pages you want to move (click to select a page, ⌘+click or Ctrl+click to select multiple pages, and Shift+click the first and last page in the continuous range). Drag the pages to a new location in the document, and release the mouse button to move the pages.

✦ If the pointer looks like a miniature page, it means that the move doesn't change the placement of other pages in the document (for example, when you move a page to the end of a document).

✦ If the pointer looks like a left-pointing or right-pointing arrow, it means that moving that particular page bumps pages to the left or to the right.

✦ If the pointer looks like a down-pointing arrow, it means that successive pages will be moved.

Using the Move Pages dialog box

If you prefer numbers to icons, you can specify which pages to move and where to move them according to their page numbers. First, identify the pages you want to move by looking at the pages themselves or at the page icons in the Document Layout palette. Then choose Page ➪ Move.

If you want to move just one page, enter its page number in the Move Page(s) field. If you want to move a range of pages, enter the first page in the range in the Move Page(s) field and the last page in the Thru field. Use the Before Page, After Page, and To End of Document controls to specify where to move the page. Then click OK to move the pages and renumber surrounding pages as necessary.

Creating Multipage Spreads

QuarkXPress lets you create layouts that span two or more side-by-side pages, called *spreads*. Spreads are made up of pages that are adjacent to each other and span a fold in the final document. A set of left- and right-facing pages is a spread, as is a set of three or more adjacent pages that appear in a folded brochure. Spreads consisting of more than two pages are called *gatefolds*. When you create a document, you can set up facing-page spreads automatically. Plus, once you're in a document, you can create spreads that span multiple pages at will.

Specifying facing pages

Facing pages are commonly used in multipage documents that have material printed on both sides of the paper, such as newsletters and magazines. You specify facing pages for an entire document when you create it by checking Facing Pages in the New Document dialog box (File ➪ New ➪ Document, or ⌘+N or Ctrl+N). Or, if you later decide to convert a document to spreads, you can check Facing Pages in the Document Setup dialog box (File ➪ Document Setup, or Option+Shift+⌘+P or Ctrl+Alt+Shift+P). Facing-page documents have both advantages and disadvantages.

Facing-page advantages

The primary advantage to facing-page documents is that the default master page automatically contains a left-facing and right-facing master page with the inside and outside margins set up as you specified. (The inside margin is usually large enough to accommodate the binding or the spreading of pages as the reader reads the document.) Then any pages you add to the document are automatically placed side-by-side on-screen for easy design.

Facing-page disadvantages

The primary disadvantage to facing-page documents is their inability to adapt to change. For one thing, converting a facing-page document to single pages is almost impossible (unless you never placed any items on the left-facing pages). Plus, when you add, delete, and move pages, facing pages can shift from left to right, picking up additional master-page items as they move. Because of this, it's important to manipulate pages as spreads rather than moving individual pages. See the "The facing-page shuffle" sidebar earlier in this chapter for more information.

Cross-Reference For more information about creating a document with facing pages, converting a document to facing pages, and setting margins for this type of document, see Chapter 7.

Creating spreads manually

Aside from the Facing Pages feature, the only other way to create spreads or gate-folds is via the Document Layout palette (View ➪ Show Document Layout, or F10 on the Mac or F4 in Windows). The process is similar to adding a page: Simply click the Blank Single Page icon or a master page icon, then drag a new page into position in the lower portion of the Document Layout palette, as shown in Figure 9-6. Using this technique, you can:

✦ Add multipage spreads to an existing facing-page spread.

✦ Create artificial facing-page spreads by dragging new pages to the left and right side of the bar dividing the Document Layout palette. (Artificial facing-page spreads don't have the "shuffling" problem that QuarkXPress-created facing-page spreads have.)

✦ Add multipage spreads to a single-sided document.

Multipage spreads can consist of as many pages as you want, but you'll need to consider output issues. Chapter 6 discusses issues with planning and printing gatefolds.

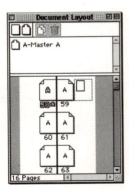

Figure 9-6: To create a gatefold in a facing-page document, drag new page icons into position in the Document Layout palette. In this example, a single-sided blank page is placed next to page 59.

Working with Master Pages

Part of the challenge of being a professional publisher is creating a consistent look throughout a document. You want what's on page 5, for example, to look connected to what's on page 10. In addition, you may want the publication name and issue date on the outer corner of each page. Perhaps you want a company logo to appear at the top of each page of an annual report. Or you may want a picture box to be placed at a specific spot on each page, ready to receive a graphic. In longer publications, you often have multiple formatting needs as well—chapter introduction pages, mini–tables of contents, body-text pages, and so on.

The QuarkXPress master pages feature is designed to help you achieve consistency. Master pages, which serve as a layout skeleton, hold the elements of a page that you want repeated on other pages in the same document. You then apply a master page to document pages as you create them (just as you apply style sheets to automatically format text). This frees you from having to create the same boxes and elements on each and every page.

Although master pages help keep documents consistent, they also allow a great deal of flexibility. You can add, modify, or delete items on master pages, and those changes automatically apply to any document pages based on that master page (unless local changes have been made to the modified elements on pages based on that master page). In addition, after master-page items are placed on document pages, you can change those items as much as necessary. Documents can have up to 127 master-page pairs.

Tip Generally, you'll create master pages after you have a good idea of the overall look of a publication and its needs. Your master pages should be included in your templates, which serve as the skeleton of an entire document. See Chapter 33 for more information.

The default master page

Whether you realize it or not, all documents are based on a master page. When you create a document, QuarkXPress creates the default master page for you. It's called *A-Master A,* and it reflects the margins and columns you set up in the New Document dialog box. All document pages are based on this master page—which you can add items to—until you create more master pages and apply them to other document pages. The items that appear on document pages from a master page, including the default master page, are called *master items.*

Designing on master pages

To design a master page, you need to leave the document and display the master page, where you can create items that you want to be repeated throughout the document. When master pages are displayed, you can design the pages as you would any other pages—the only difference is that the items aren't placed on document pages unless the master page is applied.

Displaying master pages

QuarkXPress lets you toggle between document pages and the master pages upon which they're based in the following ways:

✦ Use the Display submenu of the Page menu. To display the actual document pages on your monitor, choose Page ⇨ Display ⇨ Document. To display a master page for the document, choose Page ⇨ Display ⇨ Master (after you've established master pages, where we have used *Master,* the display will actually include a list of all master pages associated with the document; hold down the mouse button to select the master page you want to see).

✦ Press Shift+F10 (Mac) or Shift+F4 (Windows) to toggle between document pages and the default master page, A-Master A.

✦ Double-click master-page icons in the Document Layout palette (View ⇨ Show Document Layout, or F10 on the Mac or F4 in Windows).

✦ Click the Page pop-up menu in the lower-left corner of the document window, and then select a master page, as shown in Figure 9-7.

Before you start designing a master page, check the field next to the Page pop-up menu to confirm that you're displaying the master page you want.

Figure 9-7: Choosing a master page to display from the Page pop-up menu on the document window.

Adding common items to master pages

After you display a master page, you can use the typical item-creation tools to add text boxes, picture boxes, standing text and graphics, and so on, as necessary. The only thing you can't do is add text to the automatic text box on a master page. (Chapter 12 explains the automatic text box in full, including how to add an automatic text box to a master page.) Common items placed on master pages, some of which are shown in Figure 9-8, include:

✦ **Page headers and footers:** These are elements such as running heads and folios that you want to repeat from page to page. Facing-page documents often have alternating headers and footers on even– and odd-numbered pages. An example of an alternating footer is a page number; if you want the page number to print on the outside bottom corner of the page, the footers on right and left master pages differ from each other.

✦ **Automatic page numbers:** You create these by placing a Current Page Number character (⌘+3 or Ctrl+3) at the point on the master page where you want to see page numbers appear.

✦ **Page sidebars:** This is information in the outer side margins of a page that you want repeated on other pages.

✦ **Corporate logos:** Logos or other artwork that you want to appear throughout the document can also be placed on master pages.

The items you place on master pages should be appropriate for most of the document pages based on that master page. However, you can always make local changes to master-page items when they're on document pages. If you find that too many pages have too many variations, you can create additional master pages and design them differently.

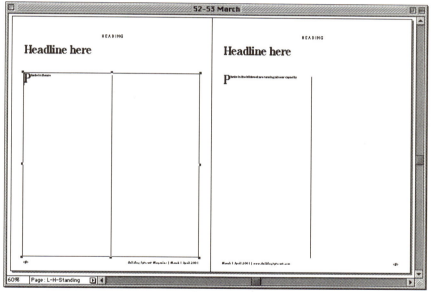

Figure 9-8: This master page from *Building Systems Magazine* contains placeholders for department headings and articles. The folios at the bottom of each page are different for the left- and right-facing pages.

Creating and naming new master pages

To add a new master page to a document, open the Document Layout palette (View ➪ Show Document Layout, or F10 on the Mac or F4 in Windows). Click the Blank Single Page icon or the Blank Facing Page icon, and then drag it down into the master-page area of the palette.

Caution Be careful not to drag it right on top of an existing master page. If you do, QuarkXPress will replace that master page with a new, blank master page.

Adding folios

Magazines and newsletters usually have straightforward headers and footers (or *folios*), composed of the page number, publication title, and issue date, or some combination of these three elements. Typically, these folios are implemented on master pages (with one folio for the left master page and one folio for the right master page), because the text doesn't vary from page to page except for the current page number (which QuarkXPress can insert automatically).

Other documents — such as manuals and books — often have more detailed headers and footers. Often, the header or footer includes information specific to the current chapter or even page. If you do want a header for each section that includes the page number and chapter name, you need to decide whether you can put this header on a master page (so that it automatically appears on each page) or whether to manually copy the appropriate text box to each page in the section. The answer depends on how you use master pages. If you have a different master page for each section, you'd have a header text box appropriate for each section on that section's master page. If you have only one master page, you need to copy the text box customized for a certain section to each page in that section.

You may, in fact, use both methods if you need further customization. For example, perhaps the footer uses the chapter name, so that it can be implemented in the section's master page, but the header uses the page's current topic. In this case, you have to manually edit that on each document page in the section.

To change the new master page's name, click on the name as you would on the desktop. Then simply type the new name, as shown in Figure 9-9. QuarkXPress will add the alphabetical prefix of A-, B-, C- to your master page name. It's always a good idea to give your master pages meaningful names such as *Features, Columns,* or *Table of Contents* instead of relying on the default names of B-Master B, C-Master C, and so on.

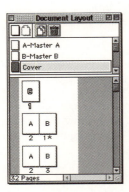

Figure 9-9: Click on a master page name to edit it.

Note If your document is single-sided, you'll only be able to add single-sided master pages to it. However, if your document is a facing-page document, you can add single-sided or facing-page master pages.

Adding new pages based on master pages

You have two options for adding new pages based on master pages. You can add one page or spread at a time using the Document Layout palette, or you can add as many pages as you want using the Insert Pages dialog box. When you add pages based on master pages, all the master items automatically appear on the document pages. To show you which master page each document page is based on, the Document Layout palette displays the master page's prefix (such as A, B, C) on the document page icons.

Using the Document Layout palette

To insert a new page based on an existing master page, open the Document Layout palette (View ➪ Show Document Layout, or F10 on the Mac or F4 in Windows). Click the icon of the master page you want the new document page to be associated with, and drag the icon into the lower part of the Document Layout palette, which shows the document pages. As you drag the page icon into position, the icon will change to an arrow or a page icon. Release the mouse when you've positioned the icon in the spot you want, as shown in Figure 9-10.

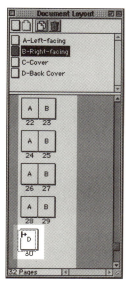

Figure 9-10: Adding a page based on master page B before the last page of the document.

Using Insert Pages

Rather than using the Document Layout palette, you can also insert a new document page based on an existing master page by choosing Page ⇨ Insert. This displays the Insert Pages dialog box. You can associate the inserted pages with a master page by choosing one of the master pages shown in the Master Page pop-up menu. To link the automatic text boxes on pages that you're inserting into the active text chain, check Link to Current Text Chain in the Insert Pages dialog box. This option is available only if a text box is active and if the pages you're inserting are set to include an automatic text box.

Applying master pages to document pages

If your document already contains pages, and you then decide to reformat a page based on another master page, you can apply the master page to that document page. But doing this can get complicated if the pages already contain items. Items from the new master page are layered on top of local items that you already created on the page. Items on the page placed by the previous master page are either deleted or retained depending on a setting in the General pane of the Preferences dialog box (Edit ⇨ Preferences ⇨ Preferences, or ⌘+Y or Ctrl+Y).

The Master Page Items preference

The default setting for Master Page Items, Keep Changes (see Figure 9-11), means that QuarkXPress keeps any items to which you've made local changes. (For example, it keeps a text box that you've already imported text into.) With this setting, you won't lose any content, but some of it may be obscured and the page won't exactly match the new master page. The other setting, Delete Changes, deletes any master items with local changes, which may cause you to lose content.

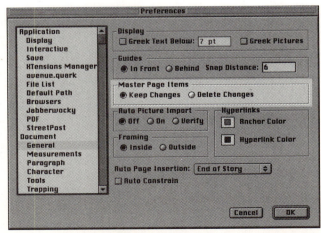

Figure 9-11: The Master Page Items preference in the General pane of the Preferences dialog box.

Tip

Regardless of your Master Page Items setting, items that you create locally on pages are retained when you apply new master pages. Therefore, applying a new master page is never guaranteed to reap consistent page formatting. Sometimes it's easier to add a new page based on the master page you want, move any content from the other page, and then delete the old page.

Applying master pages

You apply master pages to existing document pages using the Document Layout palette (View ➪ Show Document Layout, or F10 on the Mac or F4 in Windows). You cannot undo this operation, and it does have danger of losing content, so you may wish to save your document first. If applying the master page has unintended consequences, you can use the Revert to Saved option in the File menu.

✦ To apply a master page to a single page or spread, drag the master page icon on top of the document page icon.

✦ To apply a master page to multiple pages, first select all the pages (⌘+click or Ctrl+click to select discontinuous pages; Shift+click the first and last page in a continuous range of pages). Then Option+click or Alt+click the master page you want to apply.

Editing master pages

After working on a document for a while, you also may want to make changes to master pages. For example, you may decide to move the page number from the bottom center of the page to the outer margin. First, display the master page in the document window (using the Display submenu of the Page menu, the Document Layout palette, or the Page pop-up menu on the document window). Make any changes you want to the master page, and then return to the document by pressing Shift+F10 (Mac) or Shift+F4 (Windows).

The changes you make to a master page will automatically apply to master items on document pages — provided that you haven't made local edits to the master items. For example, say you change the issue date of a magazine in the folio on A-Master A. Then you switch to the document pages based on A-Master A. You'll find that if you made any local changes to a folio — such as deleting it — the new date isn't added to that folio.

Cross-Reference

To change margin and column guides on master pages, you'll use the Master Guides command in the Page menu (when a master page is displayed). See Chapter 7 for more information.

Rearranging and deleting master pages

Because you can create up to 127 master pages per document, you can easily end up with more master pages than you really need. In addition, the default order of master pages (alphabetical by prefix) may not suit your needs. To solve these problems, you can use the Document Layout palette (View ➪ Show Document Layout, or F10 on the Mac or F4 in Windows) to rearrange and delete master pages.

✦ To rearrange master pages, click the icon of the master page you want to move, and drag it into position within the top part of the palette. Release the mouse button when the arrow indicates the new position; the master page stays put.

✦ To delete master pages, first skim through the document portion of the Document Layout palette to make sure the master page is not applied to any document pages (look for the master page's prefix). If so, check out those pages and see if you're willing to lose any content from the master page on those pages. Then select the master page icon and click the Delete button at the top of the palette.

Numbering Pages and Sections

When it comes to adding page numbers to document pages, think automatic. You should, at all times, let QuarkXPress number pages for you. This gives you the luxury of adding, deleting, and reordering pages while having the page numbers update automatically. You can number pages consecutively, or you can break a document up into sections of page numbers.

Adding page numbers

To add a page number to any document page, click in a text box and press ⌘+3 or Ctrl+3. The number of that page is automatically inserted, and it takes on the formatting of surrounding text. If you move this page, this number will change.

In most cases, though, it's more useful to put a placeholder for page numbers on master pages. Then all the pages based on that master page will have a page number. To do this, again, you click in text on the master page and press ⌘+3 or Ctrl+3. On master pages, the placeholder page number shows up as the pound sign in angle brackets (<#>). You can highlight the pound sign and angle brackets, and then apply the character attributes such as font and size that you want for page numbers, as shown in Figure 9-12 (you'll have to envision how actual numbers will look, especially numbers made up of multiple digits).

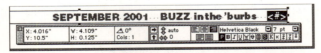

Figure 9-12: The placeholder for automatic page numbers displays as a pound sign surrounded by angle brackets (<#>) on master pages.

Tip

QuarkXPress has no other way to add automatic page numbering, so this command is worth memorizing. Fortunately, there's an easy way to remember it. The pound sign (#) displays above the 3 on the keyboard — so if you can remember that the placeholder for page numbers displays as the pound sign, you can remember the 3 in the keyboard command.

Breaking a document into sections

Sometimes you may want to number pages in a QuarkXPress document consecutively, from first page to last. Other times, such as when the document grows to an unwieldy size or when you're required to do so because of prescribed formatting standards, you may want to break the document into sections. Technical manuals or books with chapters are often broken into sections to make it easier for the reader to locate information (see Chapter 34 for more information on books and chapters).

If the document is divided into sections, you generally want the page numbers to reflect the document's structure. For example, give the 11th page in Section 5 the page number *5-11* so that readers can easily determine where pages and sections are in relation to the rest of the publication.

STEPS: Creating a section

1. Display the first page of the section in the document window. (Check the field in the lower-left corner of the document window to make sure the right page number is showing — if part of the previous page is showing, QuarkXPress will think that's the first page of the section.) You can also double-click the document's page icon in the Document Layout palette.

2. Choose Page ➪ Section. If you have selected a document page in the Document Layout palette, you can Option+click or Alt+click the page number shown in the lower-left corner of the palette to open the Section dialog box.

3. Check Section Start to create the section. You can ignore the grayed-out Book Chapter Start control, which is covered in Chapter 34.

4. Enter a prefix such as "A." or "1-" in the Prefix field, as shown in Figure 9-13. You can enter a prefix of up to four characters. If you want a space, hyphen, or other separator between the section prefix and the page number, you must enter that separator as part of the prefix name.

5. In the Number field, enter the page number for the first page in this section. For example, if you're producing a book that already has pages 1 and 2 preprinted, you want your QuarkXPress pages to begin with a page number of 3.

Figure 9-13: The Section dialog box lets you set up discrete sections of page numbers within a document.

6. Select an option from the Format menu to indicate the type of page numbers for this section:

   - Arabic numerals (1, 2, 3, 4)
   - Uppercase or lowercase roman numerals (I, II, III, IV or i, ii, iii, iv)
   - Uppercase or lowercase letters (A, B, C, D or a, b, c, d)

7. Click OK to create the section of page numbers. An asterisk (*) in the Document Layout palette indicates the start of a new section.

You can move pages around within a section, and their page numbers are updated automatically. If you move pages to within a different section, they pick up page numbering from that section.

Tip

After you have sections in a document, pages have two types of page numbers: absolute and section. An absolute page number indicates a page's actual position in the document (1 is the first page, 2 is the second page, and so on) regardless of the section page number (i, ii, iii, and so on, for example) that displays on the page. When you enter page numbers in fields (for example, to move pages), you need to enter the entire section number, including the prefix, in the fields. But you can also enter absolute page numbers by preceding page numbers with a plus sign (for example, the first page in a document is +1).

Cross-Reference

If you use a hyphen in your page number prefix, it will be difficult to enter continuous ranges of page numbers in the Pages field of the Print dialog box. That's because you would generally enter "1-5" to print the first five pages of a document, but if your prefix contains a hyphen, you might end up with "A-1-A-5." This will confuse QuarkXPress. Likewise, in the less-likely case that you use a comma in your prefix, it's difficult to enter noncontinuous page numbers to print. Both problems are solved by the Page Range Separators controls, an application preference covered in Chapter 3.

Odd– and even-numbered pages

In a facing-page document, QuarkXPress forces you to have even page numbers (2, 4, 6) on left-facing pages and odd page numbers (1, 3, 5) on right-facing pages. Therefore, if you start a section with an odd page number on a left-facing page, QuarkXPress will — without warning — make that page a right-facing page, and shuffle all subsequent pages from left to right accordingly. Although the behavior is appropriate (right-hand pages *should* have odd page numbers), the consequences of shuffling can alter the design of your document pages. So be careful to make sure you're starting odd-numbered sections on right-facing pages and even-numbered sections on left-facing pages.

Starting a document on a left-facing page

QuarkXPress doesn't like you to start a facing-page document on a left-facing page. However, needing to do this is common — for example, if your document contains a single feature story for a magazine, and the feature starts on the left. The way you accomplish this is to create a section start on the first page of the document. When you enter an even page number for the first page of the section, QuarkXPress flips the page into position as a left-facing page, as shown in Figure 9-14.

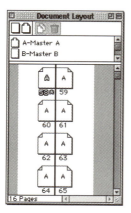

Figure 9-14: To start a facing-page document on a left-facing page, create a section start with an even page number on the first page.

Adding "Continued On" Lines

Whenever your document contains a *jump* (a place where text that cannot fit entirely on one page is continued on another, linked page), consider adding automatically generated *Continued on. . .* and *Continued from. . .* markers to the document. To use this feature, draw text boxes at the locations in the document where you want the *Continued on. . .* and *Continued from. . .* markers to appear, and make sure the two text boxes are linked (see Figure 9-15). Press ⌘+4 or Ctrl+4 (in a Continued-on box) to place the marker for the next text box's page-number character. Press ⌘+2 or Ctrl+2 (in a Continued-from box) to have the page number for the previous box holding the story automatically appear.

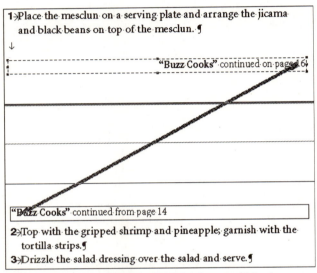

Figure 9-15: The page numbers in the two linked continued boxes here will automatically update if we move the pages.

Summary

For the ultimate in flexibility, QuarkXPress lets you add, delete, and move pages as you want. The Document Layout palette provides the most visual and interactive method for most of these changes, but you can also use commands in the Page menu. When you create documents, you can specify facing pages, and you can easily creating multipage spreads by dragging icons in the Document Layout palette.

For automatically formatting pages that you add, and to automatically reformat existing pages, QuarkXPress provides master pages. Master pages function like style sheets for document pages, even communicating changes you make on master pages to associated document pages. For easy document navigation, you can use automatic page numbers and you can break up the page numbering into sections within a document. If your stories continue from one page to the next, you can generate automatic continued-on and continued-from lines that update as necessary.

✦   ✦   ✦

Working with Layers

When you're entrenched in the publishing industry, you'll be surprised how much time you spend doing almost the exact same thing over and over. For example, you may create several different designs for the same ad to show to a client. Or you might use the same ad but flow in other text for different markets or languages. Even if you're using master pages, style sheets, libraries, and other productivity tools, you may waste valuable time repeating steps and keeping track of different versions of the same document. To streamline repetitive work and prevent confusion among multiple versions of the same document, QuarkXPress provides layers.

Layers function somewhat like the series of clear plastic overlays that teachers use in overhead presentations. The teacher might start with one overlay containing a graphic, then add another overlay with descriptive text, then add a third overlay containing a chart. Each overlay contains distinct content, but you can see through each one to the others to get the entire message. The QuarkXPress layers are somewhat like this, letting you isolate content on slices of a document. You can then show and hide layers, lock items on layers, rearrange layers, and more.

Layers provide an additional benefit for complex QuarkXPress designs that consist of many items stacked on top of other items. Layers help you isolate the items you're working on because you can control which layers display and print.

 New Feature Layers are new to QuarkXPress 5.

Understanding Layers

Each QuarkXPress document contains a default layer, Layer 1, which contains all of a document's items (including master page items) until you create and select a new layer. Items on the default layer — and any other layer for that matter — follow the standard stacking order of QuarkXPress. The first item you create is the backmost, the last one you create is the frontmost, and all the other items fall somewhere in between.

Cross-Reference   See Chapter 8 for complete information about stacking order.

Like the clear plastic overlays, the order of the layers also affects the stacking order of the items. Items on the bottom layer are behind other items, and items on the top layer are in front of other items. In Figure 10-1, the layers at the bottom of the list contain the various options for the background photograph. The Default layer contains the other design element, the circle with the drop shadow.

Figure 10-1: The Layers feature was ideal for experimenting with different photographs used on the cover of this invitation. By placing the various photographs on a separate layer, the designer could display and print several versions of the invitation for consideration without re-creating the card.

Although layers are often compared to plastic overlays, there's one big difference: Layers are not specific to individual pages. Each layer encompasses the entire document, which doesn't make much difference when you're working on a small invitation, but it makes a significant difference when it comes to a 24-page booklet. When you create layers and place items on them, it's important that your strategy consider all the pages in the document.

Finding the right tools

To work with layers, QuarkXPress provides the Layers palette, Layer preferences, and a View menu command that shows you which layers items belong to. For the most part, you'll use the Layers palette.

The Layers palette

The Layers palette (View ➪ Show Layers), shown in Figure 10-2, is your gateway to creating and manipulating layers. Buttons and icons on the palette let you manipulate the layers you create, as does the Layers palette's context menu. To display the context menu, Control+click or right-click the palette. (On the Mac, if you've changed your Interactive preferences, you may need to press Control+Shift+click to display the menu.)

Using layers strategically

To be honest, most users can get away with never touching the Layers feature. Like many features in QuarkXPress, it's intended for longer-term repetitive projects, but it's also helpful for projects that require a lot of input and collaboration. Take a look at the possibilities and see if they fit into your workflow. In the long run, learning to use layers can save time and prevent mistakes that often result when you need to track changes across multiple documents.

Say you've got an invitation with the same copy in it, but different headline and image for each city it runs in. You can place the boilerplate information on one layer and the information that changes on other layers. If any of the boilerplate information changes, you only need to change it once. To print different versions of the ad, you control which layers print.

You might use layers in the following situations:

✦ **A project with a high-resolution background image, such as a texture, that takes a long time to redraw.** You can hide that layer while designing other elements, then show it occasionally to see how it works with the rest of the design.

✦ **A document that you need to produce in several versions.** For example, you could create a restaurant ad with different prices for different cities or a cosmetic catalog featuring a different selection depending on the age group of the audience. You can place the content that changes on separate layers, then print the layers you need.

✦ **A project that includes items you don't want to print.** You might have a layer that's used for nothing but adding editorial and design comments, which is deleted when the document is final. (This can be faster than suppressing the printout of items using the Modify dialog box.)

✦ **A publication that is translated into several languages.** Depending on the layout, you can place all the common items on one layer, then create a different layer for each language's text. Changes to the common items only need to happen once — unlike if you created copies of the original document and flowed the translated text into the copies.

✦ **To experiment with different layouts of the same document.** You can show and hide layers to present different options to your supervisor or client. This strategy lets you use common elements, such as the logo and legal information, in several versions of the same design.

✦ **A complex design that contains many overlapping items, text wraps, and grouped items.** Say the background of a page consists of a checkerboard pattern made up of filled, rectangular frames. You don't want to accidentally select the blocks while you're working with other items. If you isolate complex items on their own layer, you can show only that layer to work on it, hide that layer to concentrate on other layers, lock the layer so items can't be selected, and otherwise manipulate the layer.

When determining whether to use layers or whether to place items on a separate layer, remember that layers are document-wide and not page-specific.

New Layer

Move Item to Layer

Merge Layers — Pencil icon

Delete Layer — Active Item icon

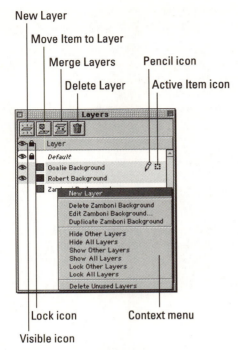

Lock icon — Context menu

Visible icon

Figure 10-2: The Layers palette.

Tip

As with other palettes, when Show Tool Tips is checked in the Interactive pane of the Preferences dialog box (Edit ➪ Preferences ➪ Preferences, or Shift+Option+ ⌘+Y or Ctrl+Alt+Shift+Y), you can find out what the controls do by pointing at them. If you know what the controls do, you can intuit a great deal of how to work with layers.

Layer preferences

You can specify some default characteristics of layers, such as whether items on the layer are locked, in Layer preferences. To access Layer preferences, choose Edit ➪ Preferences ➪ Preferences, or Shift+Option+⌘+Y or Ctrl+Alt+Shift+Y, then select the Layer pane. Layer preferences, which are the same as layer attributes, are explained later in this chapter.

Visual Indicators

While you're working with layers, it's easy to get confused about which layer an item is on. QuarkXPress provides three methods for showing an item's layer:

✦ Choose View ➪ Show Visual Indicators. This displays a small color swatch on each item; the color corresponds to the color shown to the left of each layer name in the Layers palette.

✦ If you point at a Visual Indicator, the name of the layer displays, as shown in Figure 10-3.

✦ If you select an item, the Active Item icon (a small, outlined box) displays to the right of its layer's name in the Layers palette. (If multiple items are selected, and they're on different layers, you'll see multiple Active Item icons, and it will be harder to determine which layer an item is on.)

Figure 10-3: Visual Indicators show which layer each item belongs to.

Creating Layers

You can create up to 256 layers per document, which should be plenty for any use. Once you create a new layer, it's activated automatically so you can begin working on it.

Creating a layer

To create a new layer, click the New Layer button on the Layers palette, as shown in Figure 10-4, or choose the New Layer command from the context menu. This places a new, active layer on top of all existing layers. Keep in mind that it doesn't matter which document page is displayed when you create a layer, because the layer will encompass all the pages in the document.

Figure 10-4: Creating a new layer.

Note   You cannot create layers for master pages; master page items are all stored on the default layer. If you move master page items on document pages to a different layer, they're no longer considered to be master page items, and they cannot be updated via changes to the master page.

Customizing layers

When you create a layer, it's automatically assigned a name (Layer 1, Layer 2, and so on) and a color. In addition, other attributes specified through preferences affect the layer — whether you can see items on the layer, whether the items are locked, and so on. You can change any attributes of a layer, and you can change preferences so all new layers have different attributes. To edit a layer's attributes, double-click it or select it and choose Edit Layer from the context menu. The Attributes dialog box, shown in Figure 10-5, provides name and color controls, and four check boxes that also appear in the Layer pane of the Preferences dialog box.

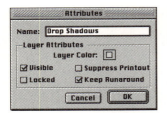

Figure 10-5: The Attributes dialog box lets you change a layer's name and the color of its Visual Indicators among other things.

Name field

Type a descriptive name of up to 32 characters for the layer. For example, if you're using layers for different versions of a design, you might have a *Flowered Background* layer, a *Striped Background* layer, and a *Text* layer.

Layer Color button

A layer's color helps you identify which layer an item is on. The color displays to the left of the layer name in the Layers palette and displays on each item's Visual Indicators (View ➪ Show Visual Indicators). By default, QuarkXPress applies a different color to each new layer, but you can customize it to something meaningful for your document and workflow (or even something more visually distinctive for you). Click the color button to select a color from your operating system's color pickers.

Visible check box

Checked by default, this control lets you specify whether items on a layer display. If the items don't display, they also don't print. This check box has the same effect as clicking the Visible (eye) icon on the Layers palette.

Locked check box

Unchecked by default, this option lets you control whether items on a layer can be edited with the mouse. Check Locked to prevent items from being accidentally resized, reshaped, or otherwise modified with the mouse (you can still modify these items using the Measurements palette and the Modify dialog box). For example, in a document containing multiple versions of text on different layers, you might lock the layer containing background images and other items that stay the same. The Locked check box has the same effect as clicking the Lock icon on the Layers palette.

Suppress Printout check box

Unchecked by default, this check box controls whether all the items on a layer print. If you want to prevent all the items on a layer from printing, check Suppress Printout. (To prevent just a few items from printing, use the Suppress Printout check box in the Modify dialog box for individual items.) If a layer isn't checked as Visible, its items won't print regardless of this setting.

Keep Runaround check box

Checked by default, this option controls whether items on layers that aren't showing still force text runaround on other layers. Check Keep Runaround if you need to see text wrap while you're working in a document, as shown in Figure 10-6. However, if you're simply editing text and the text wrap is unimportant — or if you're not planning to use the text wrap with certain layers — uncheck Keep Runaround.

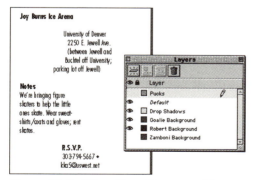

Figure 10-6: When Keep Runaround is checked, items on hidden layers still create text wraps in visible layers. In this example, graphics in the shape of hockey pucks are forcing runaround even though the Pucks layer is hidden.

Working with Items on Layers

Whether you're designing a magazine template from the ground up or modifying an existing ad, you can isolate specific types of items on layers. You can create items on a layer, move items to a layer, or copy items to a layer.

The active layer

The *active layer* is the one you're creating items on — whether you're using tools, dragging items in from a library or another document, or pasting items from other layers. A Pencil icon to the right of a layer's name, as shown in Figure 10-7, means it's the active one. Although more than one layer can be selected at a time, only one can be active. To switch the active layer to another layer, click to the right of the layer name to move the Pencil icon. To activate a layer, it must be visible.

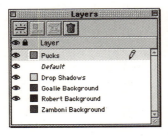

Figure 10-7: The Pencil icon indicates the active layer, which will contain any new items you create. Here, the Pucks layer is active.

Selecting items on layers

Regardless of the active layer, you can select, move, and modify items on any visible, unlocked layer. You can even select items on different layers and manipulate them at the same time. The display and locking of layers is controlled by the Visible and Lock icons on the Layers palette, respectively, and by the Visible and Locked check boxes in the Attributes dialog box.

The Layers palette helps you work with selected items in the following ways:

✦ To determine which layer an item belongs to, match the color of its Visual Indicator (View ➪ Show Visual Indicators) to a color to the left of a layer name.

✦ Point to a Visual Indicator to display its layer's name.

✦ To determine which layers contain active items, look to the right of the layer names. A small box next to a layer name, as shown in Figure 10-8, indicates that it contains an active item.

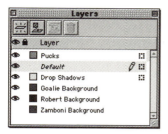

Figure 10-8: A small box to the right of a layer's name indicates that an item on the layer is selected. In this example, items are active on the Pucks, Default, and Drop Shadows layers.

Placing items on layers

To place items on a layer, the layer must be active as indicated by the Pencil icon. To place items on the layer:

✦ Use any tools to create items — text boxes, picture boxes, text paths, and lines.

✦ Use the Paste command (Edit ➪ Paste, or ⌘+V or Ctrl+V) to paste items from the Clipboard onto the layer.

✦ Drag items to the layer from a library or from another document.

Note
Items dragged from other documents bring their layers with them (except items from the Default layer). The items do not, however, bring the other items on the layer. If the layer an item brings with it has the same name as a layer in the document, an asterisk displays next to the new layer name.

Moving items to different layers

After an item is on a layer, it's not stuck there. You can copy and paste items to selected layers, or you can move them using the Layers palette. To select multiple items, remember to Shift+click them, then move them in one of the following ways:

✦ To paste items on a different layer, first cut or copy items to the Clipboard. Activate the layer you want to put the items on, then use the Paste command (Edit ➪ Paste, or ⌘+V or Ctrl+V). This method works well for moving items that reside on different layers.

✦ To move items to a different layer, drag the active item box (to the right of a layer's name) to another layer, as shown in Figure 10-9. When you use this method, it doesn't matter which layer is active. However, you can't move items from different layers to the same layer using this method. (If you select multiple items that reside on different layers, dragging the box moves only items that reside on the first layer on which you selected an item.)

✦ To pick a layer by name to move items to, select the items and click the Move Item to Layer button. The Choose Destination Layer dialog box lets you select a layer for the items.

Figure 10-9: Dragging an active item box moves the selection to a different layer. Here, we're moving an item from the Drop Shadows layer to the Pucks layer.

Manipulating Layers

Using the Layers palette, you can select and manipulate entire layers. These changes affect all the items on the layer — for example, if you hide a layer, all its items are hidden; if you move a layer up, all its items display in front of items on lower layers. Functions that affect an entire layer include hiding, locking, rearranging, merging, and deleting.

Showing and hiding layers

When you hide a layer, none of the items on that layer displays or prints. You might hide layers for a variety of reasons, including to speed screen redraw by hiding layers containing high-resolution graphics, to control which version of a publication prints, and to simply focus on one area of a design without the distraction of other areas. Note that when layers are hidden, they display temporarily while you're using Spell Check and Find/Change to edit text. To show or hide layers using the Layers palette, do one of the following:

✦ Click the Visible icon in the first column to the left of a layer's name. When this column is blank, the layer is hidden. Click in the column again to show the layer (see Figure 10-10).

✦ Double-click a layer and check or uncheck Visible in the Attributes dialog box.

✦ Choose an option from the context menu: Hide Others hides all but the first selected layer, Hide All hides every layer in the document, Show Others displays all but the first selected layer, and Show All makes all layers visible.

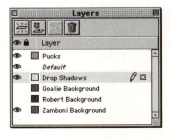

Figure 10-10: The Visible icon indicates that all items on the layer are showing. Here, the Goalie Background and Robert Background layers are hidden.

Locking items on layers

When you lock a layer, you cannot select or modify its items with the mouse — even if the locked layer is active. Generally, you'll lock layers to prevent background elements or complex drawings from accidental changes — while still allowing you to view the items in relation to the remainder of the layout. Because locking and unlocking is easy, you can lock layers while you're not working on them, then unlock them to make changes. To lock or unlock layers using the Layers palette, do one of the following:

✦ Click the blank box in the second column to the left of a layer's name. When the Lock icon is displayed, the layer is locked. Click the Lock icon to unlock the layer.

✦ Double-click a layer and check or uncheck Locked in the Attributes dialog box.

✦ Choose an option from the context menu: Lock Other Layers locks all but the first selected layer; Lock All Layers locks all items on all layers in the document.

Note When you lock a selected item to a page (Item ⇨ Lock, or F6), the item stays locked regardless of its layer's lock status. ***Remember:*** You can modify locked items and items on locked layers using the Measurements palette and the Modify dialog box.

Rearranging layers

Each layer has its own front-to-back stacking order, with the first item you create on the layer being its backmost item. You can modify the stacking order of items on a single layer using the Send commands in the Item menu. Items are further stacked according to the order in which the layers are listed in the Layers palette. The layer at the top of the list contains the frontmost items, and the layer at the bottom of the list contains the backmost items.

Dragging a layer

If you find that all the items on one layer need to be in front of all the items on another layer — throughout the document — you can move that layer up or down in the list. To move a layer, click to select it, then press Option or Alt to drag it to a new location in the layers list, as shown in Figure 10-11. (The layer will land one layer above the layer you drop it on.)

Caution When you move a layer, remember that layers are document-wide so you're actually changing the stacking order of items on all the pages.

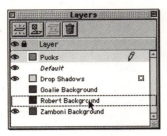

Figure 10-11: To change the stacking order of layers throughout a document, press Option or Alt while you drag a layer. In this example, the Pucks layer is moved to directly in front of the Robert Background layer.

Getting used to hiding/showing layers

You might be accustomed to moving items to the front of the stacking order to make them easily editable. Working this way, you might be tempted to bring a layer up to the top of the layer stacking order so you can edit it easily, then move it back to its original location. Try to get out of that habit, though, and into the habit of simply showing the layer you need to work on and hiding the others.

Combining layers

If you decide that all the items on one layer belong on a different layer—throughout the document—you can merge the layers. Also, when you're learning about the power of layers, it's easy to create a document that's unnecessarily complex. For example, you might put each item on a different layer and realize that the document has become difficult to work with. You can also merge all the layers in a document to "flatten" it to a single layer.

STEPS: Merging layers

1. Unlock all the layers you want to merge.

2. Select all the layers you want to merge. To select multiple layers, ⌘+click or Ctrl+click them; to select continuous layers, Shift+click them.

3. Click the Merge Layers button on the Layers palette.

4. In the Merge Layer dialog box, choose a layer from the Choose Destination Layer menu (see Figure 10-12), then click OK. All but the destination layer are deleted and all the items are moved.

Figure 10-12: In this operation, items on the Pucks layer will be merged with items on the Drop Shadows layer. The Pucks layer will be deleted.

Note When you merge layers, items on higher layers are stacked on top of items on lower layers.

Duplicating layers

If you need to create two layers containing the same items in a document, you can duplicate an existing layer. You might do this, for example, if you have two versions of text in the same document. You can duplicate the layer containing the text boxes, then import different text into the two layers. To duplicate a layer, click to select it, and then choose Duplicate Layer from the context menu.

Deleting layers

If you've carefully isolated portions of a document on different layers, then find that you won't need that portion of the document, you can delete the layer. For example, if you have two different versions of a card, and you make a final decision on the design, you can delete the layer containing the rejected design elements. Deleting unnecessary layers, rather than simply hiding those layers, will make the document size smaller and prevent any confusion that may arise in printing.

Saving items on deleted layers

When you delete layers, you have two options:

✦ Delete all the items on the layer throughout the document.

✦ Move all the items to a different layer.

To ensure that you don't need any of the items before deleting a layer, you can hide all other layers, then look at the remaining items on each page. If you will need all of them, review the document and decide which layer to place them on (consider stacking order while making your decision). If you need just a few of the items, you can drag them to the pasteboard or place them in a library.

Selecting and deleting layers

Using the Layers palette, you can delete a selected layer, multiple selected layers, or all unused layers.

✦ To delete a single layer, click on it, and then click the Delete Layer button or choose the Delete Layer command from the context menu.

✦ To delete multiple layers, ⌘+click or Ctrl+click layers to select them. If the layers are contiguous, you can Shift+click them. Then click the Delete Layer button on the Layers palette.

✦ To delete all unused layers — all the layers with no items on them — choose Delete Unused Layers from the Layers palette's context menu.

If the layers you're deleting *do* have items on them, the Delete Layer dialog box lets you decide what to do with those items. To delete all the items, click Delete Items on Selected Layer(s). To move the items to a different layer, click Move Items to Layer and choose a remaining layer from the adjacent menu, as shown in Figure 10-13.

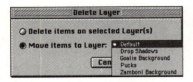

Figure 10-13: When you delete layers, you have the option of moving their items to existing layers.

Printing Layers

If you use layers to store different versions of a design or publication in the same document, you need to be sure you're printing the correct layers. ***Remember:*** Layers that aren't checked as Visible never print. So an easy way to keep layers from printing is to hide them in the Layers palette. You can also double-click a layer and check Suppress Printout for it — so even if the layer displays, it won't print.

If you're sending a document with layers to a service bureau, make sure they clearly understand which layers you intend to print. It may actually be safer to create multiple copies of the document (using File ➪ Save As, or Option+⌘+S or Ctrl+Alt+S), and then delete layers you don't want to print.

Summary

If you take the time to integrate layers into your workflow, you can save time and effort when creating multilingual publications, producing multiple versions of a document, and managing many layered items that make up an illustration or design. Until you create new layers, all the items are placed on the default layers. Although each layer has its own stacking order, the order of layers also affects stacking order.

You can create items on the active layer, and you can move items to different layers. Even though items are on layers, you can continue to modify them as you normally would — provided that the layers are visible and unlocked. Hiding layers suppresses the printout of items, in addition to preventing their display. To stream-line a document, you can merge and delete layers.

✦   ✦   ✦

Text

Text forms the backbone of a published document: critical but often not noticed by the casual observer. Without text, there's no reason to have the document (except for the rare photo or art book). After all, text is what carries the message your publication seeks to share with the world.

Text may be key to publishing, but the fact is that text creation is typically done outside a desktop-publishing program. That means you need to know how to use your word processor in a way that will create the least amount of work for moving it into QuarkXPress.

And when you've brought your text into QuarkXPress, you'll need to know how to work with QuarkXPress's own text-formatting and -editing tools to make the text look and read right. This part helps you do all those things.

◆ ◆ ◆ ◆

In This Part

Chapter 11
Working with
Text Files

Chapter 12
Flowing Text

Chapter 13
Editing Text

◆ ◆ ◆ ◆

Working with Text Files

In most publishing workflows, text is written in a word processor such as Microsoft Word or WordPerfect, and then the text files are imported into QuarkXPress documents. Among the reasons for doing this: Word processors cost less than page-layout programs, so writers and editors generally don't have QuarkXPress; in addition, word processors generally provide superior editing features such as a better spell checker and the ability to track revisions. Often, the text files contain little formatting — maybe a little bold to indicate heads and italics for emphasis — but in a more sophisticated workflow, the files might contain almost all the appropriate formatting.

Although importing text files is convenient, integrating the process into your workflow takes planning and usually a little experimentation to work out the kinks. You need to know what versions of word processors you can import from, how to save the files, what kind of formatting to include in the files, issues with special characters, and more. When you get to a point where you can easily import text files, you can also export them in the same formats. Exported text files are useful for updating existing publications. If you've made any edits to the text in QuarkXPress, writers and editors can start revising the latest files.

Preparing Text Files

You can do all kinds of formatting in word processors these days — to the point that some people think page-layout programs are unnecessary. But the features do have limits, the results are not as professional, and the formatting may not import into QuarkXPress correctly. In addition, it's probably more cost-effective for your company to have writers and editors focus on writing and editing — instead of performing any type of design work in a word processor that wasn't even designed for it. With less formatting in the text file, graphic designers can often do what they want with it in QuarkXPress more easily.

In this spirit, keep your text files as simple as possible, but with enough information for the designer to be able to figure out where the headlines, subheads, and paragraph breaks are, along with any special formatting such as italics.

Supported word processors

QuarkXPress 5 doesn't necessarily read the latest versions of Word or WordPerfect. The latest versions supported are Word 97/2000 (Windows) or 98/2001 (Mac) and WordPerfect 6 (Windows) or 3.5 (Mac). If you have a later version of Word or WordPerfect, either save your files in a supported version or see if Quark has an updated import filter on its Web site (www.quark.com). If you use those newer programs, you need to save your files in a previous format: Windows Word 97/2000 (8.0), 95 (7.0), or 6.0; Mac Word 98/2001, 6.0, 5.x, 4.0, or 3.0; Windows WordPerfect 6.x and 5.x; and Mac WordPerfect 3.x. Both versions can also import Rich Text Format (RTF), Hypertext Markup Language (HTML), and text-only (ASCII) files.

New Feature The Macintosh version of QuarkXPress no longer imports files created in WriteNow 3.0 and up, Microsoft Works 1.1 and up, or any version of Claris MacWrite Pro and MacWrite II. But it has added the ability to import RTF files.

If your favorite word processor is missing, you'll need to consider alternate options:

✦ If you have an earlier version of a supported word processor, you can save your files as ASCII, which is also called *text-only,* but you'll lose all formatting in the process.

✦ If you have a later version of a supported word processor, you can usually downsave your files into a compatible format.

✦ If you use an unsupported word processor, see if you can save text out of it in a compatible format. Use ASCII (.txt) as a last resort.

✦ Another option with an unsupported word processor is to obtain a third-party word-processing filter for it. Nisus Writer, for example, has long provided a QuarkXPress import filter for its Macintosh word processor, although when this book went to press it was unclear if it would update the filter for QuarkXPress 5.

Look for new and updated filters on the Quark Web site at www.quark.com.

Note QuarkXPress supports ASCII (text-only) files, but you should avoid using them. Plain ASCII files cannot handle any character formatting, so you must do a lot of cleanup work in QuarkXPress. Although programs must continue to support ASCII text because it's the only universally supported format, use plain ASCII as a last resort.

Word processing do's

When you're preparing text files for import, do the following, as shown in Figure 11-1:

✦ **Do make sure the graphic designer can distinguish the various levels of heads in a text file.** The best way to do this is to use boldface and different sizes on heads. In some cases, writers and editors include a small tag next to the heads: [H1], [H2], [H3], and so on.

✦ **Do use first line indents or space before/after to indicate paragraph breaks.**

✦ **Do apply any necessary formatting such as italics, underline, and bold.**

✦ **Do submit the final text file to the graphic designer.** Don't expect to keep editing it and submit an update later. After the file is imported into QuarkXPress and formatted, there's no going back.

✦ **Do type two hyphens for an em dash or go ahead and enter the special character.** QuarkXPress can convert two consecutive hyphens to an em dash. If your word processor autocorrects two hyphens to a dash, make sure it's doing it correctly for your publication.

Note that the Word for Windows default setting converts two hyphens to an en dash rather than an em dash, which is probably not what you want. In some cases, QuarkXPress for Mac will read the Word for Windows–created en dash as the æ character, which can really mess up your file, so we recommend you turn off Word's automatic conversion of two hyphens to a dash (Tools ⇨ AutoCorrect).

✦ **Do watch out for quotation marks.** QuarkXPress either converts all quotation marks to curly quotes, or it converts none. If you have a mix of inch and foot marks and quotation marks, you may need to fix these later in the layout. But if you have more foot and inch marks than quotation marks, it may be worthwhile to turn off quote conversion in the word processor and in QuarkXPress — then you'll get nice, straight quotes for foot and inch marks.

✦ **Do experiment with features that you'd really like to use.** For example, usually the automatic bullets and numbers will import properly, and they're extremely convenient. But if your document is littered with numbered and bulleted lists, check this out first.

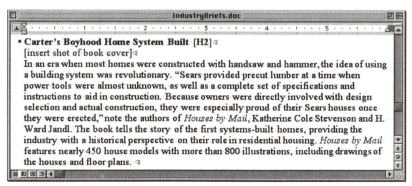

Figure 11-1: The graphic designer for *Building Systems Magazine,* Tim Giesen, appreciates the clean text files he receives from the editor. Any formatting notes are in blue and contained within graphics, and the files have no extraneous spaces or paragraph returns.

A word processing maybe: Style sheets

Granted, do's and don'ts are always open to question—just look at the back page of *Glamour* magazine. But there is one definite maybe when it comes to preparing text files in a word processor: whether to use the word processor's style sheets.

Ideally, you could set up style sheets in a word processor with the same names and the exact same formatting as the QuarkXPress template. (You could even export text from QuarkXPress with this information.) You could then apply the style sheets in the word processor. If the graphic designer imports the text file with style sheets, the text should come in fully formatted already.

This sounds good in theory, but it rarely works. Writers and editors often use PCs, while graphic designers use Macs. This means the fonts specified in the style sheets don't match—the ones the designer uses may not even be available for the PC (or the company may not want to buy them). And, as shown in the figure, word processors don't always display fonts as well as page-layout programs. The Word template used by the writers and editors at *5280* magazine calls for Concorde Nova, the magazine's main typeface for body copy. However, as you can see here, Concorde Nova is difficult to read in Word—the space between words is too small. Not only does this somewhat defeat the purpose of using a word processor, it doesn't really save the graphic designer any time. Sticking to plain fonts like Times and Arial in a word processor is usually simpler.

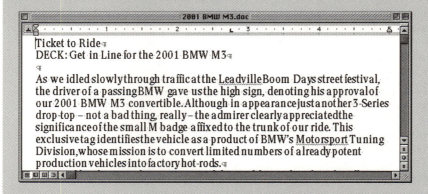

QuarkXPress style sheets can include features that word processors just don't have, such as tracking and horizontal scale. Often, the text will import properly with the right style sheet applied, but the text will retain some of its old formatting. This forces the designer to reapply the style sheet entirely—the same amount of effort it takes to simply apply it.

Using style sheets in a word processor, however, is worth exploring, especially if your formatting in QuarkXPress is on the simpler side. You can also use the base style sheets that come with the word processor—Normal, Heading 1, Heading 2, and so on—to speed what little formatting you do in the word processor. If the designer imports the text file with style sheets, he can always delete those later.

Word processing don'ts

While using a word processor to prepare text files for import, there are a few things you shouldn't do — and there are a few features you should use with careful consideration:

✦ **Don't type two spaces after a period — or anywhere for that matter.** This old typewriter convention, which has proven remarkably hard to stamp out, is unnecessary in the computer world. If you can't get out of the habit, set your word processor to autocorrect two spaces, substituting one. Or use search and replace to get rid of double spaces. If you're thinking, "But I've always used double spaces, and nobody has said anything before," well, someone has been silently cleaning up after you (and no doubt cursing you, too).

✦ **Don't use paragraph returns to add space between paragraphs.** In most cases, the designer will have to strip those out. Use the word processor's paragraph-formatting options to place space above or below paragraphs or to set a first-line indent.

✦ **Don't use spaces or tabs to indicate new paragraphs.** Spaces are the worst — five spaces may look great to you on your screen, but if it's too much space in the layout, the graphic designer will have to manually remove spaces from each paragraph. With a tab, at least the designer can set it where she wants. But if the design calls for space between paragraphs instead of an indent, the designer has to remove the tabs. Again, use your word processor's paragraph-formatting options to implement a space above or below or to set a first-line indent.

✦ **Don't enter multiple tabs to align columns of information on your screen.** This alignment may work great with the column width you're using and the current font and size. But it's not likely to make sense in QuarkXPress. What you'll end up with is jagged columns that make no sense. Type one tab between each column, then set the tabs to align the columns. The settings probably still won't work, but at least the designer won't have to strip out your extra tabs.

✦ **Don't spend too much time creating tables in your word processor.** If it's easier to separate the data, go ahead and make a table — just expect any formatting you apply to be stripped in QuarkXPress. Or just type one tab between each column and set them properly for your use.

✦ **Don't type in all caps (with the Caps Lock key down).** You may think you have something important to say — worth bellowing in capital letters — but the designer is likely to favor a more creative typographic treatment. So the designer will have to retype your text, which is a good way to introduce mistakes. When you feel a need to shout, use the character formatting options in your word processor to apply an All Caps, Bold, or Underline typestyle that the designer can easily remove.

✦ **Don't expect headers, footers, page numbers, and footnotes to import properly — if they import at all.** You may need this information while you're working, and that's fine, but if you need it to print in the final publication, work out a method with the graphic designer.

✦ **Don't make interesting choices (interesting to you, anyway) for bullets.** Just use a plain bullet and let the designer handle the final formatting. (But do enter or apply real bullets instead of hyphens or asterisks.) Ask the designers if they prefer a space or a tab after the bullet.

✦ **Don't bother with graphic features in your word processor such as colors, borders, or the ability to import inline graphics.** They're not likely to be useful to the designer and can, in fact, cause problems in production.

If you use a word processor's revisions mode or change-tracking feature, be careful. This feature is handy because it lets you see who made each change in a document. But before you import the file into QuarkXPress, be sure to use the feature's Accept All Changes command (or the equivalent). Otherwise, QuarkXPress will import the file with all the changes as well as all the original text, creating a nightmare of nonsensical text with no indication in QuarkXPress of what text should have been deleted and changed. This is true even if you set your word processor's revisions feature not to display or print deleted text.

Don't believe everything we say about using a word processor. Sure, this is a "Bible," but in the software world, things change. New versions of word processors are released with new features that may or may not import into QuarkXPress. And, periodically, Quark ships new versions of its word-processing import filters to improve existing import methods and support new word-processing features. This is an area in which experimenting with the version of word processor you actually use pays off.

See Figure 11-2 for an example of a particularly messy file for a graphic designer to handle.

The bottom line in word processing

The bottom line is to use QuarkXPress for your layout and complex text formatting (fonts, leading, and hyphenation). Use your word processor for basic text editing, style-sheet assignments (identifying headlines, body copy, and so forth), and basic character formatting (bold, italics, and other meaning-oriented formatting). Use your graphics program for creating and editing original images and photos; use QuarkXPress's graphics features to embellish your layout, rather than create original artwork. *Remember:* You're importing text, not documents.

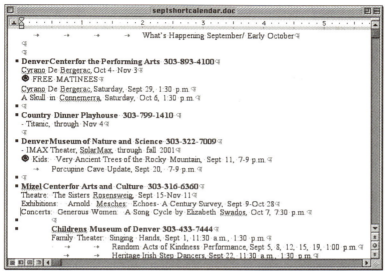

Figure 11-2: This type of file is a nightmare for a graphic designer. The headline is "centered" with tabs, blocks of information are separated with extra paragraph returns, text is aligned with a combination of indents and tabs, and the writer used dingbats from a font she owns (but the designer does not). Although it's reasonably clear how the content is organized, the designer still needs to strip a lot of extra characters and formatting.

Importing tabular data

QuarkXPress has no filters to accept files in formats such as Lotus 1-2-3, Microsoft Excel, Claris FileMaker Pro, or Microsoft FoxPro. (This is true even with the new QuarkXPress table editor.) That means you have two basic options for preparing files that contain tabular information (usually spreadsheets or databases) for import:

✦ **Option 1:** Save the files as tab-delimited ASCII text. Then import them and apply the appropriate tab stops (either directly or through styles), or use the new Text to Table feature in the Item menu, to create the desired table. Or paste the data (into a QuarkXPress text box) into your document through the Mac or Windows Clipboard. It will be pasted as tab-delimited ASCII text.

✦ **Option 2:** Use the file as a graphic by using a charting tool (such as that in Excel or Lotus 1-2-3). Export it to a format such as EPS if possible. Paste the chart via the Clipboard or use Publish and Subscribe or OLE if EPS export is not an option.

If you choose the second option, make sure that you size all charts and tables the same way so that the size of the numbers in them, when imported and placed, is consistent throughout your QuarkXPress document. Use a vector format such as PICT or EPS whenever possible to ensure the best reproduction quality no matter what size you scale the chart graphics to.

Importing Text Files

Compared to the file-preparation process, which is full of opportunity for pitfalls, importing text files is relatively easy—that is, if you save your file in the right format, with the right name, and you have the proper import filters installed.

Saving text files for import

To make it easy for you, everyone in your workflow, and even QuarkXPress to recognize the type of files you're working with, save your word-processing files with the proper file extensions:

✦ .doc for Microsoft Word

✦ .wp for WordPerfect

✦ .rtf for RTF

✦ .txt for ASCII

✦ .htm for HTML

Granted, the file extensions are unnecessary in an all-Mac-all-the-time workflow, but it's hard to guarantee that you'll never need to send a file to a PC user. Check your versions of Word and WordPerfect against the current version of the QuarkXPress import filters to be sure that you don't need to downsave your files before importing them.

Tip   If a brand-spanking-new version of your favorite word processor ships, it's not always a good idea to be the first on your block to upgrade to it. The files may not import into QuarkXPress, and it will be more difficult to share them with other users. Consider your entire workflow before upgrading any of your auxiliary software.

One last thing: If you're using Microsoft Word, the import filter for QuarkXPress cannot handle fast-saved files. If you're using fast save—which does make saving faster!—and you try to import a text file, you'll get the annoying alert shown in Figure 11-3. You need to turn the feature off and resave the file. In Windows Word 97/2000 and Mac Word 98/2001, the feature is located in the Save pane of the Preferences dialog box (Tools menu), as shown in Figure 11-4. If you prefer to allow fast saves in your everyday work, you can turn it off, resave the QuarkXPress document, and then turn it back on.

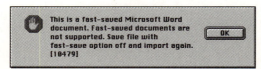

This is a fast-saved Microsoft Word document. Fast-saved documents are not supported. Save file with fast-save option off and import again. [10479]

OK

Figure 11-3: The fast-save alert in QuarkXPress.

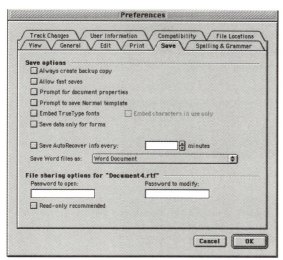

Figure 11-4: The Allow Fast Saves check box in the Microsoft Word Preferences dialog box's Save pane.

Loading import filters

By default, QuarkXPress installs the MS-Word 6-2000 filter (which also imports Word 2001 files, despite the name), the WordPerfect filter, and the HTML Text Import filter in your XTension folder so they will load with QuarkXPress. To make sure they're running, choose XTensions Manager from the Utilities menu. Skim through the alphabetical list and make sure there is a check mark next to the import filter you need, as shown in Figure 11-5. If the import filter you need isn't checked, either check the filter or select a set in which that filter is checked. Click OK, then relaunch QuarkXPress.

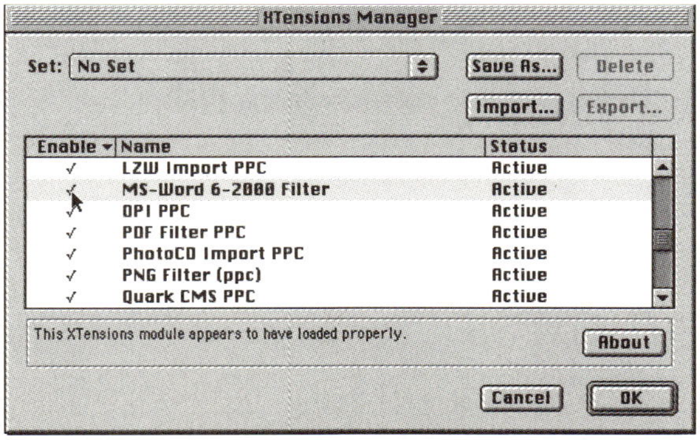

Figure 11-5: The MS-Word 6-2000 filter in the XTensions Manager dialog box.

Tip   If you purchase third-party import filters, place them in your XTension folder inside your QuarkXPress folder, then relaunch QuarkXPress to load them.

Importing a text file

Before you import a text file into QuarkXPress, it's not a bad idea to print it from the word processor. In fact, publishers require writers to submit hard copy to the designer. This way, you can review not only the content (so you know how to design it!), but the file preparation (for example, what the writer used for em dashes). With all that in mind, you can import the text file.

STEPS: Using Get Text

1. If necessary, create a text box using any of the text box tools.

Cross-Reference   See Chapter 8 for more information on text boxes.

2. Select the Content tool (the hand) on the Tool palette.

3. Click in the text box you want to import the text into:

- If you want to import the text at a specific location within existing text, click where you want it to import.

- If you want to replace existing text with imported text, highlight it (although for simplicity, you may as well delete it before importing).

- If you're going to flow the text through an entire document, you may want to select the automatic text box or have the boxes already linked.

Cross-Reference   See Chapter 12 for more information on flowing text.

4. Choose File ⇨ Get Text, or press ⌘+E or Ctrl+E (a keyboard command worth remembering, because it also opens Get Picture when a picture box is selected).

5. Navigate to the text file you want to import and select it, as shown in Figure 11-6. You can use the Type and Size areas to confirm that this is the file you want to import.

6. If you want to convert double hyphens to em dashes and convert straight quotation marks to typesetter's quotation marks, check Convert Quotes. You may need to skim the hard copy of the article to determine whether this is a good idea — for example, if you're working on a building article that's full of dimensions, you may want to uncheck it.

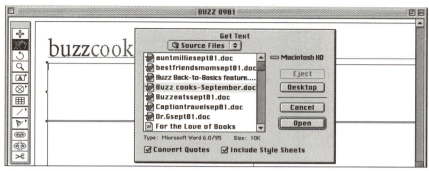

Figure 11-6: A text file ready for import into the text box, which is selected with the Content tool.

7. If you want to import style sheets from a word processor, check Include Style Sheets. This adds the style sheets to your list in the Style Sheets dialog box (Edit menu), and it leaves the style sheet applied to the text. If you uncheck this, the text is still formatted, but the Normal style sheet is applied to all the text.

If you're not planning to use the style sheets from the word processor, don't leave Include Style Sheets checked. It's a good way to clutter up your Style Sheets dialog box with unnecessary style sheets, which can end up causing confusion.

8. Click Open to import the text into the selected text box. If the text doesn't all fit, you'll see the overflow symbol (a red box with an X through it).

You may be able to simply resize the box to see all the text, but if not, see Chapter 12 for more information on flowing text.

In QuarkXPress for Windows, you can import text files by dragging a file from the desktop, into the document window, and onto a selected text box. The text will be imported at the location of the text-insertion bar. If you have trouble with this procedure, make sure the file is saved in a supported format, that the import filters are installed with QuarkXPress, and that a text box is selected with the Content tool.

Finding missing files

If the text file you want to import is not showing in the Get Text dialog box, it's probably not saved in the correct format, or the proper import filter isn't loaded. Recheck how the file was saved in the word processor, and reconfirm that the correct import filter is loaded through the XTensions Manager (Utilities menu). In Windows, also check your Files of Type pop-up menu in the Get Text dialog box and change it if necessary.

Style sheet conflicts and missing fonts

When you import text files, you typically encounter two things: style sheet conflicts and missing fonts.

If you checked Include Style Sheets, and the text file contains style sheets with the same name as those already in your QuarkXPress document, a conflict dialog box displays as shown in the figure. (Actually, this displays almost all the time, because word processors and QuarkXPress both have a Normal style sheet.) You can decide whether to use, override, or rename each style sheet with the same name. The way you handle this depends on how you use style sheets from a word processor:

✦ If you want to use the style sheets in your QuarkXPress document, because you know they're right, click Use Existing. This gives the QuarkXPress style sheets dominance over the word processor style sheets of the same name. (This is a good choice if you actually use Normal and want to use the QuarkXPress specifications — or if you don't use Normal and don't really care what happens with it.)

✦ If you want to give your word processor style sheets dominance over those in QuarkXPress, thereby overriding your QuarkXPress settings, click Use New. This is a good choice if you've put a lot of thought — and import testing — into preparing your word processor style sheets.

✦ Click Rename if you want to keep the word processor style sheets, but give them your own names. Click Auto-Rename to have QuarkXPress append a 1 to any similar names. These are good choices if you want to be able to see what style sheets were applied in the word processor and decide later whether you want to use them or delete them.

✦ If you want to handle all the style sheet conflicts the same way, check Repeat for All Conflicts before you click one of the buttons. If not, use the fields at the bottom of the dialog box to see the style sheet name and compare the formatting specifications before making a decision.

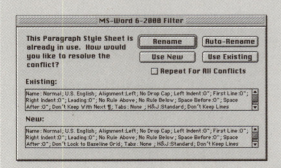

If a text file specifies a font that isn't active on your system, the Missing Fonts alert will display. You can either replace the font throughout the text file, ignore the alert and activate the font, or ignore the alert because you plan to apply an entirely different font. In many cases, the missing fonts alert is not a concern at this point because the graphic designer will use different fonts from those applied in the text file.

Importing typographic quotes and em dashes

When you check Convert Quotes in the Get Text dialog box, two things happen:

✦ **Any double hyphens (two hyphens in a row) are converted to em dashes.**
Because there is generally no other reason for a text file to contain double
hyphens — other than to be converted to em dashes — this is usually a good
thing. If you entered em dashes in the text file, they'll import fine as well.

✦ **Any straight single quotes (') and straight double quotes (") will be converted to typographic quotes (' ' and " ").** This conversion will happen
regardless of how they appear or were entered in your word processor. But
the converted quotes are not necessarily the curly ones shown in this paragraph — when QuarkXPress converts quotes, it consults a setting in the
Interactive pane of the Preferences dialog box, as shown in Figure 11-7. These
various quote types are for text in other languages. This is an Application
Preference, meaning that your copy of QuarkXPress will always convert
quotes the same way.

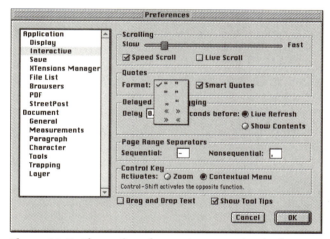

Figure 11-7: The options for quote conversion in the
Interactive pane of the Preferences dialog box.

Convert Quotes is an across-the-board setting — it converts all straight quotes
regardless of context. This is unfortunate because Americans use straight quotes
for foot and inch marks. If you know the text includes measurements, be sure to
choose Edit ⇨ Find/Change (or ⌘+F or Ctrl+F) to locate those instances. You can
manually insert straight quotes by pressing Control+' or Ctrl+' for a foot mark and
Control+Shift+" or Ctrl+Alt+" for an inch mark.

**Cross-
Reference**

QuarkXPress supports one more format for importing and exporting text: XPress
Tags. This proprietary format is actually a tagging language that you can use to for-
mat text outside QuarkXPress or simply share text from QuarkXPress with other
QuarkXPress users. XPress Tags are covered in Appendix B.

Exporting Text Files

Any time you need to get text out of QuarkXPress, you can select it and export a text file in any supported format. Exporting text is great for updating publications because you can send the very latest text back to writers and editors in a format they can use. Currently, you can export text in ASCII, HTML, XPress Tags, WordPerfect 6.0, Microsoft Word 97/98/2000/2001, and Microsoft Word 6.0/95 formats.

You can export all the text in a series of linked text boxes (called a *story*), or you can export highlighted text.

STEPS: Saving a text file

1. Select the Content tool (the hand) on the Tool palette.

2. Click in the text box containing the text you want to import. If you want to export only a portion of the text in the story, highlight it.

3. Choose File ➪ Save As or press Option+⌘+E or Ctrl+Alt+E.

4. In the Save Text dialog box, navigate to a location for the text file.

5. In the Save Text As field, type a name for the file. Make sure to use the appropriate file extension: .txt for ASCII, .html for HTML, .xtg for XPress Tags, .doc for Microsoft Word, or .wp for WordPerfect.

6. If you have highlighted text, the Selected Text option is checked. You can change your mind and click Entire Story at this point. If you haven't highlighted text, this area is grayed out.

7. Choose an option from the Format menu, as shown in Figure 11-8, to specify what type of text file you want.

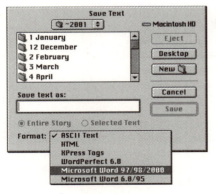

Figure 11-8: The Save Text dialog box lets you export text files in a variety of formats.

8. Click Save to create the text file.

You can send exported text files to other users for updating and editing, then reimport them into QuarkXPress.

Summary

QuarkXPress makes it easy for you to get text into — and out of — a document. This makes it easy for writers and editors to work in word processors while graphic designers focus on layout in QuarkXPress. For word processing, QuarkXPress supports the two major word processors — Microsoft Word and WordPerfect — along with ASCII, HTML, and Quark's proprietary tagging language, XPress Tags.

Your success in working with imported text files depends on several things: the preparation of the files, how the files are saved, and whether the import filters are loaded through the XTensions Manager (Utilities menu). You can export text files any time you need to use the text in another application, such as a word processor. Quark periodically updates its text-import filters, so check www.quark.com for new ones.

✦   ✦   ✦

Flowing Text

When you first learn about text boxes, your first impulse is to think, "But all my text doesn't fit in one little box." And that's fine. QuarkXPress is designed to easily flow text — whether it's typed, pasted, or imported into a text box — throughout all the pages in a document. You can do this automatically by using the automatic text box, or you can do it manually by linking text boxes. You also have options for how text flows within a box, including dividing the text into columns and positioning it.

Entering Text

As discussed in Chapter 11, the most common way to get text into QuarkXPress is to import a text file from a word processor using File ➪ Get Text, or ⌘+E or Ctrl+E. But you can also type text directly into text boxes, and you can paste text from the clipboard.

New Feature
If your design process is a little ahead of your editorial process, you can start designing with dummy text provided by Quark's free Jabberwocky XTension, now included in QuarkXPress 5.

Remember: Whenever you're working with text in QuarkXPress, you need to select the Content tool. If you're entering text in a new box or text path, the text is formatted with the Normal paragraph style sheet. Otherwise, the text picks up the attributes specified at the location of the cursor.

Typing and pasting text

Any time the Content tool is selected, you can click in a text box or text path, and simply start typing. If you click within existing text, the new text will be inserted at the location of the cursor. You can also paste text from the clipboard in any text box or on any text path.

Cross-Reference
See Chapter 13 for more information about entering text in QuarkXPress.

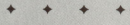

Caution

When you paste text that's copied from another program — such as a word processor or e-mail program — some special characters such as bullets are lost. In particular, note that any quotation marks in the text are pasted as straight quotes, even if you have Smart Quotes checked in the Interactive pane of the Preferences dialog box (Edit ╎ Preferences ╎ Preferences, or Option+Shift+Ô+Y or Ctrl+Alt+ Shift+Y). Text pasted from within QuarkXPress retains its special characters.

What happens when you fill the text box you're typing in? If you're working in the automatic text box and Auto Page Insertion (as it is by default), QuarkXPress inserts a new page with a new text box for you to continue in. If not, a red box with an X in it displays, as shown in Figure 12-1. This is the Text Overflow symbol, and it must be dealt with — by increasing the size of the box, decreasing the amount or size of the type, or linking the box to other boxes. The automatic text box, automatic page insertion, and linking are explained later in this chapter.

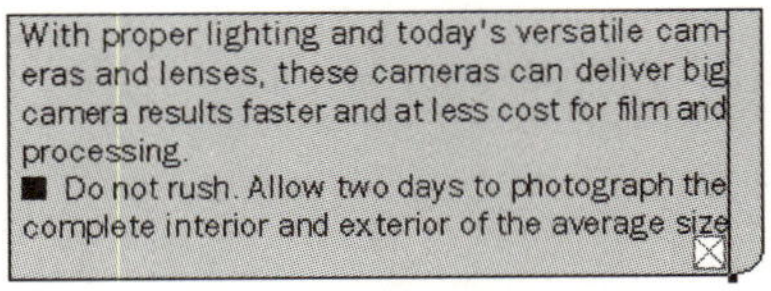

With proper lighting and today's versatile cameras and lenses, these cameras can deliver big camera results faster and at less cost for film and processing.
■ Do not rush. Allow two days to photograph the complete interior and exterior of the average size

Figure 12-1: The Text Overflow symbol, which means a text box or text path contains more text than it can display.

Working with dummy text

If you're ready to start designing, but the copy is not ready to be imported, QuarkXPress automatically generates *dummy text* with which to fill text boxes and text paths. This feature is implemented through the Jabberwocky XTension distributed with version 5 (and available for free download with previous versions). Check the XTensions Manager (Utilities ⇨ XTensions Manager) to ensure that the Jabberwocky XTension is running.

Filling boxes with dummy text

To quickly fill a selected text box or path with dummy text, choose Utilities ⇨ Jabber. The XTension generates just enough random text to fill the selection; the text is formatted according to the character and paragraph attributes at the cursor, as shown in Figure 12-2.

Editing Jabberwocky preferences and sets

By default, the random text you import is in English Prose style (paragraphs). You can change this by choosing a different topic for your dummy text (Esperanto, Klingon, Latin, or Politics Speak) from the Jabberwocky Preferences dialog box (Edit ⇨ Preferences ⇨ Jabberwocky). This dialog box also lets you choose Verse style (single lines).

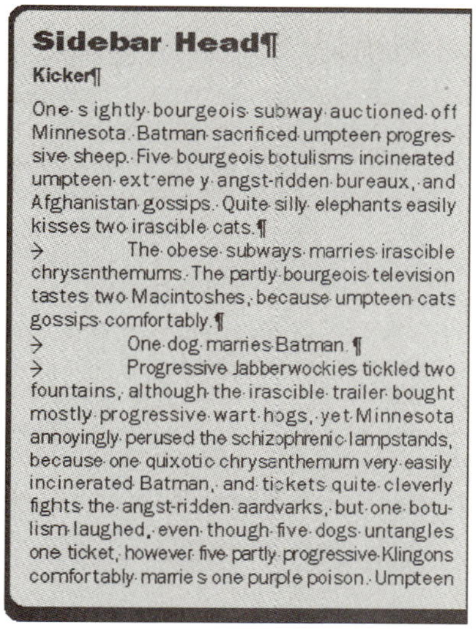

Figure 12-2: A text box filled with dummy text generated by the Jabberwocky XTension.

Jabberwocky even lets you create dummy text appropriate to your topic or industry. You do this by creating a Jabberwocky Dictionary using the Jabberwocky Sets dialog box (Edit ➪ Jabberwocky Sets). You can use this same dialog box to import and export Jabberwocky Dictionaries to share them with other users (Jabberwocky Sets do not travel with documents).

STEPS: Creating a Jabberwocky Dictionary

1. With a sample article, brochure, or magazine that reflects the terminology of the industry on-hand, choose Edit ➪ Jabberwocky Sets.

2. Click New.

3. Enter a name for your dictionary in the Set Name field.

4. Choose an option from the Part Of menu: Adjectives, Adverbs, Articles, Conjunctions, Nouns, Proper Nouns, Qualifiers, or Verbs. If it's been a while since you studied these parts of speech in grade school, the field below the menu gives you a handy refresher.

5. Type words from each part of speech in the field, then click Add, as shown in Figure 12-3. To remove any words, click Delete. (To edit the spelling of a word, delete it, then re-add it.)

6. When you're finished adding words for the various parts of speech, click Save.

7. Click Save to exit the Jabberwocky Sets dialog box.

8. To start using your new Jabberwocky Dictionary, choose it from the Jabberwocky Preferences dialog box (Edit ➪ Preferences ➪ Jabberwocky).

Figure 12-3: Adding a word to
a new Jabberwocky Dictionary.

Flowing Text through the Automatic Text Box

The automatic text box has two purposes: You can create a new document and start typing without having to draw a text box, and you can easily flow text through the pages of a document. Longer documents such as booklets and annual reports often use the automatic text box. The text inside the automatic text box is called the *automatic text chain.* Documents can have multiple automatic text chains — for example, each chapter in a book may have its own automatic text chain. However, each page can have only one automatic text chain (this means you can't have a feature story in an automatic text box and its sidebars in another automatic text box).

QuarkXPress provides two methods for creating an automatic text box: while creating a new document, or later on a master page.

Creating an automatic text box for a new document

The New Document dialog box (File ➪ New ➪ Document, or ⌘+N or Ctrl+N) includes a check box for creating an Automatic Text Box. If you check this option, QuarkXPress places an automatic text box on the default master page, called A-Master A, which is used as the basis for the first page in the document. The automatic text box is sized and divided into columns according to the information you enter in the Margin Guides and Column Guides areas of the New Document dialog box. Figure 12-4 shows a spread from *Building Systems Magazine,* which uses the automatic text box for its articles; the New Document dialog box shows the settings the designer used to place the automatic text box.

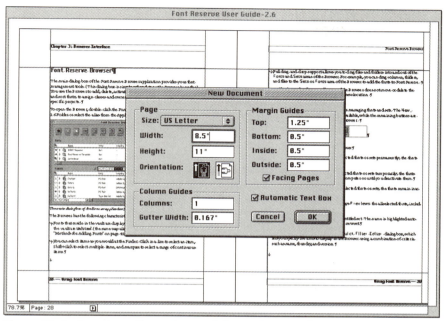

Figure 12-4: An automatic text box and the settings used to create it.

Tip

To make a global change to the size or columns of the automatic text box, you need to make the change on the master page. Display the appropriate master page (Page ➪ Display), then choose Page ➪ Master Guides. Change any of the settings in the Master Guides or Column Guides areas, then click OK to reformat the automatic text box.

Adding an automatic text box to a master page

If you create a document without an automatic text box, then decide you need it, you can easily create one for the default master page. You can also add an automatic text box to additional master pages that you create.

STEPS: Adding an automatic text box

1. Choose Page ➪ Display, then select a master page for the automatic text box.

2. Create a text box or text path of any shape. (The most practical thing is a text box that fits within the blue margin guides, but you can create a box or path of any size or shape you need.)

3. Select the Linking tool.

4. Click the Broken Chain icon.

5. Click the text box or text path, as shown in Figure 12-5.

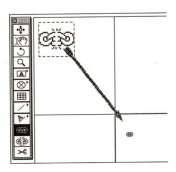

Figure 12-5: Creating an automatic text box for a new master page.

6. Select any other tool. If you're working on a facing-page document, perform these steps on both pages of the spread.

7. Choose Page ➪ Display ➪ Document to return to the document pages.

Flowing text and inserting pages

After you have an automatic text box, you can type, paste, or import text into it. If Auto Page Insertion is enabled in the General pane of the Preferences dialog box, as it is by default, QuarkXPress adds new pages as necessary to contain all the text entered into the automatic text box. (To check your Auto Page Insertion setting, choose Edit ➪ Preferences ➪ Preferences, or Option+Shift+⌘+Y or Ctrl+Alt+Shift+Y, then click the General pane under Document. Make sure that End of Story, End of Section, or End of Document is selected.)

Use it or lose it

Automatic Text Box is checked by default in the New Document dialog box, and many users never uncheck it — even if they never use it. The automatic text box just hangs in the background while the designer creates advertisements, business cards, or logos on top of it. Although the box is in the way, often getting selected by accident, the most they ever do is delete it on the document page. Some designers even resize the automatic text box and use it for their main block of copy in a design.

If you're working on a design-intensive piece such as a poster, there's really no need to create an automatic text box. Or, in a text-heavy piece such as a product brochure, where the text is spread out in various caption boxes, the automatic text box does little to help. To skip the automatic text box creation, make sure the option is unchecked in the New Document dialog box. To get rid of the automatic text box, select the box on the master page (Page ➪ Display), then choose Item ➪ Delete, or ⌘+K or Ctrl+K.

If you prefer to add pages yourself, set Auto Page Insertion to Off, then use the Page ⟹ Insert to add pages. If you insert pages based on a master page that contains an automatic text box, you can continue the text flow by checking Link to Current Text Chain in the Insert Pages dialog box. This option is preferable if you're switching master pages often.

Linking Text Boxes

The ability to link text boxes and text paths removes a possible limitation of QuarkXPress — that text is confined within the limited space of a single box or length of a path. Linking boxes has two advantages. First, you can import text from a single text file so it flows through all the boxes automatically. Second, you can manipulate the text as a unit, selecting it all to reformat it or spell checking it, for example. Text within a series of linked boxes is referred to as a text chain or story. Figure 12-6 shows the links connecting the various text boxes that make up this article.

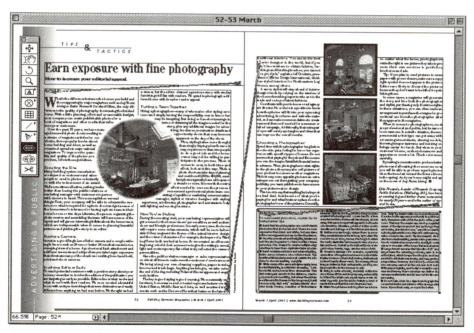

Figure 12-6: To flow text from one box to the next, when you're not using the automatic text box, use the Linking tool.

Generally, you create links when a design calls for multiple text boxes and/or paths on a single page, often of various sizes and shapes. If text flows from page to page in multiple columns, you may be better off using the automatic text box so you don't have to bother with linking. If a layout changes and a link is no longer useful, you can easily unlink two items.

Caution   Linking can be a little confusing, but don't be tempted to cut and paste text into multiple boxes to get around it—you'll lose all the benefits of working with a single story. When you get used to the feature, you'll appreciate it.

When you link text boxes, they can be on the same page or on different pages, but remember: The order in which you link text boxes is the order in which text flows. If you start with a text box at the bottom of the page and link to another text box above it or on a previous page, then you create an unnatural order (and probably nonsensical text as well). In Figure 12-6, you see two linked text boxes (between two pages).

STEPS: Linking text boxes

1. Create the text boxes and paths you want to link. They can be on the same page or on different pages, anywhere in a document.

2. Display the page containing the first box in your chain. Text flows in the order in which you link the items.

3. Click in the pasteboard to make sure no items on the page are selected.

4. Select the Linking tool—the second tool from the bottom of the Tool palette.

5. Place the pointer in the box that is to be the first in the chain. The pointer changes to look like a chain link. Click the mouse button. You see an animated dashed line around the selected box/path, indicating that it's the start of the link.

6. If necessary, navigate to the page containing the text box that is to be the next link in the chain. (Use the Page ⇨ Go To command, or ⌘+J or Ctrl+J.)

7. Place the pointer in the next box that you want in the chain and click the mouse button. The two are now linked, as shown in Figure 12-7. (You can see the link as a sort of plaid arrow whenever the Link or Unlink tool is selected.) The text flow bypasses any unlinked boxes/paths, continuing on to any others in the text chain.

8. Repeat Steps 5 through 7 (substituting the last linked box for the first box in Step 5) until all text boxes you want in the chain are linked.

Figure 12-7: Two linked text boxes.

Breaking and Rerouting Links

After you create links, you're not stuck with them. If you need to break a link—for example, because you decide to shorten a story instead of continuing it, you can do that. Or, if you simply decide to continue a story on a different page, you can reroute a link.

✦ To break the link between two items, select the Unlinking tool. This displays arrows for each link. Click on the arrowhead of a linking arrow, as shown in Figure 12-8, to break that link. If you break a link, all subsequent links are broken as well.

✦ To remove a box from within a chain of linked boxes/paths, you can delete that box or path. Text is rerouted on its own, flowing into the next box or path in the series of links.

✦ To keep the box on the page but remove it from the chain of linked boxes, you can reroute the links. Select the Unlinking tool, then Shift+click the arrowhead on the arrow that is entering the box you want to remove. Text is rerouted automatically to the next box or path in the series of links.

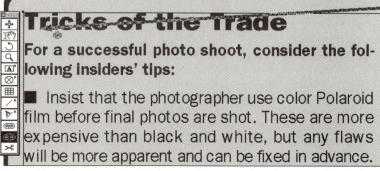

Figure 12-8: To place the sidebar to this story elsewhere, we break the link between the main story and this sidebar box.

Linking and unlinking tips

Here are a few tips and tricks for using the Link and Unlink tools:

✦ As a safety feature, the Linking and Unlinking tools revert to the Content tool or the Item tool each time you use them to prevent you from linking or unlinking more boxes than you intend to.

✦ If you press the Option or Alt key when you select the Linking or Unlinking tool, the tool remains selected until you select another tool. This lets you link or unlink a series of boxes without having to reselect the appropriate tool for each link.

✦ If you hold the Shift key while unlinking, the Unlink tool removes the selected text box and/or paths from the chain and reroutes the text flow on to the next box in the chain.

✦ The best policy is to add text to your text box after you have set the text box's links. Why? Because as you change links, any text in the box must reflow to fit the new settings, and this process takes time. Of course, if you're experimenting with different settings, it helps to have text in the text box to see what the results of the various settings look like.

✦ Note that you can't link text to a box that already contains text.

✦ You can't undo an unlinking operation—you need to relink the boxes if you change your mind. You can also save the document, then rely on Revert to Saved (File ➪ Revert to Saved).

Positioning Text within Boxes

The way text flows within a box—in columns, inset from the edges of the box, from top to bottom or bottom to top, and so on—is actually an attribute of each text box. The controls are all in the Text tab of the Modify dialog box (Item ➪ Modify, or ⌘+M or Ctrl+M). You can also open the Modify dialog box by double-clicking a text box with the Item tool selected.

Creating columns in a text box

You specify the number and placement of columns in the automatic text box in the New Document dialog box (File ➪ New ➪ Document, or ⌘+N or Ctrl+N) when you create the document. You can modify these columns by making changes in the Master Guides dialog box (Page ➪ Master Guides) when a master page is displayed in the document window (Page ➪ Display ➪ [Master Page Name]).

In addition to the automatic text box, you can create columns for any text box—of any shape—that you create. In a two-column layout, for example, you might add a three-column sidebar in a separate text box. (In QuarkXPress, the only way to vary the number of columns on a page is to create separate text boxes; the same box cannot have a varied number of columns.) To split a text box into columns:

✦ **Using the Measurements palette:** In the Cols field shown in Figure 12-9, enter the number of columns you want for the selected text box. This is the simplest method, but it gives you no control over the space between columns.

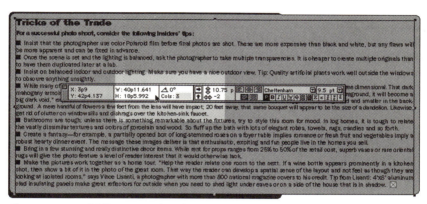

Figure 12-9: Dividing a text box into three columns.

✦ **Using the Text pane:** In the Text pane of the Modify dialog box (Item ⇨ Modify, or ⌘+M or Ctrl+M), enter the number of columns in the Column field. Then enter the amount of space between the columns in the Gutter Width field.

Note that rather than using the columns feature, some graphic designers prefer to draw two text boxes on a page, then link those two boxes. This provides an easy method for creating columns of unequal height — you simply resize one of the boxes.

Note You can create up to 30 columns in a text box, provided that it's wide enough to accommodate the columns and the gutter width. But this doesn't mean you *should* — consider readability when specifying the number of columns.

Tip If the gutter between your columns is narrow (between 0p9 and 2p0, depending on the page width and number of columns), consider adding a thin (0.5 point or smaller) vertical rule in the center of the gutter on the master page. To draw the rule, use the Orthogonal Line drawing tool, and draw the line from the top of the gutter to the bottom, midway through the gutter width. If you place the line on the master page, it will automatically appear on document pages.

Specifying text inset

Text inset is the amount of space between the outside edges of a text box (top, bottom, left, and right) and the text. Setting this value is useful for setting text off from a frame or colored background, as shown in Figure 12-10.

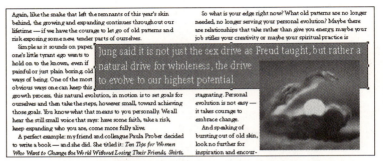

Figure 12-10: The text inset in the box containing the pull-quote helps the text stand out within the colored background.

QuarkXPress measures paragraph indents (Style ⇨ Formats ⇨ Formats, or Shift+⌘+F or Ctrl+Shft+F) from the text inset value, not from the edges of a text box. By default, QuarkXPress applies a 1-point text inset to all new text boxes, which means that text is inset from the edges of the box but not from the inner edges of any columns you create.

To change text inset, use the Text Inset area in the Text pane of the Modify dialog box (Item ⇨ Modify, or ⌘+M or Ctrl+M). For a rectangular text box, you can enter a single point value in the All Edges field, or you can check Multiple Insets, then enter different point values in the Top, Left, Bottom, and Right fields. (For nonrectangular text boxes, All Edges is your only option.)

New Feature In QuarkXPress 5, for the first time you can specify different text insets from all four sides of a rectangular text box.

Tip For layouts in which you don't want any text inset — particularly for text that makes up the body of the document — you may want to change the default inset for the Text Box tools to 0 points in the Tool pane of the Preferences dialog box (Edit ⇨ Preferences ⇨ Preferences, or Option+Shift+⌘+Y or Ctrl+Alt+Shift+Y).

Vertical alignment

Although most of the time you'll flow text from the top to the bottom of a text box, you do have other options. For example, if you're working on an invitation and you want to center the text vertically within a frame, you can do that. Or, if you want to spread text to fill a box without fiddling with leading and space between paragraphs, you can do that easily as well. QuarkXPress has four options for the way text is distributed vertically within a rectangular text box: top, centered, bottom, and justified, as shown in Figure 12-11.

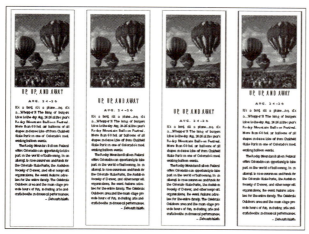

Figure 12-11: The same block of text with top, centered, bottom, and justified vertical alignment. This template specifies bottom alignment.

To change text inset, use the Vertical Alignment area in the Text pane of the Modify dialog box (Item ⇨ Modify, or ⌘+M or Ctrl+M). (The controls are grayed out for non-rectangular text boxes.) The options work as follows:

✦ Top, the default, starts text at the box's first baseline.

✦ Centered places the same amount of space above and below the block of text in a box.

✦ Bottom positions text at the bottom of a box and flows it up as you add text.

✦ Vertical spaces text evenly between the first baseline and the bottom of the text box, overriding any leading and space before and after paragraphs. If you want to have more space between paragraphs and less space between lines, you can enter a value in the Inter ¶ field. This value specifies how much space to place between paragraphs — if there's not enough room for the value you specify, it's decreased evenly between paragraphs.

New Feature

In previous versions of QuarkXPress, the Inter ¶ field was called the Inter ¶ Max field. Instead of specifying the amount of space you wanted between paragraphs as the Inter ¶ field does, the Inter ¶ Max field specified the maximum amount of space QuarkXPress could place between paragraphs to vertically justify the text.

Tip   If you plan to use Justified vertical alignment, keep in mind that you need to place picture boxes and other graphic elements outside the text box that holds the vertically justified text. The intrusion of a picture box or other graphic element with a runaround other than None automatically disables vertical justification.

Summary

You can enter text by importing text from a word-processor document (the best option), cutting and pasting it from another application, or entering it directly in QuarkXPress. Note that cutting and pasting text could cause special characters to disappear (typographic quotes, for example, are replaced with keyboard quote marks even if QuarkXPress is set to have Smart Quotes on).

To save you time, QuarkXPress has an option when you create a new document to create an automatic text box. That's great if you're creating books or magazines that have a central text area on almost every page, but if you're creating brochures, ads, and other one-of-a-kind documents, it's best to disable this box in the New Document dialog box.

You can link text boxes and text paths, so text flows from one to another. Be careful of the order in which you link the boxes and paths — that becomes the order in which text flows from one to the other, no matter their position on a page or within a document. You can also redirect text flow if you decide to change your layout and add or delete text boxes or paths.

QuarkXPress also has features to control how text appears within text boxes and along text paths. Using the Modify dialog box, you can set margins and, for text boxes only, the number of columns and the vertical alignment and spacing within the box.

✦   ✦   ✦

Editing Text

Y ou can use QuarkXPress for your primary word processor or simply to do some minor editing and touchups. Although the features are not nearly as sophisticated as a dedicated word-processing program, QuarkXPress does provide the basic text-editing features you'll need. These include cutting and pasting, checking spelling, and searching and replacing text and text attributes.

Editing in QuarkXPress

QuarkXPress provides a variety of tools for editing the words that make up your stories. As with any electronic text-editing tool, you can rearrange, delete, and insert text at will. For the most part, the editing features work exactly as you'd expect from your experiences with any text editor, from Microsoft Word to your e-mail program. As described in Chapters 10 and 11, you can get text into QuarkXPress by importing files from word processors or simply by typing into text boxes.

Text-editing tools

The only way you can edit text in QuarkXPress is to select the Content tool on the Tool palette. After you do that, you can click in any text box or text path to start editing. Here are a couple handy tools for text editing:

✦ **Invisibles:** To see what's going on in your text in terms of invisible characters such as spaces, tabs, and paragraph returns, choose View ➪ Show Invisibles, or press ⌘+I or Ctrl+I. The symbols you see are fairly standard: a tiny dot for a space, a right-facing arrow for a tab, a ¶ symbol for a paragraph return, and so on, as shown in Figure 13-1. Editing text with invisibles showing not only helps you prevent errors such as extra spaces from slipping in, but it helps you solve text-flow problems by showing new line and new column characters.

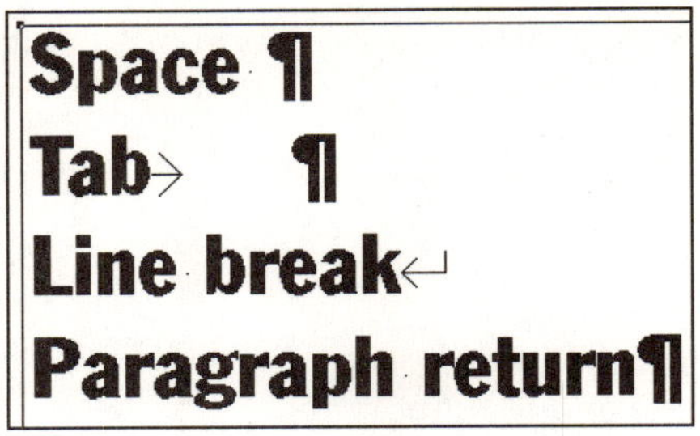

Space ¶
Tab→   ¶
Line break↵
Paragraph return¶

Figure 13-1: Choosing View ➪ Show Invisibles shows these common invisible characters.

✦ **Zooming:** The document views you use for designing the overall look of a page—Fit in Window or 100%, for example—are usually not best for editing text. Even if you can see the text well enough to edit, the smaller the text is the greater the chance of error. To zoom into the text with any tool selected, press Control+Shift or Ctrl+spacebar, then drag around the area you want to edit to increase its view scale.

New Feature

Prior Mac versions of QuarkXPress provided easy access to the Zoom tool through the Control key. The default in version 5 is that pressing the Control key gives you a context menu. If you can't get used to pressing Control+Shift for the Zoom tool, you can switch the application-wide default setting to Control for the Zoom tool and Control+Shift for the context menu using the Application pane in the Preferences dialog box (Edit ➪ Preferences ➪ Preferences, or Option+Shift+⌘+Y or Ctrl+Alt+Shift+Y).

Navigating text

To get into text to start editing it, first you need to click the Content tool inside a text box or text path. You can attempt to click it exactly where you need to edit— for example, inside a word you need to delete. After you're in the item containing text, you can move the cursor around easily by:

✦ Clicking the mouse elsewhere in the story (the text within a series of linked boxes and/or paths).

✦ Pressing the arrow keys on the keyboard to move the cursor up or down one line, and left or right one character.

✦ Adding the ⌘ or Ctrl key to the arrow keys to move the cursor one paragraph up or down, and one word to the left or right.

✦ Pressing Home or End to jump to the beginning or end of a story, respectively.

✦ Clicking directly after the last character in the box or on the path to enter text at the end of a story. As with most text editors, you can't just click in any white space and start typing.

Tip

If the box or path you need to edit is behind another box (usually with a transparent background so you can see the text through it), press Option+Shift+⌘ or Ctrl+Alt+Shift while you click until you hit the desired item.

Inserting text

After your cursor is positioned in text, you can start typing, pasting, or even importing text (through File ⇨ Get Text, or ⌘+E or Ctrl+E) at that location. All the preceding text stays in place, and all the following text reflows.

Highlighting text

To manage blocks of text — anything from a few characters to entire stories — you need to highlight (or select) the text. You can do any number of things with highlighted text, including cutting or copying it (then pasting it later) and reformatting the entire block. Your options for highlighting text are:

✦ **Select All:** Choose Edit ⇨ Select All, or press ⌘+A or Ctrl+A, to highlight all the text in a story. This is the easiest, most reliable way to select an entire story for editing.

✦ **Click-and-drag:** Click immediately before the first character, and drag to the final character. This is great for highlighting when you already have your hand on the mouse, but it's a little harder to be precise.

✦ **Double-click within a word:** For really precise mouse selections, you can double-click within a word to select it. See the sidebar "Double-click tricks" for more information.

✦ **Multiple clicks:** Triple-click to select a line, click four times to select a paragraph, and click five times to select an entire story. These methods work great for precise text selections when your hand is already poised on the mouse.

✦ **Arrow keys:** In addition to navigating text with the arrow keys, you can highlight text. Press Shift+⌘ or Ctrl+Shift to highlight one word to the right, one word to the left, to the beginning of a paragraph, or to the end of a paragraph. (Keep holding the modifier keys and pressing arrows to extend the selection.) To highlight from the current location to the beginning or end of a story, press Option+Shift+⌘ or Ctrl+Alt+Shift while you press Home or End, respectively.

Tip

If you're using QuarkXPress as your primary word processor or entering a lot of edits, using the arrows keys and the associated keyboard commands for navigating and highlighting text can be your best bet. The reason? You rarely have to lift your hands off the keyboard — saving you the time and muscle movement of reaching for the mouse.

To deselect text, select a different tool on the Tool palette or click somewhere else in text.

Double-click tricks

It doesn't seem like a big deal: Double-click in a word to highlight it. But the feature has some idiosyncrasies, some similar to word processors and others different.

✦ When you double-click within a word to select it, QuarkXPress highlights all words connected by hyphens. This is counter to Microsoft Word, which will highlight only the portion of the hyphenated compound that you're actually clicking in.

✦ If you want to select the punctuation trailing a word (such as a comma) along with a word, double-click between the word and its punctuation as shown in the accompanying figure. This is helpful when you're rearranging words in a comma-separated list. (Note that this doesn't work with invisible characters such as tabs — only characters you can see.)

"On this site in 1935," proclai
burger." A preposterous as
to hide, ashamed of its ow
of culinary glory. The who
larded up with ersatz ingredients and

✦ When you double-click to select a word, then you cut and paste the word, QuarkXPress actually includes the space after the word — even though you can't see it. This way, you don't have to worry about removing old spaces or inserting new ones as you move words. This is called *smart space,* and it actually works with any highlighted text that you cut and paste.

Replacing and deleting text

When text is highlighted, you can easily replace it by pasting text from the clipboard, typing new text, or importing text (through File ⇨ Get Text, or ⌘+E or Ctrl+E). If you want to replace an entire story, be sure to select it all by clicking the mouse five times in the story or choosing Edit ⇨ Select All, or ⌘+A or Ctrl+A.

To remove highlighted text from a document, you can highlight it and choose Edit ⇨ Clear or press Delete or Backspace on the keyboard. To use the text elsewhere, choose Edit ⇨ Cut, or press ⌘+X or Ctrl+X. (If the clipboard doesn't provide the longevity you need for saving the text for later use — or if you want to give the text to someone else — you can export the highlighted text using the File ⇨ Save Text command, or Option+⌘+E or Ctrl+Alt+E.)

If text is not highlighted, you can delete text to the right or left of the cursor. On the Mac, press Delete to delete to the left and press Del (on an extended keyboard) to delete to the right. In Windows, press Backspace to delete to the left and Delete to delete to the right.

Rearranging text

By *rearrange,* we mean the time-honored tradition of cut and paste — probably the best advantage of an electronic text editor over a typewriter. When you cut and paste, text goes to the Mac or Windows clipboard for use in any program that can receive pasted text. QuarkXPress has two methods for rearranging text: using the cut and paste commands or dragging and dropping text with the mouse.

Cutting and pasting

To cut (or copy) text and then paste it elsewhere, do the following:

1. Choose Edit ⇨ Cut (⌘+X or Ctrl+X) to cut text to the clipboard. Or choose Edit ⇨ Copy (⌘+C or Ctrl+C) to copy text to the clipboard.

2. Position the cursor elsewhere in the text (or anywhere, including a new e-mail or a word-processing file), then choose Edit ⇨ Paste (⌘+V or Ctrl+V).

Dragging and dropping

If you're addicted to the mouse — or simply have it in hand when you want to cut and paste — you can drag and drop highlighted text to a new location. (Note that drag and drop is limited to text within the same QuarkXPress story, although the text does go to the clipboard.) First, you need to turn this feature on for your copy of QuarkXPress by checking Drag and Drop Text in the Interactive pane of the Preferences dialog box (Edit ⇨ Preferences ⇨ Preferences, or Option+Shift+⌘+Y or Ctrl+Alt+Shift+Y).

When Drag and Drop Text is enabled, you can click on a block of highlighted text to "pick it up," as shown in Figure 13-2. You can then click the cursor in a new location to drop the text. If you want to copy a block of text rather than move it, press the Shift key while you drag.

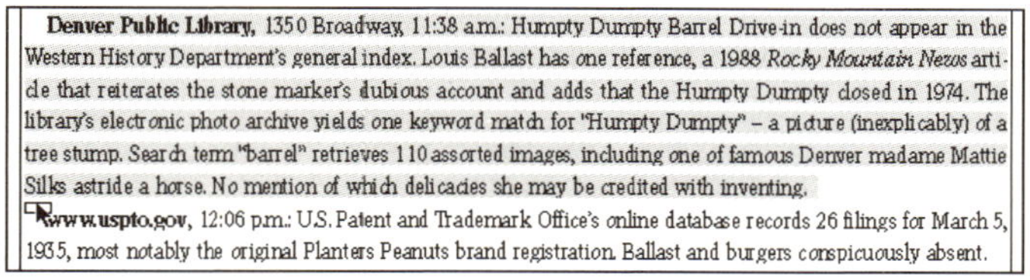

> **Denver Public Library,** 1350 Broadway, 11:38 a.m.: Humpty Dumpty Barrel Drive-in does not appear in the Western History Department's general index. Louis Ballast has one reference, a 1988 *Rocky Mountain News* article that reiterates the stone marker's dubious account and adds that the Humpty Dumpty closed in 1974. The library's electronic photo archive yields one keyword match for "Humpty Dumpty" – a picture (inexplicably) of a tree stump. Search term "barrel" retrieves 110 assorted images, including one of famous Denver madame Mattie Silks astride a horse. No mention of which delicacies she may be credited with inventing.
> www.uspto.gov, 12:06 p.m.: U.S. Patent and Trademark Office's online database records 26 filings for March 5, 1935, most notably the original Planters Peanuts brand registration. Ballast and burgers conspicuously absent.

Figure 13-2: The drag-and-drop text pointer, ready to drop text.

The cut and delete difference

Be sure to remember that cut text and deleted text are different. QuarkXPress inserts cut text automatically into the Clipboard, but it does not insert deleted text into the Clipboard. (You delete text by using the Delete key or Backspace key.)

The only way to recover deleted text is via Edit ➪ Undo Typing, or ⌘+Z or Ctrl+Z. Cut text remains in the Clipboard until you cut or copy other text or graphic elements.

Note that in QuarkXPress for Windows you can now also drag a text file from the desktop or folder into a text box. QuarkXPress 5 will import that text into the box. There is no Mac equivalent to this feature.

On the Mac, you can enable Drag and Drop Text on the fly with keyboard commands. When text is highlighted, press Control+⌘ to pick up text to drag it elsewhere. Add the Shift key to copy the text. There is no Windows equivalent to this shortcut.

Undoing text edits

If you change your mind about the last change you made in QuarkXPress (whether to text or anything else), choose Edit ➪ Undo, or press ⌘+Z or Ctrl+Z. If you then change your mind about changing your mind, you can redo your very last action by choosing Edit ➪ Redo or pressing the same keyboard commands.

Unlike many text editors, you only get one chance to undo with QuarkXPress. Sure, you can undo the last action, and redo it, and undo it over and over again. But you can't undo your second-to-last action — ever. So if you delete a block of text and then accidentally hit the spacebar, all you can undo is the addition of the space. If you're experimenting with text edits, you may want to save the document, then use File ➪ Revert to Saved to restore the original text.

Getting a Word Count

Getting a word count for a story is one of the most unintuitive features in QuarkXPress. There's only one way to do it, and it involves starting a spell check. A word count is, nonetheless, useful for communicating to writers and editors how much space they have to fill.

To get a word count, click anywhere in a story with the Content tool. Then choose Utilities ➪ Check Spelling ➪ Story, or press Option+⌘+L or Ctrl+Alt+W. The Word Count dialog box shown in Figure 13-3 displays, and the Total field tells you how many words are in the story. If you actually want to run spell check at this point, click OK. Otherwise, hit Cancel to return to the document.

Figure 13-3: The Word Count dialog box, accessed by choosing Utilities ⇨ Check Spelling ⇨ Story.

New Feature

QuarkXPress 5 lets you spell-check — and therefore get a word count for — a range of highlighted text. Simply highlight text, then choose Utilities ⇨ Check Spelling ⇨ Selection.

Checking Spelling

A finished document with spelling errors loses credibility, but the QuarkXPress spell checker is no panacea for this problem. That's partly because all electronic spell checkers rely on the user's own spelling ability — the software alerts you to possible misspellings, but it's up to you to determine if the word is actually misspelled in context and to select a correctly spelled word. The other problem is Quark's pitiful 120,000-word homegrown spelling dictionary. (By contrast, a hard-copy dictionary includes more like a million words.) The spell checker is suspicious of many plural words, most possessive terms, and many newer words (it doesn't even like *e-mail!*). Plus, the spelling dictionary cannot contain special characters, so all words with accent marks, even words as simple as *café,* show up as Suspect. Finally, spelling is all about judgment calls — some people prefer *judgement* calls — so your internal style book or preferred dictionary may not agree with the spelling dictionary. You can create your own spelling dictionaries to augment the QuarkXPress dictionary, although you can't edit the default one.

In light of all this, it's probably best to let writers and editors provide text that's already spell-checked to their standards. It still never hurts to run spell check to guard against any last-minute errors that have snuck in, such as during copyfitting. There's nothing like typing "Otober" on the cover of your magazine and having it slip through! But if you have any questions about a word that QuarkXPress doesn't like, check it out with a dictionary (www.m-w.com provides quick access to spellings in *Merriam-Webster's,* 10th Edition) or consult a copy editor.

The Check Spelling submenu

To display the spell check options, choose Utilities ⇨ Check Spelling. This menu item displays the submenu shown in Figure 13-4, which offers you the following spell-checking choices:

✦ **Word/Selection:** This option (⌘+L or Ctrl+W) checks the word containing the cursor or a range of highlighted words. This is ideal for checking one word you're not sure about or a new block of text you just added to a document.

New Feature Version 5 introduces the ability to search selected text rather than just a word, story, or document.

✦ **Story:** This option (Option+⌘+L or Ctrl+Alt+W) checks the currently active story (all the text in a series of linked text boxes/paths). Checking a story is useful for checking a newly imported story.

✦ **Document:** This option (Option+Shift+⌘+L or Ctrl+Alt+Shift+W) checks every word in the current QuarkXPress document. This option is ideal for checking all the text throughout all the disparate boxes and paths in a document.

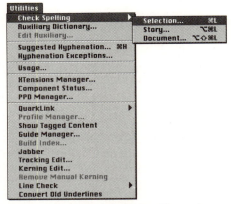

Figure 13-4: The Check Spelling submenu when a range of text is highlighted.

Tip When you spell-check, QuarkXPress shows the first instance of the Suspect word on-screen. Therefore, you may want to change the view percentage to something like 200 percent, so you can actually see the words.

Dealing with suspect words

The spelling checker displays words that it doesn't recognize (calling them *Suspect* words) one at a time, giving you an opportunity to correct or ignore (skip) all instances of the word. The spelling checker can suggest correct spellings for words that it believes are misspelled. Figure 13-5 shows the spelling checker displaying a word that is not in its dictionary.

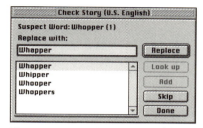

Figure 13-5: A Suspect word in the Check Story dialog box.

Looking up and replacing words

If QuarkXPress has suggested spellings for a Suspect word, the words are listed automatically. To accept a suggested replacement, click the word and the Replace button. You can also edit the word in the Replace With field yourself.

If the spelling checker suggests more than one possible spelling, QuarkXPress will jump to the one it recommends. If you highlight one of the other possibilities and decide you want to go with QuarkXPress's original recommendation, click the Lookup button (which is normally grayed out) to have QuarkXPress show that original recommendation again.

Caution

QuarkXPress has an all-or-nothing method of handling spelling corrections. So if you click Replace for a misspelled word, all instances of that word in the selection, story, or document will be replaced with the "correct" spelling. It's up to you to determine if this across-the-board correction will work for you. If not, you might jot down the word and use Edit➪Find/Change, or ⌘+F or Ctrl+F, to look at all instances of the word.

Working with auxiliary dictionaries

If you're not content with the 120,000-word dictionary in QuarkXPress—and there are many reasons not to be—you can add additional words to an auxiliary dictionary. Words of a technical nature specific to your company or industry are good candidates for an auxiliary dictionary, as are proper names.

One thing that's nice about auxiliary dictionaries is that you can pretty much put the files where you want them. In other words, auxiliary dictionaries do not have to reside in the same file as the documents accessing them. You can create as many auxiliary dictionaries as you need, you can use the dictionaries with multiple documents, and you can create copies of the dictionaries to share with other users. However, you can only use one auxiliary dictionary with a document at a time.

Creating or opening an auxiliary dictionary

If you open an auxiliary dictionary when a document is open, QuarkXPress associates the two, so when you open the document, the program has access to the auxiliary dictionary. If you want an auxiliary dictionary to be available in all documents you subsequently create, open the auxiliary dictionary when no documents are open (as explained in the following items).

To create an auxiliary dictionary:

✦ **For a specific document:** Open the document and access the Auxiliary Dictionary dialog box (Utilities ➪ Auxiliary Dictionary). Use the controls in the dialog box to locate the folder in which you want to keep the dictionary. Enter the name first, then click the New button, as shown in Figure 13-6.

✦ **For all new documents:** Make sure that no documents are open before invoking the Auxiliary Dictionary dialog box and clicking New.

If you create an auxiliary dictionary on QuarkXPress for Windows, it automatically adds the proper file name extension: .qdt. There is no reason to ever use this extension on the Mac because auxiliary dictionaries are not cross-platform.

To open an auxiliary dictionary:

✦ **In the current document:** Open your document and then open an existing dictionary from the Auxiliary Dictionary dialog box.

✦ **As the default for all new documents:** Make sure that no documents are open and then open an existing dictionary from the Auxiliary Dictionary dialog box.

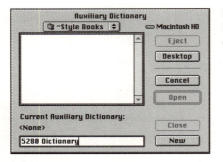

Figure 13-6: The Auxiliary Dictionary dialog box for creating an auxiliary dictionary for the open document.

Detaching an auxiliary dictionary

When an auxiliary dictionary is open for a document, but QuarkXPress cannot find the file, you cannot use spell check. This happens often when you receive documents from other users, many of whom are not likely to send the dictionary along. In this case, you need to close the dictionary, detaching it from the document. To do this:

✦ **From a current document:** Open the document and select Close in the Auxiliary Dictionary dialog box.

✦ **As the default dictionary for all new documents:** Make sure that no documents are open. Select Close in the Auxiliary Dictionary dialog box.

Tip   To prevent problems with missing auxiliary dictionaries in a workgroup, be sure everyone in the group has access to the file.

Editing an auxiliary dictionary

Before you use an auxiliary dictionary, you need to get words into that auxiliary dictionary. You can do this through spell check or through a special dialog box. First, make sure the auxiliary dictionary is selected (via Utilities ⇨ Auxiliary Dictionary).

To edit an auxiliary dictionary via spell check:

• While checking spelling, click Add to add the spelling of the current suspect word to the open auxiliary dictionary.

• If you're positive that all the suspect words in a document should be added to the auxiliary dictionary (for example, if the file you've opened contains the names of your board of directors), you can add all these words to the open auxiliary dictionary in one step. To do this, press Option+Shift or Alt+Shift while you click Done in any check spelling dialog box.

Tip   Adding all suspect words from a single document is a good way to create the same auxiliary dictionaries for Mac and Windows, given that the files are not cross-platform.

To edit an auxiliary dictionary via the Edit Auxiliary dialog box:

1. Open the Edit Auxiliary dialog box (Utilities ⇨ Edit Auxiliary), shown in Figure 13-7, to open the dictionary you want to use.

Figure 13-7: Editing an auxiliary dictionary is a simple matter of entering new words with their proper spellings.

2. If you have no auxiliary dictionaries defined, enter a name in the file name section of the dialog box, then click New (the New button will be grayed out until you enter a file name). You'll then need to reopen the Edit Auxiliary dialog box.

3. To add a word, type the word in the field below the list of current words. You are limited to typing in lowercase, but you can enter accented characters, such as é and õ in words like *entrée* and *Saõ Paulo.*

4. Click the Add button.

To delete a word, use the Edit Auxiliary dialog box. Highlight the word from the word list, or enter it in the field below the current list of words (typing the word also highlights it in the list). Click the Delete button.

Caution

Remember to click the Save button before you exit the Edit Auxiliary Dictionary dialog box. Otherwise, changes that you make are not saved. If you don't want to save your changes, choose Cancel.

Tip

When you add a word to the auxiliary dictionary, be sure to add all appropriate variations of the word such as plurals, possessives, and different tenses. For example, if you're adding *triffid,* also add *triffid's* and *triffids.*

Note

QuarkXPress doesn't allow the use of hyphens in its auxiliary spelling dictionary, so you can't enter words like *e-mail.* However, QuarkXPress won't flag *e-mail* or *m-commerce* as suspect words, because it ignores the single letters before the hyphen (they are correct "words" — letters of the alphabet — and the words that follow the hyphens happen to be standard English words). But if you had an unusual word with a hyphen, such as the brand name *e-trieve,* you would have to add *trieve* to the auxiliary dictionary and hope no one enters *i-trieve* or *o-trieve* — or simply expect to see *trieve* flagged during every spell check.

Searching and Replacing

Basic editing tools are fine for doing simple editing, but you may want to replace one piece of text with another throughout your document. Suppose, for example, that you create a catalog and you need to change a product's version number in every place that it's referenced throughout the manual. You can make the changes in the original word-processor document and then replace the text in your QuarkXPress document with the updated text (possibly losing a lot of carefully applied formatting in the process). Or you can use QuarkXPress's built-in replace function, which you access through the Find/Change dialog box, shown in Figure 13-8.You access the Find/Change dialog box via Edit ➪ Find/Change, or ⌘+F or Ctrl+F.

Figure 13-8: The Find/Change dialog box with Ignore Attributes checked.

The Find/Change dialog box lets you do simple search-and-replace operations on text, and it lets you search and replace formatting — with or without replacing text. When Ignore Attributes is checked in the dialog box, you perform standard search functions; when it's unchecked, you can include formatting such as Font, Size, and Style Sheet in a search.

Note   The Find/Change dialog box acts like a palette — it stays on-screen while letting you click into your document to edit text or perform other operations. To close the Find/Change dialog box, you must click its close box.

Searching for and replacing text

Any time you need to search for a string of text and replace it, choose Edit ⇨ Find/Change, or press ⌘+F or Ctrl+F. You can search and replace text in a portion of a story, an entire story, or an entire document. And your search can include parameters such as whole words and capitalization patterns.

Here's how the options work:

✦ **Find What:** Type or paste the text you want to search for in this field. If you want to find a word plus the space after it, make sure you enter it that way.

✦ **Change To:** Type or paste the replacement text in this field.

✦ **Scope:** To search a document from the current page forward, check Document. To check a story (all the text in a series of linked boxes/paths), uncheck Document. To search a portion of a story, click in the story at the point you want to start the search. QuarkXPress will search from that point to the end of the story.

✦ **Whole Word:** To search for text exactly as you enter it in the Find What field, check Whole Word. This will, for example, find only standalone instances of *Quark,* but not *QuarkXPress,* as shown in Figure 13-9. If you uncheck Whole Word, you'll find all instances of the text, even when it's embedded in other words.

✦ **Ignore Case:** To search and replace text regardless of capitalization pattern, check Ignore Case. To follow the capitalization patterns you enter in the Find What and Change To fields precisely, uncheck this option.

✦ **Find Next; Change, then Find; Change; and Change All buttons:** Use these buttons to search for text and replace it as necessary. Before using Change All, it's always a good idea to check the results of your settings to make sure they're working properly.

Tip   To search all the text in a document (regardless of the current page displayed) or to begin a search at the beginning of a story (regardless of the position of the cursor), press Option or Alt as you click the Find Next button. This changes the button to Find First.

Figure 13-9: Searching for *Quark* and replacing it with *QuarkXPress*. Whole Word is checked so that Find/Change only finds instances of Quark that aren't already in QuarkXPress. Ignore Case is unchecked so that the exact capitalization patterns in the Find What and Change To fields are followed.

Caution Unfortunately, when it comes to Find/Change, *all* doesn't really mean "all." When a document is displayed, QuarkXPress doesn't search master pages; when a master page is displayed, QuarkXPress doesn't search document pages. So if you're trying to search and replace something like an issue date, you'll need to search both. (Start with the master pages, and you may be able to skip the document pages.)

Searching/replacing invisible characters

In addition to searching for and replacing text and attributes, you can include invisible characters such as spaces, tabs, paragraph returns, and more in a Find/Change operation. For example, to strip a document of double spaces, you can type two spaces in the Find What field, then one space in the Change To field. You can also search for a *wild card,* any number of undefined characters with a specific pattern. For example, if you're searching for instances of *disk* and *disc,* you can search for *dis* plus the wild card code, which is \?. To enter invisible characters and the wild card, you can use shortcut combinations or textual codes, as shown in Table 13-1.

Tip You can also copy and paste invisible characters into the Find What and Change To fields.

Table 13-1
Shortcuts and Text Codes in the Find/Change Dialog Box

Character	Mac Shortcut	Windows Shortcut	Code
Wild card	Shift+⌘+?	Ctrl+Shift+?	\?
Tab	None	none	\t
Paragraph return	⌘+Return	Ctrl+Enter	\p
New line	Shift+⌘+Return	Ctrl+Shift+Enter	\n
New column	⌘+Enter	none	\c
New box	Shift+⌘+Enter	none	\b

Character	Mac Shortcut	Windows Shortcut	Code
Punctuation space	⌘+period	Ctrl+period	\.
Flex space	none	none	\f
Backslash	⌘+\	Ctrl+\	\\

Searching for and replacing text attributes

The Find/Change dialog box also lets you include formatting criteria in a search-and-replace operation. This feature is useful if, for example, you want to change all instances of the word *QuarkXPress* in 10-point Times New Roman to 12-point Palatino. To access these controls, uncheck Ignore Attributes in the Find/Change palette. When Ignore Attributes is deselected, the palette expands and offers you attribute replacement options, as Figure 13-10 shows.

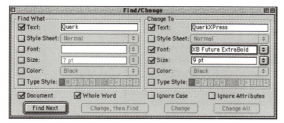

Figure 13-10: The Find/Change palette with Ignore Attributes unchecked.

In the example shown in Figure 13-10, we want to replace any text in 12-point Helvetica plain text with 13-point Arial bold text. This example shows how you can select specific text, typeface, and styles for both the search and replace functions. You specify these attributes by checking the Text, Font, Size, and Type Style check boxes in the Find What and Change To columns of the dialog box.

New Feature

QuarkXPress 5 adds the ability to search and replace color applied to text. Simply choose an option from the Color menu on the Find What and/or Change To sides of the Find/Change palette when Ignore Attributes is unchecked.

The Find What column

If you leave an option unchecked in the Find What column, QuarkXPress includes any variant (such as style) in the search. If, for example, we did not check Size in the Find What column but did check it in the Change To column, QuarkXPress would change all Helvetica italic text of any size to 13-point Arial bold text.

The Change To column

If you leave an option unchecked in the Change To column, QuarkXPress applies to the replacement text the formatting of the text that was searched. If we did not check Size in the Change To column, the size of the replacement text would be the same as the text it was replacing.

When you leave Text unchecked in the Find What column, you replace attributes only. You may do this to change all bold text to small cap text, all News Gothic bold text to News Gothic bold italic, or all 8-point text to 8.5-point text.

Type Style options

You can decide whether to include type styles (bold, italic, underline, and so on) in a search, and if you do decide to include them, you can specify which ones specifically to include. To use the type style options at all, check Type Style in the Find What and/or Change To columns. The individual style icons have three states:

✦ **Active (click once to reverse the icon):** When a type style is active on the Find What side, QuarkXPress only finds text with that type style applied. When a type style is active on the Change To side, QuarkXPress applies that type style to found text.

✦ **Inactive (click once to restore the icon to its original state):** When a type style is inactive on the Find What side, QuarkXPress only finds text *without* that type style applied. When a type is inactive on the Change To side, QuarkXPress removes that type style from found text.

✦ **Ignore (click twice to make the icon gray):** When a type style is set to ignore on the Find What side, QuarkXPress finds text whether or not this type style is applied. When a type style is set to ignore on the Change To side, QuarkXPress does not change that type style in the found text (if it's Bold it stays Bold, if it's Italic, it stays Italic, and so on).

In the example shown in Figure 13-11, the settings in the Find What column will find the words *Font Reserve* whether or not they're italicized but only if they're bold. The settings on the Change To side will remove bold in favor of the Minion SemiBold typeface, but leave the italics as applied.

Tip

When performing a search and replace for attributes, it's particularly important that you test your results by using the Change button before you launch into a Change All. It's easy to miss an important criterion and not find all instances of text you're searching for or apply the wrong replacement attributes — and there's no Undo for Change All. Before making drastic changes with Find/Change you may even want to save your document so you can use Revert to Saved in case disaster strikes.

Searching for and replacing type styles

QuarkXPress has the very handy ability to search and replace style sheets. As with other options, you can do this in combination with other text and other attributes, or you can simply find one style sheet and replace it with another. This gives you the ability to:

✦ **Apply character style sheets to text previously formatted with local formatting.** This gives you the luxury of editing the character style sheet to make global changes in the future.

✦ **Find certain words and phrases and apply a character style sheet to them.** For example, if your company name is supposed to appear in small caps at 0.5 points larger than surrounding text, you can find the company name and apply the character style sheet.

✦ **Selectively change the style sheet applied to text throughout a story or document.** This would be helpful, for example, if a designer created a new style sheet for column bylines, but not for feature bylines.

The Style Sheets dialog box (Edit ⇨ Style Sheets, or Shift+F11) does let you delete a style sheet and replace it with another. But if you want to retain the style sheet in the document but replace it selectively, Find/Change is helpful.

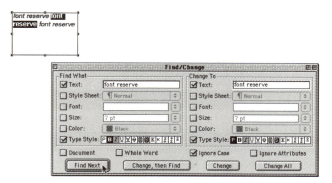

Figure 13-11: In this example, QuarkXPress will find all instances of Font Reserve with Bold type style applied — regardless of whether the words have Italic type style applied as well.

The Font Usage utility

If you need to quickly make a global change to a font used throughout a document, you can use the Font Usage utility in addition to the Find/Change dialog box. Font Usage is designed primarily to help you determine which typefaces are used in a document so that you know which typefaces you need for printing. The utility also comes in handy if you open a document that uses a typeface not available on your computer; you can replace that typeface with another.

To open Font Usage, choose Utilities ⇨ Usage, then click the Fonts pane. Use the Replace button to select a replacement font for the font selected in the list.

Note   There is no advantage to using Font Usage over Find/Change to replace fonts — in fact, you won't be able to make selective changes with Font Usage. And, as with Find/Change, Font Usage finds the font only on document pages (or only on master pages if they're displayed). So the change isn't really global.

Summary

QuarkXPress, although not a full-fledged word processor, provides the controls you need for making corrections to text, including the expected ability to cut and paste. To speed text selections for formatting and editing, QuarkXPress provides various shortcuts in addition to the tried-and-true click-and-drag method.

To help you communicate with writers and editors, the spell checker provides a Word Count feature. You can spell-check a word, text selection, story, or document, but rely on the QuarkXPress dictionary at your own risk. The dictionary includes a paltry 120,000 words, but you can augment it with your own auxiliary dictionaries.

The Find/Change feature lets you search and replace text, considering such criteria as whole words and capitalization. You can extend the search capabilities to include searching for specific attributes and replacing them with others.

✦   ✦   ✦

Typography

The typographic treatment of text can be a subtle yet powerful part of your presentation. Although you define the basic look of a document with layout and style sheets, you give it texture with the way you handle text.

With QuarkXPress, you have in your hands those tools that typographers once used to enhance the aesthetics of a document, as well as to do the nuts-and-bolts formatting. You can orchestrate the finer points of formatting on a case-by-case basis, or you can record them in character or paragraph style sheets, ready to be used again and again. With a little experimentation and a few guiding principles, you can use these typographic tools to improve the appearance and clarity of all the documents you create.

This part of the book explains typography and shows you how you can use the tools in QuarkXPress to put theory into practice. You will learn how to use these tools to control text appearance, make text fit comfortably in your document, and even produce tables.

Typography Theory

Desktop publishing has changed typography forever. In the old, old days, typefaces were available in a limited number, and then only in a limited number of sizes. You couldn't condense or expand them. And you certainly couldn't add drop shadows or make them print as outlines without hours of work in a darkroom. Desktop publishing has changed all that. By rendering type into a series of mathematical equations — curves and lines and angles — and manipulating that math with today's fast computers, type can be almost anything. In the early days of desktop publishing, that led to experimentation and a lot of bad results. That was more than a decade ago, however, and good taste in innovation has prevailed. This chapter is your guide to typographic good taste.

Understanding Typography Terms

Typography terms include words that describe the appearance of text in a document or on a computer screen. These terms refer to such aspects of typography as the size and style of the typeface used and the amount of space between lines, characters, and paragraphs.

Characters

When you're looking at the individual characters that make up a word, the following terms come into play:

✦ **Font:** A set of characters of a certain size, weight, and style (for example, 10-point Palatino Bold). This term is now used often as a synonym for *typeface,* which is a set of characters of a certain style in *all* sizes, weights, and stylings (for example, Palatino).

✦ **Face:** A combination of a weight and styling in all sizes of a font (for example, Palatino Bold Italic).

✦ **Font family:** A group of related typefaces (for example, the Franklin family includes Franklin Gothic, Franklin Heavy, and Franklin Compressed).

✦ **Weight:** Typeface thickness. Typical weights, from thinnest to thickest, are ultralight, light, book, medium, demibold, bold, heavy, ultrabold, and ultraheavy.

✦ **Style:** Type can have one of three basic stylings: Roman type is upright type; oblique type is the roman type that has been mathematically slanted to give the appearance of italic type; and italic type is both slanted and curved (to appear more like calligraphy than roman type). Type also may be *expanded* (widened), *condensed* (narrowed), or *compressed* (severely narrowed). See Figure 14-1 for examples of some of these stylings.

Syntax Medium

Syntax Medium Italic

Syntax Bold

Syntax Bold Italic

Syntax Black

Syntax Black Italic

Syntax Ultrablack

Syntax Ultrablack Italic

Figure 14-1: A sample sans serif typeface with different stylings.

Tip   Keep in mind that some of these type-style variations are created mathematically, while other fonts are created to appear a certain way. For example, you can compress a roman font, but it won't be the same as the official, compressed version of the face.

✦ **X-height:** The height of the average lowercase letter (this is based on the letter x). The greater the height, the bigger the letter looks when compared to letters in other typefaces that are the same point size but have a smaller X-height.

✦ **Cap height:** Similar to X-height, it refers to the size of the average uppercase letter (based on the letter C).

✦ **Descender:** In a letter such as q, the part of the letter that goes below the baseline is called a *descender*.

✦ **Ascender:** The part of a letter that extends above the X-height (as in the letter *b*) is called an *ascender* (see Figure 14-2).

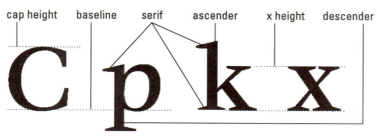

Figure 14-2: The elements of a typeface.

✦ **Serif:** A horizontal stroke used to give letters visual character. The strokes on the upper-left and bottom of the letter *p* in a typeface such as Times are serifs (refer to Figure 14-2).

✦ **Sans serif:** A typeface that does not use serifs. Helvetica is an example of a sans serif typeface.

✦ **Ligature:** A set of joined characters, such as fi, fl, ffi, or ffl. The characters are joined because the characters' shapes almost blend together by default, so typographers of yore decided to make them blend together naturally.

Automatic ligatures are available only in QuarkXPress for Mac, due to the differences between Mac fonts and Windows fonts. If you use automatic ligatures on the Mac and transfer the file to Windows, the ligatures will be replaced by the regular characters, and when the file is transferred back to the Mac, the ligatures will be automatically generated again. Note that although Windows 2000 supports OpenType fonts, which can include ligatures, QuarkXPress for Windows does not support ligatures, even in Windows 2000.

Typographic measurement units

If you've used any word processor or even a Web browser, you've probably learned that the size of text is usually expressed in points. But when it comes to measuring type, you'll probably encounter a combination of the following terms:

✦ **Pica:** A measurement unit that specifies the width and depth of columns and pages. A pica is just a little less than ⅙ of an inch (most people round it up to an even ⅙ inch).

✦ **Point:** A measurement used to specify type size and the space between lines. There are 12 points in a pica, so there are about 72.27 points to the inch. Most people round it down to 72 per inch.

✦ **Cicero:** A unit of measure used in many parts of Europe. One inch equals about 5.62 ciceros.

✦ **Agate:** Used for measuring vertical column length in classified ads. One agate equals about 5.5 points. An *agate inch* is one column wide and ¹⁄₁₄ of an inch deep.

✦ **Em, en, and punctuation spaces:** The terms *em, en,* and *punctuation space* (also called a *thin space*) are units of measurement that reflect, respectively, the horizontal space taken up by a capital *M*, capital *N*, and lowercase *t*.

Typically, an em space is the same width as the current point size; an en space is ½ of the current point size, and a punctuation (thin) space is ¼ of the current point size. In other words, for 12-point type, an em is 12 points wide, an en space is 6 points wide, and a punctuation or thin space is 3 points wide.

✦ **Figure space:** The width of a numeral, which usually is the same as an en. (In most typefaces, all numerals are the same width so that tables align naturally.)

Spacing

Spacing is a vague term that can apply to anything — the amount of space between two characters, two words, two lines. If you learn the right professional terminology, you can communicate with more precision when it comes to spacing.

✦ **Leading:** The space from the base of one line (the *baseline*) to another; also called *line spacing*. (Leading is named after the pieces of lead once used to space out lines.) See Figure 14-3 for examples of leading.

This is 14-point type set to +1 point of leading in the QuarkXPress Measurements palette. As you can see, the lines are simply too close to each other. See how the text almost overlaps between the first two lines?

This is 14-point type with the leading set to Auto in the QuarkXPress Measurements palette—the normal setting for leading. Notice how the space in between lines is more than enough to avoid text overrunning other text, but not so much that there are large gaps between lines. Note that Auto sets the leading to be 20 percent more than the point size, which usually results in the correct 1.5 to 3 points of extra space between lines (for 14-point text, that means leading of 16.8 points, or 2.8 points extra space). As text gets larger than about 18 points, you'll want to avoid Auto and use a specific leading amount (usually 2 points more than the text size). You can specify your own Auto value in the Document Preferences dialog box's Paragraph pane (⌘ + Y).

This is 14-point type with the leading set to 20 points in the QuarkXPress Measurements palette—the normal setting for leading. Notice how the space in between lines is far more than enough to avoid text overrunning other text,; in fact, it's an unusually large amount that probably looks a little strange. You might find such large leading in a kid's book, since young children need help distinguishing characters and the extra space does that. It also makes sense in very wide columns, so people can keep the long lines separated visually. You'll also find it in some layouts for parts of an introduction or other special elements that you want to call attention to. But you rarely find this amount of leading in regular body text.

Figure 14-3: The same type with different leading has a very different appearance.

✦ **Tracking:** Determines the overall space between letters within a word.

✦ **Word spacing:** Defines the preferred, minimum, and maximum spacing between words.

✦ **Letter spacing:** Defines the preferred, minimum, and maximum spacing between letters; sometimes called *character spacing*.

Note

QuarkXPress uses your preferred spacing specifications unless you justify the text or apply manual spacing adjustments; if you justify text, the program spaces letters and words within the limits you set for maximum and minimum spacing.

✦ **Kerning:** An adjustment of the space between two letters. You kern letters to accommodate their specific shapes. For example, you probably would use tighter kerning in the letter pair *to* than in *oo* because *to* looks better if the *o* fits partly under the *t*.

✦ **Pair kerning:** A table, called the *kerning table* in QuarkXPress, that indicates the letter pairs you want the publishing program to kern automatically. Kerning is used most frequently in headlines, where the letter spacing is more noticeable. See Figure 14-4 for an example of kerning.

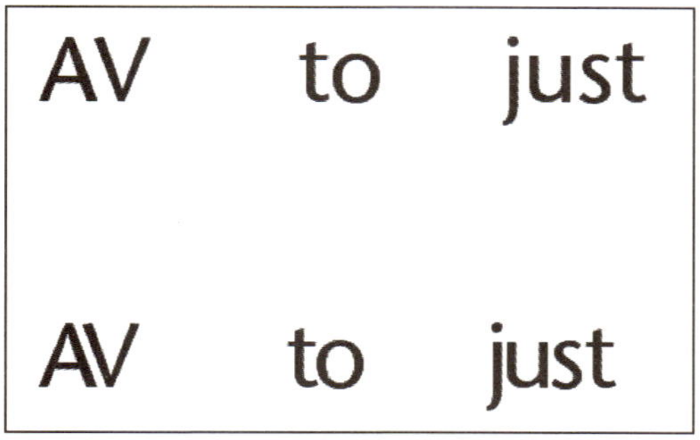

AV   to   just

AV   to   just

Figure 14-4: An example of kerned and unkerned letter pairs.

✦ **Justification:** Adds space between words (and sometimes between letters) so that each line of text aligns at both the left and right margin of a column or page. Justification also is used to refer to the type of spacing used for optimum letter and word spacing: justified, ragged right, centered, or ragged left (see the following definitions):

   • **Ragged right and flush left:** Text that aligns with a column's left margin but not its right margin.

   • **Ragged left and flush right:** Text that aligns with the right margin but not the left margin.

   • **Centered:** Text that aligns so that there is equal space on both margins.

- **Vertical justification:** Adds space between paragraphs (and sometimes between lines) so that the tops and bottoms of each column on a page align. (This term is often confused with *column balancing,* which ensures that each column has the same number of lines.)
- **Carding:** A vertical-justification method that adds space between paragraphs in one-line increments.
- **Feathering:** Another vertical-justification method that uses fractional-line spaces between paragraphs.

Paragraphs

You'll hear a variety of terms regarding how paragraphs are positioned within a column or on a page. These terms range from the simple concept of an indent to design issues such as drop caps.

✦ **Indent:** You typically indicate a new paragraph with an *indent,* which inserts a space (often an em space in newspapers and magazines) in front of the paragraph's first letter.

✦ **Outdent:** An *outdent* (also called an *extent*) shifts the first character past the left margin and places the other lines at the left margin. This paragraph alignment is typically used in lists.

✦ **Block indent:** A *block indent,* a style often used for long quotes, moves an entire paragraph in from the left margin.

✦ **Hanging indent:** A *hanging indent* is like an outdent except that the first line begins at the left margin and all subsequent lines are indented.

✦ **Bullet:** A character (often a filled circle) used to indicate that a paragraph is one element in a list of elements. Bullets can be indented, outdented, or kept at the left margin.

✦ **Drop cap:** A large capital letter that extends down several lines into the surrounding text (the rest of the text wraps around it). Drop caps are used at the beginning of a section or story. A *raised cap* is the same as a drop cap except that it does not extend down into the text. Instead, it rests on the baseline of the first line and extends several lines above the baseline.

✦ **Style sheets:** These contain named sets of such attributes as spacing, typeface, indent, leading, and justification.

✦ **Style or style tag:** A set of attributes.

Note

Essentially, styles are formatting macros. You tag each paragraph or character with the name of the style that you want to apply. Any formatting changes made to one paragraph or character are automatically reflected in all other paragraphs or characters tagged with the same style. Note that QuarkXPress uses the term *style sheet* to refer to an individual style.

Hyphenation

If you haven't been involved in professional publishing, you probably never thought about hyphenation much. But the way text is hyphenated has a significant impact on its readability. While using QuarkXPress and perfecting your type, you'll run into the following hyphenation terms:

✦ **Hyphen:** Used to indicate the division of a word at the end of a line and to join words that combine to modify another word.

✦ **Hyphenation:** Determines where to place the hyphen in words that need to be split.

✦ **Consecutive hyphenation:** Determines how many lines in a row can end with a hyphen (more than three hyphens in a row is considered bad typographic practice).

✦ **Hyphenation zone:** Determines how far from the right margin a hyphen can be inserted to split a word.

✦ **Exception dictionary:** Lists words with nonstandard hyphenations. You can add words that the publishing program's default dictionary does not recognize and override the default hyphenations for a word such as *project,* which is hyphenated differently as a noun (proj-ect) than as a verb (pro-ject).

✦ **Discretionary hyphen:** Placing a *discretionary hyphen* (also called a *soft hyphen*) in a word tells the program to hyphenate the word at that place if the word must be split. A discretionary hyphen affects only the word in which it is placed.

Identifying Typographic Color and Typefaces

Throughout the history of publishing, professional typographers have enhanced the look of documents by selecting from a variety of fonts to produce a desired look, and by increasing or decreasing character spacing. When done correctly, character spacing gives a finished look. Words set in characters that are surrounded by generous amounts of space have a light, airy feel; words set in characters that are close together feel heavier and more serious.

Typographic color

As a group, four aspects (kerning, tracking, scale, and hyphenation) determine what typographers call *color,* simply another way of describing the appearance of text on a page. If you want to see a document's typographic color, make your eyes go slightly out of focus. Here's a good way to understand the concept of typographic color: Find a magazine page that has a good amount of text on it. Stare at the page for two minutes or so. Then focus on something halfway between you and the page. You'll see the text blur. The resulting gray level and consistency is *color*. Why is a document's color so important? Because it affects both the document's mood and readability. For most publishing applications, a light to medium color is preferable because it's easier on the eye.

The influence of typeface

Factors in addition to character spacing influence color. The most fundamental factor is the typeface. An airy, light typeface such as Baskerville Old Face has a light color, while a solid, heavy typeface such as Franklin Gothic Heavy has a dark color. Figure 14-5 shows the same text in these two typefaces. Notice how the text on the right, in Baskerville Old Face, looks lighter than the Franklin Gothic Heavy text on the left. The example shown in the figure clearly demonstrates that type fonts are major contributors to typographic color. Some typefaces are light, some are heavy. Regardless of a typeface's intrinsic weight, QuarkXPress includes character spacing controls that let you modify a font's effect on typographic color.

Two decades ago, when they first began buying homes, the Donegans decided that creating a beautiful garden would be a weekend pastime they could share. "I hated boring yards!" Lorene, a writer who specializes in 19th century New York history, recalls. "Even though the yard was nearly two acres, we knew it could be a magic place."

Lorene and Joe shared a vision of natural foliage mixed with fragrant native flowers, with a border of wild raspberries. Together, the couple created a tranquil, comfortable garden that includes both annuals – many in raised beds – and perennials. Roses in many vivid colors add the final touch.

A major task for the retired couple each spring is the raking and removal of more than 100 garbage bags full of leaves, applied as a winter compost cover the previous fall to the many rose bushes. Eventually, the decomposing leaves become mulch used on perennials, except in winter, when the soil at the base of some bushes is kept bare.

Two decades ago, when they first began buying homes, the Donegans decided that creating a beautiful garden would be a weekend pastime they could share. "I hated boring yards!" Lorene, a writer who specializes in 19th century New York history, recalls. "Even though the yard was nearly two acres, we knew it could be a magic place."

Lorene and Joe shared a vision of natural foliage mixed with fragrant native flowers, with a border of wild raspberries. Together, the couple created a tranquil, comfortable garden that includes both annuals — many in raised beds — and perennials. Roses in many vivid colors add the final touch.

A major task for the retired couple each spring is the raking and removal of more than 100 garbage bags full of leaves, applied as a winter compost cover the previous fall to the many rose bushes. Eventually, the decomposing leaves become mulch used on perennials, except in winter, when the soil at the base of some bushes is kept bare.

Figure 14-5: Different typefaces produce different shades of typographic color.

Learning About Typefaces

The two basic types of typefaces are serif and sans serif. A serif typeface has horizontal lines (called *serifs*) extending from the edges of the character, such as at the bottom of a *p* or at the top of an *I*. A sans serif typeface does not have these lines (*sans* is French for "without"). There are more types of typefaces than just serif and sans serif, but these are all in the minority. Calligraphic, block, and other nonserif/non–sans serif typefaces usually have other elements that serve the purpose of serifs — extensions to the characters that add, well, a distinctive character to the typeface. Another distinct type of typeface is the *pi font,* which is a font made up of themed symbols (anything from math to Christmas ornaments). The name *pi font* comes from the Greek letter *pi* (π), a common mathematical symbol.

Typeface variations

A typeface usually has several variations, the most common of which are roman, italic, boldface, and boldface italic for serif typefaces; and medium, oblique, boldface, and boldface oblique for sans serif typefaces. Italic and oblique differ in that italics are a curved variant of the typeface, with the serifs usually heavily curved, while an oblique is simply a slanted version of the typeface. Other variations that involve type weight include thin, light, book, demibold, heavy, ultrabold, and black. Compressed, condensed, expanded, and wide describe type scale.

What's in a face?

Each of these variants, as well as each available combination of variants (for example, compressed light oblique), is called a face. Some typefaces have no variants; these are typically calligraphic typefaces, such as Park Avenue and Zapf Chancery, and symbol typefaces (pi fonts), such as Zapf Dingbats and Sonata. In Figure 14-6, you see samples of several typefaces and some of their variants. By using typeface variants wisely, you can create more-attractive and more-readable documents.

A font is a typeface by any other name

Desktop publishing programs popularized the use of the term *font* to describe what traditionally was called a *typeface.* In traditional terms, a *typeface* refers to a set of variants for one style of text, such as Times Roman. A *face* is one of those variants, such as Times Roman Italic. A *font,* in traditional terms, is a face at a specific point size, such as 12-point Times Roman Italic. (Until electronic typesetting was developed, printers set type using metal blocks that were available only in a limited range of sizes.) The word *font* today means what typeface used to mean, and almost no one uses *font* anymore for its original meaning.

The heart of a document is its typography. Everything else can be well laid out and illustrated, but if the text isn't legible and appealing, all that other work is for naught. If you don't believe type is central, then consider this: You've surely seen engaging documents with no artwork, but have you ever seen artwork carry the day if the type is ugly or scrunched? We didn't think so.

Serif Typefaces

Esprit Book *Italic*
Caslon *224 Italic*
Minion Condensed *Italic*
Americana *Italic*
Bookman Light *Italic*
Bodoni *Italic* **Bold**
Galliard *Italic* **Black**
Janson Text *Italic* **Bold**
Poppl Pontifex *Italic*
Stone Serif *Italic* **Semi Bold**
Century Oldstyle *Italic*
Garamond Condensed Light *Italic*
Industrial 736 *Italic*
Times Roman Times Ten
New Baskerville *Italic* **Bold**
Veljovic Book Medium **Bold Black**
Concorde BE *Italic* **Medium** Cond

Sans Serif Typefaces

Helvetica **Bold** *Light Italic* **Black** **Compressed**
COPPERPLATE GOTHIC CONDENSED BOLD
Gill Sans Light **Extra Bold**
Poppl Laudatio *Italic* **Bold**
Syntax Roman *Italic* **Ultra Black**
Frutiger Condensed Light **Bold** **Black** Extra
Futura Book **Heavy** Regular **Extra Bold**
Avant Garde Book **Demi**
Myriad **Bold** *Italic*
Optima **Bold**
Stone Sans *Italic* **Bold**
DIN Schriften Mittelschrift
News Gothic **Bold**
Formata **Medium** Light **Bold** Cond Cond Outline

Calligraphic/Decorative

TRAJAN **BOLD**
Sanvito Roman
Ex Ponto
ANNA
Friz Quadrata **Bold**
LITHOS **BLACK**
MACHINE BOLD
Nueva Roman **Bold Extended**
Zapf Chancery

Pi Fonts

η∓°+κ∇⊆−⊆β⊐°±÷φφϑ∩
θ.iɛ:ðɕɪɛʀyʊɪɔ'æʃʃʃ̩χɕʊʙɴɯз̩
✼➤◻◻◻✦✦✦★☀✦☛☂☺⊡✦▲✌➤☞⊠
▦❀⚘✄▤▥▦▧▨▤⊠ ℮℘&⁏◆ ♫▤☻
φℲ≅−∀:ᴧϑΔΣΞδαωΩΠ
⊛⊛Ⓔ⊕Ⓟ⊕ ▤▦▩▦▥◆▤✍℘/▮
①❷❼☆★÷×≤✂✄◻▹▸◧◸◿⊲─────➤▰◆▰◆

Figure 14-6: A variety of typefaces and their variants.

Selecting the Best Typefaces

If you've ever seen a type chart, you already know that thousands of typefaces are available, each with a different feel. Matching the typeface's feel to the effect that you want for your document is a trial-and-error process. Until you're experienced at using a wide variety of typefaces (and even then), experiment with different typefaces on a mock-up of your document to see what works best.

Understanding typeface names

The many variants of typefaces confuse many users, especially because most programs use only the terms *normal* (or *plain*), *italic* (or *oblique*), *bold,* and *bold italic* (or *bold oblique*) to describe available variations. When a typeface has more than these basic variations, programs usually split the typeface into several typefaces.

For example, in some programs, Helvetica comes as Helvetica, with medium, oblique, boldface, and boldface oblique faces; Helvetica Light/Black, with light, light oblique, black, and black oblique faces; Helvetica Light/Black Condensed, with condensed light, condensed light oblique, condensed black, and condensed black oblique faces; Helvetica Condensed, with condensed medium, condensed oblique, condensed boldface, and condensed boldface oblique faces; and Helvetica Compressed, with compressed medium and condensed oblique faces. When there are this many variations, you have to choose from among several Helvetica typefaces, and you have to know that, for example, selecting bold for Helvetica Condensed results in Helvetica Condensed Bold type.

For some typefaces, the variants are even more confusing. For example, in text, Bookman is usually printed in light face, which is lighter than the medium face. So when you select plain, you really select Bookman Light. And when you select bold, you really select Bookman Demibold. Bookman Medium and Bookman Bold are too heavy for use as body text, which is why the typeface comes in the light/demi combination of faces. Fortunately, the issue of what face a program designates as plain, italic, and the rest rarely comes into play. You usually encounter a problem only in one of the following situations:

✦ When you're exchanging files between PCs and Macs — because some vendors use slightly different names for their typefaces on different platforms. The Utilities ⇨ Usage option lets you correct this problem by replacing one typeface name with another in your document, via the Fonts pane.

✦ When you're working with a service bureau that has typeface names that are different, or whose staff uses the traditional names rather than the desktop-publishing names.

✦ When you're working with artists or typesetters to match a typeface. Typically, the problem is a lack of familiarity with the different names for a typeface. The best way to reach a common understanding is to look at a sample of the typefaces being discussed.

You may have noticed that many people use serif typefaces for body copy and sans serif typefaces for headlines, pull-quotes, and other elements. But there is no rule you should worry about following. You can easily create engaging documents that use serif typefaces for every element. All-sans-serif documents are possible, but they're rare because sans serif typefaces tend to be hard to read when used in many pages of text. (Exceptions include typefaces such as News Gothic and Franklin Gothic, which were designed for use as body text.) No matter which typefaces you use, the key is to ensure that each element calls an appropriate amount of attention to itself.

Defining a standard set

We recommend that you take the time necessary to define a standard set of type-faces for each group of publications. You may want all employee newsletters in your company to have a similar feel, which you can achieve by using common body text and headline typefaces, even if layout and paragraph settings differ. The key to working with a standard set of typefaces is to avoid limiting the set to only a few typefaces. Selecting more typefaces than any one document might use gives you enough flexibility to be creative, while providing an obviously standard appearance. You also can use the same typeface for different purposes. For example, you might use a newsletter's headline typeface as a kicker in a brochure. A consistent — but not constrained — appearance is a good way to establish an identity for your company.

Some basic guidelines

If you're feeling confused about which typeface is right for you, here are some basic guidelines:

✦ **Use a roman medium or book weight typeface for body text.** In some cases, a light weight works well, especially for typefaces such as Bookman and Souvenir, which tend to be heavy in the medium weights.

✦ **Output some samples before deciding on a light typeface for body text, because many light typefaces are hard to read when used extensively.** Also, if you intend to output publications on an imagesetter (at 1270 dpi or finer resolution), make sure that you output samples on that imagesetter, because a light font may be readable on a 300- or 600-dpi laser printer but too light on a higher-resolution printer that can reproduce thin characters more faithfully than a laser printer. (The laser printer may actually print a light typeface as something a bit heavier. Because the width of the text's stroke is not an even multiple of the laser printer's dots, the printer has no choice but to make the stroke thicker than it should be.) Although 1200-dpi laser printers are increasingly common and make more accurate proofs than a 300- or 600-dpi model, note that imagesetters are still more accurate, because they use smooth paper, which allows less distortion than the standard bond paper used in laser printers.

✦ **Use a heavier typeface for headlines and subheads.** A demibold or bold usually works well. Avoid using the same typeface for headlines and body text, even if it's a bolder variant. On the other hand, using the same typeface for subheads and headlines, even if in a different variant, helps ensure a common identity. (And if you mix typefaces, use those that have similar appearances. For example, use round typefaces with other round typefaces and squared-off typefaces with other squared-off typefaces.)

✦ **If captions are long (more than three lines), use a typeface with the same weight as body text.** If you use the same typeface as body text, differentiate the caption visually from body text. Using a boldface caption lead-in (the first words are boldface and act as a title for the caption) or putting the caption in italics distinguishes the caption from body text without being distracting. If captions are short (three lines or fewer), consider using a heavier face than body text or a typeface that is readily distinguished from your body text.

✦ **As a general rule, avoid using more than three typefaces (not including variants) in the main document elements (headlines, body text, captions, pull-quotes, and other elements that appear on most pages).** However, some typefaces are very similar, so you can use them as a group, as if they were one. Examples include Helvetica, Univers, and Arial; Futura, Bauhaus, and Avant Garde; Times and its many relatives (including Times New Roman and Times Ten); Galliard and New Baskerville; Souvenir and Korinna; Benguiat, Americana, Garamond, Stone Serif, and Cheltenham; New Baskerville and Esprit; and Goudy Old Style and Century Old Style. You can treat the individual typefaces within these groups almost as variants of one another, especially if you use one of the individual typefaces in limited-length elements such as kickers, pull-quotes, and bylines.

✦ **Use italics for kickers, bylines, sidebar headlines, and pull-quotes.**

Summary

Typography terms describe the appearance of text in a document or on a computer screen. These terms refer to such aspects of typography as the size and style of the typeface used and the amount of space between lines, characters, and paragraphs.

Kerning, tracking, scale, and hyphenation determine what typographers call *color*, simply another way of describing the appearance of text on a page. A document's color is important because it affects both the document's mood and its readability. For most publishing applications, a light to medium color is preferable because it's easier on the eye.

We recommend that you take the time necessary to define a standard set of typefaces for each group of publications you work on. You can achieve a uniform look and feel in your publications by using common body text and headline typefaces. The key to working with a standard set of typefaces is to avoid limiting the set to only a few typefaces. Selecting more typefaces than any one document might require allows for some creativity, while still providing a uniform appearance.

✦　　✦　　✦

Setting Character Attributes

◆ ◆ ◆ ◆

In This Chapter

Accessing character attributes

Specifying size and scale

Choosing fonts and type styles

Applying color and shade

Controlling character spacing

◆ ◆ ◆ ◆

When you understand the basics of good typography, you can get your hands dirty in QuarkXPress and start formatting your text. When you're setting character attributes, you're controlling formatting on a character-by-character basis, as opposed to paragraph attributes, which affect all the characters, words, and lines in a paragraph. QuarkXPress provides many options for formatting characters, including basics such as font and size along with many variations of type styles and professional controls for spacing text.

Accessing Character Attributes

To apply character attributes to text, first you need to select the Content tool (the hand) on the Tool palette. Then you either need to click in text to specify formatting for the next characters you type, or highlight some text. You have several options for selecting character attributes:

◆ The Character Attributes dialog box (Style ⇨ Character, or Shift+⌘+D or Ctrl+Shift+D) consolidates all the attributes you can apply to characters.

◆ The far-right side of the Measurements palette (View ⇨ Show Measurements, or F9) provides font, size, and type style controls.

◆ The Font, Size, Type Style, Color, and Shade submenus of the Style menu provide options for applying these character attributes.

◆ Keyboard shortcuts let you quickly try out attributes. The keyboard commands are provided in the following sections, which detail each attribute.

Cross-Reference See Chapter 13 for more information about entering and highlighting text.

 Tip If you find yourself applying the same combination of character attributes over and over again, you can save the combination as a character style sheet. See Chapter 32 for more information.

Specifying Size and Scale

You can change the point size of text in any font from 2 points to 720 points, and you can apply horizontal or vertical scaling, which is mostly used for design effects but can also be used for copyfitting.

Point size

To change point size, you can use the Size field/menu in the Measurements palette, the Size submenu of the Style menu, and the Size field/menu in the Character Attributes dialog box (Style ➪ Character, or Shift+⌘+D or Ctrl+Shift+D). To change the size of highlighted text, select a size from a menu or enter a value in the field — out to three decimal points as shown in Figure 15-1.

Figure 15-1: The Size field in the Measurements palette accepts values between 2 and 720 points.

 Tip If the Font field in the Measurements palette is active, you can tab to the Size field, enter a value, press Return to apply it, then jump back into the text. This lets you quickly change the font and point size without lifting your fingers from the keyboard.

Horizontal and vertical scales

QuarkXPress lets you change the horizontal or vertical scale of text, which influences typographic color and can create interesting effects. Scaling compresses or expands the actual characters to a percentage, ranging from 25 to 400 percent, in 0.1-percent increments. Choose Style ➪ Horizontal/Vertical Scale to open the Character Attributes dialog box with the Scale field active. First, select Horizontal or Vertical from the menu, as shown in Figure 15-2, then enter a value in the field (QuarkXPress assumes the value is a percentage).

Pay attention to the following kinds of typefaces when you scale:

✦ **Typefaces that have darker vertical strokes (the constituent components) than horizontal strokes can look odd when expanded too much.** Optima is an example of such a typeface. A sans serif typeface such as Eurostile, Helvetica, or Univers works best because its generally even shape has fewer intricate elements that might get noticeably distorted.

✦ **Many serif typefaces work fine if horizontally scaled only slightly.** Squarer typefaces such as Melior and New Century Schoolbook lend themselves best to scaling without perceived distortion. When you slightly compress wide typefaces such as Tiffany, which are normally used for headlines and other display type, they can acquire a new feel that makes them usable as body text. Finer typefaces such as Janson Text more quickly become distorted because the differences between the characters' already shallow horizontal strokes and already thicker vertical strokes become more noticeable — especially when expanded.

✦ **Avoid scaling decorative typefaces such as Brush Script, Dom Casual, and Park Avenue.** Zapf Chancery, however, can be scaled slightly without looking distorted.

Choosing Fonts and Type Styles

The font you choose is usually a specific variation of a typeface — for example, Minion Bold is a font from the Minion typeface. In addition to applying fonts, QuarkXPress lets you apply styles such as underline and shadow to further modify the look of an individual font.

Applying fonts

Before you can apply a font, first you need to activate the associated font files. (See Chapter 5 for information about acquiring and activating fonts.) All fonts active on your system are listed in the Font menu in the Measurements palette (as shown in Figure 15-4), the Font submenu of the Style menu, and the Font menu in the Character Attributes dialog box (Style ➪ Character, or Shift+⌘+D or Ctrl+Shift+D).

To apply a font to highlighted text, simply select one. The menu in the Measurements palette and the Character Attributes dialog box are also fields that let you type in font names — you need only type the first few characters of the font name until it's recognized.

Tip   If you're typing along in QuarkXPress and want to quickly change the active font, press Option+Shift+⌘+M or Ctrl+Alt+Shift+M to jump into the Font field on the Measurements palette. You can then type the first few letters of the font name until recognized, press Return to apply the font, then continue typing.

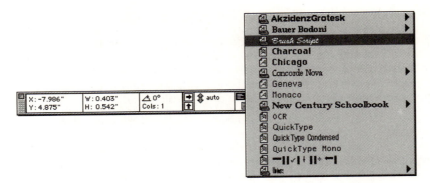

Figure 15-4: The Font menu in the Measurements palette displays all the active fonts on your system.

Applying type styles

All the type style options in QuarkXPress are shown with icons in the lower-right corner of the Measurements palette, as shown in Figure 15-5. If you point at an icon, the Tool Tip will give you its name (provided that Show Tool Tips is checked in the Interactive pane of the Preferences dialog box, Edit ➪ Preferences ➪ Preferences, or Option+Shift+⌘+Y or Ctrl+Alt+Shift+Y). Some of the type styles are mutually exclusive — for example, you cannot have text in All Caps and Small Caps at the same time.

Figure 15-5: The Type Style icons in the Measurements palette.

To apply type styles to highlighted text, you can:

✦ **Click the type style icons on the Measurements palette.** If a type style is already applied, it is highlighted.

✦ **Select an option from the Type Style submenu of the Style menu.** If a type style is already applied, a check mark displays next to it.

✦ **Check boxes in the Type Style area of the Character Attributes dialog box (Style ➪ Character, or Shift+⌘+D or Ctrl+Shift+D).** If a type style is already applied, its box is checked.

✦ **Press the keyboard shortcuts displayed in Table 15-1.** You can usually guess these commands by pressing Shift+⌘ or Ctrl+Shift along with the first initial of the type style (P for plain, I for italic, and so on).

Table 15-1		
Shortcut Keys for Typeface Attributes		
Attribute	*Macintosh Shortcut*	*Windows Shortcut*
Plain	Shift+⌘+P	Ctrl+Shift+P
Bold	Shift+⌘+B	Ctrl+Shift+B
Italic	Shift+⌘+I	Ctrl+Shift+I
<u>Underline all</u>	Shift+⌘+U	Ctrl+Shift+U
<u>Word underline</u>	Shift+⌘+W	Ctrl+Shift+W
~~Strikethrough~~	Shift+⌘+/	Ctrl+Shift+/
Outline	Shift+⌘+O (letter O)	Ctrl+Shift+O (letter O)
Shadow	Shift+⌘+S	Ctrl+Shift+S
ALL CAPS	Shift+⌘+K	Ctrl+Shift+K
SMALL CAPS	Shift+⌘+H	Ctrl+Shift+H
Superscript	Shift+⌘++ (plus)	Ctrl+Shift+0 (zero)
Subscript	Shift+⌘+- (hyphen)	Ctrl+Shift+9
Superior	Shift+⌘+V	Ctrl+Shift+V

Basic text styles

Most people are familiar with basic type styles such as bold and italics. After all, we see them routinely in newspapers, magazines, ads, and television. Despite that familiarity, these styles can be misused, especially by people experienced in producing reports on typewriters and word processors, rather than creating published (typeset-quality) documents in which these basic styles are used differently. The following is a primer on the use of basic text attributes in body text. Of course, these and other guidelines should be ignored by those purposely trying to create a special effect.

Plain as the basic style

Plain refers to the basic style for the selected typeface. Most commercial typefaces come with a roman or medium face as the basic style. But many typefaces created by do-it-yourselfers or converted via programs, such as Macromedia's Fontographer, come with each face as a separate typeface. So, for example, you may have Magazine Roman, Magazine Italic, Magazine Bold, and Magazine Bold Italic as separate typefaces in your fonts menus. If you select Magazine Bold Italic, QuarkXPress's palettes and dialog boxes show its style as plain, but it appears and prints as bold italic. This discrepancy is not a bug in QuarkXPress but simply a reflection of the fact that the basic style for any typeface is called *plain* no matter what the style actually looks like.

Bold

Bold is seldom used in body text because it's too distracting. When it's used, bold is typically applied to the lead-in words in subsections. As a rule, don't use it for emphasis — use italics instead. However, when you have a lot of text and you want people to pick out names within it easily, bolding the names may be appropriate. If, for example, you create a story listing winners of a series of awards or publish a gossip column that mentions various celebrities, you may want to bold people's names to highlight them.

Italics

Italics are used to emphasize a word or phrase in body text. For example, "You *must* remember to fully extinguish your campfire." Italics are also used to identify titles of books, movies, television and radio series, magazines, and newspapers: "Public TV's *Discovery* series had an excellent show about the Rocky Mountains." Italics can also be applied to lead-in words of subsections or in lists (these instances are described in Chapter 18).

In typewritten text, people often use underlines or uppercase as a substitute for italics. Because you have access to professional publishing tools, however, you don't need to use these substitutes in published text.

The bold and italic blues

QuarkXPress can't apply a bold style to a typeface that doesn't have one. (For example, if you have Minion and apply bold, QuarkXPress actually prints Minion Bold. If you don't have Minion Bold, or if it didn't exist, QuarkXPress wouldn't be able to bold the font when printed.) If the typeface has a bolder face, QuarkXPress is likely to use that one, assuming the typeface uses the correct internal label so that QuarkXPress knows how to do this. Similarly, QuarkXPress cannot apply an italic style to a typeface that doesn't have one. But QuarkXPress does recognize that when you select italics for a sans serif typeface, the oblique face is what you want.

If you change the face of selected text to a style (boldface or italics) not supported by the typeface in use, QuarkXPress may appear to have applied that face successfully. However, when you print, you'll see that the face hasn't really been changed (although the spacing has changed to accommodate the new face). What has happened is that QuarkXPress and the type scaler (such as TrueType or Adobe Type Manager) mistakenly create a screen font based on your request for a face change. When the text with the nonexistent face is printed, the computer finds no printer file for that face and uses the closest face it has for the typeface used: the original, regular face.

Because of this, it's always best to actually change the font of text instead of using the bold or italic type styles. For example, for emphasis you might use Garamond Bold, and for composition titles you might use Garamond Italic. To apply the font as quickly as a type style, you can create a character style sheet with a keyboard command. (See Chapter 32 for more information.)

Underline and Word Underline

Underlines are not typically used in body text in published documents. In fact, underlines are used in typewritten text as a substitute for italics. But underlines do have a place in published materials as a visual element in kickers, subheads, bylines, and tables. When used in such short elements, underlines add a definitive, authoritative feel. (Generally, these are implemented through the Rules feature discussed in Chapter 16.)

In addition to rules, QuarkXPress offers two standard type styles for underlining: regular Underline and Word Underline, both shown in Figure 15-6. Underline affects all characters, including spaces; Word Underline underlines only non-space characters (letters, numerals, symbols, and punctuation). When choosing which underline type to use, there is no right or wrong. Let the aesthetics of the document be the determining factor.

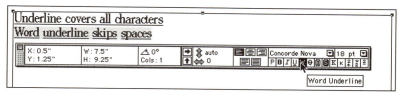

Figure 15-6: Text with Underline and Word Underline type style applied.

QuarkXPress 5 ships with an XTension called Type Tricks, which adds a custom underline feature. You can create your own styles for underlines — including color, shade, width, and offset — through the Edit ➪ Underline Styles command. You can then apply the styles to highlighted text using the Style ➪ Underline Styles submenu.

Strike Thru, Outline, and Shadow

QuarkXPress includes Strike Thru, shown in Figure 15-7, for either editing documents in progress or for special effects such as marking out a price in an ad and substituting a new, lower price. Outline and Shadow are used for design effects, but you can often achieve a superior effect using different techniques such as layering text boxes with transparent backgrounds. (See Chapter 18 for more information.)

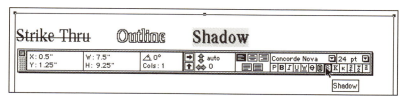

Figure 15-7: Text with Strike Thru, Outline, and Shadow applied.

All Caps

Capital letters serve both functional and decorative uses. Functionally, capital letters start sentences and identify proper names. Decoratively, they add emphasis or stateliness. Capital letters have a more stately appearance than lowercase letters, most likely because of the influence of Roman monuments, which are decorated with inscribed text in uppercase letters (the Romans didn't use lowercase much). These monuments and the Roman style have come to symbolize authority and officialism. Most government centers have a very Roman appearance, as a visit to Washington, D.C., quickly confirms. Using all capital letters has two major drawbacks:

✦ **Text in all caps can be overwhelming because uppercase characters are both taller and wider than lowercase.** In typeset materials (as opposed to typewritten), all caps looms even larger because the size difference between a capital letter and its lowercase version is greater than it is with typewriter characters, which are all designed to fit in the same space. All caps can be thought of as the typographic equivalent of yelling: READ THIS SENTENCE! Now, read this sentence.

✦ **People read not by analyzing every letter and constructing words but by recognizing the shapes of words.** In all caps, words have the same rectangular shape — only the width changes — so the use of word shape as a reading aid is lost. All caps is, therefore, harder to read than regular text.

Small Caps

The use of Small Caps typestyle can result in elegant, stately text that isn't overwhelming. The smaller size of the caps overcomes the yelling aspect of All Caps. Figure 15-8 shows an example of effective use of Small Caps. The key to using small caps is to limit them to short amounts of text where it's okay not to give readers the aid of recognizable word shapes. Small caps are effective in kickers, bylines, and labels.

Figure 15-8: The headline here shows an effective use of Small Caps type style.

The small caps expert collection

Some typefaces have a version—sometimes called an *expert collection*—that includes specially designed small caps. These caps are not merely proportionally scaled; their strokes are also modified to make them a bit darker. When you scale a character to be smaller, you make its strokes smaller, which makes the character lighter than the equivalent lowercase letter. Simulated small caps can look weaker than true small caps. This difference is usually not a problem, but for design-intensive work such as advertising, the quality difference often makes it worthwhile to get the expert-collection typeface.

Keep in mind that using the Small Caps option in QuarkXPress does not access the expert-collection typeface; you must explicitly apply the expert-collection's small cap typeface to the characters in question using the Font menu in the Measurements palette, Style menu, or Character Attributes dialog box described earlier in this chapter.

Tip

QuarkXPress lets you set the proportional size of small caps (compared to regular caps) in the Character pane of the Preferences dialog box (Edit ⇨ Preferences ⇨ Preferences, or Option+Shift+⌘+Y or Ctrl+Alt+Shift+Y). You can set the horizontal and vertical proportions separately, although they're usually the same. QuarkXPress's default setting is 75 percent, and most small caps should be set between 70 and 80 percent. If you want typographic settings to affect all future documents, open the Character pane of the Preferences dialog box with no document open.

Superscript, Subscript, and Superior

The Superscript, Subscript, and Superior type styles let you indicate notes in your text and set some mathematical notations. Although numerals are typically used for these notes, you can also use special symbols such as asterisks and daggers. These notes are in a smaller size than the rest of the text and are positioned above or below the regular baseline. A few notes about these type styles:

✦ **Superscripts and subscripts are typically used in math and other sciences**. A superscript can indicate an exponent, such as a^2 for a squared, or a notation, such as U^{235} for uranium-235.

✦ **Superscripts are commonly used for footnotes, too, but QuarkXPress also offers *superiors*, the traditional typographic method of indicating footnotes**. A superior is similar to a superscript, except that the top of a superior always aligns with the top of the text's cap height as shown in Figure 15-9. A superscript, by contrast, need not align with anything. The advantage to using a superior is that you don't have to worry about the footnote (or whatever) bumping into the text in the line above. This problem is particularly acute if you have tight leading and the superscript is positioned below a character that has a descender (such as a g or p).

✦ **If you prefer superior for footnotes, make the change in QuarkXPress.** Most word processors don't provide the Superior type style, so you'll need to use Find/Change to replace Superscript on footnotes to Superior. To do this, use the Find/Change palette (Edit ⇨ Find/Change, or ⌘+F or Ctrl+F).

Seybold, San Francisco – September 24, 2001 – DiamondSoft, Inc. announced today that it has named Modulo Systems Corporation, an industry-leading supplier of publishing software, as global distributor for its award-winning font management products: Font Reserve™ and Font Reserve Server™.

Figure 15-9: In this press release, the trademark symbol is set in Superior.

If you use additive or automatic leading (covered in Chapter 16) and your Superscript or Subscript settings cause the superscripts or subscripts to extend beyond the text's height or depth, you get uneven spacing. The uneven spacing occurs because some lines have more leading than others to accommodate the outsized or outpositioned characters. (QuarkXPress bases additive and automatic leading on the highest and lowest character in a line, not on the text's normal position.) If you can't alter your text so that none of it extends beyond the text's range — by changing either its leading or the subscript and superscript settings — don't use the additive or automatic leading options.

As it does for small caps, QuarkXPress lets you set the relative size and spacing for superscripts, subscripts, and superiors. You specify these sizes in the Character pane of the Preferences dialog box (Edit ⇨ Preferences ⇨ Preferences, or Option+Shift+⌘+Y or Ctrl+Alt+Shift+Y). You may need to experiment to derive a setting that works for all paragraph styles.

We prefer the following settings: superscripts offset 35 percent and scaled 60 percent; subscripts offset 30 percent and scaled 60 percent; and superiors scaled 50 percent. If you want typographic settings to affect all future documents, open the Character pane of the Preferences dialog box with no document open.

Shift Text Above and Below the Baseline

Baseline shift is similar to superscripting and subscripting. Baseline shift lets you move text up or down relative to other text on the line. The biggest difference between baseline shifting and superscripting or subscripting is that with baseline shift, the text size doesn't change. This effect is rarely needed, but it can come in handy when you position text for ads and other design-intensive text or when you use it with effects such as ruling lines to create reverse text. Unlike superscripts and subscripts, baseline shifts don't cause uneven leading when used with additive leading. Instead, QuarkXPress lets text overprint lines the text shifts into.

To apply shift highlighted text above or below the baseline, you can enter a point value (in 0.01-point increments) in the Baseline Shift field of the Character Attributes dialog box (Style ⇨ Baseline Shift), as shown in Figure 15-10. A positive value shifts text up; a negative value shifts text down. You can also use keyboard shortcuts for Baseline Shift, although you're limited to shifting in 1-point increments: Option+Shift+⌘+plus or Ctrl+Alt+Shift+plus shifts text up and Option+Shift+⌘+hyphen or Ctrl+Alt+Shift+hyphen shifts text down.

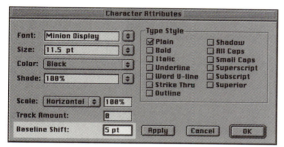

Figure 15-10: The Baseline Shift field lets you shift highlighted text up or down in 0.01-point increments.

Tip

Using the Baseline Shift feature, you can change the size of text to create superscripts or subscripts that differ from the normal settings in a document, which can be useful to scientists and engineers whose documents require several levels of subscripting or superscripting.

Applying Color and Shade

As with most special effects, you should apply color or shading to text sparingly, reserving these treatments for elements that serve as text-as-art. Good places to use color or shading include titles, bylines, pull-quotes, and ancillary elements such as page numbers. QuarkXPress lets you apply color or shading (or both) to any selected text or to any paragraph in which the style uses color or shading settings.

You can apply color and shade to highlighted text by choosing options from the Color and Shade submenus of the Style menu. Or, if you're experimenting with colors, it might be easier to use the Colors palette (View ⇨ Show Colors, or F12), shown in Figure 15-11. First, be sure to click the Text Color button at the top of the palette, then click the desired color. You can enter a shade in the field or select one from the menu.

Figure 15-11: When you click the Text Color button on the Colors palette, you can apply color to highlighted text.

Tip

Light colors and shades are best used with bold, large type because this keeps them from getting lost in the layout. They also work well when combined with other effects. Darker colors, such as blues and reds, work well in borders or as the colors of large outlined text.

Cross-Reference

To create additional colors for use in a document, use the Edit ⇨ Colors command or Shift+F12. For more information about working with color, including creating colors, see Part VII.

Controlling Character Spacing

It may sound nit-picky, but if you're a publisher, you pay attention to details such as the amount of space around individual text characters (known as *character spacing*). This attention to detail is important, because the space around characters has a profound effect on the ease with which a reader understands the text and the message the text conveys. Character spacing is a significant contributor to the quality (or lack thereof) of a printed document.

Throughout the history of publishing, professional typographers have enhanced the look of documents by increasing or decreasing character spacing. When done correctly, character spacing gives text a finished look. Character spacing is what provides the mood of a document. Words set in characters that are surrounded by generous amounts of space have a light, airy feel; words set in characters that are close together feel heavier and more serious. Character spacing gives a psychological boost to the thought conveyed by the text itself. Character spacing includes the following aspects:

✦ Tracking

✦ Kerning

✦ Scale

✦ Hyphenation

Scaling text is discussed earlier in this chapter, and hyphenation is discussed in Chapter 17.

Using tracking controls

Tracking has the greatest effect on typographic color. Also called *letter spacing, tracking* defines the amount of space between individual letters for a given section of text. The more space between letters, the looser the tracking and the lighter the color. When tracking is loosened excessively, text becomes airy and loses color. QuarkXPress sets the defaults for tracking at 0. This tells the program to use the letter spacing that the typeface's font file dictates in its width table.

QuarkXPress has several methods for tracking text:

✦ You can apply tracking on-the-fly, as necessary, to highlighted text.

✦ You can specify tracking in a character style sheet and/or paragraph style sheet.

✦ You can edit a font's tracking tables for use in a single document or for use in all QuarkXPress documents.

When to increase tracking

Are publishers more likely to decrease or increase tracking? Decreasing tracking is fairly common; increasing it is not. You'll rarely need to increase tracking. But increasing it is a good idea in two situations:

✦ **Headlines:** In headlines that use heavy fonts, the letters can look too close to each other unless you open up some space between them (typographers call this space *air*).

✦ **Special effects:** Another reason to increase tracking is to achieve a special effect that is increasingly popular: spreading out letters in a word or title so that letters are more than one character apart. This often is used with text that is short, all on one line, and used as a kicker or other secondary label. Figure 15-12 shows an example of such a type treatment. Tracking in the highlighted text is set at 90 units, a very loose tracking setting.

Understanding ems

QuarkXPress sets tracking in increments of 200ths (0.5 percent) of an em, which is the width of a capital letter *M* in the current type size. In most typefaces (decorative and symbol fonts are the main exceptions), an em is the same width as the current point size. So in 10-point Desdemona or 10-point Bookman, an em is 10 points wide. Thus, reducing tracking by 20 units (or 10 percent) makes characters set in 9-point type 0.9 point closer, 10-point type 1 point closer together, 15-point type 1.5 points closer, and so on.

In most cases, an em is equal to the width of two zeroes—the traditional em—but not in all. QuarkXPress supports both types of em spaces. You decide which definition the program uses by making a selection in the Character pane of the Preferences dialog box (Edit ⇨ Preferences ⇨ Preferences, or Option+Shift+⌘+Y or Ctrl+Alt+Shift+Y). Check the Standard Em Space box to use the traditional method, or uncheck it to use the double-zero method.

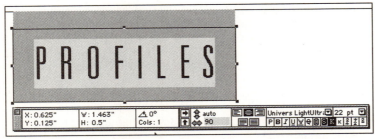

Figure 15-12: With loose tracking, the text spreads to fill the space.

The best amount of tracking is a decision based not on right or wrong, but on personal aesthetics and the intended overall feel of the document. But here are some guidelines that we like to use: If you're using small type (12 points or smaller) and placing it in narrow columns (16 picas or narrower), consider using tighter tracking. The eye more readily sees gaps between small forms and in narrow columns than it does between large forms and in wide columns. Settings from –2 to –10 should work for most common typefaces.

When to adjust tracking on-the-fly

In the following situations, you may want to apply tracking on a case-by-case basis:

✦ **Copy fitting:** Squeezing or stretching text to make it fit into a fixed amount of space is called *copy fitting*. You can do this to an entire story, but it's more commonly used to retrack widows and any lines that have only a few characters (fewer than six or so), because you gain a whole line by forcing those characters to move into previous lines.

Note You can also copy-fit by cutting out some text, but this requires the involvement of an editor, not just a production person, because the meaning of the text might be affected. Generally, you highlight one or two lines that seem to have excess space and reduce the tracking settings.

✦ **Removing widows and orphans:** When the last line of a paragraph consists of only a few characters, it's called a *widow*. This is considered typographically unsightly, particularly on a line that begins a column. How many characters constitute a widow is personal judgment. We tend to consider anything shorter than a third of a line a widow. (In Figure 15-13, we fixed a one-word widow with tracking.) An *orphan* refers to the first line of a paragraph (which is indented) that begins at the bottom of a column. Orphans are less taboo than widows. We tend to not worry about them. Even if fitting text within a certain space is not an issue, widows and orphans are frowned upon in serious publishing because they can look awkward.

✦ **Creating special effects:** Stretching a word by increasing its tracking can be a good idea, especially if you're trying to achieve a special effect. Often, stretched-out text is formatted in all caps or small caps. If you use this effect in labels or kickers, it's wise to create a style sheet with these settings, rather than apply the tracking manually.

✦ **Altering ellipses (. . .):** Many people find the ellipsis character too tightly spaced, so they use three periods instead. If you don't like the amount of spacing QuarkXPress provides when you type three periods with default tracking settings, you can change the spacing through tracking. You cannot retrack the ellipsis character itself — spacing within the character doesn't change — so if you want to define the ellipsis via tracking, use three periods instead of the ellipsis character. And be sure to use nonbreaking space (⌘+spacebar on the Mac; Ctrl+5 in Windows), so you don't have some of the periods on one line and the rest on another.

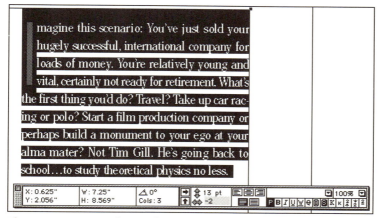

Figure 15-13: A tracking value of –2 pulled up a widow in this paragraph.

Tracking highlighted text

To apply new tracking values, highlight the text you want to track. If you want to track all the text in a story, use Edit ⇨ Select All, or press ⌘+A or Ctrl+A, to select all the text, instead of highlighting it with the mouse. (***Remember:*** Any tracking you apply manually to text is applied in addition to the tracking specified in the tracking editor.)

After you select the text, you can change the tracking values in three ways:

✦ **The fastest method is to use the appropriate keyboard shortcut.** Press Shift+⌘+} or Ctrl+Shift+} to increase tracking to the nearest ¹⁄₂₀ em (10 units); press Shift+⌘+{ or Ctrl+Shift+{ to decrease it to the nearest ¹⁄₂₀ em. Pressing Option+Shift+⌘+} or Ctrl+Alt+Shift+} increases tracking by ¹⁄₂₀₀ em (1 unit); pressing Option+Shift+⌘+{ or Ctrl+Alt+Shift+{ decreases it by ¹⁄₂₀₀ em.

✦ **The Measurements palette also provides a Tracking field, shown highlighted in Figure 15-14.** You can highlight the value in the field and enter a new value to the nearest ¹⁄₂₀ em (10 units). Or click the left arrow to decrease the tracking value by 10; click the right arrow to increase the tracking value by 10. To make the arrows work in multiples of 1 unit instead of 10, press the Option or Alt key while clicking them.

✦ **If you're setting other character attributes, you can use the Track Amount field in the Character Attributes dialog box (Style ⇨ Character, or Shift+⌘+D or Ctrl+Shift+D, or Style ⇨ Track).** Note that if no text is highlighted, this field is called *Kern Amount* and controls only the space between the current character and the next one.

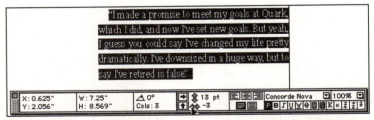

Figure 15-14: The Tracking field and arrows in the Measurements palette.

Caution

Because tracking in QuarkXPress affects the space to the right of each character, you should select all but the last character in the section of text you want to track; otherwise, you could get some variation in the tracking of the last character in the selection.

Editing tracking tables

QuarkXPress includes sophisticated tools that let you edit the tracking table that comes built into a font. This is handy if you find that with some fonts you seem to be adjusting tracking often; if so, you may want to consider editing the font's tracking table. To do this, you need to access the QuarkXPress tracking editor, which appears under the Utilities menu as Tracking Edit.

 Note   If you don't have a Tracking Edit option on your Utilities menu, it probably means you don't have the Kern/Track Editor XTension installed. Use the XTensions Manager (Utilities ➪ XTensions Manager) to activate the XTensions, quit QuarkXPress, and relaunch QuarkXPress.

When you use the QuarkXPress tracking editor, you don't make any changes to your font files themselves; you just change the way they work in QuarkXPress (not in other applications).

Adjusting the curve

With the tracking editor, you edit a curve on a graph that establishes the relationship between point size and tracking value. When you click a point in the curve, you create a turn point at which the direction of the curve can change. Figure 15-15 shows a tracking setting that loosens tracking for headline text (above 24 points in this example) to 19 units.

How QuarkXPress tracks justified text

Character and word spacing are affected by justification settings. If you *justify* text (aligning text against both left and right column margins), QuarkXPress adds space between words and characters to create that alignment. If tracking settings were the sole determinant of character spacing, QuarkXPress would be unable to justify text. Realize that justification settings influence actual tracking, so you should set them to work in conjunction with tracking settings. This will make it possible for you to meet your overall spacing goals.

When you apply tracking to justified text, you need to know the sequence that is followed by the program. QuarkXPress applies justification first, and then adjusts the tracking according to your specifications. That means if you specify tracking of −10 (equivalent to 5 percent tighter spacing) and QuarkXPress adds 2 percent more space on a line to justify it, the net spacing on that line is 3.1 percent (102 percent width for justification times 95 percent tracking: $1.02 \times 0.95 = 96.9$; and $100 - 96.9 = 3.1$ percent), or a tracking value of about −6.

Nonetheless, the Track Amount field in the Character Attributes dialog box and the Measurements palette both show a tracking value of −10. This is simply a reflection of how justified text has always been handled, even in typesetting systems that predate desktop publishing. Any publishing system ignores tracking settings if that's the only way to justify a line.

Changing tracking in one document only

When you make changes in the tracking editor, they apply not only to the document you're currently working with, but to every document you create after you make the changes. If you want your tracking changes to apply to one document only, close the document after you make the changes, then open the Edit Tracking dialog box for that font and click Reset.

Because QuarkXPress associates an edited tracking table with the document that was active when you invoked the tracking editor, when you give a service bureau your QuarkXPress document to output to negatives on an imagesetter, your tracking changes remain intact.

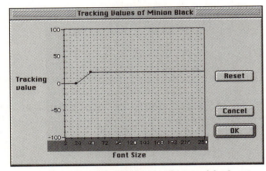

Figure 15-15: Editing the tracking table for a font.

Tip   Because the tracking editor treats each variation of a typeface—such as plain, bold, italic, and bold italic—separately, remember to make tracking adjustments in all variations of the typefaces you alter. Appropriate tracking values may be different for each typeface, especially for heavier faces such as bold and ultra.

Resetting the defaults

If you make tracking table edits and decide that you don't like the results, you can reset them to the default setting, which is defined in the typeface's font files (usually 0) by clicking the Reset button in the Edit Tracking dialog box. This works even if you've already saved your settings and exited the track editor. In another example, you may want to abandon the tracking changes that have been made to a document. Because QuarkXPress detects whether a document's settings match the defaults for that copy of the program, when you open the document, the Nonmatching Preferences dialog box gives you the option to apply the default settings by clicking Use XPress Preferences.

Using kerning controls

Often, the space between certain pairs of letters needs to be adjusted so that it looks good. This adjustment of the space between two specific letters is known as *kerning.* Kerning tells the output device — such as a laser printer, typesetter, or monitor — to add or, more typically, subtract a certain amount of space between specific pairs of letters anytime those pairs occur in a document, so that their spacing seems natural. The information on which pairs of letters to kern and how much to kern them by is stored in the font file as a kerning table.

QuarkXPress has several methods of applying kerning to text:

✦ You can use the Auto Kern Above feature, which automatically kerns text throughout documents according to the typeface designer's specifications.

✦ You can apply manual kerning between any two characters as necessary.

✦ You can edit a font's kerning tables for use in a single document or for use in all QuarkXPress documents.

When to use kerning

Without kerning, some letters may appear to be farther apart than other letters in the same word, which in some cases simply looks odd but in other cases can even trick the eye into thinking the letters are, in fact, in different words. In Figure 15-16, note the distance between the character pair *AV* in the kerned pair (top) and the unkerned pair (bottom). Kerning, which is important for all large type, adjusts the spacing to prevent such awkward spacing. The larger the characters, the larger the space between them, and thus any awkward spacing becomes more noticeable. For smaller type, kerning is often not noticeable because the space between letters is already so small.

Figure 15-16: The word *Avalanche* with kerning (top) and without kerning (bottom).

The Auto Kern Above feature

Kerning requires QuarkXPress to look at every pair of letters to see whether there are special kerning values specified within the font. QuarkXPress offers the Auto Kern Above feature, which you enable through the Character pane of the Preferences dialog box (Edit ➪ Preferences ➪ Preferences, or Option+Shift+⌘+Y or Ctrl+Alt+Shift+Y), as shown in Figure 15-17. This option tells QuarkXPress to stop kerning when text reaches a certain size. Any text at or below the size you specify is not kerned.

Preferences

	Superscript	Subscript
Application	Offset: 33%	Offset: 33%
Display		
Interactive	VScale: 100%	VScale: 100%
Save		
XTensions Manager	HScale: 100%	HScale: 100%
File List		
Browsers	Small Caps	Superior
PDF		
StreetPost	VScale: 75%	VScale: 50%
Document		
General	HScale: 75%	HScale: 50%
Measurements		
Paragraph	☐ Ligatures	
Character	Break Above: 1 ☐ Not "ffi" or "ffl"	
Tools		
Trapping	☑ Auto Kern Above: 4 pt ☐ Standard Em Space	
Layer	Flex Space Width: 50% ☑ Accents for All Caps	

[Cancel]   [OK]

Figure 15-17: The Auto Kern Above controls in the Character pane.

The cut-off size you choose for Auto Kern Above is both a personal choice based on aesthetic judgment and a technical choice based on the output device. The relatively low resolution on a 300-dpi laser printer limits how fine you can adjust spacing between characters. But on a 1270– or 2540-dpi imagesetter, there is practically no limit to how much control you have over spacing, so you should take advantage of it.

A rule of thumb is to set Auto Kern Above to between 8 and 12 points. It makes sense to set Auto Kern Above to your basic body text size, and for most documents, basic body text size falls between 8 and 12 points. If your base text is 9 points, set Auto Kern Above to 9 points. However, use a small value (8 or 9) for any text you output to a 600-dpi or finer device, regardless of the size of your body text.

On the CD-ROM You can see the kerning pairs specified within a font using the font manager, Font Reserve. A full-functioning demo copy of Font Reserve, limited to 100 font files, is included on the CD that comes with this book.

Kerning character pairs on-the-fly

You may occasionally want to manually kern specific letter pairs. For example, your document may incorporate typefaces you use so rarely that it's not worthwhile to modify the kerning table. QuarkXPress lets you modify kerning on-the-fly for any letter pairs you select. Put your text cursor between the two letters. You have three ways to change the kerning values:

✦ **The fastest way to change kerning values, especially when you want to experiment, is to use the keyboard shortcuts.** Press Shift+⌘+} or Ctrl+Shift+} to increase kerning to the nearest ¹/₂₀ em (10 units); press Shift+⌘+{ or Ctrl+Shift +{ to decrease it to the nearest ¹/₂₀ em. Pressing Option+Shift+⌘+} or Ctrl+Alt+Shift+} increases kerning by ¹/₂₀₀ em (1 unit); pressing Shift+Option+⌘+{ or Ctrl+Alt+Shift+{ decreases it by ¹/₂₀₀ em.

✦ **The Measurements palette also provides a Kerning field, shown highlighted in Figure 15-18.** You can highlight the value in the field and enter a new value to the nearest ¹⁄₂₀ em (10 units). Or click the left arrow to decrease the kerning value by 10; click the right arrow to increase the kerning value by 10. To make the arrows work in multiples of 1 unit instead of 10, press the Option or Alt key while clicking them.

Figure 15-18: The Kerning field and arrows in the Measurements palette.

✦ **If you're setting other character attributes, you can use the Kern Amount field in the Character Attributes dialog box (Style ⇨ Character, Shift+⌘+D or Ctrl+Shift+D, or Style ⇨ Track).** Note that if text is highlighted, this field is called Track Amount and controls the space between all highlighted characters.

Removing manual kerning

If you get carried away with kerning text manually, you can remove all the kerning from within highlighted text in one step. To do this, highlight the text and choose Utilities ⇨ Remove Manual Kerning. If you don't see this command, make sure the Type Tricks XTension (included with QuarkXPress 5) is running by choosing Utilities ⇨ XTensions Manager).

Editing kerning tables

The kerning table for a font may not match your preferences for some letter pairs. In some cases, the table may not include kerning information for certain letter pairs that cause you trouble. QuarkXPress includes a function that lets you edit kerning information for any TrueType or Type 1 PostScript typeface. It appears under the Utilities menu as Kerning Edit. You can modify existing settings, add new pairs, or remove existing pairs.

Note   If you don't have a Kerning Edit option in your Utilities menu, it probably means you don't have the Kern/Track Editor XTension installed. Use the XTensions Manager (Utilities ⇨ XTensions Manager) to activate the XTension, quit QuarkXPress, and relaunch QuarkXPress.

Figure 15-19 shows the Kerning Table Editor. Predefined kerning values are displayed in the Kerning Pairs list, through which you can scroll to select pairs whose values you want to change. You can delete kerning pairs by highlighting them in the Kerning Pairs list in the dialog box and clicking the Delete button. Deleting a kerning pair is the same as setting its kerning value to zero.

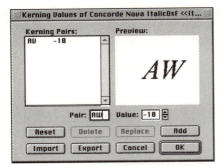

Figure 15-19: The Kerning Table Editor lets you adjust and add kerning pairs in fonts while in use in QuarkXPress.

Deleting, adding, or changing a kerning pair in the Edit Kerning Table dialog box doesn't make any changes to your font file itself; it just changes the way that pair of letters works in QuarkXPress.

STEPS: Adding kerning pairs

1. Activate the font whose kerning table you want to edit.

2. Choose Utilities ➪ Kerning Edit.

3. In the Edit Kerning Table dialog box, enter the two letters at the Pair prompt.

4. Enter the kerning value at the Value prompt. As with tracking, the unit of measurement is $\frac{1}{200}$ of an em, or roughly 0.5 percent of the current point size. Negative values decrease space between the letters; positive numbers add space. (Clicking the Reset button resets all kerning values to those stored in the font file. Any kerning pairs you've added are deleted. Import and Export buttons let you import kerning values from another file or export current ones to a new file.)

5. If you're modifying existing kerning values, select Replace; if you're adding a kerning pair, the button will be labeled Add.

6. To save changes, click OK. To cancel changes, select Cancel. (The difference between Reset and Cancel is that Reset resets all kerning pairs to the font's default and leaves you in the dialog box to make other changes, while Cancel closes the dialog box and returns you to the Edit Kerning Table dialog box.)

The Kern to Space feature

QuarkXPress also includes a Kern to Space feature. This lets you use an en space as one of the characters in a kerning pair. This kern-to-space feature comes in handy when you want to tighten the space between two items. These pairs (a character and an en space) are used just like other kerning pairs. To set up a kern-to-space pair using the Kern/Track Editor, first enter the space (Option+Space on the Mac and Ctrl+Shift+6 in Windows) into the Pair field.

Tip   The Kerning Table Editor treats each variation of a typeface — such as plain, bold, italic, and bold italic — separately, so be sure to make kerning adjustments in all faces of the typefaces you alter. And keep in mind that the appropriate kerning values are different for each face because characters are shaped differently in each face.

Enabling ligatures

In QuarkXPress for Mac, you can enable ligatures, a feature that combines the character pairs of *fi* and *fl* into a single character (fi and fl) that is available in most Mac fonts. Although this feature actually involves special characters, it does have an impact on spacing, since there is no space between the letters in ligatures. Ligatures lend a professional look to typography, so in a Mac-only environment, you should use them.

To enable this feature on the Mac, check Ligatures in the Character pane of the Preferences dialog box (Edit ➪ Preferences ➪ Preferences, or Option+Shift+⌘+Y or Ctrl+Alt+Shift+Y). The value you enter in the Break Above field is the tracking value above which you will not get ligatures. (Note that kerning always breaks ligatures.) Check Not "ffi" and "ffl" to prevent ligatures in words such as *ruffian* and *ruffle*, because in these cases ligatures may look odd.

QuarkXPress for Windows doesn't support ligatures. If they're included in a font, you can enter them as special characters, but they will trigger many spell check errors.

Changing kerning in one document only

QuarkXPress associates an edited kerning table with the document that was active when you invoked the Kerning Editor. This means that if you give your QuarkXPress document to a service bureau to output to negatives on an imagesetter, your kerning changes remain intact. If you want kerning changes to affect all documents, invoke the kerning editor with no document selected. Any future document uses the new settings.

When you make changes in the kerning table editor, they apply not only to the document you're currently working with, but to every document you create after you make the changes. If you want your kerning table changes to apply to one document only, close the document after you make the changes, then open the Edit Kerning Table dialog box for that font and click Reset.

Summary

Character attributes consist of formatting that you can apply on a character-by-character basis. These include options such as font, size, type style, and scaling. (Options such as indents and tabs affect entire paragraphs and are therefore considered to be paragraph attributes.) To apply character attributes, highlight text with the Content tool. Or you can click in text to specify attributes for the next character you type. You then apply attributes using the following methods:

✦ The Character Attributes dialog box (Style ➪ Character, or Shift+⌘+D or Ctrl+Shift+D) consolidates all the possible options for formatting characters.

✦ The Measurements palette (View ➪ Show Measurements, or F9) supplies controls in the lower-right corner for the most popular character attributes.

✦ Keyboard shortcuts exist for quickly applying or experimenting with most character attributes.

If you use a specific combination of character attributes often, you can save it as a character style sheet (Edit ➪ Style Sheets, or Shift+F11).

✦   ✦   ✦

Setting Paragraph Attributes

Paragraph attributes are formatting options that apply to an entire paragraph — from the first character to the last character followed by the paragraph symbol (¶). Most paragraph attributes are related to the spacing of text, including indents, alignment, and leading. QuarkXPress provides high-end controls to ensure that your text is spaced exactly the way you want it to be. Because character attributes and paragraph attributes are interrelated — for example, the amount of leading you specify depends on the typeface and size you use — you'll usually set both at close to the same time.

Accessing Paragraph Attributes

To apply paragraph attributes, all you need to do is click in a paragraph with the Content tool (the hand on the Tool palette) to select it. There is no need to highlight any or all of the text in the paragraph. If you want to apply attributes to a range of paragraphs, you can highlight any portion of all the paragraphs you want to select. All the paragraph attributes available in QuarkXPress are consolidated in the panes of the Paragraph Attributes dialog box (Style ⇨ Formats, or Shift+⌘+F or Ctrl+Shift+F) In this chapter, we discuss the controls in the Formats tab, shown in Figure 16-1.

For experimentation, QuarkXPress does provide Measurements palette icons and keyboard shortcuts for alignment and leading, which are discussed later in this chapter.

Copying paragraph attributes

Any time you put some effort into setting paragraph attributes — for example, setting an *outdent* (hanging indent) or changing a combination of Leading, Space Before, and Alignment — you can easily copy those attributes to other paragraphs in the same story. To do this, select the paragraphs you want to copy the new formatting to (click in one paragraph or highlight several). Then press Option+Shift or Alt+Shift while you click in the paragraph with the formatting that you like. The selected paragraphs will take on the paragraph attributes (not the character attributes) of the paragraph you click in.

Although not as efficient as using paragraph style sheets, this technique does save you time in resetting the same attributes.

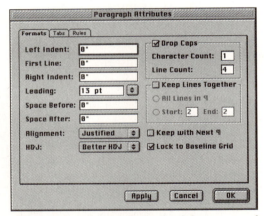

Figure 16-1: The Formats tab of the Paragraph Attributes dialog box provides most of the basic formatting options for paragraphs.

Cross-Reference This chapter covers the basic paragraph formatting options. Specifying hyphenation settings and using a baseline grid are discussed in Chapter 17, tabs are discussed in Chapter 19, and rules are discussed in Chapter 23.

Tip If you find yourself applying the same combination of paragraph attributes over and over again, you can save the combination as a paragraph style sheet. (See Chapter 32 for more information.)

Creating Indents

Designers use indents to break up a document's solid left margin. These breaks give the reader variances to notice — variances that signify a change in elements.

It's less important to break up the right margin of a document because people read from left to right and thus pay more attention to the left margin. In languages that are read from right to left, such as Farsi, Hebrew, and Arabic, the opposite is true.

You can indent text other than body text. For example, you might indent bylines or credit lines. You can indent headlines, so that the kickers overhang a little bit, or you can indent subheads. As long as you don't go overboard and end up with a seesaw pattern, using indents on a variety of elements helps keep a page visually active, even when it's filled primarily with text.

 Note

When you set indents in QuarkXPress, the selected paragraphs are indented from any Text Inset specified for the edges of the text box (Item ➪ Modify, or ⌘+M or Ctrl+M, then select the Text tab). Remember that Text Inset does not affect the inner edges of columns within a text box.

Setting first-line indents

The most basic use of an indent is to offset the first line in a paragraph. This is particularly true in multicolumn publications that use first-line indents rather than blank lines between paragraphs to indicate the start of a new paragraph.

To specify a first-line indent, enter a value in the First Line field in the Formats tab of the Paragraph Attributes dialog box (Style ➪ Formats, or Shift+⌘+F or Ctrl+Shift+F), as shown in Figure 16-2. *Remember:* Even if the document's measurement system is inches, you can enter values in points or picas by following the value with *pt* or *p*, respectively.

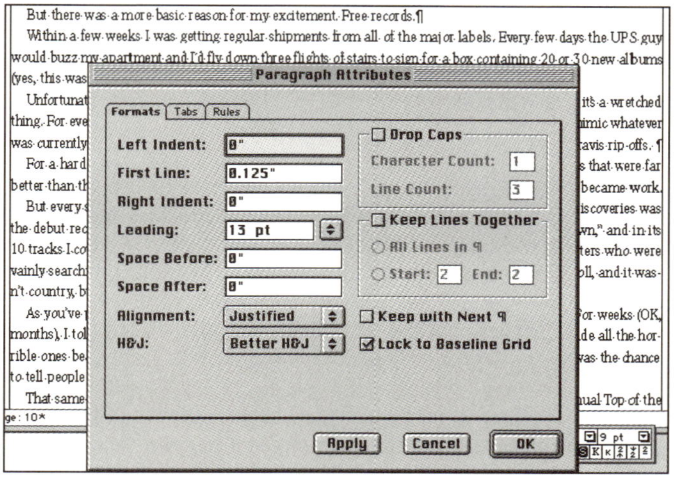

Figure 16-2: An indented paragraph, and its indent value specified in the First Line field of the Formats tab.

Make sure your first-line indents aren't too small. Usually, indents should be between one and two ems in size. An em is as wide as your current point size, so if text is 9 points, the first-line indent should be between 9 and 18 points. If columns are thin (more than three columns to a standard page), make indents closer to 9 points than 18 points. This avoids gaping indents or awkward justification in the first line of a paragraph.

Block indenting

Another form of indenting is called *block indenting*. In a block indent, the entire paragraph is indented from the left margin, right margin, or both. A typical use of block indenting — usually from the left, but sometimes also from the right — is to indicate extended quotations. Typically, these are also set in a smaller type size. Use the Left Indent and Right Indent fields of the Formats pane in the Paragraph Attributes dialog box to set block indents (Style ➪ Formats, Shift+⌘+F or Ctrl+Shift+F).

If you indent several elements in the same document, use only a few different levels of indentation — two or three at most. For example, it works well to use the same amount of indentation on bylines and kickers, even if the indentation amount differs from the amount used for the first line of body-text paragraphs. If you have too many levels of indentation, there is no pattern to help guide the reader's eye, and the resulting document appears jumbled.

Setting outdents

An *outdent,* also called an *extent* or a *hanging indent,* serves the same function as a first-line indent but moves the first line out into the margin, instead of indenting it (see Figure 16-3). It usually is reserved for bulleted lists, because it takes up space that otherwise might be used for text. Some people use outdents for sidebars, to provide a visual counterpoint to standard text; this works if the sidebars are not too long.

To create an outdent, first decide how much to indent the body of the text (for example, 0.25"), then enter that value in the Left Indent field in the Formats tab of the Paragraph Attributes dialog box (Style ➪ Formats, or Shift+⌘+F or Ctrl+Shift+F). Then enter the negative of that same value (–0.25") in the First Line field. Finally, you will need to use the Tabs pane in the Paragraph Attributes dialog box to set a tab at that same location: 0.25". To use this setup, enter a bullet character, followed by a tab, then start typing.

QuarkXPress provides a keyboard command for instant outdents. It's called the Indent Here character, and text will hang to the right of wherever you enter it. To enter an Indent Here character, press ⌘+\ or Ctrl+\. When invisibles are showing (View ➪ Show Invisibles, or ⌘+I or Ctrl+I), the Indent Here character looks like a little stick.

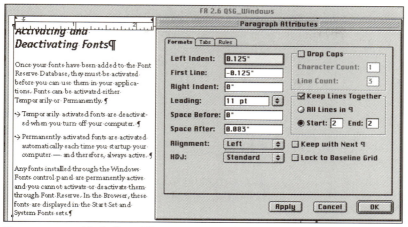

Figure 16-3: This bulleted list uses an outdent, or hanging indent, to clearly display all the text.

Specifying Leading

In traditional typesetting, *leading* (pronounced *led-ing*) is the space between lines of type. It's named for the thin strips of lead that printers used to use to separate metal type in early printing presses. Although tracking, kerning, and word spacing let you establish good typographic color horizontally, leading lets you do the same vertically.

Where to enter leading

Leading varies based on several elements: column width, type size, whether text is justified or ragged, and the total amount of text. Expressed in points, by default the leading value you specify is the amount of space placed between baselines of text. You can specify leading for selected paragraphs in the following ways:

- ✦ Enter a point value in the Leading field in the Formats tab of the Paragraph Attributes dialog box (Style ⇨ Leading, or Shift+⌘+E or Ctrl+Shift+E).

- ✦ Enter a point value in the Leading field of the Measurements palette (View ⇨ Show Measurements, or F9), as shown in Figure 16-4.

- ✦ Click the arrows next to the Leading field on the Measurements palette. Click the up arrow to increase leading by 1 point; click the down arrow to decrease it by 1 point. Press the Option or Alt key to change leading in 0.1-point increments.

- ✦ Use the following keyboard shortcuts: To increase leading by 1 point, press Shift+⌘+" or Ctrl+Shift+"; to increase leading by 0.01 point, add the Option or Alt key. To decrease leading by 1 point, press Shift+⌘+: or Ctrl+Shift+;; to decrease leading by 0.01 point, add the Option or Alt key.

Design tips for leading

Entering a leading value is easy—the challenge is entering a value that ends up with spacing that is pleasing to the eye and improves readability. Several factors help determine leading values:

✦ **Column width:** The width of a column is the most important factor affecting good leading. The wider the column, the more space you need between lines to keep the reader's eye from accidentally jumping to a different line. This is the reason why books have noticeable space between lines, whereas newspapers and magazines, which use thin columns, have very little.

✦ **Text justification:** A related concern is whether type is justified or ragged-right. Justified text usually requires more leading than nonjustified text because the ragged margin gives the eye a distinct anchor point for each line.

✦ **Leading:** For text set in multiple columns, we recommend that you set leading at the current point size plus 2 points for text 9 points and larger. For example, if the point size of the text is 12 points, set leading at 14. For text 8 points and smaller, use the current point size plus 1 point; 7-point type would get 8-point leading. This rule of thumb fluctuates somewhat according to column width. Add another 1 point or 0.5 point, respectively, if your column width is greater than 16 picas but less than 27 picas; add at least 2 more points if your text is wider than 27 picas.

Small changes in leading and point size alter the feeling of text, as you can see in the figure. This creative use of leading lets you subtly but effectively differentiate between sections or elements without resorting to extreme uses of typefaces or layout variations. Even though the typeface and justification are the same, the text on the left—set at 11 points with 16-point leading—has a very different texture than the text on the right, set at 11 points with 23-point leading.

Getting paid to find Denver's very best martinis, shoe stores, or bike trails may sound like a sweet gig, but, just like those free records, it carries a very real price. Every year at this time, our office becomes a weird blend of the Consumer Reports lab and a frat party.

Getting paid to find Denver's very best martinis, shoe stores, or bike trails may sound like a sweet gig, but, just like those free records, it carries a very real price. Every year at this time, our office becomes a weird blend of the Consumer Reports lab and a frat party.

Figure 16-4: The Leading field in the Measurements palette.

How leading values work

QuarkXPress provides an easy method for determining leading in body text: auto leading. You can change this to additive leading or absolute leading, depending on your needs. The way that leading is measured is controlled by a preference setting.

Auto leading

QuarkXPress includes an automatic leading option (use 0 or auto for the leading value), which sets leading at 120 percent of type size. This is fine for 10-point type, because it results in 12-point leading. But for 9-point type, it results in 10.8-point leading, which is an awkward size on which to base a layout grid. And at larger type sizes, leading becomes too large; for example, 43.2-point leading is set for 36-point text.

Note By default, the Normal paragraph style sheet specifies auto leading. If you prefer additive leading or absolute, you can edit Normal through the Style Sheets dialog box (Edit ⇨ Style Sheets, or Shift+F11).

Additive leading

As an alternative to auto leading, you can use additive leading. With additive leading, you specify leading to be a certain number of points more than the current type size, no matter what that size may be. Enter +2, for example, for leading 2 points more than the current type size. This additive leading option also ensures that any line with larger-than-normal type (such as a drop cap) won't overprint other lines.

Absolute leading

If you simply enter a value in the Leading field (without a plus sign to indicate additive leading and without the word *auto*), that is an absolute leading value. QuarkXPress will use the absolute leading value to measure the amount of space between lines regardless of type sizes on the line.

Setting preferences for leading

Several preferences control how leading works in QuarkXPress. The Paragraph pane of the Preferences dialog box (Edit ⇨ Preferences ⇨ Preferences, or Ctrl+Shift+Alt+Y or Option+Shift+⌘+Y) provides the following controls, shown in Figure 16-5:

✦ **Auto Leading:** The default value, 20 percent, means that QuarkXPress calculates auto leading by adding 20 percent of the current type size to the type size (for example, 10-point type will have 12-point leading because 2 is 20 percent of 10). You can enter a value between 0 and 100 percent in this field.

✦ **Maintain Leading:** Checked by default, this option ensures that leading is maintained even when items such as pull-quotes or graphics abut text, forcing text to wrap around them. When unchecked, text flows immediately below the item.

✦ **Mode:** This legacy feature, left over from an early version of QuarkXPress, controls how leading is measured. Typesetting, the default, measures leading from baseline to baseline. The only reason to switch to Word Processing, which measures leading from the ascent of one line to the ascent of the next line, is if you're trying to match the leading in a document from a version of QuarkXPress prior to 3.0.

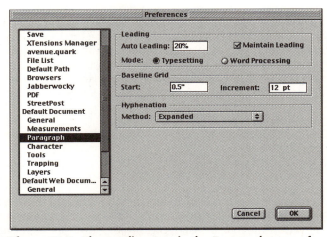

Figure 16-5: The Leading area in the Paragraph pane of the Preferences dialog box.

Tip   If you want leading settings to affect all future documents, open the Paragraph pane of the Preferences dialog box with no document open.

An additive and auto-leading drawback

Additive and automatic leading have a drawback: They are based on the highest and lowest character in a line, not on the body text's normal position. So if you mix type sizes on a line or if you use superscripts (perhaps for footnotes), subscripts, or special text or symbols that extend beyond the body text's height or depth, you get uneven leading. This is because some lines have more leading than others to accommodate the outsized or outpositioned characters.

If you can't alter your text so that none of it extends beyond the body text range, don't use these options. Instead, use absolute leading for all paragraphs and in all paragraph style sheets.

Controlling Space between Paragraphs

If you need space between body paragraphs (to indicate new paragraphs rather than indents) or space above one-line paragraphs such as subheads, you can enter values in the Space Before and/or Space After fields in the Formats pane of the Paragraph Attributes dialog box (Style ➪ Formats, or Shift+⌘+F or Ctrl+Shift+F), as shown in Figure 16-6. A good starting place for space between paragraphs is half the leading value (so if you're leading is 12 points, try 6 points between paragraphs).

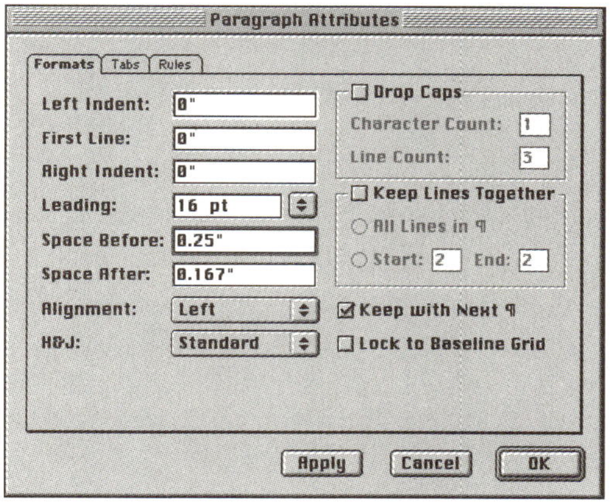

Figure 16-6: The Space Before and Space After fields in the Formats pane of the Paragraph Attributes dialog box.

Many users are tempted to place space between paragraphs by simply hitting Return as they would on a typewriter. But Space Before/After is preferable because:

✦ **When the last line of a paragraph reaches the bottom of a column or box, the Space After value is ignored; likewise, when the first line of a paragraph starts at the top of a column or box, the Space Before value is ignored.** If you use paragraph returns to add space, they can leave undesirable space at the bottom and top of columns. And when text reflows, they need to be added and removed.

✦ **The amount of space added by a paragraph return is equal to the size applied to the return character.** This size can vary depending on the size of surrounding text when you hit Return. And if you want to change the space between paragraphs, you're stuck highlighting each Return and changing its size.

Because the space between two paragraphs is equal to the space after the first paragraph and the space before the second paragraph, controlling spacing can be confusing. Because of this, many typesetters prefer to stick with setting Space Above only.

Aligning Paragraphs

Alignment controls how the lines in selected paragraphs are positioned horizontally within a box or column. Most of the options are familiar: Left (ragged right), Centered, Right (ragged left), and Justified. An additional option, Forced, justifies the last line of text (no matter how bad it looks). As with indents, text is aligned within any Text Inset specified for the outer edges of a text box in the Text pane of the Modify dialog box (Item ⇨ Modify, or ⌘+M or Ctrl+M).

Figure 16-7 shows the five types of alignment in QuarkXPress, which you can set in the following ways:

✦ Choose an option from the Alignment menu in the Formats tab of the Paragraph Attributes dialog box (Style ⇨ Formats, or Shift+⌘+F or Ctrl+Shift+F).

✦ Choose an option from the Alignment submenu of the Style menu.

✦ Click one of the Alignment icons on the Measurements palette (View ⇨ Show Measurements, F9), as shown in Figure 16-8.

✦ Press a keyboard shortcut: Left: Shift+⌘+L or Ctrl+Shift+L, Centered: Shift+⌘+C or Ctrl+Shift+C, Right: Shift+⌘+R or Ctrl+Shift+R, Justified: Shift+⌘+J or Ctrl+Shift+, and Forced: Option+Shift+⌘+J or Ctrl+Alt+Shift+J.

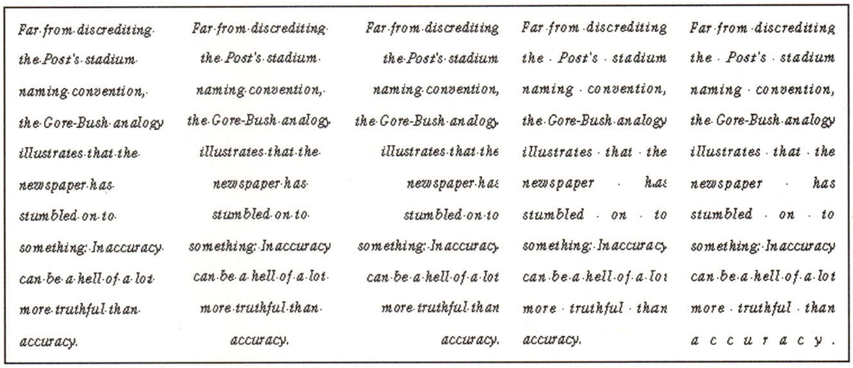

Figure 16-7: The five different options for paragraph alignment: Left, Centered, Right, Justified, and Forced.

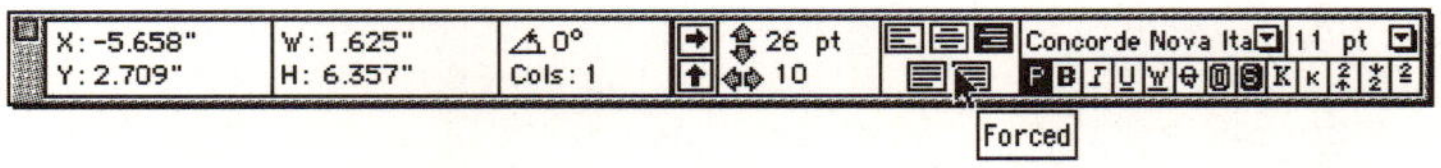

Figure 16-8: The Alignment buttons on the Measurements palette let you quickly try other alignments.

Keeping Lines and Paragraphs Together

The Formats tab of the Paragraph Attributes dialog box (Style ➪ Formats, or Shift+⌘+F or Ctrl+Shift+F) provides two automatic methods for improving how text flows from box to box and column to column. Keep Lines Together is designed to prevent *orphans* (the first line of a paragraph by its lonesome at the bottom of a column or the last line of a paragraph at the top of a column). Keep with Next Paragraph helps heads and subheads flow with their related text. These options are shown in Figure 16-9.

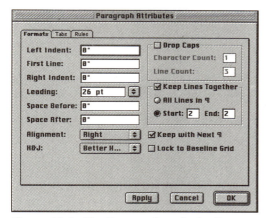

Figure 16-9: The Keep options in the Formats pane of the Paragraph Attributes dialog box.

Keep Lines Together

Generally, you will check this option for paragraphs of body text (or in your paragraph style sheet for body text) to keep them from separating undesirably at the bottom of columns. When a paragraph approaches the bottom of a column, it checks your settings to see whether and how it can break:

✦ If you want the entire paragraph to always stay together, click All Lines in ¶.

✦ If you want the paragraph to be able to break but not leave behind any orphans, click Start/End. Enter the number of lines that must remain at the bottom of a column in the Start field and the number of lines that can move to the top of a column in the End field.

Note

If you use the default settings for Start and End, 2 and 2, at least two lines must remain at the bottom of a column and at least two lines must travel to the top of the next. If the paragraph has only three lines, the entire paragraph is bumped to the next column.

Keep with Next ¶

If you want to keep one paragraph with the next — for example, to keep a subhead with the paragraph following it or to keep bulleted text together — you can check Keep with Next ¶ for a paragraph. Keep with Next ¶, which is ideal for Head and Subhead style sheets, has the effect of gluing one paragraph to the next so they always flow together.

Caution Do not overuse the Keep with Next ¶ feature. If you glue all the paragraphs in a multipage document together, for example, you end up with text overflow, because all the paragraphs are trying to stay with the next paragraph.

Summary

To apply paragraph attributes, first you need to click in a paragraph with the Content tool to select it. You can also highlight multiple paragraphs. You then apply paragraph attributes using the Formats tab of the Paragraph Attributes dialog box (Style ➪ Formats, or Shift+⌘+F or Ctrl+Shift+F). Most of the options in the Formats tab control the spacing of text:

✦ Indents and alignment control the placement of text within a column or box.

✦ Leading controls the amount of space between lines in paragraphs.

✦ Space Before and Space After values control the amount of space between paragraphs.

✦ The Keep Lines Together option prevents orphans, and the Keep with Next Paragraph helps subheads stay with related paragraphs and keeps bulleted lists together.

✦   ✦   ✦

Fine-Tuning Spacing

◆ ◆ ◆ ◆

In This Chapter

Hyphenating and
justifying text

Using special spaces

Implementing a
baseline grid

Checking lines

Fitting copy

◆ ◆ ◆ ◆

Often, you'll spot the primary differences between a
document published in a word processor and
QuarkXPress in the spacing. The precise space between
characters, words, lines, and paragraphs and the careful
alignment of text and other items on the page is a clear
indication. In Chapters 15 and 16, we cover kerning, tracking,
space before/space after, and leading—the basic methods for
character, line, and paragraph spacing. In this chapter, we
look at how to carefully control the spacing in hyphenated
text, how to clean up issues with hyphenation and spacing,
how to align text across columns using a baseline grid, and
how to adjust spacing to fit copy.

Hyphenating and Justifying Text

The spacing within a paragraph is helped immensely by
two traditional tools: hyphenation and justification. In
QuarkXPress, you specify hyphenation and justification in
concert with each other, then save them in sets called *H&J
sets* (short for—you guessed it—*hyphenation and justification
sets*). H&J sets help fit text within a certain space, while letting
the copy maintain an attractive appearance. Balancing these
paragraph spacing attributes is critical to good overall
document design and is essential if you want to keep your
readers interested. Figure 17-1 shows the difference between
using the QuarkXPress default H&J set (called *Standard*) and
a custom H&J set on the same paragraphs.

You set up H&J sets using the Edit ➪ H&Js command. Then
you apply them on a paragraph-by-paragraph basis, using the
Style ➪ Formats command. Both processes are explained in
full in this section.

Remarkably, Simmons found Victorian Denver and Bigelow's vision of Cuba an easy match, right down to the color palette. "It was amazing," he says. "We were looking for colors for the outside – bright and tropical, but not too cute. We couldn't find anything that was just right until we got out Historic Denver's color deck, and that's where we found the turquoise with yellow and white trim we chose. Standard Victorian, but also absolutely perfect for this restaurant."

Remarkably, Simmons found Victorian Denver and Bigelow's vision of Cuba an easy match, right down to the color palette. "It was amazing," he says. "We were looking for colors for the outside – bright and tropical, but not too cute. We couldn't find anything that was just right until we got out Historic Denver's color deck, and that's where we found the turquoise with yellow and white trim we chose. Standard Victorian, but also absolutely perfect for this restaurant."

Figure 17-1: The Standard H&J set, at left, specifies a six-letter minimum for hyphenated words, with three letters before the hyphen and two letters after. The H&J set designed for these narrow columns specifies a four-letter minimum for hyphenated words, with two letters before the hyphen and two letters after.

Creating H&J sets

The H&Js dialog box (Edit ➪ H&J, or Option+⌘+H or Ctrl+Alt+H), shown in Figure 17-2, lets you create H&J sets, edit H&J sets, and share them with other documents. You can create as many H&J sets as you need and edit them as necessary.

Figure 17-2: The H&Js dialog box lets you create H&J sets.

Tip If you create H&J sets with no documents open, the H&J sets become program defaults and are included with all new documents. If you create H&J sets with a document open, they're saved only with that document.

STEPS: Creating an H&J Set

1. Choose Edit ➪ H&Js.

2. Click New. (Or click Edit to modify an existing H&J set; don't be afraid to modify the default H&J set, Standard, if it doesn't suit you.)

3. In the Name field, enter a name that describes either the H&J set's characteristics or its use, as shown in Figure 17-3. It's common to see H&J sets named such things as *Body Text* or *No Hyphens*.

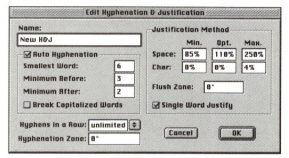

Figure 17-3: Use the Edit Hyphenation & Justification dialog box to create custom settings for hyphenating and spacing text.

4. Use the left side of the Edit Hyphenation & Justification dialog box to specify how text hyphenates. Use the right side to specify how text is spaced, especially when justified. You may need to consult the following sections to determine how to set these options.

5. Click OK to create the H&J set. If you need to create additional H&J sets, click New again.

6. Click Save to save changes made in the H&Js dialog box.

Determining hyphenation settings

Hyphenation settings determine the raggedness of *unjustified text* (text that is left-aligned, right-aligned, or centered) and the size of gaps in *justified text* (text that is aligned with both the left and right margins of a column). By varying the hyphenation settings, you can achieve a significantly different appearance, as illustrated in Figure 17-4.

The column at left has no hyphenation and therefore takes up the most space. It also has the most ragged right edge. In the middle column, hyphenation is on, but Hyphenate Capitalized Words is unchecked. Therefore the word *Westword* can't break in the second-to-last line. In the column at right, hyphenation is on and Hyphenate Capitalized Words is checked; you'll notice this column has the smoothest right edge.

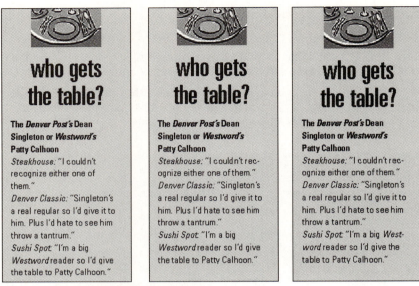

Figure 17-4: Variations in hyphenation.

Enabling hyphenation

To turn on hyphenation for the H&J set, check the Auto Hyphenation box in the Edit Hyphenation & Justification dialog box, shown in Figure 17-5. If you want to allow hyphenation in words that start with a capital letter also, check Break Capitalized Words. See the sidebar "Hyphenating capitalized words" to determine if this setting will work for your text.

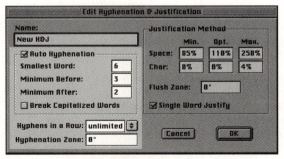

Figure 17-5: The hyphenation controls are on the left side of the Edit Hyphenation & Justification dialog box.

Setting hyphenation parameters

How QuarkXPress hyphenates is determined by word hyphenation parameters. There are three such parameters, and they're set in the Edit Hyphenation & Justification dialog box:

✦ **Smallest Word:** This determines how long a word must be before QuarkXPress hyphenates it. The default of six letters is a reasonable default, although five is acceptable as well. In narrow columns, you might even use four so you can hyphenate words such as *only*.

✦ **Minimum Before:** This determines how many characters must precede a hyphen in a hyphenated word. The default of three characters is a typical typographer's threshold, but some go with two.

✦ **Minimum After:** This sets the number of characters that must follow a hyphen in a hyphenated word. The default setting of two characters is common for newspapers and is most often seen in words ending in *-ed*, such as *blanket-ed*.

Hyphenating capitalized words

The Break Capitalized Words check box in the Edit Hyphenation & Justification dialog box controls whether QuarkXPress should hyphenate capitalized words. How do you decide? Consider the following:

✦ **If you check Break Capitalized Words, this lets the program hyphenate both proper nouns and the first word in a sentence.** Although there's generally nothing wrong with hyphenating the first word in a sentence, you may have an editorial policy against hyphenating proper nouns.

✦ **Most hyphenation dictionaries make mistakes when hyphenating proper nouns (because the letter patterns can be unfamiliar).** Depending on how many proper names you're dealing with, you might want to uncheck this feature or you might add the names to the hyphenation exceptions dictionary.

✦ **If your text frequently refers to people and places (think *People* magazine), and you don't allow hyphenation in capitalized words, you can get an abundance of awkward spacing.**

✦ **Spacing problems caused by not hyphenating capitalized words will be much more apparent in justified text.**

✦ **In narrow, justified columns, hyphenating capitalized words is almost a must.** In wide columns, you may not notice either way.

✦ **You don't have to treat the hyphenation of capitalized words the same way throughout a document.** For example, if one article has four columns and covers current events, you might want to check Break Capitalized Words in the H&J set you use. If another article has two columns and covers general topics, you might want to uncheck Break Capitalized Words.

Using Minimum Before and Minimum After

Consider changing the Minimum Before setting to 2 if you have narrow columns or large text. Although many typographers object to two-letter hyphenation — as in *ab-dicate* or *ra-dar* — it often looks better than text with large gaps caused by the reluctance to hyphenate such words. Hyphenation also makes sense for many words that use two-letter prefixes such as *in-*, *re-*, and *co-*.

Although we advocate two-letter hyphenation at the beginning of a word, we prefer three-letter hyphenation at the end. Except for words ending in *-ed* and sometimes *-al,* most words don't lend themselves to two-letter hyphenation at the end of the word. Part of this is functional — it's easy for readers to lose two letters beginning a line. We prefer two-letter hyphenations at the end of a word only when the alternative is awkward spacing. As with all typography, this ultimately is a personal or house style choice.

Regardless of the two– versus three-letter debate, words broken using minimum settings of 1 look awful. They also go against reader expectations because the norm is to have several letters after a hyphen. Never use a minimum setting of 1 for Minimum Before. If you do, you get hyphenations such as *A-sia*, *a-typical*, and *u-niform* that simply look terrible in print. They also don't provide enough context for the reader to anticipate the rest of the word. Likewise, never use a minimum of 1 for Minimum After because you get hyphenations such as *radi-o*.

Tip

The sum of the Minimum Before and the Minimum After should be less than or equal to the Smallest Word. For example, if you have a Minimum Before of three and a Minimum After of three (which equals six), but your Smallest Word is five, QuarkXPress cannot break five-letter words because it cannot leave three letters before the hyphen and carry over three letters after the hyphen.

Limiting consecutive hyphens

Text can be hard to read when it contains too many hyphens in a row. The eye gets confused about which line it's on because it loses track of which hyphen represents which line. You can avoid having an excessive number of hyphens in a row by selecting a setting in the Hyphens In A Row field in the Edit Hyphenation & Justification dialog box (refer to Figure 17-5). The more hyphens you allow, the more easily QuarkXPress can break lines to avoid awkward gaps (in justified text) or awkward line endings (in nonjustified text). A good setting for Hyphens In A Row is 3 consecutive hyphens. This gives the eye enough context to keep lines in sequence. Avoid having fewer than two consecutive hyphens as your maximum, because that typically results in awkward spacing.

Tip

Some typesetters find that you can get better hyphenation with Unlimited. Even with unlimited hyphens in a row, you get surprisingly few lines ending in multiple hyphens, and you can easily clean those up manually.

Controlling the hyphenation zone

When text is not justified (that is, when it's set flush left or flush right), you still need to be concerned about the overall appearance of the text. It's a good idea to have some consistency in how lines of text end. Typographers call the uneven line endings the *rag,* and tend to manually modify the rag to give it a pleasing shape. This is done by retracking some lines or manually inserting hyphens. A pleasing shape is usually defined as one that undulates and has few consecutive lines of roughly the same width.

QuarkXPress lets you partially control the rag of nonjustified text through Hyphenation Zone control, found in the Edit Hyphenation & Justification dialog box. A setting of 0 tells QuarkXPress to hyphenate whenever it can. Any other setting specifies the range in which a hyphen can occur; this distance is measured from the right margin.

You won't often need this feature because QuarkXPress does a decent job of ragging text on its own. But if you do use it, a setting of no more than 20 percent of the column width usually works best. No matter which setting you use, expect to occasionally override QuarkXPress through manual hyphenation to make the rag match your preferences.

Determining justification settings

When you justify text (Style ➪ Alignment ➪ Justified or Forced), QuarkXPress needs to figure out — on a line-by-line basis — how much space to add and where to add it. You provide guidance in this process through the justification controls on the right side of the Edit Hyphenation & Justification dialog box, shown in Figure 17-6.

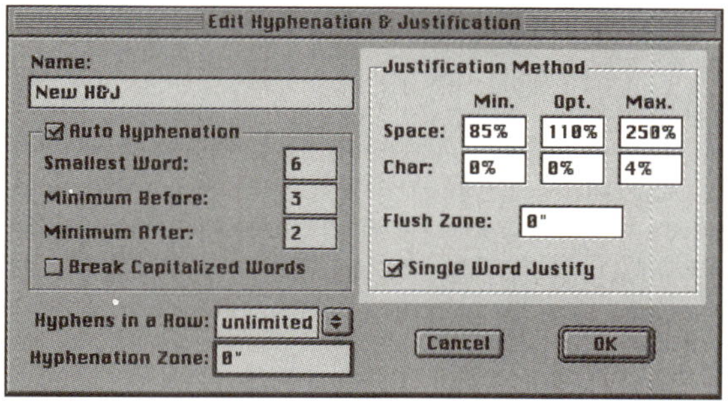

Figure 17-6: The justification controls are on the right side of the Edit Hyphenation & Justification dialog box.

Controlling space between words and characters

The Space and Char settings control how QuarkXPress adds space between words and characters to justify text. Space settings control word spacing; Char settings control letter spacing.

✦ The Min. (minimum) setting tells QuarkXPress the smallest amount of space allowed between words or characters (that is, how much it can squeeze text to make it fit in a justified line).

✦ The Opt. (optimum) setting defines the amount of space you want between words and characters, and QuarkXPress sets spacing as close to that setting as possible. Note that if text isn't justified (if it's left-aligned, right-aligned, or centered), QuarkXPress uses the optimum settings for all text.

✦ The Max. (maximum) setting sets the upper limit on space between words or characters (that is, how much it can stretch text to make it fit). QuarkXPress doesn't squeeze text more than the minimum settings allow, but it does exceed the maximum settings if it has no other choice.

Note You cannot set the optimum setting at less than the minimum or more than the maximum. If text is justified, QuarkXPress never places characters closer together than the minimum setting, but it may exceed the maximum setting if that's the only way to make the line fit.

Flush Zone

The Flush Zone setting, measured from the right margin, tells QuarkXPress when to take the text in the last line of a paragraph and force it to justify with both margins. (Normally, the last line of a justified paragraph is aligned to the left, unless you use Forced justification.) If text in the last line reaches the flush zone, it's justified; otherwise, it remains left-aligned.

We recommend that you don't use the Flush Zone feature. When the last line in a justified paragraph is left-aligned, it gives the reader a needed clue that the paragraph is complete.

Single Word Justify

This tells QuarkXPress it's okay to space out a word that is long enough to take up a single line — anywhere in a paragraph — if it's needed to justify that line. We recommend that you always turn on Single Word Justify, even though words that take up a full line are rare. When they do occur, having them left-aligned (which is what happens if this option is not selected) in a paragraph that is otherwise justified is confusing, because readers might misinterpret them as the end of the paragraph.

Working with preferred settings

Figure 17-7 compares paragraphs with two different word and character spacing options. The default settings are shown on the paragraph at left and our preferred settings are shown in action at right. We suggest 85 percent minimum, 100 percent optimum, and 150 percent maximum for word spacing; and –5 percent minimum, 0 percent optimum, and 10 percent maximum for letter spacing. We prefer minimum settings that are less than the optimum because it helps text fit more easily in narrow columns. These settings work well for most newsletters and magazines output on an imagesetter. Also, we've found that desktop-publishing programs tend to add more space than we prefer, so we typically tighten the word and letter spacing to compensate. At the same time, we usually leave the maximum word spacing at 150 percent.

STAPLETON'S REDEVELOPMENT CHALLENGE.

Federico Peña may have imagined a great city, but it was left to Wellington Webb to build it. For when the trucks lugged the last baggage cart out to DIA, Denver was left with 4,700 acres at Stapleton. What to do with all that land? Why not imagine a great city? Or at least a great new neighborhood.

Federico Peña may have imagined a great city, but it was left to Wellington Webb to build it. For when the trucks lugged the last baggage cart out to DIA, Denver was left with 4,700 acres at Stapleton. What to do with all that land? Why not imagine a great city? Or at least a great new neighborhood.

Figure 17-7: The default settings (in use at left) produce looser spacing than our preferred settings (used in the paragraph at right).

For material destined for final output on a 300-dpi laser printer, you may want to keep the defaults, because such laser printers have coarser resolution and thus cannot make some of the fine positioning adjustments our settings impose. In some cases, they move characters closer together than desired, even when the same settings work fine on a higher-resolution imagesetter.

Implementing H&J sets

After you've created H&J sets, you need to apply them to paragraphs (see Figure 17-8). To do this, you simply select the paragraphs and choose an option from the H&J menu in the Formats tab of the Paragraph Attributes dialog box (Style ⇨ Formats, or Shift+⌘+F or Ctrl+Shift+F). Any time you want to change a paragraph's hyphenation, simply choose another H&J for that paragraph.

About word spacing

Word spacing—the space between words—is another important contributor to the aesthetics of a document. Think about it: If the words in a sentence are too close to one another, comprehension may be affected because of the difficulty in telling where one word ends and another begins. If the words are too far apart, the reader might have a difficult time following the thought that's being conveyed.

Here's a design rule we like to follow: The wider the column, the more space you can add between words. This is why books tend to have more word spacing than magazines. Like all other typographic issues, there's a subjective component to picking good word spacing. Experiment to see what works best in your documents.

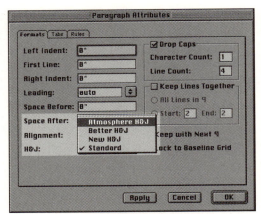

Figure 17-8: The H&J menu in the Formats tab of the Paragraph Attributes dialog box lets you apply your H&J sets to selected paragraphs.

Tip

The most consistent way to implement H&J settings is through paragraph style sheets that you apply to text. You might have one H&J for body text, bulleted text, and captions and then another H&J for subheads, for example. For more information about style sheets, see Chapter 32.

Cross-Reference

To share H&J sets among documents, use the File ➪ Append command or the Append button in the H&Js dialog box (Edit ➪ H&Js, or Option+⌘+H or Ctrl+Alt+H). For more information, see Chapter 31.

Using the Suggested Hyphenation feature

Sometimes, regardless of automatic hyphenation, you might want to manually change the hyphenation of a word to improve the look of a line break. To do this, you enter discretionary hyphens, as discussed in the "Inserting soft hyphens" sidebar. The problem with doing this is that it's hard to remember how to hyphenate every word properly.

If you need prompting, click the word in question, then choose Utilities ➪ Suggested Hyphenation (or press ⌘+H or Ctrl+H). The dialog box shown in Figure 17-9 shows the recommended hyphenation settings for the current word according to the QuarkXPress algorithm and the current H&J set. For example, if the H&J set specifies no more than two lines ending with hyphens in a row, and hyphenating the selected word would result in three lines ending with hyphens in a row, the Suggested Hyphenation dialog box shows no hyphens in the word.

Tip

Although handy as a quick reference, the Suggested Hyphenation feature doesn't replace your house dictionary as the final authority on where a word should break.

Inserting soft hyphens

There will be times when you don't want to override the H&J set for a particular paragraph. Instead, you'll want to change the place in a particular word where QuarkXPress inserts the hyphen. QuarkXPress lets you do this through its soft (or discretionary) hyphen feature. The soft hyphen works as follows:

✦ To manually insert a soft hyphen, click in the word where you want it to hyphenate, and then press the ⌘ or Ctrl key while you press hyphen. Words can contain multiple soft hyphens, which indicate places that you prefer the word to break.

✦ The advantage to using soft hyphens—rather than simply pressing the hyphen key, which results in a hard hyphen—is that soft hyphens are only used as necessary. If text reflows and the hyphen is no longer necessary, the hyphen disappears.

✦ Even if you enter a soft hyphen, QuarkXPress may still hyphenate a word in a different location if it results in better spacing.

✦ To force a word to hyphenate only where you want it to, enter a soft hyphen at the beginning of the word, then place soft hyphens at allowable places within the word.

✦ To prevent a word from hyphenating entirely, enter a soft hyphen at the beginning of the word. But don't enter any soft hyphens within the word.

One drawback to using soft hyphens is that they're invisible. You can't see them, ever, so you may be confused at times about why a word won't hyphenate or why it's hyphenating a certain way. If you suspect soft hyphens, try retyping the word.

Figure 17-9: The Suggested Hyphenation dialog box.

Inserting nonbreaking hyphens

QuarkXPress thinks that every hyphen you type in text is fair game for line breaks. But this isn't always the case: You don't necessarily want to break phone numbers, ratios, scores, and even compound words such as *follow-up*. The solution is to replace the hyphens with nonbreaking hyphens—a hyphen that can't serve as a line break. To do this, type ⌘+= or Ctrl+= in place of the existing hyphen. True, not everyone worries about whether text breaks at such points. But it's nice that QuarkXPress lets you control hyphenation precisely if doing so matters to you.

Adding words to the hyphenation dictionary

QuarkXPress uses an algorithm that looks at letter patterns when it automatically hyphenates text. Unfortunately, it's not always correct—not to mention that hyphenation is subjective in the first place. Just compare the hyphenation of words in the Webster's and American Heritage dictionaries to see for yourself. In addition, QuarkXPress itself will allow for some pretty awkward breaks, hyphenating *couldn't*, for example, as *could-n't*. For single instances, such as names that you don't use often, you can repair the break manually with soft hyphens as described in the "Inserting soft hyphens" sidebar.

If you find yourself repeatedly inserting soft hyphens into the same words, you're doing too much work. In this case, you can add your own hyphenation preferences to QuarkXPress through the Hyphenation Exception dictionary feature (Utilities ➪ Hyphenation Exceptions).

By adding words to the hyphenation dictionary, you give QuarkXPress hyphenation instructions for words the program doesn't know, hyphenates incorrectly, or hyphenates differently than your stylebook specifies. Additionally, you can prevent hyphenation of specific words by adding them to the dictionary. This dictionary can be global, affecting all documents; or local, affecting only the current document.

The Hyphenation Exceptions dialog box (shown in Figure 17-10) works as follows:

✦ As you add words to the hyphenation dictionary, indicate allowable hyphenation points by inserting hyphens.

✦ To prevent a word from hyphenating, type it in without hyphens.

✦ You can change existing hyphenation exceptions by clicking the word you want to change. The Add button is replaced with the Replace button, and the word you type in replaces the one highlighted.

✦ Be sure to enter all variations of words and their hyphenations (for example, enter plural versions of words).

✦ If you're in a document that doesn't use the standard QuarkXPress preferences, any hyphenation exceptions you enter affect only that document. To define hyphenation exceptions you want to use globally, close all active documents so that your changes are saved as default preferences.

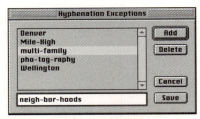

Figure 17-10: The Hyphenation Exceptions dialog box.

Checking the hyphenation method

In addition to the algorithm QuarkXPress uses to hyphenate words and your hyphenation dictionary, the program consults its own brief hyphenation dictionary. With subsequent versions of QuarkXPress, the hyphenation dictionary has been improved with the addition of a few more words — although none of the dictionaries are all that impressive. In fact, they're basically cobbled together collections of words with subjective hyphens inserted.

To see which dictionary is in use, go to the Paragraph pane of the Preferences dialog box (Edit ➪ Preferences ➪ Preferences, or Option+Shift+⌘+Y or Ctrl+Alt+Shift+Y). In the Hyphenation area, the Method menu gives you three options: Standard, Enhanced, and Expanded. Basically, Expanded is the dictionary from 4.0, Enhanced is the dictionary from 3.2/3.3, and Standard is the old dictionary. To be honest, there is no reason to change this feature from Expanded, because it provides the hyphenation dictionary with the most words.

Using Special Spaces

One way to carefully fine-tune spacing is to literally replace individual spaces with special spaces. Instead of narrowing and widening with tracking and justification settings, these special spaces maintain their widths. QuarkXPress provides the following special space options: nonbreaking spaces, en spaces and em spaces, punctuation spaces, and flexible spaces.

Nonbreaking spaces

A *nonbreaking space* glues two words together, ensuring that a line doesn't wrap between two words if you don't want it to. For example, you might want to use a nonbreaking space in *Mac OS* so Mac doesn't end on one line with *OS* starting on the next line. Nonbreaking spaces are also handy if you put spaces on either side of your dashes, as shown in Figure 17-11; they make sure a dash is glued to the word before it. The command is ⌘+space on the Mac and Ctrl+5 in Windows.

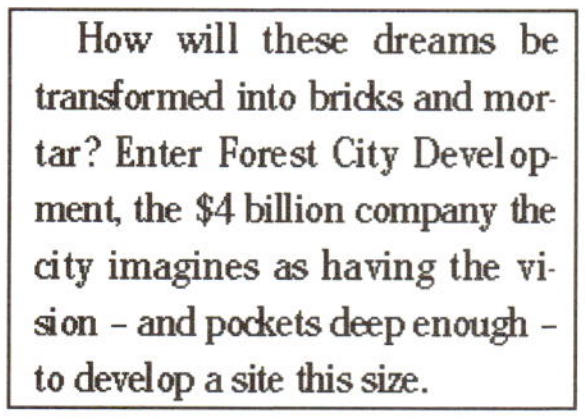

> How will these dreams be transformed into bricks and mortar? Enter Forest City Development, the $4 billion company the city imagines as having the vision – and pockets deep enough – to develop a site this size.

Figure 17-11: A nonbreaking space entered prior to the en dash on the sixth line keeps this line from starting with an en dash.

En spaces and em spaces

An en space (press Option+space on the Mac, Ctrl+Shift+6 in Windows) is often used in numbered lists after the period following the numeral. An en space makes a number more visible, because the number is more separated from the following *text* than the words in the text are separated from each *other*. En spaces also are used before single-digit numerals when a numbered list includes both single- and double-digit numerals. (In most typefaces, a numeral occupies the width of an en space. So putting an en space before numerals 1 through 9 aligns them with the 0 in the number 10.) A variation of the en space is the nonbreaking en space, accessed by pressing Option+⌘+space on the Mac or Ctrl+Alt+Shift+6 in Windows.

A common fixed space available in most desktop-publishing programs, but not in QuarkXPress, is an em space. But you can still enter an em space by simply typing two en spaces. The width of an em space is determined by a setting in the Character pane of the Preferences dialog box (Edit ➪ Preferences ➪ Preferences, or Option+Shift+⌘+Y or Ctrl+Alt+Shift+Y), as shown in Figure 17-12. When Standard Em Space is checked, the width of an em space is the width of a capital *M* in the current font and type size. When it's unchecked, the width of an em space is the width of two zeros in the font.

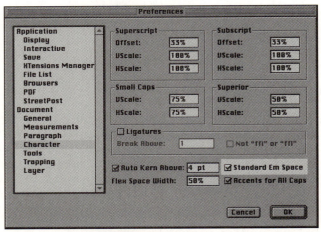

Figure 17-12: The Standard Em Space check box in the Character pane of the Preferences dialog box.

Punctuation spaces

A *punctuation space,* accessed via Shift+space on the Mac and Ctrl+6 in Windows, is the width of a period or comma. Some people call a punctuation space a *thin space;* regardless, it's generally half the width of an en space. It's typically used to ensure alignment of numerals when some numbers have commas and others don't — as in 4,109 and 142. To align the last three digits of both numbers, you place an en space and a punctuation space before 142. A punctuation space is also often used in quotes that contain an abutting internal quote: *"He asked me, 'Are you coming?' ,"* as opposed to *"He asked me,'Are you coming?'"* (no space) or *"He asked me, 'Are you coming?' "* (regular space).

A variation is the nonbreaking punctuation space, accessed via Shift+⌘+space on the Mac and Ctrl+Alt+6 in Windows.

Flexible spaces

A *flexible space* (Option+Shift+space on the Mac, Ctrl+Shift+5 in Windows) is a space you define as a certain percentage of an en space. If you define a flexible space as twice the width (200 percent) of an en space, you create an em space. You define the flexible space width in the Character pane, accessed via Edit ➪ Preferences ➪ Preferences (Option+Shift+⌘+Y or Ctrl+Alt+Shift+Y). Specify the width in percentages from 0 to 400, in increments of 0.1. For the nonbreaking variant of the flexible space, press Shift+Option+⌘+space or Ctrl+Alt+Shift+5.

Implementing a Baseline Grid

Behind each document lies a grid of lines that you can rest text on — if you want. To see these lines, choose View ➪ Show Baseline Grid or press Option+F7 or Ctrl+F7. The advantage of using the baseline grid is that text will align horizontally across columns and pages, an otherwise difficult effect to achieve when you consider the leading, space before and after paragraphs, type sizes, and other issues that affect spacing. (When text is locked to the baseline grid, QuarkXPress overrides other spacing values you've entered as necessary.) Some graphic designers and typesetters, however, sneer at the use of a baseline grid, calling it "design by the numbers."

If you choose to use the baseline grid, you can specify where it starts on the page, how much space is between grid lines, and which paragraphs actually sit on these baselines. See Figure 17-13 for an example of a document that uses a baseline grid.

Setting up the baseline grid

If you want to use the baseline grid to align text, you first need to set it up in the Paragraph pane of the Preferences dialog box (Edit ➪ Preferences ➪ Preferences, or Option+Shift+⌘+Y or Ctrl+Alt+Shift+Y). The Baseline Grid area, shown in Figure 17-14, contains a Start field for you to specify the first text baseline you want on the page. Generally, you can make this the same as the value you enter in the Increment field, which specifies the amount of distance you want between lines. Click OK to save the grid settings with the current document.

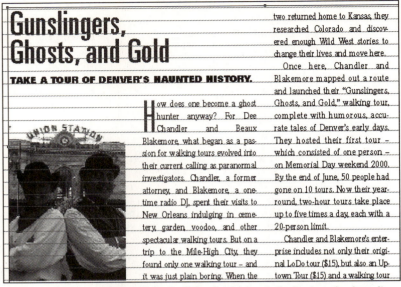

Figure 17-13: In this magazine, all the body text is locked to the baseline grid while the headlines float.

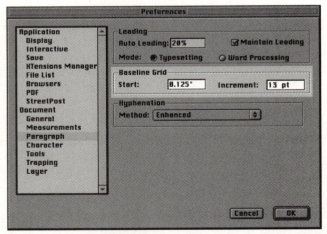

Figure 17-14: The Paragraph pane of the Preferences dialog box lets you set up the spacing for a baseline grid.

Tip   When you lock paragraphs to the baseline grid, the paragraph's leading value is ignored in favor of the Increment specified for the grid. Therefore, you might as well make the baseline grid increments and the leading the same (say 12 or 13 points).

Viewing the baseline grid

If you use the baseline grid View ➪ Show Baseline Grid, memorize the keyboard shortcuts for showing and hiding it right away: Option+F7 for Mac and Ctrl+F7 for Windows. Right off, you might consider skipping grid use when you see those hot pink lines. You can tone those down for your copy of QuarkXPress in the Display pane of the Preferences dialog box (Edit ➪ Preferences ➪ Preferences, or Option+Shift+⌘+Y or Ctrl+Alt+Shift+Y). In the Guide Colors area, click the Grid button and use the color controls to pick a more soothing color.

Locking paragraphs to the baseline grid

Setting up a baseline grid through preferences — and even displaying the baseline grid — does nothing on its own. To align text on the grid lines you have to lock paragraphs to the baseline grid. You can do this for selected paragraphs by checking Lock to Baseline Grid in the Formats pane of the Paragraph Attributes dialog box (Style ➪ Formats, or Shift+⌘+F or Ctrl+Shift+F), as shown in Figure 17-15. If you're working on a project long enough to require style sheets, you should by all means check Lock to Baseline Grid for all the appropriate paragraph style sheets.

When text is locked to the baseline grid, it rests on the closest possible baseline. For example, if you use a 12-point increment for the grid, and you lock a 16-point subhead to it, the text will skip one baseline and rest on the next. This text placement overrides leading and space before/after values.

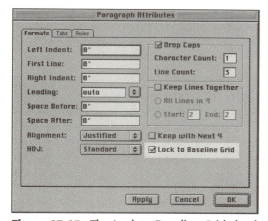

Figure 17-15: The Lock to Baseline Grid check box in the Formats pane of the Paragraph Attributes dialog box.

Tip

Note that you don't have to lock all paragraphs to the baseline grid. You can lock body text paragraphs, so they align across columns, but then not lock headlines and subheads. But if you're concerned that the baselines of all text align, *do* lock everything to the baseline grid.

To lock or not to lock

When determining whether to lock paragraphs to the baseline grid, consider the following tips:

✦ **The text you use the most in a document is body text, which is also where misalignment is most noticeable.** To avoid this kind of misalignment, set your baseline grid to be the same as the leading for body text and check the Lock to Baseline Grid option in the paragraph style sheet for that body text.

✦ **Do *not* use the Lock to Baseline Grid option on text whose style has different leading settings, because this could result in awkward spacing between lines in text of that style.** For example, if your body text has 11-point leading, but your subheads have 15-point leading, turning on the baseline lock option forces QuarkXPress to move the subhead to the next grid point, which is 22 points below the previous line of body text. This occurs even if you set the leading for the subhead style to place the subhead 15 points after the previous line of body text.

When in doubt, choose View ➪ Show Baseline Grid (or Option+F7 or Ctrl+F7) to see the pink grid lines and determine whether it will work for a paragraph.

Checking Lines

To help you review possible problems with spacing in a document, QuarkXPress 5 includes an XTension called Type Tricks, formerly available as a free download and then included with QuarkXPress 4.1. Although useful for catching issues such as text overflow and manual hyphenation — things you really need to eradicate — the XTension has limited controls, so it's certainly not a panacea for spacing problems.

Note   If you don't have a Line Check option on your Utilities menu, it probably means you don't have the Type Tricks XTension installed. Use the XTensions Manager (Utilities ➪ XTensions Manager) to activate the XTension, quit QuarkXPress, and relaunch QuarkXPress.

Specifying line-check criteria

Before you search a document for spacing issues, you can tell the XTension what to search for. Choose Utilities ➪ Line Check ➪ Search Criteria to display the dialog box shown in Figure 17-16. By default, all the options are checked. Right off, you can see how your document fares on all accounts by clicking the Count button. This shows you the number of potential problems in your document and lets you know where to concentrate your efforts.

Figure 17-16: The Search Criteria dialog box for the Line Check feature implemented through the included Type Tricks XTension.

You can check the following options to search for:

✦ **Loose Justification,** which alerts you to justified lines that exceed the Max Space or Char. settings in the paragraph's H&J set.

✦ **Auto Hyphenated** shows you lines ending in hyphens added by QuarkXPress and discretionary hyphens you add.

✦ **Manual Hyphenated** shows you lines ending in hyphens entered by someone, including hyphens in compound modifiers such as in the phrase *old-fashioned typewriter.*

✦ **Widow** shows the last line of a paragraph that falls at the top of a column.

✦ **Orphan** shows you the first line of a paragraph alone at the bottom of a column.

✦ **Text Box Overflow** shows you any instances of the text overflow symbol, which indicate that text doesn't fit in a text box or on a text path.

Whatever you set for Search Criteria is saved with the XTension, not with each document, so the settings become program defaults.

Checking each line

When you check lines for spacing and hyphenation issues, QuarkXPress highlights each line that fits your Search Criteria. But it gives you no indication of why a line is highlighted — you have to guess: Is it poor justification or the hyphen? Is the hyphen manual or automatic? Because in many cases you can't tell exactly what might be wrong with a line, it might be a good idea to search for only one or two issues at a time (by changing the Search Criteria).

STEPS: Checking lines

1. Select the Content tool.

2. Click somewhere in text, wherever you want to start the search. (If you want to search the entire document, click in text at the top of the first page.)

3. Choose Utilities ⇨ Line Check ⇨ First Line.

4. QuarkXPress highlights the first line that meets any of your Search Criteria, as shown in Figure 17-17. You can click in the text and fix any issues at that time — for example, if the text overflow symbol displays, you can expand the text box or apply negative tracking to the text.

5. To continue the search, choose Utilities ➪ Line Check ➪ Next Line, or press ⌘+; (semicolon) or Ctrl+; (semicolon). Continue checking lines and correcting problems until an alert indicates that you're finished.

Figure 17-17: The Line Check feature highlights lines with potential problems such as manual hyphenation or text overflow.

Fitting Copy

The term *copy fitting* means just what it sounds like: the process of fitting text into the layout, often by altering the spacing. If your original, unmodified text fits the layout the first time through, consider it a stroke of luck, because that's not what usually happens. Besides making pages look better, copy fitting can be a real business concern. In magazines, newsletters, and newspapers, the number of pages is set in advance, so you don't have the option of adding or removing pages to fit the lack or abundance of copy.

It's sometimes necessary to take several actions, often in concert, to make text fit in the available space. Because the usual problem is having more text than space, the goal is often to shorten text, but you can use the same procedures in reverse to expand text. Note that the following tips are given in order of preference, so use the final ones only if the first few suggestions fail to achieve the desired effect:

✦ **Edit the text.** You can remove extra lines, but be on the lookout for lines at the end of a paragraph that have only a few characters. Getting rid of a few characters somewhere else in the paragraph may eliminate these short lines, reducing the amount of page space needed while keeping the amount of text removed to a minimum.

✦ **Track the text.** This procedure results in text that occupies less space, and it eliminates short lines. Chapter 15 explains how to track text.

✦ **Tighten the leading.** You can do this by a half- or a quarter-point. This change is so small that the average reader won't notice it, and it may save you a few lines per column, which can add up quickly. See the section on leading in Chapter 16.

✦ **Reduce the point size.** Do this by a half-point. This reduction saves more space than is first apparent, because it allows you to place a few more lines on the page and put a bit more text in each line. Change point size in the style sheet or select text and use the type size controls in the Measurements palette.

✦ **Reduce the horizontal scale.** You can reduce this to a slightly smaller percentage (perhaps 95 percent) to squeeze more text in each line. The section on horizontal and vertical scale in Chapter 15 explains how to make this alteration.

✦ **Vary the size of columns.** Do this by setting slightly narrower column gutters or slightly wider margins.

Try applying these copy-fitting techniques globally to avoid a patchwork appearance. You can, however, change tracking on individual lines without ruining the appearance of your document. If you limit tracking changes to no more than –2 or –3 units, as shown in Figure 17-18, the text won't appear obviously different to your readers.

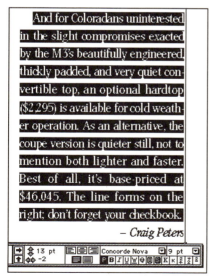

Figure 17-18: Tracking this paragraph –2 pulled up the words *your checkbook* so the story's byline would fit.

Summary

Hyphenation and justification involves a series of techniques meant to aid the readability of text by breaking words at the end of the line and determining whether text aligns against both sides of a column or just one. There is no black-and-white set of rules as to when to allow hyphenation, how many characters to require before or after a hyphen in a broken word, and whether to align text along one or both sides of a column, but it's important that a publication determine its rules and stick with them.

To help in alignment of elements, QuarkXPress includes support for several kinds of spaces, such as en spaces (often used to help align numerals), punctuation space (also used to align numerals, as well as to separate abutting quotation marks), and em spaces (often used as an indent character or as a fixed space between text and dingbats).

Implementing a baseline grid can ensure that text spacing is consistent vertically — from line to line — though it reduces flexibility for the use of various point sizes in elements like subheads.

You can use several techniques — changing leading, point size, tracking, and of course editing the text itself to be shorter or longer — to make text fit the space available. Just be sure to use the same settings on all pages of your documents; don't vary from page to page or article to article.

✦   ✦   ✦

Special Typographic Techniques

In this chapter, we'll look at ways you can pull together everything you've learned about typefaces, character formats, and paragraph formats to achieve just about any look with text. The key is to combine and apply the skills you've learned to produce special effects that not only look professional but also enhance the meaning of the text. With features such as special characters, bulleted lists, initial caps, drop shadows and reverse type, hanging punctuation, and other special effects, you can add meaning and provide readers guidance. This chapter will set you on the road to becoming a typographic special-effects expert.

Adding Bullets and Formatting Lists

Although long promised for version 5, QuarkXPress still does not include a feature for automatically adding bullets or numbers to lists. You still need to type a bullet character or numeral at the beginning of each paragraph and insert spaces or tabs to offset the text. Although this gives you complete control over the bullet or numeral's font, color, size, and placement, it's a very manual process. Fortunately, after you set up the formatting, you can automate it somewhat with both paragraph and character style sheets. In this section, we show you not only how to format a bulleted or numbered list, but how to ensure maximum readability.

Adding bullets or numerals

You have two options for adding bullets and numbers in QuarkXPress: typing them in from scratch or reformatting those that arrived with an imported text file.

Typing bullets and numerals into QuarkXPress

If you're writing in QuarkXPress, you can simply type the bullet character or number you want, then enter a space or tab to offset it from the text you type. When you're adding bullet characters, decide on the font you're going to use. You can press Option+8 or Alt+8 (in many Windows applications, but not all) for a simple, round en bullet (•) in the same typeface as the body text. Or you can choose a different character in the body text font, or pick a character in a symbol font such as Zapf Dingbats or Wingdings.

Tip   If you're editing existing text and decide to add bullets or numerals to existing paragraphs, you can paste completely formatted bullets followed by tabs or spaces at the beginning of each paragraph. You can also paste a numeral, then edit the numeral's value as appropriate.

Reformatting imported bullets and numerals

In most cases, text is delivered in the form of a word-processing file, and the writer or editor made some decisions about bullets or numerals, including:

✦ Entering an asterisk or hyphen followed by a space for a bullet

✦ Entering numerals followed by periods or parentheses and a tab or space

✦ Using the word processor's automatic bullets and numbering feature

Caution   Automatic bullets and numbers from word processors do not import into QuarkXPress. Encourage your writers and editors to number paragraphs manually.

Unless you've discussed proper formatting with the editorial staff beforehand, their bullets/numbers are unlikely to work. Fortunately, you can usually repair the text with Find/Change (Edit ➪ Find Change, or ⌘+F or Ctrl+F). Simply turn on Invisibles (View ➪ Show Invisibles, or ⌘+I or Ctrl+I) and identify the pattern used, as shown in Figure 18-1. Enter the current pattern in the Find What field, then enter the new pattern in the Change To field. If you uncheck Ignore Attributes you can specify formatting — including applying a character style sheet to bullets or numerals.

Tip   When using Find/Change to reformat existing bullets/numbering, you can replace spaces with tabs by entering a space in the Find What field and the symbol for a tab, \t, in the Change To field. If you can establish a pattern for numerals that is not used elsewhere in the document (for example, a number, a period, then a tab), you can enter that pattern in the Find What field, but use the wild card character, \?, to find any one-digit number. If your list goes to two digits, perform the Find/Change again with two wild card characters.

Bullets in Microsoft Word

Microsoft Word for Windows, versions 97 and later, don't use the keyboard shortcut Alt+8 for the en bullet (•) character. Although Word's bullet-list feature automatically inserts a bullet into text, it also inserts a tab after the bullet that you likely don't want in your QuarkXPress document.

But you can tell Word to assign a shortcut to create the bullet character. Select Insert ⇨ Symbol, then find the bullet character in the table of available characters. (You can quickly find it by selecting the General Punctuation item in the Subset pop-up menu.) Select the bullet character, then click the Shortcut Key button. In the resulting dialog box, you get the option of entering a keyboard shortcut of your choosing, as shown in the figure. We chose Alt+8 to be compatible with most Windows programs. You can, of course, choose your own shortcut, as well as use this technique for other characters you want accessible via a keyboard shortcut.

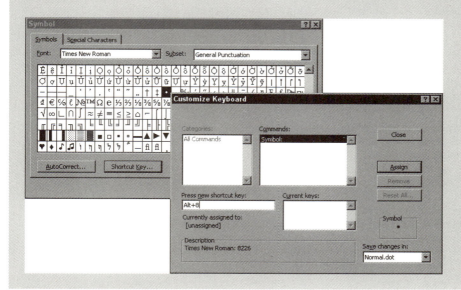

Figure 18-1: This Find/Change scheme will replace instances of an asterisk followed by a space with a square bullet character in Zapf Dingbats font followed by a tab.

Deciding on initial formatting for bullets and numerals

For bullets, you have many options, including the standard en bullet and the many special characters available in fonts. To view the characters in a font, use a utility such as the Mac KeyCaps, the Windows Character Map, or the Font Reserve Character Map. See the "Bullet character options" sidebar for more information. For numerals, you can use the font of the body text or another font, including an expert font that includes traditional numerals (see the sidebar, "Traditional numerals").

After you decide on a bullet character or font, you can use the Character Attributes dialog box (Style ➪ Character, or Shift+⌘+D or Ctrl+Shift+D) to change the color, scale, type style, and more.

Adding space between bullets or numerals

In addition to the formatting of bullets and numerals, you need to decide how text will follow them. In general, you will use fixed spaces or tabs. Figure 18-2 shows three different options for bullets. The first column shows an en bullet followed by an en space; the second column shows an en bullet followed by a tab; and the third column shows a Zapf Dingbats sideways heart used as a bullet followed by a tab and hanging indent.

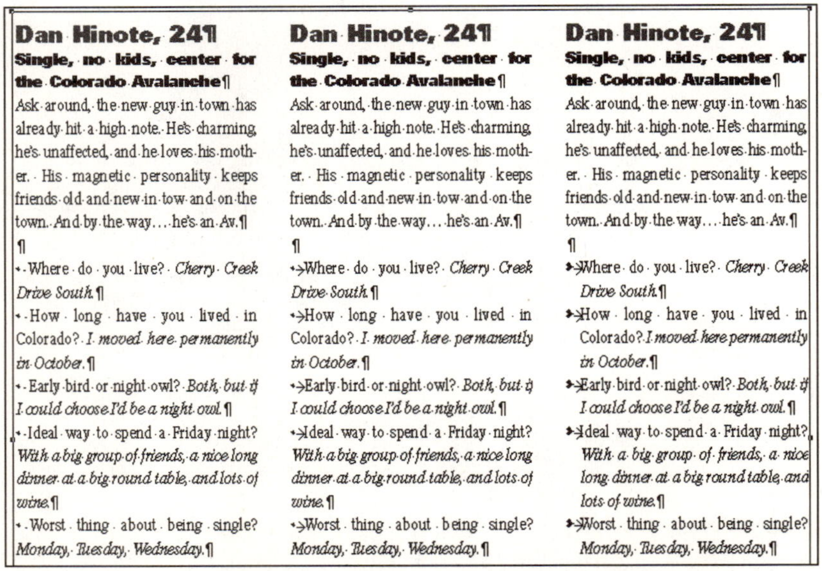
Dan Hinote, 24¶
Single, no kids, center for the Colorado Avalanche¶
Ask around, the new guy in town has already hit a high note. He's charming, he's unaffected, and he loves his mother. His magnetic personality keeps friends old and new in tow and on the town. And by the way… he's an Av.¶
¶
• Where do you live? *Cherry Creek Drive South.*¶
• How long have you lived in Colorado? *I moved here permanently in October.*¶
• Early bird or night owl? *Both, but if I could choose I'd be a night owl.*¶
• Ideal way to spend a Friday night? *With a big group of friends, a nice long dinner at a big round table, and lots of wine.*¶
• Worst thing about being single? *Monday, Tuesday, Wednesday.*¶

Dan Hinote, 24¶
Single, no kids, center for the Colorado Avalanche¶
Ask around, the new guy in town has already hit a high note. He's charming, he's unaffected, and he loves his mother. His magnetic personality keeps friends old and new in tow and on the town. And by the way… he's an Av.¶
¶
•→Where do you live? *Cherry Creek Drive South.*¶
•→How long have you lived in Colorado? *I moved here permanently in October.*¶
•→Early bird or night owl? *Both, but if I could choose I'd be a night owl.*¶
•→Ideal way to spend a Friday night? *With a big group of friends, a nice long dinner at a big round table, and lots of wine.*¶
•→Worst thing about being single? *Monday, Tuesday, Wednesday.*¶

Dan Hinote, 24¶
Single, no kids, center for the Colorado Avalanche¶
Ask around, the new guy in town has already hit a high note. He's charming, he's unaffected, and he loves his mother. His magnetic personality keeps friends old and new in tow and on the town. And by the way… he's an Av.¶
¶
➧→Where do you live? *Cherry Creek Drive South.*¶
➧→How long have you lived in Colorado? *I moved here permanently in October.*¶
➧→Early bird or night owl? *Both, but if I could choose I'd be a night owl.*¶
➧→Ideal way to spend a Friday night? *With a big group of friends, a nice long dinner at a big round table, and lots of wine.*¶
➧→Worst thing about being single? *Monday, Tuesday, Wednesday.*¶

Figure 18-2: Examples of different kinds of bullets: standard en bullets (first two columns) and a dingbat character (third column).

Bullet character options

Although you may not know what they're called, you're used to seeing en bullets, the medium-size round bullet (•) included in most typefaces. But you're not limited to using this character. You can use any character in the body text font, or you can switch to a symbol or pi font and choose a more decorative character. Consider the following:

✦ Zapf Dingbats and Wingdings are the most common symbol fonts, offering an array of boxes, arrows, crosses, stars, and check marks. Other symbol and pi typefaces have whimsical characters — ranging from skiers to leaves and everything in between — that can function as bullets when placed in the proper context.

✦ Geometric shapes are great alternatives to the traditional bullet: a solid square makes the bullet appear bolder and more authoritative; a hollow square gives a strong but silent feel; a triangle appears more distinct without being as heavy as a solid square; arrows reinforce the bullet's basic message of "Look here!"

✦ Another possibility is to use symbols with specific meanings. For example, you can use astrological signs for a horoscope column, religious symbols for a church or temple newsletter, or check marks and check boxes for election materials.

✦ You also can use a logo as a symbol if you create a typeface that uses it. (You can do this with such programs as Macromedia's Fontographer.) Using a logo is particularly effective if it's simple and readily identified with your organization.

Bullets from symbol and pi fonts can be cute and effective, but cute isn't always a good thing. If you opt for a different bullet character, make sure you have a reason and that it works well with the rest of the design. Note that you might want to reduce the size of the symbol slightly and that you might need to use different spacing values than you would use with an en bullet.

Font Reserve, a font management application, lets you sort fonts by design class such as Symbol/Pi. You can display only those fonts, then quickly display their Character Maps to pick bullet characters. A demo version of Font Reserve is included on the CD that comes with this book.

Fixed spaces

Typing a fixed space such as an en space (Option+space or Ctrl+Shift+6) ensures that text always starts in the same position in a list. If you simply type a standard space, the space can be stretched when justified or forced alignment is used. Be sure that all the spaces have the same font applied to them — either the font of the bullet/numeral or the font of the body text, or you can still get inconsistent spacing.

Single tabs

If you use a single tab after a bullet or numeral, you have the luxury of changing the amount of space between the bullet/numeral and text at will by simply changing the tab setting. If your numbers are likely to go above 10, make sure the tab setting will accommodate a double-digit number, as shown in Figure 18-3.

Figure contents:

Divorced, four kids, ↵
Littleton Fire Department Lieutenant ¶
You can't have a singles list without the American hero—and HB is one of the good guys. Clearly content to be a father and firefighter, his "life is good" frame of mind is inspiring. Not to mention he'll carry you out of a burning building if you ever get into trouble. ¶
¶
1→ Where do you live? *Northeast Denver.* ¶
2→ How long have you lived in Colorado? *Native.* ¶
3→ Dog person or cat person? *Dog (I have a dog named Teka).* ¶
4→ Early bird or night owl? *Both.* ¶
5→ Favorite pastime? *Listening to music, riding my bike, walking and watching movies.* ¶
6→ Ideal way to spend a Friday night? *Going to a show, taking in a jazz set afterwards, and then a nice dinner out.* ¶
7→ Favorite CD? *Marvin Gaye, "60 Years."* ¶
8→ Favorite author? *Agatha Christie.* ¶
9→ Best thing about being single: *I'm content and busy and I don't get very lonely because I do so much.* ¶
10→ Worst thing about being single: *If I had to say one thing, maybe it's not having that one person to share life with.* ¶

Figure 18-3: In this numbered list, the tab between the numbers and text accommodates the double-digit 10.

To change the tab setting, use the Tabs pane in the Paragraph Attributes dialog box (Style ➪ Tabs, or Shift+⌘+T or Ctrl+Shift+T). When the Paragraph Attributes dialog box is open, the ruler that displays on the active text box lets you create an *outdent* (a hanging indent) by dragging the arrows. You can also create the outdent using the Indent fields in the Formats pane of the Paragraph Attributes dialog box, as discussed in Chapter 16.

Tip   If you turn on Invisibles (View ➪ Show Invisibles, or ⌘+I or Ctrl+I) and see multiple tab characters following a bullet or numeral, use Find/Change to strip the extra tabs. (***Remember:*** Enter \t in the fields to indicate a tab.) Having only one tab to set will significantly simplify the list formatting.

Applying style sheets for numbered and bulleted lists

The combination of paragraph and character formats necessary to produce bulleted and numbered lists can be tedious to apply. You'll want to save the basic formatting as a paragraph style sheet. If the bullets or numerals have different formatting, save that as a character style sheet. Make sure to specify keyboard commands for the style sheets so you can apply them quickly.

Cross-Reference   For information about creating style sheets, see Chapter 32.

Spacing guidelines for indents and bullets

How much space goes between a bullet or numeral and the text following it? Amateur publishers or designers, who are likely to be thinking in inches rather than points or picas, are likely to use too much space. They're tempted to use 0.25", 0.125", or another nice dividend of an inch for spacing rather than a more appropriate value such as 6 points. When deciding on spacing, consider the following:

✦ First-line indents that indicate new paragraphs should generally be one or two em spaces wide. The width of an em space is equal to the point size in use—so 10-point text should have a 10- or 20-point first-line indent. Opt for less space in narrower columns to avoid awkward space and more space in wider columns so the spacing is evident.

✦ As you remember from grade-school outlines, indents help organize information, with deeper indents indicating more detail about a topic. Professional publications, though, have many organizational options—such as headlines, subheads, and run-in heads— so they rarely have a need for more than two levels of indents. You might use indents on lengthy quotes, bulleted lists, numbered lists, kickers, and bylines. If you do, stick to the same amount of indent for each so the reader's eyes don't wander.

✦ In bulleted lists, use a hanging indent for a succession of two- or three-line bulleted paragraphs in wider columns. If your bulleted items are five or six lines long, especially in narrow columns, it might work better to use labels to break up the information. (See the section "Labeling Paragraphs" for more information.)

✦ Generally, the amount of space between a bullet and its text is equal to half the point size of the text. So if you're working with 11-point text, place 5.5 points between the bullet and text.

✦ When it comes to numbered lists, you need to decide whether you're going to include a period or other punctuation after the number and whether you'll ever have two-digit numbers. Numerals in most typefaces are the width of an en space and should be followed by the same amount of space the numbers and their punctuation take up. If you have a two-digit numeral, the numbers take up one em space and so should be followed by one em space.

Although these values give you a good starting point, you might need to modify them based on the typeface, font size, column width, design, and overall goals of the publication.

To apply the style sheets to existing text, first highlight all the paragraphs, then apply the paragraph style sheet. Then you can highlight each numeral or bullet and apply the character style sheet. Make sure to apply the paragraph style sheet first and the character style sheet second, or else the paragraph formatting may wipe out your special numeral or bullet formatting.

Traditional numerals

If you look at books published early in this century or in previous eras, you'll notice that the numerals look very different than the ones you see today in books, magazines, and newspapers. Numerals used to be treated as lowercase letters, so some, such as 9, had descenders, just as lowercase letters such as *g* do. Others, such as 6, had ascenders, as do lowercase letters such as *b*. But this way of displaying numerals changed, and most modern typefaces treat numerals like capital letters: no descenders and no ascenders. This style keeps numerals from sticking out in headlines, but it also can make numerals too prominent in some text, especially in type-intensive documents such as ads, where individual character shapes are important to the overall look.

A few years back, Adobe and other type foundries resurrected the old-fashioned numerals as part of expert-collection typefaces. As you can see in the figure, which shows the two types of numerals, the traditional numerals are more stylized and have the typographic feel of lowercase letters.

0123456789

0123456789

Although they often look more elegant, old-fashioned numerals have three drawbacks that you should consider before using them routinely:

✦ **They reside in a separate font, so you must change the font for each and every numeral (or group of numerals).** Even if you apply paragraph style sheets, it can be a lot of extra work. In tables and other numerals-only text, using old-fashioned numerals is less of an issue because you can have a separate style for text that uses the expert font.

✦ **They don't have the same width.** Modern numerals are almost always the same width (that of an en space), so typographers and publishers don't have to worry about whether columns of numbers align. (Because all modern numerals are the same width, they align naturally.) But the old-fashioned numerals in expert fonts have variable widths, just like most characters, so they can look awkward in columns of numbers even if you use decimal or comma alignment.

✦ **They're unusual in modern typography, so they can call more attention to themselves than is appropriate.** For design-intensive work, this extra attention is usually not an issue, but in commonplace documents such as reports and newsletters, they can look out of place. As their popularity grows, people may become more used to seeing them.

Labeling Paragraphs

When you need to call attention to content while breaking text into lists, you can use labels to highlight the first few words of each new paragraph. These labels, shown in Figure 18-4, may be a few words that act as a mini-headline, or they may simply be the first few words of the paragraph.

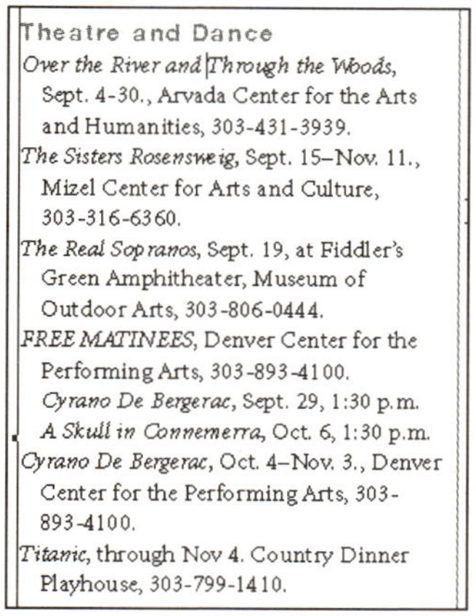

Theatre and Dance
Over the River and Through the Woods, Sept. 4-30., Arvada Center for the Arts and Humanities, 303-431-3939.
The Sisters Rosensweig, Sept. 15–Nov. 11., Mizel Center for Arts and Culture, 303-316-6360.
The Real Sopranos, Sept. 19, at Fiddler's Green Amphitheater, Museum of Outdoor Arts, 303-806-0444.
FREE MATINEES, Denver Center for the Performing Arts, 303-893-4100.
Cyrano De Bergerac, Sept. 29, 1:30 p.m.
A Skull in Connemerra, Oct. 6, 1:30 p.m.
Cyrano De Bergerac, Oct. 4–Nov. 3., Denver Center for the Performing Arts, 303-893-4100.
Titanic, through Nov 4. Country Dinner Playhouse, 303-799-1410.

Figure 18-4: In this calendar, Minion Italic is used to set the event names off from the body text in Minion Regular.

Most of the character attributes available in QuarkXPress work well for labeling paragraphs. To help you see how each looks, we've used the attributes within the following descriptions. Unless otherwise noted, these effects are available from the Type Style submenu of the Style menu, the Character Attributes dialog box (Style ➪ Character, or Shift+⌘+D or Ctrl+Shift+D), and the Measurements palette.

✦ **Boldface:** The strongest attribute, boldface often is used as a second-level subhead when the first-level subhead is a standalone headline set in a larger size and perhaps in a different typeface. It also can be used to indicate a first-level subhead in reports or newsletters when strong design is not a priority.

✦ *Italics:* This is a favorite choice. If you use boldface as a second-level subhead, italics is a natural option for third-level subheads. It also can be used after a bullet when each bulleted item contains a narrative description that benefits from a label summarizing its content.

✦ Underlines: A common choice for documents that are meant to look like word-processed or typewritten documents, underlines or rules convey a "no frills" feel. They fall between boldface and italics in terms of visual impact. If you use underlines, avoid using underlines thicker than 2 points (anywhere from 0.5 to 1.5 is usually sufficient), and stay away from special underlines such as dotted or thick-and-thin rules. Stick with single or double underlines so that you don't distract readers from the text you're trying to emphasize.

✦ SMALL CAPS: This is a classy choice for text that doesn't need a strong visual label. Small caps appear no stronger visually than regular text, so they are *not* effective if you want to make labels more visible than the surrounding text (for example, so a reader can scan the labels to see which text is relevant). But small caps provide a way to add text labels that summarize content without interfering with the overall look of the document. As with italics, small caps work well with bullets. Combining small caps with italics or boldface is an effective way to create labels that have more impact and yet retain the classy look of small caps. Don't forget to consider the small caps version of a font that comes with some expert fonts — it may be preferable to using the Small Caps type style in QuarkXPress.

✦ **Typeface change**: By changing to a typeface that is distinctly different from the current text, you can highlight labels very effectively. If you choose this option, try to pick a typeface used elsewhere in the document, so you avoid the ransom-note look. When body text is set in a serif typeface, it's typical and appealing to use a sans serif typeface for the label, but the reverse is often less effective. We used Univers Black as the typeface for the label of this paragraph.

✦ Scaled text: By scaling text horizontally or vertically, you can create a subtle label that has more visual impact than small caps and about the same impact as italics. (To access scaling features, select Style ➭ Horizontal/Vertical Scale.) Be careful not to scale text too much (we used a horizontal scale of 125 percent here), or it will look distorted. A less-effective variation is to scale the label text vertically, so that it's narrower. This technique can work if you combine it with another attribute — for example, small caps and/or boldface — to counteract the reduced visual impact of the vertically scaled text.

✦ Size change: By making text a few points larger, you can subtly call attention to labels without being too explicit about it. Don't set the label size more than a few points greater than the size of the body text, and never make label text smaller than body text. (We made the label text here 4 points larger than the body text.) As with scaling text, this technique can be combined with other techniques effectively.

Changing the horizontal scale, vertical scale, or text size are generally the *least* effective methods for indicating labels, and they can be misused easily. If you do decide to scale text or change its size, consider carefully the settings you choose.

Caution For best results in applying labels such as boldface and italics, apply the bold or italic variation of the font (such as Minion Bold or Univers Oblique) rather than using the QuarkXPress type style buttons. This ensures proper display and output, and it ensures that these variations of the fonts are collected for output. See "The bold and italic blues" sidebar in Chapter 15 for more information.

Tip To apply label formatting quickly and consistently, be sure to save the formatting as a character style sheet (Edit ➭ Style Sheets, or Shift+F11). If you need to change the label formatting — by changing the font or adding a color, for example — you can simply edit the style sheet.

Inserting Special Characters

Several characters that are not used in traditionally typed business documents—such as em dashes, typographic quotes, and trademark symbols—are used routinely in typeset documents. Don't ignore these symbols, because readers expect to see them in anything that appears to be published, whether on the desktop or via traditional means. If you're used to working only with typewritten or word-processed documents, pay careful attention to the proper use of these characters.

True quotation marks and em dashes

The most common special characters are true quotation marks and em dashes (so called because they are the width of a capital *M* when typeset). The typewriter uses the same character (") to indicate both open and closed quotation marks, and most people use two hyphens (--) to indicate an em dash when typing. Using straight quotes and hyphens in a published document is a sign of amateurism.

Converting hyphens and straight quotes

When you import text using the Get Text dialog box (File ➪ Get Text, or ⌘+E or Ctrl+E), check Convert Quotes to automatically change double hyphens and straight quotes to their typographic equivalents. Figure 18-5 shows the Convert Quotes check box.

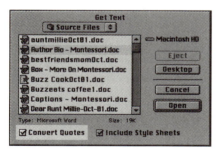

Figure 18-5: The Convert Quotes check box converts double hyphens to em dashes and straight quotes to typographers' curly quotes.

Using the Smart Quotes option

An option in QuarkXPress called Smart Quotes lets you turn on a feature that inserts typographically correct quotes as you type single and double quotes. Unfortunately, this will not translate double hyphens into em dashes as you type. Figure 18-6 shows how you specify smart quotes—and their formats—in the Interactive pane of the Preferences dialog box (Edit ➪ Preferences ➪ Preferences, or Shift+Option+⌘+Y or Ctrl+Alt+Shift+Y).

Caution   QuarkXPress provides various Formats for Smart Quotes that are intended for other languages. The Format you choose is also used when you check Convert Quotes in the Get Text dialog box, so make sure you don't choose an inappropriate format.

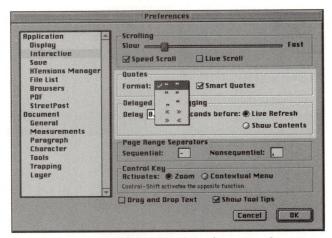

Figure 18-6: The Quotes controls in the Interactive pane of the Preferences dialog box.

Typing foot and inch marks

When Smart Quotes is checked, you can enter foot marks (') and inch marks ("), as shown in Figure 18-7, using keyboard shortcuts. Type Control+' or Ctrl+' for foot marks and Control+Shift+' or Ctrl+Alt+' for inch marks.

> "We both work at home," the buyers say, "so we created an office out of a 12'x12' sitting room and used colorful desk accessories to give the setting a casual, light and contemporary flare that truly reflects our personalities."

Figure 18-7: This magazine quotes builders often but also includes many dimensions in feet and inches. The graphic designer searches for single and double quotes and replaces them with straight quotes as necessary.

Manually creating typographic quotes

Using Smart Quotes is not always the best option — for example, if a document uses more foot and inch marks (straight quotes) than typographic quotes, you might want to turn the feature off. In this case, you can enter typographic quotes using the keyboard shortcuts shown in Table 18-1.

Table 18-1
Typographic Quote Shortcuts

Character	Macintosh Shortcut	Windows Shortcut
" (open double quote)	Option+[	Shift+Alt+[
" (closed double quote)	Shift+Option+[	Shift+Alt+]
' (open single quote)	Option+]	Alt+[
' (closed single quote)	Shift+Option+]	Alt+]
' (keyboard single quote/apostrophe)	Control+'	Ctrl+'
" (keyboard double quote)	Control+Shift+'	Ctrl+Alt+'
` (keyboard open single quote)	`	`

Caution

Do not use the keyboard open single quote key (`), in the upper-left corner of your keyboard to the left of the 1, as an open single quote. Instead, use the keyboard apostrophe ('). If you use the open single quote keyboard key, you will often get a different open single quote character than the standard typographic version — depending on how the font is set up, of course.

Typing reverse single quotes

A reverse single quote is often used to indicate an omission — for example, in *'80s* to mean the 1980s or in *'burbs* to mean suburbs. You need to enter this type of reverse quote manually at all times (whether or not Smart Quotes is in use). This is actually just a manually entered single close quote: Option+Shift+] or Alt+].

Manually entering dashes

If you want to enter dashes in text while typing directly into a QuarkXPress document, you must also use special commands, as shown in Table 18-2.

Table 18-2
Keyboard Shortcuts for Dashes and Hyphens

Character	Mac Shortcut	Windows Shortcut
— (em dash)	Option+Shift+hyphen	Ctrl+Shift+=
— (nonbreaking em dash)	Option+⌘+=	Ctrl+Shift+Alt+=
– (en dash)	Option+hyphen	Ctrl+Alt+Shift+hyphen
- (nonbreaking hyphen)	⌘+=	Ctrl+Shift+hyphen
Discretionary (soft) hyphen	⌘+hyphen	Ctrl+=

The rules of proper quoting and punctuation

Punctuating text with quotes confuses many people, but the rules aren't complicated:

✦ Periods and commas always go inside the quotation.

✦ Semicolons and colons always go outside the quotation.

✦ Question marks and exclamation marks go inside if they're part of the quote, outside if not. When the main clause is a question, but the quote is a declaration, the question mark takes precedence over the period, so it goes outside the quotes. When the main clause is a question, and the quote is an exclamation, the exclamation takes precedence, and it goes within the quotation. Look at the following examples:

  • Did he really say, "I am too busy"?

  • She asked, "Do you have time to help?"

  • I can't believe she asked, "Do you have time to help?"

  • He really did yell, "I am too busy!"

  • Did he really yell, "I am too busy!"?

✦ When a single quote is followed immediately by a double quote, separate the two with a nonbreaking space (⌘+spacebar on the Mac and Ctrl+5 in Windows).

  • He told me, "She asked, 'Do you have time to help?'"

  • He told me, "Bob heard him say, 'I am too busy.'"

  • She asked me, "Can you believe that he said, 'I am too busy'?"

For more information on these rules, refer to a grammar guide.

Tip   A nonbreaking em dash doesn't let text following it wrap to a new line. Instead, the break must occur at a spot preceding or following the dash.

Using en dashes

The en dash, so called because it is the width of a capital *N*, is a nonbreaking character, so QuarkXPress doesn't let a line break after it. Traditionally, an en dash is used to:

✦ Separate numerals, as in a range of values or dates

✦ Label a figure

✦ Indicate a negative value (a minus sign)

✦ Indicate a multiple-word hyphenation (Civil War–era)

Symbols and special characters

A typeface comes with dozens of special symbols, ranging from bullets to copyright symbols. The most common ones are accessible from QuarkXPress through the following commands (see Table 18-3 for a list of shortcuts):

✦ • En bullet: Press Option+8 on the Mac; Alt+8 in some Windows programs. (See the sidebar "Bullets in Microsoft Word," earlier in this chapter.) A bullet is an effective way to call attention to issues being raised. Typically, bullets are used at the beginning of each element in a list. If the sequence of the elements is important, as in a series of steps, use numerals instead of bullets.

✦ © Copyright: Press Option+G on the Mac; Shift+Alt+C in Windows. A copyright symbol signifies who owns text or other visual media. The standard format is Copyright © 2002 Hungry Minds. All rights reserved. For text, you must include at least the © symbol, the word Copyright, or the abbreviation Copr, as well as the year first published and the name of the copyright holder. (Note that only the © symbol is valid for international copyright.) Works need not be registered to be copyrighted. The notice is sufficient, but registering is best.

✦ ® Registered trademark: Press Option+R on the Mac, Shift+Alt+R in Windows. This is usually used in advertising, packaging, marketing, and public relations to indicate that a product or service name is exclusively owned by a company. The mark follows the name. You may use the ® symbol only with names registered with the U.S. Patent and Trademark Office. For works whose trademark registration is pending, use the ™ symbol.

✦ ™ Pending trademark: Press Option+2 on the Mac, Shift+Alt+2 in Windows.

✦ § Section: Press Option+6 on the Mac, Shift+Alt+6 in Windows. This symbol is typically used in legal and scholarly documents to refer to sections of laws or research papers.

✦ ¶ Paragraph: Press Option+7 on the Mac, Shift+Alt+7 in Windows. Like the section symbol, the paragraph symbol is typically used for legal and scholarly documents.

✦ † Dagger: Press Option+T on the Mac, Shift+Alt+T in Windows. This symbol is often used for footnotes.

Table 18-3 shows keyboard shortcuts that work for entering the most commonly used special characters in most fonts. On Windows, QuarkXPress includes additional keyboard shortcuts for the special characters you enter daily such as bullets. (In the chart, those are the commands that don't require Alt plus a four-digit number.) If a keyboard shortcut doesn't work, it's likely that the current font does not include the special character you're trying to enter. Use a character map utility, such as KeyCaps, to check. If a special character you need is listed as "not supported" below, you may still be able to find it within a dingbat font or an expert font.

Spacing em dashes — or not

Typographers are divided over whether you should put spaces around em dashes — like this — or not — like this. Traditionally, there is no space. But having space lets the publishing program treat the dash as a word, so that there is even space around all words in a line. Not having a space around dashes means that the publishing program sees the two words connected by the em dash as one big word. So the spacing added to justify a line between all other words on the line may be awkwardly large, because the program doesn't know how to break a line after or before an em dash that doesn't have space on either side. Still, whether to surround a dash with space is a decision in which personal preferences should prevail.

Table 18-3
Shortcuts for Symbols

Character	Mac Shortcut	Windows Shortcut
Legal		
Copyright (©)	Option+G	Shift+Alt+C or Ctrl+Alt+C or Alt+0169
Registered trademark (®)	Option+R	Shift+Alt+R or Alt+0174
Trademark (™)	Option+2	Shift+Alt+2 or Alt+0153
Paragraph (¶)	Option+7	Shift+Alt+7 or Ctrl+Alt+; or Alt+0182
Section (§)	Option+6	Shift+Alt+6 or Alt+0167
Dagger (†)	Option+T	Shift+Alt+T or Alt+0134
Double dagger (‡)	Option+Shift+7	Alt+0135
Currency		
Cent (¢)	Option+4	Alt+0162
Euro (€)	Option+Shift+2	Alt+Ctrl+5
Pound sterling (£)	Option+3	Alt+0163
Yen (¥)	Option+Y	Ctrl+Alt+- (hyphen) or Alt+0165
Punctuation		
En bullet (•)	Option+8	Alt+8 or Alt+0149
Thin bullet (·)	not supported*	Alt+0183
Ellipsis (...)	Option+; (semicolon)	Alt+0133

Character	Mac Shortcut	Windows Shortcut
Measurement		
Foot (')	Control+'	Ctrl+'
Inch (")	Control+Shift+'	Ctrl+Alt+'
Mathematics		
One-half fraction (½)	*not supported*	Ctrl+Alt+6 *or* Alt+0189
One-quarter fraction (¼)	*not supported*	Ctrl+Alt+7 *or* Alt+0188
Three-quarters fraction (¾)	*not supported*	Ctrl+Alt+8 *or* Alt+0190
Infinity (∞)	Option+5	*not supported*
Multiplication (×)	Option+Y in Symbol font	Ctrl+Alt+= *or* Alt+0215
Division (÷)	Option+/	Alt+0247
Root (√)	Option+V	*not supported*
Greater than or equal (≥)	Option+>	*not supported*
Less than or equal (≤)	Option+<	*not supported*
Inequality (≠)	Option+=	*not supported*
Rough equivalence (≈)	Option+X	*not supported*
Plus or minus (±)	Option+Shift+=	Alt+0177
Logical not (¬)	Option+L	Ctrl+Alt+\ *or* Alt+0172
Per mil (‰)	Option+Shift+R	Alt+0137
Degree (°)	Option+Shift+8	Alt+0176
Function (ƒ)	Option+F	Alt+0131
Integral (∫)	Option+B	*not supported*
Variation (∂)	Option+D	*not supported*
Greek beta (ß)	Option+S	*not supported*
Greek mu (µ)	Option+M	Alt+0181
Greek Pi (∏)	Option+Shift+P	*not supported*
Greek pi (π)	Option+P	*not supported*
Greek Sigma (∑)	Option+W	*not supported*
Greek Omega (Ω)	Option+Z	*not supported*
Miscellaneous		
Apple logo ( )	Option+Shift+K in Chicago font	*not supported*
Light (☼)	*not supported*	Ctrl+Alt+4 *or* Alt+0164
Open diamond (◊)	Option+Shift+V	*not supported*

When you want a long portion of text to run so that it appears as one visual block — a tactic often used for article openers in highly designed magazines — consider using symbols such as § and ¶ as paragraph-break indicators. (Frequently, they are set in larger or bolder type when used in this manner.) The symbols alert readers to paragraph shifts. *Rolling Stone* magazine is particularly partial to this effect.

Using foreign language characters

See Table 18-4 for foreign-language characters. Note that Windows shortcuts involving four numerals (such as Alt+0157) should be entered from the numeric keypad while holding the Alt key.

Table 18-4 Shortcuts for Accents and Foreign Characters		
Character	*Mac Shortcut*	*Windows Shortcut*
acute (´)*	Option+E *letter*	' *letter*
cedilla (¸)*	*see* Ç *and* ç	' *letter*
circumflex (ˆ)*	Option+I *letter*	^ *letter*
grave (`)*	Option+` *letter*	` *letter*
tilde (~)*	Option+N *letter*	~ *letter*
trema (¨)*	Option+U *letter*	" *letter*
umlaut (¨)*	Option+U *letter*	" *letter*
Á	Option+E A	' A *or* Alt+0193
á	Option+E a	' a *or* Alt+0225
À	Option+` A	` A *or* Alt+0192
à	Option+` a	` a *or* Alt+0224
Ä	Option+U A	" A *or* Alt+0196
ä	Option+U a	" a *or* Alt+0228
Ã	Option+N A	~ A *or* Alt+0195
ã	Option+N a	~ a *or* Alt+0227
Â	Option+I A	^ A *or* Alt+0194
â	Option+I a	^ a *or* Alt+0226
Å	Option+Shift+A	Alt+0197
å	Option+A	Alt+0229
Æ	Option+Shift+ '	Alt+0198
æ	Option+ '	Alt+0230 *or* Ctrl+Alt+Z

Character	Mac Shortcut	Windows Shortcut
Ç	Option+Shift+C	' C *or* Alt+0199
ç	Option+C	' c *or* Alt+0231 *or* Ctrl+Alt+comma
Đ	*not supported*	Alt+0208
đ	*not supported*	Alt+0240
É	Option+E E	' E *or* Alt+0201
é	Option+E e	' e *or* Alt+0233
È	Option+ ` E	` E *or* Alt+0200
è	Option+ ` e	` e *or* Alt+0232
Ë	Option+U E	" E *or* Alt+0203
ë	Option+U e	" e *or* Alt+0235
Ê	Option+I E	^ E *or* Alt+0202
ê	Option+I e	^ e *or* Alt+0234
Í	Option+E I	' I *or* Alt+0205
í	Option+E i	' i *or* Alt+0237
Ì	Option+ ` I	` I *or* Alt+0204
ì	Option+ ` i	` i *or* Alt+0236
Ï	Option+U I	" I *or* Alt+0207
ï	Option+U i	" I *or* Alt+0239
Î	Option+I I	^ I *or* Alt+0206
î	Option+I i	^ I *or* Alt+0238
Ñ	Option+N N	~ N *or* Alt+0209
ñ	Option+N n	~ n *or* Alt+0241
Ó	Option+E O	' O *or* Alt+0211
ó	Option+E o	' o *or* Alt+0243 *or* Ctrl+Alt+O
Ò	Option+ ` O	` O *or* Alt+0210
ò	Option+ ` o	` o *or* Alt+0242
Ö	Option+U O	" O *or* Alt+0214
ö	Option+U o	" o *or* Alt+0246
Õ	Option+N O	~ O *or* Alt+0213
õ	Option+N o	~ o *or* Alt+0245

Continued

Table 18-4 *(Continued)*

Character	*Mac Shortcut*	*Windows Shortcut*
Ô	Option+I O	^ O *or* Alt+0212
ô	Option+I o	^ o *or* Alt+0244
Ø	Option+Shift+O	Alt+0216
ø	Option+O	Alt+0248 *or* Ctrl+Alt+L
Œ	Option+Shift+Q	Alt+0140
œ	Option+Q	Alt+0156
Þ	*not supported*	Alt+0222
þ	*not supported*	Alt+0254
ß	not supported	Ctrl+Alt+S or Alt+0223
Š	*not supported*	Alt+0138
š	*not supported*	Alt+0154
Ú	Option+E U	' U or Alt+0218
ú	Option+E u	' u or Alt+0250 *or* Ctrl+Alt+U
Ù	Option+ ` U	` U or Alt+0217
ù	Option+ ` u	` u or Alt+0249
Ü	Option+U U	" U or Alt+0220
ü	Option+U u	" u or Alt+0252
Û	Option+I U	^ U or Alt+0219
û	Option+I u	^ u or Alt+0251
Ý	*not supported*	' Y or Alt+0221
ý	*not supported*	' y or Alt+0253
Ÿ	Option+U Y	" Y *or* Alt+0159
ÿ	Option+U y	" y *or* Alt+0255
Ž	*not supported*	Alt+0142
ž	*not supported*	Alt+0158
Virgule (/)	Option+Shift+1	*not supported*
Spanish open exclamation (¡)	Option+1	Ctrl+Alt+1 *or* Alt+-0161
Spanish open question (¿)	Option+Shift+/	Ctrl+Alt+/ *or* Alt+0191

Character	Mac Shortcut	Windows Shortcut
French open double quote («)**	Option+\	Ctrl+Alt+[*or* Alt+0171
French close double quote (»)**	Option+Shift+\	Ctrl+Alt+] *or* Alt+0187

* On the Mac, enter the shortcut for the accent and then type the letter to be accented. For example, to get é, type Option+E and then the letter *e*. In Windows, if the keyboard layout is set to United States-International — via the Keyboard icon in the Windows Control Panel — you can enter the accent signifier and then type the letter (for example, type ` and then the letter *e* to get è). To avoid an accent (for example, if you want the begin a quote — such as "A man" rather than have Ä man" — type a space after the accent character — for example, " then space then *A,* rather than " then *A*.

** Automatically generated if the Smart Quotes option is selected in the Interactive pane of the Preferences dialog box (Edit ⇨ Preferences ⇨ Preferences) and the French quotes are selected in the Quote pop-up menu, also in the Interactive pane.

Tip   If you apply All Caps typestyle to accented characters, your accents may disappear. If this happens — and you don't want it to — you need to check Accents for All Caps in the Character pane of the Preferences dialog box (Edit ⇨ Preferences ⇨ Preferences, or Option+Shift+⌘+Y or Ctrl+Alt+Shift+Y). This preference is checked by default.

Inserting end-of-story dingbats

A *dingbat* is a special character used as a visual marker, typically to indicate the end of a story in a multistory document like a magazine. A dingbat is especially useful if you have many stories on a page or many stories that *jump to* (continue on) later pages, because it may not be readily apparent to readers whether a story has ended or continues elsewhere. As with bullets, you can use almost any character as a dingbat. Squares and other geometric shapes are popular choices, as are logos or stylized letters based on the name of the publication or organization. Figure 18-8 shows the end-of-story dingbat for a magazine about house building.

> By making a commitment to produce better photos and allocating the resources now, you will be able to produce superb photos when the trees leaf out and the flowers bloom in the spring. And your home might end up on the cover of *Log Home Living*. ⌂

Figure 18-8: Here, a house icon is used as a dingbat to mark the end of a story.

Inserting a dingbat

To insert a dingbat, simply type the character, and then highlight it to change the font or character style sheet as necessary. If the character happens to be in Zapf Dingbats or Symbol font, you can enter a single character in that font by first typing a keyboard shortcut, then typing the character. For Zapf Dingbats, press Shift+⌘+Z or Ctrl+Shift+Z; for Symbol, press Shift+⌘+Q or Ctrl+Shift+Q.

Placing the dingbat

You have various options for the space between the end of the story and the dingbat:

✦ Set a tab for the last paragraph in the story (or within the paragraph style sheet applied to the last paragraph). Using the Tabs pane of the Paragraph Attributes dialog box (Style ⇨ Tabs, or Shift+⌘+T or Ctrl+Shift+T), set this tab to be right-aligned with the column's right margin; this is usually where dingbats are placed. (For example, if columns are 14 picas wide, set the tab at 14 picas.)

✦ A dingbat need not be aligned with the right margin. You may want to place it one em space after the last character in the paragraph, in which case you simply add two nonbreaking en spaces (Option+⌘+space or Ctrl+Alt+Shift+6) before the dingbat.

✦ Instead of manually setting the tab at the end of the story, you can also use a right-indent tab (Option+Tab or Shift+Tab) between the end of the line and the dingbat. This kind of tab automatically abuts the right margin of the box or column.

Defining a dingbat style

If you define the dingbat tab in the paragraph style sheet used for your body text, you don't have to worry about remembering to apply the right style to the final paragraph after the layout has been completed and text edited, added, or cut to fit the layout. You can also make the dingbat a character style sheet. For more information, see Chapter 32.

Formatting Fractions and Prices

To ease the pain of cookbook and ad publishers worldwide, QuarkXPress now includes a feature for properly formatting fractions and prices. Implemented through the included Type Tricks XTension, the feature automates the manual process of creating fractions and prices that look like those shown in Figure 18-9 rather than like this: 1/2, 1/3, or $9.99. If you don't like the results of the Type Tricks features, or you prefer not to run unnecessary XTensions, you can use fraction characters in expert typefaces or format fractions manually.

Note   If you don't have a Line Check option on your Utilities menu, it probably means you don't have the Type Tricks XTension installed. Use the XTensions Manager (Utilities ⇨ XTensions Manager) to activate the XTension, quit QuarkXPress, and relaunch QuarkXPress.

Mango Dressing

By Chris Kinney

Makes 2 servings for about $2^{25} each

⅔ **cup mango chunks**

¼ **cup sugar**

⅛ **cup cider vinegar**

⅛ **tablespoon red pepper, finely chopped**

⅛ **cup water**

¾ **cup olive oil**

¼ **cup canola oil**

1 Blend mango, vinegar, water, sugar and pepper.

2 Pour in the oils in a slow, steady stream.

3 Serve with Grilled Shrimp Salad.

Figure 18-9: The prices in the third line and the fractions in the recipe ingredients were formatted with the Type Tricks XTension's Make Price and Make Fractions commands.

Setting preferences for fractions and prices

The formatting applied to fractions and prices is actually a simple combination of QuarkXPress character attributes, including scaling, kerning, superior, and underline. You have some control over how those work through the Fraction/Price Preferences dialog box (Edit ➪ Preferences ➪ Fraction/Price), as shown in Figure 18-10.

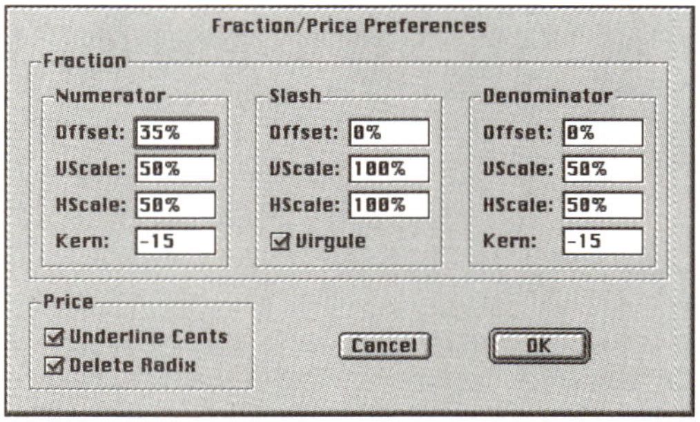

Figure 18-10: The Fraction/Price Preferences dialog box controls how fractions and prices will look.

The controls work as follows:

✦ In the Fraction area, the Numerator area controls the size and placement of the top number in the fraction and the Denominator controls the bottom number. The Slash area controls the dividing line, which typesetters call a *virgule*.

✦ In the Numerator and Denominator areas, the Offset fields are actually the baseline shift, calculated as a percentage of the original font size. The VScale and HScale fields control how much the characters are scaled in relation to the original font size. The Kern field controls how much the characters are kerned in on either side of the slash.

✦ In the Slash area, the Offset, VScale, and HScale fields work the same as in the other areas. If you check Virgule, the slash in fractions is replaced with an actual virgule character in the font, which is smaller and at more of an angle than a regular slash. (You can enter a virgule on a Mac by pressing Option+Shift+1.) The fractions in Figure 18-10 use a virgule rather than a slash.

There are no virgules available in standard Windows fonts, so the Virgule option doesn't appear in QuarkXPress for Windows.

✦ The Price feature, which you can only use on numbers with a decimal point, elevates the digits following the decimal point (refer to Figure 18-10). To have these digits underlined, check Underline Cents. To delete the decimal point in the process, check Delete Radix.

Click OK to save your changes in the Fraction/Price Preferences dialog box. These preferences are saved with the XTension, not with each document, so the settings become program defaults.

Although the default settings are a good place to start, the best settings for fractions will depend largely on the font and size you're using and the effect you're trying to achieve. You may need to experiment with the settings a little to get what you want. Because the settings are not saved with each document, you will want to write down the settings for each project.

Applying fraction and price formatting

This feature actually works like a macro, applying the formatting as you specified to highlighted numbers. The two commands for implementing the formatting — Make Fraction and Make Price — appear in the Type Style submenu of the Style menu, and they are only available when you highlight appropriate text.

✦ To create a fraction, highlight text that contains a slash character (it doesn't have to be numbers, interestingly enough). Then choose Style ➪ Type Style ➪ Make Fraction, as shown in Figure 18-11.

✦ To create a price, highlight text that contains a decimal point (it doesn't actually need to contain a dollar sign). Then choose Style ➪ Type Style ➪ Make Fraction.

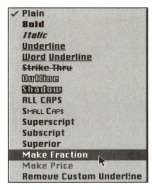

Figure 18-11: Choosing Make Fraction from the Type Style submenu automatically formats the highlighted text as a fraction.

To remove the fraction formatting, use the Character Attributes dialog box (Style ⇨ Character, or Shift+⌘+D or Ctrl+Shift+D) to reset the Size, Baseline Shift, and Kern/Track Amount (this will automatically remove any scaling). To remove the price formatting, you can highlight the text and click the Plain icon on the Measurements palette.

Using fractions from an expert typeface

Some expert typefaces include a variation, appropriately called fractions, that includes a number of common fractions such as ½, ⅓, ¼, and ¾. Adobe's Garamond Expert collection for both Macintosh and Windows includes a fractions face; examples of Mac typefaces with fraction variations include Mrs Eaves and New Century Schoolbook. To enter an expert fraction, use a utility such as KeyCaps to find the keyboard command for the fraction, then apply the appropriate typeface to the text from the Font menu in the Measurements palette. Windows fonts also provide keyboard commands for ½, ¼, and ¾, but no other fractions.

Tip

If you're dealing with a wide range of fractions in something like a cookbook, you probably won't find all the fractions you need. Because it would be difficult to format fractions such as ³⁄₁₆ exactly the same as an expert font's ¼, you might opt for formatting all the fractions with the Type Tricks XTension.

Formatting fractions manually

If you just need a quick fraction here and there, and you don't want to bother with setting preferences or finding an expert font, you can format fractions manually. You do this by applying type styles from the Measurements palette to the parts of the fraction. We usually apply Superior to the numerator, apply Superior and Subscript to the denominator, and then kern on either side of the slash. On the Mac, we replace the slash with a virgule first, using Option+Shift+1. This is also helpful when your Fraction/Price Preferences are designed for body text but you're creating a fraction in a headline.

Creating Initial Caps

Initial caps are capital letters at the beginning of paragraphs that are embellished in some way. A drop cap, for example, is an enlarged capital letter set into several lines of normal-size text. A raised cap is usually larger than the body text so it rises above the first line of a paragraph. You can even create initial caps alongside a story or screened into the upper-left corner. All these effects help draw the reader into a story, as shown in Figure 18-12, and the initial-cap design often reinforces the overall look of a publication.

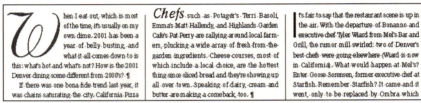

Figure 18-12: The initial cap at left, set in 99-point Nuptial Script, is in a separate text box so that the serifs on the *W* extend beyond the right margin. In the center, the word *Chefs* is in 18-point Concorde Nova Italic, rising above the 9-point Concorde Nova body text. At right, the traditional one-character drop cap, with Univers Condensed Light applied, is set three lines into the body text.

Adding drop caps

Using *drop caps* (a large letter set into several lines of normal-size text) is a popular way to guide readers through changes in topics. Drop caps also are frequently used to identify the introduction of a story. When drop caps are used in this manner, the introduction usually doesn't have a subhead, but the sections between may have subheads.

Although drop caps appear to be character attributes — given that they affect only a few characters — they're actually paragraph attributes. You can apply a drop cap to a paragraph, and even if you edit the text, the drop cap remains. This also allows you to save drop-cap formatting with a paragraph style sheet.

STEPS: Creating an automatic drop cap

1. Click in a paragraph.

2. Choose Style ➪ Formats (or Shift+⌘+F or Ctrl+Shift+F).

3. Check Drop Caps to activate the feature.

4. In the Character Count field, enter the number of characters (usually 1) to be set as drop caps.

5. In the Line Count field, enter how many lines into the paragraph you want the characters to drop (a typical setting is 3, but it can be as many as 16).

6. Click Apply if you want to preview the drop cap, as shown in Figure 18-13 (drag the Paragraph Attributes dialog box out of the way if necessary). Click OK to add the drop cap.

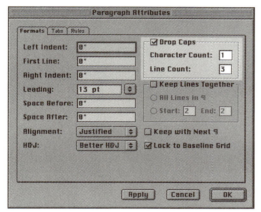

Figure 18-13: The Formats pane of the Paragraph Attributes dialog box provides controls for creating automatic drop caps.

Tip

Because you're likely to use this effect more than once, it's best to create a style sheet for any paragraphs that use it. In most cases, the settings for a drop-cap paragraph are the same as those for body text, except that the paragraph's first line isn't indented and a drop cap is defined. Rather than repeat all the settings for the body text when creating a drop cap style, you can simply follow these steps.

Applying character attributes to drop caps

To further embellish the drop cap characters, you can highlight them and apply character attributes such as a different typeface. This is optional — there is no reason a drop cap can't have the same typeface and formatting as the rest of the paragraph. But typically, a drop cap is either set in boldface or in a completely different typeface, which gives the drop cap higher visibility and usually results in a more interesting design. It's common for drop caps to be set in the same typeface as the headline or subhead or to pick up a color from other elements on the page. To change a drop cap's character attributes, highlight it and choose Style ⇨ Character (or Shift+⌘+D or Ctrl+Shift+D).

Tip

Note that you can also create a character style sheet for your drop caps, which ensures that each drop cap has exactly the same formatting as every other drop cap in your document.

Dealing with drop cap quotation marks

Should you use the open quotation character ("), the open single-quote character ('), or no character at all to indicate the start of a quote? Most typographers choose the last option to avoid having overly big quotation marks, and traditionalist stylebooks agree. (Do, however, use the close-quotation mark (") at the end of the quotation.)

Although this is an accepted practice, some people find it confusing because they don't realize they've been reading a quote until they get to the end of it. If you insist on indicating an open quote, use the single quote ('). It distracts the eye from the actual first letter less than the double quote ("). Be sure to set the drop cap's Character Count setting to 2, not 1. Otherwise, you wind up with a large quotation mark only!

Creating a raised cap

A similar effect to a drop cap is a *raised cap,* which is simply a large first letter on the first line of a paragraph. A raised cap doesn't drop into the surrounding paragraph but rises above it instead. To create this effect, simply select the first character and change its point size and, optionally, its typeface.

When you use a larger point size for a raised cap or a hybrid drop cap (see the following section on raised drop caps), the cap may extend into the text above. It's likely that you'll need to insert extra space above the cap to keep text from overprinting. One way to avoid this is to use additive or automatic leading options in your paragraph style settings.

Other hybrid drop caps

You can create yet another variation of a drop cap by moving the drop cap away from the text to make it more pronounced. Enter a kerning value in the Measurements palette to move the text away from the drop cap. In addition, you can compress or expand the drop cap with the Style ⇨ Horizontal/Vertical Scale menu option. A related variant is a hanging drop cap, in which the rest of the text aligns with the right edge of the drop cap. Use the Indent to Here character (⌘+\ or Ctrl+\) after the drop cap to set the indent position.

Other techniques for creating drop caps include using an anchored text or picture box where the drop cap would go so that you could use a graphic or a specially created letter. If you use this technique with a letter exported from an illustration program as a graphic and placed in an anchored picture box — or a letter converted to a picture box, as described in Chapter 23 — you can then use the Auto Image or Manual runaround features to have the text surrounding the drop cap follow the drop cap letter's shape.

Making raised drop caps

You also can create a hybrid between a drop cap and a raised cap. For example, you can add a drop cap that is four lines tall and drops in two lines of text. To do this, make the drop cap's line count 2, select the drop cap character, and then change its size. Note that when you do this, the Measurements palette options change from displaying actual point sizes to letting you type in percentages, such as 200 percent.

Creating Drop Shadows

QuarkXPress provides various methods for creating drop shadows behind text, an effect common in headlines and cover blurbs, as shown in Figure 18-14. Chapter 15 discusses using the Shadow type style available in the Measurements palette, but use of this type style is limited because you have no control over the color or thickness of the shadow. For display type, most drop shadows are created by layering text boxes.

Cross-Reference When you layer boxes to create drop shadows, then the text is edited, you need to edit the text in both boxes — which is kind of a hassle since it's difficult to see and select the text in the background box. You can get around this using the new Layers feature — just store each box on its own layer (see Chapter 10).

Figure 18-14: This drop shadow consists of white text (in a box with a transparent background) layered on top of black text (in a box that is offset slightly).

STEPS: Creating a drop shadow

1. Create a text box and enter the text to receive the drop shadow.

2. Using the Item tool, select the text box.

3. Choose Item ➪ Modify (or ⌘+M or Ctrl+M).

4. In the Box pane, choose None from the Color menu in the Box area.

5. Click the Runaround tab, and then choose None from the Type menu. Click OK to close the Modify dialog box.

6. With the text box still selected, choose Item ⇨ Duplicate (or ⌘+D or Ctrl+D).

7. The copied box is automatically selected. On Windows, choose Item ⇨ Send Backward (or Ctrl+Shift+F5). On a Mac, press the Option key while you choose Item ⇨ Send to Back — this changes the command to Send Backward (or Option+Shift+F5).

8. Select the text in the shadow box with the Content tool, and then change its color, shade, or other attributes as necessary to create the shadow effect you want.

9. Select the shadow box with the Item tool again. Drag it into position, as shown in Figure 18-15, or nudge it with the arrow keys.

Figure 18-15: Dragging the box containing the drop shadow to get just the right offset.

Tip

Shadows and outlines generally work best with bold type. With lighter type, the characters become obscured because their strokes may not be wide enough to be distinguished from the shadow or outline.

On the CD-ROM

To apply more complex drop shadows — to text, graphics, and items — with various options for blending, blurring, and color, try the demo ShadowCaster XTension. It's from A Lowly Apprentice Production (ALAP) and is on the book's CD.

Reversing Type

Reverse type, which features lighter text on a darker background, brightens text and pulls readers in. The effect is often used in table heads, kickers, and decorative elements, as shown in Figure 18-16. There is no automatic way to achieve reverse type — it's just a simple matter of applying a lighter color to text and a darker color to the background. You can achieve this with text boxes or with rules.

Figure 18-16: The name of the column and the pull quote for this article both stand out with the use of reverse type. The designer also picked up a spot color for the backgrounds from a graphic on the same page.

Reversing text in a box

For display type, you generally reverse all the text in a box by changing its background or placing the box on a darker background. To experiment with this effect, it's best to use the Colors palette (View ➪ Show Colors, or F12), as shown in Figure 18-17.

Figure 18-17: Dragging a different color to the background of a text box to create reverse type.

✦ With a text box selected, click the Background Color icon on the Colors palette. Click colors or drag color swatches to the box to decide on a color.

✦ Using the Content tool, highlight the text, then click the Text Color button on the Colors palette. Click a lighter color; use the Shade menu if necessary to change the intensity of the color.

✦ You can also apply None to the background of the text box, then simply drag the text box on top of any object or image with a darker background (use Item ➪ Bring to Front if necessary).

Tip　　Reverse type works best with larger type sizes and bold typefaces so the text isn't swallowed by the background. Make sure the point size of the text is large enough to print clearly on the darker background. Consider the thinnest part of characters, especially in serif typefaces, when judging the size and thickness of reverse type.

Using paragraph rules for reverse type

When the text you want to reverse is run in with other text, such as the subheads shown in Figure 18-18, you can use paragraph rules to create reverse type. A *rule* is a line that floats above or below an entire paragraph. To create reverse type, you move the rule into the paragraph.

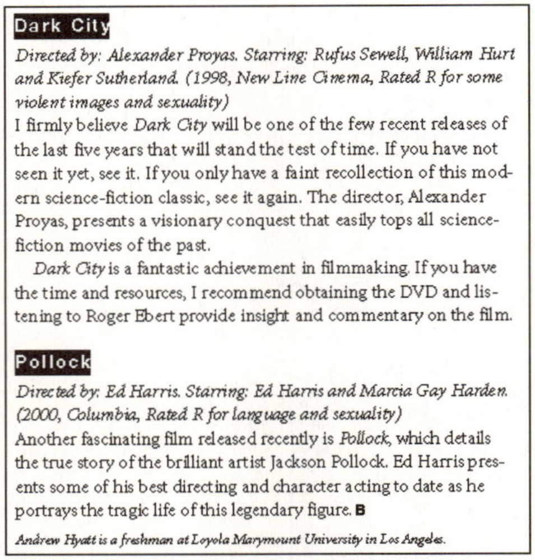

Dark City

Directed by: Alexander Proyas. Starring: Rufus Sewell, William Hurt and Kiefer Sutherland. (1998, New Line Cinema, Rated R for some violent images and sexuality)

I firmly believe *Dark City* will be one of the few recent releases of the last five years that will stand the test of time. If you have not seen it yet, see it. If you only have a faint recollection of this modern science-fiction classic, see it again. The director, Alexander Proyas, presents a visionary conquest that easily tops all science-fiction movies of the past.

　Dark City is a fantastic achievement in filmmaking. If you have the time and resources, I recommend obtaining the DVD and listening to Roger Ebert provide insight and commentary on the film.

Pollock

Directed by: Ed Harris. Starring: Ed Harris and Marcia Gay Harden. (2000, Columbia, Rated R for language and sexuality)

Another fascinating film released recently is *Pollock*, which details the true story of the brilliant artist Jackson Pollock. Ed Harris presents some of his best directing and character acting to date as he portrays the tragic life of this legendary figure. **B**

Andrew Hyatt is a freshman at Loyola Marymount University in Los Angeles.

Figure 18-18: When you use rules to create reverse type, the effect flows with the text.

STEPS: Reversing text in a rule

1. Click in a one-line paragraph and choose Style ➪ Rules (or Shift+⌘+N or Ctrl+Shift+N) to open the Rules tab of the Paragraph Attributes dialog box.

2. Check Rule Below.

3. Use the Width field to make the line thicker than the text in the selected paragraph. (Make your rule at least 2 points larger than the text to get an adequate margin.)

4. Enter a negative value in the Offset field to move the rule up into the text (the maximum allowed is half the rule size). Although the Offset is generally expressed as a percentage, you can enter point values using the abbreviation *pt*.

5. Click OK to close the Paragraph Attributes dialog box and apply the rule.

6. Highlight the text and change the color and baseline shift as necessary to fit within the rule. If necessary, modify the thickness and color of the rule using the Rules tab again.

Chapter 23 covers the paragraph rules feature in more detail.

Setting Hanging Punctuation

A technique used often in advertising is *hanging punctuation,* in which periods, commas, hyphens, and other punctuation marks fall outside the right margin. This technique is used in text that is either aligned right or justified. It doesn't make sense to hang punctuation in centered or left-aligned text because the punctuation would be too far away from the accompanying text. Hanging punctuation keeps letters aligned along the right margin but gives the text some visual flow by using the punctuation as an exterior decoration. Figure 18-19 shows an example of left-aligned text in which the punctuation hangs off the left margin. You can create hanging punctuation using tabs or using layered text boxes.

> *"Dining in Denver Peaks in 2001"*
> *Feeling flush or looking for a bar-*
> *gain? Where to find it Denver!*

Figure 18-19: Hanging punctuation adds a professional touch to display type.

Regardless of which approach you use to create hanging punctuation, if your text changes, you must manually change the line endings or punctuation positions. Because hanging punctuation is used only in small amounts of text, this is not a terrible burden. Also make sure that you turn off automatic hyphenation so that you don't get double hyphenation (one from the hyphenation feature and one from the punctuation you enter manually).

The tab approach

QuarkXPress offers no tool to handle hanging punctuation. For right-aligned text, you can create hanging punctuation by first inserting a line break at the end of each line (Shift+Return). Then insert a tab at the beginning of each line (between any punctuation and the first character), as shown in Figure 18-20.

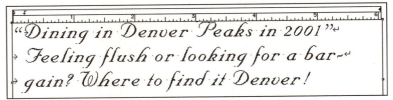

Figure 18-20: Inserting tabs to create hanging punctuation.

By positioning the tabs carefully (using the Style ⇨ Tabs command, or Shift+⌘+T or Ctrl+Shift+T), the punctuation will hang to the left of the text's margin. The advantage to this approach is that you can use the same tab settings (usually through a style sheet) for all text in which you want this effect. The disadvantage is that it does not work on justified text.

Tip Although the spacing of the tabs will depend on the particular text, size, and typeface in use, a rule of thumb is to set tabs at between one-third and one-half of the current point size. This is because the biggest punctuation symbol—the question mark—is usually about that size.

The text box approach

The other method of accomplishing this effect—and the method you must use if text is justified—is to create two text boxes, one for the text and one for any punctuation marks that end a line. The body text in the main text box will have justified alignment. In the punctuation text box, which will be slightly wider than the original text box, you can change the alignment for the punctuation as necessary. If one line has punctuation at the beginning and end, you can separate the punctuation with a right-indent tab (Option+Tab or Ctrl+Tab).

After creating the two text boxes, align them so that the punctuation appears properly spaced after its corresponding text, as shown in Figure 18-21. Select the two text boxes with the Item tool, then choose Item ⇨ Group (or ⌘+G or Ctrl+G) to prevent the two boxes from becoming separated.

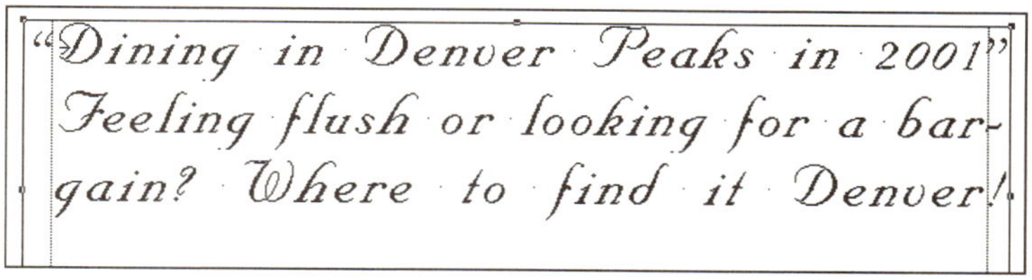

Figure 18-21: Inserting tabs to create hanging punctuation.

Applying Special Effects

QuarkXPress provides three special effects that you can apply to all the text in a text box: rotate, skew (slant), and flip (horizontal or vertical). Although rotation is probably the most common method for treating display type as artwork, skewing (slanting) and flipping text — especially when combined in interesting ways — also add to your design arsenal.

Rotating text

QuarkXPress lets you rotate an entire text box or rotate the text within the box. Rotating an entire box works well when you've already created and filled the text box but decide to angle it. Rotating text within a box works best when the box is already placed on a page — and then you decide to run text in it sideways.

✦ To rotate an entire text box, enter a value in the Angle field in the Measurements palette or in the Angle field in the Box pane of the Modify dialog box (Item ➪ Modify, or ⌘+M or Ctrl+M).

✦ You can also rotate an entire text box or text path using the Rotate tool on the Tool palette. Simply click on the item to select it (this also establishes the rotation point). Then drag in either direction to rotate the item.

✦ To rotate all the text within a box, enter a value in the Text Angle field in the Text pane of the Modify dialog box (Item ➪ Modify, or ⌘+M or Ctrl+M). Text rotated within its box is shown in Figure 18-22. The box and the text within the box can be rotated in different directions.

Flipping and skewing text

You can flip all the text in a box or on a text path horizontally, so the text not only reads from right to left, but all the characters are backward. You can also flip the text in a box vertically, which has the same sort of mirror effect of looking down into a pool of water. Skewing (slanting) also applies to all the text in a box. In Figure 18-23, we duplicated the original text box, then placed the copy under it. In the copied box, we skewed the text and flipped it vertically. The controls for flipping and skewing text are as follows:

✦ The Text pane of the Modify dialog box (Item ➪ Modify, or ⌘+M or Ctrl+M) provides the Flip Horizontal and Flip Vertical check boxes.

✦ Near the bottom of the Style menu, you'll find the Flip Horizontal and Flip Vertical commands.

✦ Arrows in the middle of the Measurements palette let you flip box contents horizontally or vertically.

✦ The Text pane of the Modify dialog box (Item ➪ Modify, or ⌘+M or Ctrl+M) provides the Text Skew field, which accepts values from 75 to –75 in degrees. You can also skew the box, independent of the contents, in the Box pane's Skew field.

Figure 18-22: Text rotated 90 degrees in a text box.

Note   When flipping all the contents of a box, select the box with the Content tool. This enables the Style menu and Measurements palette commands you need.

Figure 18-23: Combining Flip Vertical and −30° Skew creates an interesting mirrored effect.

Summary

QuarkXPress gives you the power to embellish and manipulate text in almost infinite ways. It's your responsibility to format text in ways that clarify and reinforce the content rather than simply decorate it. Using bulleted lists and paragraph labels helps break out information, and using special characters adds an air of professionalism. Initial caps draw readers into body text, while drop shadows, reverse type, and other special effects call attention to headlines, subheads, and kickers.

✦ ✦ ✦

Tabs and Tables

Aligning text is an age-old challenge in typography. After all, with characters taking different widths, and spaces varying in size because of justification and kerning, you can't just space out text like you could on a typewriter. That's why tabs were invented, to set up the alignments.

We're not talking about your grandfather's tabs here. In QuarkXPress, tabs offer sophisticated methods for aligning text — a far cry from the Tab key on the old Underwood. The key to using tabs in QuarkXPress is to pay attention to the tab characters in the text and position each tab precisely, taking advantage of options designed for aligning columns of text and numbers.

And more recently, word processors brought to the editor's portfolio table-creation tools. These tools let you set up alignments not only of individual words or numbers but of whole blocks of text by using the concept of cells to contain text and number blocks, and allow you to format those cells with shading, ruling lines, and so on. Now QuarkXPress joins the table party.

New Feature The ability to create tables is new to QuarkXPress 5.

Previously, your only option was to "fake" a table with a combination of tabs, rules, lines, boxes, and frames — a complex process that produced an inflexible table. Now you can create a table with however many rows and columns you need, import tabbed text or type in the table, include picture cells in a table, and modify the table to suit your design needs — all the while maintaining the flexibility to change the table at will. If your document already contains text suited to a table, you can easily convert it.

A Prelude to Tabs

Before you start setting tabs in QuarkXPress, you need to know a few things. Even expert users are occasionally tripped up by tabs, so pay attention to the following issues.

You can view tab characters

To see a tab setting in action, you need to actually enter a tab character in the text. Obviously, all this takes is hitting the Tab key on the keyboard. But if you're working with someone else's text, actually seeing the tab characters is helpful. To do this, choose View ➪ Show Invisibles, or press ⌘+I or Ctrl+I. Any tabs in your text look like right-facing arrows, as shown in Figure 19-1. As discussed later in this chapter, you should never have two tabs doing the job of one — so keep an eye out for two or more tab characters in a row.

Store→	Glue→	Scissors→	Tape→	Compass→	Ruler¶
→	Elmer's, 4 oz.→	child's→	Scotch's, small→	various→	12" wood¶
King Soopers→	.99→	1.75→	1.65→	.99→	.49¶
Long's Drug→	1.39→	2.59→	.99→	1.29→	.89¶
Office Depot→	.99→	1.99→	.99→	.99→	.99¶

Figure 19-1: The right-facing arrows shown here are tab characters.

Tabs are paragraph attributes

In QuarkXPress, tabs are *paragraph attributes* — meaning that, when you set them, they apply to all the text in selected paragraphs rather than to selected lines or characters within a paragraph. So if you want different tab settings on different lines of text, make sure there's a paragraph return at the end of each line (refer to Figure 19-1).

Default tabs are invisible

Word processors and page-layout programs, including QuarkXPress, seem to believe you'll be confused by actually viewing the tabs they've set for you. So when you start looking at tabs for the first time, it appears that none are set. This isn't true. In QuarkXPress, by default, invisible, automatic tab stops are located every 0.5 inch. Regardless of the measurement system your rulers are set to, when you hit the Tab key, you'll jump 0.5 inch to the right.

Tip If the default tab settings don't work for you, you can edit the tab settings in the Normal paragraph style sheet, which specifies the default formatting for all text. You can't actually tell QuarkXPress how far apart to space the default tabs, but you can set as many tabs as are generally useful for you. For example, you may set the first five tabs at 0.25 inch apart, then not worry about the rest, which will revert to the default setting. To edit the Normal paragraph style sheet, use the Edit ⇨ Style Sheets command or press Shift+F11. If no documents are open, you can edit Normal for all future documents.

Your tabs override default tabs

As soon as you set a tab stop of your own, it overrides any of the automatic tab stops to its left. The automatic 0.5-inch tab stops remain to the right until you override all of them. Again, this is mysterious because the tab controls look the same to the left and right of your tab settings, as shown in Figure 19-2.

Figure 19-2: The first tab set here is at 1.5 inches, followed by another tab at 3 inches. Although you can't tell, there is a default tab at every 0.5-inch after the 3-inch tab stop.

Text Inset affects tabs

When you set a tab, you're specifying a distance from the left edge of a box or column. But if you've specified Text Inset from the left edge of a box, tabs will actually be measured from there. To see if a selected box has a Text Inset set for it, choose Item ⇨ Modify, or press ⌘+M or Ctrl+M, then click the Text tab. By default, the text box tools create text boxes with a 1-point inset on all edges.

Fewer tabs are better

"Less is more" definitely applies to the use of both tab stops and tab characters. The easiest way to align text is to use one tab that is set where and how you need it to be. But at least half the time, when you turn on invisibles in QuarkXPress documents, what you'll find is an amalgam of multiple tabs and spaces used to fudge text into place. It's a mess, and it doesn't always print right. In Figure 19-3, compare the text on the right (set up properly) to the text on the left (set up with multiple tabs and spaces). You can clean up these messes by stripping the multiple tabs and spaces, then resetting all the tabs.

Store→	Glue→	Scissors→	Tape→	Compass→	Ruler¶
→	Elmer's, 4 oz.→	child's→	Scotch's, small→	various→	12" wood¶
King·Soopers→	···99→ →	1.75→	1.65→ →	···99→	.49¶
Long's·Drug→	1.39→ →	2.59→	··99→ →	1.29→	.89¶
Office·Depot→	··99→ →	1.99→	··99→ →	···99→	.99¶
Wal-Mart→	··.25→ →	···.76→	·.82→ →	···.97→	.27

Store→	Glue→	Scissors→	Tape→	Compass→	Ruler¶
→	Elmer's, 4 oz.→	child's→	Scotch's, small→	various→	12" wood¶
King·Soopers→	.99→	1.75→	1.65→	.99→	.49¶
Long's·Drug→	1.39→	2.59→	.99→	1.29→	.89¶
Office·Depot→	.99→	1.99→	.99→	.99→	.99¶
Wal-Mart→	.25→	.76→	.82→	.97→	.27

Figure 19-3: In the table at the top, the designer tried to align the text with a combination of default tabs and spaces; at the bottom, the text is aligned with one decimal tab per line.

Setting Tabs

QuarkXPress provides six different types of tabs, each shown in Figure 19-4:

✦ **Left:** The default tab stops are Left tabs (left-aligned), which means that the left side of the text touches the tab stop as if it were a left margin. Most tabs you create for text will be left-aligned.

✦ **Center:** Centered tab stops are like centered paragraph alignment, with text dividing itself evenly on either side of the tab stop. Center tabs are often used for table headings.

✦ **Right:** When you set Right tabs (right-aligned), the right edge of text touches the tab stop. This is commonly used for aligning numbers that don't include decimals or for the last column in a table.

✦ **Decimal:** Decimal tabs position the first period within text on the tab stop; if no periods exist, QuarkXPress pretends there is one after the last character.

✦ **Comma:** Comma tabs position the first comma in text on the tab stop; if no comma exists, QuarkXPress pretends there is one after the last character.

✦ **Align On:** Align On tabs let you specify the character for positioning the text (such as a percent symbol). Text is then positioned on that character as with Decimal and Comma tabs.

Preparing text files for tabs and tables

To set effective tabs for columns of information, each line of information should be its own paragraph, and each column of data should be separated by only one tab character. If there's only one tab between each column, you only need to set one tab stop per column, and you can more carefully control a single tab stop rather than several. The same goes for text you're planning to import into a QuarkXPress table or convert to a table—if you have multiple tabs between columns of information, or extra paragraph returns between lines, you'll end up with empty table cells.

The following image shows an example of a "table" typed into Microsoft Word by a novice publisher. Although each row of the table is its own paragraph, the columns of information are separated by varying numbers of tabs and even spaces. Although the text lines up somewhat on-screen, it will not align at all when printed or imported into QuarkXPress.

```
Store  →        Glue →       →   Scissors→    →   Tape →      →   Compass   →   Ruler¶
  →        →    Elmer's, 4 oz. →  child's→      →   Scotch's    →   various→   →   12" wood¶
King Soopers →  .99 →       →   1.75 →     1.65 →      →   .99 →       .49¶
Long's Drug →   1.39 →       →   2.59 →     .99 →       →   1.29 →      .89¶
Office Depot →  .99 →       →   1.99 →     .99 →       →   .99 →       .99¶
Office Max  →   .99 →       →   1.97 →     .99 →       →   .88 →       .99¶
Rite Aid   →   1.49 →       →   1.99 →     1.19 →      →   1.19 →      .49¶
Super Kmart →   .79 →       →   1.39 →     .89 →       →   .99 →       .99¶
Target →       .79 →       →   .99 →     .96 →       →   1.49 →      .27¶
Wal-Mart   →   .25 →       →   .76 →     .82 →       →   .97 →       .27¶
¶
```

With a file like this, you would need to use a search/replace function in the word processor or in QuarkXPress to replace the multiple spaces with tabs and replace multiple tabs with single tabs. (In QuarkXPress, use Edit ⇨ Find/Change, or ⌘+F or Ctrl+F. Enter the code \t to search for a tab.)

The resulting word processing file actually looks worse, as shown in the next image, but will work significantly better in QuarkXPress. Because the text is not in its final font or text frame, the current tab placement doesn't matter. But if necessary, an editor or writer can change tab settings in Word to align the columns for proofreading or editing purposes.

```
Store →  Glue →  Scissors→    →   Tape →  Compass   →   Ruler¶
  →     Elmer's, 4 oz. →  child's→  Scotch's    →   various→12" wood¶
King Soopers →  .99 →   1.75 →   1.65 →   .99 →   .49¶
Long's Drug →   1.39 →   2.59 →   .99 →   1.29 →   .89¶
Office Depot →  .99 →   1.99 →   .99 →   .99 →   .99¶
Office Max  →   .99 →   1.97 →   .99 →   .88 →   .99¶
Rite Aid   →   1.49 →   1.99 →   1.19 →   1.19 →   .49¶
Super Kmart →   .79 →   1.39 →   .89 →   .99 →   .99¶
Target →.79 →   .99 →   .96 →   1.49 →   .27¶
Wal-Mart   →   .25 →   .76 →   .82 →   .97 →   .27¶
```

↵ As with multiple tab stops, if extra paragraph returns are between the rows of information or if each line ends in a soft return (shown at left) rather than a paragraph return (¶), you should fix these with search and replace in your word processor or Find/Change in QuarkXPress. (In QuarkXPress, use the code \p to search for paragraph returns.)

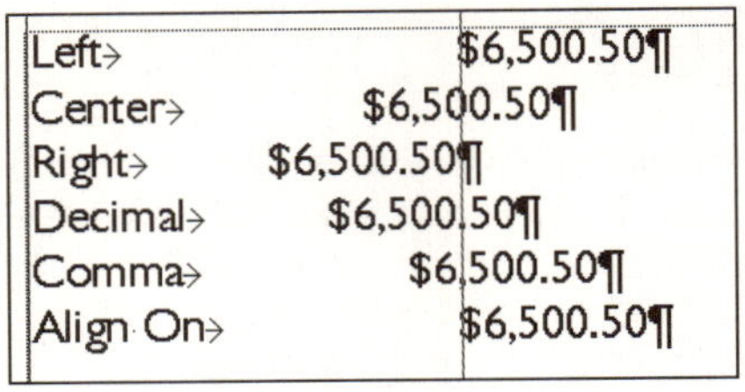

Left→		$6,500.50¶
Center→		$6,500.50¶
Right→		$6,500.50¶
Decimal→		$6,500.50¶
Comma→		$6,500.50¶
Align On→		$6,500.50¶

Figure 19-4: Here, each one-line paragraph has a tab set at 1.5 inches (we placed a guide on the tab to show you where it's set). However, each tab has a different alignment, and text aligns on it very differently. The Align On tab is set to align text on any dollar signs ($) in the text.

When you set tabs, you can also specify a *fill character,* which is the character used to fill the empty space that usually precedes a tab stop. Often, this is something like the dots used to separate a table of contents entry from its text. (QuarkXPress actually lets you specify two characters, as discussed later in this chapter.)

Using the Tabs pane

To set tabs, first you need to click in or highlight paragraphs with the Content tool. This lets QuarkXPress know where to apply the tab settings. Then choose Style ➪ Tabs, or press Shift+⌘+T or Ctrl+Shift+T.

On the Mac, when the Tabs pane is open, the tab ruler displays at the very top of the text box containing the selected text, as shown in Figure 19-5. The tab ruler will also display within a text cell in a table. When you're dealing with text paths, the tab ruler displays within the Tabs pane. In Windows, the tab ruler always displays within the Tabs pane.

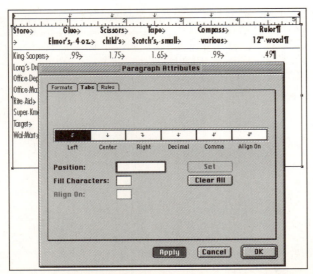

Figure 19-5: The Tabs pane of the Paragraph Attributes dialog box and the tab ruler.

Seeing what you're doing

To see how your tab settings affect your selected paragraphs, click the Apply button in the Tabs pane. But for true interactivity, Option+click or Alt+click the Apply button. This makes the Apply button stick, so any changes you make in the Tabs pane or using the tab ruler happen right before your eyes.

Starting over

If the current settings in the Tabs pane are not going to work, you can easily start over. Simply click the Clear All button. This reverts the tabs to the default settings. You can also Option+click or Alt+click the tab ruler to delete all tab settings.

Sharing your tab settings

After you click OK in the Tabs pane, you'll be surprised to find out how many times you need those same tab settings in another paragraph. Sometimes this is simply because you forgot to highlight one of the affected paragraphs. Other times it's because the formatting turns out to be used often. If you forgot to highlight a paragraph, simply click in it to select it, then Option+Shift+click or Alt+Shift+click the paragraphs with the correct tabs. (Note that this copies all the paragraph attributes to the selected paragraph.) If you need the tab settings frequently, save them in a paragraph style sheet.

 See Chapter 32 for information about creating and applying paragraph style sheets.

Setting tabs by the numbers

If you know exactly where you want your tab stops positioned, you can enter their precise positions numerically. If, on the other hand, it doesn't matter where the tabs go — just that all the text fits — you might set tabs using the tab ruler.

STEPS: Setting a tab

1. Using the Content tool, select the paragraphs you want to set tabs for. (It helps if the text already contains tab characters — this way, you can see your tabs in action.)

2. Choose Style ⇨ Tabs, or press Shift+⌘+T or Ctrl+Shift+T, to open the Tabs pane.

3. Click one of the six tab icons to indicate the type of tab you want to set: Left, Center, Right, Decimal, Comma, or Align On. (If you select Align On, the Align On field becomes active so you can enter a character. You might, for example, align a dollar sign [$], cents symbol [¢], or opening or closing parentheses [(and)] in text with the tab.)

4. Enter a value in the Position field for the tab. You can use the currently selected measurement system, or you can enter values in other measurement systems by including their abbreviations (such as 6 pt for 6 points). ***Remember:*** The tab stop is measured from the left edge or text inset of the box, and it removes all default tab stops to the left of it.

5. If you want to fill the white space between the tabs — for example, with periods as you see between a table of contents entry and its page number — use the Fill Character field. You can type or paste two characters to alternate, including spaces and special characters. Fill characters are also called *tab leaders,* because they lead your eye across the page.

6. Click Set to create the tab stop.

7. To see how your tab works with the selected text, click Apply. If necessary, drag the Paragraph Attributes dialog box out of the way.

If you need to change the position of the tab, click its icon on the tab ruler and drag it, as shown in Figure 19-6. (To change the alignment of a new or existing tab, also click its icon on the tab ruler and then select the new alignment in the Tabs pane. You can also drag the tab off the ruler, then create a new one in the same position.)

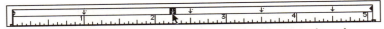

Figure 19-6: To change a tab's position, click its icon on the ruler and drag it.

8. Repeat Steps 3 through 7 to create any additional tabs, then click OK.

Calculating tab stops

As with other fields in QuarkXPress, the Position field can perform mathematical computations for you. So you can set a tab at half of 0.125 inches by entering /2 after 0.125". Or, you can move a tab by adding to or subtracting from its current value. It may seem unlikely that you would ever do this, but it's extremely handy for changing tab settings so they're, say, half as far apart as they used to be. Or half as far apart but 2 points over. The following example will move the tab at 2.25 inches over 6 points to the right.

Position: `2.25"+6 pt`

The operands for performing math in fields are + (plus), - (minus), * (multiply), and / (divide). If you want to combine these operands — for example, add 5 then subtract 2 — you'll have to remember back to ninth grade Algebra class to enter the operands in the correct order. Here's a hint: Computations are performed in the following order: multiply, divide, add, then subtract.

Using the Tab ruler

For a more visual method of creating and editing tabs, you can use the tab ruler, which displays above the current text box or within the Tabs pane. To create a tab, click one of the alignment options, then click on the tab ruler — the Position field shows the exact location of the tab. You can also select any tab on the ruler to change its characteristics, or you can drag a tab off the ruler to delete it.

The tab ruler has the following characteristics:

✦ It displays in the same measurement system as the document, as shown in Figure 19-7.

✦ Icons that match the tab styles display on the rulers to show you where and what type of tabs are already set. You can drag these around to reposition existing tabs.

✦ The ruler provides arrows for controlling and displaying the selected paragraph's first-line, left, and right indents, which you specify in the Formats tab of the Paragraph Attributes dialog box. Dragging the two left arrows changes both the paragraph's first-line and left indent, while dragging the top arrow changes only the first-line indent. Dragging the arrow at right changes the right indents. These arrows help you see indents in relation to tabs that you're setting.

Figure 19-7: The tab ruler displays icons for tabs and arrows for the first-line, left, and right indents.

Entering a right-indent tab

If you need a tab flush with the right margin, for example to position a dingbat at the end of the story, you don't need to set a tab. You can simply press Option+Tab or Shift+Tab while you're typing — this automatically takes you to the right edge of the column or text box. However, if you're in a workgroup and you're concerned about members' ability to remember this keyboard shortcut, you can always set a right-aligned tab at the right margin.

Working with Tables

In prior versions of QuarkXPress, if you wanted a table in a document, you had to combine tabs, rules, vertical lines, and multiple boxes. You could create a nice-looking table, but it was difficult to change the size or number of rows and columns, and it was difficult to change the formatting. QuarkXPress 5 introduces a tables feature that changes all that. You can now create tables with a tool or convert existing text to a table. After you have a table, you can fill it with text, pictures, colors, and blends. You can format the text with all the Style menu options you're accustomed to, including paragraph style sheets and character style sheets, and you can format pictures as usual.

Tables are designed for flexibility, letting you easily change contents, add rows, add columns, combine cells, and more. In addition, you have complete control over the size and placement of the table and the look of the grid lines that make up the table.

Understanding table construction

A QuarkXPress table actually consists of a collection of rectangular text boxes, picture boxes, and/or no-content boxes, all grouped together to function as a single unit, as shown in Figure 19-8. Each box is called a *cell* and can have its own content that you format with the Style menu and its own properties that you specify in the Modify dialog box. Although the feature makes it easy to format with data, it is by no means bringing you the power of a spreadsheet program such as Microsoft Excel to QuarkXPress (for example, you cannot add columns of data in QuarkXPress).

Back to School Bargains				
Store	Glue Elmer's, 4 oz.	Scissors child's	Tape Scotch's, small	Compass various	Ruler 12" wood
King Soopers	.99	1.75	1.65	.99	.49
Long's Drug	1.39	2.59	.99	1.29	.89
Office Depot	.99	1.99	.99	.99	.99
Office Max	.99	1.97	.99	.88	.99
Rite Aid	1.49	1.99	1.19	1.19	.49
Super Kmart	.79	1.39	.89	.99	.99
Target	.79	.99	.96	1.49	.27
Wal-Mart	.25	.76	.82	.97	.27

Figure 19-8: In this table, the top row is a single picture cell. The table heading, consisting of two grouped text boxes (one for the text and one for its drop shadow) is placed on top of the picture cell. In the top row of text cells, the paragraphs are center-aligned. In the remaining rows of text cells, containing the prices, the cells contain a decimal tab to align the prices.

Creating tables

The new Table tool lets you draw a rectangular table that is approximately the dimensions you need. When you've drawn the table, you can specify how many rows and columns of information you need. (Therefore, looking at your data before drawing the table is a good idea.) QuarkXPress automatically determines the size of the cells based on the height and width of the table and the number of rows and columns.

STEPS: Creating a table

1. Click the Table tool on the Tool palette.

2. Click and drag anywhere on the page to create a table. Use the rulers and Measurements palette to judge the size and placement. (If you want to create a square table, press the Shift key while you drag.)

3. Release the mouse button to display the Table Properties dialog box, as shown in Figure 19-9.

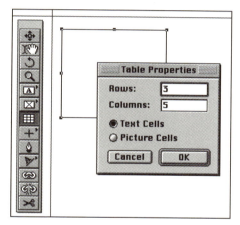

Figure 19-9: Here, the Table tool is selected, the dimensions of the table are complete, and the Table Properties dialog box is open so you can specify the number of rows and columns.

4. In the Rows field, specify the number of horizontal rows your table needs (be sure to include a row for table headings at the top).

5. In the Columns field, specify the number of vertical columns your table needs (be sure to include a column for the table headings that usually appear on the left side).

6. In the Cell Type area, click Text or Picture to specify whether the table cells should be text boxes or picture boxes (you can change individual boxes later).

7. Click OK to complete the table.

Changing Table tool preferences

As with other tools, you can modify preferences for the default behavior of the Table tool. To do this, double-click the Table tool to open the Tools pane of the Preferences dialog box. Click Modify to change defaults for the table tool — the options you'll get are shown in Figure 19-10.

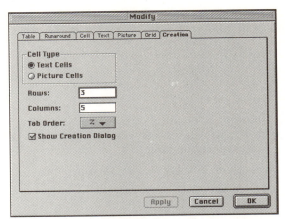

Figure 19-10: The Modify dialog box that displays when you're editing preferences for the Table tool.

The Creation pane lets you specify the default number of Rows and Columns, the Cell Type, and the Tab Order (the order the boxes are linked in). If all the tables you create are the same, you can uncheck Show Creation Dialog so that Table Properties never opens.

Note   Remember that changes to a tool's preferences affect the active document; if no documents are open, the changes affect all future documents.

Whether to create or convert

QuarkXPress gives you two options for tables: Create one from scratch then enter information in each cell, or convert existing text to a table. Each has its place:

✦ If you're planning to type your table text directly into QuarkXPress, create a table from scratch. You specify how many rows and columns you want, and you end up with a table of empty, linked cells. You can then type information into each cell, then press Shift+⌘+Tab or Ctrl+Shift+Tab to jump to the next cell. But what you can't do is import text into the entire table with Get Text. All the text does is fill the first cell, and you'll have to manually move it from cell to cell.

✦ If your table text already exists, you should import the text into QuarkXPress (using File ➪ Get Text, or ⌘+E or Ctrl+E), and then convert it to a table. (If you have data in a spreadsheet program, export it as a tab-delimited text file, then import it into a QuarkXPress text box for use in a table.)

What you don't want to do is spend a great deal of time creating and formatting an empty table, then expect to flow an existing text file into it. As mentioned, flowing text from cell to cell in a table is difficult.

Filling tables

When you create a new table, all the cells are empty. Filling the cells is easy—it's just like filling any other text boxes or picture boxes. Figure 19-11 shows a table that contains both text and picture cells.

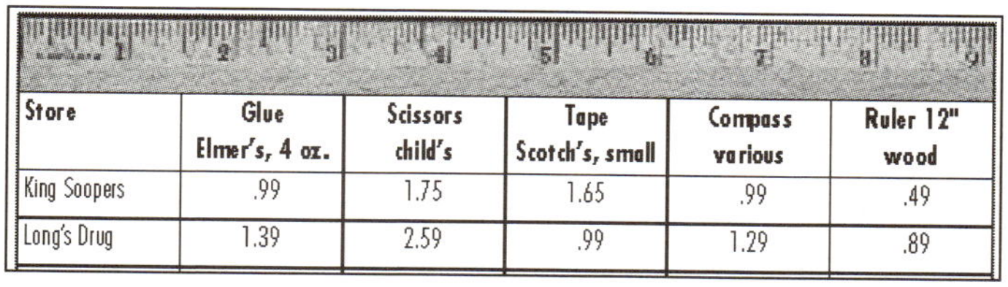

Store	Glue Elmer's, 4 oz.	Scissors child's	Tape Scotch's, small	Compass various	Ruler 12" wood
King Soopers	.99	1.75	1.65	.99	.49
Long's Drug	1.39	2.59	.99	1.29	.89

Figure 19-11: In the top row of this table, all the text cells were combined into a single cell, and the resulting cell was converted to a picture cell. The remaining cells are text cells, which contain a decimal tab for aligning the prices.

Adding text

To enter a text in a text cell, click in it with the Content tool and start typing. You can click in any cell and start typing or editing. Or, if you're entering data in order, you can jump from one cell to the next by pressing Control+Tab or Ctrl+Tab. (To jump back to the previous tool, press Shift+Control+Tab or Ctrl+Shift+Tab.) By default, you travel through the cells from left to right and top to bottom. If you need the cells linked in a different order, you'll have to change the Table tool's preferences before you create the table.

Tip

You're forced to throw in the modifier key to tab between cells because QuarkXPress actually lets you type standard tab characters inside cells. This means you can have decimal tabs, for example, within cells to align columns of data properly.

Adding pictures

To add pictures to picture cells, first click in one with the Content tool (the Item tool selects the entire table). You can then paste a picture from the Clipboard or use File ➪ Get Picture, or ⌘+E or Ctrl+E, to import an image file.

Tip

It's rare that you'll have an entire table full of images. Generally, you'll have mostly text cells with a few table cells. If that's the case, create a table full of text cells, then select the cells you want to contain pictures. With the cells selected, choose Item ➪ Content ➪ Picture.

Converting Text to Tables

If the text you're planning to put in a table already exists, import it into a text box. You can then convert this text into a table. In fact, due to the tedious nature of entering text into a completed table, you may want to simply type your table text into a text box—with tabs between columns and a paragraph return at the end of each row—and convert it to a table.

Understanding what happens to converted text

When you convert highlighted text to a table, the following things happen:

✦ By default, tabs in the text mark new cells and paragraph returns mark new rows. Tabs and paragraph returns are then stripped from the text inside the cells. (You can specify the actual characters used to separate your data during the conversion process.)

✦ Any character attributes, including character style sheets, are retained.

✦ Paragraph attributes are retained except those specified in the Tabs and Rules panes of the Paragraph Attributes dialog box (Style ➪ Formats, or Shift+⌘+F or Ctrl+Shift+F).

✦ Any lines or text paths anchored in text will end up in the text's cell.

✦ Any picture boxes anchored in text will become picture cells in the table.

✦ The text you convert to a table is copied—not cut—from the document. Therefore, you'll still need to delete the text from its original text box after creating the table.

Converting selected text

To convert text to a table, first analyze how the text is set up. To do this, choose View ➪ Show Invisibles, or press ⌘+I or Ctrl+I. If you see tabs (right-facing arrows) between each column of data and paragraph returns (¶) at the end of each line, you're good to go. If you see spaces, line breaks, or other characters, you may want to jot them down so you'll remember what's going on in the text. To create the table, highlight all the affected text with the Content tool (note that the text must fit on one page). When the text is highlighted, choose Item ➪ Convert Text to Table. The Convert Text to Table dialog box, shown in Figure 19-12, displays.

Specifying separation characters

Use the Separate Rows With menu to specify the character used at the end of each horizontal line in your text. This is usually the default option, Paragraphs, meaning paragraph returns (¶). But you can change this to Tabs, Space, or Commas. Use the Separate Columns With menu to specify the character used between each vertical column of data. Again, this is usually the default, Paragraphs, but you can change it to Paragraphs, Space, or Comma. These two menus, obviously, must have different settings.

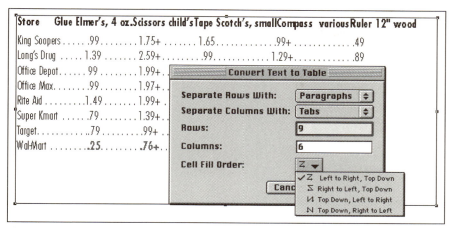

Figure 19-12: The Convert Text to Table dialog box, along with text highlighted and ready for conversion.

Changing the number of rows and columns

QuarkXPress automatically determines the number of rows and columns you need for the highlighted text. You can, however, increase these numbers to leave place-holder cells in your table by entering different values in the Rows and Columns fields. Or you can leave out data at the far right or bottom of your table by decreasing the number of cells.

Changing Cell Fill Order

If, for some reason, the text you highlighted is not in the same order as you want the data to be in your table, you can change the way the text fills the table. For example, if your data is in ascending order from left to right (say, least expensive to most expensive), but you want it in the reverse order (say, most expensive to least expensive), you can change the Cell Fill Order from Left to Right, Top Down to Right to Left, Top Down. The options are not only self-explanatory but are accompanied by an arrow showing the direction the text will flow.

Converting tables back to text

If you decide not to use text as a table, you can convert it back to text. This copies the text out of the table, separating the columns and rows with the characters you specify. If you want, you can delete the table while converting it back to text. In some cases, if table text needs a lot of editing, it may even be easier to convert it back to text. You can then edit it easily and convert it back to a table.

STEPS: Converting a table to text

1. With the Content tool, click anywhere in a table to select it. (You have to convert the entire table.)

2. Choose Item ⇨ Table ⇨ Convert Table to Text. The Convert Table to Text dialog box, shown in Figure 19-13, displays.

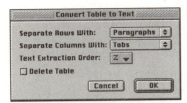

Figure 19-13: The Convert Table to Text dialog box.

3. To specify the characters inserted at the end of each row, choose an option from the Separate Rows With menu. This is usually the default, Paragraphs, meaning paragraph returns (¶).

4. To specify the characters inserted between each column of data, choose an option from the Separate Columns With menu. This is usually Tabs.

5. If you want the converted text to be in a different order than it was in the table, choose an option from the Text Extraction Order menu. You might do this if, for example, you want to make the text's columns be the rows in the table and the rows be the columns. You might do this because it fits better having the axes switched. Similarly, you might want to reverse the order of the columns so what had been the last is now the first, the second to last now the second, and so on.

6. Check Delete Table to delete the table after converting the text.

7. Click OK to place the converted text in a new text box, which is the size of the table.

Working with Table Content

When the Content tool is selected, you can edit and format the text and pictures within table cells much the same way you work with text and pictures in boxes. The advantage to working with a table is that you can highlight multiple rows and columns and apply the same attributes in one step.

Working with table text

When you're working with text in a table, it's similar to working with text in a single text box. You simply select the text or the cells, then use options in the Style menu or Modify dialog box (Item ⇨ Modify, or ⌘+M or Ctrl+M) to modify the text or the cell.

 Note   Because text cells are limited to one column each, the columns controls are disabled in the Text tab of the Modify dialog box and in the Measurements palette.

To select text in a table or table cells:

✦ To enter or edit text in a cell, click in it.

✦ To navigate within a cell or to the next cell, use the arrow keys.

✦ To select text in a single cell, click and drag to highlight a range or use Edit ⇨ Select All (⌘+A or Ctrl+A) to select all the text in a cell. You can also click the mouse to select text: Click twice to highlight a word, three times to highlight a line, four times to highlight a paragraph, and five times to highlight all the text in the cell.

✦ To select a range of text in several cells, click and drag.

✦ To highlight the text in a row, click the right or left edge of the table. Figure 19-14 shows a selected row.

✦ To highlight the text in a column, click the top or bottom edge of the table.

✦ To highlight the text over several rows or columns, click and drag along an edge of the table.

| Target | .79 | .99 | .96 | 1.49 | .27 |
| Wal-Mart | .25 | .76 | .82 | .97 | .27 |

Figure 19-14: Clicking outside the table with the Content tool lets you select entire rows and columns.

A few common changes you might make to table cells include:

✦ Changing the Text Inset in the Text pane of the Modify dialog box (to move the text in from the edges)

✦ Changing the Vertical Alignment of text within the cell using the Text pane of the Modify dialog box

✦ Inserting a tab, then positioning it, to align columns of data

Working with table pictures

When table cells contain pictures, you can select them with the Content tool and modify the picture size, placement, and more with the usual options: the Style menu for Pictures, the right side of the Measurements palette, and the Picture tab of the Modify dialog box (Item ⇨ Modify, or ⌘+M or Ctrl+M). If an entire row or column contains picture cells, you can click outside the table to select them all, then change their formatting at the same time.

Converting cell type

Any time you need different content within a cell, you can convert its type. To do this, select the cells, then choose an option from the Content submenu of the Item menu: Text, Picture, or None. Use None for cells that will contain only background colors or blends. You can select multiple cells for conversion as well: Using the Content tool, Shift+click to select multiple cells or click along the edges of the table to select columns or rows.

Modifying Tables

Once a table is finished, you're not stuck with it. You can resize rows and columns, change the number of rows and columns, apply colored backgrounds to cells, format the grid lines and frame, combine cells, and more. The tools you'll use to accomplish these tasks include the following:

✦ The Content tool lets you work inside a table: selecting cells, rows, and columns; dragging grid lines; and editing cell contents.

✦ The Item tool lets you work with the entire table: moving it, resizing it, and scaling it.

✦ The Modify dialog box (Item ⇨ Modify, or ⌘+M or Ctrl+M) provides the Table pane for positioning the table, the Runaround pane for controlling how the table affects surrounding text, the Grid pane for formatting the lines and frame, the Cell pane for formatting cells, and the Text or Picture pane for working with cell contents. As with other items, the controls in the Modify dialog box vary according to what you've selected in the table.

✦ The Measurements palette lets you size and position a table using the X, Y, W, and H fields. When text within a table is selected with the Content tool, you can format the text with the Measurements palette, including setting the font, size, alignment, leading, tracking, and style, as well as flipping the text within the cell horizontally and vertically

✦ The Table submenu of the Item menu gives you commands for adding and deleting rows and columns and for combining or splitting cells.

✦ The context menu, which you can display by Control+clicking or right-clicking anywhere in the table, provides all the options applicable to the part of the table you click on. For example, if you click on a picture cell when the Content tool is selected, you'll have options for modifying the graphic in addition to gaining access to commands for formatting the table. Figure 19-15 shows the context menu for a text cell. (***Mac users:*** Note that if you changed your Control Key preferences in the Interactive pane of the Preferences dialog box, you may need to press Control+Shift to display the context menu.)

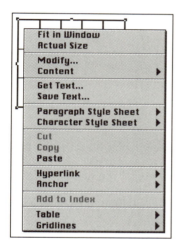

Figure 19-15: The context menu for a text cell.

Read on for information about selecting parts of a table to modify and about the modifications you can make to tables.

Selecting table elements

Before you can work with anything in a table, you need to select it. The biggest thing you need to remember about working with tables is that the Content tool lets you work with what's inside of the table, while the Item tool lets you work with the entire table.

Using the Item tool, click to select an entire table. Using the Content tool:

✦ Click to select a cell.

✦ Click the right or left edge to select a row.

✦ Click the top or bottom edge to select a column.

✦ Click and drag to select multiple rows or columns.

✦ Shift+click to select multiple cells, as shown in Figure 19-16.

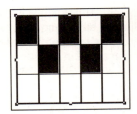

Figure 19-16: To select multiple cells, Shift+click them with the Content tool.

Tip

Working with cells in a table is the same as working with individual items within a group. If you want to modify a single item in a group, you need to select it with the Content tool.

Working with the entire table

When you select an entire table with the Item tool, you can move it, resize it, specify how text wraps around it, and format its horizontal and vertical lines.

Caution

You cannot, however, specify a background blend or graphic for an entire table — the only thing you can do is give each cell the same background color. Because this color cannot be None, you can't even place boxes containing graphics or blends behind the table. This limits your ability to give tables backgrounds composed of a single blend or a single image (such as a silhouette) — a disappointing limitation.

Moving a table

To move a table, the simplest thing to do is to select it with the Item tool and drag it to a new location. You can also cut and paste the entire table to move it to a different page. While you're dragging the table, use the rulers and X and Y fields in the Measurements palette for precision placement. You can also enter placement values in the X and Y fields in the Measurements palette or in the Origin Across and Origin Down fields in the Table pane of the Modify dialog box (Item ⇨ Modify, or ⌘+M or Ctrl+M).

Resizing a table

Resizing a table is like resizing any other item — select it with the Item tool and drag any handle. The table, rows, columns, and cells are resized automatically as you drag the handle. For more control, press the following keyboard commands while dragging:

✦ To constrain the table shape to a square, press Shift.

✦ To resize cell contents and borders along with the table, press ⌘ or Ctrl.

✦ To constrain the shape to a square and resize contents and borders, press Shift+⌘ or Ctrl+Shift.

✦ To resize cell contents and borders proportionally, press Option+Shift+⌘ or Ctrl+Alt+Shift.

You can also resize a table by entering new values in the W and H fields in the Measurements palette or in the Width and Height fields in the Table pane of the Modify dialog box (Item ➪ Modify, or ⌘+M or Ctrl+M).

Specifying Runaround for a table

Unlike all other items, QuarkXPress has a runaround rule for tables: Text must wrap around the outside edges of tables. (This means that you can't lay a table on top of other text, which is understandable because you wouldn't be able to read the table or the underlying text.) To specify runaround for a table selected with the Item tool, use the Runaround pane in the Modify dialog box (Item ➪ Modify, or ⌘+M or Ctrl+M). Although you can't choose a runaround type, you can specify a runaround value for the Top, Left, Bottom, and Right edges of the table.

Cross-Reference For more information about wrapping text around items, see Chapter 23.

Formatting a table's grid lines

When a table is selected with the Item tool, the Modify dialog box (Item ➪ Modify, or ⌘+M or Ctrl+M) includes the Grid pane. The Grid pane lets you change the look of all the horizontal and vertical lines (including the outside edges) that make up the table. Oddly enough, you cannot specify a frame for the table — all the horizontal and vertical lines must look the same.

Tip Limitations in the table feature mean that you can't frame a table or specify a thicker line below the heading row. What you can do is place a framed box with a background of None and a runaround of None on top of the table. You can also draw thicker lines and place them on top of your table. But since you can't group items to tables (Item ➪ Group, or ⌘+G or Ctrl+G), if you need similar effects, you may want to wait until your layout is almost finished to add them.

STEPS: Using the Grid pane

1. Select a table with the Item tool.

2. Double-click the table to open the Modify dialog box, then click the Grid tab.

3. Click one of the three buttons at right to specify (from top to bottom) whether to format all grid lines, horizontal grid lines only, or vertical grid lines only, as shown in Figure 19-17.

4. Use the Width field to specify the thickness of the grid lines.

5. Use the Style menu and the Line and Gap areas to specify the look of the grid lines. Your changes show up right away in the Preview area.

6. If you want to make the horizontal and vertical grid lines different, you can click another grid button at any time (without closing the dialog box and starting again).

7. When you're finished formatting grid lines, click OK.

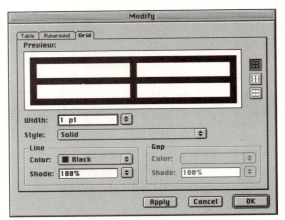

Figure 19-17: The Grid pane of the Modify dialog box.

The Width, Style, Line, and Gap controls in the Grid pane are the same as those found in the Frame pane. For more information about using these controls, see Chapter 8.

Anchoring tables in text

If you've got a table that needs to flow with text — for example, a small chart that supports the paragraph before it — you can anchor the table in text. This works the same as anchoring any other item. Using the Item tool, select the table and choose Edit ⇨ Cut, or press ⌘+X or Ctrl+X. Switch to the Content tool, click in text, and choose Edit ⇨ Paste, or press ⌘+V or Ctrl+V. You'll need to be sure the column or text box you're anchoring the table in is wide enough to accommodate the table. It's also helpful to place the table in its own paragraph, and give that paragraph auto leading so it has enough space above it. See Figure 19-18 for an example of an anchored table.

Working with rows and columns

Any time the data in your table changes, or you want to change its design, you can change its rows and columns accordingly. You can resize rows and columns, add them, and delete them.

Resizing rows or columns

To resize an individual row or column, all you need to do is grab its grid line with the Content tool. The pointer lets you drag the grid line up and down as shown in Figure 19-19. When you drag grid lines, the remaining rows or columns are resized accordingly.

If you're looking for school supplies, check out our chart of the best prices in town.¶

Store	Glue ↵ Elmer's, 4 oz.	Scissors ↵ child's	Tape ↵ Scotch's, small
King Soopers	→ .99	→ 1.75	→ 1.65
Long's Drug	→ 1.39	→ 2.59	→ .99
Office Depot	→ .99	→ 1.99	→ .99
Office Max	→ .99	→ 1.97	→ .99
Rite Aid	→ 1.49	→ 1.99	→ 1.19
Super Kmart	→ .79	→ 1.39	→ .89
Target	→ .79	→ .99	→ .96
Wal-Mart	→ .25	→ .76	→ .82

X: 1" Y: 0.5" W: 4.012" H: 7.5" ∠ 0° Cols: 1 auto 0 Helvetica 12 pt P B I U W @ 0 S K

Figure 19-18: This anchored table occupies its own paragraph, and the paragraph has auto leading specified in order to place enough space above the table.

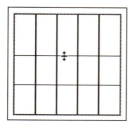

Figure 19-19: Dragging a grid line to enlarge a row.

For more precision in resizing rows and columns, you can use the Cells pane of the Modify dialog box.

STEPS: Resizing tables and rows numerically

1. Using the Content tool, select the rows or columns you want to resize. (You can even Shift+click outside the table to select both rows and columns.)

2. Choose Item ➪ Modify, or press ⌘+M or Ctrl+M, then click the Cells pane (see Figure 19-20).

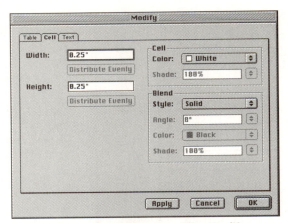

Figure 19-20: The Cells pane of the Modify
dialog box.

3. To specify a fixed width for selected columns, enter a value in the Width field. To create columns of equal size, click the Distribute Evenly button. (If the button is unavailable, the columns are already the same size.)

4. To specify a fixed width for selected rows, enter a value in the Height field. To create rows of equal size, click the Distribute Evenly button. (If the button is unavailable, the rows are already the same size.)

5. Click Apply to confirm your changes, then click OK.

Inserting rows and columns

If you need to include more information in a table than you originally thought, you can add horizontal rows and vertical columns as necessary. You can insert rows or columns above or below the currently selected one. To make insertions in the table, you'll use the Item ➪ Table ➪ Insert Rows or Item ➪ Table ➪ Insert Columns command. The resulting dialog box, Insert Table Rows or Insert Table Columns (see Figure 19-21), lets you specify how many to insert and where to place them.

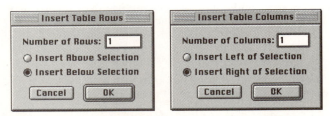

Figure 19-21: The Insert Table Rows and Insert Table
Columns dialog boxes let you expand an existing table.

By default, when you add rows or columns, the table becomes wider or taller as necessary. If you prefer to keep the table the same size, and instead resize the existing rows and columns, check Maintain Geometry in the Table tab of the Modify dialog box (Item ⇨ Modify, or ⌘+M or Ctrl+M).

Deleting rows or columns

If rows or columns of data are no longer applicable, you can delete them at any time. Simply select the rows or columns with the Content tool, then choose Item ⇨ Table ⇨ Delete Row or Delete Column. This deletes not only the selected rows or columns, but their contents as well. There's no alert, so fortunately you can undo this action (Edit ⇨ Undo, or press ⌘+Z or Ctrl+Z).

Working with cells

Aside from filling cells with text and pictures (and using the Text and Picture panes of the Modify dialog box to adjust them), you can apply colored backgrounds and blends to selected cells. You can also combine cells so they span several rows or columns.

Applying backgrounds to cells

To fill the background of cells with a color or blend, first select the cells with the Content tool. Then use the Cell and Blend areas of the Cells pane in the Modify dialog box (Item ⇨ Modify, or ⌘+M or Ctrl+M) to specify the color or create the blend. You can also use the Colors palette (View ⇨ Show Colors, or F12). Note that if you specify a blend for multiple cells, a new blend appears in each cell — the blend will not span multiple cells.

For more information about applying colors and creating blends, see Chapter 21.

Combining cells

To have cells that span more than one row or column, you can combine cells. This is handy if you want to place a graphic across the top of a table or down one side. To do this, Shift+click multiple cells with the Content tool. (The selection needs to consist of a rectangular selection of adjacent cells — you can't skip around in the table.) Then select Item ⇨ Table ⇨ Combine Cells. If you change your mind about the combined cells, select the resulting cell and choose Item ⇨ Table ⇨ Split Cells.

Summary

The control you have over tabs and tables is important for organizing information in QuarkXPress. The use of both features is improved by your ability to prepare clean text files that don't include extraneous tabs, spaces, and other characters to separate information. When working with both features, here are a few things to keep in mind:

✦ Choose View ➪ Show Invisibles (⌘+I or Ctrl+I) to display tabs, paragraph returns, spaces, and other hidden characters in text. These will help you set tabs and convert text to tables.

✦ Tabs apply to entire paragraphs and are set using the Tabs pane of the Paragraph Attributes dialog box (Style ➪ Formats, or Shift+⌘+T or Ctrl+Shift+T). You can also set tabs visually using the tab ruler that displays above text boxes or inside the Tabs pane.

✦ The Table tool on the Tool palette lets you create tables from scratch. You can then enter text into them. It's difficult, however, to import text into an entire table.

✦ You can convert selected text into a table, and convert a selected table back into text using commands in the Table submenu of the Item menu.

✦ Tables are made up of grouped text boxes, picture boxes, and/or no-content boxes. You can fill and modify these boxes as you do with any other items.

✦ The Modify dialog box, the Table submenu of the Item menu, and the context menu that displays for tables give you control over the placement, size, and formatting of tables.

✦   ✦   ✦

Graphics

Graphics are a vital part of page design. Often the most glamorous parts of a document, pictures and other graphics play a major role in attracting the reader's eye. Like text, they are largely created outside of QuarkXPress, so it's critical to know how to create them properly for the best and simplest use in QuarkXPress.

When they're in your layout, graphics do much more than make a document look better — graphics convey meaning and tone. So, it's important to treat the visuals with the same care as you use with the text or layout itself. To help you do so, QuarkXPress offers a solid set of graphics tools to let you import, create, and modify pictures.

This part explains how to prepare pictures for import, how to manipulate imported pictures, how to work with bitmapped images like scanned photos, and how to make text and graphics work together through text wrap and text-picture integration.

Working with Graphic Files

Most of the graphics you'll use in QuarkXPress — photographs, charts, graphs, and illustrations — actually come from outside the program. They generally exist as separate files created in applications such as Adobe Photoshop, Adobe Illustrator, and Macromedia Freehand. Your success in importing these images and printing them with QuarkXPress documents depends on their preparation. You can also output images, in EPS form, from QuarkXPress pages for use in other QuarkXPress documents.

Preparing Graphic Files

QuarkXPress offers support for the most-used formats of graphics files. Some formats are more appropriate than others for certain kinds of tasks. The basic rules are as follows:

✦ **Save line art in a format such as EPS or PICT.** These object-oriented formats support vector data. Vector files are composed of instructions on how to draw various shapes.

✦ **Save bitmaps (photos and scans) in a format such as TIFF, Photo CD, or PICT.** These pixel-oriented formats support raster data. Raster files are composed of a series of dots, or pixels, that make up the image.

✦ **PICT and EPS files can be in vector or bitmap format depending on the original image and the program in which it was created or exported from.** If you enlarge a PICT image and it begins to look blocky, it is a bitmap. (This technique does not work for EPS files, though, because all you can see of them in QuarkXPress is their low-resolution bitmap preview, which always looks blocky when scaled up.)

✦ **If you output to high-end PostScript systems, make EPS and TIFF file formats your standards.** EPS files can use PostScript fonts; can be color-separated if produced in a program such as Adobe Illustrator, CorelDraw, Macromedia FreeHand, or Deneba Canvas; and can support an extremely large set of graphical attributes. You also can manipulate grayscale TIFF files in QuarkXPress to apply custom contrasts, line screens, and other photographic effects.

Supported file formats

QuarkXPress imports the following file formats. If your program's format is not on this list, chances are high that it can save as or export to one of these formats. In the following list, the code in italics is the file name extension common for these files on PCs:

✦ BMP, the Windows bitmap format. *.BMP, .DIB*

✦ EPS, the Encapsulated PostScript vector format favored by professional publishers — also Adobe Illustrator's native format. *.EPS, .AI* (QuarkXPress also supports the DCS color-separated variant of EPS, whose full name is Document Color Separation.)

✦ GIF, the Graphics Interchange Format common in Web documents. *.GIF*

✦ JPEG, the Joint Photographers Expert Group compressed bitmap format often used on the Web. *.JPG*

✦ PCX, the PC Paintbrush format very popular in DOS programs and common still in Windows. *.PCX*

✦ Photo CD, the Kodak format used for photo finishing on CDs and popular for image catalogs. *.PCD*

✦ PICT, the Mac's native graphics format (it can be bitmap or vector); little used in professional documents but common for inexpensive clip art. *.PCT*

✦ Portable Document Format (PDF), also known as Acrobat format, a variant of EPS that is commonly used for distributing formatted documents. *.PDF*

✦ Portable Network Graphics (PNG), a recent bitmap format from Adobe Systems that's designed for use on the Web. *.PNG*

✦ RLE, Run Length Encoded bitmap, the OS/2 variant of BMP. *.RLE*

✦ Scitex CT, the continuous-tone bitmap format used on Scitex prepress systems. *.CT*

✦ TIFF, the Tagged Image File Format, the bitmap standard for professional image editors and publishers. *.TIF*

✦ WMF, the Windows Metafile Format native to Windows but little used in professional documents. *.WMF*

Additions to QuarkXPress's graphics import support in version 5 are the PDF and PNG formats. The ability of Mac QuarkXPress to import GIF files is new in version 5; the Windows version supported it back in version 4.

 The Windows Metafile format is supported only by QuarkXPress for Windows. All other graphics formats can be imported by both the Mac and Windows versions of QuarkXPress.

 Several import filters use Required Components or XTensions. QuarkXPress will not run without Required Components (which include GIF and JPEG import), but you can run QuarkXPress without XTensions. So if you're unable to import PDF, Photo CD, PNG, or compressed TIFF files, make sure the PDF Import, PhotoCD Import, PNG Import, and LZW Import XTensions are installed.

Issues with EPS files

EPS files come in several varieties, and not every EPS file is the same. You see the most noticeable differences when you import EPS files into QuarkXPress. The following sections explore these issues.

Preview headers

The preview header is a displayable version of the EPS image; because the Mac and PC don't use PostScript to display screen images, they can't interpret a PostScript file directly, which is why many programs add a preview header to the EPS files they create. At first you may not see anything but a big, gray rectangle and the words *PostScript Picture* when you import an EPS file. The file either has no preview header or its header is in an unreadable format. Although the image prints correctly, it's hard to position and crop because you must repeatedly print your page to see the effects of your work. This condition is typical for EPS files transferred from the Mac to the PC, because EPS files use a different header format on each platform (PICT or JPEG on the Mac; TIFF or WMF on the PC).

When you first get the picture, you can see whether there is a preview by checking the Preview box. As you click a file, a preview appears; if the preview is gray, there is either no preview or the preview is in an incompatible format. QuarkXPress for Mac can read all three types of preview headers, but QuarkXPress for Windows can only read a TIFF preview header. The Type field under the list of file names tells you what sort of file the selected image is.

Creating a preview header

If your picture lacks a usable preview header, use this workaround: After you print an EPS graphic, use the Item ⇨ Shape menu to convert the picture box to a freehand box and reshape the box to match the outline of the graphic you printed. If possible, convert the EPS file to a format such as TIFF and import that TIFF file into the box so you can more easily create the outline. You're able to see the TIFF file on-screen, rather than use a printout of the EPS file as a guide. When you're finished, replace the TIFF file with the original EPS file.

Whether you use QuarkXPress for Mac or for Windows, to generate an acceptable image header in an EPS file created on the Mac you need to save the file with a TIFF header when possible. This is the default for most Mac programs. For Windows programs, look for a Mac preview option and use it; if there is no such option, look for a TIFF preview option and use that instead. (An exception to this use-the-TIFF-preview rule applies for Adobe Illustrator files: Use the PC image header if you're using the files in Windows QuarkXPress.)

A few exceptions

As the major illustration and imaging programs have become cross-platform, with file formats that work on both platforms, the EPS header issue is less of a problem because the programs' designers account for use of their files on both platforms. You're therefore likely to have header problems only with older versions of your software. Here are some exceptions:

✦ **Early versions of the major Windows programs cannot generate the appropriate Mac EPS header.** During export, CorelDraw 5 generates a low-resolution black-and-white preview (even with the high-resolution option selected) for its color EPS files. Adobe Illustrator 4.0 generates no Mac-compatible preview. Like CorelDraw, the defunct Computer Support Corporation's Arts & Letters Graphics Editor generates only a black-and-white preview, and then only if you select TIFF for the preview format (use the Setup button in the Export dialog box).

✦ **In Adobe Illustrator 5.0 and 6.0, the default is to have no header.** If you are using Mac QuarkXPress, change that to Color Macintosh when saving in Illustrator 5.x and to 8-Bit Macintosh in Illustrator 6.0 or later. If you're using Windows QuarkXPress, use the 1-Bit PC option. If you're using both platforms' versions of QuarkXPress, use the PC preview header, because both platform versions of QuarkXPress display it. (Note that Illustrator 5.x's native format is EPS, so don't look for an export or save-as option. In Illustrator 6.0 and later, save as Illustrator EPS.)

✦ **If you're planning to print an EPS file from Windows, make sure you save it with ASCII encoding instead of binary encoding.** If you save the EPS file with binary encoding, you may not be able to print it from Windows.

Color issues

If you create color images in an illustration program, make sure that you use the CMYK color model or named spot colors. If you use CMYK the color is, in effect, pre-separated. With QuarkXPress, any colors defined in an EPS file are automatically added to the Colors palette for your document and set as a spot color. (You can change a color to a process color via Edit ➪ Colors or via the Colors palette's context menu; see Chapter 28 for details.)

To take advantage of QuarkXPress's color-separation features for imported EPS files, you need to create the colors correctly. (If you intend to print your file on a color printer rather than have it separated, don't worry about the instructions given in this section.)

Color separations

If your program follows Adobe's EPS specifications (as Adobe Illustrator, CorelDraw, and Macromedia FreeHand all do), QuarkXPress color-separates your EPS file, no matter whether it uses process or spot colors. Canvas automatically converts Pantone spot colors to process colors in your choice of RGB and CMYK models. For other programs, create your colors in the CMYK model to be sure they print as color separations from QuarkXPress.

PANTONE colors

Most artists use Pantone to specify desired colors, so keep a Pantone swatch book handy to see which CMYK values equal the desired PANTONE color. (One of the available Pantone swatch books — *The PANTONE Process Color Imaging Guide CMYK Edition* — shows each PANTONE color next to the CMYK color build used to simulate it.)

The *CV* after the PANTONE MATCHING SYSTEM color number in the QuarkXPress (and other programs') dialog boxes stands for *computer video,* which is Pantone's way of warning you that what you see on-screen may not be what you get in print. Because of the different physics underlying monitors and printing presses, colors cannot be matched precisely, even with color calibration. This is true for other color models, such as Focoltone and Trumatch.

If you don't have the Pantone swatch book, you can define the color in QuarkXPress as a PANTONE color and then switch color models to CMYK. QuarkXPress immediately converts the PANTONE color to CMYK, and then you know which value to use in your illustration program (if that program doesn't itself support PANTONE). Many high-end illustration programs, including Adobe Illustrator, support PANTONE and can do this instant conversion as well. If the option is available (as it is in QuarkXPress), use the PANTONE Process color model because it is designed for output using CMYK printing presses.

 For more information on defining colors and working with color images, see Chapter 28.

Calibrated color

With the bundled Quark CMS XTension installed, QuarkXPress color-separates non-CMYK files. (*CMS* stands for Color Management System.) It also calibrates the output colors (whether printed to a color printer or color-separated for traditional printing) based on the source device and the target output device.

Importing color files

When importing color files, be sure to change the color profile assigned by Quark CMS (if you're using this XTension) for images created by devices other than the default source. For example, your default profile for RGB images may be NEC MultiSync 1.5 Gamma, because the TIFF and PICT files you usually use were created on a Mac with this type of monitor. But if you're importing a scanned image, you should change the profile to match that particular scanner. You do so by choosing the appropriate file from the pop-up menu in the Get Picture dialog box. Note that it may take a moment for QuarkXPress to display that pop-up menu, because first it scans the image to see if it contains a profile of its own (called a Metric Color Tag, or MCT). You can also change an image's profile after it's imported (via Utilities ➪ Usage, and then selecting the Profiles tab, or in the Profile Information palette).

DCS and DCS2

The Document Color Separation (DCS) variant of EPS is a set of five files: an EPS preview file that links together four separation files (one each for cyan, magenta, yellow, and black). Use of this format speeds printing and ensures correct color separation when you output negatives for use in commercial printing. These files are often preferred over standard EPS files by service bureaus that do color correction. (The DCS2 file format is the same as the DCS format except that it combines all the plates into one file and supports spot colors as well as CMYK.)

Dealing with fonts

When you use fonts in text included in your graphics files, you usually have the option of converting the text to curves (graphics). This option ensures that your text prints on any printer.

If you don't use this conversion before making an EPS file, make sure that your printer or service bureau has the fonts used in the graphic. Otherwise, the text doesn't print in the correct font (you'll likely get Courier instead). Remember that QuarkXPress doesn't show fonts used in graphics in the Fonts pane of the Usage dialog box (Utilities ➪ Usage), so your layout artists and service bureau have no way of knowing which fonts to have available unless they run a Collect for Output report (see Chapter 36).

Working with bitmap formats

Bitmap (also called *raster*) formats are simpler than vector formats because they're made up of rows of dots *(pixels),* not instructions on how to draw various shapes. But that doesn't mean that all bitmaps are alike. The following sections cover the differences.

TIFF

The most popular bitmap format for publishers is TIFF, the Tagged Image File Format developed by Aldus Corporation (later bought by Adobe Systems) and Microsoft Corporation. TIFF supports color up to 24 bits (16.7 million colors) in both RGB and CMYK models, and every major photo-editing program supports TIFF on both the Macintosh and in Windows. TIFF also supports grayscale and black-and-white files. The biggest advantage to using TIFF files rather than other formats that also support color, such as PICT, is that QuarkXPress is designed to take advantage of TIFF. QuarkXPress can work with the contrast settings in grayscale TIFF images to make an image clearer or to apply special effects — something QuarkXPress can't do with any other bitmap format (see Chapter 21).

TIFF comes in several variants and no program, including QuarkXPress, supports all of them. Here are our recommendations for how to save TIFF files for optimal use in QuarkXPress:

✦ You should have no difficulty if you use the uncompressed and LZW-compressed TIFF formats supported by most Mac and Windows programs. If you do have difficulty with compressed TIFF files, we recommend that you use uncompressed TIFF files.

✦ If you want to color-separate your QuarkXPress document, it's best to save your TIFF file in CMYK format (Adobe Photoshop supports this format) because QuarkXPress cannot color-separate non-CMYK files unless the Quark CMS XTension is installed.

✦ Save the alpha channel for 24-bit TIFF images, because this comes in handy for creating a clipping path in QuarkXPress, as Chapter 22 explains.

✦ Save the clipping path, if you created one, for graphics files in QuarkXPress. With this path, QuarkXPress can do contoured text wraps around your image, if you so desire.

New Feature Note that QuarkXPress 5 can work with multiple clipping paths in an image. Previous versions supported just one.

✦ If you do color calibration in Photoshop 2.51 or later, or otherwise use a program that saves calibrated color in the Metric Color Tags format, be sure to save with the Metric Color Tags option enabled. This will help QuarkXPress's color-management system better reproduce your image.

✦ Use the byte order for the platform that the TIFF file is destined for. Macs and PCs use the opposite byte order — basically, the Mac reads the eight characters that comprise a byte in one direction and the PC reads it in another. Although QuarkXPress reads both byte orders, other programs may not, so why invite confusion? Of course, if only QuarkXPress and Photoshop users will work on your TIFF files, the byte order doesn't matter.

PCX

Like TIFF, PCX supports color, grayscale, and black-and-white images.

PICT

The standard Macintosh format for drawings, PICT (which stands for *Picture*) also supports bitmaps and is the standard format for Macintosh screen-capture utilities. QuarkXPress imports PICT files with no difficulty. Colors cannot be color-separated unless the Quark CMS XTension is installed and active. Because fonts in vector PICT graphics are translated to curves, you need not worry about whether fonts used in your graphics are resident in your printer or available at your service bureau.

Photo CD

Like other bitmap formats, no special preparation for this file format is necessary—which is great, considering that users have no control over the image format because it is created by service bureaus converting 35mm film to digital images via Kodak's proprietary process. With the Quark CMS XTension, QuarkXPress can color-separate Photo CD files.

JPEG

The JPEG (Joint Photographers Expert Group) compressed color-image format is used for very large images and the individual images comprising an animation or movie. Images compressed in this format may lose detail, which is why TIFF is preferred by print publishers. But JPEG is fine for the relatively coarse resolution of a monitor, and its file sizes are much smaller than TIFF files, so it's very popular in Web documents.

GIF

The GIF (Graphics Interchange Format) is a very simple bitmap graphic format with a limited color palette and resolution, designed to take little file space. It's very popular on the Web, because of its small file size.

PNG

The PNG (Portable Network Graphics) format is designed by Adobe as a potential replacement for GIF. It has a richer color palette and supports higher resolution but still takes relatively little file space. Because it's just a few years old, it isn't widely used on the Web.

Importing Graphic Files

Placing pictures in boxes is easy. Simply select a box and press ⌘+E or Ctrl+E, or use File ➪ Get Picture. You get a standard Open dialog box in which you move through your drives and folders to get to where the file is. Figure 20-1 shows the dialog boxes on Mac and Windows for both text and pictures. If you import a picture into a box that already has a picture, that picture will be replaced.

If you hold the ⌘ or Ctrl key when importing a color image, it will be converted to grayscale during import.

In QuarkXPress for Windows, you can also import graphic files by dragging a graphic file's icon from the desktop or from a folder onto a selected picture box on a QuarkXPress page.

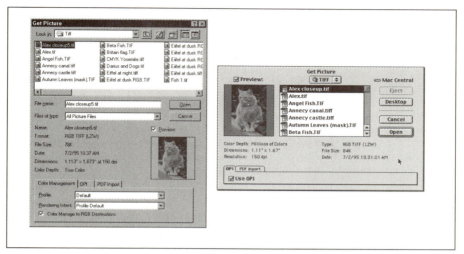

Figure 20-1: The Get Picture dialog boxes in Windows (left) and Macintosh (right).

Maintaining Links

You can bring graphics into QuarkXPress documents in two ways: You can import them through the File ➪ Get Picture menu (or ⌘+E or Ctrl+E) or use the Macintosh or Windows Clipboard to copy a graphic from another application directly into QuarkXPress. Both methods have their advantages:

✦ **The import method:** The primary advantage to using the import method is that you can create a link to the original graphic in case the graphic is changed or moved.

✦ **The Clipboard method:** The primary advantage to using the Clipboard method is that you can copy into a document graphics that QuarkXPress ordinarily cannot import. The Clipboard translates them to a format (PICT on Mac, Windows Metafile on Windows) that QuarkXPress can read. (Note that the PICT and Windows Metafile formats have limits in terms of output resolution and the image controls that QuarkXPress can apply to them.

Cross-Reference For information about positioning, scaling, and otherwise manipulating imported picture files, see Chapter 21.

When you open a document

When you open a QuarkXPress document, QuarkXPress can check the links to any imported graphic. These links are created automatically when you import the file; no special effort on your part is needed. QuarkXPress looks for two things: Is the file where it's supposed to be? And has the file changed since the last time it was accessed? (QuarkXPress looks at the file's date and time stamp to determine the second factor.)

If you've set your general preferences (Edit ➪ Preferences ➪ Preferences, or Option+Shift+⌘+Y or Ctrl+Alt+Shift+Y) in the General pane so that the Auto Import Picture option is set to Off (the default), QuarkXPress does not alert you to missing pictures. We recommend you set this preference to On, which automatically updates pictures with later versions, or Verify, which gives you the choice of doing so when you open a QuarkXPress document. Of course, if a file is missing or has been deleted, none of these options can update the file. You have to do that manually, as explained later. Figure 20-2 shows the General pane of the Preferences dialog box.

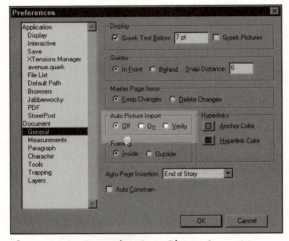

Figure 20-2: By setting Auto Picture Import to Verify (in the highlighted area of the Preference dialog box's General pane), you can have QuarkXPress notify you when a graphic is missing or has been modified.

The Verify option had been called On (verify) in earlier versions of QuarkXPress.

If the file is missing or has been modified, QuarkXPress displays the alert box shown in Figure 20-3. You can select Cancel, which tells QuarkXPress not to worry about the problem, or you can choose OK to invoke the Missing/Modified Pictures dialog box (see the next section, "Finding missing graphics"). (A file might be missing because the file was deleted, moved to a different disk — perhaps for backup — or renamed.)

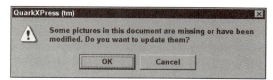

Figure 20-3: The alert box can show if a graphics file is missing or modified.

Finding missing graphics

The Missing/Modified Pictures dialog box (see Figure 20-4) gives you several pieces of information about the graphics that are missing or have been modified. These include:

✦ The full file name, including the last known location.

✦ The page that each graphic appears on. A dagger (†) with the page number indicates that it appears in the adjacent pasteboard.

✦ The type of graphic format, such as TIFF or EPS.

✦ The graphic's status (OK, Missing, or Modified). OK appears only after you update a graphic.

✦ The graphic's print status. If a check mark appears, the graphic will print. By unchecking a graphic, you can suppress its printing. You toggle between having a check mark and not having one by clicking under the Print column in the row for the desired graphic. (Chapter 35 covers printing issues in more detail.)

You can get more details on a specific image by selecting it with the mouse and ensuring that the More Information box is checked at the bottom of the dialog box.

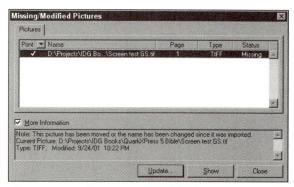

Figure 20-4: The Missing/Modified Pictures dialog box.

When you update

When you update a graphic, QuarkXPress checks the folder in which the graphic was located to see if other missing graphics are in it (because a common reason for missing graphics is that they have been moved). If it finds other missing graphics, it displays a dialog box that gives you the chance to simultaneously update all the missing files in that folder. If you need to see the graphic to remember what its file name refers to, select the file name, and then choose Show in the Missing/Modified Pictures dialog box. QuarkXPress displays the screen version of the graphic on the page on which it occurs.

You should be in a normal (100 percent) or reduced view so that you can see enough of the image when QuarkXPress displays it. Because you can't change the view after you're in the dialog box, close the dialog box (click Done on the Mac; Close in Windows), change your view, and bring the dialog box back via Utilities ⇨ Usage, and then switch to the Pictures pane.

When you don't update

If you don't update files when you open your document (by selecting Cancel in response to the alert box or by not making selections in the Missing/Modified Pictures dialog box), you still see the graphics in your document. What you see is a copy of your graphic that QuarkXPress creates when importing a graphic. For TIFF, Scitex CT, and all vector formats, this preview is a low-resolution copy that isn't appropriate for printing and shouldn't be used in place of the real thing. It exists only to show you what graphic you placed in case you don't remember the graphic by name. For PICT, PCX, BMP, GIF, PNG, and Windows metafile graphics — formats that use a fairly low resolution to begin with — you can print acceptably using just the print preview copy.

If you decide not to update a graphic link when you first load your document, you can do so later through the Utilities ⇨ Usage dialog box's Pictures pane. This pane works the same way as the Missing/Modified Pictures dialog box. You can also use the Picture Usage dialog box (Utilities ⇨ Usage) to substitute new graphics for missing graphics because QuarkXPress doesn't know (or care) whether the new links are to the same graphics.

Updating missing and modified graphics

When you've discovered that a graphic is missing, you'll want to update its link. You may also want to update a modified graphic or remove a link from a missing graphic you no longer want to use. This and the following sections cover all these issues. If you want to update a link to a missing graphic, the following steps tell you how to get the job done.

STEPS: Updating the link to a missing graphic

1. Select the file name.

2. Choose Update, and then move through the drives and folders available through the Find dialog box. Only files that match the file type of the missing file (such as TIFF) appear in the Find dialog box's file list. You cannot use this dialog box to replace one type of file (say, TIFF) with another (say, EPS). The way to perform this kind of change is to simply use File ⇨ Get Picture, or ⌘+E or Ctrl+E, to load the new image into the appropriate picture box.

3. QuarkXPress uses the standard Mac and Windows Open dialog boxes to search for missing graphics. When you find the missing graphic, select it and choose OK to update the link to the graphic and return to the Missing/Modified Pictures dialog box.

4. You see confirmation of your selection in the dialog box and can update any other files. After you've found the file, it is no longer labeled "Missing," but it may be labeled "Modified," if the newly located file is older than or more recent than the original or has a different name. (For more information on dealing with modified files, see the following section.)

5. Click the Update button again in the dialog box to update the link to the file.

As long as your graphic files use the proper PC file extension (such as .TIF or .EPS), both the Mac and Windows versions of QuarkXPress can recognize them and display them in the Get Picture dialog box. If you transfer graphics files from a Windows computer to a Mac, you don't need to change their file types in a program such as ResEdit or DiskTop (to, say, TIFF or EPSF), but you should make sure their DOS file extensions are correct.

Updating modified graphics

The process for updating a modified graphic is simpler than updating a missing graphic because QuarkXPress already knows where the graphic is located. To update a graphic, select the file name and choose Update. QuarkXPress prompts you with a dialog box and asks you if it's okay to update the file. (You can also cancel the update through this dialog box.) If you choose OK, QuarkXPress creates a new low-resolution screen representation and updates its link to the modified graphic. You also see the graphic's status change to OK in the Missing/Modified Pictures dialog box.

Only if you've selected Verify as the option for Auto Picture Import in the General pane of the Preferences dialog box (Edit ⇨ Preferences ⇨ Preferences, or Option+Shift+⌘+Y or Ctrl+Alt+Shift+Y) are you prompted to update modified pictures when you open a QuarkXPress document.

Deleting a missing link

If a graphic is missing because you no longer want to use it and have deleted it from your computer, you can remove the link to it either by cutting the box or boxes that contain the picture or by clearing the picture from any boxes that contain it.

Before you cut a box, the Item tool must be active; use ⌘+X or Ctrl+X, or Edit ➪ Cut. The Content tool must be active to clear a box; use Edit ➪ Clear. Alternately, to clear a box, select it with either the Item or Content tool and use the new Item ➪ Content ➪ None menu option. In any of these cases, use the Show feature in the Missing/Modified Pictures dialog box or the Pictures pane in the Usage dialog box to find these boxes.

Completing the update process

When all missing or modified graphics are updated, their names disappear from the Missing/Modified Pictures dialog box or acquire a status of OK in the Pictures pane of the Usage dialog box. When you are done and exit the dialog box, remember to save your document. If you don't save your document, none of the updates are saved.

Understanding links

QuarkXPress supports several types of links to source files, particularly graphics. The terms used to describe links can be confusing, especially because people tend to use the word *link* generically, no matter what kind of link they're referring to. Links in QuarkXPress fall into two classes: static links to files and dynamic links to objects.

✦ **Static links:** These are the standard links common to most publishing programs. When you import a graphics file, QuarkXPress records the location of the file and its date and time stamp. The next time you open a document, QuarkXPress looks to see if the graphic is in its expected location and if its date and time stamp has changed, assuming you checked Verify for Auto Picture Import in the Preference dialog box's General pane. (If so, the graphic itself has been changed in some way since the last time QuarkXPress checked the file upon opening the document.) QuarkXPress makes these checks for two reasons:

  • By linking to the original graphic, QuarkXPress needs to make only a low-resolution image for use on-screen, which keeps the document size manageable and screen-redraw time quick. (When printing, QuarkXPress substitutes the actual high-resolution graphic.)

  • By checking the links, QuarkXPress gives the layout artist the opportunity to use the latest version of a graphic. QuarkXPress lets you choose to always load the latest version of a graphic, ignore any updates to a graphic; or decide whether to update the graphic. If the graphic is not where QuarkXPress expects it to be, the program asks you to find the graphic.

✦ **Dynamic links:** These are possible with a capability on the Mac called Publish and Subscribe, and with a capability called OLE in Windows. (Note that Publish and Subscribe, like OLE, opens the originating program, which means you need sufficient RAM for both.) Dynamic links differ from static links in two significant ways:

  • They are links to objects (called *editions* by Publish and Subscribe), not entire files. You might, for example, have a link to a range in a spreadsheet or to part of a graphic.

  • The links can be updated any time, not just when you open a document. Dynamic links are managed through a Mac technology called Apple Events that lets programs communicate with one another and share objects among themselves in the background without user intervention or management. OLE uses a similar mechanism within Windows.

There are two basic types of dynamic links: live (automatic) and manual:

✦ **Live dynamic links:** With live dynamic links, there is regular communication between QuarkXPress and the program that created the object. If the linked object is changed in its original program, the new version is automatically sent to QuarkXPress, which automatically updates the object in the layout document to which it is linked.

✦ **Manual dynamic links:** With manual dynamic links, either the publisher or the subscriber must update the link by clicking the Send Edition Now button in the publishing program or the Get Edition Now button in the subscribing program. (In QuarkXPress, you double-click a picture box that contains a picture to get the dialog box that lets you click that button, as shown here. You also choose whether to make the link manual or automatic.) Either way, the subscriber always has the option of launching the original program with the original file so that modifications can be made. OLE has similar functions, as described elsewhere in this chapter.

Whether you were working with missing or modified graphics (or both), you may be puzzled about how to leave the Missing/Modified Pictures dialog box, because it doesn't offer an OK button. Instead, a Done button (on the Mac) or a Close button (in Windows) functions how the OK button usually does: It accepts the changes and closes the dialog box. Alternately, you can click the close box in the dialog box's upper-left (Mac) or upper-right (Windows) corner.

Using Publish and Subscribe

The Mac's System 7 brought with it a powerful feature called *Publish and Subscribe* that lets you create live links directly between applications. Mac OS 8 and 9 keep this capability. This feature ensures that when you make changes to text or graphics in the program in which you originally created them, the text or graphics are instantly and automatically updated in other programs that use them. Through object embedding, you can launch the application that created the graphic in QuarkXPress and work on the graphic.

Windows and OLE

Windows users may recognize Publish and Subscribe as similar to Microsoft's OLE capability (which stands for Object Linking and Embedding and is pronounced like the Spanish word *olé*). OLE and Publish and Subscribe accomplish the same thing. The main difference is that the user of a source application on a Mac must explicitly publish a file to make it available for subscribing, whereas the user of a Windows source application needs only to copy or cut a graphic or text to put it in the Windows Clipboard for linking.

Another difference is that OLE is implemented on both the Mac and in Windows, so that some programs (such as Microsoft Excel) can have cross-platform links, but Publish and Subscribe is a Mac-only feature. Unfortunately, QuarkXPress supports OLE only in its Windows version, so you cannot have such cross-platform links. See the sidebar "The perils of OLE" for more on OLE in QuarkXPress for Windows.

Creating live links

The first step to creating a live link is to create an *edition,* which is the result of publishing all or part of a file in its originating program. This edition file contains the link to the original file and program as well as a copy of the data itself (so that if the original file is lost, you still have a static image of it). Use the following steps to create a live link with the Mac's Publish and Subscribe feature. Figure 20-5 shows an example of how the Publish options work in two applications.

STEPS: Creating a live link

1. Select the element(s) in the originating program that you want to publish. Most programs, such as Excel, require that you select the element(s). Refer to Figure 20-5 to see the dialog boxes in Microsoft Excel 98 and Adobe Illustrator 8.0. Excel's is accessed via Edit ⇨ Publishing ⇨ Create Publisher, while Illustrator's is accessed via Edit ⇨ Publishing ⇨ Create Publisher.

   Most programs offer publish options that determine file format and degree of information published. For example, in Excel we clicked the Options button to get the Publish Options dialog box (below it), which lets us determine the file format and the resolution. Illustrator has a similar options dialog box, as Figure 20-5 shows. (Because QuarkXPress can subscribe only to graphics, make sure that you publish your data as graphics. For example, the published Excel data will be used as a picture, not as a textual table. Also, make sure that you publish the data in PICT or EPS format—QuarkXPress cannot subscribe to other formats.)

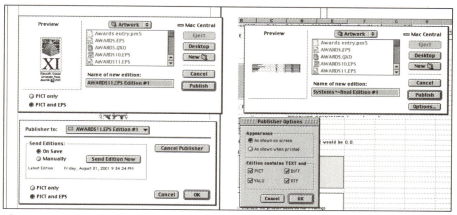

Figure 20-5: The Publish feature in Adobe Illustrator (left) and Microsoft Excel (right), along with their options dialog boxes.

2. In QuarkXPress, create or select the picture box that you want to put the edition into. Make sure you selected the box with the Content tool, and then choose Edit ⇨ Subscribe To. The dialog box is similar to the Get Picture dialog box (see Figure 20-6). Note that the preview image may be distorted for wide images.

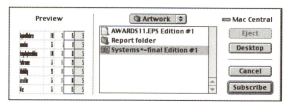

Figure 20-6: The Subscribe To dialog box in QuarkXPress.

The downside of the live-linking

We don't believe Publish and Subscribe's live-link feature is significantly useful for most QuarkXPress users to be worth the hassle and system memory requirements. QuarkXPress's own graphic-links updating features handle most of what Publish and Subscribe offer.

We do see a use for people publishing changing data, such as prices from an Excel table. But because the data must be published as a graphic, users must choose between printing data graphically (when they'd most likely want to format the data in QuarkXPress so that it looks like the rest of their document) or manually reimporting the updated data when it's changed. Of course, someone will have to tell them that the data has changed, or they'll have to check it themselves before finalizing their layout. For these people, a better bet is an XTension like Em Software's Xcatalog, which translates database files into formatted QuarkXPress layouts. (For more on XTensions, see Chapter 41.)

Updating live links

After you've subscribed to an edition, you can control when it's updated via Edit ⇨ Subscriber Options (see Figure 20-7). The options are described in the following list. *Note:* If the Content tool is active and you double-click a subscribed-to picture, the Subscriber Options dialog box automatically appears.

✦ **Get Editions:** The Get Editions portion of the dialog box offers you the choice of Automatically or Manually. The default option is Automatically, which means that whenever the source object is altered, the new version will be placed into QuarkXPress.

✦ **Get Edition Now button:** No matter which choice you make (Automatically or Manually), you can click the Get Edition Now button to update the link to the source.

✦ **Cancel Subscriber button:** Clicking the Cancel Subscriber button breaks the link to the edition. The current image remains in your document unless you remove it from the picture box.

✦ **Open Publisher button:** Clicking the Open Publisher button launches the source application so that you can modify the source object. Note that the application will likely not appear over your current application. If you use the Mac OS applications menu, you'll see the application and be able to select it, bringing it to the foreground with the linked file already loaded. The applications menu is the list of open applications you get at the far right of the menu bar (look for the icon of the currently active program) — you won't see a menu item named *Applications* anywhere.

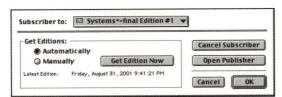

Figure 20-7: The Subscriber Options dialog box in QuarkXPress.

Deleting and finding an edition file

The publishing program has a menu item called Publisher Options (in the Edit menu) to cancel the publisher (shown in Figure 20-5 for Illustrator and Excel), which deletes the edition file. If the publisher is canceled, a static copy of the last version is retained in your document.

You can locate the edition file by clicking and holding the mouse over the file name at the top of either the Subscriber Options or Publisher Options dialog box; the folder hierarchy displays.

The perils of OLE

In Windows, QuarkXPress lets you use Microsoft's OLE (Object Linking and Embedding) technology to import pictures. This technology is not as good as the Mac's Publish and Subscribe, which is why many programs don't publish their information via OLE. Here's why you'll probably want to avoid using OLE import (via Edit ➪ Insert Object):

✦ Only objects imported via OLE can be dynamically updated from your QuarkXPress layout. (On the Mac, any imported picture can be dynamically updated.) Pictures imported through the Get Picture command (Ctrl+E) must be updated by reimporting the pictures or by reopening the QuarkXPress file and having the Auto Picture Import option set to On or Verify in the General pane of the Preferences dialog box (accessed via Ctrl+Alt+Shift+Y).

✦ OLE takes a lot of RAM, and you'll often get error messages when trying to import or update OLE objects — even if you have 64MB or more of RAM. That's because OLE is not entirely stable and because many programs don't implement OLE well (because programmers found it to be very complex).

However, if you do want to use OLE, the way to do it is to select a picture box with the Content tool and use Edit ➪ Insert Object to get the Insert Object dialog box shown here. You need to select the object type from the list and select either Create New (to create a new object in the appropriate program) or Create from File (to import an existing object). If you choose Create from File, use the Browse button (it appears under the Filename field) to find an existing file, and be sure to check the Link box to ensure that the OLE file has a live link so that any updates to it are made to your QuarkXPress layout. Don't be surprised if it takes several minutes for the link to be made.

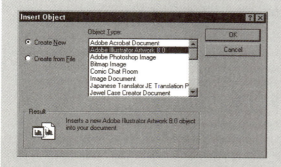

Continued

Continued

If you're creating a new object, OLE launches the appropriate program. After you're done creating the object, use the program's File menu to make the object available to QuarkXPress.

Whenever you want to update the OLE link from within QuarkXPress, select the picture box and use Edit ➪ [program name] Object. (For example, if the object is a Media Clip, you'd see a Media Clip Object menu item in the Edit menu. That menu in turn will have a submenu with options specific to the data you imported. For a media clip, the submenu would list Play, Open, and Edit, while for a graphic, it would list Open, Update, and Edit.) This menu item appears only if you've selected an OLE object. Selecting this menu option launches the originating program.

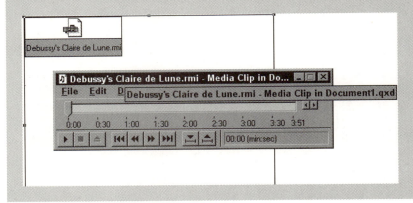

Launching source applications

A simpler way to use the Subscribe feature is to launch the application that created a graphic used in a QuarkXPress layout. To do this, you don't have to use Publish. Any graphic imported into QuarkXPress — via Edit ➪ Subscribe To or File ➪ Get Picture (or ⌘+E or Ctrl+E) — may have its originating application launched so that you can work on the graphic.

STEPS: Launching an application

1. Use the Edit ➪ Subscriber Options (refer to Figure 20-6) — either the Content tool or Item tool may be active — and select the Open Publisher button. (If the Content tool is active, you can simply double-click the picture box to get this dialog box.)

2. Select Open Publisher to load the program with the source file open in it. Note that the application will likely not appear over your current application.

3. Use the Mac OS applications menu to select the application and bring it to the foreground. (The other options in the dialog box are irrelevant, and clicking them will have no effect.)

Saving Pages as EPS Files

QuarkXPress has a nifty feature that lets you, in effect, take a picture of a page in a document and turn the picture into an EPS file. You can then use the EPS file as an illustration for another document. A catalog of brochures is a good example of an application of this feature. You might create several brochures, make an EPS file of each brochure cover, and then create a marketing piece that shows all the brochure covers.

STEPS: Saving a page as an EPS file

1. Open the document that contains the page you want to save.

2. Choose File ➪ Save Page as EPS (Option+Shift+⌘+S or Ctrl+Alt+Shift+S) to display the Save Page as EPS dialog box, shown in Figure 20-8.

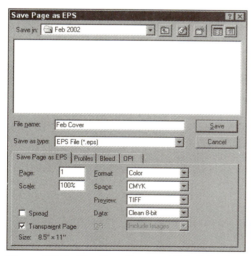

Figure 20-8: The Save Page as EPS dialog box.

3. Enter a name for the new EPS file in the Save Page As box (Mac) or File Name box (Windows).

4. In the Save Page as EPS pane, enter the page number of the page you want to save as an EPS file in the Page box.

5. If you want to modify the scale of the page as you save it, enter a percentage value in the Scale text box; 50 percent reduces the page to half its original size.

6. Click the appropriate format for the file type in the Format list box. Choices include B&W (black-and-white), Color (generates a color EPS file), DCS (the Document Color Separation form of EPS, used when outputting negatives for four-color process printing), and DCS 2.0 (a version of the DCS format that includes process and spot colors).

7. The new Space pop-up menu lets you choose between CMYK and RGB output for the EPS file. Choose CMYK for an EPS file that will be color-separated.

8. Unless your service bureau has specifically asked for the output files to be in ASCII format, make sure that the Data field is set to Clean 8-Bit, not ASCII, unless you know you'll only be printing the EPS file from Macintosh computers directly to the printer (that is, you know you won't be using any Windows spoolers).

9. Choosing an option from the Preview pop-up menu lets you choose a preview format for the EPS file. Choices are PICT, TIFF, or None. (In Windows QuarkXPress, your options are TIFF and None.) Choose TIFF if the EPS file will be used in a Windows environment; otherwise, choose PICT. (The ability to choose a preview format for the EPS file is a new feature.)

10. To save all the pages in the current spread as an EPS file, check the Spread check box.

11. If you want the page to have a transparent background, check the new Transparent Page option. Anything that doesn't contain an image or that has a background other then None will be transparent in the EPS file.

12. When you save a page as an EPS file, the picture box is clipped to the exact size of the page. But you can enter a value in the Bleed pane to cause a picture larger than the page size to be captured in the resulting EPS file. QuarkXPress 5 has enhanced these options to include two bleed types: Symmetric, where the bleed is the same on all four sides of the page, and Asymmetric, where you specify the amount of bleed separately for each side.

13. If you're using Open Prepress Interface, choose one of the following options in the OPI pane. Your selection determines how pictures and comments are included with a page saved as an EPS file. (If you aren't using OPI, just use the default setting of Include Images.)

   • OPI Active: This enables the feature, letting you temporarily disable OPI settings to create an EPS file. That can minimize the size of the EPS file, because the very-high-resolution images stored on an OPI server for substitution during printing won't be placed into the EPS file if OPI is turned off.

   • Include Images: The TIFF and EPS sections of the pane both have this option for you to decide whether to include the high-resolution TIFF and EPS files in the document into your exported EPS file, or to use the low-resolution preview images (unchecked).

- The TIFF section also has an option for Low Resolution, which uses the lower-resolution working file rather than the high-resolution version stored on the OPI server when generating the EPS file. If you're producing a cover repeat for, say, the table of contents of a magazine, it's a good idea to check this option to save file size. After all, the very high resolution of the OPI file will be wasted on such a small version of the image.

New Feature The Save Page As EPS dialog box has several additions in QuarkXPress 5: the Space pop-up menu, the Transparent Page option, and the ability to bleed pages asymmetrically in the Bleed pane.

Summary

QuarkXPress imports most common graphics formats, but it's best to stick with TIFF and EPS for images you'll use in printed pages. The GIF, PNG, and JPEG formats are fine for Web publishing. TIFF files also can be manipulated in QuarkXPress to change the appearance of color in them and to apply shades and hues.

QuarkXPress can monitor the use of graphics, alerting you when a graphic file has been modified or is missing. And there's a dialog box to let you find or update graphics files. QuarkXPress also supports the Publish and Subscribe linking functionality on the Mac and the OLE linking functionality on Windows, but both have limitations that should keep most publishers from using them.

Finally, QuarkXPress can output its own pages into an EPS graphic, which you can then use in other layouts or in illustration programs. A common use would be to show a small version of the cover in a table of contents or maybe a miniature of an opening spread in an article that generated a lot of letters to the editor.

✦　　✦　　✦

Modifying Graphics

In Chapter 8, we explain how to create a picture box and fill it with an imported picture. We also explain how to make changes to the size and position of a picture box. After you create, position, and size a picture box, you may want to make some changes to its contents — the picture itself. This chapter shows you how to alter the contents of an active picture box by changing the values in the Measurements palette and by adjusting the controls in the Modify dialog box, as well as several of the Style menu options. There's also a section on how you can achieve faster printing and screen displays in graphics-intensive documents.

QuarkXPress offers sophisticated ways of controlling bitmap images, and this is particularly true for grayscale images. An important part of traditional publishing, grayscale images are usually scanned photographs, but they can also be original artwork created by paint programs. This chapter covers all the bases: bitmap formats, negative images, contrast, halftones, and dithering. We also cover the QuarkXPress image controls for color bitmap images.

Finding the Right Tools

As you work with graphics, you'll probably find yourself using all the tools at your disposal, including keyboard shortcuts and palettes. There's no single right mix, but the information in this chapter will help you find the right balance for your working style. Here's a quick overview:

◆ **The Measurements palette:** This is the best place to make most modifications of size, placement, scale, and box settings. Why? Because not only does the Measurements palette contain the most common functions, it's almost always on your screen. Using it doesn't require you to open a dialog box that often blocks the view of what you're working with.

✦ **The Modify dialog box:** If you need a function that's not on the Measurements palette, you have to use the Modify dialog box. The Modify dialog box is also convenient when you're applying multiple settings, because they're all in one place.

✦ **The Style menu:** Most of the relevant items in the Style menu affect output for bitmapped images or for color images. Almost all these techniques work with text boxes as well; Chapters 15 and 18 cover these functions, from a text perspective, in detail.

Positioning Graphics

Often, imported pictures are not positioned within the box as you want them to be. The focal point of a picture might be too far to the left, too far to the right, or too high or low within the box. To fix this, you need to adjust the *offsets* — how far the picture is offset from the edges of the box — in one of three ways:

✦ Drag the image with the Content tool or nudge it with the arrow keys

✦ Enter values in the Offset fields in the Measurements palette

✦ Enter values in the Offset fields in the Picture pane of the Modify dialog box

You can also change the angle and skew of the picture within the box.

Tip   You may need to resize, then reposition, several times until the graphic is right. That's because until you experiment with these two aspects of the graphic, it's hard to visualize how it will actually look in the layout. This is particularly true when you're *cropping* an image (showing just part of it) within the picture box.

Understanding offsets

Picture offsets aren't relative. They're absolute positions based on the upper-left corner of the picture box. Thus, moving an object 6 picas from an original position of 3p means adding 6p to the original 3p (or subtracting 6p to move in the opposite direction). The math can get tricky, so let QuarkXPress do it for you. Just add or subtract the distance in the Offset Across and Offset Down dialog boxes.

For example, if the Offset Across is 3p7 and you want to shift the image to the right 6p6, tack on +6p6 after 3p7 (so it reads 3p7+6p6). QuarkXPress will do the math and come up with the correct 10p1 offset. Use a minus sign (−) to go to the left. When moving vertically, adding to the current value moves down, while subtracting from the current value moves up. You can also multiply the current value by using * (such as 3p*6 to get 18p) and divide by using / (such as 3p/2 to get 1p6).

Dragging or nudging images

An easy (although less precise) way to position a picture within a picture box is to use the Content tool. First select the Content tool. If you then place the cursor over the active picture box, it turns into a grabber hand that lets you shift the picture into place by holding the mouse button while moving the mouse.

When the Content tool is selected, using the keyboard's arrow keys with the Content tool active does exactly the same thing as using the Measurements palette's shift handles: in 1-point increments. Hold the Option or Alt key to move the picture within the box by 0.1-point increments.

There are several ways adjust an image's position:

✦ **Enter values for the image to be shifted within the picture box in the Measurements palette:** Enter the numbers in the fields to the right of X+: and Y+:. Or you can click the arrows next to the fields in the Measurements palette as follows:

  • Click the horizontal arrows to move an image from side to side within the picture box. Each click moves the image in 1-point increments (0.014 inches, 0p1, and so on). If you hold the Option or Alt key when clicking an arrow, you move the picture in 0.1-point increments (0.0014 inches, 0p0.1, and so on).

  • Click the vertical arrows to move an image up and down within the picture box in the same way as the horizontal arrows described in the preceding bullet.

✦ You can also use the keyboard arrow keys (cursors) to move the image within the picture box, as described for the Measurements palette's shift handles.

✦ Use the Style ⇨ Center Picture option, or the keyboard shortcut Shift+⌘+M or Ctrl+Shift+M, to center the picture in the middle of the picture box.

✦ Use the shortcut Option+Shift+⌘+F or Ctrl+Alt+Shift+F, or the new Fit Picture to Box (Proportionally) menu item in the Style menu. This both repositions and resizes the image.

Using the Measurements palette

To use the Measurements palette to modify the contents of a picture box, you must first make the picture box active. (If the box is active, its sizing or reshaping handles are visible around the edge of the box.) You also must display the Measurements palette. (To display the palette, choose View ⇨ Show Measurements, or use the shortcut F9.) In Figure 21-1, you see a page containing a picture box. (The Measurements palette appears at the bottom of the screen.) The figure shows the page just after we filled the picture box with a picture. We used the Rectangular

Picture Box tool to draw the picture box, and we filled the box with the picture by choosing File ➪ Get Picture (or press ⌘+E or Ctrl+E). Note the sizing handles on the borders of the box: They indicate that the box is active.

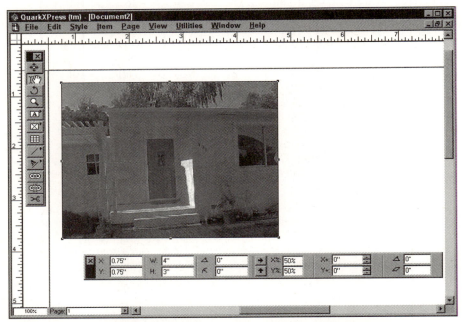

Figure 21-1: A picture imports at its full size, whether or not that picture box matches that size.

Using the Picture pane

You can position the picture — in a precise, numerical fashion — by entering values in the Offset Across and Offset Down fields in the Picture pane of the Modify dialog box. In Figure 21-2, we adjusted the offset to the left by entering an Offset Across value of –6 picas. This change moves the picture box's contents 6 picas to the left. (A positive number would move it to the right.) Compare this to the position in Figure 21-3, which shows the image's original offset.

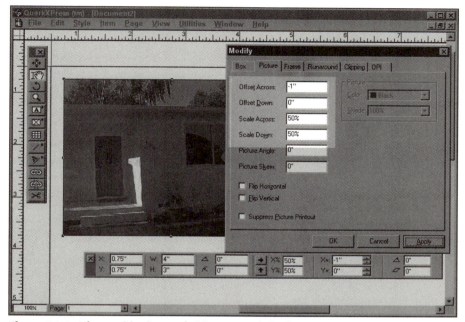

Figure 21-2: The positioning and sizing controls in the Picture pane of the Item dialog box.

Resizing Graphics

Images rarely fit the picture box's dimensions — in Figure 21-1, for example, it's larger than the picture box. QuarkXPress loads an image in its actual size and doesn't try to fit the image to the picture box size. That's why, as you work with QuarkXPress, you'll probably frequently use the scale options to resize graphics. In fact, it's one of the handiest items in the entire program, especially if you create documents that include graphics. It's rare that a graphic has the size you want it to be when you first import it, which is why the ability to change the size (scale) is so important. And you'll often adjust the size of your pictures even after getting them to fit initially, as you adjust the size and position of your picture boxes and other elements.

There are several ways to resize images:

✦ Use the Style menu commands and keyboard shortcuts.

✦ Use the Measurements palette's controls.

✦ Use the Modify dialog box's Picture pane.

✦ Use the mouse.

Using Style menu commands and keyboard shortcuts

To resize a picture within its box, you can use Style menu commands and keyboard shortcuts. The commands work as follows:

✦ Style ➪ Fit Picture to Box, or Shift+⌘+F or Ctrl+Shift+F, stretches or shrinks the picture to the borders of the picture box without keeping the picture's aspect ratio — it will distort the image if necessary to make it fit the box.

✦ Style ➪ Fit Picture to Box (Proportionally), or Option+Shift+⌘+F or Ctrl+Alt+Shift+F, fits the picture as close as it can to the picture box but maintains the picture's aspect ratio. Keeping a picture's aspect ratio means that you keep its proportions the same as you enlarge it or reduce it. Keeping aspect ratio means keeping equal scale-across and scale-down percentages, such as 50 percent horizontally (X%), 50 percent vertically (Y%), and so on.

✦ The keyboard shortcut Option+Shift+⌘+< or Ctrl+Alt+Shift+< decreases Scale Across and Scale Down values to the next smallest 5 percent.

✦ Option+Shift+⌘+> increases Scale Across and Scale Down values to the next highest 5 percent.

New Feature

QuarkXPress 5 adds a new set of menu options in the Style menu: Center Picture, Fit Picture to Box, Fit Picture to Box (Proportionally), and Fit Box to Picture. The first three are existing features previously accessible only via keyboard shortcuts, while Fit Box to Picture (which has no keyboard shortcut) is a new function in QuarkXPress. Figure 21-3 shows these new menu options.

Using the Measurements palette

You can also change the size of an image within the box, not just change the size of the box. The setting in the X% and Y% fields in Figure 21-2 is 61.2 percent. Changing the percentage values in the X% and Y% fields reduces or enlarges the picture in the picture box. To keep the proportions of the picture the same, enter the same value in the X field as you enter in the Y field. Unfortunately, you cannot link the two so that if you change one, the other automatically changes with it to keep the picture's proportions consistent.

In the first illustrations presented in this chapter, we used a picture at 62.1 percent scale across and down. Figure 21-4 shows the same illustration scaled at 105 percent along both dimensions, which is about 50 percent larger than the size used up until now.

Using the Picture pane

In the Modify dialog box's Picture pane, you can change an image's size by entering new values in the Scale Across and Scale Down fields. You can specify a size from 10 to 1,000 percent of the picture's original size. You can enter scale values in increments as small as 0.1 percent. You don't have to enter the same values for Scale Across and Scale Down; you can enter different values for each field to distort the picture.

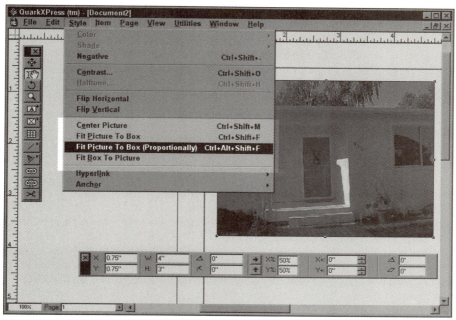

Figure 21-3: The new sizing options in the Style menu.

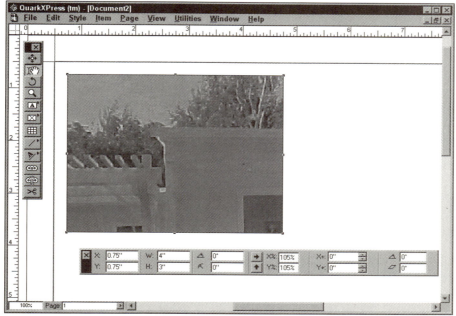

Figure 21-4: The image in Figures 21-2 and 21-3 resized to 105 percent.

Resizing via mouse

If you hold the ⌘ or Ctrl key when dragging a picture box's handle, the image is automatically resized as you resize the box. Hold the Shift key in addition to ⌘ or Ctrl to resize the box and its image proportionally.

Fitting the box to the picture

Tip

You may occasionally want to place a graphic when you aren't sure what size the picture box should take. What you should do is create the picture box, import the picture, and then resize the picture box to fit the graphic.

In addition to making the picture fit the box you imported it into, you can of course make the box fit the picture. We recommend that you start by making the picture box the size you want the picture to take—that's a better approach in a layout for something like a magazine or newspaper that has standard sizes. But even if you do so, you may decide that the picture works better in a different-size box once you see how the image looks in the layout. In more free-form layouts like ads, you often don't know the size you want an image to be until you've experimented in its placement and size.

Here's how:

✦ The easiest approach to making a picture box the size of its image is to use the new Fit Box to Picture option in the Style menu.

✦ You can also simply drag a corner of the picture box and drag it to resize the box by hand.

✦ You can use the Measurements palette W: and H: fields to enter new widths and heights for the box, or the similar controls in the Modify dialog box's Box pane.

Tip

Often, you'll use a combination of the fitting-image-to-box and resizing-the-box options to get the optimal size, placement, and cropping of the image.

Adjusting Image Angle, Skew, and Flip

Most designers will focus on resizing and repositioning graphics, but QuarkXPress has other controls to adjust the image's appearance.

Adjusting the picture angle

When you first place a picture into a picture box, it's oriented at the same angle it had in its source graphics program. Occasionally, you may want to change the angle of the picture without changing the angle of the picture box itself. In the Picture pane of the Modify dialog box or in the Measurements palette (on the right side), enter a value in the Picture Angle field to rotate the picture within the box. The picture is rotated around the center of the picture box as it was created in the original graphics program. The angle of the box stays the same; only the contents rotate. You can enter Picture Angle values from –360 to 360 degrees, in increments as small as 0.001 degrees. Figure 21-5 shows the effect of changing the Picture Angle from 0 degrees to 40 degrees.

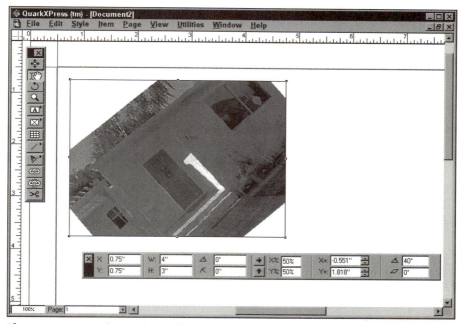

Figure 21-5: Rotating a picture by 40 degrees.

 Entering any value except 0 in the Rotate field (the icon shown here) on the *left* side of the Measurements palette rotates the picture *box* by that many degrees. Because the box in Figure 21-5 is not rotated, the value in the field is 0 (zero) degrees. If you use negative numbers, you rotate the box counterclockwise; positive numbers rotate the box clockwise. Entering any value except 0 in the Rotate field located at the *right* side of the palette rotates the picture *within* the picture box by that many degrees. (The current value for the picture box in Figure 21-3, for example, is 0, which means the image is not rotated within the box.)

Skewing the picture

Another special effect you can try with QuarkXPress is *skewing,* or slanting, a picture within its box. You do this by entering a value in the Picture Skew field of the Modify dialog box or the Measurements palette. You can enter values from –75 to 75 degrees, in increments as small as 0.001 degrees. If you enter a positive value, the picture skews to the right; if you enter a negative value, the picture skews to the left. Figure 21-6 shows the effect of skewing our picture 40 degrees.

 Entering any value except 0 in the Skew field (the icon shown here) slants the contents of the picture box. In Figure 21-3, the picture-box contents are not slanted. If you use negative numbers, you slant the box to the left; positive numbers slant the box to the right.

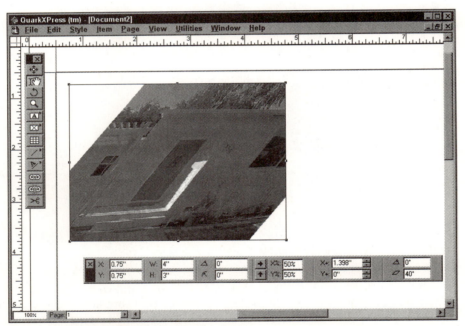

Figure 21-6: Skewing a picture by 40 degrees.

Flipping pictures

QuarkXPress also lets you flip an image, mirroring it from right to left or top to bottom. This is handy, for example, if you have a picture of a person that is looking in one direction but would look better in the layout if she were looking in the opposite direction, perhaps at a headline. (Of course, you should be careful that any flipping doesn't make text or other elements, such as wedding rings, read the wrong way or be in an obviously incorrect location.)

As with rotate and skew functions, the flip features are available in the Modify dialog box's Picture dialog box and the Measurements palette. The style menu also has flip options: Flip Horizontal and Flip Vertical.

In the Measurements palette, clicking the Horizontal Flip icon (shown here) flips the image along the X axis. The horizontal arrow's direction changes (as shown here) to let you know whether a picture has been flipped.

Clicking the Vertical Flip icon (shown here) flips the image along the Y axis. The vertical arrow's direction changes (as shown here) to let you know whether a picture has been flipped.

Applying Photographic Effects

QuarkXPress offers sophisticated ways of controlling bitmap images, and this is particularly true for grayscale images. An important part of traditional publishing, grayscale images are usually scanned photographs, but they can also be original artwork created by paint programs. This chapter covers all the bases: bitmap formats, negative images, contrast, halftones, and dithering. We also cover QuarkXPress's image controls for color bitmap images.

Tip You can convert an image from color to grayscale during import by holding the ⌘ or Ctrl key when clicking the Open button in the Get Picture dialog box (File ⇨ Get Picture, or ⌘+E or Ctrl+E).

Exploring the controls

The bitmap controls in QuarkXPress fall into the following basic classes of image-manipulation techniques:

✦ **Output control:** This feature lets you fine-tune the output of an image for best reproduction, such as lightening an overly dark image or enhancing contrast.

✦ **Image alteration:** This lets you change the image's appearance to achieve a visual effect, such as coloring a grayscale image or removing subtle details in a photo to give it a more drawn appearance.

The Style menu is where QuarkXPress keeps its image-manipulation functions, which it groups in three dialog boxes, each of which has its own version of the following entries in the Style menu:

✦ **Negative:** Lets you create a photographic negative.

✦ **Contrast:** Lets you adjust the contrast and brightness of images. You can use this to fine-tune an image for clarity or to apply special effects to it.

✦ **Halftone:** Lets you adjust how an image is printed — its coarseness and the shape of the elements used to create it (photos and other bitmaps are usually printed as a series of fine dots; QuarkXPress lets you choose the size of those dots and use other shapes, such as lines, rather than dots, to reproduce the image).

The several menu items for image manipulation in the Style menu are grouped into three dialog boxes in QuarkXPress. To apply these tools, you may have either the Content or Item tool selected.

Working with image formats

Table 21-1 shows what controls can be applied to specific image formats. You can apply contrast settings to all supported grayscale and color images except vector formats such as EPS, PDF, and Windows metafile.

Table 21-1 Image Controls Available for Graphics					
Image Type	*Negative*	*Contrast*	*Halftone*	*Color*	*Shade*
BMP					
color	yes	yes	no	no	no
gray	yes	yes	yes	yes	yes
black-and-white	yes	no	yes	yes	yes
EPS, DCS	no	no	no	no	no
GIF					
color	yes	yes	no	no	no
gray	yes	yes	yes	yes	yes
JPEG					
color	yes	yes	no	no	no
gray	yes	yes	yes	yes	yes
MacPaint 1	no	no	yes	yes	yes

Image Type	Negative	Contrast	Halftone	Color	Shade
PCX					
color	yes	yes	no	no	no
gray	yes	yes	yes	yes	yes
black-and-white	yes	no	yes	yes	yes
Photo CD	yes	yes	no	no	no
color	yes	yes	no	no	no
gray	yes	yes	yes	yes	yes
PICT					
color bitmap	yes	yes	no	no	no
8-bit gray bitmap	yes	yes	yes	yes	yes
low-gray bitmap 2	no	no	no	no	no
black-and-white bitmap	no	no	yes	yes	yes
vector	no	no	no	no	no
PNG					
color	yes	yes	no	no	no
gray	yes	yes	yes	yes	yes
Portable Document Format (PDF)	no	no	no	no	no
Scitex CT					
color	yes	yes	no	no	no
gray	yes	yes	no	no	no
TIFF					
color	yes	yes	no	no	no
gray	yes	yes	yes	yes	yes
black-and-white	yes	no	yes	yes	yes
Windows Metafile	no	no	no	no	no

1 Format not supported in QuarkXPress for Windows

2 A low-gray image is one with fewer than 256 levels of gray (8-bit) but more than black-and-white (1-bit).

Creating negative images

The simplest feature to use is the Negative feature. Just select an item and use Style ➪ Negative or the keyboard shortcut Shift+⌘+hyphen or Ctrl+Shift+hyphen. Figure 21-7 shows the effect in action. For gray and black-and-white images, this feature exchanges white for black and black for white. For color images, this exchanges each primary color (red, blue, and yellow) for the opposite color (green, magenta, and cyan, respectively).

Figure 21-7: The effects of the Negative control (bottom).

Adjusting contrast

When you adjust contrast with the Picture Contrast Specifications dialog box (accessed via Style ⇨ Contrast, or Shift+⌘+C or Ctrl+Shift+C), you get the dialog box shown in Figure 21-8. At the left of the dialog box is a line that shows how values in the image are mapped to the output. Typically, it's a straight line at a 45-degree angle, which means that the input and the output settings are the same — no adjustment to the image. It's this contrast line, which is technically called a *gamma curve,* that you adjust to change the contrast of the image as it is output.

Using the filters

The simplest way to adjust output is to use one of the following predefined adjustments (often called *filters*) on the dialog box's left side:

✦ Normal ensures that the image prints with its original, unadjusted values.

✦ High Contrast essentially replaces the midtones with either black or white, with the separation happening at the 30-percent gray (or hue, for a color image) mark. (Any part of the image darker than 30 percent becomes black, while any part lighter than 30 percent becomes white.) Figure 21-9 shows the result.

✦ Posterize bands the grays (or hues) together, so similar grays get changed into the same gray. For example, all parts of the image that are 0 to 10 percent gray become pure white, while all parts of the image that are 10 to 20 percent gray become 20 percent gray, and so on. Figure 21-10 shows the result.

✦ You can check the Negative box or the Swap Axis icon to create a photographic negative of the image. Note that this feature works with any other settings. For example, if you posterize an image and click the Swap Axis icon, you will get both effects applied. Note that if you check the Negative box, your contrast line doesn't change, but if you click the Swap Axis icon, it does. Either way, the output is the same.

Because you can fundamentally alter the character of an image by editing its gray-level map, QuarkXPress lets you preview the effects of your edits via the Apply button.

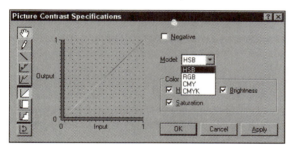

Figure 21-8: The Picture Contrast Specifications dialog box.

Color contrast adjustments

For a color image, there is also one line that adjusts all the colors equally when you open the Picture Contrast Specifications dialog box. To adjust colors individually, uncheck the color attributes you don't want to affect and then adjust the line for the remaining color channel(s). For example, if you have an RGB image and you uncheck Blue and Green, any changes to the line will affect just the red component of pixels in the image. For a CMYK image, you can manipulate four channels: cyan, magenta, yellow, and black. You can change color settings for each color channel separately by changing which colors are checked. Figure 21-11 shows an example.

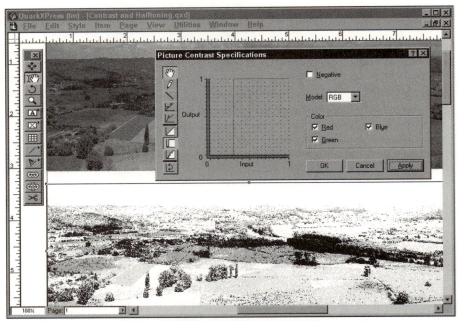

Figure 21-9: The High Contrast filter applied (bottom) to an image.

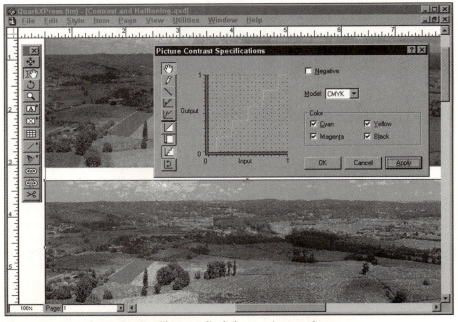

Figure 21-10: The Posterize filter applied (bottom) to an image.

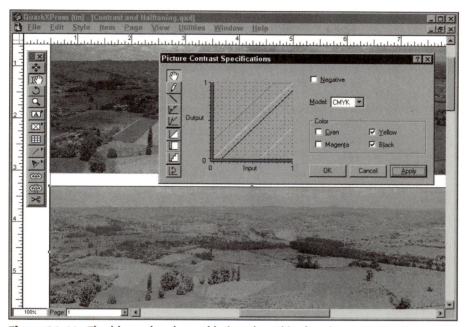

Figure 21-11: The blue color channel being altered in the Picture Contrast Specifications dialog box (results shown in bottom image).

Photo-editing programs like Photoshop offer many more sophisticated options for image manipulation. Most people use Photoshop, and an excellent resource is *Macworld Photoshop 6.0 Bible* by Deke McClelland (published by Hungry Minds, Inc.).

Manually adjusting contrast

The dialog box also has controls that let you adjust the contrast line manually. From top to bottom, the icons and their uses are as follows:

✦ The grabber (hand) icon lets you move the entire contrast line in any direction, which is useful for shifting all color mappings at once. For example, shifting the line upward darkens the entire image because lighter input values are mapped to darker output values. Moving the line with the grabber hand results in a consistent image even though color levels are shifted; however, the darkest and lightest hues may get chopped off.

✦ The pencil icon lets you draw your own line, which is handy if you want to experiment.

✦ The line icon lets you add straight segments to the contrast curve by clicking and dragging. This can be useful for smoothing out curves that have been drawn with the pencil icon.

✦ The constrained step icon lets you select increments on the line and move them as a group up or down. The selected segment between two points on the line moves. This icon is helpful when editing posterization settings.

✦ The constrained line icon causes node points on the line to appear so that you can move them. Then you can select any node on the line and move it up or down. Like the constrained step icon, this icon is helpful for editing existing lines, particularly if the changes are not discontinuous.

Customized contrast settings

You can use several different tools to edit the same line. Figure 21-12 shows an example of customized contrast lines.

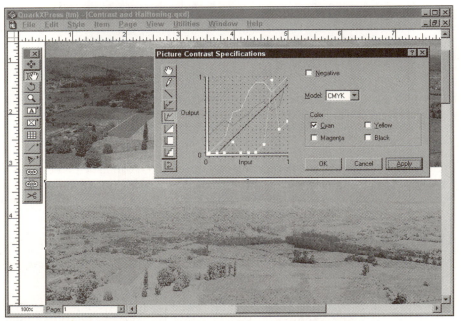

Figure 21-12: The Picture Contrast Specifications dialog box lets you adjust the contrast line for all or individual colors (results shown in bottom image).

Returning to a common contrast-level map

If, after editing a contrast-level map, you want to return the image to a more common contrast-level map, you can reenter the dialog box and use one of the default-setting icons (Normal, Posterized, or High Contrast). This kind of change is possible because QuarkXPress doesn't actually modify your source image but simply retains a set of instructions generated by your contrast settings. It applies these settings to the output image while printing but never applies them to the source image itself.

What's in a hue level?

The number of hue levels determines how natural an image looks. Each level is a percentage: the more levels there are, the more percentages of the hue are used to display an image.

Having two levels means the image is black-and-white (or blue-and-white, or red-and-white, and so on). Having 16 levels means that there is enough shading to make an image recognizably detailed. Having 256 shades is enough to make an image look realistic. Another way to think of it is like this: With 16 levels of hue, you can represent 0 percent black, 6.7 percent, 13.3 percent, 20 percent, and so on, up through 100 percent black (and so on for the other colors in an RGB or CMYK color image). With 256 levels, you can represent 0 percent black, 0.4 percent, 0.8 percent, 1.2 percent, and so on, up through 100 percent black.

The human eye can barely detect such subtle jumps, which is why 256 levels is the most you'll find for grayscale, whether it be for the images themselves or for the levels a monitor (even a color one that supports millions of colors) will display. The illustration shown here demonstrates the same images at several popular hue levels (256, 128, 64, and 16) to make the differences apparent. You'll see the subtleties that higher hue levels allow. For color images, which combine hues, 256 levels per hue provides decent fidelity, but higher levels are needed to look photorealistic.

The maximum number of levels corresponds to the image's bit depth, or color depth. Having 8 bits gives the computer 2^8 possible shades, or 256 levels. Having 4 bits gives it 2^4, or 16 levels. For color images, 2^{16} possible shades (65,536 hues) per color is needed for photorealism, and 2^{24} (16.8 million possible shades) is common.

Note that an image in 8-bit format, such as a TIFF file saved in grayscale mode in Adobe Photoshop, may have fewer than 256 levels of gray if effects like posterization were applied to it. In other words, if some gray levels are unused in an 8-bit file, the file nonetheless remains an 8-bit file. (*Posterization* is the removal of gray levels, as shown in the images.) The bit depth determines the maximum number of levels; the image's visual characteristics determine how many levels are actually used.

Regulating halftones

Printers use line screens to convert a continuous-tone image like a photograph into the series of spots, called a *halftone,* which is required to reproduce such an image on most printing presses. (Color images use four sets of spots — one each for cyan, magenta, yellow, and black. The process of filtering out each of these colors is called *four-color separation,* which is described more fully in Part VII.) Take a magnifying glass to a printed photo — either color or black-and-white — in a newspaper or magazine, and you'll see the spots that the photo is made of. These spots are usually dots, but they can be any of several shapes. Most people never worry about line screens. (In fact, many desktop publishers don't know what they are.) They can have a profound effect, however, on how your bitmap images print. Many artists use line-screen controls to add a whole new feel to an image. The following sections show you how it's done.

Making line screens with QuarkXPress

When your source image is electronic, how do you create the series of spots needed to mimic continuous tones? Desktop publishing programs use mathematical algorithms that simulate the traditional piece of photographic line screen. Because the process is controlled by a set of equations, desktop publishing programs such as QuarkXPress offer more options than traditional line screens, which come in a fixed set of halftone frequencies and with a limited set of elements.

Seeing is believing when it comes to special graphics effects, so you'll want to experiment with line-screen settings before going to press with your document. In most cases, you should use the default screening values, which are the defaults for all imported images. The default line-screen frequency is set in the File menu's Print dialog box through the Frequency option in the Output pane (Figure 21-13 shows the settings). The default screen angle is 45 degrees, and the default halftone dot shape is a dot; neither of these defaults can be changed.

Some special graphics effects are available only for PostScript printers because other types of printers (such as QuickDraw and PCL printers) don't have the correct controls in their internal computers to do the calculations required to achieve these effects.

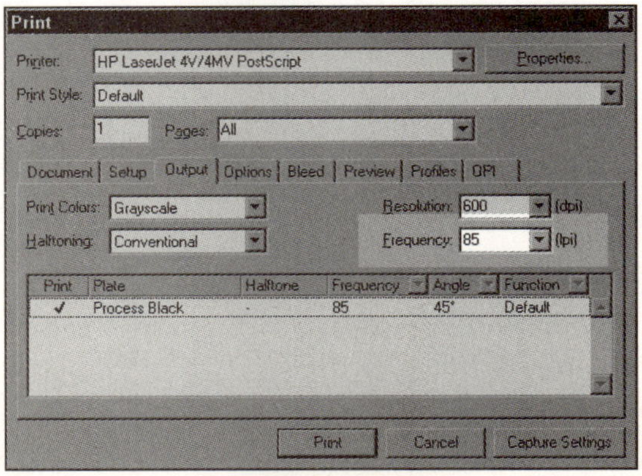

Figure 21-13: The Frequency option in the Print dialog box's Output pane.

A line-screen primer

In traditional printing, a *line screen* is an acetate mask with a grid of holes. This line-screen mask is then placed on top of a piece of photographic paper (such as Kodak's RC paper, used for decades in traditional photography). The continuous-tone original is then illuminated in a camera so that the image is projected through the mask onto the photographic paper. The high-contrast photographic paper is exposed only where the mask is transparent (in the grid holes, or spots), producing the spots that make up the image to be printed. The size of each spot depends on how much light passes through, which in turn depends on how dark or light each area of the original image is. Think of a window screen through which you spray water: the stronger the spray, the bigger the spots behind the screen's holes.

The spots that make up the image are arranged in a series of lines, usually at a 45-degree angle for grayscale images (this angle helps the eye blend the individual spots to simulate a continuous tone). The number of lines per inch (or *halftone frequency*) determines the maximum dot size as well as the coarseness *(halftone density)* of the image (thus, the term *line screen*). The spots in the mask need not be circular—they can be ellipses, squares, lines, or more esoteric shapes like stars. These shapes are called *halftone dot shapes*. Circular dots are the most common type because they result in the least distortion of the image.

Halftone special effects

When you want to do something special, you can. As a rule, most people using line-screen effects prefer coarser halftone frequencies to make the image coarser but bolder. They usually also change the halftone dot shape to a line or other shape to alter the image's character. Use Style ➪ Halftone or the shortcut Shift+⌘+H or Ctrl+Shift+H to get the Picture Halftone Specifications dialog box, shown in Figure 21-14. (Halftone settings won't affect an image when displayed on the Web.)

Note
This halftoning feature doesn't work on color images or on vector images such as EPS. It works only on grayscale bitmap images.

You cannot see on-screen the effects of the settings you make. That's because QuarkXPress has the option of using its own halftoning algorithm or passing on the work to your imagesetter. Because it doesn't know what your imagesetter might do with halftone settings, QuarkXPress no longer displays them on-screen—even if you choose the QuarkXPress default halftoning algorithms. You'll need to print the images to see the effects.

Caution
The halftoning functions are easily subverted. Not only can you disable any halftones set by simply telling QuarkXPress to use the Printer setting in the Halftoning option in the Print dialog box's Output pane, but if you output the file to a PostScript file (raw PostScript, EPS, or PDF), halftone settings are also lost. The only safe way to ensure your intended halftone settings are printed is to print directly to the target printer and ensure Conventional is chosen as the Output pane's Halftoning option.

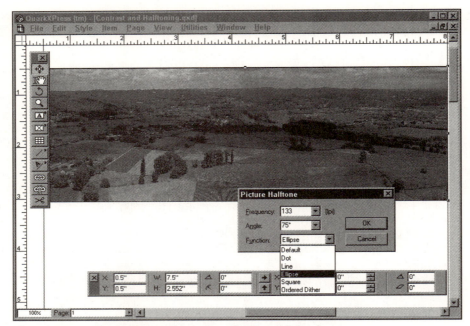

Figure 21-14: The Picture Halftone Specifications dialog box.

To gauge the effects of different halftone dot shapes, compare the sections within
Figure 21-15. Except for the first (set using printer defaults), all are set at 15 lpi so
that the differences are magnified. The rest show the five screen element shapes:
dot, line, ellipse, square, and ordered dither. In all examples, the halftone screen is
arranged at a 45-degree angle.

We recommend that you create a sample page that has a series of strips set for
different line screens and line elements. You can use the resulting guide to see the
effects of various line-screen settings on the entire range of gray values, from
white to black. You can also create a similar guide using a sample grayscale photo.
To create a sample page, use the following steps:

1. In an image-editing program, create a grayscale TIFF file that has a smooth
   gradient from white to black. The image in this file should be shaped like a
   long rectangle, either horizontal or vertical, with the gradient going from one
   end to the other along the longest axis.

2. Import this object into a QuarkXPress document's picture box and then
   duplicate that box several times, placing each duplicate next to the previous
   one. You now have a series of gradient strips.

3. Use the Style ➪ Halftone (Shift+⌘+H or Ctrl+Shift+H) option to set each strip
   at a different line-screen setting. We recommend that you do this at least for
   common line-screen frequency settings (such as 20, 30, 60, 85, 110, 120, 133,

and 150). You can then copy all these picture boxes to a new page and change the halftone dot shape for each (which you must do one at a time). Likewise, you can do the same for different screen angles.

4. Output these pages on a 2540-dpi imagesetter.

Understanding line per inch (lpi)

When you're talking about an output device, lines per inch (lpi) and dots per inch (dpi) aren't related, because the spots in a line screen are variable-sized, whereas dots in a laser printer are fixed-sized. (Because newer printers using techniques like Hewlett-Packard's Resolution Enhancement Technology or Apple Computer's FinePrint and PhotoGrade use variable-sized dots, the distinction may disappear one day.) Lines per inch specifies, in essence, the grid through which an image is filtered, not the size of the spots that make it up. Dots per inch specifies the number of ink dots per inch produced by the laser printer; these dots are typically the same size. A 100-lpi image with variable-sized dots will therefore appear finer than a 100-dpi image.

Depending upon the size of the line-screen spot, several of a printer's fixed-sized dots may be required to simulate one line-screen spot. For this reason, a printer's or imagesetter's lpi is far less than its dpi. For example, a 300-dpi laser printer can achieve about 60-lpi resolution; a 1270-dpi imagesetter can achieve about 120-lpi resolution; a 2540-dpi image-setter about 200-lpi resolution (that is, if you want a reasonable number of gray shades). Resolutions of less than 100 lpi are considered coarse, and resolutions of more than 120 lpi are considered fine.

But there's more to choosing an lpi setting than knowing your output device's top resolution. An often overlooked issue is the type of paper the material is printed on. Smoother paper (such as glossy-coated or super-calendared) can handle finer halftone spots because the paper's coating (also called its *finish*) minimizes ink bleeding. Standard office paper, such as that used in photocopiers and laser printers, is rougher and has some bleed that is usually noticeable only if you write on it with markers. Newsprint is very rough and has a heavy bleed. Typically, newspaper images are printed at 85 to 90 lpi; newsletter images on standard office paper print at 100 to 110 lpi; magazine images are printed at 120 to 150 lpi; calendars and coffee-table art books are printed at 150 to 200 lpi.

Other factors affecting lpi include the type of printing press and the type of ink used. Your printer representative should advise you on preferred settings.

If you output your document from your computer directly to film negatives (rather than to photographic paper that is then shot to create negatives), inform your printer representative. Outputting to negatives allows a higher lpi than outputting to paper because negatives created photographically cannot accurately reproduce the fine resolution that negatives output directly on an imagesetter have. (If, for example, you output to 120 lpi on paper and then create a photographic negative, even the slightest change in the camera's focus will make the fine dots blurry. Outputting straight to negatives avoids this problem.) Printer representatives often assume that you're outputting to paper and base their advised lpi settings on this assumption.

Figure 21-15: Examples of halftone settings. At top left is the standard output for a 600-dpi printer. The next four images are at 15 lpi with dot, line, ellipse, and square screen element. The final image is set to ordered dither. Note that the ordered dither doesn't have an lpi option and uses the printer defaults.

Dealing with dithering

An effect related to halftone screening is called *dithering*. Dithering means replacing gray levels with a varying pattern of black and white. This pattern doesn't attempt to simulate grays; instead, it merely tries to retain some distinction between shades in an image when the image is output to a printer that doesn't have fine enough resolution to reproduce grays (through the fine grid of dots used in screening to reproduce each gray shade).

How dithering works

Dithering uses coarse patterns of dots and lines to represent the basic details in a grayscale image. A set of mathematical equations determines how the dithered pattern appears for each image. The basic technique is to replace dark shades with all black, medium shades with alternating black and white dots or lines, and light shades with a sparse pattern of dots or lines.

With dithering, there are no controls available for halftone frequency or screen-element angle because these elements are determined by the dithering equations.

Calculating halftone scans and output

One of the most difficult concepts to implement in black-and-white publishing is picking the right dpi setting when scanning grayscale (and color) artwork. You scan in fixed-sized dots per inch (dpi), but you output to film in lines per inch (lpi) composed of variable-sized dots. There's also a relationship between both the dpi and the lpi and the number of gray levels you can scan and print, respectively. Here's how it works:

✦ First, figure out the right scan resolution (dpi) for your scans: The simplest way is to multiply the screen frequency (lpi) you plan to output to by 2: lpi × 2 = dpi. This assumes that you're scanning in the image at the same size it will be reproduced. If you intend to change the size, the math gets trickier: Multiply the longest dimension of the final size (lf) by the screen frequency (lpi), and multiply this result by 2. Divide the result by the longest dimension of the original size (lo): lpi × lf x 2 ÷ lo = dpi. (If the number is not a whole number, round up to the nearest whole number; for example, treat a dpi result of 312.32 as 313.) Note that if you're outputting to coarse paper, such as newsprint, you can use a smaller multiplier than 2. But don't go lower than ^{2} (equal to about 1.4).

✦ Second, figure out the needed resolution from your imagesetter to achieve the output screen frequency (lpi) your printing press is set for: lpi × 16 = imagesetter's required dpi. Thus, for magazine-quality frequencies of 133 and 150 lpi, you would need to ensure the imagesetter outputs at 2540 dpi (the 133-lpi setting requires an output dpi of 2128 dpi—that's 133 × 16 = 2128—and the 150-lpi setting requires 2400). So why 2540 dpi? Because that's the standard high-resolution setting for most imagesetters; the other standard setting, used mostly for text-only documents, is 1270 dpi. At 2540 dpi, the highest lpi you can achieve is 158¾.

✦ Last, figure out how many gray levels you'll actually get when printing, based on the imagesetter's output resolution (dpi) and output screen frequency (lpi): (dpi ÷ lpi)^2 + 1 = gray levels. Thus, an imagesetter set for 2540 dpi and a QuarkXPress document set up for a 133 lpi screening frequency can theoretically produce 365 levels of gray (in reality, 256 levels is the top limit)—more than enough for most images. To get that number, the math is (dpi ÷ lpi) + 1, (2540 ÷ 133)^2 + 1, or 19.1^2 + 1, or 364.7 + 1, or 365 after rounding. At 150 lpi, that theoretically means 287 gray levels (again, 256 levels in reality). At an output resolution of 1270 dpi, you would get 92 gray levels at 133 lpi and 72 gray levels at 150 lpi. It may seem counterintuitive that the higher lpi setting results in fewer grays, but it's true. The trade-off you make is that at the higher lpi settings, the image seems smoother, but lower lpi settings give you greater grayscale fidelity.

QuarkXPress limits the number of grays used by a graphic or blend to 256. This should be just fine, however, unless you're creating a blend that's unusually long. In that case, create the blend in Adobe Photoshop, Adobe Illustrator, or CorelDraw.

Working with ordered dithering

There are many sets of dithering equations; QuarkXPress uses one called *ordered dithering,* which you select by choosing Ordered Dither in the Picture Halftone Specifications dialog box's Function pop-up menu. Figure 21-15 shows an image to which ordered dithering is applied. To apply other dithering equations, you must dither the image in a paint or graphics program that supports dithering before importing the image into QuarkXPress.

You can use dithering to simulate a wood-cut or pointillism effect. Otherwise, use dithering only if your printer has less than a 300-dpi resolution.

Applying Color and Shade

Even if you don't alter gray levels or screening, you can still alter the way in which grayscale and black-and-white bitmap graphics print by using QuarkXPress color and shade controls, available through the Style menu, the Picture pane, and the Colors palette. You use this effect to tint a monochromatic image, such as taking a black-and-white photo and giving it a sepia-brown tint to suggest an old photo, or lightening a grayscale image so it can be placed on the background behind text. You can change a picture's color or shade only if it is one of the following basic types:

✦ Black-and-white BMP, GIF, JPEG, MacPaint (Mac only), PCX, Photo CD, PICT, PNG, and TIFF bitmap images

✦ Grayscale BMP, GIF, JPEG, PCX, Photo CD, PICT, PNG, and TIFF bitmap images

You can combine the color and shade options. You can print an image at 30 percent magenta, for example, over a solid cyan background (for the picture box), which would give you a surrealistic blend of magenta and cyan. You can also apply other effects, such as gray-level filters and screen settings, to the same image.

Through three mechanisms — the Colors palette, the Style menu, and the Modify dialog box's Picture pane — you can replace the black parts of an image (including grays, which, after all, are simply percentages of black) with a color. In all three options, any colors defined in the document appear in the list of colors. (Part VII describes colors in depth.)

Using the Colors palette

To use the Colors palette to change the color or shade of a grayscale image, make sure the Content tool is selected. Then select the background icon in the palette (the box with an X), and then choose the color from the list of colors and the shade from the pop-up menu at the upper left of the palette, as shown in Figure 21-16. Select Other to enter a specific shade in 0.1-percent increments rather than the options in the pop-menu.

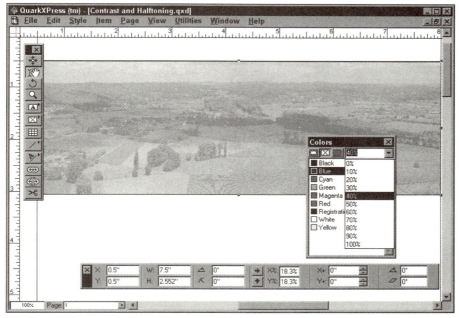

Figure 21-16: Applying color and shade via the Colors palette.

The Style menu

Through the Style menu's Color option, Figure 21-17 shows the secondary menu that appears when you highlight the Color option on the Style menu while a box containing a grayscale image is selected.

Likewise, you can make an image lighter by applying a shade through Style ➪ Shade. This technique is handy when you want to have a background image behind text that leaves the text readable. You aren't limited to the shade percentages displayed in the Shade drop-down menu. By choosing Other, you can set any percentage from 0 to 100, in 0.1-percent increments.

Using the Picture pane

You can also use the Picture pane in the Modify dialog box (Item ➪ Modify, or ⌘+M or Ctrl+M) and select the shade and/or color in the Picture section, as Figure 21-18 shows.

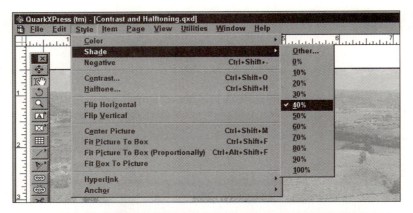

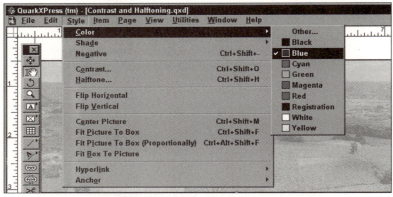

Figure 21-17: Applying color and shade via the Style menu.

Figure 21-18: Applying color and shade
via the Picture pane.

Achieving Faster Printing and Display

A document chock-full of pictures can be slow to print and display on-screen. Fortunately, QuarkXPress has a variety of settings to speed up your work. The rest of this chapter tells you how to use them.

Picture suppression

The Box and Picture panes on the Modify dialog box (Item ⇨ Modify, or ⌘+M or Ctrl+M, or double-click the picture box with the Item tool) have two similar items: Suppress Printout in the Box pane and Suppress Picture Printout in the Picture pane. In these two fields, you can select options that speed document printing — something you may want to consider when you print proofs or rough copies. Here's how they work:

✦ **Suppress Picture Printout:** If you select Suppress Picture Printout, the frames or backgrounds of picture boxes print, but the contents of the picture boxes do not. If you use frames around picture boxes, we recommend that you print proof copies with Suppress Picture Printout selected. This lets you see the size and placement of the frames.

✦ **Suppress Printout:** Selecting Suppress Printout takes this option one step further. It prevents picture box frames, backgrounds, and contents from printing.

To choose either option, check the box next to the option label. If you select one of these options, remember to go back into the Modify dialog box and uncheck the box before printing final copies of the document.

Be careful with this feature, because there's no option when you print to force all suppressed boxes and pictures to print. If you want to find out which pictures in a document are set to print and which pictures are suppressed, open the Usage dialog box (Utilities ⇨ Usage), click the Pictures tab, and look in the Print column to see if the picture is checked or not.

You can make a suppressed picture print from the Usage dialog box's Pictures pane by clicking the Print pop-up menu and selecting Yes, as Figure 21-19 shows. You can also simply click in the column to toggle the check mark on and off.

Display quality

For on-screen time savings, you can set several options that don't let pictures get in the way of your moving speedily about. The absolute fastest is to check the Greek Pictures item in the General pane of the Preferences dialog box (Edit ⇨ Preferences ⇨ Preferences, or Option+Shift+⌘+Y or Ctrl+Alt+Shift+Y). With this option checked, pictures will appear as gray boxes on-screen unless they're selected. (They will print normally.) Figure 21-20 shows the option. (In publishing, *greeking* has always meant to use random text as a placeholder in layouts and now also means to use a gray or black box as a placeholder for an image.)

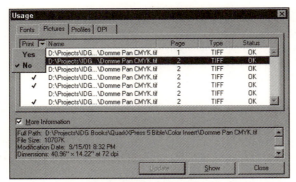

Figure 21-19: Overriding a suppressed picture via the Usage dialog box's Pictures pane.

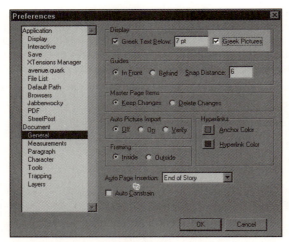

Figure 21-20: Check Greek Pictures in the Preferences dialog box to speed up redisplay time on-screen.

If you keep your pictures visible on-screen, you still have the following time-saving settings at your disposal:

✦ In the Display pane of the Preferences dialog box (Edit ➪ Preferences ➪ Preferences, or Option+Shift⌘+Y or Ctrl+Alt+Shift+Y), set Color TIFFs and Gray TIFFs to the minimum resolutions (8-bit and 16 levels, respectively). The truer the color, the more data QuarkXPress has to keep in RAM (and the larger your QuarkXPress files will be as well). It sure looks better when set at 32-bit color and 256 levels of gray (at least if your monitor supports thousands or millions of colors), but if you're feeling mired in mud, give up the detail. Figure 21-21 shows the Display pane.

✦ In the Interactive pane (shown in Figure 21-22), make sure Speed Scroll is checked. It will temporarily greek pictures when you're scrolling through your pages.

✦ In the Interactive pane, keep Live Scroll unchecked, to prevent pages from displaying while you're dragging the scroll box in the scrollbar. If you want the pages to display while you drag the box, just hold down the Option or Alt key. (The Option or Alt key also turns off Live Scroll when it's enabled.)

✦ Also in the Interactive pane, choose Show Contents rather than Live Refresh in the Delayed Item Dragging section. Live Refresh has QuarkXPress update text flow and item layering as you drag items, something you'll rarely need to see and don't need to have QuarkXPress make you wait for. Note that to activate either Show Contents (which keeps the picture visible, but only at minimum color depth) or Live Refresh, you must click and hold the mouse button for half a second (or whatever number you enter in the Delay Seconds field). Otherwise, you get normal movement — which is fine for most object movements and faster to boot.

New Feature

Gone in version 5 is the ability to speed screen display by unchecking the Accurate Blends item in the General pane of the Preferences dialog box.

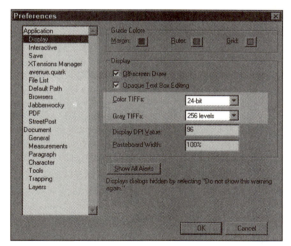

Figure 21-21: Set the Color TIFFs and Gray TIFFs pop-up menus to their lowest settings to speed on-screen display.

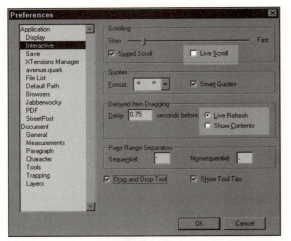

Figure 21-22: Uncheck Live Scroll and select Show Contents instead of Live Refresh to speed on-screen display.

Summary

Use the combination of picture positioning and sizing options in the Measurements palette, Modify dialog box, and Style menu to make pictures fit their boxes, make the boxes fit the picture size, and to crop and resize both the picture box and its picture. The Style ➪ Fit Picture to Box (Proportionally) and Style ➪ Center Picture options are the most convenient of these for basic sizing and positioning, while the ability to nudge a picture's position and size through keyboard shortcuts and the Measurements palette are the most convenient for fine adjustments.

QuarkXPress also offers controls to slant (skew), rotate, and flip (mirror) images, accessible most easily through the Measurements palette, as well as through the Style menu and the Modify dialog box.

For grayscale bitmap images, QuarkXPress lets you apply colors and shades, as well as change the halftoning. For all bitmap images, you can also have QuarkXPress make a photographic negative or change the contrasts for any or all basic colors in the picture. But note that halftoning settings are easily overridden during output, so it's best to use them only when outputting directly to a printer.

Finally, you can speed display on-screen by turning off high-resolution previews and live scrolling, as well as suppress picture printout and display. Suppressing picture printout also speeds creation of mockup layouts.

✦   ✦   ✦

Working with Clipping Paths

22

CHAPTER

✦ ✦ ✦ ✦

In This Chapter

Importing clipping paths with images

Creating clipping paths in QuarkXPress

Creating paths in Photoshop

Modifying clipping paths

✦ ✦ ✦ ✦

A *clipping path* is an invisible boundary used to mask certain parts of a picture and reveal other parts. In QuarkXPress, with TIFF files, you can select from different clipping paths created in image-editing programs (to display or hide various parts of an image), and you can create your own clipping paths. You might use a clipping path, for example, to isolate a flower from its background or to isolate an individual within a crowd. The advantages of using clipping paths — as opposed to editing out undesirable content — are that you often save time and the image remains flexible, allowing you to change your mind about what you want to show in it.

 Cross-Reference In addition to creating and selecting clipping paths in QuarkXPress, you can also wrap text around these paths. Text wraps are covered in detail in Chapter 23.

Importing Clipping Paths with Images

One of the neatest features of QuarkXPress is its ability to let you wrap text around images, which creates a dynamic interaction between text and imagery that's a hallmark of sophisticated documents. QuarkXPress 5 has several ways to let you wrap text around graphics, such as drawing your picture box in the shape of the image. You can also use these capabilities to create shapes that follow an object's own shape to remove backgrounds from images or to do other forms of knockouts and cameos. Figure 22-1 shows an example of this technique.

Figure 22-1: The use of clipping paths lets the designer have the petals at upper left overprint the *2* in the logo but not the *8*.

There are two ways to create these outlines, called clipping paths: Use a clipping path within the source image or, in some cases, create one from the image during export into QuarkXPress. There are pros and cons to the various approaches:

✦ Having QuarkXPress create the clipping path is fast, but the program can't handle very fine paths, such as around blades of grass or shafts of hair. It also will have trouble detecting what you want the clipping path to be in objects with multihued backgrounds.

✦ Use Photoshop or another image-editing tool to create the path, then have QuarkXPress use that path during import. This gives you absolute control over the path, and even lets you set multiple paths so you have multiple options in your layout for text wrap and knockouts.

QuarkXPress has several methods of selecting the boundaries for a text wrap or knockout, as Figures 22-2 and 22-3 show.

✦ Draw a picture box in the shape you want to wrap the text or knock out the image, as described in Chapter 25.

✦ Using the Runaround pane (Item ➪ Runaround, or ⌘+T or Ctrl+T) of the Item dialog box, select one of the runaround types from the Type pop-up menu. Text wrap options are discussed in Chapter 23.

✦ Using the Clipping pane (Item ➪ Clipping, or Option+⌘+T or Ctrl+Alt+T) of the Item dialog box, select one of the clipping-path types from the Type pop-up menu. The next section, "Creating Clipping Paths in QuarkXPress," covers these options.

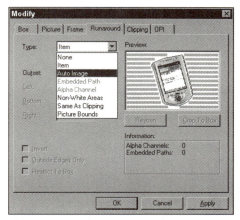

Figure 22-2: The Runaround pane's runaround options.

Figure 22-3: The Clipping pane's clipping options.

The runaround and clipping options are very similar, and in many cases you can use the two features interchangeably. For example, both the runaround and clipping options will let you create the outline for text runaround and image knockouts. Technically, you should use the runaround options for text runarounds and the clipping options for knockouts. Figure 22-4 shows the two effects.

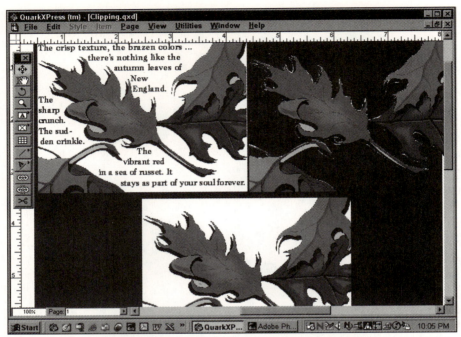

Figure 22-4: Text runaround (upper left), image clipping or knockout (upper right), and the same image without a runaround or knockout (bottom).

But you can also use both tools on the same image, setting a different runaround than clipping path so you can have text run around the image along one outline while knocking out the background through another. Typically, the knockout has to closely follow the image shape, while the text runaround avoids such precision so text doesn't get stuck in little nooks and crannies.

Cross-Reference   See Chapter 23 for more on text runarounds and using text and graphics together.

Creating Clipping Paths in QuarkXPress

You can apply runarounds and clipping paths to pretty much any image. But the more sophisticated clipping paths require an image that has one of several kinds of embedded paths — alpha channels and clipping paths — created in a program like Adobe Photoshop.

Choosing a Clipping option

After you import an image, you can get the following options from the Clipping pane (Item ⇨ Clipping, or Option+⌘+T or Ctrl+Alt+T). Items that don't apply to the selected image will be grayed out.

✦ **Embedded Path:** This setting uses a Bézier shape called a *clipping path* that is part of the image (programs like Photoshop can create such clipping paths in EPS and TIFF files) and uses that as the boundary for wrapping text or creating the knockout.

✦ **Alpha Channel:** This setting lets you wrap around an invisible irregular shape created within the program that created the image (Photoshop users will be familiar with this term). It's typically used to accomplish the same goal as a clipping path.

 New Feature

QuarkXPress 5 lets you select from multiple paths in an image — not just the first path defined in it. If an image has more than one embedded clipping path or alpha channel, the Path pop-up menu lets you select which one you want. (If you have selected Alpha Channel, the Path pop-up menu changes to the Alpha pop-up menu.)

✦ **Non-White Areas:** Another way to achieve an irregular or form-fitting wrap is to have QuarkXPress ignore the white background of an image, under the presumption that the white area is not actually part of the image. If the image is placed on some other color background in its originating program, this wrapping effect won't work in QuarkXPress. Note that most bitmap files such as scanned photos have a white background. This option offers a Tolerance area, described later, to help fine-tune the runaround or clipping path creation.

✦ **Picture Bounds:** Picture Bounds simply selects the image's original dimensions. That rectangle may be larger than the picture box if the picture itself exceeds the picture box's size.

The Runaround pane has the same options as the Clipping pane, plus the following:

✦ **Auto Image:** The Auto Image feature creates both a runaround and a clipping path, neither of which are editable, based on the shape of the image. Auto Image looks for differences in colors to detect the image border. You set the amount of visual contrast to seek in the Tolerance section of the dialog box, as described later.

✦ **Same as Clipping:** This uses whatever option is selected in the Clipping pane.

✦ **None:** This turns off text wrap, so any text would overprint the image.

✦ **Item:** This uses the picture box's boundaries.

Using the Tolerance section options

The other clipping options, in the Tolerance section of the Clipping and Runaround panes, control the degree of precision in determining the clipping path. They work as follows:

✦ **Noise:** This setting lets you tell QuarkXPress to ignore parts of the picture that are below a certain size (the default is 2 points). This is useful if the image contains small dots around the edges that may be overlapped by the text. For a *strict* (exact) runaround, set this value to 0 points.

✦ **Smoothness:** This setting lets you tell QuarkXPress how closely to follow the outline of the nonwhite area. The higher you make this value, the smoother — and potentially less exact — the runaround or clipping path is.

✦ **Threshold:** This setting lets you specify what shades of the image qualify as "nonwhite." At the default setting of 10 percent, anything 10-percent colored is considered nonwhite. To exclude all nonwhite pixels, change this setting to 0 percent. For runarounds, you can let the text intrude upon parts of the image that are lighter in color by raising this value to 20 percent or 30 percent. For clipping paths, however, raising this value can result in odd-looking clipping.

Additional clipping options

In addition to all these options, there are up to three additional options and two buttons you can apply in the Clipping pane. Not all options are available for all clipping types; those that aren't available are grayed out. You can use these singly or in combination. Figure 22-5 shows them all, in this case in the Clipping pane. These options work as follows:

✦ **Invert:** This makes the QuarkXPress runaround area or clipping path the opposite of what it would otherwise be. For example, if you have a circle image with a runaround around it, normally the text would run around the outside of the circle. With this option selected, the text would run inside the circle.

✦ **Outside Edges Only:** For a shape that has a "hole" in it, this option ignores the hole and keeps the clipping path away from it.

✦ **Restrict to Box:** When a picture is cropped by the picture box, the clipping path normally extends beyond the box edge. To prevent that — stopping the path at the box edge — select this option.

✦ **Rescan button:** This rebuilds the runaround or clipping path used by QuarkXPress for the selected image.

✦ **Crop to Box button:** This removes any part of the QuarkXPress runaround or clipping path that is outside the picture box boundaries. Crop To Box does the same thing as the Restrict to Box check box, except that to undo Crop to Box, you have to click the Rescan button.

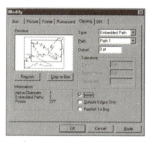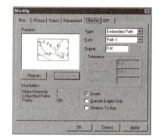

Figure 22-5: The standard clipping settings, as well as the effects of the Invert, Outside Edges Only, Restrict to Box, and Crop to Box options. The selected picture is intentionally sized and cropped so that the full picture exceeds the picture box's dimensions.

Creating Paths in Photoshop

Although this isn't a book about Adobe Photoshop, it's helpful to know how to create alpha channels and clipping paths in this nearly universally used image editor, because chances are you may have to create paths in Photoshop for use in QuarkXPress. For the full details, see *Adobe Photoshop 6 Bible* by Deke McClelland (Hungry Minds, Inc.).

There are several ways to create a path in Photoshop, but you start by going to the Paths pane (Window ➪ Show Paths). Then do one of the following steps:

1. Using the Lasso tool and/or Marquee tool, draw the shape that you want to be your path.

2. Using the Magic Wand tool, select color(s) on your image to highlight the part of the image you want to be the basis for the path.

3. Click Work Path in the Paths pane's pop-up menu. You'll see an outline of the path display in the pane.

4. Make sure the outline of the path is highlighted, then select Save Path from the same menu and give it a name.

Figure 22-6 shows the pane and pop-up menu. You can create as many paths as you like.

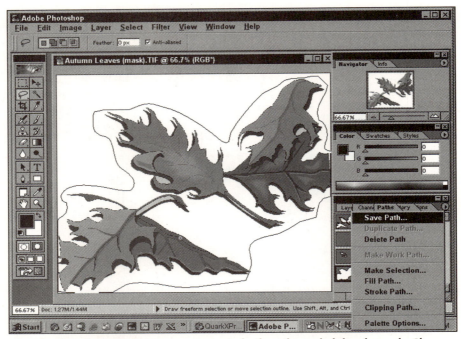

Figure 22-6: In Photoshop, you can create both paths and alpha channels. Shown here is a path being created from a rough outline created through the Lasso tool. The bottom path in the Paths pane is the one just created; the others were done earlier by using the Magic Wand tool to select portions of the leaves and creating paths from those selections.

If you want to designate one of the paths as the clipping path (for programs that see only that one path), choose the Clipping Path option from the Paths pane's pop-up menu. Then select the path you want to make the clipping path from the resulting dialog box's pop-up menu.

Creating alpha channels is similar. Use the Channels pane's pop-up menu and its New Channel option to make a channel. Make sure the eye icon is selected for the new channel in the Channels pane. Now use the painting and pen tools to draw the mask — anything in black will be part of the channel's shape. You could, for example, use the Magic Wand tool to select part of an image, then use the Paint Bucket tool to fill it in black; the result is an alpha channel that is the shape of the selected and painted-in area. (You're not actually painting in the image itself, just the channel "layer.")

Any paths and alpha channels you create in your saved TIFF file will be available in QuarkXPress's Runaround and Clipping panes.

Modifying Clipping Paths

Finally, you can further edit the runaround or clipping path. After you've applied a runaround or clipping path to a picture in the Runaround or Clipping pane, exit the Modify dialog box and select the picture box with either the Content or Item tool, then select the Edit menu option. Figure 22-7 shows the resulting submenu and, at left, the editable nodes. You can also use the following shortcuts to edit the runaround or clipping path:

✦ **Runaround:** ⌘+F4 or Ctrl+F10

✦ **Clipping path:** Option+⌘+F4 or Ctrl+Shift+F10

You can now edit the path just as you would any Bézier or freehand box, using the techniques described in Chapter 25.

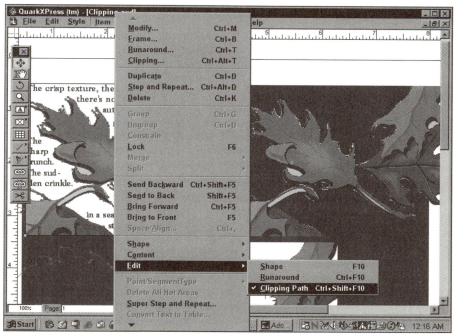

Figure 22-7: QuarkXPress lets you edit a runaround or clipping path's shape using the Bézier and freehand tools described in Chapter 25.

Tip

When you're editing runaround and clipping paths with guides showing (View ⇨ Show Guides, or F7), by default the item displays with a blue boundary, the runaround path is green, and the clipping path is pink. These colors correspond to your Display preferences in the Interactive pane of the Preferences dialog box as follows: the Margin color equals the item color, the Ruler color equals the runaround color, and the Baseline Grid color equals the clipping path color. To open the Display pane and change these colors for your copy of QuarkXPress, choose Edit ⇨ Preferences ⇨ Preferences, or press Option+Shift+⌘+Y or Ctrl+Alt+ Shift+Y, then click the Display tab.

Summary

Runarounds and clipping paths are invisible boundaries that an imported TIFF image might contain or that QuarkXPress can create from many types of images. You then use those boundaries to allow close-fitting text wraps or to knock out an area of an image from its background. A new feature lets you select from several paths in a TIFF image that has clipping paths or alpha channels.

QuarkXPress lets you control how these paths are created through a series of options in the Runaround and Clipping panes of the Modify dialog box.

It's best to use a program like Photoshop to create custom paths or paths in objects with complex backgrounds, but QuarkXPress does a fine job in tracing paths for many images, assuming the background is white or a light color.

You can edit a path in QuarkXPress as if it were any other illustration created in the program.

✦   ✦   ✦

Combining Text and Graphics

As we suggest in previous chapters, text can be used graphically, not just to convey information. That's why typography is so important to successful publications and why QuarkXPress includes so many tools to provide graphical treatment to text. (Chapter 18 covers these effects.) And top-notch layout artists and publication designers know the interplay between text and graphics is key to a successful look and feel. For the reader, the publication is a unified package, and treating text and graphics as separate issues defeats that unity. Much of the unification is based on how you position and size text and graphics relative to each other — essentially, how you lay out the various elements. QuarkXPress offers several tools and techniques to facilitate that unification and interplay, and that's what this chapter covers.

Using Text Runaround

The most obvious interplay between text and graphics is the text runaround. A *runaround* is an area in a page's layout where you don't want text to flow. *Text runaround* lets you place copy around an active element (such as a text box, picture box, or line), fitting the text as close to the contours of the element as you want.

Text runaround is often used in advertisements and other design-intensive documents. Like other special effects, text runaround is most effective when not overused. Done correctly, this technique can add a unique, polished look to a page layout.

To set the specifications for text runaround, select the text box, picture box, or line that holds the contents that you want the text to run around. Choose Item ➪ Runaround, or use ⌘+T or Ctrl+T, to display the Runaround pane in the Modify dialog box. In the dialog box, you can control the type of runaround as well as the distance between the object and the text running around it. The effects of the options available in the dialog box depend upon the type of element you select.

See Chapter 22 to understand how to create and work with clipping paths and alpha channels, which are used to define text-runaround areas.

The preview feature within the Runaround pane lets you see the effects of your runaround choices before you implement them. You'll see this preview window in the screen shots that show the various runaround settings.

Two options create a clipping path automatically: Auto Image and Non-White Areas. The Alpha Channel, Embedded Path, and Same as Clipping settings can achieve custom wraps, but you must create the path or channel first in a program like Adobe Photoshop, as Chapter 22 describes.

QuarkXPress offers a variety of runaround options. They are determined by both the type of active element and by what you enter in the Type field. You have a choice of types that varies depending on whether you run text around boxes or lines. The choice of types are as follows, with the first two applying to both picture and text boxes and the rest only to picture boxes:

✦ **None:** This setting causes text behind the active item to flow normally, as if there were no object in the way. Figure 23-1 shows the overprint that occurs when you select None.

✦ **Item:** Choosing Item as the runaround mode causes text to flow around the box that holds the active element. Figure 23-2 shows the effect of Item runaround. Note how the background text flows around the item by a set amount of offset; in this figure, the offset is 6 points. (The default is 1 point, but you usually want a larger offset than this; we tend to use 6 points or more.)

✦ **Picture Bounds:** This mode automatically determines the shape of the image in the picture box and how text flows around it. The picture bounds will vary from image to image, but in most cases it is simply an invisible rectangle that contains the image (even if the image appears to be nonrectangular). If the picture doesn't fill the picture box, or if it extends past the picture box boundaries, selecting this item will cause the text to wrap around the picture's actual dimensions regardless of the picture box's dimensions. Figure 23-3 shows an example of this, without the Restrict to Box option checked. (We'll cover Restrict to Box and the other options a bit later.)

QuarkXPress 5 brings back the Auto Image option that was dropped in version 4.

✦ **Auto Image:** Used only for picture boxes, this option automatically determines the shape of the image in the picture box and how text flows around it. The runaround follows the shape of the active item while maintaining the offset you specify. Figure 23-4 shows an example.

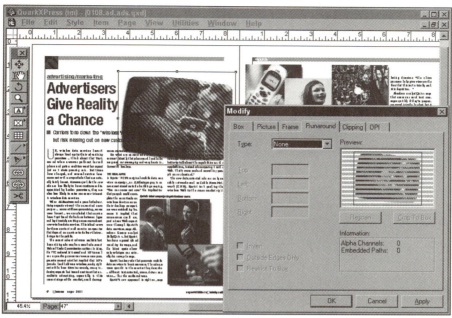

Figure 23-1: With runaround set to None, text and pictures overprint each other if their boxes overlap.

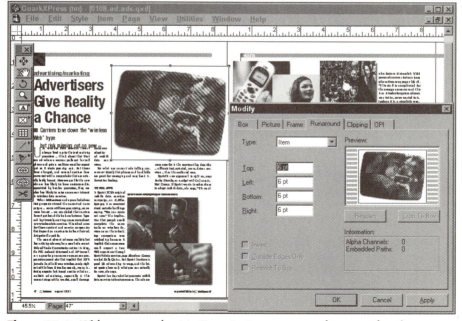

Figure 23-2: With runaround set to Item, text wraps around any overlapping boxes' edges.

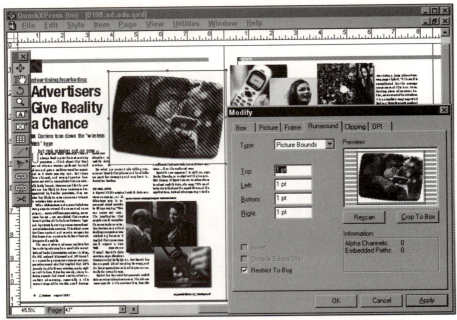

Figure 23-3: With runaround set to Picture Bounds, text wraps around the actual size of the image, even if it extends past or falls short of the picture box's edges.

✦ **Embedded Path:** This setting uses a Bézier shape called a *clipping path* that is part of the image (programs like Photoshop can create such clipping paths) and uses that as the boundary for wrapping text.

✦ **Alpha Channel:** This setting lets you wrap around an irregular shape by ignoring a color that is placed in its own color channel, called an *alpha channel,* within the program that created the image (Photoshop users will be familiar with this term). It's typically used to accomplish the same goal as a clipping path.

✦ **Non-White Areas:** Another way to achieve an irregular or form-fitting wrap is to have QuarkXPress ignore the white background of an image, under the presumption that the white area is not actually part of the image. If the image is placed on some other color background in its originating program, this wrapping effect will not work in QuarkXPress. Note that most bitmap files such as scanned photos have a white background.

✦ **Same as Clipping:** This applies the settings from the Clipping pane, which appears in the Modify dialog box only if the selected picture box has a picture in it. The Clipping pane is shown in Figure 23-5. The difference is that the Clipping pane is where you determine what part of the picture appears on the page, while the Runaround pane determines how text runs around the image.

Typically, these would be set as the same, because you'd want the text to run around the object as it appears on the page. But if for some reason you want, for example, the image to have a clipping path but the runaround to be the same as the box size, you could set the runaround as Item in the Runaround pane and still select a clipping path in the Clipping pane.

To find out whether your image has an alpha channel or an embedded path, look at the Information section of the Runaround or Clipping pane—it will indicate any alpha channels or embedded paths.

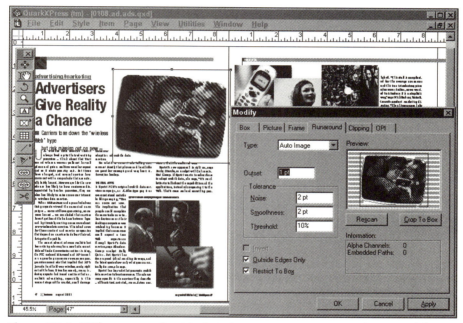

Figure 23-4: With runaround set to Auto Image, text wraps around a curve (often called a *clipping path*) that QuarkXPress creates by looking for solid colors next to a continuous light background to judge where the image's internal outline lies.

In addition to all these options, there are up to three additional options you can apply in either the Runaround or Clipping panes. Not all options are available for all runaround types; those that aren't available will be grayed out. You can use these singly or in combination, as Figure 23-6 shows.

✦ **Invert:** This makes the QuarkXPress runaround area the opposite of what it would otherwise be. For example, if you have a circle image with a clipping path around it, normally the text would run around the outside of the circle. With this option selected, the text would run inside the circle.

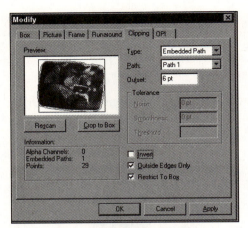

Figure 23-5: The Clipping pane.

✦ **Outside Edges Only:** For a shape that doubles in on itself, this option ignores the doubled-in areas and keeps the clipping path away from them. For example, a clipping path of a doughnut would have the outside and the inside sections; Outside Edges Only would ignore the doughnut hole. For text wraps, you'd almost always use this setting if the path or alpha channel has such interior outlines.

✦ **Restrict to Box:** When a picture is cropped by the picture box, the clipping path normally extends beyond the box edge. To prevent that — to stop the path at the box edge — select this option.

There are also two buttons to note in these panes: Rescan, which rebuilds the clipping path used by QuarkXPress for the selected image, and Crop to Box, which removes any part of the QuarkXPress clipping bath that is outside the picture box boundaries. Crop to Box does the same thing as the Restrict to Box check box, except that to undo Crop to Box, you have to click the Rescan button.

The other clipping options, in the Tolerance section of the Runaround and Clipping panes, control the degree of precision in determining the clipping path or alpha channel. The higher the Noise, Smoothness, and Threshold numbers, the more jagged the path will be. As the Noise and Threshold values increase, the greater the chances that the clipping path won't match the image boundary, because you're in essence telling QuarkXPress to take more chances on what is and is not part of the image.

Cross-Reference   You can edit the clipping path or alpha channel, as Chapter 22 explains.

The final kind of runaround is not in the Runaround or Clipping panes. You may recall the Run Text Around Sides option in the Modify dialog box's Text pane. Figure 23-7 shows it in action. At top is the default behavior, in which a box placed wholly within a text box has the text wrap to one side but not both. If the enclosed box is in the right half of the enclosing box, the enclosed box will have no text to its right; if the enclosed box is in the left half of the enclosing box, the enclosed box will have no text to its left.

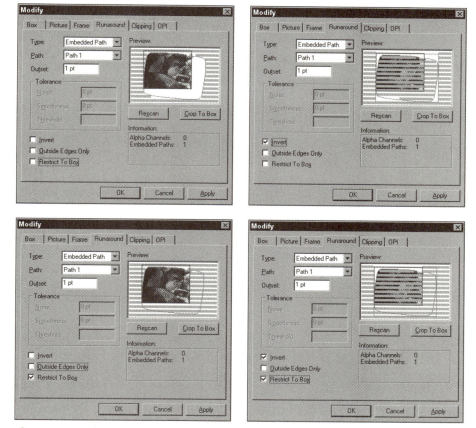

Figure 23-6: The standard settings for the Clipping and Runaround panes, as well as the effects of the Invert, Restrict to Box, and Crop to Box options. The selected picture is intentionally sized and cropped so that the full picture exceeds the picture box's dimensions.

With the Run Text Around All Sides option selected, however, this changes, and the text wraps around both sides, as the bottom of Figure 23-7 shows. Remember that you specify this option in the enclosing text box, not in the box that is inside it.

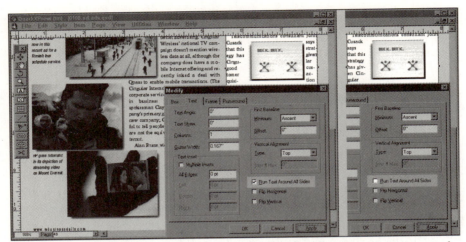

Figure 23-7: The normal wraparound method (far right) and the Run Text Around All Sides option.

Caution   The Run Text Around All Sides option is unusual and counterintuitive for most readers. They've been trained to move to the next line when a column ends or text runs into another object (sort of a forced column end), so if you use this new technique, they may not realize that the text continues on the other side of the intervening box. Use this tool sparingly, if at all. The best place to use it is when the intervening boxes are very small — such as picture boxes containing small icons — so the reader can easily see that the text continues on the same line.

Anchoring Items

Another way to have interplay between text and graphics is using the anchoring feature. QuarkXPress lets you select a text box, picture box, line, or text path and *anchor* it (attach it) to the text that surrounds it. You may want to do this to keep a graphic with a certain passage of text. Anchored items *flow* with the text to which they are anchored, even during the most massive edits. One common application of anchored items is to create a page that incorporates icons as small graphic elements in a stream of text. A movie guide that uses a different graphic to indicate the critic's opinion and a design that uses icons as paragraph breaks are examples of layouts that would benefit from using anchors. Figure 23-8 shows an example of an icon used with article subheads.

QuarkXPress treats anchored elements as individual characters of text. After you anchor them, you can cut, copy, paste, and delete these items just as if they were single characters of text. To anchor a text box, picture box, line, or text path, just follow these steps:

1. Using the Item tool, select the box, line, or path to be anchored into text.

2. Cut or copy the box, line, or path in the same way that you cut or copy any single text character (use Edit ⇨ Cut or Edit ⇨ Copy or the keyboard shortcuts ⌘+X or ⌘+C, or Ctrl+X or Ctrl+C).

3. Using the Content tool, position the cursor at the location where you want to anchor the item and paste in the item (select Edit ⇨ Paste, or ⌘+V or Ctrl+V).

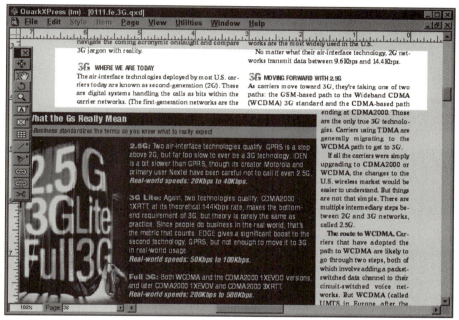

Figure 23-8: Anchored picture boxes used as dingbats in section titles in a story.

After the item becomes an anchored item, you can modify it by selecting it and then choosing Item ⇨ Modify, or using ⌘+M or Ctrl+M. For a box, you'll get the Box pane; for a Line, the Line pane; and for a text path, the Text Path pane. Figure 23-9 shows the Box pane, which is slightly different from the standard Box pane for a picture or text box. What's different is the Align with Text section, which tells QuarkXPress how to align the text that follows the anchored box. Lines and Text Path have the same Align with Text sections.

You have two options in the Align with Text section of the pane:

✦ Ascent, which has the top of the text align with the bottom of the anchored box.

✦ Baseline, which has the text align to the next baseline as set in the document's baseline grid (covered in Chapter 4). If you select Baseline, you can also add space after the anchored box by using the Offset field to indicate how much space you want.

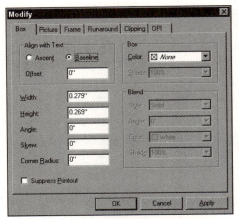

Figure 23-9: The Box pane's Align with Text options for anchored boxes.

Because an anchored box is a box, you can use the standard panes in the Modify dialog box — Runaround, Clipping, Frame, and Picture or Text, depending on whether the anchored box is a text box or picture box. Thus, you can specify a runaround margin to determine the space above, below, and to the sides of the anchored box. Similarly, you have the standard panes for lines and text paths.

And because the anchored graphic is part of a paragraph, you can apply several paragraph formatting commands in the Style menu and Measurements palette. Examples include making its paragraph centered or indented, or flipping the box. You cannot raise the baseline or do character formatting — although these Style menu and Measurements palette options are available, they affect the invisible anchor character, not the anchored item.

Note   Anchored items may only have a runaround of Item, so the only thing you can set in the Runaround pane is the amount of margin around the anchor item. If you're working with a box, you can of course use or create a clipping path for the item in the Clipping pane. But your text will wrap around the box, not the clipping path.

New Feature   You can adjust an anchored item's size in any direction. If you extend the item past the boundaries of the text column, QuarkXPress will reposition the box so it fits within the column, moving it to a different line if necessary. (In QuarkXPress 4, doing so created unpredictable placement of text.)

Caution   Don't make the anchored item wider than your column — that essentially prevents the text from appearing, and if you don't immediately undo the sizing (via Edit ⇨ Undo, or ⌘+Z or Ctrl+Z), you cannot make that text reappear.

Converting Text into Graphics

Text can be beautiful, thanks to some of the innovative, engaging letterforms that type designers have created, as Chapter 14 shows. So it makes sense to think of type as an art element, not just a medium with which to convey information. A technique prized by high-end designers has been to use text as the outline of an image — masking the image within the confines of a letter's shape. But the work to do that historically has been very great, limiting its use to publications with the time and money to achieve it. But the miracles of computer technology have taken what had been an arcane technique and made it commonplace.

Creating text-based boxes

QuarkXPress lets you convert text into a box — a picture box or a text box. That means you can take an image and have it form the background of a letter, word, or phrase. Or you could even create a text box in the shape of text. Figure 23-10 shows an example.

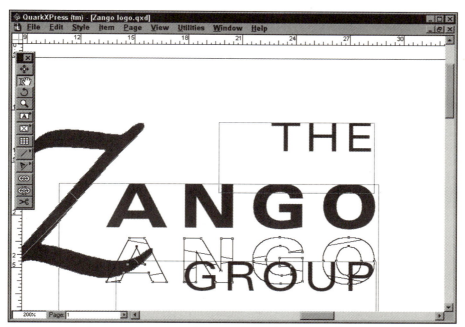

Figure 23-10: Text *ango* converted into a picture box (immediately below the text) as part of creating a Bézier logo from text. (The Z was previously converted.)

The process is very simple:

1. Format the text with the exact typeface, style, size, scale, tracking, kerning, and so forth.

2. Using the Content tool, select the text. (You can covert only one line at a time, not multiple lines.)

3. Use Style ⇨ Text to Box to change the text into a Bézier picture box. The picture box will appear on-screen (your test is also retained in its original text box, as Figure 23-10 shows.

4. If you want the picture box to be a text box, use Item ⇨ Content ⇨ Text to convert it.

You can now modify the text-based box as you would any box, as described in Chapters 28 and 32. Note that even though the box is composed of several distinct letters, the group of letters form one Bézier picture box, not a separate picture box for each letter. (If you want a separate box per letter, use the split feature described in Chapter 26, or create the boxes one letter at a time.)

Caution   Note that you cannot convert a text-based box back into text.

Fitting text to curves

Another desirable but difficult technique involving the use of text as graphics is the ability to have text follow a curve. Once again, QuarkXPress 5 makes this easy.

The Text-Path tools let you create one of four line types — straight line at any angle, *orthogonal line* (fully vertical and fully horizontal), freehand, and Bézier — and have text follow along the curve. Figure 23-11 shows an example, as well as the four Text-Path tools. After you draw the text path, you simply click on the line and start typing. You can format the text as you would any other text (see Part IV and Chapters 13, 15, and 18). Again, it's that simple.

About the only thing you can't do in QuarkXPress when it comes to treating text as graphics is define a shape and have QuarkXPress make the text distort to fit the contours of the shape. (It gives you a reason to keep using Adobe Illustrator, Macromedia FreeHand, or CorelDraw!)

Figure 23-11: Text along a Bézier curve, plus the four Text-Path tools.

Working with Dashes, Stripes, and Underline

Dashes, stripes, and underlines give emphasis to text. Dashes and stripes embellish lines, text paths, and the frames of text boxes (as well as lines and picture boxes), while underlines accent selected text.

Working with Dashes and Stripes

QuarkXPress has 11 predefined line styles in the Measurements palette and via the Style ⇨ Line Style submenu; Figure 23-12 shows the Measurements palette. These same 11 styles are available for boxes' frames as well in the Frame pane of the Modify dialog box (Item ⇨ Modify, or ⌘+M or Ctrl+M).

Although QuarkXPress does have 11 predefined line styles, artistically inclined users will want even more styles available to them, which is why QuarkXPress includes the Dashes and Stripes feature, which lets you create your own line styles. These line styles can be used both in box frames and for independent lines created with one of the line tools.

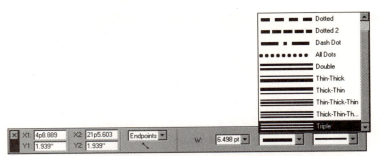

Figure 23-12: QuarkXPress has 11 predefined dashed and striped line patterns, 10 of which are shown here.

You get the Dashes & Stripes dialog box shown in Figure 23-13 via Edit ⇨ Dashes & Stripes. With it, you can create lines made up of multiple lines — what QuarkXPress calls *stripes* — and dashed lines made up of line segments.

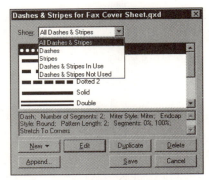

Figure 23-13: The Dashes & Stripes dialog box.

New Feature   Gone from QuarkXPress 5 is the Frame Editor tool that had been available only for the Macintosh version. That tool let you create bitmaps that could serve as frame borders. However, QuarkXPress keeps — in both the Mac and Windows versions — some predefined bitmap frame styles available via the Frames pane, as Figure 23-14 shows. You cannot edit them or create new ones.

The Dashes & Stripes dialog box shows the existing line styles at the top; you scroll through the list to see those not visible in the list window.

Dashed lines

When you create a new line style, you first choose whether you want to create a stripe or a dash. We'll create a dash first. Figure 23-15 shows the Edit Dash dialog box, which you would also see if you edited an existing dash line style.

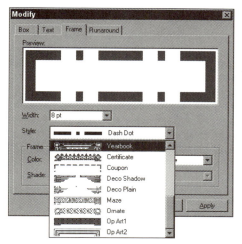

Figure 23-14: Bitmap frame styles available via the Frames pane.

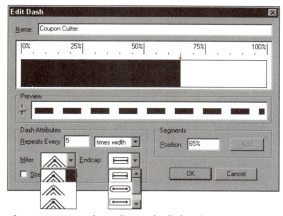

Figure 23-15: The Edit Dash dialog box.

Here are the steps:

1. The first thing to do is give your new dash a name, which you do in the Name field.

2. Now choose your dash attributes, in the Dash Attributes section of the dialog box. The key one to choose at this point is the Repeats Every attribute. The default setting is Times Width, which makes the pattern repeat in increments of the line width. Thus, the thicker the line, the longer the segments, and the smaller the number you enter, the finer the dash elements — compare the two dashes in Figure 23-16, one that has a repeat of 1 and one that has a repeat of 9. Use the Preview slider to see the effects at different line widths.

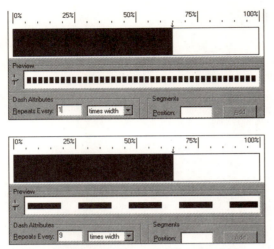

Figure 23-16: The effects of different width settings.

Tip   If you pick Points as the width, the dash pattern will fit within the specified width.

3. To create the actual dashes, move your mouse to the top section of the dialog box that has the ruler. The default is that the line is solid. To change that, click to where you want the first segment to end. The rest of the dash will become empty.

4. You add the next segment by clicking the mouse on the ruler (like adding a tab). If you hold down the mouse button when adding a segment, you can drag the segment to the desired width. (You can also enter the ruler location in the Position field and click the Add button.)

5. You resize an existing segment by clicking and holding the mouse on one side of the segment boundaries *on the ruler* and dragging to expand or contract the segment.

6. Finally, you can move a segment by dragging it to the left or to the right within the windows (the mouse should be on the segment itself, not on the ruler).

7. Now you can finish specifying the dash attributes. First, we recommend that you select the Stretch to Corners check box, which ensures that no corner has a segment only in one direction. Figure 23-17 shows the effects of having the box checked and unchecked.

8. Set the miter type. A *miter* is the connection method for lines at a corner, and your choices are for the corner to be a right angle (the default), curved, or beveled. For fine lines (2 points and narrower), all three options look the same, so you may as well leave the option set to a right angle for such lines. Figure 23-15 shows the options.

Figure 23-17: The effects of the Stretch to Corners check box (bottom).

9. Choose the *endcap,* which is the shape of the dash segment at the beginning and end. The default is that the endpoint of the dash segment is where the dash ends. But you can also set a rounded endcap, which adds a curve at the end of the dash segment — extending slightly past the dash's endpoint. Another option is a squared-off endcap, which adds a rectangle at the end of the dash segment — again, extending slightly past the dash segment's endpoint. Figure 23-15 shows the options.

Frankly, the squared-off endcap makes little sense because all it does is make your dashes a bit wider — something you could more precisely do by just making the dashes wider to begin with.

10. Click OK when you're done, then click the Save button in the Dashes & Stripes dialog box to save all your changes.

If you want to start over again with a solid line, Option+click or Alt+Click anywhere on the line or ruler while in the Edit Dash dialog box.

You can create true dots with the Dashes & Stripes feature. Typically, your "dots" will simply be squares. But if you choose a rounded endcap, your square becomes a circle. You can also edit the dotted line that QuarkXPress comes with. Possible modifications include changing the spacing by changing the Repeats Every value and changing the dots into rounded dashes by adding a dash segment. We recommend you duplicate the All Dots line style and work with that duplicate rather than edit the original style, so you don't lose the default settings.

Striped lines

Creating stripes is similar to creating dashes, although there are fewer settings to worry about. Figure 23-18 shows the Edit Stripe dialog box. Note that rather than have a horizontal ruler, you have a vertical one. You use it to create and modify the stripe's constituent ruling lines just as you would modify a dash in the Edit Dash dialog box.

1. To create the actual stripes, move your mouse to the top section of the dialog box that has the ruler. The default is that the stripe is solid. To change that, click to where you want the first segment to end. The rest of the stripe will become empty.

2. You add the next segment by clicking the mouse on the ruler (like adding a tab). If you hold down the mouse button when adding a segment, you can drag the segment to the desired width. (You can also enter the ruler location in the Position field and click the Add button.)

3. You resize an existing segment by clicking and holding the mouse on one side of the segment boundaries *on the ruler* and dragging to expand or contract the segment.

4. Finally, you can move a segment by dragging it up or down within the windows (the mouse should be on the segment itself, not on the ruler).

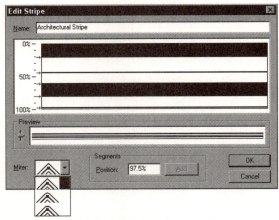

Figure 23-18: The Edit Stripe dialog box.

The management of dashes and stripes

Like similar dialog boxes for creating style sheets and colors, the Dashes & Stripes dialog box lets you duplicate existing line styles to create variants of existing ones (with the Duplicate button), as well as edit existing styles (with the Edit button) and delete existing styles (with the Delete button).

Remember that you must click the Save button to save any changes you make to dashes and stripes, and that any dashes and stripes created, edited, duplicated, or deleted when no QuarkXPress document is open become the default settings for all future QuarkXPress documents.

Any documents that use these new and modified line styles will print and display them properly when opened in other copies of QuarkXPress (such as when sharing files with other users or with service bureaus). You can also import line styles created in another document by using the Append button in the Dashes & Stripes dialog box.

You can fine-tune your view of stripes and dashes via the Show pop-up menu (refer to Figure 23-13). This is a handy way to see what line styles are used in your document.

Using underline styles

Finally, you can create your own format of underline, so you can determine the color, size, and offset from the text. (A negative offset moves the underline below the text, a positive value moves it up into the text.) You do so via Edit ➪ Underline Styles or Style ➪ Underline Styles ➪ Custom, which produces the dialog box shown in Figure 23-19. Give the style a name, fill in the settings, then click OK. Be sure to click Save when done to save the style.

The Underline Styles feature is new to QuarkXPress 5.

You cannot create or apply underline styles if text on a text path is selected. Underline styles can be applied only to selected text in text boxes.

You apply the underline via Style ➪ Underline Styles, selecting the style from the submenu. (Figure 23-19 shows the resulting line applied to the word *Hot.*) There is a predefined style named *default* that is a 1-point black rule with no offset.

If you use the standard underline commands in the Style ➪ Type Style submenu, via the Measurements palette, or via the keyboard shortcut Shift+⌘+U or Ctrl+Shift+U, QuarkXPress will use the standard underline style. You can apply both the standard underline and an underline style at the same time; the standard underline will appear underneath the underline style if they overlap.

You can import and export underline styles via the Import and Export buttons in the Underline Styles dialog box. But you cannot use the Append dialog box to import underline styles from other documents as you can colors, style sheets, dashes and stripes, H&J sets, and lists.

Figure 23-19: The Underline Styles dialog box, with a custom underline applied to the word *Hot.*

Summary

Text wraps provide a visually dynamic way to create interplay between text and graphics by letting you have the text follow the shape of an image. QuarkXPress provides a runaround tool to let you choose from several types of runarounds. If you use embedded paths or alpha channels in your image editor, you can even more precisely control how the text wraps.

QuarkXPress has one wrap feature, Run Text Around All Sides, that you should avoid. It lets text wrap around all sides of a box wholly within the text column, but that creates an unnatural break and usually hinders readability, even if it looks nice visually.

Another way to intermingle text and graphics is by anchoring images into text. Essentially, you can paste a picture frame, line, or text path into text, so the pasted element — called an *anchored element* — flows with the text. This is handy for using images as bullet characters or dingbats, as well as for inserting special symbols and icons in text, such as for engineering symbols.

QuarkXPress also has a neat feature that converts text (as long as it takes just one line) into picture boxes, so you can create logos from text or picture boxes that are the shape of text (for example, you could have a field of flowers appear within the letters of the word *Flowers*).

Dashed and striped lines are often used to accent text, such as by indicating a coupon with a dashed line or a certificate with an ornate border. QuarkXPress has a set of tools to create custom dashes and stripes. QuarkXPress for Mac no longer includes the Frame Editor tool to create ornate bitmap frames for boxes (the Windows version never had this feature), but both platform versions of QuarkXPress now include a selection of such bitmap frames, although you cannot edit them or create new ones.

An addition to QuarkXPress 5 is that of underline styles, which let you create underlines of any color, thickness, and offset from the text. You still have the regular underline feature as well, and you can use both simultaneously.

✦   ✦   ✦

Illustrations

◆   ◆   ◆   ◆

◆   ◆   ◆   ◆

QuarkXPress is not an illustration tool. Well, maybe it is. Its ability to create shapes of any sort and fill them with lines, colors, and so forth gives it much of the basic capabilities of an Adobe Illustrator or CorelDraw. Of course, there are techniques in those professional tools that QuarkXPress can't match, so you should continue to make them an essential part of your publishing work. But we suspect you'll find yourself doing a fair amount of basic illustration right in QuarkXPress rather than switching back and forth from page layout to illustration.

This part shows you what the QuarkXPress illustration tools can really do and how to use them to best effect.

Drawing Tools and Terms

Although the illustration tools in QuarkXPress aren't going to win awards from Adobe Illustrator or Macromedia FreeHand users — who are busy drawing labyrinths and illustrations of carburetors using their favorite drawing application — that's not really why Quark gave you these tools in the first place.

When it comes to Quark's illustration tools, the most helpful benefit lies in your ability to take simple tasks that you've *always* performed in QuarkXPress — such as importing pictures — and elevate those tasks to a higher level of design. Learn the illustration tools, and you'll be able to draw any shape you want for the picture boxes, text boxes, text characters, clipping paths, and runaround paths that form an inseparable part of your layout.

Another great advantage to using illustration tools in QuarkXPress is that your drawings remain scalable directly in the finished layout, both on-screen and at printout time. Unlike EPS files, illustrations made with these tools need *not* be imported into a picture box and subjected to low-resolution screen previews!

Illustration Terminology

Before we get started, it's important that you understand some of the terminology we'll be using. The following sections identify the key terms you'll want to know.

Bézier

Bézier is an industry-standard way of defining curved paths. Bézier technology relies on *curve handles* (Quark's term for what the industry calls *control points*) to manipulate the curvature of each segment in a path. Zero, one, or two curve handles may extend from any one point.

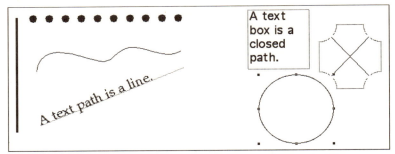

Figure 24-4: On the left are examples of open paths, called *lines.* On the right are closed paths, called *boxes.*

Segment

A *segment* is part of the actual path. It always resides in between two adjacent points. Therefore, the number of segments and the number of points are always equal for any path. When you select a segment, both of its points are selected along with it. Likewise, when you select two adjacent points, the segment is said to be selected as well. Dragging a segment changes its shape, as shown in Figure 24-5.

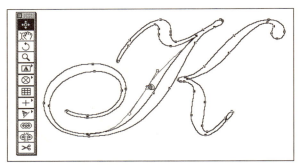

Figure 24-5: Dragging a curved segment will bend it. QuarkXPress is luxurious in this respect, because the program is sensitive to the exact location from which you start dragging the segment. Consequently, bending segments feels very intuitive — like bending a piece of wire.

Illustration Tools

The term *illustration tool* refers here to any tool that lets you create Bézier shapes. Use them to create, for example, triangular text boxes, amoeba-like picture boxes, jagged lines, squiggly paths, and so on. (Ovals, circles, and rectangles may be used in illustrative ways as well, but we cover these in Chapter 8.)

Most of the illustration tools in the QuarkXPress Tool palette can be placed into one of the following three categories:

✦ Freehand versus Bézier tools

✦ Box versus line tools

✦ Text versus picture tools

We cover each of these in the following sections.

Freehand versus Bézier tools

All the tools covered in this section create Bézier objects. The difference between a tool named *freehand* and one named *Bézier* lies in how each tool initially creates an object. See Figure 24-6 for an example of a freehand item and a Bézier item.

✦ *Freehand* tools quickly auto-trace the movements of your mouse (or other input device) as you click and drag to create a new item.

✦ *Bézier* tools let you draw curved and polygon shapes in a more hands-on way, point by point.

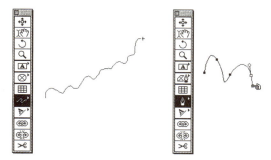

Figure 24-6: On the left, the artist uses a freehand tool while QuarkXPress quickly auto-traces the movement. On the right, the artist draws an item point-by-point using a Bézier tool.

Box versus line tools

Although you may think of a rectangle when you hear the word *box,* QuarkXPress uses this term to refer to *any* single item consisting of one or more closed paths. In Quark lingo, even doughnut shapes can be called boxes, because they have no discernible endpoints.

A *line* is just the opposite. A line can be any shape, but it always has two endpoints. Line tools are used to create open paths. You can stroke lines with a color, but you cannot "fill" them with a background color, blend, or picture.

Text versus picture tools

Each illustration tool creates a shape that defaults to a certain type of content (picture, text, or none). For example, the Freehand Text Path tool draws lines that can hold text as shown in Figure 24-7.

Figure 24-7: If you ever use text paths, you may want to learn Bézier technology.

Tip

In addition to picture boxes and text boxes, QuarkXPress provides "no content" boxes to use for frames and background colors. Normally, you need to convert a text box or a picture box to a no-content box using the Item ⇨ Content ⇨ None command. But if you use no-content boxes often, you can add a row of no-content box tools to the Tool palette. To do this, press Option+Shift+⌘ (Mac OS) or Ctrl+Alt+Shift (Windows) while you click the Default Tool Palette button in the Tools pane of the Preferences dialog box. The no-content tools work the same as the picture box tools, but the boxes you create cannot contain pictures.

Knowing which tool to use for the job

Table 24-1 lists all the irregular drawing tools by name, icon, and characteristics. Decide which characteristics are necessary for what you're trying to draw. (Don't worry: If you choose the wrong tool, you may be able to change the item characteristics later.)

Table 24-1
A Guide to What Each Tool Does

Name of Drawing Tool	Icon	Auto-Traces Initial Drawing Movement	Closed Path	Open Path	Text-Ready	Picture-Ready
Freehand Picture Box tool			x			x
Freehand Text Box tool		x	x		x	
Freehand Text Path tool		x		x	x	
Freehand Line tool		x		x		
Bézier Picture Box tool			x			x
Bézier Text Box tool			x		x	
Bézier Text Path tool				x	x	
Bézier Line tool				x		

Point and Segment Types

As discussed in the "Illustration Terminology" section of this chapter, Bézier paths are made up of points and segments. Now it's time to explore points and segments a little deeper.

There are three types of points (corner, smooth, and symmetrical), and two types of segments (straight and curved).

Corner points, shown in Figure 24-8, are used to create sharp transitions. A triangle has three corner points. A figure-8 has no corner points, consisting entirely of *smooth points*.

Figure 24-8: The left side of the *B* consists of corner points.

Smooth points, shown in Figure 24-9, are used to change the direction of a path in a smooth way, with no sharp corners. An *S* shape has three smooth points: one at the start of the path, one at the end, and one in the middle, where the two arches join.

If you click on a smooth point, you will see two curve handles extending from it, both forming a straight line through the point. If you drag to revolve one of these curve handles around its point, its partner curve handle will revolve along with it. This restrictive behavior is what preserves the smoothness of the transition.

Figure 24-9: The curves on the *B* are examples of smooth points.

Symmetrical points, shown in Figure 24-10, are specialized smooth points. Not only do the curve handles revolve together around a point, they also remain equidistant from the point. Move one curve handle closer to a symmetrical point, and its partner will move closer as well.

Try drawing a curved path using the Bézier Picture Box tool. Click and drag to create each point. As you do so, you will notice the curve handles behaving in the symmetrical way described above, but this is only temporary. If you try to go back and move a curve handle after a point has already been created, you will notice that QuarkXPress defaults points to the *smooth* state. If you want to change the state of the point back to a symmetrical point, select it later and press Option+F3 or Ctrl+F3.

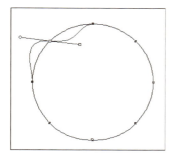

Figure 24-10: Examples of symmetrical points.

Straight segments, shown in Figure 24-11, are most easily created using a Bézier tool (as opposed to a Freehand tool). To draw curved segments while using a Bézier tool, simply click without dragging as you create the points of the shape. This produces corner points that have fully retracted curve handles. The result: straight segments.

If you change your mind later and want the straight segment to be curved, first make sure that Item ⇨ Edit ⇨ Shape is checked, then select the segment in question and press Option+Shift+F2 or Alt+Shift+F2.

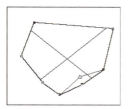

Figure 24-11: Examples of straight segments.

Curved segments, shown in Figure 24-12, are what it's all about! To draw them while using a Bézier tool, simply click and drag to create each point in the shape. This produces smooth points that have fully extended curve handles. The result: curved segments.

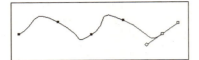

Figure 24-12: Examples of curved segments.

If you change your mind later and want the curved segment to be straight, first make sure that Item ⇨ Edit ⇨ Shape is checked. Then select the segment in question and press Option+Shift+F1 or Alt+Shift+F1.

Shape-Editing Tools

After using one of the illustration tools (covered in the preceding sections) to create an item, you'll probably need to edit the shape. Or perhaps you have a fancy Bézier clipping path or *runaround path* (a path to wrap text around); these are not items per se, but their shapes can be edited nonetheless.

On the Tool palette, you'll find three tools that will help you edit Bézier shapes. One of these tools was brand new to QuarkXPress 4.1, and the other two have existed for eons.

Scissors tool

There is now a Scissors tool, introduced in QuarkXPress 4.1, that lets you sever a path.

To sever a path using the Scissors tool, simply click directly on an existing path. Although no immediate results may be visible, you'll notice the split if you move things around.

If the Scissors tool is used on an open path, two paths are the result. If it's used on a closed path, an open path is the result.

Item and Content tools

When it comes to Bézier editing, the Item and Content tools are interchangeable. As soon as you finish drawing a shape, QuarkXPress selects one of these tools for you.

If Item ⇨ Edit ⇨ Shape is checked, you can begin editing the completed shape immediately. You'll just need to know the proper keyboard commands before you can be very effective at this (see Table 24-2).

Table 24-2
Shortcuts for Shape Editing

Function	Mac OS Command	Windows Command
Change point to a corner point	Option+F1	Ctrl+F1
Change point to a smooth point	Option+F2	Ctrl+F2
Change point to a symmetrical point	Option+F3	Ctrl+F3
Toggle state of point between smooth and curved	Control+drag curve handle	Ctrl+Shift+drag curve handle (ineffective for shapes in progress)
Change curved segment into a straight segment	Option+Shift+F1	Ctrl+Shift-F1
Change straight segment into a curved segment	Option+Shift+F2	Ctrl+Shift-F2
Add point	Option+click segment	Alt+click a segment
Delete point	Option+click point	Alt+click a point
Constrain a curve handle or point to 45-degree movement	Shift+drag	Shift+drag
Select all points in a single-path item	Double-click a point	Double-click a point
Select all points in a multiple-path item	Triple-click a point	Triple-click a point
Retract curve handles	Control+Shift+click a point	Ctrl+Shift+click a point
Expose curve handles	Control+Shift+drag from a point	Ctrl+ Shift+drag from a point
Edit shape in progress (you can combine this modifier with most of the commands listed above)	⌘ key	Ctrl key

Tip

The last command listed in Table 24-2 is also the most useful! Edit a shape in progress by holding down the ⌘ or Ctrl key with any of the other commands listed in the table, and if you're talented, you'll have your shape 90 percent perfected before you've even finished creating it.

Also, make sure the correct part of your item — whether it's a point or a segment — is selected before you try to use a particular command.

Summary

If you have drawing talent and a mastery of the tools, QuarkXPress can provide useful illustration tools. Some useful points to remember:

✦ Curved boxes and lines in QuarkXPress are made using Bézier technology. These shapes can be used to contain text or pictures, so they're useful for much more than simple line drawings.

✦ When creating shapes initially, use a freehand tool when speed is most important, but use a Bézier tool (for more hands-on control) when smoothness is most important.

✦ Bézier paths are composed of points and segments, with curvature determined by the curve handles that extend from points. To make points visible in a shape, make sure Item ⇨ Edit ⇨ Shape is checked. To make curve handles visible, make sure a point is selected in the shape.

✦   ✦   ✦

Creating Illustrations

This chapter builds on the tools and terminology you learned about in the previous chapter. You'll need to be especially familiar with the terms *Bézier, path, point, curve handle,* and *segment,* because we use those terms quite frequently here. We also suggest you have at least a rudimentary grasp of the difference between the Bézier tools and the freehand tools before we delve into specific applications for these tools.

Keep in mind: The illustration tools in QuarkXPress will no sooner make you an illustrator than the design tools will make you a designer. Your success with mastering the illustration tools is somewhat based on your understanding of and need for them. And, unfortunately, if you have no artistic talent, you may have difficulty understanding or needing the tools.

Drawing with Straight Segments

Drawing with straight lines is the simplest way to illustrate in QuarkXPress. The program gives you several ways of going about it, but because most of these methods involve tools described in Chapter 8, we'll limit ourselves here to the Bézier tools introduced in the previous chapter.

Out of the four Bézier tools in QuarkXPress, the Bézier Picture Box tool is probably the most widely used, so if you're keen to experiment, this is the tool we recommend. Just keep in mind that most of the basics associated with this tool apply to the other three Bézier tools as well.

To use one of the four Bézier tools to draw a shape consisting of straight segments only, as shown in Figure 25-1, simply click (without dragging), in succession, where you want each segment to join the next. A new Bézier *corner point* will be created wherever you click. The curve handles associated with each of these points will be fully retracted, ensuring that your segments remain straight even if you later move them. (In fact, the only way to induce curvature in a straight segment is to click on the segment with Edit ⇨ Shape checked in the Item menu, then click the Curved Segment button in the Measurements palette.)

When you're ready to create the last point in the shape, double-click. QuarkXPress will then complete the shape and automatically select the Item or Content tool. Alternatively, if you've already single-clicked to create the last point in the shape, you can either click on the start point, or you can manually select the Item or Content tool to complete the shape.

Figure 25-1: This triangular text box was created in only four clicks using the Bézier Text Box tool.

Constraining points as you draw

QuarkXPress lets you use the Shift key to constrain segments to 45-degree increments. Notice we said *increments,* and not *angles.* This means that 45-degree angles, 90-degree angles, 135-degree angles, and 180-degree angles are all fair game when you're holding down the Shift key.

Constraining angles might seem pointless if you're drawing curved segments, but the technique can come in handy for straight segments — particularly when you need two or more segments to appear parallel. To constrain segments to 45-degree increments, as shown in Figure 25-2, simply hold down the Shift key as you click to create each new point in the shape.

Using guides to draw

The technique of constraining segments to 45-degree angles has numerous limits. It may, for example, help you create a schematic for a piece of electronic equipment, but when the aesthetics of alignment and symmetry become more important, what you really need are *guides* — lots of guides.

Figure 25-2: This abstract shape was created by Shift-clicking with the Bézier Picture Box tool. Shift-clicking constrains all straight paths to 45-degree increments. (QuarkXPress makes an exception for the last segment in a closed path, which must join the first and last points at all costs.)

If you were one of those kids who used graph paper in the fifth grade to draw mazes or dungeons, you'll be at home with the QuarkXPress Guide Manager (Utilities ➪ Guide Manager), a feature added to version 4.1 of the program. By entering a few simple values into the Guide Manager dialog box, as shown in Figure 25-3, you can quickly cover your work area with a grid of "snappable" guides. Just make sure that Snap to Guides is checked in the View menu, or the guides will have no effect. Also, be sure to choose View ➪ Show Guides (or use the shortcut F7) to make the guides visible.

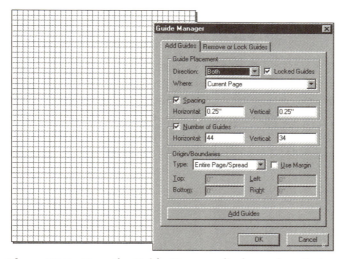

Figure 25-3: Here, the Guide Manager displays values that cover an 8.52-x-11-inch page with a grid of quarter-inch-spaced guides. Drawing on such a grid makes it much easier to create alignment and symmetry among segments, points, paths — you name it.

Tip

Make sure that Locked Guides is checked in the Guide Manager dialog box to prevent your guides from being moved.

The Guide Manager is invaluable when symmetry is required, because you have the ability to know, at a glance, the exact length and angle of every segment you create (see Figure 25-4).

Figure 25-4: In this house shape, the artist wanted perfect symmetry. While drawing, rather than spend a half hour measuring out the various line lengths and angles required, he simply snapped each point to a grid that he created using the Guide Manager.

Tip

The Guide Manager isn't just useful for drawing straight segments—it's useful as the basis for any illustration in which alignment and/or symmetry are important. Even curve handles will snap to a guide if there's one nearby!

Drawing Freehand

Drawing with any of the four freehand tools is no more complicated than knowing how to identify the tools. When you know the difference between the Freehand Picture Box tool, the Freehand Text Box tool, the Freehand Line tool, and the Freehand Text Path tool, you're ready to go.

Cross-Reference

If you're not sure which tool is which, refer to Chapter 24.

All you have to do is select the appropriate tool from the Tool palette, then click and drag on the page to define the path. QuarkXPress auto-traces the movement of your mouse (or other input device). When you've defined the entire path, let go of the mouse button, and—voilà!—a new Bézier path is born (see Figure 25-5 for an example of a freehand box created in QuarkXPress).

You can edit freehand paths in the same way that you edit any curved path in QuarkXPress. To edit the shape, use the Item or Content tool with the keyboard commands described in Chapter 24, and make sure that the Edit ➪ Shape option is checked in the Item menu.

Figure 25-5: By auto-tracing your mouse movement, freehand tools let you draw loosely defined curves in seconds.

Drawing Curves with Bézier Tools

The Bézier tools are more challenging than the freehand tools, but they offer much more control over the smoothness and symmetry of your artwork. To draw a curved shape using Bézier tools, you should do more than simply click where you want each point to go. You should actually drag to create each smooth point. Doing so exposes the curve handles, thereby creating curved segments as you go along.

Basically, you have two methods for creating Bézier items — we call them "Draw It Ugly, Edit Pretty" and "Draw it Pretty." The difference, as you might guess, is in your initial precision in drawing the item. The two methods are described in detail in the following sections.

Cross-Reference The QuickStart at the beginning of this book provides a quick tutorial on drawing Bézier shapes.

The "draw it ugly, edit pretty" method

If you have a good feel for where to plot points and where not to plot them, you'll have a significantly enhanced ability to perfect your shapes during the editing stage. Even if the shape initially looks far removed from what you envision, don't let that discourage you. All you need are some basic Bézier editing skills.

Let's walk through the example of the half-guitar shape shown in Figure 25-6. For now, assume that it exists only as a pencil sketch on a physical piece of paper.

Knowing how many points you'll need

It takes an uncommon amount of practice and know-how to draw curved objects that are, from the moment of creation, exactly the shape you want them. Although you may not be able to attain this level of Bézier expertise, you should at least learn where to plot points and where not to plot points if you hope to attain results good enough to allow for efficient shape editing afterwards.

The first rule of drawing with traditional Bézier tools is this: If you plot too many points, you won't have enough smoothness. The second rule: If you create too few points, you won't have enough control.

So how many points is the right amount? Assuming every part of your envisioned shape is curved, the idea is to have one segment for every shallow to medium-depth "arch." An S-shape, for example, would consist of two such arches, and therefore two segments (three points).

Continued

Continued

Here are specific guidelines to give you a better idea of what we mean. They aren't strict rules, but they do represent a nice balance between smoothness and control.

✦ Corners (sharp transitions), shown in the following figure, are best represented by one point per corner. If you envision sharp transitions in your shape, plan on putting one point per corner.

✦ Straight segments, as shown in the next figure, should always have a point on each end and no points in between. If you envision straight segments in your shape, make sure there's a point on each side of every straight segment.

✦ Whenever a curve shifts direction (like the way a letter *S* shifts direction at its center), include one point (see the next figure). If you envision sine waves or other types of curves that "shift direction," plan to place a point where the shift in direction occurs.

✦ This last tip is a little trickier to describe. Envision, if you will, any ellipse, circle, or egg shape. If you cut such an ellipse in half, you're left with an arch that requires two endpoints *only* as shown in the last figure. If a given arch has a more bulbous depth than this (as would be the case if we were dealing with *more* than half an ellipse), include an extra point for added control. In the figure, the arches on the left have an amount of curvature equal to or less than half of an ellipse. Two endpoints are all that are needed for such curves. The arches on the right are deeper and more bulbous, requiring an additional point for proper control.

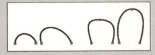

Figure 25-6: You can sketch a shape similar to this half of a guitar, then perfect the shape later.

Your first job is to figure out where to put the points. In the "Knowing how many points you'll need" sidebar, we mention that corners (sharp transitions) always get one point each. If you count the amount of corners in the half-guitar shape, you should come up with a total of six corner points: four that go near the headstock, one that goes where the neck joins the body, and one more at the far upper right of the drawing.

But six points alone won't suffice, because there's also a continuous curve in the drawing that's too complex to be considered a simple arch. ***Remember:*** Complex continuous curves should be broken apart until there is one segment describing every shallow- to medium-depth arch in the path. It looks as though the main curve in the half-guitar shape is composed of at least three such arches, so you'll need to add two more points (*smooth* points, to be specific) to break up this segment.

Figure 25-7 shows what we now envision, with points numbered to make our description easier to follow.

Figure 25-7: This half-guitar shape needs at least eight points. Points 1 through 5 and 8 are all corner points. Points 6 and 7 are the only smooth points.

To get started drawing the half-guitar shape shown in Figure 25-7, follow these steps:

STEPS: Drawing a Bézier shape

1. Select the Bézier Picture Box tool from the Tool palette.

2. When using the "draw it ugly, edit pretty" method described here, it's best to simply click (without dragging) where you envision corner points. So, click in the appropriate areas to create points 1 through 5. (Click clockwise, in succession.) Hold down the Shift key as you're creating point 5, and you should wind up with a nice straight line across the top.

3. When you get to point 6, click and drag toward the upper left to create it. Don't bother trying to shape the curve properly just yet.

4. When you get to point 7, click and drag toward the lower left to create it.

5. Point 8 is another corner point, so don't drag. Simply click to create it.

6. Click on the start point to complete the shape. You should now have a shape that looks something like Figure 25-8.

Figure 25-8: Don't expect this method to produce perfect results right off the bat. The basic idea is to click for corner points, drag for smooth points, then fix the exact shape during the editing stage.

Note If you don't see the points in your shape but instead see a rectangular perimeter of resizing handles, press F10 to turn the Edit ⇨ Shape ability on. (This switch is also available from the Item menu.)

7. Move your pointer over the completed shape and notice how the pointer changes depending on whether a point or a segment is underneath.

8. When your cursor is over a point that you want to move, click and drag to move it. When your cursor is over a straight segment that you want to move, click and drag to move it. Last but not least (and this is one of the best illustration features that QuarkXPress offers), when your cursor is over a curved segment that you want to reshape, click and drag to reshape it.

9. When you're fairly happy with the basic positions of the points and curve handles, double-click a point to get a better view of the end result. This tells QuarkXPress to select all the points in the shape simultaneously so that you can see every point and curve handle all at once. The result might look something like Figure 25-9.

Figure 25-9: If you double-click a point in a Bézier shape, all the points become selected, and all the curve handles become visible at once.

By now, you'll have noticed that whenever a point adjoining a curve is selected, its associated curve handles become visible. When a curve handle is visible, you can drag it. This gives you a more accurate level of control over the curvature of adjoining segments.

Tip Notice that there is no difference between having two adjacent points selected and having a single segment selected.

Now let's take a look at the Measurements palette's role in all this.

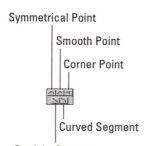

Symmetrical Point

Smooth Point

Corner Point

Curved Segment

Straight Segment

Figure 25-10: Bézier editing buttons become visible in the middle of the Measurements palette whenever a point or segment is selected. Clicking a button changes the state of the active point(s) or segment(s).

If you follow the advice given here and always click (without dragging) to create corner points, you'll run into a snag when you have two corner points that must be connected by a curved segment. That's because Quark creates a rigid, straight segment whenever you click twice in succession using a Bézier tool. Even if you drag on such a segment, it won't bend.

To change a rigid, straight segment into one that can be bent, select the segment and click the Curved Segment button in the Measurements palette.

The other Bézier editing buttons on this palette work in a similar way: Select the point or segment whose state you want to alter, then click the appropriate palette button.

Tip   You can add or delete points after the fact using the Option or Alt key along with the mouse.

The "draw it pretty" method

After you've had a bit of experience with the "draw it ugly, edit pretty" method, if you're a hard-core power user, you may want to learn a method that supports keyboard commands for on-the-fly Bézier editing. This will let you perfect the shape as you draw it initially, rather than perfect it later.

There are two key secrets to this method:

✦ Holding down the ⌘ key (Mac) or Ctrl key (Windows) while using a Bézier tool lets you edit shapes on the fly, as you create them. For example, you can reposition points and curve handles, and you can bend curved segments, even though your shape is incomplete. Just make sure you don't keep holding down the key when you're ready to create the next point in the shape.

✦ Pressing Option+⌘+F1 or Ctrl+F1 changes the active point into a corner point.

This second secret is especially important for you power users, so read it again! Remember how, in the "draw it ugly, edit pretty" method, you had to click to create corner points? And remember how this approach initially prevented you from creating a corner point that connected to a curved segment? Well, if you master this keyboard command, you can transcend those limitations and create corner points with independently movable curve handles before you've even completed the shape.

Summary

When it comes to creating illustrations in QuarkXPress — just like illustrating in real life — you may not get it right the first time. That's why there are plenty of methods for editing the points and curves that make up your shapes. Some useful points to remember:

✦ To draw straight lines using a Bézier tool, simply click (without dragging) wherever you want each segment to join the next.

✦ To draw Bézier shapes in a more freehand fashion, use one of the four freehand tools.

✦ The Guide Manager (Utilities ⇨ Guide Manager) can help you create a snappable grid that might prove useful when your artwork requires a certain amount of alignment or symmetry.

✦ To use one of the four traditional Bézier tools, try the "draw it ugly, edit pretty" method, which requires you to click for corner points, drag for smooth points, then perfect the shape with the Item or Content tool after the shape has been initially created.

✦ Power users can periodically press the ⌘ (Mac) or Ctrl (Windows) key while creating a shape with a Bézier tool to edit their shapes on the fly.

✦   ✦   ✦

Creating Composite Illustrations

◆ ◆ ◆ ◆

In This Chapter

Merging items

Splitting items

Scaling multiple-item illustrations

◆ ◆ ◆ ◆

Whether you're trying to create a shape so complex that it cannot be drawn with the traditional Bézier tools, or you're looking for an alternate method that takes less time than drawing point by point, the QuarkXPress compositing features may be just the ticket.

By *compositing features,* we're referring mainly to the Merge and Split commands in the Item menu. But as you'll see, QuarkXPress has at least one more trick up its sleeve when it comes to compositing.

Merging Items

The Merge submenu of the Item menu offers a selection of commands that instantly create a single Bézier box to replace two or more selected items. The commands work by analyzing the shapes of these items. Although shapes created using the Merge commands are Bézier in nature, the shapes that you start with can be almost anything — even standard (rectangular) boxes and lines!

This fact can save you time drawing. Suppose you want to import a picture into a box that's shaped like the view through a pair of binoculars. Instead of painstakingly trying to draw such a box using the Bézier tools, you could simply merge two circles together using the Union command.

Selecting items to merge

Merge commands aren't available unless you have at least two items selected. So if you're not familiar with the concept of drag-selecting or Shift+clicking to select multiple items, see Chapter 8.

Your selection may include lines as well as boxes, but keep in mind that a single box will always be the end result of any Merge command. The one exception is Join Endpoints — a command designed exclusively for use with lines. You can see a Merge command, Union, in action in Figure 26-1.

Figure 26-1: Why waste time drawing a picture box shape like this from scratch when you can simply merge two circles together?

Tip   If items in your selected stack contain color, frames, text, or a picture, you may lose these items after performing a Merge command. Only the contents of the item in back will be retained. So, when you're using Merge commands, always think of the item in back as the safe deposit box for anything you want to keep.

You can choose from seven Merge commands, explained on the following pages.

Intersection

Intersection looks for any areas that overlap the item in back, retains these areas, and eliminates the remainder.

Sample Usage: You want to draw the shape of a single slice of pie. Start by drawing a circle, then draw a triangle on top of the circle as shown on the left side of Figure 26-2. Select both items, and choose Item ➪ Merge ➪ Intersection. You'll be left with a single pie slice as shown on the right side of Figure 26-2.

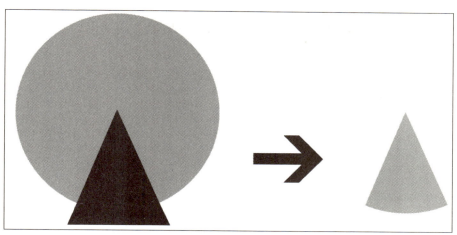

Figure 26-2: The Intersection command in action.

Union

Union combines all the selected shapes into one, with any overlapping areas melting into a seamless whole. (If the items don't overlap, the resulting item will consist of multiple paths.)

Sample Usage #1: You want a single picture to appear behind all the circular picture boxes shown on the left side of Figure 26-3. Select all the circles, and choose Item ➪ Merge ➪ Union. Then import the picture you want as shown on the right side of Figure 26-3.

Figure 26-3: A Union command resulting in a multiple-path box.

Sample Usage #2: You want a keyhole shape. Start by drawing a circle. Then draw a triangle on top of the circle, as shown on the left side of Figure 26-4. Select both items, and choose Item ➪ Merge ➪ Union. You'll end up with a single picture box, as shown on the right side of Figure 26-4.

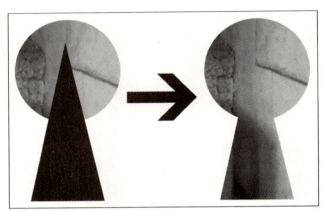

Figure 26-4: A Union command resulting in a single-path box.

Difference

When using the Difference command, only the shape at the very back of the stack is retained, minus any areas of that shape that are overlapped. This can be useful for deleting unwanted parts of an existing shape.

Sample Usage: You want a circular pie shape with one piece of pie missing, as shown on the right side of Figure 26-5. Start by drawing a circle, then draw a triangle on top of the circle, as shown on the left side of Figure 26-5. Select both items, and choose Item ➪ Merge ➪ Difference.

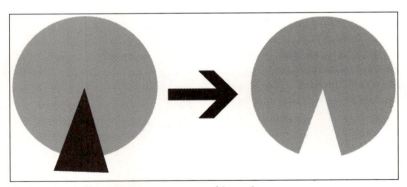

Figure 26-5: The Difference command in action.

Reverse Difference

Reverse Difference fuses everything together the same way Union does, but with one exception: The shape at the back of the stack acts like a flame that burns a hole into whatever was stacked on top of it.

Sample Usage: You want to draw something resembling the goal posts on an American football field. The first thing you would draw would be a rectangle representing the space between the goalposts. Overlapping this would be a larger rectangle to produce the posts themselves, and then a third rectangle to represent the base pole. When you perform a Reverse Difference on all these items, the backmost rectangle will conveniently "burn away" the area where you wanted the empty space to go (see Figure 26-6).

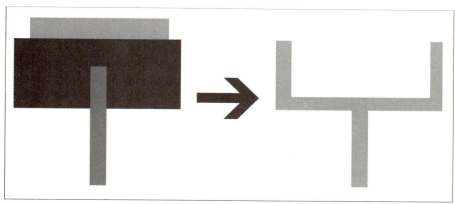

Figure 26-6: The Reverse Difference command in action.

Exclusive Or and Combine

On first glance, these two commands produce nearly identical results, but there *is* a subtle difference, as you'll discover in a moment. Exclusive Or and Combine both delete all overlapped areas while retaining all non-overlapped areas. (QuarkXPress's overlapping in this case is performed among every object in the stack.)

The difference between the two commands becomes apparent only when you reshape. If there were any overlapping segments in your original selection, the Exclusive Or command would create two new Bézier points at each one of those crossroad locations, so you could more easily modify them later if you chose. The Combine command adds no such points.

Sample Usage: These two commands are mainly useful for special effects. Figure 26-7 shows a checkerboard effect created using the Combine command.

Join Endpoints

The Join Endpoints command simply fuses together two overlapping line endpoints (don't worry about them being exactly overlapped — QuarkXPress will give you a bit of breathing room). If you're using the command to fuse two separate lines, the result is a single Bézier line. If you're using it to merge the endpoints of a single open path, the result is a closed path.

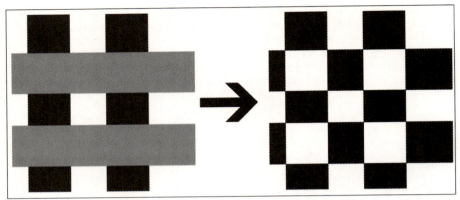

Figure 26-7: The Exclusive Or or the Combine command would produce this result.

Sample Usage: Join Endpoints is especially useful when you're dealing with thick lines. That's because the thickness magnifies the ugliness of any haphazardly formed junctures. Join Endpoints makes these junctures into a thing of beauty (see Figure 26-8).

Figure 26-8: The Join Endpoints command in action.

Tip   You may have noticed that moving Bézier lines can, at times, seem like a hassle in QuarkXPress. Do you have to turn off Item ⇨ Edit ⇨ Shape every time you want to move a Bézier line? Thankfully, no. There are two alternatives. First, on a Mac, simply press the ⌘ key; in Windows, press Ctrl (you should get a Mover pointer). The second alternative is useful if you need to snap *one* of the item's points to a guide without reshaping any part of the item: Simply double-click a point to select all the points in the shape. You can then snap the entire item to a guide according to any point you drag.

Splitting Items

Instead of making one item from several (as the Merge commands do), the Split commands make several items *from one*. How is it possible to split one item into several? Well, don't forget that an item need not consist of one path alone. Multiple-path items do exist, and that's where Split commands shine. (Split commands can also be used when a single path crosses over itself like a figure-8.)

If an item is selected that fits this description, QuarkXPress will let you choose between two Split commands, explained in the following sections.

Outside Paths

Outside Paths makes a separate box for every path in the original item, with one exception: If a path is encompassed by another path (for example, a doughnut hole), the hole will remain a hole, so to speak. (Read about the All Paths command in the following section for a description of the opposite behavior.)

Sample Usage: You've just performed a Text to Box command on a word (see Chapter 23), but all your letters are clumped together as one multiple-path item, and you want to treat each letter separately. Simply choose Item ➪ Edit ➪ Outside Paths, and your box will split so you can apply different formatting, as shown in Figure 26-9.

Figure 26-9: The Outside Paths command in action.

All Paths

The All Paths command works the same as Outside Paths, but this time even doughnut holes are turned into boxes.

Sample Usage: You've performed a Text to Box command on the letter *e* and applied a circular blend, but now you want to create a slight 3-D effect and have the hole in the *e* pop out with its own circular blend (see Figure 26-10).

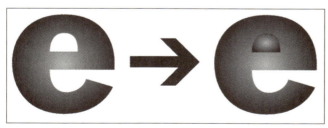

Figure 26-10: The All Paths command in action.

Scaling Multiple-Item Illustrations

Not many users know about this trick, but it's extremely important, so we've devoted a whole section to it. Suppose you've drawn an illustration that consists of 50 separate items, only to discover afterward that your production department has decided to shrink the page size so drastically that your illustration will no longer fit.

Does this mean that you have to scale everything on the page separately? And if so, what about the text that's incorporated? And the line weights? And the scaling percentages on the imported pictures? Ugh!

There are two possible solutions:

✦ You can use the Save Page as EPS feature (described in Chapter 20), then import the EPS into a picture box. However, this method is *not* viable if you want to be able to edit the illustration later from within QuarkXPress.

✦ The second alternative is a trick that snuck into QuarkXPress 4 without much fanfare. It consists of resizing a group.

STEPS: Resizing a group

1. Select all the items in your illustration (drag-select or Shift+click the items).

2. Choose Item ➪ Group, or press ⌘+G or Ctrl+G.

3. You'll see a bounding box with resize handles. Click and hold one of the corner resize handles. As you're holding the mouse button down, press all three of the major modifier keys: On the Mac, press Option+Shift+⌘; in Windows, press Ctrl+Alt+Shift.

4. You should now be holding down three modifier keys along with the mouse button. Now simply drag to scale the entire group. All text, pictures, line weights, boxes — you name it — will be scaled proportionally.

Summary

QuarkXPress includes several tools to merge and split items. This is handy when working with illustrations you create within QuarkXPress that are initially composed of multiple boxes and/or lines — after you've composited your illustration, it makes sense to convert it into one set of Bézier paths for easier editing later. QuarkXPress has several options when combining items to determine exactly how the items are merged together.

Conversely, if you've converted text to boxes, you'll likely want to split the text so each letter is its own shape, which you can also do in QuarkXPress. You'll also find it useful to split illustrations done in QuarkXPress so that, for example, interior elements are separate objects so you can work with shading and so forth just for that portion. You'll find two options for splitting items that let you determine whether to use only the outside part of the shape or all curves within the shape for the split.

The Item ➪ Merge and Item ➪ Split commands let you handle both needs.

You can also group items together with the Group command (Item ➪ Group, or ⌘+G or Ctrl+G), and resize grouped items using the keyboard shortcut Option+Shift+⌘ or Ctrl+Alt+Shift while resizing the grouped items with the mouse.

✦   ✦   ✦

Color

O ne of the trickiest sets of issues in desktop publishing has to do with color. Today, applying color to a document is very easy, but getting the colors you really want is very hard. What you see on-screen doesn't match what a printing press can produce, and different screens and presses provide different results, so the complexity is almost infinite when you factor in all the variables that affect what color you actually get.

Fortunately, QuarkXPress knows how to handle color. Its color-creation, application, calibration, and trapping tools will let you create the colors you really want — at least as close as is humanly possible.

This part explains how to create colors, what the issues are that affect output, how to minimize differences between intended and printed color, and how to ensure that the colored objects don't have unsightly gaps or overlaps on the printing press.

To help you better see the color issues this part of the book covers, we've included Chapters 27, 28, and 30, as well as the color insert, as PDF files on the CD for you to view on-screen or print in color.

Color Fundamentals

In This Chapter

Understanding
color terms

Understanding
process and
spot color

Working with
color models

We see color every day, so it seems so natural. But color is a complex issue in printing, involving both physics and chemistry. The inks that produce color are chemically designed to retain those colors and to produce them evenly, so your images don't look mottled or faded. How light passes through these inks and reflects to your eye determines the color you see, and many factors can affect the physics of how the light carries the color, particularly different textures of paper.

You also have implementation issues to consider: How many colors can your printing press produce, and how much will it cost? When do you decide to go for the exact pure color, and when do you decide to go with a close-enough version that's cheaper to print?

The rest of this chapter will explain the basic theory behind color and QuarkXPress's use of it. Although color is natural, it requires some thinking and solid understanding to look the way you want in your printed pieces.

Understanding Color Terms

Color is an expansive (and sometimes confusing and esoteric) concept in the world of publishing. The following definitions, however, should start you on your way to a clear understanding of the subject.

+ **Spot color:** This is a single color applied at one or more places on a page, such as for a screen or as part of an illustration. You can use more than one spot color per page. Spot colors can also be process colors.

+ **Process color:** A process color refers to any of the four primary colors in publishing: cyan, magenta, yellow, and black (known as a group as CMYK).

✦ **Color model:** A color model is an industry standard for specifying a color, such as CMYK and PANTONE.

✦ **Swatchbook:** The printer uses a premixed ink based on the color model identifier you specify; you look up the numbers for various colors in a table of colors (which is often put together as a series of color samples known as a swatchbook).

✦ **Four-color printing:** This is the use of the four process colors in combination to produce most other colors.

✦ **Color separation:** A color separation is a set of four photographic negatives — one filtered for each process color — shot from a color photograph or image. When overprinted, the four negatives reproduce that original image.

✦ **Build:** A build attempts to simulate a color-model color by overprinting the appropriate percentages of the four process colors.

✦ **Color space:** This is a method of representing color in terms of measurable values, such as the amount of red, yellow, and blue in a color image. The color space RGB represents the red, green, and blue colors on video screens.

✦ **CIE LAB:** This standard specifies colors by one lightness coordinate and two color coordinates — green-red and blue-yellow.

✦ **CMYK:** This standard specifies colors as combinations of cyan, magenta, yellow, and black. These four colors are known as *process colors*.

✦ **RGB:** This is the standard used by monitors, and the abbreviation from the three colors in it: red, green, and blue. One of the biggest hurdles to producing color documents that look as you'd expect is that computers use RGB while printers use CMYK, and the two don't always produce colors at the same hue.

✦ **Color gamut:** This is the range of colors that a device, such as a monitor or a color printer, can produce.

✦ **High-fidelity color:** This is a form of process color that builds from more than the four CMYK plates. QuarkXPress includes the PANTONE Hexachrome high-fidelity color model, an ink set that includes orange, green, and black, along with enhanced versions of cyan, magenta, and yellow inks.

Cross-Reference   Chapters 28, 29, and 30 cover color in greater detail.

Understanding Process and Spot Color

Before we launch into a discussion of the practical aspects of working with color in QuarkXPress, let's briefly explore the differences between spot and process colors. If you're already familiar with these concepts, you can skip ahead to the section on defining color, but if you're new to the subject, it's important that you understand them before you move on.

Reviewing the methods of color printing

Several forms of color are used in printing, but the two most-used ones are process color and spot color.

Process color refers to the use of four basic colors — cyan, magenta, yellow, and black (known as a group as CMYK) — that are mixed to reproduce most color tones the human eye can see. A separate negative is produced for each of the four process colors. This method, often called four-color printing, is used for most color publishing.

Spot color refers to any color — whether one of the process colors or some other hue — used for specific elements in a document. For example, if you print a document in black ink but print the company logo in red, the red is a spot color. A spot color is often called a second color even though you can use several spot colors in a document. Each spot color is output to its own negative (and not color-separated into CMYK).

A new kind of process color, called Hexachrome, was introduced by Pantone in 1995 and is slowly but surely gaining popularity among very–high-end publishers. It uses six process colors — the four CMYK colors plus orange and green — to produce a wider range of accurate colors.

Exploring spot color

Using spot color gives you access to special inks that are truer to the desired color than any mix of process colors can be. These inks come in several standards, and QuarkXPress supports them all (see the section on working with color models, later in this chapter). Basically, spot-color inks can produce some colors that are impossible to achieve with process colors, such as metallics, neons, and milky pastels. You can even use varnishes as spot colors to give layout elements a different gleam than the rest of the page. Although experienced designers sometimes mix spot colors to produce special shades not otherwise available, it's unlikely that you'll need to do so.

Mixing spot and process colors

Some designers use both process and spot colors in a document — known as using a *fifth color.* Typically, the normal color images are color-separated and printed via the four process colors, while a special element (such as a logo in metallic ink) is printed in a spot color. The process colors are output on the usual four negatives; the spot color is output on a separate, fifth negative and printed using a fifth plate, fifth ink roller, and fifth inkwell. You can use more than five colors; you're limited only by your budget and the capabilities of your printing plant. (Most commercial printers can handle six colors for each run through the press, and larger ones often can handle as many as eight.)

Converting spot colors to process colors

QuarkXPress can convert spot colors to process colors. This handy capability lets designers specify the colors they want through a system they're familiar with, such as PANTONE, without the added expense of special spot-color inks and extra negatives (see the section on standard color models, later in this chapter). Conversions are never an exact match, but there are now guidebooks that can show you in advance the color that will be created. And with PANTONE Process variation (which QuarkXPress supports), designers can now pick a PANTONE color that will color-separate predictably.

You can set QuarkXPress to convert some spot colors in a document to process colors while leaving others alone. Or you can leave all spot colors as spot colors.

Working with Color Models

When you understand color terminology — and the difference between process and spot colors — you can start thinking about the type of colors you create in QuarkXPress. You'll define colors in the Edit Color dialog box, which appears when you choose New, Edit, or Duplicate in the Colors dialog box (Edit ➪ Colors or Shift+F12). The color models fall into two broad classes:

   ✦ Those that let you define a color by selecting a color from a color wheel, which represents a spectrum of available colors, or by entering specific values for the color's constituent colors. These include CMYK, RGB, HSB, LAB, and Multi-Ink (see the following section on standard color models).

   ✦ Those that have a predefined set of colors, which you select from a palette of swatches. These include the four variants of PANTONE, the two variants of Hexachrome, Focoltone, Trumatch, DIC, and Toyo (again, see the following section on standard color models).

Keep in mind that the colors displayed are only on-screen representations; the actual color may be different. The difference will be particularly noticeable if your monitor is running in 8-bit (256 hues) color mode. Check the actual color in a color swatchbook for the model you're using. (Art and printing supply stores usually carry these swatchbooks; see the sidebar on swatchbooks for lists of other sources.)

Standard color models

QuarkXPress supports several color models, which are ways of representing colors. Figure 27-1 shows the options in the Edit Color dialog box.

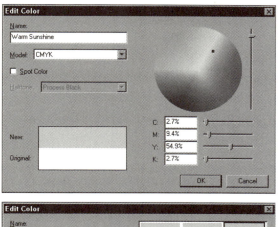

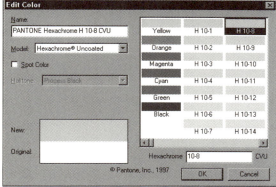

Figure 27-1: The Edit Color dialog box with a color wheel (top) and with a swatch (bottom). The color model selected will determine whether a color wheel or swatch appears.

The supported models include the following:

✦ **CMYK:** The standard process colors used in professional printing.

✦ **DIC (Dainippon Ink & Chemical):** A spot-color model used in Japan.

✦ **Focoltone:** Another CMYK-based spot-color model popular in Europe.

✦ **Hexachrome:** A six-color process model created by Pantone for high-fidelity color output (of which two variants are supplied: one for coated paper, one for uncoated paper).

✦ **HSB (Hue, Saturation, Brightness):** Typically used in creating paints.

✦ **LAB (Luminosity, A axis, B axis):** An international standard for colors.

✦ **Multi-Ink:** Lets you mix a new color by taking percentages of any combination of colors from any combination of CMYK or Hexachrome process color models — including colors defined in other models as process colors.

New Feature QuarkXPress 5 has changed the PANTONE color models. New are specific swatchbooks for coated, matte, and uncoated paper, as well as a new process-compatible swatchbook for uncoated paper. The former ProSim swatchbook is now called PANTONE Solid to Process, and the former PANTONE swatchbook is now renamed PANTONE Coated.

✦ **PANTONE:** A spot-color model with a range of inks (of which five variants are supplied: one for coated paper, one for matte paper, one for uncoated paper, one for when your printer uses other manufacturers' brands of process-color inks, and two for PANTONE colors that can be accurately translated to CMYK process).

✦ **RGB (Red, Green, Blue):** Used in monitors.

✦ **Toyo:** A Japanese color model.

✦ **Trumatch:** A CMYK-based set of spot colors designed for accurate color separation.

New Feature QuarkXPress 5 adds two Web-oriented color models.

✦ **Web-Named Colors:** A set of colors for use on the Web by current Windows and Mac Web browsers.

✦ **Web-Safe Colors:** A set of colors designed to reproduce accurately on any Web browser.

New Feature QuarkXPress 5 has dropped the POCE color model introduced in version 4. The PANTONE Open Color Environment had included several color models redundant with those offered natively by QuarkXPress — including CMYK, HLS and HSV (variants of HSB), PANTONE, PANTONE CMYK (a variation of PANTONE Process), and RGB — as well as two unique color models: Crayon (60 popular crayon colors) and HTML (colors supported by the Web's Hypertext Markup Language color specifications).

You can convert a color defined in any model to CMYK, RGB, LAB, or HSB models simply by selecting one of those models after defining the color. But note that colors defined in one model and converted to another may not reproduce exactly the same because the physics underlying each color model differs slightly. Each model was designed for use in a different medium, such as paper or a video monitor.

Paper variation models

Both the standard PANTONE and PANTONE Hexachrome color models recognize that the type of paper you print on affects how a color appears, so they have variations based on popular paper types. Here's how they work:

✦ **PANTONE Coated:** Use this when your printer will use actual PANTONE-brand inks (as spot colors) when printing to coated paper stock. Colors in this variant will have the code CV (computer video) appended to their names.

✦ **PANTONE Matte:** This is the same as PANTONE Coated but for paper with a matte finish. Colors in this variant will have the code CVM (computer video matte) appended to their names.

✦ **PANTONE Uncoated:** This is the same as PANTONE but for uncoated paper. Colors in this variant will have the code CVU (computer video uncoated) appended to their names.

✦ **PANTONE Solid to Process:** Use this when you color-separate PANTONE colors and your printer uses other manufacturers' brands of process-color inks. Colors in this variant will have the code CVP (computer video process) appended to their names.

✦ **PANTONE Process:** Use this when you color-separate PANTONE colors and your printer uses the standard PANTONE-brand process-color inks on coated paper. Colors in this variant will have the code S (SWOP, or single-web offset printing) added to their names.

✦ **PANTONE Process Uncoated:** This is the same as PANTONE Process but for uncoated paper. Colors in this variant will have the code S (SWOP, or single-web offset printing) plus the code CVN (computer video no-coat) added to their names

✦ **Hexachrome Coated:** Use this when your printer will use actual PANTONE Hexachrome-brand inks when printing to coated paper stock. Colors in this variant will have the code CVC (computer video coated) appended to their names.

✦ **Hexachrome Uncoated:** This is the same as Hexachrome Coated but for uncoated paper. Colors in this variant will have the code CVU (computer video uncoated) appended to their names.

When printing on uncoated stock with any colors designed for use on coated stock, you will usually get weaker, less-saturated color reproduction.

Color wheel models

Figure 27-2 shows a color being defined through the CMYK model, the standard model used in the publishing industry. After selecting the model from the Model pop-up list, we entered values in the Cyan, Magenta, Yellow, and Black fields. If you prefer, define the color values by using the slider bars or by moving the black spot on the color wheel to the desired color. (The bar to the right of the color wheel adjusts brightness.) Or use any combination of these three techniques.

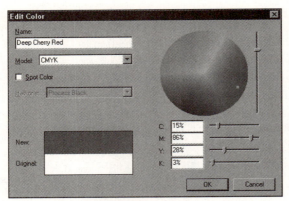

Figure 27-2: Defining a color in the CMYK color model using the color wheel.

Swatch models

Figure 27-3 shows a PANTONE color being added to the QuarkXPress color list. As you can see, the fields in the Edit Color dialog box change depending upon which color model you use. When you use a spot-color model such as PANTONE, QuarkXPress replaces the color wheel with a series of color swatches and their identifying labels. If you know the label, you can enter it in the field at the bottom right; alternately, you can scroll through the list of labels.

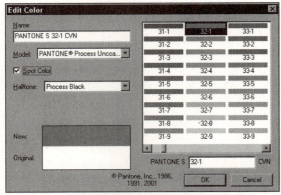

Figure 27-3: Defining a color in the PANTONE color model using the swatchbook.

Using color swatchbooks

Anyone who uses a lot of color should have a color swatchbook handy. You probably can get one at your local art supply store or from your commercial printer (prices typically range from $50 to $100, depending on the color model and the type of swatchbook). But if you can't find a swatchbook, here's where to order the most popular ones:

✦ **PANTONE:** There are several PANTONE swatchbooks, including ones for coated and uncoated paper, and for spot-color output and process-color output. If you're converting (called *building* in publishing parlance) PANTONE colors to CMYK for four-color printing, we particularly recommend the PANTONE Process Color Imaging Guide: CMYK Edition or the PANTONE Process Color System Guide swatchbooks. Pantone, 590 Commerce Boulevard, Carlstadt, NJ 07072-3098; phone: 866-726-8663 or 201-935-5500; fax: 201-896-0242; Web site: www.pantone.com.

✦ **Hexachrome:** Pantone also created the Hexachrome standard and sells Hexachrome swatchbooks, as well as the $299 HexWare software that adds Hexachrome output capability to Adobe Photoshop and Illustrator.

✦ **Trumatch:** Based on a CMYK color space, Trumatch suffers almost no matching problems when converted to CMYK. There are variants of the swatchbooks for coated and uncoated paper. Trumatch, 50 East 72nd Street #15B, New York, NY 10021; phone: 800-878-9100; fax: 212-517-2237; Web site: www.trumatch.com.

✦ **ANPA:** Designed for reproduction on newsprint, these colors also are designed in the CMYK color space. Although QuarkXPress doesn't have an ANPA color library predefined, you can create these colors using the swatchbook's definitions. Newspaper Association of America, 1921 Gallows Road #600, Vienna, VA 22182; phone: 703-902-1600; Web site: www.naa.org.

✦ **Focoltone:** Like Trumatch, this color model (used primarily in Europe) is based on the CMYK color space. A&P Publishing Network, No. 6 Aljuneid Avenue 3 #01-02, Singapore 389932; phone: 65 746-0188, fax: 65 746-1890; Web site: www.apmedia.com.

✦ **Dainippon:** Like PANTONE, this is a spot-color–based system. Dainippon Ink & Chemical Americas, 222 Bridge Plaza South, Fort Lee, NJ 07024; phone: 201-592-5100, fax: 201-592-8232; Web site: http://dicwww01.dic.co.jp/index-e.html.

✦ **Toyo:** Similar to PANTONE in that it's based on spot-color inks, this model is popular in Japan. Toyo Ink America, 710 West Belden Addison, IL 60101; phone: 800-227-8696; Web site: www.toyoink.com.

Simulating other color models

Although QuarkXPress supports many color models — Trumatch, DIC, Toyo, Focoltone, and several variants of PANTONE and Hexachrome — there are other color models in use, such as the ANPA color model. (ANPA stands for the American

Newspaper Publishers Association, which several years ago renamed itself the Newspaper Association of America — but the color model's name hasn't changed.) You can still use such color models in QuarkXPress by using the following techniques, which apply to any color model, not just the ANPA example used here:

✦ **Using spot color:** If you're using spot color, in which the ANPA color prints on its own plate, just define a color with the ANPA name you want the printer to use. The printer doesn't care if you actually had the right color on-screen. Knowing what color you want and having a plate for that color are all that's needed.

✦ **Using process color:** If you're using process (CMYK) color, create the ANPA colors using the CMYK color model. That means you'll need to know the CMYK values for the ANPA colors you want to use; you can get these values from the swatchbook you use to select colors or from your commercial printer.

You can also use RGB values to enter the colors and then switch the model with QuarkXPress to CMYK. This may result in some altered colors, because you're converting colors twice: once to RGB and then again to CMYK. Any conversion between color models may result in color differences because of the physics involved in reproducing color.

Tip   If there are certain ANPA colors you use repeatedly, create them in the Colors dialog box (Edit ➪ Colors or Shift+F12) with no document open. They'll then be available for all future documents. If different types of documents use different sets of colors, define them in the template for each type of document. Doing so will save a lot of redefinition.

Summary

Colors come in several forms, called color models. QuarkXPress supports several of these models, including all the standard ones used in printing and for the Web. Because a color can look different depending on what kind of paper it's printing on, the most widely used color model, PANTONE, has six variants to accommodate different kinds of paper.

In QuarkXPress, you can define a color easily by selecting a new one from a color wheel or from a swatchbook. The new color can be made available to all documents or just to the current one, depending on whether a document is open when you define the color. The color can also be set as a process color — to be color-separated — or as a spot color — to be printed separately. Colors reproduced via separation don't always look like the original color, but having more than a couple spot colors becomes very expensive.

✦   ✦   ✦

Creating and Applying Colors

Color is becoming more accessible to all publishers. Whether you want to produce limited-run documents on a color printer, create newsletters using spot colors, or publish magazines and catalogs using process colors and special inks, QuarkXPress offers the tools that you need to do the job well. If you're doing professional-quality color production, such as a color catalog printed on a standard web offset printing press, QuarkXPress includes the Quark CMS (color management system) XTension that lets you calibrate the output against the input source (such as monitor or scanner) and the output target (such as the printing press or color printer). Chapter 29 covers color matching and other high-end color issues in depth. This chapter concentrates on how to create and apply colors within QuarkXPress.

Defining Colors

You can use color in your graphics or apply colors to text and layout elements (such as bars along the edge of a page). Or you can use color in both ways. To a great extent, where you define and apply color determines what you can do with it. But before you can apply any colors — whether to bitmap images or to layout elements — you must first define the colors (see Chapter 30 for information on defining color trap values).

Using the Colors dialog box

To define colors, select Edit ➪ Colors or use the keyboard shortcut Shift+F12 to open the Colors dialog box, shown in Figure 28-1.

Figure 28-1: The Colors dialog box.

Alternately, if you've selected a box and the Colors palette is visible (use View ⇨ Show Colors or the shortcut F12), you can ⌘+click or Ctrl+click any color in the Colors palette to bring up the dialog box. From the Colors dialog box, you can make the following selections:

✦ **New:** Select New to add colors.

✦ **Edit:** Choose Edit to edit any color you add. You can also edit the blue, green, red, and registration colors that come with QuarkXPress.

✦ **Append:** Select Append to import colors from another QuarkXPress document.

✦ **Duplicate:** Select Duplicate to duplicate an existing color for editing purposes.

✦ **Delete:** Choose Delete to remove a color. You cannot delete the white, black, cyan, magenta, yellow, or registration colors that come with QuarkXPress.

✦ **Edit Trap:** Select Edit Trap to edit color trapping values, as explained in Chapter 30.

Some of the choices you'll have to make depend on the color model you'll be using. You may want to review the following section on working with color models before you make your selections.

New Feature You can also create a new color, edit, duplicate, or delete a selected color, or change the current color from process to spot or vice versa using the new context menu in QuarkXPress 5. Just Control+click or right-click a color name in the Colors palette, as shown in Figure 28-2.

Caution For your changes to take effect, you must also choose Save in the Colors dialog box after you finish defining colors. Choose Cancel to undo any changes you make.

Color tips and tricks

You can name a color anything you want, provided that you stay within the character limit of the Name field. To make it easier to remember what a defined color looks like, either use descriptive names (such as Grass Green) or use names based on the color settings. For example, if you create a color in the CMYK model, give it a name based on its mix, such as 51C 0M 87.5Y 0K for our green color—composed of 51 percent cyan, 0 percent magenta, 87.5 percent yellow, and 0 percent black. (Believe it or not, this naming convention is how professionals typically specify colors.) The same system applies to the RGB, HSB, and LAB models. With this naming convention, you can look at the Colors palette and immediately tell what color you'll get.

If you edit an existing color, the old color is displayed in the box to the right of the word *Original* in the Edit Color dialog box. As you define the new color, you see the new color to the right of the word *New*. If you define a color for the first time, no color appears in the Original field.

Because regular black can appear weak when it's next to black that has been overprinted by other colors, many designers create what printers call *superblack* by combining 100 percent black and 100 percent magenta. You can define superblack as a separate color or redefine the registration color as 100 percent of all four process colors, and use that as an even richer superblack. Note that on thinner paper, black composed of 100 percent each of cyan, magenta, yellow, and black inks could oversaturate the paper, bleeding through. Check with your printer before creating a superblack that rich.

Figure 28-2: The QuarkXPress context menus let you change color definitions from the Colors palette.

Tip

If no document is open when you create, edit, or delete colors, the new color palette becomes the default for all future documents. (The dialog box will be titled Default Colors.)

Working with the predefined colors

QuarkXPress comes with several predefined colors: black, blue, cyan, green, magenta, red, registration, white, and yellow. (Registration is a color that prints on all negatives and is primarily used for crop and registration marks.) You cannot edit cyan, black, magenta, yellow, or white. You can duplicate any of the predefined colors except registration and then edit the duplicates. (You can, for example, use green as both a spot color and as a process color, perhaps with one version named Green Spot and the other named Green Process.)

Tip Feel free to delete red, green, and blue if you're not going to use them. Although they come with QuarkXPress, they're rarely used in commercial publications, because designers typically create specific shades of these colors as needed, rather than using the basic colors that QuarkXPress offers.

Working with color models

You define colors in the Edit Color dialog box, which appears when you choose New, Edit, or Duplicate in the Colors for Document Name dialog box.

Cross-Reference See Chapter 27 for more on color models.

Using Spot Colors

You may have noticed the Spot Color check box in the Edit Color dialog box and its accompanying Halftone pop-up menu. Simply stated, checking the Spot Color option means that the color you define (no matter what model it was defined in) will print on its own plate when you color-separate the file during printing. In professional printing, each color is printed from a separate plate that has the image in only that color. In most cases, you'll not have Spot Color checked. Exceptions are when you want a spot color on its own plate, such as for colors that don't reproduce well or at all when converted to process color. Examples of these are metallics, neons, and pastels from Pantone, DIC, or Toyo. Using a separate plate for Focoltone or Trumatch colors makes little sense, because they're based on CMYK mixtures to begin with and color-separate reliably.

New Feature QuarkXPress now lets you know whether a color is a spot color or a process color by using a symbol in the Colors palette. In Figure 28-2 (shown earlier in this chapter), Cyan (the selected color) has the four-triangle symbol for process colors, while Green has the target symbol for spot colors.

Choosing and editing screen angles

The reason for choosing a different screening angle when mixing a spot color is complex, but the reason for not using the angle for yellow boils down to the fact that the other colors overpower it when viewed by the human eye. The screen angles for other colors overprint each other less. If you choose the yellow values for your screening angle, there's a greater chance your spot color will have many of its dots overprinted by black, changing the mix of the two colors.

The rule of thumb is that darker colors should be at least 30 degrees apart from each other, and lighter colors should be at least 15 degrees apart from other colors. You can see that each plate's angle for your output device is defined via the Output pane in the Print menu (File ⇨ Print, or ⌘+P or Ctrl+P), as described in Chapter 35.

You or your service bureau may have to manually edit your screen angle settings in the PostScript file. To create a PostScript file with a Level 1 driver (LaserWriter or PSPrinter 7.x), select PostScript File as the destination in the Print dialog box (File ⇨ Print, or ⌘+P or Ctrl+P). To create a PostScript file with a Level 2 driver (LaserWriter or PSPrinter 8.x), select File as the destination, and make sure (in the dialog box that appears after you click the Save button) that you've chosen the PostScript Job option from the Format pick list and selected the ASCII option. Editing settings in a PostScript file requires a fairly intimate knowledge of the PostScript language. Don't expect your service bureau or printer to do this work for you automatically—consult with them first.

The Halftone pop-up menu

The Halftone pop-up menu lets you use the halftone screen settings of cyan, magenta, yellow, or black for a spot color. (Figure 28-3 shows the menu.) It doesn't replace that color plate but simply uses the same screen angle as that standard color plate. For example, if you assign a color like Toyo 0385pc to the cyan plate, QuarkXPress will generate both cyan and Toyo 0385pc film negatives for use in creating the printing press's color plates. But the Toyo 0385pc color will have the same screen angle as the cyan plate. In process printing, each plate's dots are offset from each other so the color dots don't overprint each other any more than necessary, which is why there are different screen angles for each plate. (Chapter 35 covers screen angles in more depth.) If the Spot Color box is unchecked, the color is converted to process color, divided among the four CMYK or six Hexachrome plates (depending on which color model is selected for output).

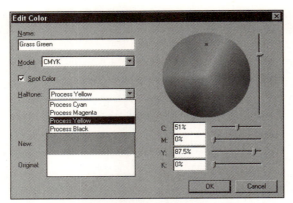

Figure 28-3: The Edit Color dialog box lets you define not only colors but whether they print as process colors or spot colors. If you print them as spot colors, you choose what screen angle to assign in the Halftone pop-up menu.

Mixing spot colors

Many designers use spot colors because they can't afford four-color (CMYK) printing, but they want more than just black and their spot color. Thus, many will create new colors by mixing the spot color with shades of black. In other cases, you may want to mix both spot and process colors to achieve the desired result. Here are a couple rules of thumb to avoid unexpectedly displeasing results:

✦ **Mixing spot colors and black:** If you mix spot colors and black, make sure you change the spot color's screening angle, because the default angle for spot colors is the same as for black. By choosing a different screening angle, you ensure that the dots making up the two colors don't overprint unnecessarily, resulting in a muddy image. Choose either the magenta or cyan angles, not yellow (refer to Figure 28-3). The sidebar "Choosing and editing screen angles" covers this in more detail.

✦ **Mixing process and spot colors:** When you're working with both process and spot colors, picking the right screening angle is tougher. Pick the screen angle of a process color that is never or rarely used with the spot color, or make sure that the spot color knocks out (see Chapter 30). If a screening-angle conflict can't be avoided and you can't knock out the spot color, consult your printer or service bureau for advice.

When working with scanned images, use black as the screening angle, because that results in a 45-degree angle that often avoids moiré patterns, which are annoying kaleidoscope-like patterns. If you must use a different screening angle (perhaps because you have other spot colors defined or you're using black mixed with the spot color), consult your service bureau or printer.

Using Multi-Ink Colors

The QuarkXPress Multi-Ink feature lets you create new colors by mixing together other colors—the basic CMYK or Hexachrome process colors plus any spot colors previously defined. You cannot use other non-spot colors. With the Process Inks pop-up menu, you determine whether a multi-ink color can use CMYK or Hexachrome process colors. Figure 28-4 shows the Edit Color dialog box with the Multi-Ink model in use. Here, we've mixed a color from the selection of CMYK process colors and spot colors previously defined. To get the percentages of each color, first select the color(s) you want to have a specific percentage, then click the Shade drop-down menu to choose from a predefined percentage or to choose the Other option to define your own shade percentage.

Tip   You can select multiple colors by ⌘+clicking or Ctrl+clicking them; Shift+clicking selects all colors between the first one selected and the color that has been Shift+clicked.

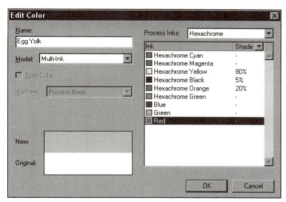

Figure 28-4: The Multi-Ink feature lets you combine process colors (CMYK or Hexachrome) with other colors defined in your document.

Applying Colors

Now that you've defined your colors, you can use them in the following ways:

✦ Apply color to specific text.

✦ Apply color to imported gray-scale and black-and-white bitmaps (see Chapter 21).

✦ Add color backgrounds to text boxes and picture boxes, including blend patterns.

✦ Add color borders to boxes.

✦ Apply color to ruling lines associated with text and to lines drawn with the line tools.

In addition, by using *empty boxes* (boxes with no pictures or text imported into them) as shapes, you can create both simple and complex graphics to which you can apply colors.

Most dialog boxes for text and items contain a color list option, as do many options in the Style menu. All colors defined in a document appear (in alphabetical order) in any of these color lists. But a universal way to add color is through the Colors palette, which you make visible via View ➪ Show Colors or the shortcut F12. Figure 28-5 shows the Colors palette. This palette gives you a handy way to quickly apply colors to lines and to picture box and text box backgrounds, frames, and, in some cases, contents.

You can apply colors to any contents except color pictures and pictures saved in EPS format. If you apply color to the contents of a text box or text on a line, any selected text and any text you subsequently enter into the text box or line takes on the applied color. Existing non-selected text is unaffected.

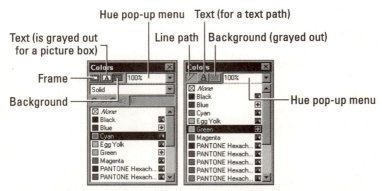

Figure 28-5: The Colors palette and the buttons that let you select where a color is applied to in the current element, as well as the pop-up menu to let you choose a hue of the desired color. At right, note that Frame icon changes to a diagonal line if a line is selected rather than a box, and the Text icon changes to a different form if text on a text path is selected.

Directing the color application

The Colors palette displays a list of available colors. The palette also contains icons that let you direct how QuarkXPress applies colors to the selected box. Note that the icons will change depending on whether a picture box, text box, or line is selected. From left to right, the Colors palette icons are as follows:

✦ **Frame:** If you select this icon, QuarkXPress applies the selected color to the box frame. If no frame is defined for the box, no color appears. As soon as a frame is defined, it takes on the color you applied. If you select a line, this icon changes to a line and lets you specify the color of the line.

✦ **Line:** If you select a line, you'll get a Line icon instead of the Frame icon.

✦ **Contents:** The contents icon changes depending upon which element is currently selected. Choosing an icon applies the selected color to the contents of the box or the text (if any) on the line. (The Content tool must be selected for this option to be available. If the Item tool is selected, the contents icon is grayed out.) The various icons look like the following:

  • A picture box, if the selected item is a picture box

  • A text box (an *A* in a box), if the selected item is text

  • An underlined *A,* if the selected element is text on a text path

✦ **Background:** Use the background icon to change the background color of a picture or text box. (This option is grayed out for lines.)

Tip

A very simple way to change the color of a frame, box background, or line is to drag a color onto the box border (to change the frame's color); into the box's interior (to change the box's background color); or onto the line. Just click and hold on the desired color square in the Colors palette and drag it to the appropriate location. This technique doesn't work to change the text color or picture color.

Determining a shade percentage

You can apply the color at different shades by editing the number in the field located at the upper right of the Colors palette. Enter any value from 0 to 100 percent, in 0.1-percent increments. You can access common percentages (multiples of 10) through the pop-up menu to the right of the field.

You can also assign color to box backgrounds, frames, and lines using the Modify dialog box. To do so, simply select an item, choose Item ⇨ Modify (or press ⌘+M or Ctrl+M), and then switch to the Box, Frame, or Line pane.

Applying a blend

Using the Colors palette, you also can apply a *blend,* which is a smooth transition from one color to another. QuarkXPress's Cool Blends Required Component provides six blend choices: linear, mid-linear, rectangular, diamond, circular, and full circular. Figure 28-6 shows the pop-up menu enabled and an example diamond blend.

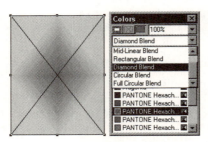

Figure 28-6: The pop-up menu with the QuarkXPress blend options.

Adding blends to pictures or text boxes

You can apply a blend to a selected picture box or text box. To perform this task, select the background icon from the Colors palette and then select from the pop-up menu of blend options below the row of icons. (The current list selection will likely be Solid, which is the default.) The two radio buttons and a numeric field are where you specify the blend's colors and angle (see Figure 28-7). They work as follows:

✦ **The #1 radio button:** This is selected by default, and the current background color is highlighted. (The color is white if you didn't apply a color to the box.) You create the blend from the selected color; change the color if necessary.

✦ **The #2 radio button:** Click this button and select the color you want to blend into. In the field to the right of the #2 button, enter the angle of the blend. You can enter any value from –360 to +360 degrees, in increments of 0.001 degrees. For a linear blend, a setting of 0 degrees blends the two colors from left to right; a setting of –90 degrees blends the colors from top to bottom.

For black-only publications, you can create a one-color blend by using white as one of the blend colors and black (or a shade of gray) as the other.

Figure 28-7: The radio buttons (highlighted) let you specify the color, shade, and angle settings for the two colors that make up a blend. Button #1 specifies the beginning color and button #2 specifies the ending color.

The effect of applied blends

Figure 28-8 shows the use of the six blends. For the top six, an angle of 30 degrees was chosen to show the effects of this feature. The bottom-right two show the effects of the angle on circular blends: a smaller angle results in a more-compact circle. The bottom-left box has no blend applied to its background.

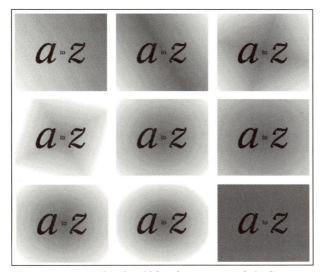

Figure 28-8: Six kinds of blends. From top left: linear, mid-linear, rectangular, diamond, circular, and full circular, all set at 30 degrees. On the bottom row, the first two show circular blends with different angles (70 and 5), and the final example has no blend applied.

Managing Colors

When you create colors, you'll find it easy to go overboard and make too many. You'll also find that different documents have different colors, each created by different people, and you'll likely want to move colors from one document to another. QuarkXPress provides basic tools for managing colors in and across documents.

Deleting colors

If you delete a color used in your document (through the Delete button in the Edit Color dialog box or by Control+clicking or right-clicking a color in the Colors palette and choosing the Delete option), you get the dialog box shown in Figure 28-9. This dialog box lets you substitute any other color for the removed one. If the color being deleted is not used in your document, this dialog box doesn't appear. In either case, you also have the option of canceling the delete operation by picking the Cancel button in the Colors dialog box (you would click Save to accept the change). When removing a color used in your document, you can also click the Cancel button in the dialog box asking you if it's okay to delete the color.

Figure 28-9: The warning you get when deleting colors in use in your document.

Appending colors

When you click the Append button in the Edit Color dialog box, you'll first get a standard Open dialog box in which you find the QuarkXPress document that you want to copy colors from. When you've selected that document, the Append Colors to Default Document dialog box appears (see Figure 28-10). Here, you can manage specifically which colors are moved through the Append Colors to document name dialog box.

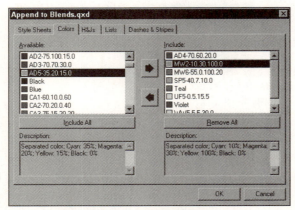

Figure 28-10: The Append Colors dialog box.

The Available list shows all the colors in the selected document. You can move them over one at a time or in groups by selecting the colors and clicking the right-arrow icon at top. (Shift+clicking lets you select a whole block of colors, while ⌘+clicking or Ctrl+clicking lets you select multiple, nonadjacent colors.) Use the left-arrow icon to remove colors from the Including list at right, which shows the colors you've marked for copying to your current document. You can also use the

Color Techniques

QuarkXPress offers sophisticated color features and controls. Chapter 28 shows you how to create, edit, and apply color, while Chapter 29 shows you how to use the Quark-XPress color-management features. This special 16-page color insert was created in QuarkXPress 5 and, where noted, with the assistance of Adobe Photoshop.

Literally thousands of colors are available using the various color models in QuarkXPress 5. Here is a photo of the standard PANTONE color swatchbook, fanned out to show the many available colors.

Color Models Revealed

QuarkXPress supports a range of color models, including CMYK and several variants of the industry-standard PANTONE MATCHING SYSTEM, as well as the new high-fidelity Hexachrome system from Pantone. Shown here are the color wheels for CMYK and RGB, as well as sample swatches for the other color models supported by QuarkXPress. Note that this book was output on a CMYK standard web-offset printing (SWOP) press, so not all the colors reproduce accurately from other color models. That's a reality in color publishing. We did have the Quark Color Management System (CMS) active, so the colors are as close as they can possibly be.

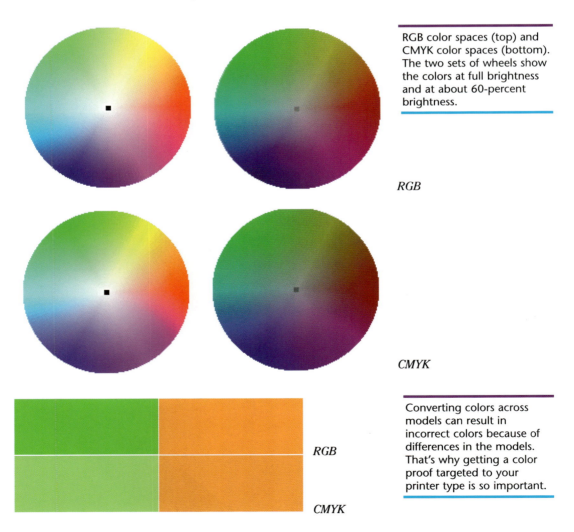

RGB color spaces (top) and CMYK color spaces (bottom). The two sets of wheels show the colors at full brightness and at about 60-percent brightness.

RGB

CMYK

Converting colors across models can result in incorrect colors because of differences in the models. That's why getting a color proof targeted to your printer type is so important.

RGB

CMYK

Samples from the various spot-color models in QuarkXPress 5. Note that the PANTONE Process, PANTONE Solid to Process, Focoltone, and Trumatch models are all based on CMYK and thus should reproduce most accurately on a printing press. The other spot-color models, as well as the Hexachrome process colors, are designed to reproduce best with special inks.

Purple	Process Yellow	HEXACHROME...
Violet	Process Magenta	HEXACHROME...
Blue 072	Process Cyan	HEXACHROME...
Reflex Blue	Process Black	HEXACHROME...
Process Blue		HEXACHROME...
Green		HEXACHROME...
Black		

PANTONE Coated

Yellow	Violet	Process Yellow
Orange 021	Blue 072	Process Magenta
Warm Red	Reflex Blue	Process Cyan
Red 032	Process Blue	Process Black
Rubine Red	Green	
Rhodamine Red	Black	
Purple		

PANTONE Solid to Process

#009900	#00CC00	Green
#009933	#00CC33	#00FF33
#009966	#00CC66	#00FF66
#009999	#00CC99	#00FF99
#0099CC	#00CCCC	#00FFCC
#0099FF	#00CCFF	Cyan

Web Safe

1-1	2-1	3-1
1-2	2-2	3-2
1-3	2-3	3-3
1-4	2-4	3-4
1-5	2-5	3-5
1-6	2-6	3-6
1-7	2-7	3-7
1-8	2-8	3-8
1-9	2-9	3-9

PANTONE Process

Purple	Process Yellow	100
Violet	Process Magenta	101
Blue 072	Process Cyan	102
Reflex Blue	Process Black	Yellow
Process Blue		103
Green		104
Black		105

PANTONE Uncoated

Yellow	H 10-1	H 10-8
Orange	H 10-2	H 10-9
Magenta	H 10-3	H 10-10
Cyan	H 10-4	H 10-11
Green	H 10-5	H 10-12
Black	H 10-6	H 10-13
	H 10-7	H 10-14

Hexachrome Coated

18-a1	18-a2	18-a3
18-b1	18-b2	18-b3
18-c1	18-c2	18-c3
18-d1	18-d2	18-d3
18-e1	18-e2	18-e3
18-f1	18-a5	18-a6
18-g1	18-b5	18-b6
18-d5	18-c5	18-c6

Trumatch

0281pc*	0291pc*	0301pc*
0282pc*	0292pc*	0302pc*
0283pc	0293pc*	0303pc*
0284pc	0294pc	0304pc*
0285pc*	0295pc*	0305pc*
0286pc	0296pc	0306pc*
0287pc	0297pc*	0307pc*
0288pc*	0298pc	0308pc*
0289pc*	0299pc	0309pc*
0290pc*	0300pc	0310pc*

Toyo

Yellow	H 10-1	H 10-8
Orange	H 10-2	H 10-9
Magenta	H 10-3	H 10-10
Cyan	H 10-4	H 10-11
Green	H 10-5	H 10-12
Black	H 10-6	H 10-13
	H 10-7	H 10-14

Hexachrome Uncoated

1073	1076	2285
1083	1082	2291
2250	2249	3458
3417	3416	3464
		3470

Focoltone

1p	11p*	21p
2p	12p*	22p
3p	13p*	23p
4p*	14p*	24p
5p*	15p*	25p
6p*	16p*	26p*
7p	17p*	27p
8p	18p*	28p
9p	19p*	29p*
10p	20p	30p*

DIC (Dainippon)

Working with Traps

If you don't have your QuarkXPress documents output to negatives or directly to plate and have them printed on a SWOP press, you don't need to worry about trapping. But if you do such professional output, trapping is an issue you should be aware of. Simply put, trapping manages how different colors print when they abut or overlap. Many printing presses use four or more plates, each with its own ink. With modern high-speed printing presses, computers keep the plates aligned, but most presses still can have slight variations in the plates' positions, which leads to gaps between colors. Thus, QuarkXPress lets you determine how much slippage your printing press may have and adjusts image borders accordingly, reducing the risk of gaps. The default settings in QuarkXPress work for most presses, but you should talk with your service bureau or printer first to see what settings they recommend.

A negative number in a trapping setting *chokes* the foreground color, which makes the surrounding color bleed in. A positive number *spreads* the color, which makes the inside color bleed out. (It's best to have the lighter color bleed into the darker color.) An *overprint* lets the colors mix together (without knocking cut the foreground from the background).

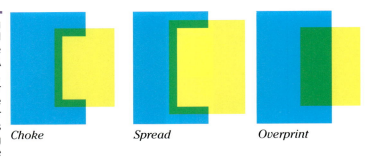

Choke   *Spread*   *Overprint*

The effects of text on a multicolored image. The default is to trap the text, rather than overprint or knock out.

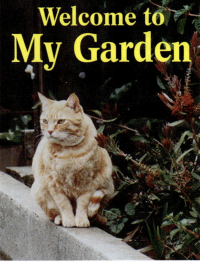

Default (trap of 0.144 points)

Overprint

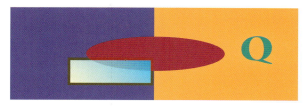

Defaults: backgrounds overprint, text has 0.144-point trap, white knocks out, frames have 0.144-point trap.

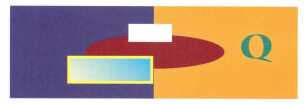

Everything overprints.

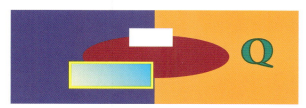

Everything knocks out.

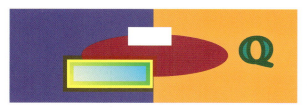

Backgrounds overprint, text has 1.0-point trap, white knocks out, oval has Auto Amount (+) trap, navy-blue box has Auto Amount (−) trap, outside frame has −0.5-point trap, inside frame has 0.5-point trap.

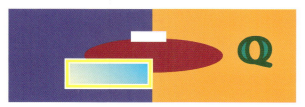

Backgrounds overprint, everything else has a 3.0-point trap.

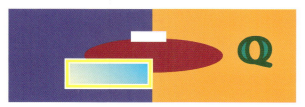

Backgrounds overprint, everything else has a −3.0-point trap.

Working with Clipping Paths

QuarkXPress 5.0 adds the ability to import clipping paths in images, as well as to create clipping paths by ignoring any white part of an image. A clipping path is essentially a runaround area, and besides using a clipping path on an irregular object to create a text wrap that fits that object's shape (or at least the shape of its clipping path), you can also use a clipping path as a *mask* — an area that is transparent, so whatever color is behind the image shows through. Typically, you create your clipping path in Adobe Illustrator or Photoshop, and then save the file as an EPS or TIFF file. Use the Clipping pane (Item ⇨ Clipping, or Option+⌘+T or Ctrl+Alt+T) to activate the clipping path, as described in Chapter 22. Now you can place a graphic over a background color or blend and have that background show through.

The image at left has no clipping path. Notice the mottled, dark background. In the image below it, we created a clipping path in Photoshop that removed the background (the Clipping pane is shown below as well), and then applied a colored background to the picture box.

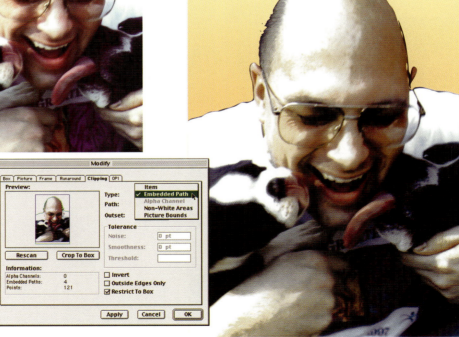

Include All and Exclude All buttons to copy over all colors or to undo the copying of all colors. If the active document contains colors with the same names as the colors you're importing, you'll be given a chance to resolve the conflict in the Append Conflict dialog box. Click OK when you're done.

To add colors to all future documents, open the Edit Color dialog box with no document open (it will be entitled Default Colors) and append colors from other documents. Those copied colors will be available to all future documents.

Displaying color groups

When you define lots of colors, you can easily lose track of what's in your document. The Show pop-up menu in the Colors dialog box is designed to take the effort out of that task.

The Colors dialog box (accessed via Edit ➪ Define Colors or by ⌘+clicking or Ctrl+clicking a color in the Colors palette) has a Show pop-up menu (see Figure 28-11) that lets you select the kinds of colors displayed in the Colors scroll list. Your choices are All Colors (the default), Spot Colors, Process Colors, Multi-Ink Colors, Colors in Use, and Colors Not Used. The last option is handy when you want to delete unused colors from a document but can't quite remember which colors were used.

Figure 28-11: The Show pop-up menu in the Colors dialog box.

Working with Color Pictures

When you work with imported graphics, whether they're illustrations or scanned photographs, color is part of the graphic file. So the responsibility for color controls lies primarily with the creator of the picture. If you're planning to separate your document for CMYK printing, it's best to use color files in CMYK EPS or DCS format (for illustrations) or CMYK TIFF format (for scans and bitmaps). These standards are de facto for color publishing, so QuarkXPress is particularly adept at working with them. (See Chapter 20 for details on preparing graphics files for import.) After you import a non-EPS color graphic, you can adjust its hues with the QuarkXPress contrast controls and create a negative of the image, as described in Chapter 21. You can, of course, resize and crop the image. The following sections cover these issues in detail.

Caution   Color files pasted via the clipboard should print properly after they are pasted into a QuarkXPress picture box. But problems, such as dropped colors or altered colors, do sometimes occur, depending on the applications involved and the amount of memory available.

EPS files

QuarkXPress automatically imports color definitions from EPS files, so you'll see any spot colors in them show up in your Colors palette and in menus and dialog boxes that display color lists. If you create files in EPS format, do any required color trapping in the source application. (Trapping for elements created in QuarkXPress is covered in Chapter 30.) Not all programs encode color information the same way. If you create EPS files in some illustration programs, colors may not print as expected. Any of the following three things can happen:

✦ Each color prints on its own plate (as if it were a spot color), even if you defined it as a process color.

✦ A spot color is color-separated into CMYK even when you define it as a spot color in both the source program and in QuarkXPress.

✦ A color prints as black.

There is no easy solution, because the problem is how the illustration program manages color internally. The only safe bet is to use a program that uses standard color-definition methods; these include the latest versions of Adobe Illustrator, CorelDraw, and Macromedia FreeHand.

TIFF files

Color TIFF files don't cause such peculiarities. QuarkXPress can color-separate both CMYK and RGB TIFF files, though the Quark CMS XTension must be active to color-separate RGB files.

Other files

QuarkXPress does not import color definitions from other image formats. All such images will be imported as RGB files or CMYK files for the few formats that support that (such as PDF).

Summary

QuarkXPress lets you define colors in several models and apply them to text, box backgrounds, lines, and box frames. Those colors can be either spot or process colors, depending on what you specified when you created them in the Edit Colors dialog box.

The Colors palette is a handy way to apply colors to layout elements, as well as to apply blends between two colors. The palette also shows you which colors are process and which are spot, and it has a context menu that lets you edit, duplicate, delete, or convert between process and spot.

You can import colors from other QuarkXPress documents using the Append command in the Edit Colors dialog box. Colors defined in EPS files are automatically imported into QuarkXPress.

✦   ✦   ✦

Color
Management

Color isn't always what it seems to be. As we mentioned in Chapter 27, how light passes through inks on the page and reflects to your eye determines the color you see, and many factors can affect the physics of how the light carries the color, particularly different textures of paper. This variability is made even more difficult by the fact that we view our QuarkXPress layouts on a computer monitor, which uses an entirely different method to produce an image, one with its own physics. The monitor's electron guns send pulses of colored light — red, green, and blue — to the screen phosphors, which then glow when struck. The combined colors mix in your brain, appearing as multiple shades, similar to how the four process colors — cyan, magenta, yellow, and black — mix in your brain when you see them on the printed page.

But they mix differently. In print, red and green become brown, while on-screen, they become yellow. That's because reflective light, such as from ink on a page, is *additive* — the two colors combine — while light from a light source, such as a monitor, is *subtractive* — where the lightwaves intersect, information (color) is removed.

The different physics of RGB and CMYK also mean that the colors they can produce don't always match. RGB tends to create brighter colors and does well in the orange and green ranges, while CMYK tends to create deeper colors and does poorly with greens and oranges but very well with subtle dark shades like eggplant and indigo. Therefore, the color you create on-screen may look little like the one that ends up on your printed page. There's really no way around that, other than to use colors that are similar in both models. That's where a color-matching system comes in — it does its best to make what you see on-screen and on paper match, or at least be close.

Setting Up Your System

To achieve the best reproduction of printed colors on-screen, you need a closely controlled environment for your computer. Most people don't bother, relying instead on their brain's ability to mentally substitute the print color for what they see on-screen after they've had experience seeing what happens in actual printed documents. But the more you do to control the color-viewing environment, the closer the match between what you see on-screen and see on the page.

We've ordered these tips on setting up your system from simplest to most complex:

✦ **Dim the lights.** Most people turn the brightness of their monitors too high, which distorts colors by overdoing the blues and underdelivering on the reds. Turn the brightness lower, to between 60 and 75 percent maximum. To make sure you can still see the screen, lower the amount of light in your workspace by using lower-wattage bulbs, turning off overhead lighting right above your monitor, and/or using translucent shades in nearby windows.

✦ **Change the color temperature of your monitor to 7200 degrees on the Kelvin scale, something that most monitors have on-screen controls to do.**

✦ **If your monitor came with a color profile, use it.** On the Mac, the Monitors control panel has an option for setting color to a profile (stored in the ColorSync Profiles folder in the System Folder), or you can use the ColorSync control panel to set profiles for several devices. In Windows, use the Display control panel; the Settings pane has an option called Advanced that will open a dialog box that has a Color Management pane. The profiles are stored in the Color folder in the System folder in the Windows folder. Some monitors or video cards come with their own color-setup software.

✦ **Use a calibration tool, such as ColorVision's Monitor Spyder, Monaco Systems' Monaco Sensor, or X-Rite's Monitor Optimizer, to calibrate your monitor and create a color profile specifically for it.** These calibrators cost $375 to $600, so they're typically purchased by graphics departments, not individual designers. Note that color calibration software without a hardware calibrator device is worthless — without being able to measure what colors actually come from your monitor, there's no way they can meaningfully adjust the colors your display shows. Also note that monitors vary their color display over their lifetime (they get dimmer), so you should recalibrate every six months. For most users, the variances in monitor brightness, color balance, and contrast — coupled with the varying types of lighting used in their work space — mean that true calibration is impossible for images created on-screen and displayed on-screen. Still, using the calibration feature will make the on-screen color closer to what you'll print, even if it's not an exact match.

✦ **Work in a color-controlled room, where the lighting is at 5000 degrees Kelvin, so the light reflecting off your color proofs matches that of a professional prepress operation.** (There's long been a standard, whose latest version is called ISO 3664, that has set 5000 degrees Kelvin as the industry standard for proofing color printing. Basically, 5000 degrees is filtered daylight where the red, green, and blue components are equal. The International Prepress Association (www.ipa.org) has a lot of standards information and resources related to color accuracy.) Monitors should also be set with a white point of D65 (something done with calibration hardware and software). Also try to buy monitors with a neutral, light gray shade — or paint them that way — so your brain doesn't darken what you see on-screen to compensate for the off-white monitor frame right next to the screen image. Similarly, all furnishings should be neutral, preferably a light gray. Avoid having anything with a strong color in the room — even clothes.

Defining color models

Whether you define colors in QuarkXPress or in your illustration or paint program, the method you use to define them is critical to ensuring the best possible output. It's best to define all colors in the same model as the target output device. Use the following guidelines:

✦ If your printer is RGB, use the RGB model to define colors.

✦ If your printer is CMYK (like an offset printer), use CMYK to define colors.

✦ If you are using PANTONE colors for traditional offset printing, pick the PANTONE or PANTONE Uncoated models if using PANTONE inks. Pick PANTONE ProSim (also called PANTONE Solid to Process) if your printer is using inks from companies other than Pantone.

✦ If you're using Hexachrome colors for high-fidelity offset printing, pick the Hexachrome model.

✦ If you're using PANTONE colors for traditional offset printing, pick the PANTONE Process model if you will color-separate those colors into CMYK.

✦ Trumatch and Focoltone colors were designed to reproduce accurately whether output as spot colors or color-separated into CMYK. Other models (such as Toyo and DIC) may or may not separate accurately for all colors, so check with your printer or the ink manufacturer.

✦ If you're using any PANTONE, Focoltone, Trumatch, Toyo, or DIC color and outputting to a desktop color printer (whether RGB or CMYK), watch to ensure that the color definition doesn't lie outside the printer's gamut, as explained in the next section.

✦ Never rely on the screen display to gauge any non-RGB color. Even with Quark CMS's monitor calibration, RGB monitors simply cannot match most non-RGB colors. Use the on-screen colors only as a guide, and rely instead on a color swatchbook from your printer or the color ink's manufacturer.

✦ Quark CMS does *not* calibrate color in EPS files. If you use EPS, we strongly recommend that you use the DCS (preseparated CMYK) variant.

See Chapters 27 and 28 for more details on color models and defining color.

Setting Up the CMS XTension

With the Quark Color Management System (CMS) XTension, QuarkXPress can help you ensure accurate printing of your colors — both those in imported images and those defined in QuarkXPress. What Quark CMS does is track the colors in the source image, the colors displayable by your monitor, and the colors printable by your printer. If the monitor or printer doesn't support a color in your document, Quark CMS alters the color to its closest possible equivalent.

To activate the Quark CMS, make sure the Quark CMS XTension is active (use the XTensions Manager, described in Chapter 41, to do so) and the Color Management is on. In Windows, you'll see a pop-up menu in the Color Management Preferences dialog box (Edit ⇨ Preferences ⇨ Color Management) that can be set to Disabled or Kodak Digital Science CMM, as shown in Figure 29-1. On the Mac, there's a check box to enable color management; QuarkXPress for the Mac uses whatever model is selected in Apple's ColorSync control panel.

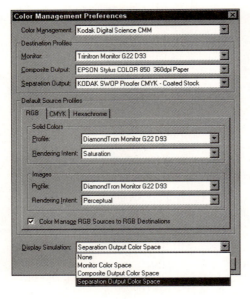

Figure 29-1: The Color Management Preferences dialog box. Note that the Mac version has a check box for Color Management, while the Windows version has a pop-up menu.

How Quark CMS works

Note that we do not characterize Quark CMS's capabilities as color *matching*. It is impossible to match colors produced in an illustration or paint program, or via a scanner, with what a printer or other output device can produce. The underlying differences in color models (how a color is defined) and the physics of the media (screen phosphors that emit light versus different types of papers with different types of inks that reflect light) make color matching impossible. But a calibration tool like Quark CMS can minimize differences.

The mechanism that Quark CMS uses is the profile that contains the information on color models and ranges supported by a particular creator (such as an illustration program or scanner), display, and printer. Quark CMS includes several predefined profiles and uses a device-independent color space to match these profiles against each other. A color space is a mathematical way of describing the relationships among colors.

By using a device-independent model (Kodak CMS or, on the Mac, whatever is set in ColorSync), Quark CMS can compare *gamuts* (the boundaries within, or range of, a color space) from other device-dependent models (like RGB and the others). What this means is that Quark CMS can examine the colors in your imported images and defined colors, compare them against the capabilities of your monitor and printer, and adjust the colors for the closest possible display and printing.

Adjusting On-Screen Display

The Quark CMS XTension comes with profiles for several monitors, including models from Apple, NEC Technologies, and Sony. Here's how it works:

✦ To have color calibration in effect for a monitor, you must be displaying thousands of colors (16-bit color depth) or more colors (or a higher color depth, such as 24-bit). On the Mac, use the Monitors & Sound control panel to change your monitor's bit depth. (On older Mac systems, use the Monitors control panel.) In Windows, use the Display control panel.

✦ You select the monitor in the Monitor area of the Color Management Preferences dialog box, accessed via Edit ➪ Preferences ➪ Color Management (refer to Figure 29-1). The monitor that you select will tell Quark CMS how to display imported images and colors defined within QuarkXPress.

✦ You select the output devices in the Composite Output and Separation Output pop-up menus. Composite Output is for a proofing printer you may have in your office, while Separation Output is for the imaging device used at your prepress bureau to create the actual color separations. These are covered in more detail later in this chapter.

✦ You also need to tell QuarkXPress what to correct the on-screen display for, which you do with the Display Simulation menu at the bottom of the dialog box. Here, you decide whether to simulate the color space of your monitor, your composite printer, or your separation printer. Or you can just turn off on-screen simulation. Typically, you would choose whatever output device your pages are finally destined for.

✦ You need to tell QuarkXPress which color models to apply the display correction to. There are three panes, one each for RGB, CMYK, and Hexachrome. In each, you set the profile and rendering intent for the source of two types of Graphics: Solid Colors and Images. We explain these options later in the chapter.

New Feature   QuarkXPress 5 has changed the Color Management Preferences dialog box considerably, although the features are largely the same as in version 4.

The on-screen appearance

It's possible to have a different on-screen appearance than Quark CMS expects. For example, your brightness and contrast settings affect how colors display, but Quark CMS has no way of gauging their settings. Likewise, in Mac OS 8.x you can change the color temperature characteristics (the *gamma*) of your display in the Monitors & Sound control panel's Monitor pane. (Note that Mac OS 9.x and Windows do not have controls for the monitor's gamma settings, although some graphics cards come with software that adds this feature via a control panel on the Mac or into the Windows Display control panel.) But you can set these with most monitors' on-screen controls, as noted earlier.

Calibrations from other programs

Other programs may have similar settings for calibrating their display against your type of monitor. For example, Adobe Photoshop offers such an option (via Edit ➪ Color Settings), as Figure 29-2 shows. If you're creating colors in a program and importing those colors into QuarkXPress, it's important to have them calibrated the same way, or at least as closely as the different programs will allow.

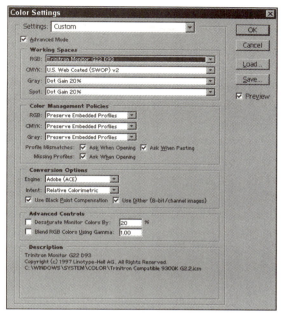

Figure 29-2: Programs like Photoshop can also set display calibration. It's best if all programs use the same settings.

Using Output Profiles

In addition to selecting the monitor profile and on-screen color correction, you can also set the output profiles in the Color Management Preferences dialog box. The Composite Print and Separation Printer pop-up menus let you select which printers you use for your output. Obviously, you need to choose an output device in the Composite Printer and/or Separation printer pop-up menus for the Quark CMS to have any effect when trying to calibrate on-screen color to match the color of the target output device. Here's what the options mean:

✦ **Composite printer:** This printer is typically a proofing printer, such as a dye-sublimation printer, used to see colors before outputting to negatives, or an output process like 3M's Matchprint service that produces a laminated image meant to simulate the colors that the printing press will produce.

✦ **Separation printer:** This is a web offset or other printing press that uses multiple color plates to produce the output. A separation printer can also be a printer like the Xerox Tektronix Phaser line of dye-sublimation printers that actually outputs each of the CMYK colors separately, creating, in essence, separate negatives.

Setting the default source profiles

The last set of profile information to select is for the default source profiles, also in the Color Management Preferences dialog box. There are three panes (RGB, CMYK, and Hexachrome) and two menu areas for each (Solid Colors and Image). For each color model used, select the source profile as follows:

✦ **Solid Colors:** Use this to select the device in which you plan to define the majority of your colors. This is typically a monitor for RGB colors and a printer for CMYK colors (the printer you intend to output to). In the RGB pane, use the profile that matches your monitor (or your artist's monitor), since the intent here is to calibrate colors created on your computer in QuarkXPress or in an illustration program.

✦ **Image:** Use this to select the device that created the majority of images you plan to import. This is typically a scanner or printer for RGB colors but could be a monitor if you create original artwork in QuarkXPress, Photoshop, Illustrator, or some other program. For CMYK images, this is typically a printer (the one you intend to output to).

Make sure that you use the same color profiles wherever possible in all the programs you use to create images and colors — QuarkXPress, your image editor (such as Photoshop, Corel Photo-Paint, or MetaCreations Painter), and your illustration program (such as Illustrator, FreeHand, or CorelDraw). Almost every professional program supports the Kodak CMM. Therefore, such consistent color model use should be easy to achieve.

Setting the default rendering intents

New Feature The ability to set rendering intent is new to QuarkXPress 5.

The options you choose in the Rendering Intent menus determine how QuarkXPress translates the color in imported graphics files to the gamut (color range) of the output device. Basically, this determines how QuarkXPress maps one model to another, based on your intent of keeping colors in the same relative range or of forcing an exact match for each color even if that leaves gaps in the color spectrum that may result in odd color shifts on some images.

If the picture is a scanned photograph, choose Perceptual. The other options — Saturation, Relative Colorimetric, and Absolute Colorimetric — are appropriate for images that contain mostly areas of solid color, such as Illustrator EPS files that have been opened in Photoshop and saved as TIFF files. When in doubt, choose the Profile Default option. Here's what each option does in detail:

✦ **Perceptual** tries to balance the colors in an image when translating from the original color range to the output device's color range under the assumption that it's a photograph and, thus, needs to look natural. This is appropriate for photographs.

✦ **Saturation** tries to create vivid colors when translating from the original color range to the output device's color range — even if doing so means some colors are printed inaccurately. This is appropriate for charts and other slide-like graphics whose colors are intended for impact rather than naturalness.

✦ **Absolute Colorimetric** makes no adjustments to the colors during output. So it allows, for example, an image that uses two similar colors to end up being output as the same color because of the printer's limited color range.

✦ **Relative Colorimetric** is the same as Absolute Colorimetric except that it will shift all the colors to compensate for the white point of the monitor as set in the monitor profile (essentially, adjusting the brightness of the output to compensate for any dimness or excess brightness in the monitor).

Tip

Depending on what kinds of documents you produce, you'll likely want Perceptual as your document-wide default for Images, and Saturation as your document-wide default for Solid Graphics.

Calibrating Imported Colors

When you load an image into QuarkXPress, the Quark CMS XTension applies the default settings defined in the Color Management Preferences dialog box (these are described earlier in this chapter). You can change these settings, however, as you import each file by using the Color Management pane in the Get Picture dialog box, shown in Figure 29-3. *Remember:* Color correction is an *attempt* to match colors, not a guarantee. Here are your options:

✦ The Profile menu lets you select a profile for the source of the image. For example, if you've set QuarkXPress to default to a monitor profile under the assumption that most images are created on the computer but the particular image now being imported was scanned in on a Hewlett-Packard scanner, you'd select the profile for that scanner. Note that if the image has its own color profile (which images from Photoshop and other image editors can have), the menu will default to the Embedded option, which you should almost always leave as is — someone embedded that profile for a reason, after all.

✦ The Rendering Intent menu lets you override the document-wide setting you selected in the Color Management Preferences dialog box.

✦ There's also a check box to color-manage the image to RGB, CMYK, or Hexachrome destinations, depending on whether the file is RGB, CMYK, or Hexachrome. This option tells QuarkXPress whether to calibrate the image to its ultimate destination (output device). Typically, you'd leave this alone, letting the document-wide settings dictate how the image is handled.

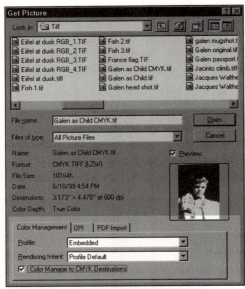

Figure 29-3: You can override color management settings during file import for specific graphics.

Note   You may need to wait a few seconds for the Color Management pane's settings to appear because Quark CMS must read the file to determine what options are valid.

Changing profiles after import

You can also change profiles after you import an image by selecting a picture box and using the Profile Information palette (View ➪ Show Profile Information). Figure 29-4 shows the resulting dialog box. Note that this option won't appear if Quark CMS isn't installed and active.

If you open a QuarkXPress document with a copy of QuarkXPress that doesn't have the Quark CMS XTension installed, your profile information is retained for the next time you open it in a copy of QuarkXPress that has Quark CMS installed.

Figure 29-4: You can override color management settings after file import for specific graphics using the Profile Information palette.

Determining and updating profiles

If you're unsure of which profiles a document uses (perhaps someone else put together the document that you're working on), you can use the Usage dialog box (Utilities ➪ Usage, and then click the Profiles tab) and click the Replace button to get the dialog box shown at the bottom of Figure 29-5. You can also use this dialog box to update any missing profiles or to change to a new profile after you've installed it in your system.

Figure 29-5: Use the Usage dialog box to replace a profile used throughout the document with another.

Note that the Usage dialog box replaces the profile for all images using a particular profile, while the Profile Information palette replaces the profile for the selected image only.

Setting printing options

By setting the Quark CMS profiles when defining colors or importing images, you've done most of the work needed to calibrate your colors for optimal output. Still, you have the following options:

✦ In the Print dialog box's Profiles pane (use File ➪ Print, or @cmd+P or Ctrl+P, to get the Print dialog box), you can choose a profile for output other than the one used as the default for your document. This is handy when printing to a different printer than usual. Figure 29-6 shows the Profile pane.

✦ In the same pane, you can also have QuarkXPress try to make a composite proof look like the ultimate separated output by checking the Composite Simulates Separation check box. Use this when you're printing proof copies on a printer or other device before outputting the final pages to negatives for use on a SWOP press.

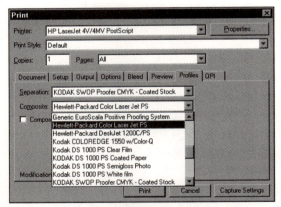

Figure 29-6: In the Print dialog box's Profile pane, you can change the color profile. This is handy if you're outputting to a different printer than usual and want QuarkXPress to recalibrate the output to that device.

Summary

Although exact color matching is impossible because the laws of physics simply won't allow what's on a monitor to be reproduced exactly via ink on paper, color calibration and management systems can make the printed appearance as close as possible.

You can help make what you see on-screen translate to print by using monitor calibration hardware, adjusting your monitor brightness, and adjusting the surrounding light.

Within QuarkXPress, you can ensure the most accurate color reproduction if you use the Quark CMS XTension, which lets you tell QuarkXPress what devices your graphics were created on and what devices you intend to print to. You can also specify the method by which QuarkXPress maps (or renders) colors from one device's capabilities to another. Although these are global settings, QuarkXPress lets you change the color profile and rendering intent on an image-by-image basis during import or after import. You can also adjust the profiles used document-wide during printing, as well as replace one profile globally for another.

✦ ✦ ✦

Trapping

Color trapping, which controls how colors overlap and abut when printed, is one of the most powerful features available in QuarkXPress. It's also one that novice users can abuse terribly. If you don't know much about trapping, leave the features of the program at the default settings. Before you use QuarkXPress trapping tools, study some books on color publishing, talk to your printer, and experiment with test files that you don't want to publish. If you're experienced with color trapping — or after you become experienced — you'll find the QuarkXPress trapping tools a joy to use.

In This Chapter

Understanding trapping

Setting traps

Setting default color traps

Overriding traps

Note The illustrations and figures in this chapter are in black and white. You'll need to look at your color monitor to see the effects of what's described here, or check out the TIFF screenshot files on the CD for this chapter. Also, take a look at the examples in the special 16-page color insert, which covers color techniques in color.

Understanding Trapping

Who needs trapping? If you're printing to a color laser, dye-sublimation, ink-jet, or thermal wax printer, don't worry about trapping. You're not getting the kind of output resolution at which this level of image fine-tuning is relevant. But if you're outputting to an imagesetter (particularly if you're outputting to negatives) for eventual printing on a web-offset or other printing press, read on. In either case, you'll also want to understand the color-calibration features in the Quark CMS XTension (covered in Chapter 29), because it will help you get the best color fidelity possible with your images and output devices.

If you do need to get involved with trapping, use the trapping tools in the illustration program with which you create your EPS graphics. These tools will help you to finely control the settings for each image's specific needs. Also, if you're using a service bureau that does high-resolution scanning for you and strips these files into your layout before output, check to make sure that the bureau isn't also handling trapping for you with a Scitex or other high-end system. If it is, make sure you ask whether and when you should be doing trapping yourself.

Choking versus spreading

So what is trapping, anyway? *Trapping* adjusts the boundaries of colored objects to prevent gaps between abutting colors on the final printed page. Gaps can occur because of misalignment of the negatives, plates, or printing press — all of which are impossible to avoid. Colors are trapped by processes known as *choking* and *spreading*. Both make an object slightly larger — usually by a fraction of a point — so that it overprints the abutting object slightly. The process is called *choking* when one object surrounds a second object, and the first object is enlarged to overlap the second. The process is known as *spreading* when you enlarge the surrounded object so that it leaks (or bleeds) into the surrounding object.

The difference between choking and spreading is the relative position of the two objects. Here's how it works:

✦ **Choking:** Think of choking as making the hole for the inside object smaller (which in effect makes the object on the outside larger).

✦ **Spreading:** Think of spreading as making the object *in the hole* larger.

The object made larger depends on the image, but you generally bleed the color of a lighter object into a darker one. If you did the opposite, you'd make objects seem ungainly. Thus, choke a dark object inside a light one, and spread a light object inside a dark one. If the objects are adjacent, spread the light object.

Figure 30-1 shows the two types of trapping techniques. Spreading (at left) makes the interior object's color bleed out; choking (at right) makes the outside color bleed in, in effect making the area of the choked element smaller. The dashed lines show the size of the interior object; as you can see in the image on the right, when you choke a darker object into a lighter one, the effect is to change its size (here, the interior object gets smaller).

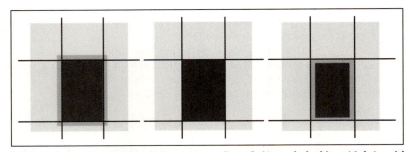

Figure 30-1: Two kinds of traps: spreading (left) and choking (right), with an untrapped image in the center that was misregistered during printing.

Knocking out and overprinting

In practice, trapping also involves controlling whether colors *knock out* or *overprint*. The default is to knock out — cut out — any overlap when one element is placed on top of another. If, for example, you place two rectangles on top of each other, they print like the two rectangles on the right side of Figure 30-2. If you set the darker rectangle in this figure to overprint, the rectangles print as shown on the left side of the figure. Setting colors to overprint results in mixed colors, as on the left, while setting colors to knock out results in discrete colors, as on the right.

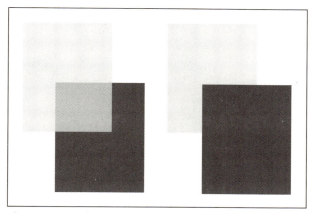

Figure 30-2: The two kinds of untrapped options: overprint (left) and knockout (right).

Setting Traps

You define trapping settings for separate colors in the Trap Specifications dialog box, shown in Figure 30-3. (To open the dialog box, select Edit ➪ Colors or use the shortcut Shift+F12, select a color, and then click the Edit Trap button.) However, you define default trapping settings in the Trapping pane of the Preferences dialog box, accessed via Edit ➪ Preferences ➪ Preferences, or Option+Shift+⌘+Y or Ctrl+Alt+Shift+Y (see the later section on setting trap defaults).

Working with object and background colors

The title of the Trap Specifications dialog box shows the color for which you're defining trapping values — the *object color*. (In Figure 30-3, trapping values are being defined for yellow.) In the Background Color list, you see all defined colors except registration, white, and the selected color. You don't need to trap these colors as background colors because registration completely obscures any color spread into it. Also, white doesn't "mix" with other colors — it's just paper with no ink on it — and thus causes no unsightly gaps or color artifacts due to misregistration.

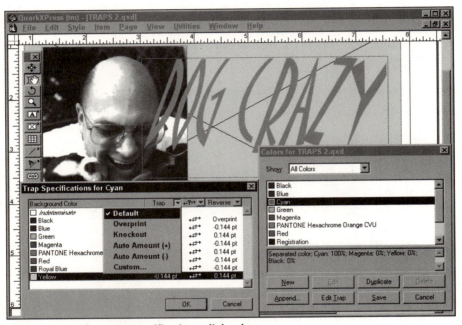

Figure 30-3: The Trap Specifications dialog box.

The list of background colors includes one color not defined via Edit ⇨ Colors: Indeterminate. This item is not exactly a color but a special case used by QuarkXPress to handle multicolored backgrounds (such as a color photo or multiple-color objects abutting) for which trapping information is unavailable or is conflicting.

Using the background color option

You set options in the Trap Specifications dialog box by first selecting the background color for which you want to define the trap relationship and then selecting the corresponding Trap menu. What you are defining is the relationship between the color name in the dialog box's title (yellow in Figure 30-3) and the color selected in the dialog box's Background Color list. The relationship is for cases when the object whose color is in the dialog box overlaps an object whose color is selected (brick in Figure 30-3). In the case of Figure 30-3, we're defining the traps for cases when yellow objects are in front of objects of all other colors.

Setting the amount of trapping

The six options on the Trap pop-up menu (refer to Figure 30-3) set the actual amount of trapping between the selected colors. The options are as follows:

✦ **Default:** This means QuarkXPress chooses the amount of trap and whether the object color spreads or chokes. The settings in the Trapping pane of the Default Document Preferences dialog box form the parameters under which QuarkXPress makes these decisions.

   QuarkXPress will let you know when you have specified a trap other than the default by adding an asterisk (*) to the end of the trap settings in the Trap and Reverse lists (see the following section on the Reverse pop-up menu).

✦ **Overprint:** This means to print the color over the background color, in essence mixing the inks. Note that the object color must be of a darker shade than specified in the Trapping pane's Overprint Limit option in the Default Document Preferences dialog box.

✦ **Knockout:** This cuts a hole in the background object and has no trapping. Thus, a slight misalignment in the printing press could cause a gap between the two colors.

✦ **Auto Amount (+):** This means QuarkXPress spreads the object color into the selected background color. The actual trapping amount is specified in the Default Document Preferences dialog box.

✦ **Auto Amount (–):** This means QuarkXPress chokes the object color with the selected background color. The actual trapping amount is specified in the Default Document Preferences dialog box.

✦ **Custom:** This is where you specify your own trapping amount.

Entering a negative trapping number chokes the object color with the background color. Entering a positive number spreads the object color into the background color. The difference between the two is subtle (as described earlier and shown in Figure 30-1) and usually comes into play for fine elements such as text and lines. If the object using the background color is thin or has a light hue, a good rule of thumb is to spread; otherwise, choke.

Using the Relationship option

The Relationship option lets you choose whether a trap is dependent or independent.

A dependent trap is shown via the symbol at the left.

An independent trap is shown via the symbol at the left.

A dependent trap is one in which QuarkXPress figures out automatically, based on the settings defined in this dialog box, how to trap the same color combination when the dialog box's color is behind the selected background color. For example, if you define a trap for cases when cyan overlaps blue, having a dependent relationship means that QuarkXPress automatically defines the trap for cases when blue overlaps cyan, based on the approach you took for cyan overlapping blue. An independent relationship means you manually choose the trap settings for each direction.

The Reverse menu

When you've given a color pair an independent relationship, use the option in the Reverse pop-up menu to choose the trapping for the reverse relationship. For example, if you set traps for cyan overlapping blue and you want to set traps for blue overlapping cyan independently, make the relationship independent and then select a trapping method here for blue overlapping cyan. The reverse pop-up menu has the same options as the Trap pop-up menu, listed in the "Setting the amount of trapping" section earlier in this chapter.

If you choose an option from the Reverse pop-up menu for a color pair that has a dependent relationship, QuarkXPress will adjust the original relationship accordingly. The relationship is dependent, so a change to one direction automatically affects the settings for the other.

Setting Default Color Traps

In the Trapping pane in the Preferences dialog box, shown in Figure 30-4, you set the defaults that Default represents in the Trap Specifications dialog box. There are several options to set in this pane, covered in the following sections.

Trapping Method

This setting determines whether QuarkXPress uses the trapping values specified in the Auto Amount option or whether it adjusts the trapping based on the saturation of the abutting colors. If you choose Absolute, the program uses the values as is. If you choose Proportional, QuarkXPress calculates new trapping values based on the value entered in Auto Amount and the relative saturation of the abutting colors. The third option is Knockout All, which does no trapping. The default is Absolute.

Process Trapping

This option controls how trapping is handled when you output to CMYK negatives. If Process Trapping is set to On, QuarkXPress examines each color plate as a whole when determining the trapping settings. For example, if you place a light blue object on a dark blue background, both objects will use cyan ink when color-separated to

CMYK negatives. Because of that, QuarkXPress doesn't have to worry so much about trapping, because the cyan in both objects is on one plate and couldn't be misregistered. But the other three CMYK colors used to create the colors could misregister, because they're on their own plates, so QuarkXPress will still figure out trapping for those in relationship to the cyan plate. In other words, QuarkXPress will trap entire plates, not individual colors, with this option on.

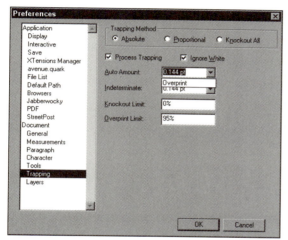

Figure 30-4: The Trapping pane of the Preferences dialog box lets you set defaults for trapping.

By contrast, if the two blues were PANTONE spot colors and thus printed on separate plates, QuarkXPress would need to worry about the registration of the two colors, because each would be on its own plate. There really is no reason to turn this setting to Off.

Ignore White

If you check this option box, QuarkXPress traps an object based on all nonwhite objects abutting or behind the object. Otherwise, QuarkXPress calculates a trap based on the smaller of the Indeterminate settings and the trap specification for any other colors (including white) abutting or behind the object. This option is checked as a default, because it makes little sense to trap to white (because there is nothing to trap to).

If you choose Absolute as your trapping method and also have Process Trapping turned on, QuarkXPress will divide the Auto Amount value in half and apply that to the darker shade in each plate. Thus, if the Auto Amount is 0.144 point and you have two blue objects, one with more cyan than the other, the dark object's cyan component will be choked by 0.077 point, rather than 0.144 point.

Auto Amount

This option specifies the trapping value with which the program calculates automatic trapping for the Default, Auto Amount (+), and Auto Amount (−) options in the Trap Specifications dialog box. You can enter values from 0 to 36 points, in increments of 0.001 point. If you want the amount to be infinite (so that colors overprint), select the Overprint option in the pop-up menu. The default setting is 0.144 point.

Indeterminate

The Indeterminate setting tells QuarkXPress how to trap objects that abut multicolored or indeterminate-colored objects, as well as imported color graphics. As with Trapping Method, this setting applies only to colors set at Default in the Trap Specifications dialog box. Valid options are 0 to 26 points, in 0.001-point increments, as well as Overprint. The default is 0.144 point.

Knockout Limit

This value tells QuarkXPress when to automatically knock out a color object from its background (this, in effect, turns off trapping for that knocked-out object). The default is 0 percent, meaning that the object won't knock out of the background unless it's white (0 percent of the darkness of the background color). Ordinarily, you would want to leave this setting at 0 percent. However, if you want trapping to be turned off for sufficiently light-colored objects against sufficiently dark-colored backgrounds (to preserve object shapes where trapping isn't really necessary), you may want to increase this value slightly.

Overprint Limit

This value tells QuarkXPress when to overprint a color object. You can specify any percentage from 0 to 100, in increments of 0.1. If you enter 50 percent, QuarkXPress specifies an overprint for any color whose trap specification is set as Overprint and whose saturation is 50 percent or greater; otherwise, it traps the color based on the Auto Amount and Trapping Method settings. This limit affects black objects regardless of whether black is set at Auto or Overprint. The default is 95 percent.

Overriding Traps

Because trapping depends as much on the elements being trapped as on their colors, trapping tools based solely on relationships among colors would be insufficient. That's why QuarkXPress offers the ability to override trapping settings for selected objects.

When to use independent trapping tools

The QuarkXPress trapping tools are great for making sure color elements — lines, type, and backgrounds — created in QuarkXPress print well. But for some types of elements you'll need to go outside QuarkXPress for the right tools. For example, if you create a logo as an EPS file and place it over a TIFF photo (perhaps for a cover), QuarkXPress's trapping settings won't be applied. That's because QuarkXPress can't work with the EPS file at that level of detail. In many cases, your document will print fine, but if you see the need for trapping when you look at the match print or final output, it's time for a professional trapping tool.

One solution is to use a program like ScenicSoft TrapWise (www.scenicsoft.com) that lets you do trapping on the EPS or DCS files you create from QuarkXPress. Of course, if you're not a trapping expert, you should have your service bureau do the trapping.

QuarkXPress's Trap Information palette lets you set the trap for any element in a selected object: the background, frame (inside, outside, and, for multiline frames, the middle), gaps (inside multiline frames), picture, and text. Note that the bottom option will display Text if text is selected and Picture if a picture is selected. A line has slightly different options, because it has no background.

To override trapping locally, you must first invoke the Trap Information palette, which is accessible via View ➪ Show Trap Information, or Option+F12 or Ctrl+F12. The contents of this palette depend on the type of object selected, but no matter what the contents, the palette works the same way. Figure 30-5 shows the Trap Information palette for a framed picture box.

Looking at the default settings

In Figure 30-5, the two picture-box elements for which trapping is appropriate are set at Default (shown in the middle column), which means that they take on whatever settings were made globally in the Trap Specifications dialog box and the Trapping pane of the Preferences dialog box. Because there are so many possible combinations of colors, no one can be expected to remember how every color combination traps. Recognizing this, QuarkXPress displays what the default setting is in the column at right. Thus, in Figure 30-5, the defaults are as follows:

✦ The default for trapping the frame color with the color of the image inside the frame and/or the box background is 0.144 point (which happens to be the setting for automatic trapping in this document).

✦ The default for trapping the frame color with the color of the object outside (abutting) the frame is overprint, because the background object is white, so there is no need to trap the frame color.

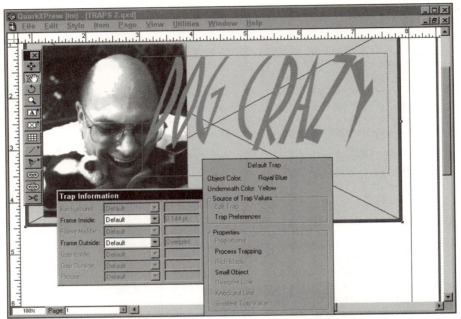

Figure 30-5: The Trap Information palette lets you override trapping preferences in selected items.

The trapping rationale

To further explain trapping settings, QuarkXPress describes the current trapping rationale if you select the question mark icons in the Trap Information palette. Refer to Figure 30-5 for an example explanation for the selected picture box. (In the explanation, the relevant rationales are in black; the grayed text isn't relevant to the particular item's trap settings.)

Summary

Trapping — ensuring that abutting colors print without gaps — is something best left to the prepress experts, whose intimate knowledge of colors and printing gives them the ability to ensure the highest-quality production of your images without unsightly gaps due to misregistration, or awkward-looking images due to excess overlap during trapping. QuarkXPress's default settings also handle the needs for basic color elements like frames, backgrounds, and illustrations created within QuarkXPress.

If you do have a need to adjust the QuarkXPress trapping settings, you'll find the tools to do so in the Color palette for individual colors and in the Preferences dialog box for document-wide settings. You can also modify the trapping for individual elements with the Trapping Information palette.

✦　　✦　　✦

Managing Projects

Desktop publishing can be a one-person affair, and there are plenty of designers who work just fine that way. But in most cases, publishing is a collaborative effort, combining the expertise and talents of diverse people.

Harnessing that talent, though, can be tricky. After all, the final result needs to be seamless, presenting a unified vision and message despite the many contributors. A strong editor and a strong design director can ensure that happens with the actual content, but strong vision doesn't eliminate the technical difficulties in managing projects on which multiple people work. But QuarkXPress can. It has a series of tools meant specifically to smooth the interaction of people working together on a document or set of documents. For very large operations, the Quark Publishing System offers even more file-management capabilities, but most publishers will find themselves with all or nearly all the capabilities they need in the standard version of QuarkXPress.

This part shows you how QuarkXPress can help you manage the workflow and technical consistency in workgroup projects. But even if you don't work in a workgroup, the consistency and standardization they encourage can help do-it-all designers ease their workloads as well.

Communicating in a Workgroup

◆ ◆ ◆ ◆

In This Chapter

Sharing electronic files

Gathering QuarkXPress program files

Sharing project files and document elements

◆ ◆ ◆ ◆

Publishing is rarely a single-person enterprise. Chances are high that the creators of your text and graphics are not the same people who do your layout, so publishing programs must support workgroups. And the key to successful workgroup publishing is communication — especially in this day of widespread office campuses and telecommuting. When your collaborators aren't sitting right next to you, it's important that you're all working with the same information and the same standards. QuarkXPress lets you create your own balance between the individual and the workgroup by allowing you to share common files over a network and import other essential elements from document to document.

Sharing Electronic Files

When you're working on a project in a workgroup, the first thing to consider is how to share files electronically. Generally, this will be through a networked server, but you can also share files through an FTP site, you can distribute files via e-mail, or you can share a set of master CDs containing all common elements. Make sure all the users have appropriate access, know where the files are, and know their passwords — providing this information to users upfront can save hours of hassles and delays during the course of projects. All these project files should be backed up, and the backup files should be updated regularly.

Tip

In smaller environments, the temptation is to give everyone in the workgroup the same access to all the files in the company. Even if you trust everyone, this isn't necessarily the best strategy. With software and fonts, for example, you may be violating a license agreement by providing free access to everything.

Cross-Reference

See Chapter 5 for information about networks and sharing files between platforms.

Organizing files

While you're setting up your project folders on your server or other shared media, you may organize files by project, by file type, by user, and more. If, for example, your company produces only one or two publications, you may have a folder for each publication (containing a subfolder for each issue), a folder for shared graphics, a folder for ads, a folder for shared fonts, and a folder for site-licensed utilities such as Suitcase. Figure 31-1 shows the networked Mac server that 5280 Publishing uses; off-site workers access the server over the Internet via AppleShare on their Macs.

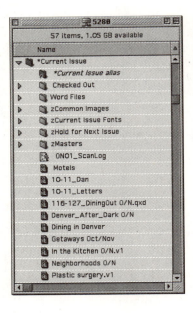

Figure 31-1: The 5280 server contains a folder for the current issue of *5280 Magazine,* which contains all the QuarkXPress files along with subfolders for images, fonts, and more. Other folders on the server house shared templates and software, ads, and database files.

Naming files

The way you name your folders, directories, and files can significantly improve — or inhibit — access by a workgroup. First, the names need to be meaningful to the people who look at them. Using the file name "Cover" or "CoverFinal" or worse yet, "CoverFinalFinal," communicates very little. But the file name "Buzz Cover 09/01.qxd" indicates a QuarkXPress file that's the cover for the September 2001 issue of the *Buzz* newsletter.

It's also important that files conform to the standards of your operating system, Mac or Windows. Unless you're producing final output in a single-platform environment, though, you can never be sure that your files will not be opened on the other platform. The simplest way to ensure that you won't have problems with transferring files is to use a naming convention that satisfies both Mac and Windows standards, including:

✦ **Keeping file names to 27 characters or less.**

✦ **Always including the PC file extension (which adds 4 characters to the full name, hitting the Mac limit of 31).** Use .QXD for documents, .QXT for templates, .QDT for auxiliary dictionaries, .QPJ for printer styles, and .KRN for kerning tables. Typical extensions for cross-platform graphics are .TIF for TIFF, .EPS for Encapsulated PostScript, .AI for Adobe Illustrator, .PCT for PICT, .PCX for PC Paintbrush, .BMP and .RLE for Microsoft bitmap, .GIF for Graphics Interchange Format, .PDF for Acrobat Portable Document Format, .WMF for Windows metafile, .PSD for Adobe Photoshop, .CDR for CorelDraw, and .SCT or .CT for Scitex. For text documents, they are .DOC for Microsoft Word, .HTM for HTML, .WPD for WordPerfect, .RTF for Rich Text Format, and .TXT for Text-only (also called ASCII).

✦ **Never using the pipe (|), colon (:), period (.), asterisk (*), double quote ("), less-than symbol (<), greater-than symbol (>), question mark (?), slash (/), or backslash (\ ) characters.**

For more on cross-platform system issues, see Chapter 5 and Appendix D.

Gathering QuarkXPress Program Files

After you have a method for sharing files — network, Internet, CD, and so on — you need to collect the files you want to share. First, you should collect any shared fonts, graphics, and software that you can freely distribute. When it comes to QuarkXPress, some program files can be stored in a central location and easily accessed from a common folder: XPress Preferences, color management profiles, kerning tables, and auxiliary dictionaries.

Unfortunately, not all program preference files are cross-platform.

Using XPress Preferences files

The XPress Preferences file, which resides in the Preferences folder inside your QuarkXPress folder (see Figure 31-2), contains many default preferences and other information, including:

✦ Settings in the Application section of the Preferences dialog box (Edit ➪ Preferences ➪ Preferences, or Option+Shift+⌘+Y or Ctrl+Alt+Shift+Y), which control how QuarkXPress features such as Smart Quotes and Auto Save work.

✦ Settings made when no documents were open in the Document section of the Preferences dialog box (Edit ➪ Preferences ➪ Preferences). These settings control features such as Auto Page Insertion, Auto Leading, and Trapping.

✦ Any style sheets, colors, H&J sets (hyphenation and justification settings), lists, and dash and stripe patterns created when no documents were open.

✦ Changes to the default kerning and tracking tables, hyphenation exceptions, and the default auxiliary dictionary.

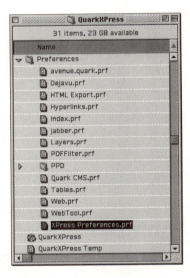

Figure 31-2: The XPress Preferences file.

If it's important that all users share the same preferences, you can store a master copy of the XPress Preferences file on a server. All users will need to drag a copy to their Preferences folders in their QuarkXPress folder (the file cannot be aliased). If you're working in a multiplatform environment, you'll need to maintain a Mac and Windows version of the XPress Preferences file, because it isn't cross-platform.

Tip If you keep the XPress Preferences file current with all your preferences, you can apply these preferences to all previously created documents. To do this, open each document and click the Use XPress Preferences button in the Nonmatching Preferences dialog box. (Newly created documents always use the current XPress Preferences settings.)

Quark CMS profiles

When you open a document, QuarkXPress checks to see whether a Quark CMS color profile that isn't on your system was used. If so, a dialog box shows you which images are affected, letting you replace the profile if you want. You'll need to add the profile before printing if you want that particular color calibration applied.

But if you intend to move the document back to the system that has the missing profile, don't worry. The reference to the missing profile is retained (unless you replace it).

On the Mac, color profiles are stored in the ColorSync Profiles folder in the System Folder's Preferences folder. In Windows, the profiles are stored in the `SYSTEM\COLOR` directory in the directory that contains the Windows operating system. Color profiles on Mac and Windows are also not interchangeable, so if you work in a cross-platform environment and add profiles on one platform, be sure to ask the manufacturer for the profiles for the other platform.

You can also store color profiles in a second folder of your choice, which you select via the Auxiliary Profile Folder option in the Profile Manager dialog box (Utilities ⇨ Profile Manager). This second folder is a great place to store color profiles specific to your work, rather than mixing them up with the default color profiles.

Kerning tables

Unlike many other preferences, changes to kerning tables are stored in the XPress Preferences file and used for all subsequently created documents, whether a document is open or not when they are made. They aren't used for previously created documents, though, unless you click Use XPress Preferences when you open them. QuarkXPress also provides a method to export and import kerning tables, so that you can move kerning information between documents that have already been created.

After you've changed kerning values for a particular typeface, you can export the new values as a text file that can be imported into other documents. Figure 31-3 shows the Edit Kerning Table dialog box (accessed via Utilities ⇨ Kerning Edit and then clicking the Edit button after selecting the font whose kerning values you want to change). At the bottom of the dialog box is the Export button, which creates the kerning file, and the Import button, which loads in previously created kerning files. If you choose Export, another dialog box appears that lets you select the name and location of the kerning file. Importing kerning tables gives you a similar dialog box. When you select a kerning table to import, its values will display in the Kerning Pairs list in the Edit Kerning Table dialog box.

By periodically exporting kerning tables and then importing them into QuarkXPress when no documents are open, you can update the global preferences set in XPress Preferences so that all future documents use these new kerning values.

 Kerning files are the same on both platforms, so you can import kerning pairs from Mac to Windows and vice versa. In Windows QuarkXPress, make sure that you've selected All Files as the file type, or that you've added the extension .KRN to the kerning file on the Mac, so that it appears in the import dialog box.

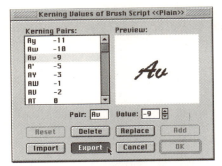

Figure 31-3: Exporting kerning information for a font.

Auxiliary spelling dictionaries

Auxiliary dictionaries are separate files used to supplement the QuarkXPress spelling dictionary. You can create an auxiliary dictionary using the Utilities ➪ Auxiliary Dictionary dialog box, add all the words specific to a project to it, then share the file with other users. The other users can copy the dictionary to their hard drive and open it for documents they want to use it with (again, through Utilities ➪ Auxiliary Dictionary).

Cross-Reference   For more information about creating and using auxiliary dictionaries, see Chapter 13.

QuarkXPress auxiliary dictionaries are simply text files in which all the words are listed, one after the other in alphabetical order, with a return after each word. This makes it easy for you to use a word processor to edit or merge together multiple auxiliary dictionaries. For QuarkXPress to recognize an auxiliary dictionary, it must have a creator code of XPR3 and file code of XDCT (on the Mac) or end with .QDT (on Windows).

Platform Difference   Auxiliary dictionaries aren't compatible across platforms, so you can't import dictionaries from Mac to Windows and vice versa.

Sharing Project Files and Document Elements

After you have all the software issues worked out, you can start collecting the content files (graphic and text files) and layout files (QuarkXPress templates, documents, libraries, and so on) necessary for your project. After you place the files in a shared location, be sure to update them—and notify other users to obtain updated files as necessary. Figure 31-4 shows a project folder and all the pieces for pulling the project together.

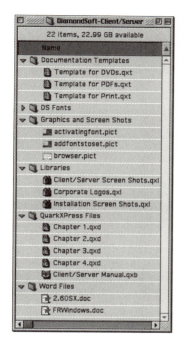

Figure 31-4: A project folder may include the templates, libraries, fonts, graphics, and text files used to create the project.

Graphics and text files

Perhaps the most obvious elements to standardize are the source elements — the text and graphics that you use in your documents — especially if you have common elements such as logos that are used in multiple documents. The simplest method of ensuring that the latest versions of these common elements are used is to keep them all in a standard folder (either on each computer or on a network drive). This method works well when first using a text or graphic element, but it doesn't ensure that these elements are updated in QuarkXPress documents if the elements are changed after being imported.

Tip   If the graphics and text are formatted extensively, you may want to place them in a library or template. See Chapter 33 for more information.

Standardizing text files

For text files, there is no easy solution to the updating problem, because QuarkXPress has no text-link feature. But you can put common text contained in a QuarkXPress text box into a library (see the following section on libraries), which should handle most needs, such as mastheads, postal information, and standard sidebars (for example, "How to contact the company").

Standardizing graphics files

For graphics files, using Publish and Subscribe on the Mac, OLE in Windows, or regular links — when combined with the approach of keeping common elements in a common location — can ensure consistency across documents. You can also use libraries to store commonly used graphics.

Chapter 20 covers Publish and Subscribe and OLE in more detail, showing their pros and cons.

Fonts

If you're working on a single platform, and you have an appropriate license agreement, you can store all the fonts for a project in a shared location. Users can then copy all the fonts to their hard drives, or grab the ones they need when they need them. (To guarantee consistency, it's important that all members of a workgroup use the exact same fonts — the same type and version from the same foundry. It's not okay to use just any version of Helvetica. If one person uses a TrueType Helvetica from Apple and another uses a PostScript Helvetica from Adobe, text can easily reflow.) As with other project pieces, if you update a font, notify all the users.

In a cross-platform environment, fonts become more complicated, because text doesn't always flow the same, even if you're using the same font from the same foundry. See Appendix D for more information.

Templates

In the course of creating documents, you're likely to evolve templates that you want to use over and over. A template is a document that serves as a preformatted starting place for new documents of similar design — for example, each issue of a magazine probably starts from a template. Although the optimal approach is to design a template before creating actual documents, the truth is that no one can foresee all possibilities. Even if you create a template (and you should — with style sheets, colors, H&J sets, standing text and artwork, and master pages intended for use in all new documents), you can expect to modify your template as your work on real documents creates the need for modifications and additions.

In QuarkXPress, the only difference between a template and a document is that a template forces you to use Save As rather than Save in the File menu, so that you do not overwrite the template but instead create new documents based on it. QuarkXPress supports the use of templates over a network. Each time a template is accessed, the user accessing it is given a local copy. Thus, multiple users can access the template simultaneously, and even a single user can have several documents based on the same template open at once.

The Mac and Windows versions of QuarkXPress read each other's template files, so you can have master templates available for all your users in a cross-platform environment. Just make sure your template files have names that end in .QXT if you want to use them in Windows.

For more information about using templates, see Chapter 33.

Master pages

Although templates should include the master pages you need for a project, occasionally you'll need to use a master page from an existing document. Chapter 33 describes a technique for sharing master pages among documents.

Libraries

QuarkXPress libraries are a great aid to keeping documents consistent. Because libraries are stored in their own files, common libraries can be put in common folders. You can even access them across the network. If you want, you can keep an alias to a library elsewhere on the network or on your computer's local drive.

For many people, libraries offer more flexibility than just linking to graphics files, because all attributes applied to graphics and their picture boxes are also stored in the library. Graphics in libraries also retain any links — either regular import links or Publish and Subscribe (Mac) or OLE (Windows) links — so you don't have to worry about this information being lost for graphics stored in libraries.

Unfortunately, QuarkXPress libraries on Macs and Windows are not compatible, so you'll need to maintain two sets of libraries if you work in a cross-platform environment.

Style sheets, colors, H&J sets, lists, and dashes and stripes

When you're working on longer projects in a workgroup, you'll generally want to keep style sheet, color, H&J, list, and dash and stripe definitions consistent across documents. This consistency helps you ensure that corporate-identity colors, typography, and design are used instead of someone's approximations. These definitions are usually included in templates, but they may need to be updated or added to with information from existing documents.

To append a definition, you use the global Append dialog box (File ➪ Append, or Option+⌘+ A or Ctrl+Alt+A), shown in Figure 31-5. You can also append one type of definition at a time using the Append buttons in the Style Sheets, Colors, H&Js, Lists, or Dashes & Stripes dialog boxes, all available through the Edit menu.

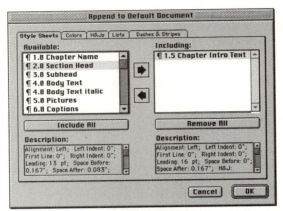

Figure 31-5: The Append dialog box lets you share style sheets, colors, H&J sets, lists, and dashes and stripes among documents.

Tip

When you append any type of definition (such as style sheet), any definitions it specifies (such as a color) are appended as well.

The Append dialog box lets you selectively import style sheet, color, H&J, list, and dash and stripe definitions from existing documents, templates, or libraries. If a document is open when you use Append, the definitions are imported into that document and saved with it. If no documents are open, the definitions are stored in the XPress Preferences file and included with all new documents. If you want all users to have the same default style sheets, colors, H&J sets, lists, and dashes and stripes included with all new documents, you can share the XPress Preferences file, as described earlier in this chapter.

Cross-Reference

For more information about appending colors, style sheets, H&J sets, lists, and dashes and stripes, see Chapters 8, 17, 28, 32, and 34.

Print styles

Print styles store information about output settings that are specific to QuarkXPress. These are handy to share when you want to be sure that everyone is printing the same documents the same way—whether it's color-separated film at a service bureau or black-and-white laser prints with graphics suppressed for text proofing. You may have many print styles for use with different projects and printers. After you figure out the print settings that work, you can share them with other users.

Print styles aren't saved in preferences and can't be appended. Rather, you can export them from one copy of QuarkXPress and create a file that you can share with other users. The other users import the print style. To do this, use the Import and Export buttons in the Print Styles dialog box (Edit ➪ Print Styles).

The file extension difference

Windows QuarkXPress and Mac QuarkXPress can append each other's style sheet, color, H&J, lists, and dashes and stripes definitions. To ensure that Windows QuarkXPress displays your Mac QuarkXPress files in the Append dialog box, be sure to select the file type All File Types, or add the extension .QXD to the Mac QuarkXPress document's file name.

The difference between All Append Sources and Display All Files is that All Append Sources displays only files with the .QXD, .QXT, .QXL, and .ASV file extensions. That's fine if you're in a Windows-only environment, because Windows QuarkXPress automatically adds these file extensions to the files you create.

But Mac QuarkXPress doesn't add such file extensions, so to display Mac files in the Windows QuarkXPress Append dialog box, you need to have Display All Files selected as the file type. (On Mac QuarkXPress, the Append dialog box shows all Mac-created QuarkXPress documents, templates, libraries, and auto-saved files, as well as all PC-created files — those without a Mac file type and file creator ID embedded in them — as long as they have an acceptable file extension.)

 Print style files are the same on both platforms, so you can import print styles from Mac to Windows and vice versa. In Windows QuarkXPress, make sure that you have selected All Files as the file type, or that you have added the extension .QPJ to the print style file on the Mac, so that it appears in the import dialog box.

Summary

When you're working in a workgroup, it's important that all members of the group have appropriate access to all the files they need. This includes:

✦ Software and utilities

✦ XPress Preferences files, color management profiles, kerning tables, and auxiliary dictionaries

✦ Graphics, text files, and fonts

✦ Templates (including master pages) and style sheets, colors, H&J sets, lists, and dashes and stripes

✦ Libraries and print styles

In a cross-platform environment, some of these project elements can be shared, whereas others need to be re-created for the other platform.

✦　　✦　　✦

Using Style Sheets Effectively

Style sheets are like macros for formatting text. With one click you can change all the attributes of a selected paragraph: the typeface, alignment, leading, indents, and more. And, with one click, you can change the formatting of selected characters and words: the typeface, size, color, scaling, tracking, type style, and more. After you apply style sheets, you can apply additional formatting, called *local formatting,* to text as necessary.

Any lengthy projects that include a lot of text — such as annual reports, newsletters, magazines, and books — should rely on style sheets almost exclusively for formatting text. Style sheets provide many advantages, including the following:

✦ They guarantee quick, consistent formatting across projects.

✦ Their specifications can be updated to automatically reformat text.

✦ In a workgroup, carefully named style sheets can communicate to other users how to format text.

When you start using style sheets, you'll wonder how you got along without them.

Planning Style Sheets

If you work alone, even on a continuing project such as a newsletter, you can create style sheets on the fly and name them whatever you want. And you may only have style sheets for the most obvious needs: headlines, bylines, and body text, for example. But in a workgroup, when multiple users are working on the same project, it's important that you carefully consider the style sheets you create and how you name them. This way, it will be obvious from a look at the Style Sheets palette which style sheets go where—and if any formatting, anywhere in the document gets messed up, it's easy to restore with one click. Figure 32-1 shows the difference between a rough set of style sheets and a well-considered set.

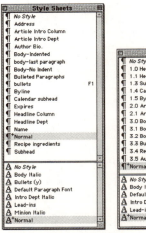 

Figure 32-1: While developing a new template, the graphic designer worked up the rough set of style sheets at left. But before putting the new template to work, a production artist helped fine-tune the set for use by other designers.

Formatting sample text

Before you start creating style sheets, you have to know what kind of text you're dealing with and how you want it to look. You can do this with the first issue of a publication, an early draft, or even dummy text. Try to include all the basic elements that will appear in the document—but don't worry if you can't account for every situation. You can always add more style sheets later.

Elements in a newspaper, for example, include body text, headlines, bylines, captions, and page numbers (folios). In addition, lead text, pull-quotes, biographies, subheads, sidebar heads, bulleted lists, and other more specialized types of formatting may be necessary. You might want to use a character style sheet to format end-of-story dingbats or to format all your company's acronyms in italics.

Make sure the length of the sample text you're formatting is representative of the final text. You don't want to base formatting on the best-case scenario (such as a two-word headline) rather than a worst-case scenario (such as a two-line headline). In a newsletter, you might have distinct formatting for the following elements:

✦ The headline

✦ The *kicker* (the small headline above the headline that identifies the type of story)

✦ The byline

✦ The body lead (which has a drop cap but otherwise is like the body text)

✦ The body text

✦ Captions

✦ Folios (page numbers), which typically run at the top or bottom of each page

✦ The publication name, which typically runs at the top or bottom of each page

✦ The publication date, which typically runs at the top or bottom of each page

✦ Subheads

✦ Sidebar heads

✦ Drop-cap character formatting

✦ End-of-story dingbat formatting

 Tip Some of these elements, like the folios and page headers, may be included on your master pages. But that doesn't mean they don't require style sheets, especially if a workgroup is using your templates. If formatting is inadvertently messed up, a click on a style sheet can bring it back in line quickly.

After you've defined the formatting for the basic elements of your publication, you'll know what style sheets you need. Any elements with any differences in formatting, no matter how small, should have a different style sheet. This guarantees consistency.

Deciding on style sheet names

Creating a set of style sheets that's easy for anyone to use depends on clear naming conventions. Names that mean something to you — heads, heads2, body, body2, and so on — may not be as clear to other users in your workgroup. (*You* might even forget what they mean.)

The based-on advantage

When you create style sheets for a document, you'll probably have several similar styles, and some may be variations of others. For example, you might have a body text style plus a style for bulleted lists that is based on the body text style. Fortunately, QuarkXPress uses a technique called *based-on formatting* in its styles. You can tell QuarkXPress to base the Bulleted Text style on the Body Text style, in which you defined typeface, point size, leading, justification, hyphenation, indentation, tabs, and other attributes. You then modify the Bulleted Text style to accommodate bullets — by changing the indentation, for example.

The great thing about based-on formatting is that later, if you decide to change the typeface in Body Text, the typeface automatically changes in Bulleted Text and in all other styles that you created or edited based on Body Text — saving you a lot of work in maintaining consistency of styles.

To start thinking about names, print out your sample document. Using your printout, define groups of style sheets that go together: heads, subheads, and details heads, for example, or lead-ins and body text. As obvious as it seems to name your headline style sheet something as simple as *Heads,* this is not what you want to do. The problem is that QuarkXPress can only list style sheets alphabetically in the Style Sheets palette. So your palette ends up containing a jumbled list of styles that you may need to scroll through to find your next style, as shown in Figure 32-2.

Figure 32-2: A long list of style sheets, listed alphabetically, becomes confusing in the Style Sheets palette.

But there is a way to organize style sheets in the palette: Simply include numbers in the names. In this way, you can create a hierarchy within the Style Sheets palette. If your document includes only a few style sheets, you might number the style sheets in order of use: 1 Headline, 2 Kicker, 3 Byline, 4 Lead Paragraph, 5 Body Text, and 6 Author Bio, for example. If your document is more complex, including many variations of standard formatting, you might include decimals with the numbers: 1.0 Heads, 1.1 Subheads, 1.2 Details Heads, and so on. This gives you the luxury of inserting additional style sheets without having to renumber your existing styles. If you need to go into double digits on your style sheets names, be sure to include zeros with the names: 01, 02, 03, . . . 10, 11, 12, and so on. Figure 32-3 shows a set of numbered style sheets with names that indicate their usage.

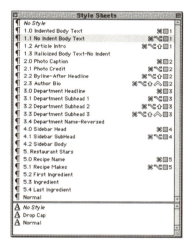

Figure 32-3: Preceding style sheet names with numbers lets you create a hierarchy in the Style Sheets palette.

Some designers are tempted to name style sheets according to *their* specifications: 12-point Helvetica or 36-point Univers. These names, however, are only useful to a person who knows what those specifications mean in relation to the template. The *designer* may know that 36-point Univers is for heads, but another user of the template may not.

Looking at your style sheet options

While creating your style sheet strategy, it helps to know what your options are. You can, for example, embed character style sheets in paragraph style sheets, which gives you the option to change the typeface used in a group of style sheets with one quick change. Your options include the following:

✦ Creating paragraph style sheets to change all the formatting of selected paragraphs.

✦ Creating character style sheets to change the formatting of selected characters or words.

✦ Deriving character attributes for paragraph style sheets in one of two ways: by simply specifying attributes in the style sheet or by embedding a character style sheet.

✦ Basing one style sheet on the attributes of another. For example, if the only difference between your body text style sheet and your bulleted text style sheet is the indent, you can quickly create the bulleted style sheet by basing it on the body text style sheet.

✦ Assigning keyboard commands to both types of style sheets for quick application.

✦ Importing style sheets from a word processor, along with formatted text, if you want. See Chapter 11 for more on this.

Using Default Styles: Normal and No Style

QuarkXPress documents always include three "style sheets" by default: Normal paragraph style, Normal character style, and No Style. We put *style sheets* in quotes because No Style is, as it sounds, not really a style sheet. When you're creating and using style sheets in QuarkXPress, it's important to understand why these three options are there and how to use them. (Actually, if you're using style sheets effectively, you're not likely to use *any* of them.)

Normal paragraph style sheet

The Normal paragraph style sheet is the default style sheet provided with all QuarkXPress documents. If you create a new text box or text path, and then start typing, the Normal style sheet is automatically applied to the text. If you import unformatted text into a text box, Normal is applied as well. In this way, Normal is considered to be the default text formatting.

The Normal paragraph style sheet has the following characteristics:

✦ The formatting is basic: left alignment, automatic leading, tabs at every half-inch, no indents.

✦ The character attributes — by default, 12-point Helvetica on Mac and 12-point Arial in Windows — are actually specified by the Normal character style sheet, which is permanently embedded in the Normal paragraph style sheet.

✦ You can edit paragraph attributes of the Normal paragraph style sheet. To edit its character attributes, you need to edit the Normal character style sheet (which you can do while editing the paragraph style sheet).

✦ You can edit the Normal paragraph style sheet for all new documents by editing it when no documents are open.

Normal character style sheet

The Normal *character* style sheet's primary purpose is to give the Normal *paragraph* style sheet its character attributes. The Normal character style sheet has the following characteristics:

✦ The default formatting is 12-point Helvetica on the Mac and 12-point Arial in Windows with no modifications to the scale, baseline shift, tracking, or type style.

✦ The Normal character style sheet is permanently embedded in the Normal paragraph style sheet — the only way to change the character attributes of the Normal paragraph style sheet is to edit the Normal character style sheet.

✦ You can apply it to selected characters and embed it in other paragraph style sheets.

✦ You can edit the Normal character style sheet for all new documents by editing it when no documents are open.

No Style

No Style is not a style sheet — it's more like the absence of one. When it comes to applying style sheets, No Style represents a clean slate because:

✦ When you apply a style sheet to text bearing No Style, all existing formatting is wiped out and replaced with the precise specifications in the style sheet.

✦ When you apply a new style sheet to a paragraph in Normal (or any other style sheet), any local formatting in that paragraph (such as bold words or adjustments in leading) is preserved.

No Style can be a good thing or a bad thing, depending on your perspective. Sometimes, you want to maintain local formatting when applying style sheets, so starting with No Style is undesirable. Other times, you want to cleanly apply your style sheets, so starting with No Style *is* desirable. Unfortunately, there's no middle ground in QuarkXPress — you can't maintain some local attributes and not others. So, often you need to apply No Style first for a clean style sheet application, and then reapply the local formatting.

QuarkXPress provides a No Style for paragraphs and a No Style for characters. When No Style is applied to a paragraph, and you apply a new paragraph style sheet, all local formatting in the paragraph — including any character style sheets applied — is wiped out.

Tip   QuarkXPress provides a handy shortcut for applying No Style, then applying a new style sheet — this is a clean apply of a style sheet. Simply Option+click or Alt+click a style sheet name in the Style Sheets palette.

Avoiding Normal and No Style

The mark of a sloppy document is often liberal use of local formatting piled on top of text sporting Normal and No Style. This is typical of shorter pieces—ads, signs, short brochures—but it's a bad idea for longer projects or projects that go through periodic revisions. The problems arise because of the following:

✦ Because word processors have a Normal paragraph style sheet, if you import text with style sheets, you end up having to handle conflicting versions of Normal. If you don't use Normal, you don't have to care about the conflict.

✦ Normal retains local formatting. So if you apply a new style sheet to text in Normal, any formatting that has been changed doesn't pick up attributes from the new style sheet (for example, if you already centered the text, it stays centered). Unfortunately, this is often undesirable because generally you want the text to be formatted exactly as the style sheet specifies. The only way out of this is to apply No Style first (or Option+click or Alt+click the style sheet in the Style Sheets palette). What this means is that you can't quickly and cleanly apply style sheets with keyboard commands alone—you have to rely on the mouse and the Style Sheets palette.

✦ The Normal paragraph style sheet is just one style sheet, so if you're using it, you should only be using it on text with one set of formatting such as all body copy. That way, if the body copy specifications change, you can just edit Normal. This means Normal should not be on any heads, bylines, subheads, or special treatment to introductory paragraphs.

✦ Normal cannot be renamed, so it's harder to fit it into a well-thought-out naming scheme for style sheets.

✦ If most of your body copy is in Normal, and your heads and subheads also have Normal applied (with local formatting), when you edit your body copy in Normal, you may inadvertently change the heads and subheads as well.

✦ Using No Style is even worse than using Normal. For one thing, if you accidentally click on another style sheet in the Style Sheets palette, all your carefully applied local formatting is lost. Also, you can't automatically update formatting by editing a style sheet—because it's not a style sheet.

Although Normal has its place (text has to look like something by default!) and No Style does, too (using it is the only way to cleanly apply a new style sheet), a document that uses style sheets effectively should have few instances of either one.

Local formatting

When you're dealing with style sheets, the concept of local formatting comes up often. *Local formatting* is formatting you've applied to text that is in addition to the formatting specified by the style sheet. For example, if the Normal paragraph style sheet is applied to a paragraph, and then you center the paragraph, the Centered paragraph alignment is considered to be local formatting. Many shorter documents consist almost entirely of local formatting—and that's okay. It is not, however, okay for longer documents, especially those produced in workgroups. Without style sheets, there is no way to guarantee consistency in locally formatted documents. That said, it is almost inevitable that documents will have some local formatting. For example, you might track a paragraph slightly to improve the rag.

Working with Style Sheets

All the style sheet creating and modification you will do starts in the Style Sheets dialog box. To open it, choose Edit ⇨ Style Sheets; you can also press Shift+F11 or ⌘+click or Ctrl+click on the Style Sheets palette. The Style Sheets dialog box gives you access to the two dialog boxes where the actual style sheet creation occurs: Edit Paragraph Style Sheet and Edit Character Style Sheet.

When you create style sheets, they are all listed in the Style Sheets palette and in the Character Style Sheets and Paragraph Style Sheets submenus of the Style menu.

Tip If you create style sheets with no documents open, the style sheets become program defaults and are included with all new documents. If you create style sheets with a document open, they're saved only with that document.

Understanding the Style Sheets dialog box

The Style Sheets dialog box, shown in Figure 32-4, provides all the options you need for editing paragraph and character style sheets.

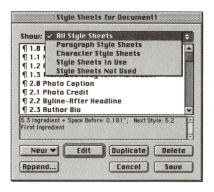

Figure 32-4: The Style Sheets dialog box for creating and editing style sheets.

Using the Show menu

The Show menu lets you specify which style sheets are listed in the Style Sheets dialog box:

✦ All Style Sheets lists all your character and paragraph style sheets.

✦ Paragraph Style Sheets lists only paragraph style sheets.

✦ Character Style Sheets lists only character style sheets.

✦ Style Sheets In Use lists only style sheets applied to text in the active document.

✦ Style Sheets Not Used lists only style sheets that are not applied to text in the active document.

Choosing Style Sheets Not Used is helpful for cleaning up the style sheets list in a document. You can look through the list of unused style sheets, decide which ones don't belong in the document or that you're never likely to use, and then delete them.

Looking at your editing options

Your options for editing style sheets in the Style Sheets dialog box are as follows:

✦ **New:** This option is a menu that lets you specify whether to create a new paragraph style sheet or a character style sheet. You can create a new style sheet by specifying all the formatting, by using the attributes of the currently selected text in the document, or by basing the new style sheet on an existing style sheet.

On the Mac, click the New button quickly to bypass the menu and create a new paragraph style sheet. In Windows, you have to use the New button's pop-up menu.

✦ **Edit:** This option lets you change the name and attributes of a style sheet selected in the list.

✦ **Duplicate:** This option copies all the attributes of an existing paragraph or character style sheet and gives the duplicate style sheet the name *Copy of style*. You can then change any attribute settings, including the style sheet name.

✦ **Delete:** This option lets you delete an existing paragraph style sheet or character style sheet. This option is grayed out when Normal is selected because you cannot delete the Normal style.

If you try to delete a paragraph style sheet or character style sheet that has been applied to text, an alert displays. You can then choose a replacement style sheet to be applied to the text, or you can delete the style sheet and have No Style applied to the affected text.

✦ **Append:** This option lets you copy one or more style sheets from another QuarkXPress document or library.

✦ **Save:** This option lets you save all the style sheet additions, deletions, and changes you make in the Style Sheets dialog box. You *must* save your work when leaving the Style Sheets dialog box for changes to take effect.

✦ **Cancel:** This option instructs QuarkXPress to ignore all style sheet additions, deletions, and changes you made in the Style Sheets dialog box since you last opened it.

The Style Sheets palette provides a context menu, shown in Figure 32-5, for you to Edit, Duplicate, or Delete a style sheet. To display the menu, Control+click or right-click on a style sheet name. To create a new paragraph style sheet, Control+click or right-click in the top portion of the palette and choose New. To create a new character style sheet, perform the same steps in the lower portion of the palette.

Figure 32-5: The context menu in the Style Sheets palette.

Understanding the Edit Paragraph Style Sheet dialog box

If you choose New ⇨ Paragraph, or you select a paragraph style sheet and click Edit or Duplicate, the Edit Paragraph Style Sheet dialog box shown in Figure 32-6 displays. This dialog box contains the General pane, which provides several basic style sheet controls, and the Formats, Tabs, and Rules panes, in which you define the actual attributes of the style sheets.

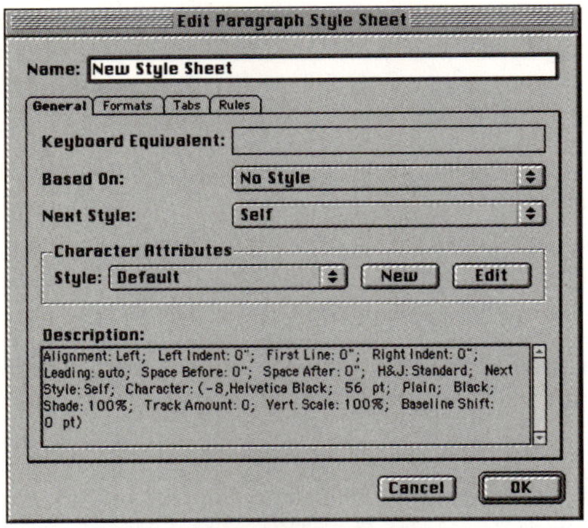

Figure 32-6: The Edit Paragraph Style Sheet dialog box.

Name

This field defaults to New Style Sheet if you selected New. Remember to enter names that indicate a style sheet's purpose, such as Column Heads, rather than a style sheet's attributes.

Keyboard Equivalent

This field lets you press a *hot key,* or a keyboard shortcut, that you can use to apply the style sheet. You can use a combination of modifier keys along with keys on the numeric keypad or the function keys on an extended keyboard.

The allowable shortcuts differ on Mac and Windows.

The allowable hot keys differ in Mac and Windows as follows:

+ **Mac:** You may use the Option, Shift, Control, and ⌘ keys with the number keys on the numeric keypad. For the F1 through F15 function keys on an extended keyboard, you may use only Shift, Control, and ⌘ — not Option.

+ **Windows:** You may use the Ctrl and Shift keys both with the numbers on the numeric keypad and with the function keys F1 through F12.

Note that a Mac QuarkXPress document moved to Windows will lose any hot keys that include Option or Control. Hot keys that use ⌘ will use Ctrl instead on Windows, while Windows QuarkXPress files with Ctrl in a hot key will be translated to use ⌘ instead when transferred to the Mac.

See the sidebar "Notes about keyboard equivalents," later in this chapter, for important notes.

Based On

The Based On menu lists No Style (the default) along with all your other paragraph style sheets. The Based On option lets you select an existing style sheet as a starting point for building a new style sheet. For example, if all the attributes of the new style sheet are the same as an existing style sheet — except for the tab settings — you can select the existing style sheet, then change the tabs in this one. If you modify the style upon which this style sheet is based, the changes will affect both style sheets — except the tab settings, which are different.

Next Style

This Next Style menu comes in handy when you're entering text directly into QuarkXPress because it lets you establish a chain of linked style sheets. For example, you can specify that a headline style sheet is followed by a byline style sheet, which is followed by a body text style sheet. The body text style sheet is generally followed by itself. Here's how this nifty feature works: As you type text, each time you hit return, QuarkXPress automatically applies the Next Style. (Unfortunately, Next Style only works as you're typing in QuarkXPress — it doesn't function as an autoformat feature for imported text.)

Character Attributes area

Paragraph style sheets always contain character attributes. These are applied to all the characters in the paragraph each time you apply the paragraph style (except where you've applied character style sheets or local formatting). There are two methods for assigning character attributes to paragraph style sheets:

✦ **Setting character attributes for this paragraph style sheet, independent of character style sheets.** To do this, select Default from the Style menu, then click Edit to specify your character attributes.

✦ **Embedding a character style sheet by selecting one of your existing character style sheets from the Style menu.** This lets you specify character attributes — font, size, style, and so on — through a character style sheet that you've already created. If you modify the character style sheet, the changes will affect the paragraph style sheets that it's embedded in.

Tip

To create a new character style sheet for this paragraph style sheet, click New. You can also select a character style sheet from the Style menu and click Edit — but recognize that you're changing the entire character style sheet, not just an instance used by this paragraph style sheet.

Notes about keyboard equivalents

Whether you're specifying keyboard equivalents for paragraph style sheets or character style sheets, keep the following in mind:

✦ If you assign a function key (F1 through F15 on the Mac, F1 through F12 in Windows), with a modifier key like ⌘ or Ctrl, as a keyboard equivalent for a style sheet, the setting will replace the QuarkXPress default setting for that function key — but only when text is selected with the Content tool. For example, if you use F7 for a style sheet's keyboard equivalent, you won't be able to Show/Hide Guides with F7 if text is selected with the Content tool, but the Show/Hide Guide shortcut will work normally if you have, say, the Zoom tool selected. On the Mac, which never uses the Control key as a modifier for function keys, you can add the Control key to distinguish style sheet keyboard equivalents from built-in QuarkXPress commands.

✦ On the Mac, the Keyboard control panel will try to launch when you choose a function key that's already in use by the Mac OS or QuarkXPress. You can turn off that feature in the dialog box that appears.

✦ If you used numbers in your style sheet names to establish a hierarchy, you can synchronize the numbers to the style sheet keyboard shortcuts. For example, you might have Ctrl+1 for the style sheet 1 Headline and Ctrl+2 for the style sheet 2 Subhead. Or, if your style sheets are more sophisticated, you might have Ctrl+1 for 1.0 Headline, Ctrl+Alt+1 for 1.1 Subhead, and so on.

✦ If you're creating style sheets for a template that will be used in a cross-platform environment, use only the ⌘ or Ctrl and the Shift keys.

Formatting panes

You'll find three other panes in addition to the General pane in the Edit Paragraph Style Sheet dialog box: Formats, Tabs, and Rules. You can use them in any order and ignore ones that don't apply to the current style sheet (often, Rules and Tabs are ignored). The Formats, Tabs, and Rules panes let you invoke the appropriate controls for each major part of the style sheet, as follows:

✦ **Formats:** Here you can select formats for paragraph attributes such as leading, H&J, and indentation.

✦ **Tabs:** These options let you define tab stops and tab types.

✦ **Rules:** This is where you can choose options for ruling lines associated with paragraphs.

For more information about the Formats pane, see Chapter 16. For the Tabs pane, see Chapter 19. And for Rules, see Chapter 23.

Understanding the Edit Character Style Sheet dialog box

If you choose New ➪ Character, or you select a character style sheet and click Edit or Duplicate, the Edit Character Style Sheet dialog box shown in Figure 32-7 displays. The options work as follows:

✦ **Name:** The Name field is where you name a new character style sheet, or rename an existing one. In our example, we've created a character style named *End-of-Story Dingbat.*

✦ **Keyboard Equivalent:** This field lets you pick a *hot key,* or a keyboard shortcut, that you can use to apply the style sheet, as described earlier.

✦ **Based On:** This menu allows you to base one character style sheet on an existing character style sheet. If you modify a style sheet upon which another style is based, the changes you make affect *both* style sheets. The default for Based On is No Style.

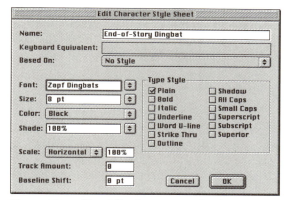

Figure 32-7: The Edit Character Style Sheet dialog box.

Creating Style Sheets

If you're planning to embed character style sheets within paragraph style sheets — that is, to derive the character attributes for a paragraph style sheet from an existing character style sheet — you should plan to create your character style sheets first. Likewise, if you're planning to use Based On, create the most basic style sheets first so they're available in the menus. *Remember:* If you create style sheets with no documents open, they become program defaults and are included in all new documents.

STEPS: Creating a character style sheet

1. If you're in a document that already contains the formatting for the character style sheet, highlight a word in that text. If not, make sure you know all the character attributes the style sheet is supposed to include.

2. Choose Edit ➪ Style Sheets, or press F11.

3. Click the New button to display the menu, then choose Character.

Tip

For a shortcut to creating a new character style sheet, remember you can Control+click or right-click the lower portion of the Style Sheets palette to display the context menu. Choose New to go directly to an Edit Character Style Sheet dialog box.

4. Type a name in the Name field.

5. Click in the Keyboard Equivalent field, then press the keys for the keyboard shortcut you want to use.

6. If you want to base this style sheet on an existing one, choose an option from the Based On menu.

7. If you have highlighted formatted text, all the character attribute options are already set for you. You might skim through to confirm them, though. If not, change any of the settings for Font, Size, Type Style, and so on.

8. Click OK to create the character style sheet, then click Save to save it with the document (or with the program defaults).

STEPS: Creating a paragraph style sheet

1. If you're in a document that already contains the formatting for the paragraph style sheet, click in a paragraph to select it. If not, make sure you know all the paragraph and character attributes the style sheet is supposed to include.

2. Choose Edit ➪ Style Sheets, or press F11.

3. Click the New button to display the menu, then choose Paragraph.

Tip

For a shortcut to creating a new paragraph style sheet, remember you can Control+click or right-click the lower portion of the Style Sheets palette to display the context menu. Choose New to go directly to an Edit Paragraph Style Sheet dialog box.

4. Type a name in the Name field.

5. Click in the Keyboard Equivalent field, then press the keys for the keyboard shortcut you want to use.

6. If you want to base this style sheet on an existing one, choose an option from the Based On menu.

7. In the Character Attributes area, leave the setting at Default to specify attributes specific to this paragraph style sheet. Click Edit to confirm the attributes in a selected paragraph or to specify them from scratch. When you're finished, click OK. To embed a character style sheet, choose an existing one from the Style menu or click New to create one.

8. Use the Formats, Tabs, and Rules panes to format your style sheet appropriately. If you've selected an appropriately formatted paragraph in the document, all you need to do is confirm these settings. (For example, if you're creating a body text style sheet, you may have forgotten to apply the correct H&J set to the sample paragraph.)

9. Click OK to create the character style sheet, then click Save to save it with the document (or with the program defaults).

Tip

At the bottom of the General pane on the Edit Paragraph Style Sheet dialog box is a description of the attributes for the selected style. This is a handy way to see what the current settings are, as well as to verify that you set the options you intended. The same description is also displayed in the Style Sheets dialog box when a style sheet is selected.

Modifying style sheets

You can make changes to a style sheet definition any time. These changes are automatically applied to text with that style sheet applied, except where local formatting exists.

To edit a style sheet, choose Edit ➪ Style Sheets, or press F11. Select the style sheet, then click Edit. As a shortcut to this point, Control+click or right-click a style sheet name anywhere in the Style Sheets palette, then choose Edit from the context menu, as shown in Figure 32-8. Either way, you end up in the Edit Paragraph Style Sheet or Edit Character Style Sheet dialog box for that style sheet. Make any changes you want, click OK, then click Save.

Figure 32-8: Choosing Edit from the Style Sheets palette's context menu.

Comparing style sheets

The Style Sheets dialog box lets you display a quick comparison of two style sheets, which can be helpful when you're creating and editing lots of them. To do this, select the first style sheet, then ⌘+click or Ctrl+click to select the second one. Press Option or Alt to change the Append button to Compare, then click it. The Compare dialog box displays the differences between the style sheets in bold.

Applying Style Sheets

Applying style sheets is easy—you select text, then select a style sheet. To apply a paragraph style sheet, you can click in a single paragraph or highlight any portion of a range of paragraphs. To apply a character style sheet, highlight the characters. (To select all the text in a story, choose Edit ⇨ Select All, or use ⌘+A or Ctrl+A.) You have three options for applying the style sheet from here:

✦ **Style menu:** You can choose a style sheet from the Character Style Sheet or Paragraph Style Sheet submenu of the Style menu. This is pretty inefficient but can be useful for applying a single style sheet when you've already got your hand on the mouse and you don't have the Style Sheets palette open.

✦ **The Style Sheets palette, shown in Figure 32-9:** Choose View ⇨ Show Style Sheets or press F11 to open this palette, and keep it open any time you're applying a lot of style sheets. To apply a style sheet to selected text, all you need to do is click on one.

✦ **A keyboard shortcut:** If you defined a keyboard shortcut for a style sheet, press it to apply it to selected text. Although this option is the fastest method, it's best for very commonly used style sheets because you have to remember the shortcuts or consult the Style Sheets palette.

Style Sheets palette anatomy

The Style Sheets palette is divided into two sections: paragraph style sheets on the top and character style sheets on the bottom. You can drag the divider line between the two to show or hide more of each. Within each section, all your style sheets are listed in alphanumeric order.

If the palette is wide enough, any keyboard shortcuts you assigned display next to the style sheet names. (If necessary, widen the palette by dragging the lower-right corner.) If a keyboard shortcut includes a key on the numeric keypad, it's indicated by a small box (Mac) or the abbreviation *KP* (Windows), as shown in Figure 32-10.

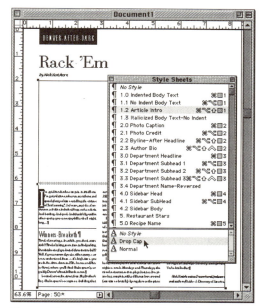

Figure 32-9: The Style Sheets palette.

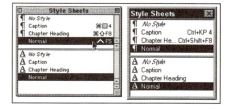

Figure 32-10: The keyboard shortcuts shown here include keys on the numeric keypad (Mac at left, Windows at right).

The sign of local formatting

Depending on where the text came from and how it was previously formatted, when you apply a style sheet it doesn't always take completely. This is because of local formatting. When a style sheet is already applied to text, and you then apply additional formatting to the text, that is called *local formatting*. QuarkXPress thinks that any local formatting you apply is purposeful and should be maintained.

Say, for example, you have a paragraph in Normal style sheet and you change the font used in that paragraph. Then you apply a paragraph style sheet that specifies a different font. What do you get? You get the font applied through local formatting. You can tell this by looking at the Style Sheets palette — a little plus sign displays next to the name of the style sheet you just applied, as shown in Figure 32-11. This plus sign indicates that local formatting still exists in the selected text.

Figure 32-11: When selected text has any formatting that deviates from the specifications of its style sheet, a plus sign displays next to the style sheet name in the Style Sheets palette. In this example, the book name is in plain face so it stands out from the italic introductory text.

If what you really want is the font specified in the style sheet you just applied, you need to perform a *clean apply* of the style sheet. To do this, first apply No Style to the text by clicking it in the paragraph or character section of the Style Sheets palette. Then reapply the new style sheet. (This also wipes out any local formatting that you do need, such as italics on a book name, so you'll need to reapply that.) The shortcut for a clean apply is to Option+click or Alt+click a style sheet name in the palette. Unfortunately, there is no way to get a clean apply when using your style sheets' keyboard shortcuts.

The plus sign can be an indication that something has gone horribly wrong — someone has entirely changed the proper formatting of text. Or it can be an indication of a simple change such as tracking. There's no way to know. Often, you have to perform a clean apply just to see what you should have had. Style sheet purists consider the plus sign insidious and shoot for a document with almost none. This means all text is perfectly formatted according to style sheets. Others don't care about the plus sign.

Note   When you apply character style sheets to a few selected words within a paragraph, and then you select that paragraph, you'll see the plus sign next to the paragraph style sheet name. This is because the application of character style sheets is considered local formatting on top of the paragraph style sheet.

Managing Style Sheet Sets

QuarkXPress lets you import style sheets into a document from another document, from a library, or from an XPress Tags file. You can also import style sheets from a word processor when you import a formatted text file.

Cross-Reference   For information about importing style sheets with a text file from a word processor, see Chapter 11.

Choosing a file to append from

Any time you need to add style sheets from another QuarkXPress file to a document, choose File ➪ Append, or press ⌘+Option+A or Ctrl+Alt+A. You can also click
the Append button in the Style Sheets dialog box. A directory dialog box displays,
allowing you to choose a QuarkXPress file from which to append. Select any
QuarkXPress document, library, or XPress Tags file (all of which need to be from
version 3.3 or greater). Then the Append dialog box displays, as shown in Figure
32-12. (If you get to Append from the Style Sheets dialog box, your only option is to
append style sheets, so the Append dialog box you see is a little more limited.)

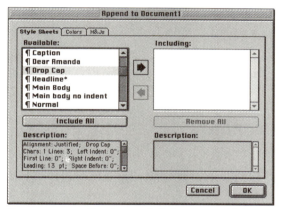

Figure 32-12: The Append dialog box, which
displays after you select a QuarkXPress file to
append attributes from.

If no documents are open, you can append style sheets to the QuarkXPress
program default settings. Then these style sheets will be included with all new
documents.

Selecting style sheets to append

The Available list in the Append dialog box lists all the style sheets defined in the
source file (the file from which you're appending). You can select style sheets in the
Available list and click the right-facing arrow to send them to the Including list:

✦ To select an individual style sheet, click on it.

✦ To select multiple style sheets, ⌘+click or Ctrl+click them.

✦ To select a continuous range of style sheets, click the first style sheet in the
range, then Shift+click the last one.

✦ To select all the style sheets, click the Include All button. (This not only
selects all the style sheets but sends them to the Including list automatically.)

When you're finished selecting style sheets and you've clicked the right-facing arrow to send them to the Including list, click OK. (If you change your mind about any style sheets in the Including list, select them and click the left-facing arrow to send them back to the Available list.) The first thing that happens is that QuarkXPress notifies you that the style sheet will include any colors, H&J sets, and so on, that are not already in the document. This is a good thing, because otherwise the style sheet may not arrive completely, so you'll generally click OK.

At this point, you may need to resolve some conflicts between style sheets that already exist in the document and those you're appending. If you're appending all, for example, you'll almost always encounter a conflict with the Normal paragraph and character style sheets.

Tip
If you're not sure whether you want to include a style sheet, click on it to see its attributes in the Description fields at the bottom of the dialog box. To see the descriptions of two different style sheets at the same time, ⌘+click or Ctrl+click to select both at the same time. Then press Option or Alt to change the Append button to Compare. Click Compare to see both style sheets at once.

Resolving style sheet conflicts

If you append a style sheet that has the same name as a style sheet in the active document, but with different attributes, an Append Conflict dialog box appears. The attributes that differ between the two style sheets are displayed in bold as shown in Figure 32-13. The Append Conflict dialog box gives you the following options for resolving style sheet conflicts:

✦ **Rename** displays a dialog box that lets you rename the style sheet you're appending. After entering the new name, click OK. This is a good choice if you're not sure what you want to do with the two style sheets and want to decide later.

✦ **Auto-Rename** puts an asterisk at the beginning of the name of the appended style sheet — also a good choice if you want to resolve this conflict later.

✦ **Use New** causes the appended style sheet to replace the existing style sheet of the same name. This is helpful if you're appending a set of updated style sheets to a document or template.

✦ **Use Existing** keeps the existing style sheet in the document and doesn't import the new version. Use this in instances when you know the style sheet in the document is correct but you're not sure about the imported one (this is often a good choice for handling Normal).

If you're appending a set of updated style sheets, from a new template for example, you might want to handle all conflicts the same way. If that's the case, check the Repeat for All Conflicts box in the Append Conflict dialog box.

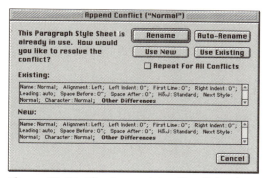

Figure 32-13: The Append Conflict dialog box.

Summary

Any time you're developing a template for a project that you have to produce more than once—especially if a workgroup will be involved—style sheets are essential. With carefully named and created style sheets, you can guarantee quick, consistent formatting from any user involved in the project.

The Style Sheets dialog box provides controls for managing all the style sheets in a document. This includes access to the Edit Paragraph Style Sheet and Edit Character Style Sheet dialog boxes, which let you create and edit style sheets. The Style Sheets palette lets you apply style sheets to selected text with a single click.

✦ ✦ ✦

Using Libraries and Templates Effectively

When you're working with long-standing clients or on continuous projects, you'll find yourself spending hours creating that perfect logo or the ideal newsletter. And you'll want to use both again, placing the logo in other documents at will and using the newsletter as a starting place for the next issue. Obviously, in this electronic world of cut-and-paste, you won't need to re-create the work. QuarkXPress provides two features to streamline the multipurposing of your content and designs: libraries and templates.

A *library* is a floating palette designed to hold formatted items such as blocks of text and graphics until you need them. A *template* is the shell of a document — the basic structure — that is used as a starting place for new documents. Using both libraries and templates provides convenient access to designs you've already created, while guaranteeing consistency among documents.

Planning Libraries and Templates

Libraries and templates are simply another kind of QuarkXPress file — easy to create and begin using. But for the best use of both, you may want to think about who will use them and how they will be used. This will help you decide on the contents and structure of your libraries and templates.

Library issues

When you're creating libraries, you don't want to jump in, create one, and then add every item you think you might use again to it. You could easily end up with too many libraries containing a confusing mish-mash of contents. First, think about the following:

✦ In general, it's best to create one library for each client or — if the client has many projects — one for each project. Although you can have multiple libraries open, figuring out which one you need can get confusing.

✦ Libraries can be opened across a network, meaning that multiple users can share the same file. If you plan to work this way, one user needs to be in charge of the library contents to be sure they remain consistent.

✦ You can give library items names, called labels, to identify them. This is particularly helpful when many users are accessing the same library.

✦ If multiple users are accessing the same library, make sure to store the file on a server that users have access to. Also, you'll need to provide the users with any fonts and graphic files used in items in the libraries.

 Libraries are one of the few QuarkXPress file types that aren't cross-platform. You can't open a Mac OS library on Windows and vice versa, so if you work in a cross-platform environment, you'll need to create two different libraries.

Take a look at libraries in action — 5280 Publishing, for example, produces *5280: Denver's Mile-High Magazine* and *Mile-High Weddings*. The art director has a library for all the ad placeholders for both magazines, because the ad sizes are the same. Then the art director has a different library for each magazine's standing artwork — pictures of the columnists, logos, and so on. All three libraries, shown in Figure 33-1, are stored on the server at the all-Mac shop so the publisher, production artist, and editors can access them. The folder containing the library also contains the fonts and graphic files used in items in the libraries. The art director updates the libraries when things change.

Figure 33-1: The library at right, Ad Placeholders, is used for two magazines, each of which has its own library: 5280 Art and Mile-High Weddings Art.

Template issues

Many graphic designers, to be honest, don't bother with templates. When they start a new issue of a newsletter or design the second in a series of brochures, they simply save over an old document. Then they delete any contents they don't want and start popping in new contents. This strategy — or lack thereof — has many pitfalls, including the following:

✦ Every document carries with it formatting and adjustments specific to its content. For example, the document might contain a spot color derived from the color of a model's lips on the cover. Or the text boxes might have been lengthened slightly or a style sheet modified to fit text from a particular story. These changes are probably not appropriate to the next issues.

✦ When you're replacing old content with new content, you can easily miss something. So you end up with last month's date on the footers, last month's writers in the credits, or even an incorrect photograph on a column.

✦ The older a document is, and the more you do to it, the more chances of corruption. If any page items become corrupt, you're carrying them around from issue to issue.

Due to these issues, you should definitely plan to create a template as soon as you have a design finalized. If it's a newsletter, for example, start with the first issue and strip out anything that isn't likely to repeat. When you create your template, keep the following in mind:

✦ Keep (or create) a master page for any type of page you might need — ever. In a newsletter, this might mean the cover, table of contents page, feature pages, and department/column pages.

✦ If your document is usually the same length, with similar content, you can leave blank pages based on master pages inside the document. If the document's length varies or has completely different content, delete the interior pages and drag new pages in — based on the appropriate master page — when you start a new issue.

✦ Make sure the *master pages* (pages that remain in the document) include headers, folios, and anything else that repeats from issue to issue.

✦ Carefully consider each item on each page. Is this specific to this issue and will it remain on this page? If so, leave it in the template. If not, put it in a library. For example, if the inside front cover of your newsletter always contains four ads, you can leave placeholder picture boxes for them. If, on the other hand, it contains a conglomeration of ads in any size, put the placeholders in a library and leave the page blank in the template.

✦ Make sure the document contains paragraph style sheets and character style sheets for any formatting you plan to use again. This means everything from headlines and author bios to table of contents listings and page footers. This guarantees that you can quickly reapply formatting without having to go back to an old document.

✦ If multiple users will use your template, pay careful attention to the way you name master pages and style sheets. (This applies to lists, H&J sets, and colors as well, but it's particularly important for these basic elements.) The names should be obvious to anyone who opens the template—not just you.

✦ Go through the document and strip out anything that was created for content specific to the current issue. This includes colors, style sheets, H&J sets, and master pages along with page items.

✦ When you name the template, include the date. That way, if you update the template, you'll know you're using the latest one.

✦ Templates are cross-platform, and they can be opened over a network. If the template will actually be used in a cross-platform environment, make sure it specifies fonts available for both Mac OS and Windows (preferably the same version of the font, from the same vendor).

When you have a document stripped down to a shell and ready for use as a template, you can go on to save it as a template. See Figure 33-2 for an example of a completed template.

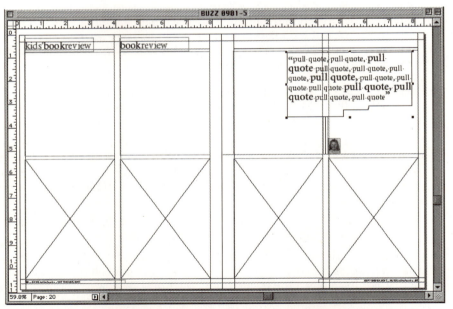

Figure 33-2: After completing a major redesign of a newsletter called *Buzz in the 'Burbs,* the graphic designer created a template from the first issue to use for the second issue.

Working with Library Files

A powerful layout-management feature that originated with QuarkXPress is the ability to create libraries of items such as text boxes, picture boxes, lines, and groups. This feature is a great aid if you reuse items throughout a set of publications. For example, you can have a library containing your corporate logos, photos, and such standard text as mastheads and postal statements.

QuarkXPress does more than let you create libraries; it lets you create multiple libraries — any or all of which may be open at a time (as long as you don't already have 25 files open). QuarkXPress also lets you group library items to make them easy to find. The libraries themselves are separate files that can reside anywhere on your hard disk (or network). Because the libraries aren't part of any document, any document can use them. After items are in a library, you can manage their order and add or remove unwanted items. The following sections show you how.

Creating libraries

Before you can use a library, you need to create one. To do this, select File ➪ New ➪ Library or press Option+⌘+N or Ctrl+Alt+N. In the New Library dialog box, shown in Figure 33-3, navigate to a location for the library file. Enter a name in the New Library field (QuarkXPress for Windows adds the .qxl extension for libraries automatically). Click Create, and a new, empty library palette displays.

Figure 33-3: Creating a library in the New Library dialog box.

You can resize the palette by selecting the resize icon in the lower-right corner, or you can click the full-size icon in the upper-right corner to have the library expand to cover the full screen (if you click that icon again, the palette returns to the original size).

Opening, closing, and saving libraries

You handle library files much the same way you handle other QuarkXPress files. The process of opening, closing, and saving libraries is covered in more detail in Chapter 4, but here's a quick recap:

✦ To open a library, use the Open dialog box (File menu) or double-click a library file at the desktop. You can recognize library files by their icon, shown in Figure 33-4, and on Windows the names have a .qxl extension. Libraries stay open until you close them — even reopening automatically when you launch QuarkXPress.

✦ To close a library, click its close box.

✦ By default, changes are saved to libraries automatically as you make them. To confirm, make sure Auto Library Save is checked in the Save pane of Application Preferences (by selecting Edit ⇨ Preferences ⇨ Preferences, or Option+Shift+⌘+Y or Ctrl+Alt+Shift+Y). Changes to libraries are always saved when you close the library or quit QuarkXPress.

Figure 33-4: The icon for a library file and the open library palette.

Working with Library Items

Libraries accept only items — not loose contents. This means you can add text boxes, picture boxes, no-content boxes, lines, text paths, and groups of any of these into a library. And these items can contain any level of formatting you desire. But you cannot include text or a picture that is not in a box in a library. All attributes applied to items — including frames, backgrounds, and colors — are retained when you copy the boxes to libraries. Pictures include all cropping, sizing, and other such information; text includes all formatting, including style sheets, H&J sets, and colors.

Libraries are especially helpful for items and contents created through a variety of special effects. For example, if you create a logo using text converted to a box, merged Bézier items, and reverse type, it's unlikely that you'll want to make it again. Or, if you drop shadow and color a word as shown in Figure 33-5, you might want to use that effect again — even if you end up entering different words. By placing such special-effects text in the library, you save yourself the work of later applying those special effects.

Figure 33-5: A special effect such as this drop shadow is ideal for placement in a library.

After copying a library item into a document, you can easily change its specific attributes to something else while retaining all the formatting of the original item. This technique is also handy for special lines like arrowheads and for picture boxes that have intricate frames, special color blends, or odd shapes.

Adding items to libraries

When a library is open, you can add items to it from any document or from any other open library. Because libraries stay open until you close them, you can add items to them as you open and close other documents and libraries.

STEPS: Adding an item to a library

1. Select the Item tool.

2. Click on the item in an open document that you want to add to the library. This can be any type of box, line, text path, or group. You can even Shift+click to select multiple items, then add them to the library as a group. (You can also click on an item in another library.)

3. Drag the selected item into the library palette. The pointer changes to a pair of eyeglasses to indicate that you can add the item to the library.

4. Release the mouse button to add the item. If you want to add the item somewhere in particular in the library, drag it around until the pointer is where you want it, as shown in Figure 33-6. Then release the mouse button.

Figure 33-6: Dragging an item from a document into an open library.

Repeat this process to add any other items to the library. The library palette displays little thumbnail versions of the items you place in it, flowing them from left to right (assuming the palette is wide enough to hold two or more items) and then from top to bottom.

Tip

In addition to dragging items into library palettes, you can cut and paste them or copy and paste them. To do this, select an item in a document or another library, and then choose Edit ⇨ Copy (⌘+C or Ctrl+C) or Edit ⇨ Cut (⌘+X or Ctrl+X). Click on the library palette to select it, then choose Edit ⇨ Paste (⌘+V or Ctrl+V).

Adding master pages to libraries

If you create a variety of similar projects, you may find that you use similar master pages. Rather than create the master pages over and over again, or copy the items from other pages, you can have a simulation of master pages on hand in a library. We say *simulation* because you can't actually store pages in libraries — but you can store all the page items, then place them in the same position on a new master page in a new document. This can be tricky because QuarkXPress offers no feature explicitly designed to perform this task. But you can move master pages by taking the following steps.

STEPS: Moving master pages to libraries

1. Open or create a library to hold the master pages.

2. Open the document that contains the master page you want to copy. Display the master page by selecting Page ⇨ Display.

3. Select the Item tool and then select all items (choose Edit ⇨ Select All or use the shortcut ⌘+A or Ctrl+A). If you plan to place the items in the same position on a new master page, jot down the X and Y coordinates showing in the Measurements palette.

4. Drag (or copy and paste) the items into an open library and release the mouse button.

5. Open the document into which you want to copy the master page (ideally, the document should have the same page size as the document from which you're copying the master page). Close the other document, if you're finished with it.

6. Insert a new blank master page in the second document.

7. Drag (or copy and paste) the library item containing the master-page items to the new master page, as shown in Figure 33-7, and position it where you want it. Choose View ⇨ Fit in Window or press ⌘+0 (zero) or Ctrl+0 (zero) to see the entire page or spread its items better.

8. Use the Document Layout palette to display the master pages, and rename the new master page so that you can remember what it contains.

Figure 33-7: Dragging master page items from a library to a new master page.

Using library items in documents

After you create and fill your libraries, it's easy to move the library items into your documents. With any tool selected, simply click on a library item and drag it into your document. You can also select an item in the library, copy it, click in the document, then paste it.

Library items always paste into documents at their original size, as shown in Figure 33-8, not the smaller version displayed in the library. After you place an item into a document, you can modify it as you do any other item.

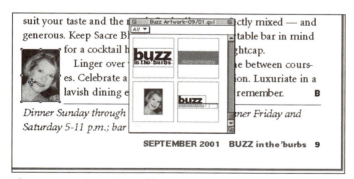

Figure 33-8: Dragging a library item into a document.

Tip

In some cases, when you add a library item to a document, you introduce fonts that aren't active — and maybe not even present on your computer. You can also add pictures for which you don't have the actual picture file. For proper display, you'll need to locate and activate the fonts used in the new items (a program like Extensis Suitcase or Adobe Type Manager might do this for you automatically if installed). For proper output, you'll need to locate any picture files as well.

Note   When you add library items to documents, all the style sheets, colors, H&J sets, list definitions, and dashes & stripes patterns used in the items are added to the QuarkXPress document as well. In the case of any name conflicts (for example, a style sheet with the same name), the items and text remain formatted as they are, but the specifications are not added.

Rearranging library items

The order of items in a library depends on where you drop them or where the pointer is when you paste them. If you want to rearrange the order, select the item you want to move, hold down the mouse button, and move the pointer to the new position in the library palette. Release the mouse button when you reach the desired location (the triangles that appear as you move the item are the insertion points).

Deleting library items

Your libraries will evolve over time as your document items change. As a result, you'll occasionally need to delete library items. To delete an item in a library, click on it to select it. Then choose Edit ⇨ Clear. If you want to use the item one last time, choose Edit ⇨ Cut (⌘+X or Ctrl+X) to remove it from the library and place it on the Clipboard. You can then paste the item into another document or library.

Labeling library items

Labels are names that you can give to library items — either because the thumbnails in the library palette are too small to see, your library palette contains too many items to scroll through, or you're just super-organized. You can give the same label to multiple items, to create a category of items such as "head shots," or you can give each item a distinct label. But you don't need to label everything — some can remain as Unlabeled. You can then limit the display of items in the library palette to those with specific labels.

Before you begin labeling, think about the labeling scheme you want to use: whether you're naming items according to their use (such as Ads or Features), content (Columnist Head Shots or Legal Text), or placement (TOC Art or Spine). Or you might use a combination of these labels. If you like things nice and tidy — as most people in publishing do — decide whether to enter library names in all caps, *title case* (important words capitalized), or *sentence case* (first word capitalized).

STEPS: Labeling a library item

1. Double-click the item you want to label. The Library Entry dialog box appears.

2. In the Library Entry dialog box, type a new label in the field (as shown in Figure 33-9) or select an existing label from the menu (multiple items can have the same label).

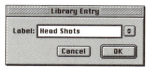

Figure 33-9: Creating a new label.

3. Click OK.

The label does not display with the item in the library palette. Any time you need to see an item's label, double-click the item.

Displaying items by label

After you label items, you can start filtering items in the library palette according to label. To do this, choose an option from the Labels menu, as shown in Figure 33-10. You can choose more than one option at a time, to show items that have a couple different labels applied, if you want. To hide items with a specific label, simply choose that option again.

Figure 33-10: Displaying items by label.

The Labels menu provides the following options:

✦ All, which displays all the items in the library, regardless of their labels.

✦ Unlabeled, which displays only items with no label.

✦ The names of any labels you create. Select any labels whose items you want to display.

Using multiple libraries

Although labels are a great way to keep the list of library items manageable, they are no substitute for creating different libraries to hold distinct groups of items. Don't let the label feature be an excuse for having an unwieldy library. When the items in a library become too diverse, it's time to create a new library and move some items into it. There are three ways to move items from one library to another:

Option 1: Drag the item into the new library. This option copies the item from the first library into the second while leaving the original item intact in the first library.

Option 2: Use the copy command in the first library and paste a copy of the item into the second library. This option also copies the item from the first library into the second while leaving the original item intact in the first library.

Option 3: Use the cut command in the first library and paste the item into the second library. The item is removed from the first library.

Another benefit of creating multiple libraries is that you can more easily find the library items that a specific document requires if you use logical file names for your libraries, such as Corporate Logos or Garden Photos.

Working with Templates

A *template* is a formatted document that is protected from *overwriting* (saving over the original). The only difference between a template and a document is that a template forces you to use Save As rather than Save in the File menu so that you don't overwrite the template but instead create new documents based on it.

Templates are ideal for projects that use a similar look but different content. For example, suppose you have an assignment to create a dozen customer success stories for your company. Each story will be different, but all the individual stories need to have a consistent appearance. The best way to do this is to create a template and then pour the individual stories into the template.

Designing templates

Although the optimum approach is to design a template before creating actual documents, the truth is that no one can foresee all possibilities. Even if you create a template (and you should) that contains all the standing art and the style sheets, colors, H&J sets, and master pages intended for use in all new documents in a related series, you can expect to modify your template as your work on real documents creates the need for modifications and additions. As discussed at the beginning of this chapter, most designers actually create templates by stripping an existing document down to the basics.

Tip When you design templates, be sure to use graphics and text that represent worst-case — or at least standard — scenarios. For example, say you're creating the introduction page for a bimonthly magazine's calendar. You design it so the words "May/June" take up the first two columns, leaving the third column for text. How do you expect to fit "September/October" in that same space?

Saving documents as templates

As you're working on a template, continue to save it as you would any other document so you don't lose any work. When you're satisfied with a document and ready to start using it as a template, you can save it that way.

STEPS: Saving a template

1. Choose File ➪ Save As, or press Option+⌘+S or Ctrl+Alt+S.

2. In the Save As dialog box, navigate to a location for the template file.

3. Type a name for the file in the Save Current Document As field (Mac) or the File Name field (Windows). Windows adds the appropriate file extension to the name; on Macintosh, add the .qxt file extension if you want.

Tip Because templates get updated often, it's helpful to include the date in the file name.

4. Choose Template from the Type menu (Mac) or Save As Type menu (Windows), as shown in Figure 33-11.

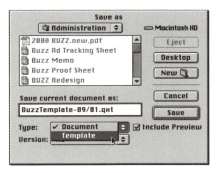

Figure 33-11: Choosing Template in the Save As dialog box.

5. On the Mac, check Preview. This displays a thumbnail version of the template, which is helpful for identification, in the Open dialog box. (The Windows version of QuarkXPress doesn't offer this feature.)

6. Click Save to create the template. The template remains open on-screen with the new name, but you can no longer save changes to it directly, so you might as well close the file.

To make changes to an existing template, open the template, modify it, and save it again using File ⇨ Save As. If you give it the same name and save it in the same location, an alert will ask you to confirm whether you want to replace the existing template; if so, click Replace. However, we recommend that you include dates with template names, so each revision of a template will have a new name.

Opening templates

You can open a template—whether it's on your hard drive or a server—using the Open dialog box (File menu) or by double-clicking the template's file icon. Either way, a local copy of the template opens on your computer in the form of a new, unsaved document. Multiple users can open the same template, and you can open multiple copies of the same template at the same time. When you do any meaningful work in a new document that is based on a template, be sure to name and save the document. Figure 33-12 shows the work a designer has started on a newly opened template.

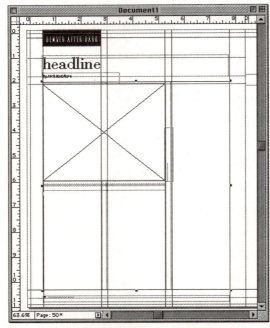

Figure 33-12: Starting a new document from a template.

Summary

Libraries and templates are special types of QuarkXPress files designed to streamline the process of designing many similar pieces. Both types of files can be stored on a network and opened by multiple users, which makes them convenient for use in workgroups. Libraries, however, are not cross-platform. Although templates are cross-platform, you need to make sure the fonts and graphics used in them are available for both platforms as well.

Libraries can contain items — text boxes, picture boxes, lines, and so on — but no loose contents such as just text. Adding items to libraries is a simple drag-and-drop process, as is using library items in documents. Generally, you store items that you need frequent access to in libraries.

Templates can contain anything a document contains, but they usually contain just the shell of a document. When you save a document as a template, you can no longer save changes directly to the file. Each time you open a template, it opens as a new, unsaved document.

✦   ✦   ✦

Using Long-Document Features

When you're working on any type of longer
document — a saddle-stitched booklet, a magazine,
a perfect-bound textbook — you can easily spend more time
on tracking project files, communicating with your workgroup,
and manually creating tables of contents and indexes than
you spend designing the publication. Longer projects such as
these generally consist of multiple QuarkXPress documents,
which lets multiple users work on the project and creates
smaller, more manageable documents. If you're working on
this type of document, by yourself or in a workgroup,
QuarkXPress provides the Book feature for managing the
document files, updating page numbers across documents,
and ensuring consistency in the book.

For longer projects, QuarkXPress also provides its Lists feature,
which lets you create and update automatically formatted
tables of contents, figures lists, and more. These lists are compiled from text formatted with specific paragraph style sheets
(heads, subheads, and so on). If your publication needs an
index, you can tag words throughout your text, then generate
an automatically formatted index. The Lists and Index features both work in single documents and for an entire book
(and they both transfer to documents exported in PDF form).

**New
Feature** New to version 5 is the ability to create lists from text with
certain character style sheets applied. This lets you generate
a list from more discrete chunks of text within a document.

Managing Multiple Documents with Books

In QuarkXPress, a book is a special type of file that you create to track multiple documents for yourself or for a workgroup. A book file displays as a palette, and it lists each QuarkXPress document — called a *chapter* — that you add to the book. Using the book palette, you can add, open and edit, rearrange, and print chapters of the book. Although the book feature is intended for workgroups — and indeed, multiple users can open the same book and access chapters — it works best in a single-user environment. See the sidebar "The pros and cons of books" for more information.

Planning your book

If you decide that the book feature is appropriate and useful for a project, you'll want to do some planning before you even create a book. Use the following guidelines before you begin building your book in QuarkXPress:

✦ **Organize your chapters in advance by deciding on the number, names, and order of the chapters.** You can make changes to a chapter's number, name, and order at any time, but figuring out these basics ahead of time will save you time in the long run.

✦ **Make decisions about the format of the book (style sheets, colors, H&J sets, lists, pagination style, and so on) at the chapter level, beginning with the first chapter.**

✦ **Pay attention to formatting.** Formatting is important, because the first chapter you add to the book palette will become the master chapter (see the later section on working with master chapters), and attributes of that document will form the basis for the other chapters you add to the book.

✦ **Use templates and style sheets to format the chapters uniformly.**

✦ **Decide where to store the book file itself (this must be a shared server for a workgroup); store the documents in this folder as well.** Set up the appropriate sharing through your operating system.

✦ **Make sure members of the workgroup have access to any templates, libraries, graphics, fonts, XTensions, and so on necessary to work on the project.**

 Cross-Reference If you decide to use the book feature in a workgroup, be sure to review Chapter 31 for information about implementing standard preferences, templates, and more.

Creating and opening books

To create a new book, choose File ➪ New ➪ Book. The New Book dialog box, shown in Figure 34-1, lets you specify a location for the book and give it a name. If you're on a Mac, and creating a book that may be used in Windows, add the .qxb extension to the file name (it's added automatically by QuarkXPress for Windows). Click OK to create and open the book.

The pros and cons of books

Although designed for workgroups, the implementation of the book feature in QuarkXPress has some fatal flaws that may discourage you from using it that way. The problem is with how multiple users access book chapters:

✦ **For a workgroup to access a book, the book itself must be stored on a shared server.** Users then open the book across the network and leave it open while they're working. To work on a document in the book, the user opens the document across the network as well. Not only can opening and saving the file be slow, but it leaves documents vulnerable to any instability in your network. (While you're working on the document, there is no local copy of it.) For years, Quark has strongly recommended that users not open documents across the network, yet the book feature implementation essentially requires you to do so.

✦ **To have multiple users access the same book, the users must all follow the same file path to opening the book.** This means that the book cannot be stored on the computer of a user who also needs to access the book — because that user would have a different file path to the book. Basically, you need a computer that acts as a dedicated server.

✦ **Books are ostensibly cross-platform files, but users on Macs and PCs cannot open the same book at the same time.** So to use a book in a cross-platform environment, you'd have to make sure that all Mac users worked on it at one certain time, then have PC users work at a different time.

✦ **The ability to update page numbers only works with documents that have continuous page numbering — it doesn't affect section starts that you create.** If you're working on a magazine in which each article starts on a left-facing page (which you can only do by creating a section start), you won't benefit from the page-numbering feature in books.

Despite these drawbacks, the book feature does provide advantages in a workgroup situation that may outweigh any concerns you have. These include the abilities to:

✦ See who is working on each chapter and when.

✦ Update style sheets, colors, H&J sets, and more, across documents for consistency.

✦ Update page numbers across multiple documents.

✦ Create a table of contents, other lists, and an index for multiple documents. (In fact, using a book is the only way to generate these for multiple documents.)

✦ Easily print all the chapters of a book with the same settings.

If you need some of the benefits of using a book (such as a table of contents for multiple documents), but you can't live with one of the drawbacks (such as the cross-platform limitation), you can start out with separate documents. Then, once the documents are in close-to-final form, you can combine them into a book on one computer and finish up the project in book form.

Continued

Continued

None of this is meant to discourage the single user from managing longer projects through the book feature. If you're producing a book by yourself, and it consists of multiple QuarkXPress documents, by all means take advantage of the book feature. The only consideration is whether your output provider can handle the book file or will require you to combine the documents into a single document. (This may also be an issue if you're creating a PDF form of the document.)

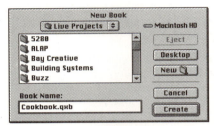

Figure 34-1: To create a new book, choose File ➪ New ➪ Book.

To open an existing book, use the File ➪ Open command (⌘+O or Ctrl+O). If you're opening a book from a shared server, make sure to mount the server on your desktop first. You can also double-click a book's icon, as shown in Figure 34-2, which also shows the open book palette. To close a book, simply click its close box.

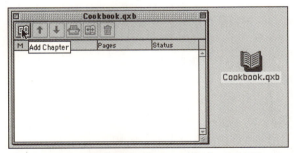

Figure 34-2: The book palette, with the Add Chapter button selected, and the icon for its book file.

Tip   Multiple users can open the same book palette at the same time. If another user makes changes to the book, those changes will show up in your copy of the book when you click on the palette.

Adding chapters to books

New book palettes are empty—you need to add your carefully prepared documents to them. To do this, click the Add Chapter button, the first button on the left side of your book's palette. Use the Add Chapter dialog box, shown in Figure 34-3, to locate and select the first chapter you want to add. Click the Add button to make this the first chapter in the book. Repeat this process to add to the book all the chapters you have ready (you can also add more later).

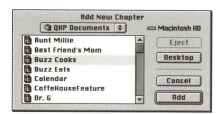

Figure 34-3: The Add New Chapter dialog box lets you select documents to become chapters of the active book.

Working with master chapters

The first chapter you add to the book is, by default, the master chapter as indicated by the *M* to the left of its file name. If the chapters of your book don't share common formatting, you don't need to worry about this feature. But with a book, that's rarely the case—usually you want the text formatting, colors, and so on to remain the same. The master chapter in a QuarkXPress book defines the style sheets, colors, H&J sets, lists, and dash and stripe patterns that are common to all the chapters in the book. When you use the Synchronize feature, discussed later in this chapter, QuarkXPress makes sure that the common style sheets, colors, H&J sets, and so on in each chapter in the book match those in the master chapter.

If you decide to make a different chapter the master chapter, all you need to do is click in the column to the left of that chapter's file name. This moves the *M,* indicating the master chapter, to that chapter (see Figure 34-4).

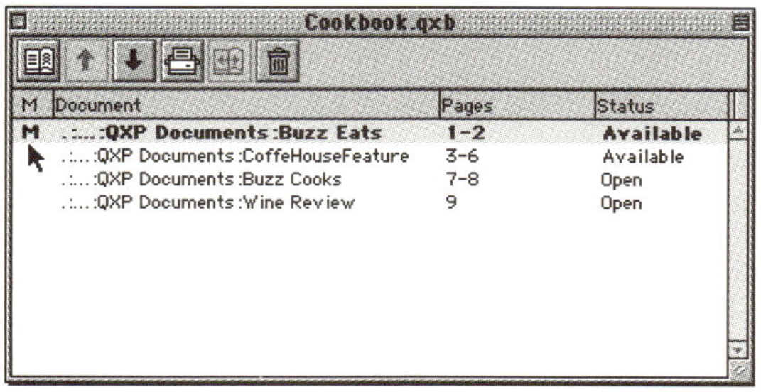

Figure 34-4: The *M* to the left of a chapter's file name indicates the master chapter.

Opening and editing chapters

To work on a chapter in a book, first open the book. Then double-click the chapter name in the book palette. The chapter will open in QuarkXPress just like any other QuarkXPress document opens. Note that to open a chapter, it must have the status of Available, as discussed in the next section. When you're finished editing a chapter, save and close it as usual. Note that if you close a book, all the open chapters will close as well.

Note   If you need to take a chapter home and work on it, you can edit a chapter outside the book. To do this, first move the chapter's file to a different folder so the chapter displays as Missing in the book palette. This will keep other users from editing it while you have it. When you finish editing the file, place the edited file back in its original folder. The book palette will show this chapter as Modified.

Book palette status reports

If you're using the book palette in a workgroup, it provides helpful status reports about each chapter, as shown in Figure 34-5. The statuses include:

✦ **Available:** The chapter can be opened, edited, or printed. Only one user at a time can open a chapter.

✦ **Open:** You have the chapter open and can edit it or print it. Nobody else can open the chapter at this time.

✦ **[User Name]:** If you see the name of another user in your workgroup, it means that user has the chapter open. In this case, you cannot edit or open the chapter.

✦ **Modified:** The chapter has been changed since the last time you opened the book palette. Simply click on the book palette to update it.

✦ **Missing:** The chapter's file has been moved since it was added to the book. Double-click the chapter name to open a Find File dialog box and locate it.

Book palette buttons

Buttons across the top of the Book palette give you control over the chapters. The buttons (refer to Figure 34-5) work as follows (from left to right):

✦ The Add Chapter button lets you locate chapters and add them to the book.

✦ The Move Chapter Up and Move Chapter Down buttons (the two arrows) let you move the selected chapter up or down in the book.

To speed things up, you can also move a chapter in the list by pressing the Option or Alt key and clicking and dragging the chapter up or down.

✦ The Print Chapters button lets you print all available chapters with the same settings.

✦ The Synchronize button makes sure that definitions (colors, style sheets, H&J sets, lists, and dashes and stripes) in all the chapters match those in the master chapter.

✦ The Delete button removes selected chapters from the book. The document files themselves are not deleted, but the chapters are no longer linked to the book.

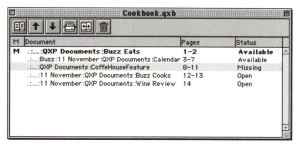

Figure 34-5: The Status column shows which chapters are open on your machine, which are available to be opened, and which are missing. If you were in a work-group and other members had chapters open, the Status column would identify the users by their computer's name.

Synchronizing chapter formatting

To help you make sure that common formatting remains consistent across the document, the book palette provides a Synchronize button. Before you use the Synchronize button, be sure you're satisfied with the styles in the master chapter and that all chapters are available for editing. Clicking Synchronize will:

✦ Compare the style sheets, colors, H&J sets, lists, and dash and stripe patterns in the master chapter to those in each chapter.

✦ If anything is different, the information in the chapter will be updated to match the master chapter. This means that if someone changed the typeface in a style sheet in a chapter, it would revert to the typeface specified in the master chapter.

✦ If anything is missing from a chapter — for example, if you've just added a list to the master chapter — that information is added to each chapter.

What clicking Synchronize results in is that each chapter will have the same basic set of style sheets, colors, H&J sets, lists, and dashes and stripes as the master chapter. We say *basic set* because you can still add more of these specifications to each chapter. When using Synchronize, you need to keep in mind:

✦ Synchronize will *not* move additional style sheets, colors, H&J sets, and so on with different names in chapters. Therefore, you can implement different formatting needs in a chapter by creating an additional style sheet in that chapter.

✦ Synchronize *cannot* solve any problems related to using the template or style sheets incorrectly, or change any local formatting applied to text (such as font changes or italics) or local changes to master page items.

Clearly, Synchronize is no cure-all for the renegade formatting that often occurs when multiple users work on the same project. Be sure everyone knows what the standards are for the design, how to implement the standards properly, and how to make local changes appropriately.

New Feature In QuarkXPress 5, you can synchronize selected chapters rather than all chapters. To do this, Shift+click a range of continuous chapters or ⌘+click or Ctrl+click non-contiguous chapters. After the chapters are selected, click Synchronize.

Printing chapters and books

If you want to print multiple chapters in the book with the same settings, you can print through the Book palette. You can print any chapters with the status of Available or Open.

STEPS: Printing chapters

1. To print the entire book, make sure no chapters are selected. To print a continuous range of chapters, Shift+click them. To print noncontiguous chapters, ⌘+click or Ctrl+click the chapters to select them.

2. Click the Print button to open the standard QuarkXPress Print dialog box.

3. To print all the pages in all the selected chapters, leave the Pages field setting at All. To print a range of pages from selected chapters, enter the page numbers in the field. (QuarkXPress will print the pages in that range for each chapter, such as the first five pages.)

4. Click OK to print the chapters.

Tip Specify pages to print as you do any other time. This means you can enter section page numbers such as "iii-vii" or "5.1, 5.5" or you can enter absolute page numbers, which indicate a page's position in a document, by including a plus sign (+) as in "+1-+5."

Handling chapters with sections

When working with books, you have two choices for numbering pages: You can let the Book palette number pages consecutively from one chapter to the next. Or you can add sections of page numbers, which carry through the book until you start a new section. In long documents, section page numbering is common because it lets you have page numbering such as 2.1-2.14 in, say, Chapter 2. (Plus, creating a section start is the only way to start a document on a left-facing page, which is often necessary in magazines.)

Numbering pages consecutively

If the chapters you add to a book have no sections in them, you end up with consecutive page numbering, as shown in Figure 34-6. The first page number of each chapter follows the last page number of the previous chapter (so if one chapter ends on page 16, the next chapter starts on page 17). QuarkXPress calls this a Book Chapter Start, and if you open the Section dialog box (Page ➪ Section), you'll see that Book Chapter Start is checked (but grayed out).

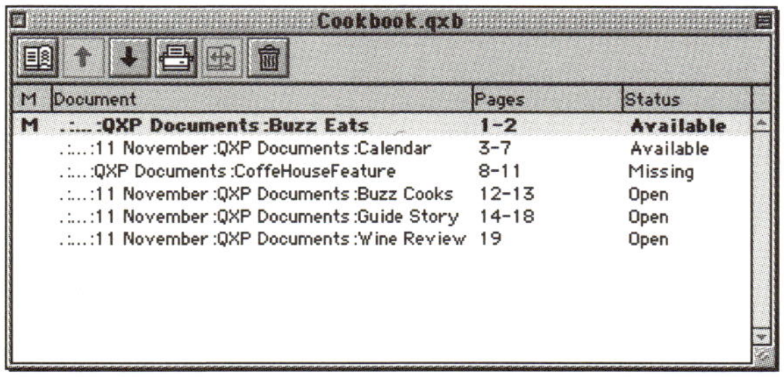

Figure 34-6: Without sections of page numbers, pages in a book are numbered consecutively across chapters.

The consecutive page numbering works as follows:

✦ Whenever you add a chapter with no sections to a book, QuarkXPress numbers pages consecutively throughout the book.

✦ As you add and delete pages from chapters, the page numbers are also updated.

✦ The Book Chapter Start check box is only available if a chapter is opened independently of its book. This lets you remove the book page numbering from the document while you're working on it.

✦ In facing-page documents, chapters always start on a right-facing page with an odd page number (even if the previous chapter ends on a right-facing page). In this case, QuarkXPress "skips" the even page number (so one chapter might end on page 15 and the next chapter will start on page 17, leaving you to add a blank page 16 to the previous chapter for proper pagination).

Numbering pages with sections

If any chapters you add to books already contain sections of page numbers (implemented through the Page ⇨ Section command), the section page numbering overrides the book's consecutive page numbering. The section page numbering carries through chapters of the book until QuarkXPress encounters a new section start. So if one chapter ends on page *iv,* the next page starts on page *v* unless you start a new section. In the Book palette, section page numbering is indicated by asterisks, as shown in Figure 34-7.

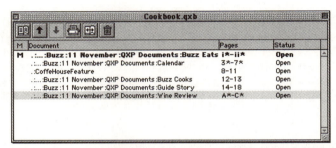

Figure 34-7: Section page numbers are indicated by asterisks in the Book palette. In this example, the first chapter includes a section with pages *i–ii*. The second, third, and fourth chapters encompass pages 3–18, while the last chapter contains a section with pages A–C.

You can add a section within a chapter any time using the Page ⇨ Section command. This works the same as adding a section to any other document with a single exception: The Book Chapter Start command is unchecked for you.

Cross-Reference

Using the options in the Section dialog box is covered in Chapter 9.

Creating Tables of Contents and Other Lists

Long documents lend themselves to lists, which help to keep information organized. A table of contents is a list, as is a list of figures or tables. In QuarkXPress, a *list* is actually nothing more than a list of paragraphs or words that are formatted with the same style sheets. After you've created a book (or even a single document), QuarkXPress can build a list by scanning the chapters for the style sheets you specify. For example, if you create a book and have a paragraph style sheet named *Figure* that you apply to figures in the document, you can generate a list of figures by asking the program to list all paragraphs that use the style sheet named *Figure*.

Version 5 of QuarkXPress introduces the ability to generate lists from character style sheets in addition to paragraph style sheets. This give you the opportunity to extract all the text with a specific character style sheet applied — for example, all the names of stocks in a business magazine — and create an alphabetical list from it. Lists can include text in both paragraph and character style sheets at the same time.

Planning a list

Before you start whipping up a list in QuarkXPress, decide what the content of your list will be: All the text in your Head and Subhead paragraph style sheet? All the text in your Famous People character style sheet? *Remember:* You'll need to be sure style sheets are applied consistently to generate a list (so if you're not sure about that, look through the documents or chapters).

After you decide what will be in your list, use a little bit of dummy text to format a sample list. Your formatting should include any indents for different levels in your list and it should include tabs and fill characters as necessary. When you're satisfied with the formatting of your sample list, create paragraph style sheets from it. Be sure to use clear names such as TOC-Level 1.

To make things easy on yourself, limit the formatting of a completed list to paragraph style sheets. If you add local formatting such as a color or different typeface on page numbers, you'll have to add that manually when you're finished.

Defining a list

In QuarkXPress, a list defines the text you want in a table of contents (or other list), what order it appears in, how page numbers are added, and how the list is formatted. Because you specify the list's final formatting through paragraph style sheets, it's best to create those style sheets before you define the list (as discussed in the preceding section). To create a list, you use the Edit ➪ Lists command.

STEPS: Creating a list

1. To create a new list, choose Edit ➪ Lists. If you're working in a book, make sure you do this in the master chapter.

2. Click New. Enter an obvious name such as *Table of Contents* in the Name field.

3. To specify what text belongs in your list, click the first style sheet in the Available Styles list, and then click the right arrow to transfer the style to the Styles in List area. Although the Styles in List do not need to be in the same order as they will appear in your final list, it will be easier for you to decipher what's going on in the Edit List dialog box if you do so. You can include up to 32 style sheets in a list, which should be plenty.

4. For each style sheet you add to the list, choose an option from the Level menu to indicate its position in the list hierarchy. For example, if you're including chapter heads, they might be level 1, and section heads might be level 2. QuarkXPress provides levels 1 (highest) to 8 (lowest).

5. Use the Numbering menu shown in Figure 34-8 to specify whether and how page numbers are listed for each item in the list. A traditional table of contents might use the Text...Page # option, but you might use Text Only for chapter names so page numbers are not listed for chapter introduction pages. You can also place page numbers prior to text in your list by choosing Page #...Text.

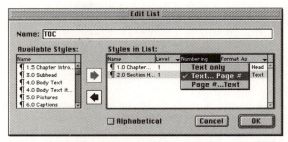

Figure 34-8: The Edit List dialog box lets you define which style sheets to include in your list and how to format the final list.

6. Now it's time to use those paragraph style sheets you created for your sample list. Use the Format As menu to select the paragraph style sheets to be applied to your formatted list. For example, text in your Chapter Heads style sheet might be formatted with TOC-Level 1. It's through these paragraph style sheets that text in your list is indented and that tabs are placed — if you don't select well-created paragraph style sheets, your list could end up making no sense.

7. If you want the text in your list to be alphabetical (rather than sequential through the document or book), check Alphabetical. This will override any levels you've specified — you will not get alphabetical lists within each level.

8. If you change your mind about including any styles in your list, select the style sheet and click the left-facing arrow to send it back to the Available Styles area. When you're satisfied with your list definition, click OK, and then click Save.

After you've defined a list, you can go to the Lists palette and display it. If you're working on a book, and the list is not included in all the book's chapters, be sure to synchronize the chapters, as covered earlier in this chapter. This will add the lists from the master chapter to all other chapters.

Don't be surprised if you need to come back and edit your list — you may have included too much information to start with, resulting in a list that's too long, or you may not like the page numbering you've selected. Using the Lists dialog box (Edit ➪ Lists), you can always edit an existing list. (Again, if you're working in a book, synchronize to update the list throughout the chapters.)

Compiling a list

To view a list, you use the Lists palette (View ➪ Show Lists) shown in Figure 34-9. The Lists palette works as follows:

✦ The Show List For menu lets you display a list for the current document or for an entire book. (To create an accurate list for all the chapters in a book, the chapters need to be available.)

✦ The List Name menu shows all the lists you've created for the current document. Pick one to display it. In the palette, QuarkXPress indents each level of your lists. Note that the list will only include the first 256 characters of a paragraph (it's unlikely, though, that you'll include in a list style sheets that are used for such long paragraphs).

✦ In a longer list, use the Find field to locate specific text within the list. All you have to do is type in the field to jump to the first instance of that text in the list.

✦ Click the Update button any time you modify text in the document, add new chapters to a book, modify your list definition, or make any other change that affects the content of your list. Lists don't update dynamically as you work.

✦ Double-click any item in the list to jump to that location in the document. If the location is in another chapter in a book, the chapter will be opened to that location (provided that the chapter is still available).

The prerequisites for lists

If you want to use the List feature—and you should if you're creating lists for documents more than 20 or so pages long—you have to use style sheets. Not only do style sheets guarantee consistent formatting but they tell QuarkXPress what text you want to include in your list. The other thing to keep in mind for lists: They are linear, listing from top to bottom the text in the order it appears in a document (or in alphabetical order). If your final list is not meant to be linear, the Lists feature may not be for you.

The first table of contents shown here is ideal for the Lists feature (in fact, it was created with a list). The list is linear, and it reflects text in specific paragraph style sheets in the order the text appears in a booklet. But the second table of contents shown would be difficult to produce with the lists feature. The information is broken up according to columns, departments, and features rather than the order in which it appears in the magazine. Columns and departments use the same paragraph style sheets, while features are designed individually with local formatting.

Continued

Continued

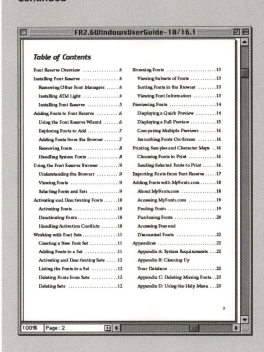

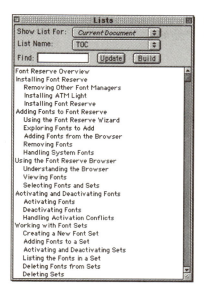

Figure 34-9: The Lists palette displays the Table of Contents list for the current document.

 If you used the Lists palette in version 4, you'll notice some welcome improvements in version 5. The Lists palette can now display special characters, which were previously replaced by small boxes. So you can now view text such as *entrée*. In addition, the list no longer includes blank lines inadvertently formatted with a list style sheet (a paragraph return or next box character with a section head style sheet applied, for example, used to create empty lines in lists).

Flowing a formatted list

When the Lists palette is open, you can flow a formatted list, with up-to-date page numbers, into any selected text box. Before you do this:

✦ **Make sure you've saved space in the document for the list.** This should consist of a single text box or a series of linked text boxes. You can also use the automatic text box as long as you set Auto Page Insertion to End of Story in the General pane of the Preferences dialog box (Edit ➪ Preferences ➪ Preferences, or ⌘+Y or Ctrl+Y). If you don't, your list might start on one page and end at the end of the document. When you're creating a table of contents for a book, it might be useful to flow the table of contents into its own chapter.

✦ **Click Update and skim through the Lists palette to make sure the list content looks right.** (If not, use the Edit ➪ Lists command to modify the list and fix any problems with style sheets incorrectly applied to text.) If you're working in a book, be sure all the chapters are available while updating and building your list. If you change the list definition at all, be sure to do so in the master chapter and to synchronize the book.

When you're satisfied with the contents of your list, select the Content tool and click in the text box in which you want to place the list. On the Lists palette, click Build. An updated, formatted list is shown in Figure 34-10. If you want to apply any local formatting to the list, such as colors or typeface changes, be sure you're working with the final version of the list or be prepared to do it again.

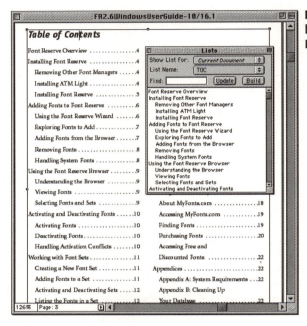

Figure 34-10: When we build the TOC list in the Lists palette, it looks like this.

Note   If you see a dagger † (Mac) or the letters PB (Windows) rather than a page number in your list, that means the text referenced by the list is on the pasteboard and will not print in your document.

Caution   Make sure that you don't change page numbering when you flow your list. For example, if you add five pages to the beginning of a document to flow a table of contents, the page numbers listed may be five pages off (if your pages are numbered sequentially). If you do need to update page numbering after flowing a list, simply rebuild the list.

Updating and rebuilding a list

If you edit a list definition, document, chapter, or entire book after building a list, you need to rebuild the list. There is no link between the text you've flowed into the document and the list in the Lists palette. To do this, all you need to do is click Update on the Lists palette, then click Build. Because you've already built the list, QuarkXPress prompts you to replace the existing list. Click Replace. If you want to

Stripping the space

When QuarkXPress builds a list, it separates the text in the list from the page number with a space and then a tab. If you're using a dot leader (...) as a fill character for the tab, the space preceding the tab can leave an annoying gap, as shown in the figure. If this bothers you, you can strip it out using Find/Change (Edit ➪ Find/Change, or ⌘+F or Ctrl+F). Search for a space followed by a tab character (\t) and replace it with only a tab character. Make sure you do this when your list is completely final or you'll have to do it again.

change the location of your list in the document or book, you can delete the original list and click Insert to flow the new list at the location of the cursor.

Tip   If you rebuild a list right before completing a project, you can be sure the page numbers in it are up to date and that the contents of your list exactly match the spelling and capitalization of text in your document. Therefore, you can skip this part of the proofing process — it's truly a waste of time to proof page numbers generated by the Lists feature.

Indexing Documents and Books

If you've ever been unable to find information in a book that you knew was there, you'll appreciate how important a good index can be. Short, simple documents can get by fine without indexes. But long books almost always need indexes to help the reader locate specific information. Indexing used to be a laborious process, involving lots of index cards. Now, QuarkXPress makes indexing much easier, while still relying on you to make key decisions about how the index will be formatted. The following sections show you how to do your part.

Note   The indexing features are implemented through the Index XTension, which comes with QuarkXPress. To make sure the Index XTension is running, use the Utilities ➪ XTensions Manager command. If you never intend to index a document — which is the case with many graphic designers — feel free to disable this XTension. However, when you're working with documents that may be indexed, it's best if you have the XTension running.

Creating lists from character style sheets

Most lists you'll create will be generated from paragraph style sheets. But the ability to create lists from text formatted in a specific character style sheet does offer some interesting possibilities. For example, if you use a character style sheet to format the names of famous people in your gossip column, you can create an alphabetized list of people from the column. The figure below shows an alphabetical list of wines created from an article of wine recommendations. The separate, alphabetical wine list is printed elsewhere in the magazine so users can cut it out and take it into the store. This type of list can actually take the place of an index in many simpler publications.

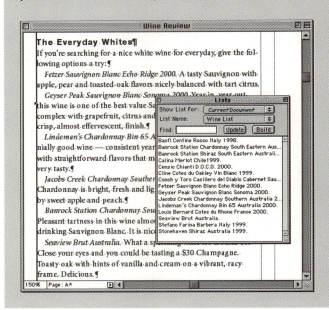

Choosing an indexing style

Your approach to developing an index depends on the indexing style you want to use. Large publishers usually have their own house style guides for indexes. If you don't have a style guide for indexes, we recommend that you read through the indexing guidelines in *The Chicago Manual of Style*. Another option is to use an index you like as a model and then take the steps necessary in QuarkXPress to achieve that index style. Before you begin indexing your document, ask yourself the following questions:

✦ Do you want to capitalize all levels of all entries, or do you just want initial caps?

✦ Should headings appear in boldface?

✦ What type of punctuation will you use in your index?

✦ Will you capitalize secondary entries in the index?

✦ Should the index be nested or run-in style (see the sidebar "Nested or run-in index?")?

Once you make these decisions, it's a good idea to make a small dummy of your index. From the dummy, create a master page for index pages, paragraph style sheets for letter headings (A, B, C, and so on in the index), paragraph style sheets for each level of the index (including indents as appropriate), and character style sheets for any special formatting you want on page numbers or cross-reference text. QuarkXPress doesn't do any of this for you — if you don't set up style sheets for your index, your multilevel index will simply look linear when it's built.

Using the Index Preferences dialog box

The Index Preferences dialog box (Edit ➪ Preferences ➪ Index), shown in Figure 34-11, lets you choose the color of *index markings* (the markers that indicate text is part of the index) and the punctuation (called *separation characters*) used in your final, built index. The following sections explain how the options in the Index Preferences dialog box work.

Figure 34-11: The Index Preferences dialog box.

Changing the index marker color

To add words to an index in QuarkXPress, you need to *mark* the words in the chapters of your book that you want to use as index entries. These markers appear as colored brackets around the entry. To change the color of the index markers, click the Index Marker Color button; this will display a system color picker. Use the controls in the color picker to define the new color for index markers. Click OK to close the color picker, and then click OK in the Index Preferences dialog box to complete the process.

Choosing separation characters

The Index Preferences dialog box also lets you choose the characters and spaces used to separate entries in the index. The options in the Separation Characters section of the dialog box work as follows:

✦ **Following Entry:** This defines the punctuation that immediately follows each index entry — usually a colon (:). For example, the index item *Fonts: vi, 14, 21–23* uses a colon and space following the index entry *Fonts*.

✦ **Between Page #s:** This defines the characters or punctuation that separate a list of page numbers — usually a comma (,) or semicolon (;). For example, the index item *Fonts: vi, 14, 21–23* uses a comma and space between page numbers.

✦ **Between Page Range:** This defines the characters or punctuation that indicate a range of pages — usually the word *to* or an en dash. For example, the index item *Fonts: vi, 14, 21 to 23* uses the word *to* plus a space on either side of the word between numbers indicating a range of pages.

✦ **Before Cross-Reference:** This defines the characters or punctuation that appear before a cross-reference — usually a period and space or a semicolon. For example, the index item *Fonts: vi, 14, 21–23. See also Typefaces* uses a period and a space before the cross-reference.

✦ **Cross-Ref Style:** This lets you select a character style sheet to apply to the cross-reference part of an index item. For example, in the index item *Fonts: vi, 14, 21–23. See also Typefaces,* the word *Typefaces* would be formatted with the character style sheet selected here. (Note that the entire *see also* phrase does not take on the Cross-Ref Style.)

✦ **Between Entries:** This defines the characters or punctuation between entry levels in a run-in index — usually a period or a semicolon. For example, the index item *Fonts: vi, 14, 21–23; Adding: 15–16; Deleting: 19* uses a semicolon between entry levels.

Tip   You may need to create a few lines of a sample index to determine your Index Preferences. As with lists, if the first index you generate doesn't work for you, you can easily change settings and try again.

Nested or run-in index?

There is no right way to index, but common sense should be a guide. Determine which index format you use by the number of levels in the index's hierarchy. If the index has only two levels, a run-in format works well, but an index with three or more levels requires a nested format for the sake of clarity.

Nested indexes look like this:

Kitchen Hardware

Buying, 191

Cost estimates, 242–248

Design guidelines 92–94, 96, 99–101

Hiring contractors, 275–284

Installation, 180–195

Sizing, 91–99

Standards, 24–28, 98, 133

Tools, 199–203, 224, 282–283

Run-in indexes look like this:

Kitchen Hardware: Buying, 191; Cost estimates, 242–248; Design guidelines 92–94, 96, 99–101; Hiring contractors, 275–284; Installation, 180–195; Sizing, 91–99; Standards, 24–28, 98, 133; Tools, 199–203, 224, 282–283

Although QuarkXPress doesn't force you to make this decision until you actually build the index, you really need to make it before you get started. If you tag words for a four-level index, but then build a run-in index, your index will have some logic problems.

Using the Index palette

When a chapter or document is ready to be indexed, open the Index palette (View ➪ Show Index). You use this palette to add words to the index in up to four indent levels, edit or delete index entries, or create cross-references. The Index palette appears in Figure 34-12.

The Entry section

The controls in the Entry section of the Index palette control the text that displays in your index. They work as follows:

✦ **Text:** The Text field in the Entry section of the Index palette is where you type in an index entry or where the text appears that you've tagged with index markers. When you have the Index palette open and you highlight text in the open document, the first 255 characters of the highlighted text appear automatically in the Text field and are ready to be captured as an index entry.

In version 5 of QuarkXPress, you can automatically reverse the text in the Text field as you add it to the index. For example, you can change *Adding fonts* to *Fonts, adding.* All you need to do is press the Option or Alt key while you click the Add button or the Add All button.

✦ **Sort As:** Entries in the Sort As field override the default, alphabetical sorting of the index entry. For example, you may want *2-byte fonts* to be indexed as if the entry were spelled *Two-byte fonts,* and you could accomplish this by entering the spelling *Two-byte fonts* into the Sort As field.

✦ **Level:** This menu lets you control the order and structure of index entries. A nested index can have up to four levels, and a run-in index can have only two levels. (Granted, QuarkXPress doesn't know what type of index you're creating, so your run-in index can have four levels, too, but it doesn't make any sense visually to use more than two.)

Figure 34-12: The Index palette.

The Reference section

The controls in the Reference section of the Index palette control the page numbers or cross-references associated with each index entry. Generally, you will have multiple references for the same index entry.

The Style menu lets you apply a character style sheet to the page numbers for the current index entry. You can also override the Index Preferences for the character style sheet applied to the cross-reference text. For example, you might apply a boldface character style sheet to page numbers that indicate where an index entry is defined.

The Scope menu, shown in Figure 34-13, lets you specify how much text an index entry encompasses, which determines the page numbers listed for it:

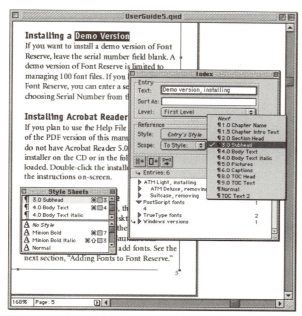

Figure 34-13: The Scope menu lets you specify the range of text that an index entry covers. In this example, the entry *Demo version, installing* has a scope of *To Style: 3.0 Subhead*. This means the index entry will list the page numbers until the 3.0 Subhead style sheet appears again (here, it occurs prior to the next paragraph).

✦ Selected Text is the most common option; it lists the page numbers the marked text falls on.

✦ Selection Start, another commonly used option, lists the page number the beginning of the selection is on.

✦ To Style lists the page numbers from the start of the selected text until a different paragraph style sheet is applied (you get to specify which one). This is handy if you know that the Subhead style sheet indicates a topic change so the index entry covers all the text until Subhead is used again.

✦ Specified # of ¶'s (that's QuarkXPress's apostrophe, not ours) lets you enter how many paragraphs the index entry covers — a risky choice because text may change.

✦ To End Of lists page numbers from the start of the selected text to the end of the Document or Story (your choice).

✦ Suppress Page # Scope is useful for multilevel indexes in which the first level is simply serving as a topic head such as *Fonts*.

The indexing buttons

New to version 5 are mysterious icons on the indexing buttons instead of nice, plain words.

From left to right, the buttons on the Index palette work as follows:

✦ **The Add button:** This lets you add an entry to the index. Option+click or Alt+click this button to add the reverse of the text in the Text field (for example, *Anton, Robert* instead of *Robert Anton*).

✦ **The Add All button:** This lets you add all instances of the text in the Text field to the index. The entries will all have the same settings, so be sure the Scope is appropriate for wherever this text appears (usually Selected Text will work for this). As with Add, you can Option+click or Alt+click this button to reverse the text as you add it.

✦ **The Find Next Entry button:** This finds the next occurrence of an index entry in the active document. Basically, you'll use this to jump through a document and look at what you've indexed.

✦ **The Edit button:** This lets you change the selected index entry's text, sorting, or level. If you click the triangle next to an index entry in the lower portion of the palette, then click on a page number, you can edit the index entry's scope or style.

✦ **The Trash button:** You can delete a selected index entry or page number reference by clicking the Trash button. If you delete an entry with subentries, the subentries are deleted as well.

Creating an index entry

When you create an index entry, you need to carefully consider the text in the field, how it sorts, what level it appears at in the index, and how much text it covers.

If you're indexing an entire book, note that the Index palette is only able to show the index for one chapter at a time. This can lead to consistency problems such as different wording for what is essentially the same index entry as well as cross-references that don't go anywhere. To prevent problems such as this, you can generate mini-indexes for each chapter for reference (you can print them, then delete them from the document).

STEPS: Adding an index entry

1. Highlight the text you want to add to the index. The text appears in the Index palette's Text field. You can also simply click in text where the index entry starts (as long as you're not planning to use the Scope of Selected Text). If the text you highlight has already been added to the index, but you want to list it again, you need to click next to the text rather than highlighting it.

2. If you want to edit the text, do so at this time. For example, if you highlight the word *font,* you can capitalize it and make it plural so it appears in the index as *Fonts.* Don't worry about reversing proper names though — to change *Sammy Sosa* to *Sosa, Sammy* for example. You can do that automatically when you add the text.

3. If you want to change the way this entry sorts in the index, enter the proper sorting in the Sort As field.

4. If you're creating a first-level index entry, choose Level ➪ First Level. If you're creating a subentry, first click next to an existing index entry in the palette. An arrow indicates where the subentry will go. Then choose Second Level, Third Level, or Fourth Level from the Level menu. (Third Level is only available if you click next to a Second Level entry, and Fourth Level is only available if you click next to a Third Level entry.)

5. If you want the page numbers for this entry to display differently in the index, choose one of your character style sheets from the Style menu.

6. Choose an option from the Scope menu to specify how much text this index entry covers. (The Scope options were described previously.)

7. When you're sure all the settings are correct, click the Add button, as shown in Figure 34-14. To reverse an entry, press Option or Alt while you click Add.

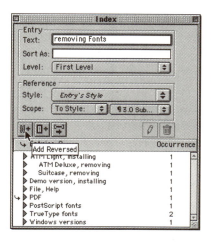

Figure 34-14: Here, the entry *removing Fonts* will be added as a First Level entry with a Scope of To Style. We Option+clicked or Alt+clicked the Add button to change it to Add Reversed, which changed the entry to *Fonts, removing.*

Although all this sounds tedious for a simple one– or two-level index, it's really not. Most of your index entries will be the same level and have the same scope — probably Selected Text. So you can easily run the cursor through a document, look for text you want to index, highlight it, and click Add.

Tip   To add highlighted text with the current settings in the Index palette, you can press Option+Shift+⌘+I or Ctrl+Alt+Shift+I. In addition, you can display the text box's context menu and choose Add to Index.

Editing an index

If you delete text that contained index markers, the associated entry is deleted from the index automatically. But you will often want or need to change the wording of an index entry, the sorting, the level, and the scope. Generally, after you build an index once and skim through it, you'll find changes you want to make so the index is more consistent and more useful. You edit the information in the Entry and Reference sections of the palette separately.

Editing an entry

If you want to change the text, sorting, or level of an entry, click on the entry's text in the lower portion of the Index palette. Then click the Edit button (the pencil icon). You can also double-click the entry to enter editing mode. This activates the Entry portion of the Index palette, where you can:

✦ Edit the entry in the Text field.

✦ Enter or edit text in the Sort As field.

New Feature   The ability to change an index entry's level is new to version 5. Previously, you had to delete an entry and re-create it if there was a problem with the level.

✦ Elevate a subentry to a First Level entry by selecting that option from the Level menu.

✦ Move a subentry to a different entry, but keep it at the same level, by clicking the arrow in the palette to another location.

✦ Change an entry's level by clicking the arrow next to the entry you want to place it under, then choosing the appropriate option from the Level menu (see Figure 34-15).

You'll notice that nothing is happening to the entry shown in the Index palette while you're making changes. To implement your changes, click the Edit button again to exit editing mode.

Editing an entry's page numbers

In the Index palette, if you click a triangle next to an index entry, you can see the page numbers and any cross-references associated with it. The numbers or cross-references listed for each instance of an index entry are controlled by the Scope. If you find that a Scope you used is incorrect, you can change it, and you can change the character style sheet applied to that page number in the index.

To edit a page number or cross-reference, click on it and click the Edit button — or double-click it. This activates the Reference area and takes you to that occurrence of the index entry in your document or book. Here, you can change the information in the Style and Scope menus as shown in Figure 34-16. Click the Edit button again to save your changes.

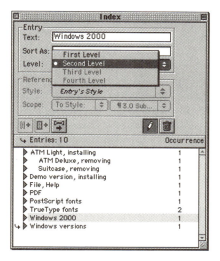

Figure 34-15: In this example, we selected the *Windows 2000* entry and clicked the Edit button. Then, we clicked next to the *Windows versions* entry and selected Second Level. This will make *Windows 2000* a subentry of *Windows versions*.

Figure 34-16: Here, the first instance of the *Windows 2000* entry has the wrong scope. It's covering pages 4–5, while the text is really only on page 4. We double-clicked the entry and selected Selection Text for the new scope.

Creating cross-references

Cross-references enhance an index because they give the reader another way of finding pertinent information. In QuarkXPress, a cross-reference is just another scope — a roundabout way of showing you the page numbers for a listing. You can have index entries that include page numbers and a cross-reference and you can have index entries that include only a cross-reference.

STEPS: Creating a cross-reference

1. If you're creating a new index entry, highlight the text in the document and make sure the Text, Sort As, and Level field settings are appropriate. If you're adding a cross-reference to an existing entry, click on that entry in the index to place its information in the Text field.

2. From the Scope menu, choose Cross-Reference, and then choose an option from the adjacent menu: See, See Also, or See Herein (as shown in Figure 34-17). Use See to point readers to the appropriate index entry; use See Also to point the readers to additional useful information elsewhere in the index; use See Herein to point readers to a subentry for this index entry.

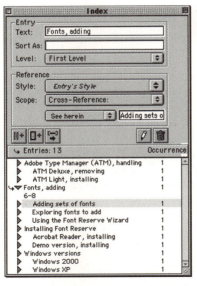

Figure 34-17: In this example, we cross-reference the index entry *Fonts, adding* to its own subentry *Adding sets of fonts.*

3. To point readers to another index entry, you have two choices: You can either type an index entry's text in the field or you can click on an existing entry in the Index palette. If the entry you're referencing is in another chapter, you have no choice but to enter its text in the field. You may want to refer to the other chapter to make sure you get the wording exactly right.

4. Within your cross-reference, you can change the formatting of the text for the referenced index entry. For example, if your cross-reference is *See also Fonts Control Panel,* you can change the formatting of *Fonts Control Panel* to italics. A setting in the Index Preferences dialog box controls the default character style sheet applied to cross-reference text, but you can change it by selecting an option from the Style menu.

Building an index

When you're finished marking words for the index in a document or book, you can build a formatted index for an entire book or document. Before you do this, check into the following:

✦ Confirm the punctuation you've specified for the index in the Index Preferences dialog box (Edit ➪ Preferences ➪ Index). If you're working in a book, be sure to check this in the chapter that will actually contain the index.

✦ Make sure you have a master page ready for the formatted index. The only requirement is that the master page have an automatic text box, but you may want to include more columns for the index pages and appropriate headers and footers as well.

✦ Check to see if you created all the paragraph style sheets you need for the formatted index, including any letter headings you add (A, B, C, and so on) and for each level of the index. You need to be sure your paragraph style sheets include deeper indents for each level of the index.

✦ Confirm that it's okay to add pages to the very end of the current chapter or document — because that's where QuarkXPress will place the index. For example, if you've already placed a cover on the back page, you'll have to move it at some point. For a book, it's a good idea to flow the index into its own chapter at the end of the book.

✦ If you're indexing a book, make sure all the book chapters are available.

If you don't make these preparations upfront, don't be surprised if you end up canceling out of the Build Index dialog box because you can't set everything in it. In fact, the Index XTension will not even let you build an index without a master page containing an automatic text box.

STEPS: Building an index

1. Choose Utilities ➪ Build Index to open the Build Index dialog box shown in Figure 34-18. This command is only available when the Index palette is open.

2. In the Format area, click Nested or Run-in. (See the sidebar "Nested or run-in indexes?" at the beginning of this section to help you make a decision.) If you choose Run-in, be sure your index entries are all First Level or Second Level.

3. If you're building an index for the open book (and all the chapters are available), check Entire Book.

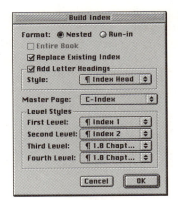

Figure 34-18: The Build Index dialog box.

4. Check Replace Existing Index to overwrite the existing index with the most current version. To compare a newer version of an index with its predecessor, uncheck Replace Existing Index. Then when you build the index, it won't replace the previous version.

5. In long indexes, it's helpful to divide the index alphabetically, so that all the index entries that begin with *A* are in a category with the heading *A*. Check Add Letter Headings to make this happen, and select a paragraph style sheet for the formatting.

6. Choose the master page you want to use for the index from the Master Page menu. Only master pages containing automatic text boxes are listed. For long indexes, you should consider developing a master page just for that purpose.

7. The Level Styles menus let you choose the paragraph style sheets you want to apply to the various index levels. If you select the Run-in format, all the index levels flow into one paragraph, so only the First Level menu will be available.

8. When you've made your choices in the Build Index dialog box, click okay to generate the formatted index. Figure 34-19 shows a final index generated by the Index XTension.

Indexing is an iterative process, and it's very likely that you'll need to build an index a few times through the course of a project. The first index is usually a good draft for reviewing your master page, style sheets, and punctuation choices — along with the contents of your index. You're likely to see things you want to change, but don't change them in the document. Go back and change your Index Preferences, master page and style sheets, and entries in your index — and then build the index again.

Tip   Each time you edit text in a document or book chapter, it's a good idea to rebuild the index so the page numbers in it are updated. There is no dynamic link between a flowed and formatted index and the index markers in text.

A

Activate Permanently command (**Edit** menu), 61
Activate Temporarily command (**Edit** menu), 61
Activating fonts
  Automatically, 63
    Disabling auto-activate feature, 63
  Handling conflicts, 65–66
    Font ID conflicts, 65
    Menu name conflicts, 65–66
  Keeping all your fonts active, 56
  Methods for, 56–59
    Activating copies of fonts, 58–59
    Activating fonts "in place," 57
  Permanently, 60
  Reaching the Mac OS limit, 59
  Selecting fonts to activate/deactivate, 60–61
  Setting toggle preferences to activate/deactivate fonts, 62
Activity log, 44–45
Add Ownership command (**Owners** menu), 72, 120
Add time is last scan (**Filter** criteria), 84
Adding fonts
  Activating simultaneously, 41–42
  Drag-and-drop, 36
  Methods for, 32–33
    Alias method, 33, 35, 37
    Vault method, 32–33, 35, 37
  Scan Folder command (**File** menu), 36
  Scanning fonts to add, 37–38
    Add phase, 38
    Match phase, 38
    Pausing or stopping, 38
  Setting preferences for adding fonts, 34–35
  Temporarily, 39–40
    Specifying, 39–40
    Using DropSet for, 40
Adding Fonts panel (**Preferences** dialog

Figure 34-19: This simple, two-level index for a 178-page user manual includes local formatting (bold) on software command names. The bold was added when the index was final.

Incorporating indexing into a workflow

If you're working on a document by yourself, or you're creating a fairly simple index in a workgroup, you can pretty much index as you go. Or you can plan some time at the end of the editorial cycle to go through a document or chapters to index them. But if your publication requires professional indexing—as would be the case for the multilevel index of a long book such as this one—it's hard to decide when to send your original QuarkXPress files out for indexing. You might do it one chapter at a time, right after editorial approval and right before the file goes to production. Or you might send each chapter out for indexing before the last round of edits. What you can't do is continue working on one copy of your QuarkXPress documents while another copy is being indexed—there is no way to move the index tags to another file.

On a tight schedule, you may be tempted to move your QuarkXPress documents into production while another copy of your files is indexed. You then generate the index, send that file to production, then send the whole thing to print. The index is trapped in QuarkXPress documents that aren't final—unfortunate, because the next time you edit the document, you would like to have the index tags in it. If you have to work this way, you'll need to decide whether to re-index the publication or redo the production work.

Summary

The books, lists, and indexing features of QuarkXPress can significantly streamline longer projects, especially those consisting of multiple documents. Although the book feature's implementation limits its use by a workgroup — primarily because it requires you to open and save documents over a network — it's ideal for a single user to combine multiple documents into a single publication. In fact, the only way to create a table of contents (or other list) or an index for multiple documents is to combine the documents into a book.

The lists feature makes it easy to generate tables of contents, figures lists, author lists, and more from text formatted with paragraph and character style sheets. The indexing feature, on the other hand, can only be considered easy by people with knowledge of the indexing process. Implemented through the Index XTension, you can make use of the simpler features — such as adding a First Level entry that consists of text highlighted in the document — but the more complicated your index, the more you may need a professional indexer. If you do need a professional, be sure your schedule considers time for the indexer to take possession of your QuarkXPress files.

✦   ✦   ✦

Output

P A R T

✦ ✦ ✦ ✦

In This Part

Chapter 35
Printing Documents

Chapter 36
Working with a
Service Bureau

✦ ✦ ✦ ✦

For print publishers, the ultimate goal is getting a printed version of the document. QuarkXPress, of course, ensures that's what you get. But printing is not as simple as pressing a button, even if the program lets you do just that. When you print, you need to consider many issues to ensure the result is what you intended and that you're taking full but appropriate advantage of your output device — whether it be a laser printer, imagesetter, or color thermal wax proofer.

This part explains how to control and optimize the print output for your layouts, as well as how to work with a service bureau to make sure they produce the film negatives that will give the commercial printer the best material from which to print your magazines, books, brochures, or other high-volume, high-quality documents.

Printing Documents

This chapter deals with putting the efforts of your work on paper — an exciting prospect after hours, days, and sometimes weeks of intensive labor. Like any other aspect of using QuarkXPress, there are a few tricks to be learned on the way. But by and large, the printing process is pretty straight-forward. One of the first decisions you have to make (and hopefully you've made it before you created the documents you want to commit to paper) is the type of printer you want to use. This topic, as well as the options specific to Macintosh, to Windows, and to QuarkXPress itself, are all dealt with in this chapter. You'll also find a section on creating print styles.

Choosing the Right Printer

Choosing the right printer (the hardware, not the nice people who put ink on paper) is an important part of the publishing process. QuarkXPress documents can be printed on a wide variety of printers, from dot matrix printers to imagesetters. Here is a very simple overview of your choices.

Inkjet printers

Inkjet printers print by ejecting dots of ink onto paper. The appearance of images printed on inkjet printers is generally smoother than that of those printed on dot matrix printers. The reason is that the dots of ink applied to paper by inkjet printers tend to blend together, instead of remaining separate dots, as on a dot matrix printer. Inkjet printers have come a long way in recent years. You can now buy color inkjet printers that provide 720-, 1,440-, and 2,880-dpi resolution for about $200 ($500 for a version with an Ethernet connection, and $1,000 for a version with both PostScript and an Ethernet connector). Black-and-white inkjets have all but disappeared. These make great color-proofing printers, except for one thing: very slow speed. Inkjets are fine for do-it-yourself color documents and as an adjunct to a laser or other high-end printer. Canon, Epson, and Hewlett-Packard make most inkjet printers.

Dye-sublimation and thermal-wax printers

Dye-sublimation and thermal-wax printers print by using dry color media and heating them onto a page. A dye-sub printer uses film with embedded dyes and heat-transfers the image from the film onto paper. A thermal-wax printer melts colored waxes and lays the wax onto the page similar to how an inkjet printer sprays paper with its ink nozzles. Both are used for professional color output, although usually to create comps, not final output or rigorous color proofs. (These printers' colors approximate, but do not match, final color output from a printing press.) They can cost from $5,000 to $15,000. Hewlett-Packard and Xerox Tektronix make most such printers.

Laser printers

Laser printers print by making a laser-light impression of the page image on a drum, adhering toner to that image, and then transferring the toner image to paper. The output quality from a laser printer is about equal to that of inkjet printers, largely because laser printers print at a high resolution (typically 600 dots per inch), which is great for black-and-white and grayscale output. Color laser printers do exist and are getting cheaper, but they're not in the same league yet as inkjets or more established color technologies like dye sublimation. Pages produced on a black-and-white laser printer are great for proofing. Some people use laser output for their camera-ready pages; whether this is a good idea is a judgment call. Laser output is very useful for proofing work before you send it to your service bureau. It's also adequate for documents such as correspondences, simple newsletters, or price sheets. But laser output doesn't have a high enough quality for high-end publications such as newspapers and magazines. If you want your document to have a polished, professional appearance, we recommend that you have it produced on an imagesetter. Apple Computer, Brother, Hewlett-Packard, Lexmark, and Xerox are major suppliers of such devices.

Imagesetters

Imagesetters are high-end output devices that produce your document pages on film or photo paper, ready to be printed. Imagesetter resolution ranges between roughly 1,200 and 4,000 dots per inch. When you send a document to a service bureau, it's output on an imagesetter. Pages produced on an imagesetter and then printed professionally have a professional look that is well worth the small expense involved. We strongly recommend outputting your final pages to an imagesetter.

Setting Up a Printer

Because printers can have such a variety of features, they usually require setup beyond plugging them in to the computer or network. Making sure your Mac or PC is configured to take full advantage of your printer's capabilities is important. Otherwise, QuarkXPress can't do so. Note that sometimes you'll set up printers you don't actually have attached; this is typically done for imagesetters and other final-output devices that your document may use and for which you want to output to via output files rather than through a direct printer connection.

Mac and Windows printer setup differs considerably, so we cover them in separate sections in this chapter.

Setting up Macintosh printers

Although you choose the printer type in the Setup pane of the Print dialog box, you still need to set up the printer on your Mac before you can use it. To do that, the Mac has a program called the Chooser, which appears in the Apple menu. The Chooser will list drivers for all sorts of printers — PostScript, inkjet, fax modems, whatever is installed. Make sure the printer you want to set up is connected to your Mac and turned on. (If you're using a network printer, make sure the Mac is connected to the right network port, through the AppleTalk and TCP/IP control panels [depending on what network protocol(s) you use]; called the Network control panel on older Macs.) Choose the appropriate driver, then select the printer from the list at right, as shown in Figure 35-1.

Next, click the Setup button and configure the printer through the dialog box that then appears (this dialog box generally has several buttons for different options and differs from printer to printer).

Note You may need to install a PPD (PostScript Printer Description) file that contains specific details on your printer; this file should come on a disk or CD with your printer; otherwise, download it from the printer maker's Web site. These files should reside in the Printer Descriptions folder inside the Extensions folder in your System Folder. The Mac OS installs some for you, particularly those for Apple-branded printers.

Close the Chooser when you're done. Your printer is now set up.

Tip   We recommend you set Background Printing to On, so your Mac can print while you're working on other stuff. And to print on a networked printer, make sure AppleTalk is set to Active (even if you use TCP/IP).

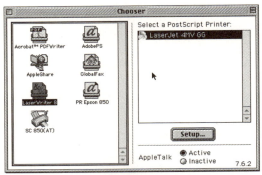

Figure 35-1: The Mac's Chooser lets you select printer drivers (Acrobat PDFWriter, AdobePS, LaserWriter 8, PR Epson 850, and SC 859(AT) are available here) and get a list of available, supported printers when clicking them, as shown at right.

Drag-and-drop printing

Drag-and-drop printing is also called *desktop printing*. Versions 7.5 and later of the Mac OS let you create icons for each installed printer and place these icons on your desktop. You can drag a file onto a printer to have it printed; the Mac will launch the program needed to print the file. If you double-click a printer icon, you'll get a list of any print jobs in progress or on hold, as shown in Figure 35-2. If a printer icon is selected, the Printing menu appears in the Finder desktop, letting you start and stop print queues and specify the default printer. (The default printer is the one that will appear in your program's Print dialog boxes. You usually need to change the default printer through the Printing menu if you want to change printers, although some programs let you change printers in their Print dialog boxes.)

The default printer is different than the Printer Description set in the Print dialog box's Setup pane. You could select a completely different printer in the Setup pane than you're actually printing to. This usually results in no or garbled output, because the printer is getting instructions designed for a different device (the printer whose printer description was selected).

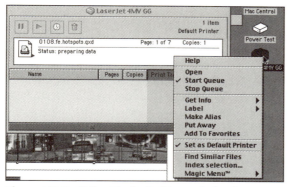

Figure 35-2: If the Mac's desktop printing is enabled, you can open a print job dialog box by double-clicking the printer icon or using the Open command in the context menu for that icon.

Setting up Windows printers

To set up a Windows printer, use Start ➪ Settings ➪ Printers. You'll then see a window with a list of existing printers and an icon labeled Add New Printer. Double-click the printer to set up, or double-click Add New Printer (you'll likely need a disk that came with the printer, or the Windows CD-ROM if you add a new printer, because Windows will need information specific to that printer). When you open an existing printer, use Printer ➪ Properties to get the dialog box like that shown in Figure 35-3.

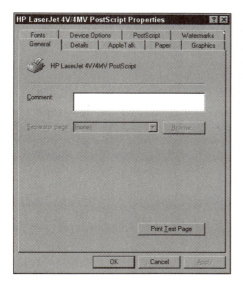

Figure 35-3: The Properties dialog box for a Windows printer. (Not all panes will appear for all printers, depending on the printer type chosen and the network protocols installed.)

Here are two panes that matter most:

✦ **Fonts pane:** This pane lets you specify what happens to non-PostScript fonts when printing to a PostScript printer. The best setting is to have the printer translate TrueType fonts to PostScript (via the Outlines option in Send TrueType Fonts) and to substitute the standard PostScript fonts for the basic TrueType fonts, such as Arial and Times New Roman (via Substitute Printer Fonts for TrueType Fonts When Available), as shown in Figure 35-4. Be sure to select Add Euro Currency Symbol to PostScript Fonts as well.

✦ **Device Options pane:** This pane lets you configure items such as RAM amount, as shown in Figure 35-5. Make sure this is set correctly, based on your printer's actual configuration.

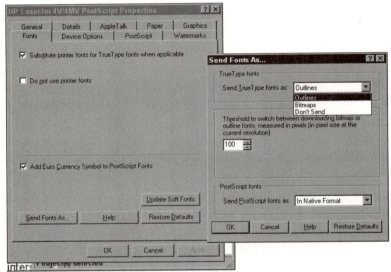

Figure 35-4: The Fonts pane in Windows set up for PostScript devices.

Tip   We recommend you use Adobe's PostScript driver rather than Microsoft's. The Microsoft driver often doesn't send fonts to the printer, and it often prints extra blank pages at the end of a job. The Adobe Universal PostScript driver doesn't have these issues. You can download the Adobe driver from www.adobe.com/support/downloads in the Printer Drivers section. When you install the driver, it will give you the option of converting your existing PostScript printers to the Adobe driver. You must run this program again to install new printers using the Adobe driver — using the Add Printer wizard will automatically install the Microsoft driver for those new printers.

Setting the default printer

To set a printer as the default printer, right-click the printer in the Printers window (Start ➪ Settings ➪ Printers), and select Set Default Printer from the context menu that appears.

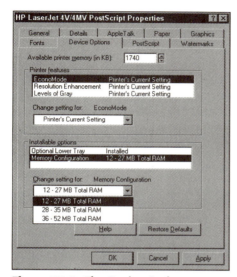

Figure 35-5: The Device Options pane in Windows for a Hewlett-Packard LaserJet 4MV printer.

Getting Ready to Print

When you're ready to print a QuarkXPress document, first make sure that the Document Setup dialog box and Setup pane in the Print dialog boxes are set up the way you'd like them to be. These dialog boxes let you change the size of the document and control the way that it prints. They also let you specify paper size, the orientation of images on the page, and the page image size.

The Document Setup dialog box is where you set the size of your printed page. The dimensions set here determine where the crop marks appear, if you print registration and crop marks (as described later). To display the Document Setup dialog box, shown in Figure 35-6, use File ➪ Document Setup, or use the shortcut Option+Shift+⌘+P or Ctrl+Alt+Shift+P.

Figure 35-6: The Document Setup dialog box.

You control printer– and page-specific options through the menu item File ⇨ Page Setup or the shortcut Option+⌘+P or Ctrl+Alt+P. These bring you to the Print dialog box's Setup pane, where you set basic output settings, and let you access more printer options through the dialog box that appears when you click the Page Setup button (on the Mac) or Properties button (in Windows) to set up the printer. Figures 35-7 and 35-8 show the Setup pane and the printer dialog boxes for Macintosh and Windows, respectively.

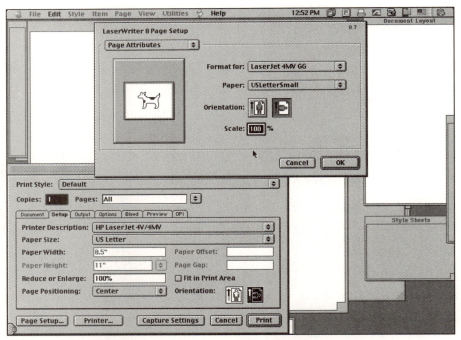

Figure 35-7: The Setup pane and printer options dialog box on the Mac.

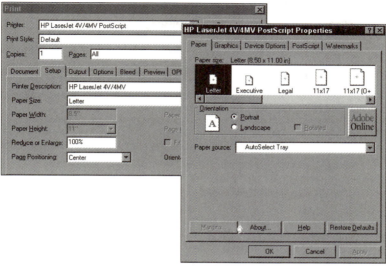

Figure 35-8: The Setup pane and printer options dialog box in Windows.

Options you can set in the Printer dialog box's Setup pane include the following:

✦ **Printer Description:** This is a pop-up menu that lists the printers for which a PostScript printer description file (PPD) is available. On the Mac, these files are installed in the Printer Descriptions folder (in the Extensions folder, which is in the System Folder), although QuarkXPress will also find them if they're in a folder named "PPD" within the QuarkXPress folder. In Windows, these files are typically installed in the System folder inside the folder that contains the Windows OS (usually called Windows or WinNT). Printers should come with a disk that contains these files and installs them in the appropriate Mac or Windows location. QuarkXPress has printer descriptions appropriate for common printers and imagesetters.

✦ **Paper Size, Width, and Height:** For Paper Size, choose the size of the paper that will be used in the printer. The size of the paper you'll be using doesn't always correspond directly to the trim size of your final document. Note that if you select a printer that's able to print on nonstandard pages (such as an imagesetter), the Paper Width and Paper Height fields of the dialog box become active so that you can specify the size of the paper.

✦ **Paper Offset and Page Gap:** The Paper Offset and Page Gap fields are controls used in imagesetters; don't change them unless your service bureau directs you to. But do ask what the service bureau prefers the first time you work with them.

Tip

If you have elements that bleed off the page and you're printing with a commercial printing press, make sure the paper size is larger than the document size by at least ¼ inch wide and ¼ inch tall (⅛ inch on each side).

✦ **Reduce or Enlarge:** You can scale a page before you print it by entering a value between 25 percent and 400 percent. Printing at reduced scale is particularly useful if your document's page size is large and if you can get by with a reduced version of the document for proofing purposes.

✦ **Page Positioning:** This pop-up menu lets you align the page within the paper it's being printed on. Your choices are Left Edge (the default), Center (centers both horizontally and vertically), Center Horizontal, and Center Vertical.

✦ **Fit in Print Area:** This calculates the percentage of reduction or enlargement necessary to ensure that the document page fits fully within the paper size. Almost every printer has a gap along at least one edge where the printer grasps the paper (usually with rollers) to move it through the printing assembly. The printer can't print in this gap, so a document as large as the paper size usually has part of it cut off along one or more edges of the paper. Checking this option ensures that nothing is cut off.

✦ **Orientation:** Click on the icon that looks like a portrait to get vertical orientation of the document (taller than wide). The horizontal icon produces pages with a landscape orientation (wider than tall).

The printer-specific dialog boxes available through the Printer and Properties buttons will vary by printer, but here are the common options (some duplicate features in QuarkXPress's Print dialog box) first for Mac and then for Windows.

Mac-specific options

In the Mac, the typical panes (accessible via the pop-up menu below the printer name) are:

✦ **General,** which lets you set paper sources, page ranges, and number of copies

✦ **Background Printing,** which lets you control the priority of print jobs

✦ **Color Matching,** which lets you choose between color and black-and-white printing, as well as select a color profile to adjust color output

✦ **Cover Page,** which lets you select whether a special cover page is printed

✦ **Font Settings,** which lets you control handling of PostScript and TrueType fonts

✦ **Job Logging,** which lets you control how errors are reported and whether a job report is printed

✦ **Layout,** which lets you control page printing order, whether a border prints, and *n*-up printing (having multiple pages print on one sheet, a user-specified thumbnails feature)

✦ **Save as File,** which lets you control whether pages are printed to a file and, if so, how fonts are handled and what version of PostScript is used

✦ **Printer-Specific Options,** which lets you specify options specific to the selected printer

There are also setup options specific to the Mac, as shown in Figure 35-9. In Mac QuarkXPress, you get one set of these options by clicking the Page Setup button in the Print dialog box and then the Options button, and a second set of these options by clicking the Printer button and then the PostScript Options option in the pop-up menu. The special Mac options are listed under the Image & Text heading.

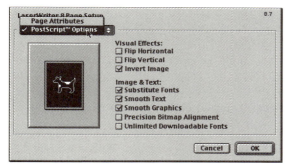

Figure 35-9: The PostScript Options dialog box accessible via the Printer button.

The controls will vary from printer to printer, but here are the basic options:

✦ Check the Substitute Fonts box to substitute Times for New York, Helvetica for Geneva, and Courier for Monaco. Leaving it unchecked means that the printer will print bitmap versions of these system fonts instead (unless the appropriate TrueType or PostScript Type 1 versions are installed).

✦ To smooth the printing of bitmap fonts for which no PostScript or TrueType font is installed, check Smooth Text. You should usually leave this option unchecked, as you will probably have the PostScript or TrueType versions of most of the bitmap fonts you use.

✦ To smooth printed bitmap images, check Smooth Graphics. You may want to avoid this option if you're printing screen shots, because it may make text in dialog boxes look strange or hard to read.

♦ To print bitmap images faster, check Faster Bitmap Printing. This is usually unnecessary, however.

♦ If you use many fonts, check Unlimited Downloadable Fonts in a Document. This may make printing take a bit longer, but it will help to make sure all of your text prints in the correct font (especially text in imported EPS pictures).

♦ Check Precision Bitmap Alignment or Larger Print Area (Fewer Downloadable Fonts) only if requested by your service bureau or printing expert.

Avoid setting anything in these platform-specific dialog boxes that you can also set in QuarkXPress. It's better to set up local printer settings within your QuarkXPress documents than to use these global settings.

Windows-specific options

In Windows, the typical panes accessed from the Properties button are:

♦ **Paper,** which lets you choose paper source (for multi-tray printers), size, and orientation

♦ **Graphics,** which lets you choose output dpi resolution (if the printer supports multiple resolutions), scaling, negative creation, and *n*-up printing (having multiple pages print on one sheet, a user-specified thumbnails feature)

♦ **Device Options,** which lets you specify options specific to the selected printer

♦ **PostScript,** where a pop-up menu lets you choose between fast output, more compatible output (for printing to file), EPS output, and archival output (a version of PostScript that strips out printer-specific commands so the document can be used on any PostScript devices)

♦ **Watermarks,** which lets you have text, such as "Confidential," appear on the backgrounds of pages

To print to file in Windows, you must set up a separate printer that sets the output port to FILE: using the Add Print Wizard (Start ⇨ Settings ⇨ Printers). For example, you might add an imagesetter as a printer and choose FILE: as its port so you can create output files for that imagesetter. If that imagesetter is also available on the network and you want to be able to print directly to it, you'll need to add the imagesetter again through the wizard but this time choose the network location for it. (If you have a direct connection to the device, you would choose a local port rather than a network connection.) Figure 35-10 shows where you set the output to be FILE:.

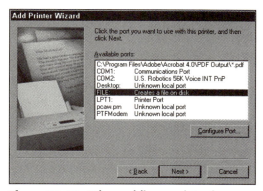

Figure 35-10: When adding a printer in Windows, select FILE: in the Add Printer wizard to be able to print to file in that printer's format. This means you may have two instances of a printer in Windows: one to print to the printer and one to print to file for it. (Note that this is the Windows 98 screen for the Add Printer wizard; the Windows 2000 and XP versions look slightly different, though they have the same options.)

Printing Options in QuarkXPress

After the page is set up for printing and the printer is set up for printing, you're ready to actually print the document. To print a document, select File ➪ Print (or the shortcut ⌘+P or Ctrl+P) to open the Print dialog box, which has seven panes (or eight, if you have the Quark CMS XTension installed), as well as several options common to all the panes. (One of those panes is the Setup pane, covered in the previous section.) Change any options, choose OK, and QuarkXPress sends your document to the printer (or file, if you're printing to a PostScript file).

New Feature QuarkXPress 5 adds two panes to the Print dialog box — Bleed and OPI — for functions available in other panes previously. The Color Management pane has also been renamed Profiles.

Purely PostScript no more

In QuarkXPress 5, many new output options are available for non-PostScript printers; in earlier versions they were grayed out in the Print dialog box. Today, all that's changed. More and more non-PostScript printers are being used by designers and publishers for proofing purposes, particularly inexpensive color inkjet printers.

Heeding the call, QuarkXPress has added several new enhancements for non-PostScript printers to QuarkXPress 5. For example, you can now print pages as thumbnails to non-PostScript printers. Also, the Reduce or Enlarge field, the Page Positioning pop-up menu, and the Fit in Print Area check box features are now non-PostScript-friendly.

QuarkXPress 5 now lets you print RGB composite picture files to non-PostScript printers, and you can print rotated TIFF pictures at full resolution to non-PostScript printers. Another cool non-PostScript enhancement is the addition of print styles for non-PostScript printers.

Probably more significant, though, you can now use the Frequency field in the Print dialog box's Output pane to control the line frequency for imported pictures when printing to a non-PostScript printer. Before, these sorts of sophisticated, professional print features were thought worthy only of PostScript printers.

It's doubtful that PostScript output devices will be dethroned by non-PostScript devices anytime soon. And PostScript still remains the official language (printing language, that is) of the high-end publishing world. Still, it would seem that while PostScript is still far from being on its way out, there are now some solid, less expensive alternatives out there — making a home publishing system even more attainable than ever before.

Some common options

No matter what pane is open, the following options are always available:

- ✦ **Print Style:** You choose the *print style* — a saved set of printer settings — from this list. Print styles are covered later in this chapter.

- ✦ **Copies:** Enter how many copies of the document you want printed.

- ✦ **Pages:** Choose which pages to print. You can enter a range, such as 3–7; a single page, such as 4; a set of unrelated pages, such as 3, 7, 15, 28; or a combination, such as 3–7, 15, 28–64, 82–85. Select All from the pop-up menu to print all pages, or type All.

 If you'd prefer to use something other than a hyphen (-) to indicate a sequential range and a comma (,) to indicate nonsequential, separate pages, go to the Interactive pane of the Preferences dialog box, accessible via Edit ⇨ Preferences ⇨ Preferences, or Option+Shift+⌘+Y or Ctrl+Alt+Shift+Y, go to the Range Separators section, and substitute your preferred symbols.

- ✦ **Capture Settings:** This button remembers the current Print dialog box settings and returns you to your document. This way, you can make a change and return to the Print dialog box later without having to reestablish your settings.

✦ **Print:** This button prints the document.

✦ **Cancel:** This button exits the Print dialog box without printing.

✦ **Page Setup:** This button opens the Mac's Page Setup dialog box, covered earlier in this chapter.

✦ **Printer:** This button opens the Mac's Printer dialog box, covered earlier in this chapter.

 Windows QuarkXPress doesn't have the Page Setup or Printer buttons. But, as described earlier in this chapter, it does have the Properties button, which opens the properties for the current printer, and the Printer pop-up menu, in which you choose the printer to use. (On the Mac, you use the Chooser, a desktop printer icon, or the Finder's Printing menu to select the printer, as described earlier in this chapter.)

The Document pane

In this pane, shown in Figure 35-11, you set up the basic page attributes.

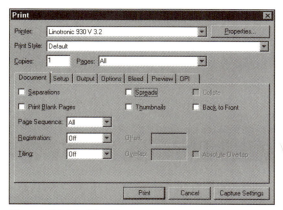

Figure 35-11: The Document pane.

The following items describe the options in the current version of QuarkXPress and how to use them:

✦ **Separations:** Prints color separations, putting each color on its own sheet (or negative), for use in producing color plates.

✦ **Include Blank Pages:** Sometimes you want blank pages to print, such as when you're outputting pages to be photocopied, where you want the blank pages used as separators between sections of your document. Check this option to output blank pages, uncheck it to print only pages with text or graphics on them.

✦ **Spreads:** If your printer can print facing pages on one sheet of paper (such as if you have an 11-x-17-inch printer and your pages are 8½ x 11 inches or smaller) and you want them printed that way, check this option.

Caution

If you have bleeds, you may not want to use the Spreads option when outputting to an imagesetter, because there will be no extra space for the bleed between the spreads. If you use traditional *perfect-binding* (square spines) or *saddle-stitching* (stapled spines) printing methods, in which facing pages aren't printed contiguously, don't use this option.

✦ **Thumbnails:** To get a miniature version of your document printed several pages to a sheet, select this option.

✦ **Collate:** This option remains grayed out unless you're printing more than one copy. If checked, it will print a full copy of the document and then repeat for as many times as copies are specified. If unchecked, this option will print the number of copies of each page before going on to the next page (such as ten copies of page 1, followed by ten copies of page 2, and so on). Collating takes longer for a printer than not collating, but it may save *you* time.

✦ **Back to Front:** If checked, this reverses the printing order, so the last page comes first, followed by the next-to-last page, and so on. This is handy for output devices that print with the pages facing up, rather than facing down.

✦ **Page Sequence:** You can select All, Odd, or Even, which will print the specified type of pages from whatever range you select in the Pages box. Thus, if you select Odd and specify a page range of 2–6, pages 3 and 5 will print. Note that this option is grayed out if you've checked the Spreads option.

✦ **Registration:** This adds registration marks and crop marks, which you'll need if your document is being professionally printed. A printer uses the registration marks to line up the page correctly on the printing press. Registration crop marks define the edge of the page (handy if you're printing to paper or negatives larger than your final page size). If you print color separations, enabling registration marks also prints the name of each color on its negative and includes a color bar in the output, so that the printing press operator can check that the right colors are used with the right plates. You can choose to have registration centered, off-center, or turned off. If you check Registration, you have the added option of selecting Centered or Off Center registration marks. Centered is the default.

Tip

Use the Off Center registration option when your page size is square or nearly square. Choosing Off Center makes it easy for the press operator to tell which sides of the page are the left and right sides and which are the top and bottom sides, thus reducing the chances that your page will be accidentally rotated.

✦ **Tiling:** For documents that are larger than the paper you're printing them on, select Manual or Automatic to have QuarkXPress break your page into smaller chunks that fit on the page; you can then stitch those pages together. QuarkXPress will print marks on your pages to help you line up the tiles. Here's how the options work:

- If you choose Auto, QuarkXPress determines where each tile breaks. You can select the amount of tile overlap by entering a value in the Overlap field. You can enter a value between 0 and 6 inches.

- If you enter a value in the Overlap field, QuarkXPress will print that over-lapped area on both adjacent tiles, giving you duplicate material that you can overlap the tiles with to help with alignment.

- If you check the Absolute Overlap option, QuarkXPress will make sure the overlap is always exactly the value specified in the Overlap field. If it's unchecked, QuarkXPress will center the tiled image on the assem-bled pages, increasing the overlap if necessary.

- If you choose Manual, you decide where the tiles break by repositioning the ruler origin in your document. For all pages selected, QuarkXPress prints the tiled area whose upper-left corner matches the ruler's origin. Repeat this step for each tiled area. Choose the Manual tile option if cer-tain areas of your document make more logical break points than others.

The Output pane

The Output pane, shown in Figure 35-12, is where you set many attributes for print-ing to an imagesetter, whether you're producing black-and-white documents or color-separated documents. You also use this pane for printing to a standard printer and to set resolution and color modes. The following two sections explain the options for both types of printers.

Using the section-numbering feature

If you use the QuarkXPress section-numbering feature to create multiple sections in your document, you must enter the page numbers exactly as they're labeled in the document. (The label for the current page appears in the lower-left corner of your document screen.) Include any prefix used and enter the labels in the same format (letters, Roman numerals, or regular numerals) used in the section whose pages you want to print.

Alternately, you can indicate the absolute page numbers by preceding the number with a plus sign (+). For example, suppose that you have an eight-page document with two sec-tions of four pages each. You label pages one through four as AN-1 through AN-4 and label pages five through eight as BN-1 through BN-4. If you enter BN-1 through BN-4 in the Pages field of the Print dialog box, QuarkXPress prints the first four pages in the section that uses the BN- prefix. If you enter +5 through +8, QuarkXPress prints document pages five through eight—which again includes BN-1 through BN-4.

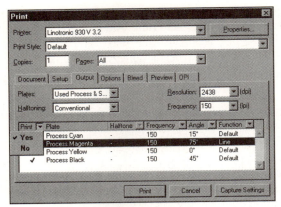

Figure 35-12: The Output pane.

QuarkXPress offers several advanced printing options designed for professional publishing users. Options not available for non-PostScript printers (such as color options) are grayed out in the Print dialog box.

Here's how the settings work in the Output pane of the Print dialog box:

✦ **Print Colors:** This pop-up menu (available only if the Separations option is not checked in the Document pane) lets you select Black & White, Grayscale, and, on a color printer, Composite RGB and, for some printers, Composite CMYK. The Grayscale option is handy for printing proof copies on non-color printers. It's also helpful if you have a color image that you cannot otherwise convert to grayscale for use in a black-and-white document. If the Black & White option is checked, colors may appear as solid whites or blacks if printed to a non-color printer. The Composite RGB and Composite CMYK options print color images in color.

The choice of RGB and CMYK composite output is new to QuarkXPress 5.

✦ **Plates:** Appearing where the Print Colors pop-up menu does if the Separations option is checked in the Document pane, you use this pop-up menu to deter-mine whether all spot and process (CMYK) colors are output to their own individual plates (All Process & Spot, which had been called Spot & Process in QuarkXPress 4) or if all the spot colors (such as PANTONE) are converted into the four process plates (Convert to Process). The answer depends on the capabilities of your printing press and the depth of your budget; typically, you'd choose Convert to Process.

A new option in QuarkXPress 5 is the Used Process & Spot item in the Plates pop-up menu. This outputs only plates for each color actually used in the document (so default colors that come with QuarkXPress are not automatically output onto plates as in previous versions).

✦ **Halftoning:** Use this pop-up menu to choose the halftone settings specified in QuarkXPress (the Conventional option) or to use the defaults in your printer. For black-and-white and composite-color printing, you'd typically choose Printer, unless you used halftoning effects in the QuarkXPress Style menu. For color separations, only Conventional is available, because QuarkXPress has to do the halftoning calculations itself so it can also figure out the color trapping.

✦ **Resolution:** Select the dpi (dots per inch) at which the imagesetter will be printing the document. The minimum resolution for most imagesetters is 1270 dpi. If you choose a lower setting in QuarkXPress than the printer is set for, all images will be halftoned at the lower resolution.

✦ **Frequency:** Specify the lines per inch (lpi) for your target printer. QuarkXPress will choose an initial setting based on the Resolution field's setting, but you can also select from the pop-up menu's other popular frequencies.

Screening angles explained

Normally, you'd probably never worry about the screening angles for your color plates. After all, the service bureau makes those decisions, right? Maybe. If you have your own image-setter, or even if you're just using a proofing device, you should know how to change screen angles for the best output. If you're working with spot colors that have shades applied to them, you'll want to know what the screen angles are so that you can determine how to set the screening angles for those spot colors.

Screening angles determine how the dots comprising each of the four process colors—cyan, magenta, yellow, and black—or any spot colors are aligned so they don't overprint each other. The rule of thumb is that dark colors should be at least 30 degrees apart, while lighter colors (for example, yellow) should be at least 15 degrees apart from other colors. That rule of thumb translates into a 105-degree angle (also called −15 degrees; it's the same angle) for cyan, 75 degrees for magenta, 90 degrees for yellow, and 45 degrees for black.

But those defaults sometimes result in moiré patterns. (*Moiré* is pronounced *mwah-ray* or *more-ay.*) With traditional color-separation technology, a service bureau would have to manually adjust the angles to avoid such moirés—an expensive and time-consuming process. With the advent of computer technology, modern output devices, such as image-setters, can calculate angles based on the output's lpi settings to avoid most moiré patterns. (Each image's balance of colors can cause a different moiré, which is why there is no magic formula.) Every major imagesetter vendor uses its own proprietary algorithm to make these calculations.

PostScript Printer Description (PPD) files contain printer-specific, optimized settings, including for screen output and resolution. (Many of these PPD files come bundled with various programs, including QuarkXPress, and are also often available from the manufacturer's Web as well as from the downloads sections of `www.adobe.com`.) QuarkXPress automatically uses the PPD values to calculate the recommended halftoning, lpi, and frequency settings shown in the Output pane of the Print dialog box.

In QuarkXPress 5, you can override the frequency, angle, and function (screen element) for specific color plates. If you're outputting separations, you can also select which plates print. Select the plate from the list in the pane, then use the pop-up menus that the Print, Halftone, Frequency, Angle, and Function headings become. (These headings don't function as pop-up menus unless color printing is selected; the Resolution and Frequency settings elsewhere in the pane, plus any halftoning set through the Style menu, will be used instead.) Figure 35-12 shows this new feature in use.

The Options pane

The Options pane is almost exclusively designed for people using an imagesetter to create film negatives. Typically, your service bureau will adjust these settings or tell you how they want you to set them. Figure 35-13 shows the pane.

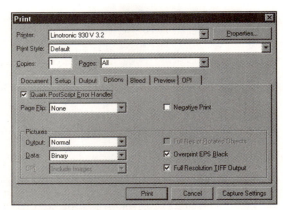

Figure 35-13: The Options pane.

The Page Flip and Negative Print options determine how the film negatives (or positives) are actually produced. The Output, Data, OPI, Overprint EPS Black, Full Res of Rotated Objects, and Full Resolution TIFF Output options determine how pictures are printed. The following list describes how each option works:

    ✦ **Quark PostScript Error Handler:** This check box enables a neat utility that will help you diagnose output problems on a PostScript printer. PostScript is a language, and sometimes programs use it incorrectly, or at least differently from what the printer expects, which leads to incorrect output or often no output at all. If this option is checked, QuarkXPress will print a report when it encounters a PostScript error and will even print the problem page to the point where the error occurred, helping you narrow down the problem (it may be in an imported image, for example).

✦ **Page Flip:** This pop-up menu lets you mirror your page; your options are Horizontal, Vertical, and Horizontal & Vertical. You would use this feature if your service bureau requests that the page be flipped. Otherwise, leave this option at the default None setting. Reasons to flip a page have to do with what's called reading and emulsion. *Reading* is the direction on which the page prints on a negative (to the left or to the right), while *emulsion* is the stuff on the negative that holds the image. Different printing presses expect the reading to be different ways and the emulsion to be on a specific side of the negative. The Page Flip settings let your service bureau adjust how the pages print in anticipation of these needs.

✦ **Negative Print:** This check box will print an inverse image of your pages, exchanging black with white, and dark colors with light ones. Your service bureau uses this option if it has imagesetters that can print both positives and negatives (so the service bureau can have the correct output based on what it's printing on). Have your service bureau tell you when to use this option.

When both Negative Print is checked and a page is flipped either horizontally or vertically, the result is that the page is printed right-reading, emulsion side down, which is the typical setting in the United States for printing presses.

✦ **Output:** The default is Normal, but you can also choose Low Resolution or Rough from this pop-up menu. Normal means the pictures print normally; Low Resolution means the pictures print at the screen resolution (usually 72 dpi); Rough means the pictures don't print at all. You use the last two when you're focusing on the text and layout, not the images, because Low Resolution and Rough greatly accelerate printing time.

✦ **Data:** Typically your service bureau will tell you which of the three settings to use: Binary (smaller file sizes, faster printing, but not editable), ASCII (larger file sizes, slower printing, but editable), and Clean 8-Bit (a "hybrid" of binary and ASCII, somewhere between the two in size, that can safely be sent to PC-based output devices).

✦ **OPI:** If you *don't* use an Open Prepress Interface (OPI) server, leave this option at the default setting of Include Images. If you use OPI, choose Omit TIFF if your OPI server has only high-resolution TIFF files (the most common type of OPI setup), and choose Omit TIFF & EPS if your OPI server contains both EPS and TIFF files. (An OPI server stores the original high-resolution image files on a server and lets your designers keep smaller, low-resolution versions of images on their local computers. This makes the layouts load and display faster when being designed.)

✦ **Full Res of Rotated Objects:** This option ensures that rotated objects are printed at their full resolution on non-PostScript printers. This takes more imaging time (since the printer must recalculate all the pixel positions in the image because the rotation has moved them to perhaps suboptimal patterns for printing) and will slow down printer output, but it makes for the most accurate output of these images. (PostScript devices will output rotated images at their maximum resolution, so this option is grayed out when they're used.)

✦ **Overprint EPS Black:** Normally, QuarkXPress prints black using the trapping settings set in the Trap Specifications dialog box (accessed via the Edit Trap button in the Colors dialog box, which you open via Edit ➪ Colors, or Shift+F12). But EPS files may have their own trapping settings for black defined in the program that created the EPS file. If you check the Overprint EPS Black option, QuarkXPress forces all black elements in EPS files to overprint other colors. This doesn't affect how other black elements in QuarkXPress print.

✦ **Full Resolution TIFF Output:** This option overrides the Frequency setting in the Output pane when TIFF images are printed. (Other elements are not affected.) If checked, it sends the TIFF image to the printer at the highest resolution possible based on the Resolution setting in the Output pane. You use this when you want your TIFF images (typically photos and scans) to be as sharp as possible. Sharpness is more of an issue for bitmapped images than for text and vector images, which is why QuarkXPress offers this feature.

New Feature The Full Res of Rotated Objects option is new to QuarkXPress 5.

The Bleed pane

This pane, shown in Figure 35-14, is where you tell QuarkXPress how much room to leave around the document edges for elements that bleed off. This is useful when printing to a file or to an imagesetter to ensure that the bleed is not inadvertently removed or shortened. A value of ⅛ inch (0.125 inch) suffices for most work.

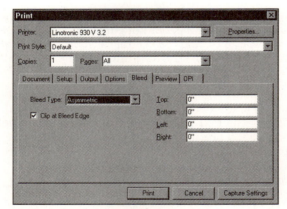

Figure 35-14: The Bleed pane.

New Feature The pane is new to QuarkXPress 5, although the ability to set bleeds is not (it used to be done in the Document pane). QuarkXPress 5 broke out the Bleed pane because it has added new Bleed options.

Previous versions provided only one bleed setting for the document, but QuarkXPress 5 lets you control whether the bleed setting is the same for all sides of the page or varies for each. If you select the Symmetric option in the Bleed Type pop-up menu, the bleed amount applies to all four sides. If you choose Asymmetric, you can set the bleed individually for each side. The Page Items option makes the page boundary the bleed boundary (no bleeds).

There's also a new Clip at Bleed Edge check box. If checked, it prevents anything outside the bleed rectangle from printing, even if it's within the imageable area of the output device. When Clip at Bleed Edge is unchecked, QuarkXPress prints all objects that are at least partially within the bleed rectangle *if* they fit within the imageable area.

The Preview pane

It's easy to set up your Print dialog box and print your job, only to find out that something was offbase after your pages printed. Use the Preview pane (which Quark has enhanced in QuarkXPress 5, after first introducing it in version 4) to ensure that margins, crop marks, bleeds, and other element-fitting issues actually work with your target paper size.

Figure 35-15 shows an example Preview pane in which the document exceeds the right side of the page boundaries.

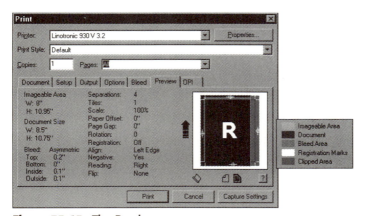

Figure 35-15: The Preview pane.

 New Feature The Preview pane has new enhancements to indicate the type of paper used and the page position relative to the spine.

The Preview pane shows the document area, bleed area, imageable area, and any clipped areas using specific colors. You can get a list of these colors by clicking the ? icon below the preview. There are other new icons below the preview, including one that indicates whether the output is to a roll of paper (as shown in Figure 35-15) or to sheets of paper (the icon would change to a stack of pages).

Two new icons, the Right of Spine and Left of Spine icons, appear below the preview *only* if you have an asymmetric bleed specified for a document with facing pages. Clicking on the Left of Spine and Right of Spine icons should give you a different preview for the left and right pages, adjusting its position based on those asymmetric bleed settings and their relationship to the inside page margin (spine).

The other visual indicators are the big *R* that indicates the reading order for the text and the big arrow that indicates the direction the paper feeds into the output device. The rest of the pane gives all the specific output settings.

The Profiles pane

If color management is active (via Edit ➪ Preferences ➪ Color Management), you'll get a Profiles pane, as Figure 35-16 shows.

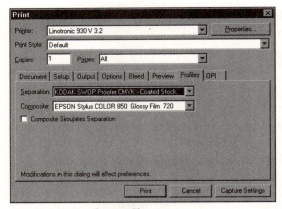

Figure 35-16: The Profiles pane.

The pane lets you select the color profile for RGB and CMYK output, a well as determine whether the composite output, such as to an inkjet printer for proofing, tries to simulate the CMYK output.

> ✦ **Separation Profile:** Here, you choose the output device (such as a printing press) that QuarkXPress should color-correct all images for when creating color separations. The default profile is whatever you specified in the Color Management dialog box.

✦ **Composite Profile:** Here, you choose the output device (typically an inkjet printer, thermal-wax printer, color laser printer, or dye-sublimation printer, but sometimes a proofing system or a CMYK output device) that QuarkXPress should color-correct all images for when printing colors on a single page (rather than color-separating them). The default profile is whatever you specified in the Color Management dialog box.

✦ **Composite Simulates Separation:** If you check this box, QuarkXPress will alter the colors on your composite printer to make them match the separations printer as closely as possible. Use this when you're proofing color on a local composite printer before sending the final document out for color separations.

The OPI pane

This new pane, which appears only if the OPI XTension is active, lets you turn on the Open Prepress Interface feature, letting you store high-resolution images on a remote server or at a service bureau while you work on lower-resolution, more manageable-size versions. During printing, the high-resolution images are substituted from the OPI server, and your QuarkXPress settings are applied to them. Figure 35-17 shows the pane.

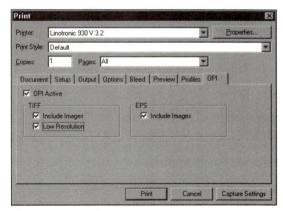

Figure 35-17: The OPI pane.

In the pane, you also determine whether OPI is active for TIFF and EPS images (by clicking Include Images) and whether to substitute a low-resolution version of the TIFF file in local printing. By selecting Include Images, you ensure that the PostScript output contains any special instructions in the master OPI image. By clicking Low Resolution, you speed up printing because QuarkXPress sends only a 36-dpi version of the TIFF file with any functions applied in QuarkXPress rather than the full image. When you output the final document, the OPI server will substitute the high-resolution TIFF image and apply any QuarkXPress instructions to it, so checking this option will *not* downgrade the quality of the final document, though any proofing copies made could be at low resolution.

Printing Color Separations

It's very easy to accidentally use spot colors such as red and PANTONE 111 (say, for picture and text box frames) in a document that contains four-color TIFF and EPS files. The result is that QuarkXPress outputs as many as six plates: one each for the four process colors, plus one for red and one for PANTONE 111. You might expect the red to be separated into 100 percent each of yellow and magenta (which is how red is printed in four-color work). And maybe you expect QuarkXPress to separate the PANTONE 111 into its four-color equivalent (11.5 percent yellow and 27.5 percent black). So why doesn't QuarkXPress do this? Read on.

Using the Edit Color dialog box

By default, each color defined in QuarkXPress — including red, green, and blue, which are automatically available in the Edit ⇨ Colors menu — is set as a spot color. And each spot color gets its own plate, unless you specifically tell QuarkXPress to translate the color into process colors. You do so when defining a new color by unchecking the Spot Color box in the Edit Color dialog box, described in Chapter 28.

Regardless of whether a color was defined as a process or spot color, you can also choose the Convert to Process option in the Print dialog box's Output pane's Plates pop-up menu when printing to convert all spot colors to process colors (refer to Figure 35-12). However, this technique is no good if you want to print a mixture of process colors and spot colors — for example, having red color-separated as 100 percent yellow and 100 percent magenta but PANTONE 111 printed on its own plate as a spot color.

New Feature That's where the new option in the Plates pop-up menu — Used Process & Spot — comes in very handy. It will output plates just for the colors used.

Of course, this Used Process & Spot won't prevent a common human error: If you used one of the QuarkXPress default spot colors, such as Red, and intended to make it a process color instead so it would be separated, but you forgot, you'd get the unwanted red plate instead of having it separated into its yellow and magenta constituent plates.

The advantage to setting the colors to process — either in the Edit Color dialog box or via the context menu in the Colors palette — is that the colors are permanently made into process colors; the Convert to Process option must be used each time you print (which you can automate via print styles, as described later in this chapter).

If your work is primarily four-color work, either remove the spot colors such as blue, red, and green from your Colors dialog box or edit them to make them process colors. If you make these changes with no document open, they become the defaults for all new documents.

Transferring duplicate color sets

If you do some spot-color work and some four-color work, duplicate the spot colors and translate the duplicates into process colors. Make sure that you use a clear color-naming convention, such as Blue P for the process-color version of blue (which is created by using 100 percent each of magenta and cyan). The same is true when you use PANTONE colors (and Hexachrome, Trumatch, Focoltone, Toyo, DIC, and multi-ink colors). If you check the Spot Color box in the Edit Color dialog box (choose Edit ➪ Colors ➪ New), these colors are output as spot colors. Again, you can define a PANTONE color twice, making one of the copies a process color and giving it a name to indicate what it is. Then all you have to do is make sure that you pick the right color for the kind of output you want.

Mixing spot and process colors

You still can mix process and spot colors if you want. For example, if you want a gold border on your pages, you have to use a PANTONE ink because metallic colors cannot be produced via process colors. So use the appropriate PANTONE color, and don't uncheck the Spot Color box when you define the color. When you make color separations, you get five negatives: one each for the four process colors and one for gold. That's fine, because you specifically want the five negatives. (Just make sure that any other colors you created from spot-color models were turned into process colors in the Edit Color dialog box; otherwise, each of these spot colors will print on its own negative, too.)

Setting imagesetter color separation options

If you're printing color separations to an imagesetter, you may want to adjust the output options at the bottom of the Output pane. You'll see a list of plates used in your document. If you chose the Convert to Process option in the Plates pop-up menu, you'll see only the CMYK or Hexachrome plates. You can adjust the characteristics for each plate by selecting a plate and then using the pop-up menus (with the triangle after their names in the column header) to choose a new setting. Figure 35-18 shows this section of the Output pane.

The pop-up menus work as follows:

✦ **Print:** Your options are Yes and No, but it's easier to just click the check mark in this column to suppress printing of a particular plate (if the check mark is visible) or enable printing (if the check mark is not visible).

✦ **Halftone:** Available only for non-CMYK plates, this lets you choose which CMYK plate's halftone settings (the screen frequency, angle, and element) to use. (You can also set each spot color's halftone assignment in the Edit Color dialog box. Use the Output pane to override that setting.) If you have spot colors blending into each other, make sure they use different CMYK colors' halftone settings to avoid poor print quality.

✦ **Frequency:** This lets you set the lines per inch for the specific plate. Typically, it is set for the same plate as is used for the Halftone setting, although you can enter a specific value via the Other option in its pop-up menu.

✦ **Angle:** This option determines the angle on which the dots making up the color-separated pattern align. Light spot colors should use the settings of the yellow (Y) plate, medium-light colors the settings of the cyan (C) plate, medium-dark colors the settings of the magenta (M) plate, and very dark colors the settings of the black (K) plate. You can enter any value — not just the common 0-, 15-, 45-, and 75-degree angles — but do so only after discussing the settings with your printing-press operator or service bureau. Figure 35-18 shows this pop-up menu when a spot color is selected; if you select a process color, you get a dialog box to enter a specific value.

✦ **Function:** This pop-up menu lets you set the halftone dot shape — the shape that comprises the dots that make up an image — for each plate. They should almost always be the same, unless you're trying to achieve a special effect and know what you're doing. Figure 35-18 shows the available dot patterns; one is *tridot,* which is a fine dot pattern not available in the halftone settings in the Style menu.

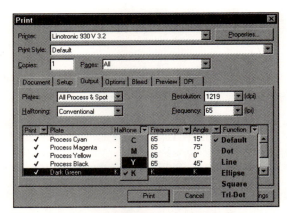

Figure 35-18: Options for overriding halftone and screen element settings in the Output pane.

Printing to a File

Although you'll print mostly to a printer connected to your computer or to the network, there are times you'll want to print to a file. Typically, this happens when you want to output a file exactly as you have created it for output on a service bureau's imagesetter. The imagesetter is probably miles away and is certainly not connected to your computer. But you don't want the service bureau to open your QuarkXPress files directly and print from their computers because you're concerned that settings might be changed accidentally. Or maybe you use XTensions they don't have and thus your files won't print from their computers. Another reason to print a file is as the first step of creating a PDF file via Adobe's Acrobat Distiller program, which converted PostScript files to PDF. (You can also use QuarkXPress 5's new PDF output capability, described in Chapter 40.)

Printing to a file from a Mac

To print to a file from a Macintosh, use the following steps:

STEPS: Printing to a file on the Mac

1. Click the Printer button in the Print dialog box, and then click the File button in the resulting dialog box's Destination section or choose Printer from the Destination pop-up menu.

2. Click the Save (or Print) button, which displays the dialog box shown in Figure 35-19.

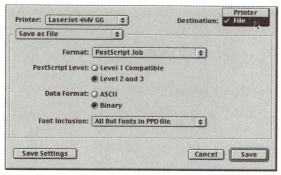

Figure 35-19: Settings for saving output to a file on the Mac.

3. From the Format pop-up list, select PostScript Job. (You would choose EPS or Acrobat PDF if you want to create files in those formats directly; some service bureaus prefer those formats for file-based output.)

4. From the PostScript Level radio buttons, choose Level 1 Compatible or Level 2 and 3. Select the Level 1 Compatible option unless you're sure the output device uses PostScript Level 2 (devices from 1995 and later are almost assuredly Level 2–compatible). You won't lose any capabilities by selecting Level 1 Compatible, although a Level 1 file can take longer to print on a Level 2 or 3 printer.

5. From the Data Format radio buttons, choose ASCII or Binary. If you select the ASCII option, your service bureau will be able to edit some of the defaults (which a savvy service bureau will sometimes do to correct a printing problem), but the file could be very large. If you select Binary, the file is much smaller but uneditable. Ask your service bureau which option it prefers.

6. Select the appropriate option — None, All, All But Standard 13, or All But Fonts in PPD File — from the Font Inclusion pop-up list. The All But Standard 13 option includes font files for all but the 13 faces included with most PostScript printers: the regular, bold, italic, and bold italic faces in the Helvetica, Times, and Courier fonts, as well as the single face in the Symbol font. Most people should select None, because it is easier and faster for the service bureau to download the fonts used into the printer memory (your files will get very large if you include your fonts). But choose All But Standard 13 or All But Fonts in PPD File if you use unusual or custom fonts that the service bureau is unlikely to have.

Printing to a file from Windows

Some Windows programs have a Print to File option in their Print dialog boxes. But QuarkXPress does not, which forces you to create a separate virtual printer in Windows. The process is not difficult, but it's not something that most people generally need to do.

To print to a file from a PC, use the following steps:

STEPS: Printing to a file in Windows

1. Use Start ➪ Settings ➪ Printers to open the Printers window. Double-click the Add New Printer icon. This will launch the Add Printer Wizard.

2. Go through the dialog boxes, selecting the appropriate printer (the one that your print files will ultimately be output on). You may need the Windows CD-ROM or a disk from the printer maker; if so, Windows will tell you. *Note:* When asked whether the printer is a local or network printer, choose local.

3. When you get to the dialog box that lists available Ports, as shown in Figure 35-20, be sure to choose FILE:, not a port like LPT1: or COM1:. This is the key to creating a virtual printer.

4. Complete the installation (skip the printing of a test page). Make sure you name the virtual printer something like printer name To File so you'll know what it is later. From now on, select this printer in the QuarkXPress Print dialog box's Printer pop-up list when you want to print to a file. (It will be available in all Windows programs' Printer pop-up lists.) You may need to create multiple virtual printers if you or your service bureau uses different output devices for which you want to generate print files.

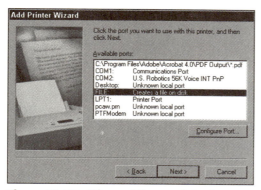

Figure 35-20: When adding a printer in Windows, select FILE: in the Add Printer wizard to be able to print to file in that printer's format. This means you may have two instances of a printer in Windows: one to print to the printer and one to print to file for it. (Note that this is the Windows 98 screen for the Add Printer wizard; the Windows 2000 and XP versions look slightly different, though they have the same options.)

Setting the PostScript level

In mid-1993, Apple Computer and Adobe Systems released the long-awaited PostScript Level 2 specification, for which Microsoft has included a driver since Windows 95 and NT 4.0. If you use this driver to print to a file, make sure the device you're using is Level 2–compatible. (The Adobe PostScript driver we recommended earlier in this chapter instead of the Microsoft driver is Level 2–compatible. It's also compatible with the Level 3 version introduced in 1997 that extends Level 2's color capabilities. But the Adobe driver is not compatible with Level 1 devices.) To set the PostScript level for your printer, use the following steps:

STEPS: Setting the PostScript level in Windows

1. Use Start ➪ Settings ➪ Printers to open the Printers window.

2. Double-click your PostScript printer, and then choose File ➪ Properties.

3. Select the PostScript pane and then click the Advanced button. You'll see a pane like that shown in Figure 35-21.

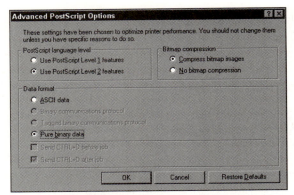

Figure 35-21: Clicking the Advanced button in the PostScript pane displays a dialog box similar to this one.

4. Select the Use PostScript Level 1 Features option in the PostScript Language Level option list unless you're sure the output device uses PostScript Level 2 (devices from 1995 and later are almost assuredly Level 2–compatible). You won't lose any capabilities by selecting Use PostScript Level 1, although a Level 1 file can take longer to print on a Level 2 or 3 printer. If you select the ASCII Data option in the Data Format options list, your service bureau will be able to edit some of the defaults (which a savvy service bureau will sometimes do to correct a printing problem), but the file could be very large. If you select Tagged Binary Communications Protocol or Pure Binary Data, the file is much smaller but uneditable. Ask your service bureau which option it prefers.

Using Print Styles

The ability to create print styles is very handy. It lets you save settings for specific printers and/or specific types of print jobs. To create a print style, use Edit ➪ Print Styles to get the dialog box shown in Figure 35-22.

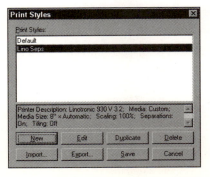

Figure 35-22: The Print Styles dialog box lets you save print settings; you can then select a print style in the Print dialog box.

Print styles tips

It's common to have multiple printers in your office or in your service bureau — laser print-ers for basic business use and quick proofing of layouts, color printers for color proofing, and an imagesetter for final film output. Rather than specify the various settings for each printer each time you print your document — an exercise prone to mistakes given the com-plexity of the QuarkXPress Print dialog box — use print styles to save all these settings. Then just select the printer setting you want to use from the Print dialog box. Here are a couple of additional print style tips:

✦ You can share print styles with other users by using the Export button to save your styles to a file that your colleagues can then import via the Import button.

✦ If you select a print style in the Print dialog box and make changes to the various panes, you'll see the name of the print style change: a bullet (•) will precede the name. This is meant to remind you that you have changed the print style's settings for this particular print session. It does not change the print style itself, so the next time you use that print style, its original settings will be in effect.

When you choose to edit an existing style or create a new style, you get the Edit Print Style dialog box (refer to Figure 35-22). It contains four of the Print dialog box's panes: Document, Setup, Output, and Options. These panes are the same as in the Print dialog box, so set them here as you would there. When you've set the print style's options, click OK, and then click Save in the Print Styles dialog box.

Caution   Unfortunately, QuarkXPress (still!) does not let you take Print dialog box settings and create a print style from them. You must re-create them in the Print Styles dia-log box. So be sure to write them down first.

Summary

QuarkXPress has a broad range of printing controls, letting you determine virtually every aspect of output, from number of pages to bleed areas, from color profiles to halftone screens, from collation to registration marks. The Print dialog box's eight panes (two of which appear only if specific XTensions are active: Profile and OPI) contain all the controls.

When you've determined the best print settings for your document, you can save those settings in a print style that — like a style sheet, color definition, or H&J set — lets you save future work and even share settings across documents.

Beyond QuarkXPress's controls, Windows and the Mac OS have their own printer controls, aimed mainly at setting up printer defaults such as paper trays and installed fonts, that you must also set up so QuarkXPress can tap into those features. Some of the Mac and Windows controls duplicate QuarkXPress's, and you should use QuarkXPress's wherever such duplication occurs.

Printing involves not just working with a printing device, but also printing to file, for use by a service bureau or other program. The Mac and Windows have very different approaches to enabling printing to file.

✦　　✦　　✦

Working with a Service Bureau

Service bureaus — companies that provide high-end output to prepare your files for professional printing — are great. They keep and maintain all the equipment, know the ins and outs of both your software and your printing press requirements, and turn around jobs quickly — at least most of the time. Working with a service bureau involves commitment and communication between both parties. They need your business; you need their expertise and equipment.

To ensure that you get what you want (fast, accurate service) and that the service bureau gets what it wants (no-hassle clients and printing jobs), make sure that you both understand your standards and needs. As a customer, keep in mind that the service bureau has many other customers, all of whom do things differently. Service bureaus likewise must not impose unreasonable requirements just for the sake of consistency, because customers have good reasons for doing things differently.

Terms You'll Encounter

Many specialists have their own terminology, and service bureaus are no exception. Anyone with experience working with service bureaus knows that consistent terminology is one of the key factors in a project's success. By *consistent terminology,* we mean that the words you use to discuss a project should have one definition. Using the correct terms reduces chances of misunderstanding and makes it more likely that your project will turn out the way you want it to.

Color terms

Color is an expansive (and sometimes confusing and esoteric) concept in the world of publishing. The following definitions, however, should start you on your way to a clear understanding of the subject:

✦ **Spot color:** This is a single color applied at one or more places on a page, such as for a screen or as part of an illustration. You can use more than one spot color per page. Spot colors can be special inks such as PANTONE or one of the standard process colors.

✦ **Process color:** A process color is any of the four primary colors in publishing: cyan, magenta, yellow, and black (known as a group as CMYK).

✦ **Color model:** A color model is an industry standard for specifying a color.

✦ **Swatch book:** The printer uses a premixed ink based on the color model identifier you specify; you look up the numbers for various colors in a table of colors (which is often put together as a series of color samples known as a *swatch book*).

✦ **Four-color printing:** This is the use of the four process colors in combination to produce most other colors.

✦ **Color separation:** A color separation is a set of four photographic negatives — one filtered for each process color — shot from a color photograph or image. When overprinted, the four negatives reproduce that image.

✦ **Build:** A build tries to simulate a color-model color by overprinting the appropriate percentages of the four process colors.

✦ **Color space:** This is a method of representing color in terms of measurable values, such as the amount of red, yellow, and blue in a color image. The color space RGB represents the red, green, and blue colors on video screens.

✦ **CIE LAB:** This standard specifies colors by one lightness coordinate and two color coordinates: green-red and blue-yellow.

✦ **CMYK:** This standard specifies colors as combinations of cyan, magenta, yellow, and black.

✦ **Color gamut:** This is the range of colors that a device, such as a monitor or a color printer, can produce.

✦ **High-fidelity color:** This is a form of process color that builds from more than the four CMYK plates.

✦ **PANTONE Hexachrome:** A high-fidelity color model with an ink set that includes orange, green, and black, along with enhanced versions of cyan, magenta, and yellow inks.

Cross-Reference   Part VII of this book covers color in great detail.

Production terms

The following definitions refer to some of the terms you need to know when you're preparing documents for printing.

✦ **Registration marks:** These tell a printer where to position each negative relative to other negatives (the registration marks must line up when the negatives are superimposed). Registration marks also help printers keep different-colored plates aligned with one another on the press.

✦ **Crop marks:** These show a printer where to trim pages down to their final size. An image or page element may extend past the area defined by the crop marks, but anything beyond that area is cut away by the printer. Crop marks are used both to define page size and to indicate which part of an image is to be used.

✦ **Screen:** A screen is an area printed at a particular percentage of a color (including black). For example, the border of a page may have a 20-percent black screen, which appears light gray if printed on white paper.

✦ **Trapping:** This refers to the technique of extending one color so that it slightly overlaps an adjoining color. Trapping is done to prevent gaps between two abutting colors. Such gaps are sometimes created by the misalignment of color plates on a printing press.

For more information on these and related subjects, see Chapter 35.

Collecting for Output

If you've ever had the experience of giving a document to a service bureau, only to be called several hours later by the person who is outputting your document because some of the files necessary to output it are missing, you'll love the Collect for Output feature in QuarkXPress. This command, which you access by choosing File ➪ Collect for Output, copies all the text and picture files necessary to output your document into a folder. It also generates a report that contains all the information about your document that a service bureau is ever likely to need, including the document's fonts, dimensions, and trapping information.

With QuarkXPress 5, Collect for Output is more useful than ever because it also copies fonts, color profiles, and embedded pictures into the collection folder. Previously, you had to review the Collect for Output report and then check to make sure you'd assembled all the files you needed to send to the service bureau.

How it works

The Collect for Output feature generates very useful things to take to your service bureau:

✦ A folder that contains the document and, depending on the options you select, every file used by your document (linked pictures, embedded pictures, color profiles, and fonts)

✦ A report listing all the specifications of the document

To use Collect for Output, begin by saving the document (File ➪ Save, or ⌘+S or Ctrl+S). Then choose File ➪ Collect for Output (see Figure 36-1) and specify the location where you want to place the folder with the document's collected files.

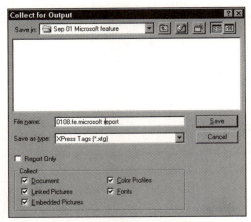

Figure 36-1: The Collect for Output dialog box.

Tip   Before doing a full Collect for Output, it's a good idea to first generate a report about the document so you can review it for errors. To do this, check the Report Only box in the Collect for Output dialog box. This generates a report about the document without actually collecting the files.

Select the options you want in the Collect for Output dialog box:

✦ **Report Only** (see the next section) is unchecked by default. A shortcut that automatically opens the Collect for Output dialog box with Report Only checked is to press Option (Mac) or Alt (Windows) while, at the same time, choosing File ➪ Collect for Output.

✦ **Document** copies the document to a specified folder.

✦ **Linked Pictures** copies imported pictures into the "Pictures" folder inside the collection folder.

✦ **Embedded Pictures** copies pictures, such as .PICT files on the Mac and .BMP and .WMF files on Windows, that are embedded in the documents.

✦ **Color Profiles** (available only when the Quark CMS QuarkXTensions software is loaded) copies color profiles associated with the document itself, or with pictures imported into the document, into the "Color Profiles" folder inside the collection folder.

The Collect for Output dialog box has different font options for Mac and Windows.

✦ **Screen Fonts** (Mac only) copies any screen fonts that are necessary for displaying the document into the "Fonts" folder inside the collection folder.

✦ **Printer Fonts** (Mac only) copies any printer fonts that are necessary for printing the document into the "Fonts" folder inside the collection folder.

✦ **Fonts** (Windows only) copies any fonts that are necessary for printing the document into the "Fonts" folder inside the collection folder.

After you've made the selections in the Collect for Output dialog box, click Save.

Dealing with missing files

If a picture file is missing or has been modified, an alert is displayed. Click List Pictures to display the Missing/Modified Pictures dialog box. Note that if you click OK, and continue with Collect for Output without updating missing or modified pictures, Collect for Output will be unable to collect all the necessary files to output your document correctly. Select each modified picture and click Update to automatically update the picture file. Select each missing picture and click Update to display the Find dialog box. Locate the missing picture file, select it, and click Open. Click OK in the Missing/Modified Pictures dialog box to continue with Collect for Output.

Tip

If your document is linked to picture files that are in various locations on your computer and you'd like to collect them, uncheck Document and check Linked Pictures and Embedded Pictures, then click Save. This will collect all those stray picture files into one collection folder.

The document report

Collect for Output creates a document Report file and places it in the same folder as the copy of the document and its associated font and picture files. The Report file is in XPress Tags format and contains the following information:

✦ Document name, date, total pages, width, and height

✦ The document's original location and the location to which it is copied

✦ Version of QuarkXPress, file size, required XTensions, and active XTensions

✦ A list of any necessary color profiles (if the Quark CMS XTension is active)

✦ Names of the fonts used (remember that sending the actual font files to the service bureau is potentially a violation of your font license)

✦ Pictures used (including size, box/picture angle, skew, path name, type, fonts in EPS, and location in document)

✦ Resolution of pictures

✦ The names of style sheets and H&J sets

✦ Each color created and information to reproduce custom colors

✦ Trapping information

✦ Color plates required for each page

Using the Output Request Template

QuarkXPress provides the Output Request Template (called Output.qxt in Windows) to contain the Report file (it's placed in your QuarkXPress folder when you install the program). This template is shown in Figure 36-2. Open the template (File ➪ Open, or ⌘+O or Ctrl+O) and customize the template to suit your needs. Click on the text box on the lower half of the template and choose File ➪ Get Text, or ⌘+E or Ctrl+E, to import the Collect for Output report. Make sure Include Style Sheets is checked.

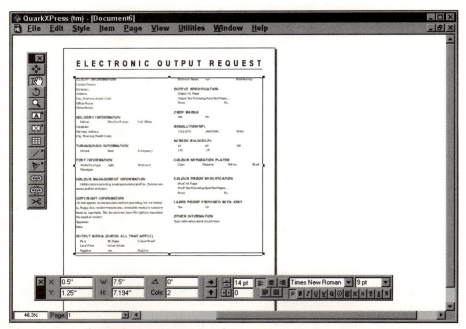

Figure 36-2: The Output Request Template.

Going beyond Collect for Output

Although Collect for Output is a big help, don't let it make you complacent. Relying only on this feature to make sure you're giving the service bureau all the files they need can be risky. A file that looks good on-screen and is capable of being processed by Collect for Output is not necessarily one that will be processed smoothly at the service bureau. Two additional steps you can take to avoid problems are, first, reviewing the document's separations and, second, using a separate preflight software application.

Before collecting the files for output in QuarkXPress, take a close look at the color separations, rather than the on-screen or printed composite. Doing so could save you from sending off a file with an underlying error, one you may otherwise find out about only after paying for film or, worse yet (if no one catches the error on the film), not until after the job has been printed. Make sure that every element on each separation is supposed to be there. Also check that nothing is missing. Even the most experienced publishers find many errors by taking the time to do this type of review.

Another precaution to take before sending the file to your service bureau is to use an after-market software program such as Extensis's Preflight Pro. Preflight programs check your document against a predefined and customizable list of common errors and mistakes. Like the updated (with version 5) QuarkXPress Collect for Output feature, these programs gather all the files (graphics file, fonts, and so on) associated with the document and place them into a folder for you to send to your service bureau. But the real value of preflight programs is that they also check for errors that might otherwise be missed. Remember to first check the printed or PDF color separations of the document before running the preflight program.

We strongly recommend using the Collect for Output feature. It ensures that your service bureau has all the necessary files and information to output your document correctly.

Sending documents versus output files

Now that you have Collect for Output, do you give the service bureau your actual QuarkXPress documents or do you send a PostScript output file? The answer depends on the following things:

✦ A document file, even if the graphics files are copied with it, takes less space than a PostScript file created from your document, which means fewer disks or cartridges to sort through and less time copying files from your media to theirs.

✦ A document file can be changed accidentally, resulting in incorrect output. For example, a color might be changed accidentally when the service bureau checks your color definitions to make sure that spot colors are translated to process colors. Or document preferences might be lost, resulting in text reflow.

✦ The service bureau cannot edit most attributes in a PostScript file. So the service bureau can't come to your rescue if you make a mistake such as forgetting to print registration marks when outputting the PostScript file or specifying landscape printing mode for a portrait document.

✦ PostScript files cannot contain QuarkXPress trapping information, so any trapping settings you create in QuarkXPress for the document will be lost.

✦ Many service bureaus and printers are starting to request PDF files for pre-press rather than document, graphic, and font files. This topic is covered in Chapter 40.

Basically, the question is whom do you trust more: yourself or the service bureau? Only you can answer that. But in either case, there are two things that you can do to help prevent miscommunication: Provide the Collect for Output file and report to the service bureau, and provide a proof copy of your document. The service bureau uses these tools to see if its output matches your expectations — regardless of whether you provided a document file or PostScript file.

Ensuring correct bleeds

Bleed is the term used to describe items that are printed to the edge of a finished page. You create a bleed by extending an item from the document page onto the pasteboard. The Custom Bleeds QuarkXTension, which ships with QuarkXPress, gives you control over how items will bleed.

When you create an image that bleeds, it must actually print beyond the area defined by the crop marks. There must be enough of the bleeding image that, if the paper moves slightly in the press, the image still bleeds. (Most printers expect ⅛ inch, or about a pica, of trim area for a bleed.) In most cases, the document page is smaller than both the page size (specified in QuarkXPress through the File ⇨ Document Setup option) and the paper size, so that the margin between pages is sufficient to allow for a bleed. If your document page is the same size as your paper size, the paper size limits how much of your bleed actually prints: Any part of the bleed that extends beyond the paper size specified is cut off. (This problem derives from the way PostScript controls printing; it has nothing to do with QuarkXPress.)

Make sure that your service bureau knows that you're using bleeds and whether you specified a special paper or page size, because that may be a factor in the way the operator outputs your job.

Sending oversized pages

If you use a paper size larger than U.S. letter size (8½ x 11 inches), tell the service bureau in advance, because the paper size might affect how the operator sends your job to the imagesetter. Many service bureaus use a utility program that automatically rotates pages to save film, because pages rotated 90 degrees still fit along the width of typesetting paper and film rolls. But if you specify a larger paper size to make room for bleeds, or if your document will be printed at tabloid size, this rotation might cause the tops and/or bottoms of your document pages to be cut off.

We've worked with people in service bureaus who forgot that they loaded this page-rotation utility, so they didn't think to unload it for our oversized pages. It took a while to figure out what was going on, because we were certain that we weren't doing the rotation (the service bureau assumed we had) and the service bureau had forgotten that it was using the rotation utility.

Summary

To ensure fast, accurate service and to ensure that the service bureau gets a no-hassle printing job, make sure that you both understand your standards and needs. Using terms (to describe the project) that both you and your service bureau understand reduces the chances of a misunderstanding and makes it more likely that your document will turn out the way you want it to.

The Collect for Output feature generates a report that contains all the information about your document that a service bureau is likely ever to need, including the document's fonts, dimensions, and trapping information. It also lets you collect all the actual document, font, and picture files into a folder that you can give to your service bureau. Before collecting the files for output, review the color separations. Doing so could save you from sending off a file with an underlying error, one you may not otherwise find out about until it's too late in the process.

✦　　✦　　✦

Interactive and Web Publishing

P A R T

◆   ◆   ◆   ◆

In This Part

Chapter 37
Web Publishing
Basics

Chapter 38
Creating Basic
Web Documents

Chapter 39
Creating Interactive
Documents

Chapter 40
Exporting Documents
as PDF Files

◆   ◆   ◆   ◆

In recent years, the rapid growth of the World Wide Web has had a dramatic affect on the way information is distributed. The Web has made it possible for any company to make information available to a worldwide audience without having to deal with many of the issues — and costs — that print publishers face. There's a benefit for readers, too: They get tell-me-what-I-want-to-know-now resources that also offer interactivity, easy navigation, and concise information.

Recognizing this emerging need, QuarkXPress adds several tools to create online documents, for the Web, CD-ROM, and the computer. You can create basic Web pages, output Portable Document Format (PDF) files, and convert your QuarkXPress content into a database format called XML that can then be used and reformatted for any medium.

That's where the chapters in this part help: They show you the basic issues in using QuarkXPress to publish Web, PDF, and XML documents. They also let you know when you have to go beyond QuarkXPress and into more specialized tools. QuarkXPress may have Web and interactive-document capability now, but it's no more a Web-publishing system than Microsoft Word is a desktop-publishing system. QuarkXPress's role in Web and interactive publishing is to extend the program's core print functionality where it makes sense to do so, and to lay the groundwork for the appropriate set of tools where it doesn't.

Web Publishing Basics

QuarkXPress 5, for the first time in its history, is breaking out of the print-only world. The software now includes an entirely separate type of document called a *Web document*. With a Web document, your design and typography options are limited by what makes sense on the Web, but you can include interactive elements such as hyperlinks. You can then export documents in Hypertext Markup Language (HTML) format, the standard format for Web documents. As in the past, you can also convert existing QuarkXPress documents into HTML using third-party XTensions such as BeyondPress. Your success in producing and converting documents for use on the Web, however, depends as much on your background knowledge of Web publishing as on the features in the software.

This chapter endeavors to fill any gaps you may have in your knowledge of issues that affect Web publishing. But keep in mind that producing a document in HTML format is a relatively small task compared to the bigger picture — establishing and maintaining a Web site. We don't attempt to cover that issue in this book. Instead, we confine our coverage to issues specific to QuarkXPress. The publisher of this book, Hungry Minds, offers several good books on HTML and Web publishing, for those who want to dive deeply into Web issues.

Web Publishing Terms

To get started in Web publishing, at the very least you'll want to be familiar with the following terms:

✦ **Home page:** A home page is an HTML page (a Web page) that usually summarizes what your Web site, or entire group of Web pages, offers.

✦ **HTML:** Hypertext Markup Language (HTML) is a page-description language that's interpreted (turned into page images) by HTML browsers.

✦ **Browsers:** HTML browsers are separate programs, such as Netscape Communicator, Opera Software's Opera, and Microsoft Internet Explorer, that interpret HTML codes so formatted pages display properly on-screen. Browsers and HTML are designed to give users some power over how pages display. Generally, browsers come preinstalled with operating systems and computers.

✦ **Links and jumps:** A link (also known as a *hyperlink*) or jump is an area in a Web page that takes users to a different location on a Web page or to an altogether different Web page. Links often consist of an icon, button, or underlined word, and users click on them to activate them.

Learning About HTML

HTML (Hypertext Markup Language) is a semantic markup language that assigns meaning to the various parts of a Web-page file. An HTML document might contain a headline, a number of paragraphs, an ordered list, a number of graphics, and so on. HTML documents are *linear* in structure, meaning that one element follows another in sequence. In general, the elements that make up a Web page are displayed from left to right and from top to bottom in a browser window, although the rigid structure that limited the appearance of early Web documents has evolved in recent years to give Web-page designers more control over the way HTML documents look on-screen.

How the World Wide Web works

The World Wide Web is a means of distributing information on the Internet, and it provides anybody with an Internet connection point-and-click access to documents that contain text, pictures, sound, video, and more. The Web was developed at the European Particle Physics Laboratory (CERN, the Centre Européen pour la Recherche Nucléaire) in the early 1990s as a way for physicists to exchange information in a more collaborative way than was possible with simple text documents.

Web documents are text files that contain embedded HTML codes that add formatting to the text, as well as hyperlinks, which let a viewer access other Web pages with just a mouse click. How the various elements in an HTML document are displayed on a computer monitor is determined in large part by the *browser,* a program that lets computer users view Web documents. Different browsers render a single HTML document slightly differently. (See the sidebar "A brief look at browsers" for information about the most commonly used browsers.)

Free access to information

Despite the linear structure of HTML documents, viewers are free to access information in whatever order they want. That's because the hypertext links embedded in Web pages let viewers choose their own path through information. Think of it this way: Everybody enters a museum through the same door, but after they're inside, viewers are free to meander from exhibit to exhibit in any sequence they want. Surfing the Web offers the same freedom. When you're connected, you can linger as long as you want on a particular page or jump to other pages by clicking on a hyperlink.

Where content is king

HTML's greatest strength is its versatility. Web pages can be viewed on a wide range of computer platforms with any monitor using a variety of browsers. Granted, a particular document may look a bit different when viewed under different circumstances, but that's considered a minor inconvenience in a publishing environment where content — not design — is king.

Web pages by design

For many designers of printed publications, who are accustomed to having absolute control over the appearance of the final printed page, the idea of creating pages that will look different depending on the browser that's used to display them and the personal preferences of the person viewing them is a bit disconcerting. However, when designers understand the limitations of HTML, they can use its strengths to create effective Web pages. Freed from the burden of fine-tuning the look of the pages they create, Web-page designers can focus on organizing the content of their publications so that viewers can access and digest it easily.

The creation process

The first generation of Web pages was built using word processors or even simple text editors. The HTML codes that identified the different components of Web pages had to be inserted manually. As was the case with old, non-WYSIWYG typesetters, Web-page builders didn't know what the codes would actually produce onscreen until they opened the text files in a browser. A single errant character could produce strange results.

The Web-publishing features in QuarkXPress and in third-party XTensions are designed to spare users the headache of learning and entering HTML codes. If you're the curious type and would like to see what HTML codes look like, import an HTML text file into a QuarkXPress text box. You'll see lots of cryptic formatting codes that — mercifully — you don't have to understand. If you're the really curious type and want to learn more about HTML codes, tons of information is available on the Web. For starters, try NCSA's Beginner's Guide to HTML (www.ncsa.uiuc.edu/General/Internet/WWW/HTMLPrimer.html).

Seeing the Differences

Most QuarkXPress users are aware of the fundamental differences between publications that are printed on paper and publications that are displayed on a computer monitor. After all, QuarkXPress users spend long hours staring at their monitor while creating pages that will ultimately be printed. The following sections explore some of the most significant differences you'll encounter as you bridge the gap between print and Web publishing.

A brief look at browsers

In 1993, the National Center for Supercomputing Applications (NCSA) at the University of Illinois released a program called Mosaic. This was the "killer app" that got the Web rolling. You don't see much of Mosaic these days. Now, the most popular browsers are Netscape Communicator (formerly called Netscape Navigator), Microsoft Internet Explorer, and America Online (which uses a version of Internet Explorer).

It's important to understand that a Web page will look different when displayed with each of these browsers. It will also look different when displayed on older versions of the browsers. To add to the confusion, pages displayed on Macintosh computers look different than pages displayed on Windows computers. (Different Mac browser appearances for the same page — Communicator, Internet Explorer, and America Online — are shown here.)

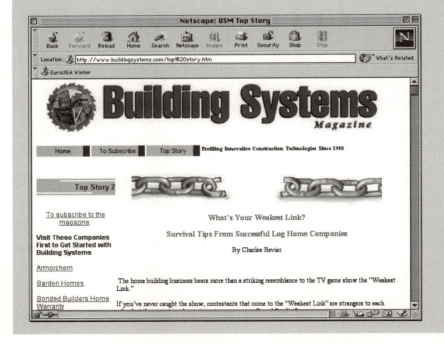

Not only are there differences between browsers, but each browser includes display-related preferences that can be customized by each user to control how Web pages look in the browser window. For example, most people are accustomed to seeing Web pages that use the Times New Roman font extensively. This is because Times New Roman is the default display font specified in most browsers. However, a Web surfer who doesn't like Times New Roman is free to choose any available font for text display. In addition, users can increase font sizes to better suit their own vision. Similarly, most Web pages are displayed with gray backgrounds, but that's a browser preference that's easily changed.

The bottom line is that fonts, font sizes, background color, and other formatting may vary depending on the hardware and software being used to view a particular Web page. This means that no matter how careful you are when you produce Web pages — whether from a dedicated HTML editor or from QuarkXPress — and no matter how much subsequent tweaking you do, you have little control over the way individual viewers see the pages.

Due to these issues, Web publishers need to decide which operating systems, browsers, and versions to support. Typically, if you design your pages to work with the latest version of Communicator, Internet Explorer, and AOL on both operating systems, you'll be fine. You may want to consider supporting the previous version of each browser as well.

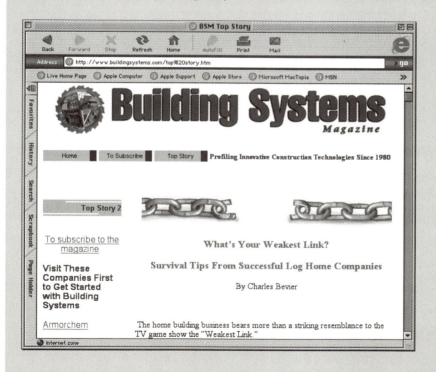

Continued

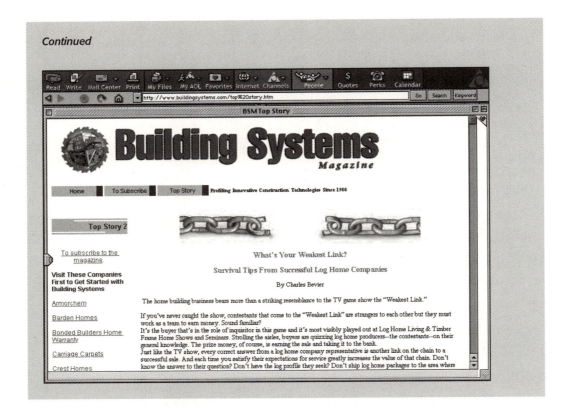

Continued

The CMYK/RGB difference

All you have to do is look at a printed version of a color publication to see the differences between it and the one you saw on-screen during production. For example, QuarkXPress users who've done spot-color publishing have probably held a Pantone swatchbook next to their monitor and mused, "Hmmm. They're close, but they're not the same." That's mostly because the colors that can be created on paper by mixing cyan, magenta, yellow, and black inks aren't the same as the colors that can be produced on a computer using red, green, and blue light. The differences between the CMYK and RGB color models is one of the big differences between print and Web publishing, but it's not the only one.

The conceptual difference

If you decide to become a Web publisher in addition to a print publisher, you should be aware of the basic differences between print and Web publishing — and you should take advantage of the strengths of each media. For print publishers, this means being open to some new concepts in communication, covered in the following sections.

 Chapter 38 covers the difference between QuarkXPress print and Web documents in more detail.

Making the information jump

Most print publications are designed to be read from beginning to end. But on the Web, stories can contain hyperlinks that let readers instantly jump to related information. The idea of reading stories from top to bottom, beginning to end, is a print-based concept. On the Web, hyperlinks provide publishers with a different paradigm for presenting information. An effective Web publication uses hyperlinks to present information in discrete chunks and make it easy for viewers to access information.

Losing control

Most print designers are accustomed to having absolute control over the look of the publications they produce. They specify the fonts, design the pages, create and apply the colors, and print proofs to make sure that what they get is what they want. But the designers of Web pages don't have this level of control. That's because many display options are controlled by the viewer of a Web page — and more specifically, by the viewer's browser. As a QuarkXPress user, whether you're creating Web pages from scratch or converting existing documents to HTML, you'll need to become comfortable with relinquishing some of the design control they've enjoyed while creating printed publications.

Creating without columns

QuarkXPress users are accustomed to pages that contain multiple columns, complex text runarounds, layered items, and so on. Not all these page-layout options are available to designers of Web pages, and some of the design options that are available for both print and Web publishing behave differently. You have to be careful about using multicolumn formats for Web pages. For one thing, if a story is presented in two columns — one long one and one short one — the reader may have to do considerable scrolling to read everything. For another, if the columns are fixed-width, viewers with small monitors may have to deal with a truncated column.

Redefining the page

The meaning of the term *page* is very different in a QuarkXPress environment from the Web. For QuarkXPress users, a page is a finite area with specified height, width, columns, and margins. The number of text boxes, picture boxes, and lines you place on a QuarkXPress page is limited by the physical size of the page (and your tolerance for crowding). On the Web, a page is a single HTML file and all its embedded elements — pictures, sound, video, and so on. A Web page can contain very little information or a whole lot of information. Its size is determined by the amount of information it contains, and its width by the size of the browser window in which it's displayed. This is a pretty foreign concept for print designers. Think of it as a bonus: Free from the size limitations imposed by printed pages, Web-page designers can rest assured that all their pages will be exactly the appropriate size for the information they contain.

If you create Web pages from scratch in QuarkXPress, or if you end up converting your existing documents using an XTension, you'll learn firsthand the differences between print publishing and Web publishing. You'll also have to make some decisions about how you want to deal with the differences.

Navigating with headers and footers

Another difference between print and Web publishing is the nature and appearance of headers and footers. In printed publications, headers and footers inconspicuously inform readers of their location within the publication. However, in Web pages, headers and footers play multiple roles. In addition to informing viewers of their current location, a Web page's header also must function as an attention-grabber and often as a navigation tool.

Keeping minimum monitors in mind

While surfing the Web, you may have landed on pages that were designed with a minimum monitor in mind. Such pages contain fixed-width items and often multicolumn layouts that look fine when displayed on monitors wide enough to hold the elements or columns, but that get clipped when viewed on small monitors. It's never a bad idea to let the viewer control the width of your Web pages and to make sure that design elements, image maps, and pictures aren't too wide to be displayed on most monitors.

A good rule of thumb is to design Web pages for 800-pixel widths, because that's the default resolution for a 17-inch monitor (the most popular size of monitor). Although the trend is to buy larger monitors, or to run 17-inch monitors at higher resolutions, the 800-pixel width is a safe, inclusive bet. And for those with more resolution, that width will do no harm, because unless you make every element in your page fixed-width, column widths and so on will automatically adjust for their bigger screen areas.

Keeping it simple

While you're making the leap from thinking about print publishing to Web publishing, keep simplicity in mind. Yes, you can include sound, video, and other interactive features in Web pages (using QuarkXPress or a third-party conversion XTension). But before you venture into multimedia Web publishing, ask yourself two questions:

✦ Do you have the resources to do it?

✦ Will adding sound and video significantly improve the quality of your content?

Getting Ready for the Web

As a QuarkXPress user, we assume you're currently involved in print publishing — and you have existing content that you'd like to use either exclusively on the Web or that you'd like to reuse on the Web. From this point, you need to decide which documents or content you want to use online. A book publisher, for example, probably wouldn't want to put all its books online, because reading long tracts of text on a computer monitor is no fun. But if the company produces a catalog of its titles, converting the catalog into a Web page makes perfect sense. After you decide what will work online, you need to decide how the content fits into the bigger picture of your existing Web site.

If you're starting a Web site from scratch and you intend to incorporate pages from QuarkXPress, you should decide on the overall structure of the site before you begin creating or converting documents. If possible, get the corporate portion of the site up and running before you start adding publications. It's much easier to add a document exported from QuarkXPress as HTML to an existing Web site — all you have to do is provide a link from an existing page — than to do everything at once.

Using QuarkXPress as an HTML-authoring tool

If you're *not* a print publisher, but instead you're considering launching a Web site or Web-based business, QuarkXPress is probably not the tool for you. The advantage to using QuarkXPress for creating or converting Web pages is that it's a known quantity — but only to print designers. They can leverage existing page-layout skills and designs in a Web-publishing environment.

But QuarkXPress is not a full-fledged HTML-authoring tool. Many powerful WYSIWYG Web-authoring tools are available — for both hobbyists and professionals — that do not rely on existing QuarkXPress content or skills. Although these additional programs can be expensive, buying and learning a dedicated tool will save you money in the long run over using a less effective tool. If your business is exclusive to the Web, you'll also want to hire Web masters (people with experience developing Web pages and sites) rather than print designers.

Getting ready

Before you even get started with QuarkXPress features, or any other software, think about the following issues in relation to the creation and maintenance of a Web site:

✦ What content will the site contain?

✦ Who will its audience be?

✦ How will the content be produced and how often?

✦ What tools and skills will be required to produce it?

✦ Will all work be done in-house, or will parts be outsourced?

✦ What are the cost issues?

✦ What will the site look like? How will design elements be incorporated to give the site a unified look?

Establishing a structure

Web sites offer even greater flexibility than printed publications. A viewer can bounce from place to place within a page, or jump to another page that's part of the same Web site or even across the world. Still, a good Web site, like a good printed publication, has a logical structure that provides a viewer easy access to the information.

Making a map

You're probably already familiar with creating flowcharts for printed publications. Do the same thing with your Web site and your individual Web pages. Sit down with printed versions of all the possible information that you may include on your Web site. For a corporate site, all your content may not come from QuarkXPress — much of the content may be in the form of simply formatted Microsoft Word documents, for example. Then decide what elements to include and create a map using page icons to represent Web pages and arrows to represent basic links.

After you identify content that is coming from QuarkXPress, you can decide whether it makes sense to create new Web documents and reuse the content or whether converting the documents to HTML with a third-party XTension would be easier. In addition, you need to review the content to see what makes sense on the Web. Figure 37-1 shows the structure for a Web site, which uses content from a variety of programs.

Maintaining a look and feel

Again, because we assume you're a print publisher in addition to being a Web publisher, it's likely that your company already has an established look. No doubt you have corporate fonts, colors, and a logotype at the very least. Whether you're creating new Web pages in QuarkXPress or converting existing documents, you'll want to maintain your company's look as much as possible.

✦ When you're creating Web documents in QuarkXPress, be sure to create a simulation of your corporate colors that lies within the Web-safe color palette (covered later in this chapter). In areas of the page where it's important to reinforce your company identity, you have the option of converting text boxes to graphics so the typefaces don't change.

✦ When you're converting QuarkXPress documents to Web pages, you can maintain some of the original structure of the printed pages. You can do this by creating a title page for the Web version that includes a scaled-down reproduction of the printed cover alongside a table of contents that contains hyperlinks to individual articles. Chances are, each of the articles is a separate QuarkXPress document. Under these circumstances, you would create a separate Web page out of each QuarkXPress document.

Tip

If Web publishing is new to you, start small before you get big. You may have grandiose plans to convert many of your QuarkXPress content — back issues and all — into Web pages; to add sound and video; to add search capabilities and database connectivity; to boldly create the greatest Web site of all time. That's fine. But start small.

Making a prototype

After determining the overall content and look of your Web site, or even an individual Web page, it's always a good idea to rough it out. You may want to rough out an entire Web site using placeholder files, replacing each file as the final file is produced in HTML format. For Web pages, you can draw a sketch or whip something up on-screen to guide you as you produce the page or convert an existing document.

Getting to work

When you're finally ready to jump into the software to create a Web document or convert a print document, first gather copies of all the content you'll need. And we mean *copies* — never use original print files for Web publishing, because you risk losing valuable information. Also, be sure the content has been through any approval processes — design, editorial, fact checking — before you start working with it. Although making changes in QuarkXPress files is easy, it's more difficult to handle an error that makes it all the way to your Web site. (In the first place, it's often hard to communicate where an error is — you have to figure out the name of the page it's on and what line the error is in, for example. Then, when an error is corrected, you have to replace the Web page while your site is up and running.)

Cross-
Reference

The actual steps you'll take to create Web documents in QuarkXPress are covered in Chapter 38.

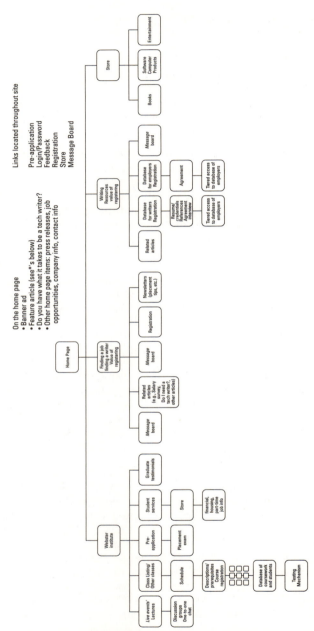

Figure 37-1: A flowchart is a good way to organize a new Web site or incorporate new pages into an existing Web site.

Creating Colors for the Web

Because nearly everybody who uses a computer these days has a color monitor, most Web-page designers use color freely. But printing color on paper and displaying color on a computer monitor are different. In the following sections, we look at some of the differences between printed color and color displayed on a monitor and discuss how these differences affect the Web pages you export from QuarkXPress.

Web-safe palette

Regardless of the colors you apply to text, images, and backgrounds in any program — QuarkXPress, Photoshop, Illustrator, an HTML editor, and so on — if the colors end up in a Web page, the viewers will only see the colors their browsers and monitors can display. With the variations in hardware, operating systems, and browsers out there, how can you guarantee consistent color from Mac to PC, from browser to browser, and from monitor to monitor? The answer is to use the 216-color Web-safe palette that's new in QuarkXPress 5; these are the colors that most PC and Mac browsers support.

When you create colors in QuarkXPress Web documents, you can easily limit the colors to the Web-safe palette. Simply select Web Safe Colors or Web Named Colors from the Model menu in the Edit Color dialog box (Edit ➪ Colors). Figure 37-2 shows the Edit Color dialog box for creating a Web Safe Color.

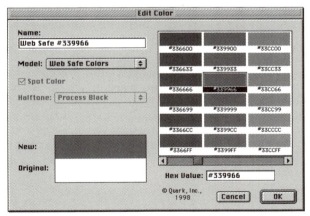

Figure 37-2: In QuarkXPress Web documents, the Edit Color dialog box includes Web Safe Colors and Web Named Colors.

Beware the WYSIWYG approach

The QuarkXPress Web-publishing features — and many other Web-publishing tools — let you see your Web pages as you create them. But this WYSIWYG — what-you-see-is-what-you-get — approach has its pitfalls. You must make assumptions about the circumstances under which your pages will be viewed, such as the minimum monitor size and the browsers in use.

The assumption that what you see is what the reader will see may be appropriate if you're certain that all viewers will be accessing the pages under the same conditions — platform, browser, and monitor. For example, if all viewers will access your pages over a corporate intranet using the same hardware and software, you can design your pages so that they look good under these controlled circumstances.

The monitor-to-monitor difference

Depending on the capabilities of a monitor, and how many colors it's set to display, colors can vary. But if you set your monitor to display 256 colors while working with Web pages, which will encompass the 216-color Web-safe palette, you're likely to see what your viewers see. Previewing anything you're creating for the Web in a browser is always a good idea, though, so you can check the actual color.

Typographic Issues

When it comes to typography, the biggest difference between designing for print and designing for the Web is the limitations in typefaces. In print design, you can use any typeface that you own the font for. In Web design, you're limited to the fonts your potential viewers own. If you know who your viewers are (for example if you're creating Web pages for a corporate intranet), you can make sure they have the fonts you design for them. But most of the time, you have no control over the fonts your viewers have — just like you have no control over the browser they're using, how they have it set up, their monitor, and more. In addition to typeface issues, you're faced with special characters, character attributes, and paragraph attributes that may not convert.

Tip   If you're creating Web pages in QuarkXPress, you're protected — the software turns off features that won't transfer to HTML (but it still lists fonts that are unwise to use). Unless you set a text box to export as a graphic, expect to see many options grayed out.

Handling the typeface limitation

Deprived of your usual free-for-all with typefaces, you have two ways to handle the typeface limitation in Web publishing:

✦ **Limit your typeface use to those that you can expect users to have.** In general, this is Times, Times New Roman, Arial, Helvetica, and Courier. But even if you specify these fonts, keep in mind that the users may have their browser preferences set to use different fonts. Still, you shouldn't totally avoid using multiple fonts from that short list of universal ones; for example, if you use a sans serif font for heads and a serif font for body text, even substituted fonts are likely to help you achieve the same look across different operating systems and browsers, even if they're not the same fonts you used.

✦ **Convert text to graphics so the typefaces display as you intended.** Because this requires users to download the graphics — consuming time and bandwidth — you should limit the use of this technique to places where the correct typeface is necessary for the overall look or message. Typically, this is for logos and major headings such as page titles and, of course, ads.

Working with limited character attributes

Unlike in QuarkXPress, there's no fine-tuning of character spacing through kerning, tracking, and H&J sets in Web publishing. Point sizes are fairly standard on the Web (6, 8, 9, 10, 12, 14, 18, 24), and you can't use fractions of point size. In addition, type styles are generally limited to bold, italic, underline, superscript, subscript, and all caps. Again, as with typefaces, if you really need to maintain the look of text for communication purposes, convert it to a graphic.

On the Web, special characters won't all display reliably. Just because Macs and PCs support many special characters, that doesn't mean that all Web browsers support them. They don't. The good news is that, in general, all the characters you see on your keyboard, such as the percent sign and the dollar sign, are exported intact. The bad news is that special characters created using a Ctrl, Alt, Option, or ⌘ key combination may not survive. To complicate matters further, different fonts offer different sets of special characters. Table 37-1 shows the special characters that can be used safely in an HTML document.

Working with limited paragraph attributes

Other than paragraph alignment, you can forget about most of the paragraph formatting you've done in QuarkXPress when you export Web documents to HTML. HTML does support left–, right–, or center-aligned text, and left and right indents. Justified and forced-justified text are converted to left-aligned text. Most other paragraph attributes — first-line indents, tabs, space before and after, and so forth — are ignored, depending on the browser. Box-based attributes, such as rotate, skew, and flip don't convert to the Web either.

Table 37-1
Special Characters That Export to HTML

Character	Windows	Macintosh
Accented Characters Ä À Â Á Ã Â ä à â á ã å Ä Ç ç Ë È Ê É ë è ê é Ï Ì Î Í ï ì î í Ñ ñ Ö Ò Ô Ó Õ Ø ö ò ô ó õ ø Š š Ü Ù Û Ú ü ù û ú Ý ý Ÿ ÿ	all but Š š Ý ý Ÿ ÿ*	all but Š š Ý ý
Diphthongs Æ æ Œ œ	Æ æ Œ œ	Æ æ Œ œ
International Punctuation ¿ ¡ « »	¿ ¡ « » £ ¥ €	¿ ¡ « » £ ¥ €
International Currency £ ¥ €	£ ¥ €	£ ¥ €
Legal Symbols © ® ™	© ® ™	© ® ™
Ligatures fi fl	none	none
Mathematical Symbols ± × ÷ ≠ ≈ ∞ √ ¼ ½ ¾	± × ÷ ¼ ½ ¾	± × ÷
Miscellaneous Symbols ¢ °	¢ °	¢ °
Text Symbols † ‡ § ¶	† ‡ § ¶	† ‡ § ¶
Typographic Characters – — … ' ' " "	quotes as keyboard " '	quotes as keyboard " '

*Many Windows fonts don't support Š or š.

Choosing Graphic File Formats

The main decision you must make when you include pictures in Web pages—
created in QuarkXPress or converted from existing documents—is the file format

used for the exported picture files. Regardless of the original file type of any picture you export (be it TIFF, EPS, PICT, or whatever), when you create Web pages you must choose between two standard Web graphic formats: GIF and JPEG. (Another format, PNG, is increasingly supported by Web browsers and is now supported by QuarkXPress, but we recommend you not use it until it's universally supported.)

Using the GIF format

The GIF format works best for relatively small images that don't have much detail. The biggest advantage of the GIF format is its relatively small file size. As the amount of material available on the Web proliferates and Internet traffic grows, users are growing increasingly impatient waiting for Web pages to download. Keeping image files small goes a long way in keeping viewers happy and interested. The GIF format works well for simple images, such as logos and vector graphics created with programs like Adobe Illustrator, Macromedia FreeHand, and CorelDraw, and for text that you choose to export as a graphic. The GIF format lets you use color palettes in a variety of ways but will not let you use more than 256 colors in one image file.

Using the JPEG format

Sometimes, using the GIF format for an exported picture produces an image file that's prohibitively large. Pictures such as large scanned images that contain a wide range of colors and considerable detail don't always work well when they're converted into GIF files. The alternative is to use the JPEG format. Unlike the GIF format, the JPEG format compresses a file by tossing out some of the detail. But the JPEG format retains true 24-bit color and generally produces a smaller file than the GIF format for complex images. Because it's a highly compressed format — more so than the GIF format — JPEG has become the format of choice on the Web for scanned photographs and other large images.

Interlaced GIFs

If you choose to export images using the GIF format, QuarkXPress and the Web-export XTensions also provide the option to create interlaced GIF images. An interlaced GIF image looks exactly the same as a non-interlaced GIF image and is the same file size. However, when an interlaced GIF image is displayed in a browser window, a low-resolution version of the image is first displayed, and then as the rest of the file is downloaded, the resolution is steadily enhanced until the entire image is displayed with maximum possible clarity.

Non-interlaced GIF images are drawn at maximum resolution from top to bottom as the file is downloaded. Interlaced GIF images appear to draw faster than non-interlaced GIF images, although the total screen display time is the same for both. Interlacing GIF images, particularly those that are fairly large, softens the download experience for the viewer and also lets the viewer begin examining any surrounding text while the picture is drawn. It's usually a good idea to select this option for exported GIF images.

Deciding what's best

No matter how you develop your Web pages, the learning process should begin with plenty of fiddling around. The best way to learn about the options for exporting pictures is to import a variety of pictures into a test Web document, and then start exporting to HTML and experimenting with different image-export settings — GIF versus JPEG, interlaced GIF versus non-interlaced GIF, and so on. Switching back and forth between your Web browser and QuarkXPress as you try different file formats is easy.

Summary

The overall process of publishing on the Web is the same as publishing in print — you need to plan your resources, content, navigation tools, and formatting to publish on time with a consistent look. That's about where the similarities end. In Web publishing, you'll need to consider the following:

✦ Keep in mind that viewers have different browsers, operating systems, fonts, and monitors that affect how your Web pages look.

✦ Take advantage of the strengths of the Web by adding hyperlinks and image maps for navigation. Consider your resources and audiences before delving too deeply into multimedia features.

✦ For a consistent look, limit colors to the Web-safe colors provided in QuarkXPress and limit typography to basic typefaces such as Times, Times New Roman, Helvetica, Arial, and Courier.

✦ Face the fact that most of the character attributes and paragraph attributes you use freely in QuarkXPress won't transfer to the Web. Where it's important to your message, you can preserve typefaces and fine-tuning by saving text as a graphic.

✦ Experiment with the two graphic file formats universally supported on the Web — JPEG and GIF — to see which works best for your images. Be sure to preview images, colors, and pages in the minimum browsers you decide to support.

The Web-publishing basics in this chapter apply whether you're creating Web documents in QuarkXPress, converting QuarkXPress documents to HTML using a third-party XTension, or using another HTML-authoring tool entirely. You may end up using all three methods to create and maintain a Web site.

✦   ✦   ✦

Creating Basic Web Documents

Web-page creation using the Hypertext Markup Language (HTML) in recent years has moved from a weird effort by green-haired kids in the basement to a standard part of publishing. What magazine or book publisher doesn't have a companion Web site? Very few these days—not to mention all the Web-only content providers and commerce sites. Until now, QuarkXPress designers couldn't partake of the Web efforts using QuarkXPress unless they bought an XTension. QuarkXPress 5 adds Web-page creation tools drawn from a variety of sources, including new capabilities from Quark, as well as the integration of the previously separate Avenue.Quark Web-posting and QuarkImmedia interactive-document tools.

New Feature New to QuarkXPress 5 is the ability to create Web pages. But that's not to say QuarkXPress is the best Web-creation tool. Plenty of dedicated HTML editors are optimized for Web-page creation, and you should use those tools if your core business is Web-page creation. The QuarkXPress Web tools come in handy in a print-oriented environment that's creating occasional Web pages, where the QuarkXPress-experienced designers can use their QuarkXPress skills in a new medium.

Starting Out

You create a QuarkXPress Web page the same way you create a QuarkXPress print document—you choose File ➪ New. To let you create those Web pages, QuarkXPress 5 has several new options in the File ➪ New pop-up menu, one of them being Web Document. This displays the New Web Document dialog box Document shown in Figure 38-1 (you can also use Shift+Option+⌘+N, or Ctrl+Alt+Shift+N).

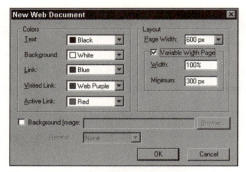

Figure 38-1: The New Web Document dialog box.

QuarkXPress 5 doesn't let you convert QuarkXPress print documents into Web format. Instead, you must create a new Web document and then copy the elements from the print document into it. Use a tool like Extensis's BeyondPress to convert existing QuarkXPress documents into Web format.

The New Web Document dialog box looks like the standard New Document dialog box at first, though it has fewer options.

Colors

The first thing in the New Web Document dialog box is the Colors section. This is where you decide the default colors for several of the items in your Web page. They are as follows:

✦ **Text:** Use this pop-up menu to decide what color the text in your Web page will be. Resist the temptation to use arbitrary colors like green and orange here. Instead, we suggest you opt for something more traditional like black or dark blue — if you use the default colors, your readers will see the same colors they do on most Web sites. If you're using a dark background, you may want to choose a nonstandard text color such as white and consider adjusting other colors so they'll be more visible on the dark background than the other standard Web text colors would be.

✦ **Background:** Use this pop-up menu to decide what color the background of your Web document will be. You may want to choose a background color before you pick a text color, because the color of your text will depend largely on the color you choose for your background. Typically, you should pick a light color for the background.

✦ **Link:** Use this pop-up menu to decide what color your hyperlinks will be. Blue is the standard used by most Web sites. This color applies to text hyperlinks only. *Image maps* (links from a graphic) won't be affected by your choice; they remain invisible.

✦ **Visited Link:** Many times, people like to choose a different color for hyperlinks that have already been clicked on, or visited. That way they know they've already been there. You can choose any color in this pop-up menu, although we recommend you use either the standard purple or a lighter shade of the color you chose in the Link pop-up menu. This gives the visited link a grayed-out appearance, making it easier for visitors to make the association between visited links and unvisited ones.

✦ **Active Link:** Use this pop-up menu to choose a color for the link you're currently visiting. This may sound a bit ridiculous at first. After all, you just clicked on the link that got you where you are now. You should have no trouble remembering which one it is, right? But you'll be surprised at how easy it is to forget how you got to where you are.

Colors on the Web

When you open the pop-up menus in the New Web Document dialog box, you'll notice that QuarkXPress has already chosen a nice palette of colors for you to work with, in case you aren't quite ready to make your own color choices yet. But if you want to dive right in and pick your own colors, choose Other... at the top of the menu; this opens the Edit Color dialog box, where you'll find all your favorite color-matching systems in the Model pop-up menu. Ignore these systems — they won't do you any good on a Web page, because they're for print documents. Monitors don't bother matching colors like printers do. Instead, they just display whatever equivalent is at hand — and in many instances, that color won't be the same as the color you picked.

Instead, choose the new Web Safe Colors color palette at the bottom of the list. These colors have been created specifically for Web pages. As the figure shows, the naming is a little weird — blues, for example, have bland tags like #000066 and #0033CC. (The numbers are the hexadecimal codes for the 256 possible shades each of red, blue, and green, so 000000 means 0 percent red, 0 percent blue, and 0 percent green, while FFFFFF means 100 percent red, 100 percent blue, and 100 percent green. FF is the hexadecimal numeral for 255; in hexadecimal, A equals 10, B equals 11, C equals 12, D equals 13, E equals 14, and F equals 15. So FF means 16 times 15 (the first F: 15 values of 16) plus 15 (the second F: 15 values of 1). This sounds weird but decimal works the same way: 99 is 9 values of 10 (the first 9) plus 9 values of 1 (the second 9).

Continued

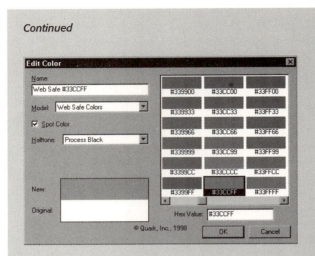

Continued

If hexadecimal numbers really confuse you, try the Web Named Colors color palette. This palette isn't nearly as extensive as the Web-safe palette, but the names are much more user-friendly. Some are even kind of cute: How do PeachPuff and PapayaWhip grab you?

Layout

The layout section of the New Web Document dialog box lets you decide the width of your Web page. There is no default measurement for length, because there is no need for one. Theoretically, a Web page is bottomless — the only thing hampering its length is the amount of memory on the visitor's computer and their level of patience. After all, who wants to scroll through a page of text 15 miles long? Here is a rundown of the choices in the Layout field:

✦ **Width:** The width choices in this section are very limited. And for good reason. Even though Web browsers have both horizontal and vertical scroll bars, most people find it annoying to scroll from left to right while reading a page, particularly if they're already scrolling from top to bottom. So QuarkXPress limits your width options to four choices: 600px, 800px, 1024px, and 1268px (*px* means pixels) — the standard widths of most monitor screens on the market. We recommend you use either 600px or 800px. The other two widths are for widescreen monitors. And although *you* may have a widescreen monitor, the people who will be reading the page may not. Using 600px or 800px assures that those people with smaller monitors can read the full width of your page, too.

✦ **Variable Width:** When Variable Width is checked, your page will expand or contract to fit the width of the reader's Web browser. To make the page a variable width page, check Variable Width Page, and then enter values for the following fields:

- The Width field lets you specify the percentage of the viewable browser area that the page will occupy.

- The Minimum field lets you specify a minimum page width. If the reader's browser window is made smaller than this width, items will stop being resized.

Note The Variable Width feature is a great fix for readers with varying monitor widths, with a couple exceptions. First, this feature is not compatible with all Web browsers, particularly older ones. Second, if the reader's monitor is much larger than your specified page width, the page will "stretch" to fit the larger monitor, but doing so will make very wide areas of text that can create huge gulfs between images on the left of the page and those on the right, which end up getting moved farther apart.

Background

Not to be confused with the Background pop-menu in the Colors section, the last series of choices in the New Web Document palette have to do with the background of your document. One of the neat (or sometimes, not-so-neat) features of HTML is its ability to take a Web-format graphic (JPEG, GIF, or PNG) and turn it into a wallpaper-like background for your Web document. If used wisely, this wallpaper affect can add depth and dimension to a Web document, but more often than not these backgrounds are just annoying and interfere with the rest of the items in your document. For an example of this background effect, see Figure 38-2.

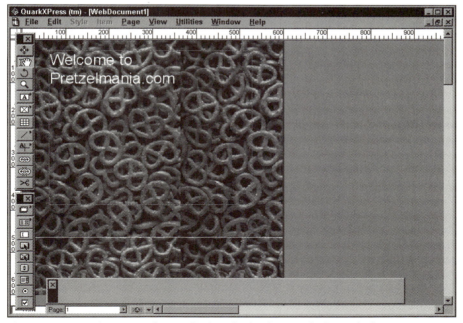

Figure 38-2: A picture can be applied to the background of a Web document — often with mixed results.

Most Web sites that have image backgrounds use a tiled background, where the image is repeated in tiles in the background of the page (refer to Figure 38-2). That ensures the graphic is shown throughout the page. Be sure to use a background image designed to tile well, where the "seams" aren't obvious. If you set Repeat to None, the image comes in at its size. If that's smaller than the final page, the reader will see blank space elsewhere on the page's background — that clearly wouldn't work if you had set the text color to white so it stands out from the background image, only to have the white text be invisible against the white background on the rest of the page outside the image. In the Repeat pop-up menu, you can also choose to repeat the image either vertically or horizontally. For a fixed-width Web site, repeating the image vertically can make sense as long as the image is as wide as the page.

Tip If you want to use a background image and aren't worried about making the page too big to download in a reasonable time, your best bet is to create a very large, very light image, select it using the New Web Document commands, and choose None in the Repeat pop-up menu. This produces the effect of a background image that bleeds on all four sides of the Web browser, not unlike if you were to use a large background image on the cover of a brochure or catalog. This effect has its pitfalls, too, however. The major one is the huge file size of such a graphic. A large picture like the one described can take a long time to download — especially for those still using a 56 Kbps modem. Still, with some experimentation, you may be able to come up with some striking effects using the background features in the New Web Document dialog box.

After you've made your choices, click OK. You now have a brand-new canvas on which to build your first QuarkXPress Web page.

Tip To change any of these settings in an existing Web document, use Page ➪ Page Properties, or Option+Shift+⌘+A or Ctrl+Alt+Shift+A, to open the Page Properties dialog box.

Differences for Web documents

Although the familiar QuarkXPress interface, menus, and palettes remain when you work on Web documents, the program does modify itself to add new relevant features and to gray out irrelevant features. For example, you cannot shift the baseline of text in a Web document. The Page Setup, Document Setup, Collect for Output, and Save Page as EPS functions in the File menu are unavailable, as are the object-linking functions and Print Styles function in the Edit menu and the Underline Styles function in the Style menu. In the Utilities menu, the PPD Manager and Profile Manager functions are unavailable. And the Trap Information, Profile Information, and Index palettes aren't available.

Figure 38-3 shows a blank new Web document in QuarkXPress. Among the key changes are those covered in the following sections.

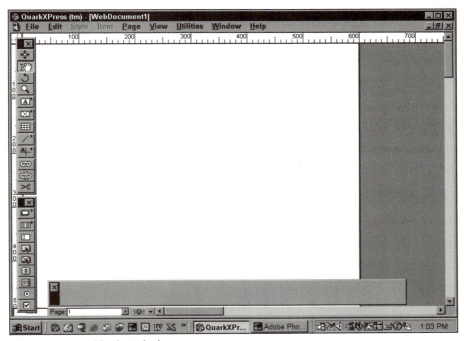

Figure 38-3: A blank Web document.

The Web Tools palette

When you open a Web document in QuarkXPress 5, Show Tools in the View menu turns into a submenu, namely the Tools submenu. There you'll find two choices: Show/Hide Tool and a new choice, Show/Hide Web Tools. The Web Tools palette is an extension of sorts of the regular Tool palette. In fact, it looks very similar to the Tool palette, with the obvious exception that the nine tools in the Web Tools palette are completely different from those in the regular Tool palette.

Note

Both the Tool Palette and the Web Tools palette can be open at the same time within a Web document. We recommend you have both open at the same time; otherwise, you'll be switching back and forth between the two constantly while you're working.

Figure 38-4 shows the Web tools' names. Here's what each does in brief (full details are covered later in this chapter and in Chapter 39):

✦ **Image Map:** The Image Map tool has three versions, for different shapes of image maps. An image map is a graphic that, when clicked on the Web, has a hyperlink to bring the user to a new Web page.

✦ **Form Box and File Selection:** These two tools let you create two kinds of forms for Web pages. The Form Box tool creates a standard fill-in-the-blank form for Web users to fill in information, such as subscription information. The File Selection tool creates a dialog box that lets users select a file for downloading.

✦ **Text Field:** The Text Field tool is essentially a one-line version of the Form Box tool.

✦ **Button and Image Button:** These tools let the Web page designer create buttons the user can click to perform an action. The Button tool creates a button, while the Image Button tool creates a picture box that acts as a button.

✦ **Pop-up Menu:** The Pop-Up menu tool creates a pop-up menu from which the Web user can make a selection.

✦ **List Box:** The List Box tool creates a box in which a user can enter a list of items, such as for filling in a database over the Web.

✦ **Radio Button and Check Box:** These tools let users select options on a Web page. The Radio Button tool makes the user choose just one option in a list, while the Check Box tool lets users elect multiple items from the list.

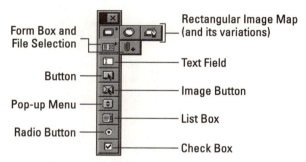

Figure 38-4: The Web-oriented QuarkXPress tools.

Chapter 39 covers most of the Web Tools palette's tools (the Image Map tool is covered in this chapter).

New preference options

In the Preferences dialog box (Edit ⇨ Preferences ⇨ Preferences, or Option+Shift+⌘+Y or Ctrl+Alt+Shift+Y), the Document preferences change to Web Documents, and there are subtle changes in each of the panes:

✦ **The General pane** gains an Image Export Directory option in which you specify where Web-document images are exported (the program that you will use to deliver the Web page to the World Wide Web will need to know where to access these images from). The default is image, which means to get them from their source. If you enter a path, it is similar to using the Collect for Output feature on a print document. The Site Root Directory specifies where the home page files are stored. For Web page delivery, all files and folders should be within a specific directory or folder known as the *root*. The Auto Page Insertion option is gone, though you can manually add pages through the Page ⇨ Insert command. (Note that each page in your document will export as a separate Web page.) The Hyperlink Color option is also missing, because you now set that in the Page Properties mentioned in the "Starting Out" section earlier.

✦ **The Measurements pane** loses its Item Coordinates option, because you can't have spreads on Web pages.

✦ **The Trapping pane** doesn't appear for Web documents.

✦ **The Layers pane** grays out the Suppress Printout option — you don't really print a Web document.

The other panes are unaffected.

The Export pane

The Modify dialog box gets a new pane called Export for picture boxes, text paths, and lines. This pane, shown in Figure 38-5, lets you determine the format and location for exported graphics. QuarkXPress will export both imported and QuarkXPress-created pictures, as well as lines and text on text paths, as graphics so they look correct on the Web. Because the Web can't duplicate most of QuarkXPress's image– and text-manipulation features, converting them to a Web-compatible graphic format is the only way to retain their settings.

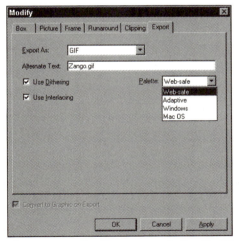

Figure 38-5: The Export pane in the Modify dialog box (here, for a picture box; similar panes appear for lines and text paths as well).

Browser selection

Another change to QuarkXPress when you create a Web document is the insertion of a pop-up menu with a globe icon next to the Page pop-up menu at the bottom of the screen (you can see it in Figure 38-3). This lets you open a Web browser (click the globe) to preview your current Web document as it would appear online. If you have more than one Web browser installed, select which to open via the pop-up menu. You specify which browser(s) you want accessible via the Browsers pane in the Application section of the Preferences dialog box (Edit ⇨ Preferences ⇨ Preferences, or Option+Shift+⌘+Y or Ctrl+Alt+Shift+Y), as Figure 38-6 shows.

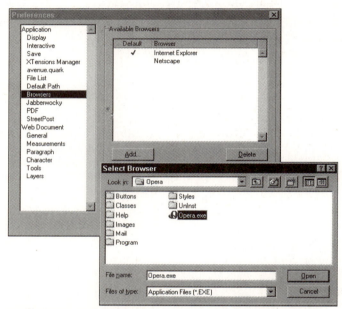

Figure 38-6: The Browsers pane in the Preferences dialog box, as well as the dialog box to open a new browser link.

Tip

We recommend you have the latest and next-to-latest versions of Microsoft Internet Explorer, Netscape Navigator/Communicator, and Opera browsers installed on at least one testing system on Mac and one testing system on Windows to see how your Web documents will look in the real world—browsers don't always show the same thing. All three browsers are free downloads from their respective sites (www.microsoft.com or www.microsoft.com/mac, www.netscape.com, and www.opera.com).

File name and icons

A QuarkXPress Web document has a slightly different icon than a QuarkXPress print document: The circle is blue, not red, and the icon is shaded, not white. In Windows, the file name also has the .qwd file name extension rather than .qxd.

Web-oriented palettes

Web documents have several unique palettes. These are covered in detail later in this chapter, but here are summaries of what they accomplish.

✦ **Hyperlinks palette:** The Hyperlinks palette, shown in Figure 38-7, contains a list of hyperlinks to Web pages and to document pages used in the current QuarkXPress Web document. A hyperlink is an area that, when clicked, opens a new page or a new location on the existing page.

Figure 38-7: The Hyperlinks palette.

✦ **Placeholders palette:** The Placeholders palette, shown in Figure 38-8, is used in creating Extended Markup Language (XML) files, a database language used to produce structured Web content. It shows the records defined in a particular XML file.

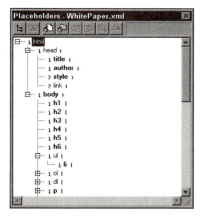

Figure 38-8: The Placeholders palette.

Chapter 39 covers XML in more detail.

✦ **Sequences palette:** The Sequences palette, shown in Figure 38-9, builds a list of objects to be displayed or linked to in a Web page. The sequence created in this palette is essentially a mini-program to display certain items in a certain order.

Figure 38-9: The Sequences palette.

Constructing a Document

Web pages can be simple or complex, and QuarkXPress offers tools to handle most levels of complexity. We cover them from least to most complex, which typically corresponds to most and least used as well.

Note   The construction of pages in a Web document is the same as for a print document, except as noted earlier. You place your pictures and text in boxes as appropriate for your layout goals. (We do suggest you avoid using multicolumn text boxes, however, because these are hard to follow on a browser screen that requires scrolling.) So we don't cover these basic layout issues here.

We recommend that you put all related pages in one QuarkXPress document, so you can easily create the links between pages.

Exporting text as an image

When you're working in a Web document, many of the higher-end typographic features are disabled. In character attributes, this includes kerning, tracking, baseline shift, and type styles such as shadow, small caps, and superior. In paragraph attributes, this includes H&J sets and tab settings. But you may want to use some of these features, especially in image maps — and you can.

All you need to do is export a text box as a graphic. To do this, select the text box and check Convert to Graphic on Export in the Box tab of the Modify dialog box (Item ⇨ Modify, or ⌘+M or Ctrl+M). This enables all the typographic controls for that text box. Remember that graphic files take longer for users to download than text, so use this feature judiciously. Consider whether you really need the special formatting to communicate your message.

Tip   When you're creating a Web document, you'll likely bring in existing text boxes from print documents. You can do this by dragging items between documents, pasting, or using a library. No matter how you do it, the typography won't change. QuarkXPress will automatically check Convert to Graphic on Export for these text boxes. For boxes containing body text, it's probably a good idea to uncheck this.

Creating hyperlinks

A *hyperlink* is an area of text or an area of an image that, when clicked, opens a new Web page or moves you to a different location on the current Web page. It's one of the most powerful features of the Web and underpins its easy navigation.

The process is simple: Highlight the text to be linked, or select the picture, and then choose Style ⇨ Hyperlink ⇨ New or click the Link icon (the chain) in the Hyperlinks palette (View ⇨ Hyperlinks). Figure 38-10 shows the palette and the Edit Hyperlink dialog box that appears. You can type in a URL (a Uniform Resource Locator, or Web address) manually or click Browse to select an existing HTML file on your computer. Or, if you've already created a hyperlink, simply click that link in the Hyperlinks palette after selecting the graphic or text to jump from.

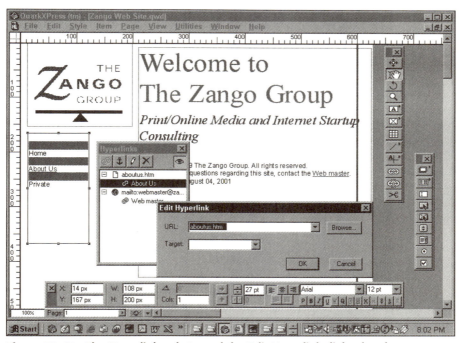

Figure 38-10: The Hyperlink palette and the Edit Hyperlink dialog box let you set hyperlinks for selected text or pictures.

You don't have to enter the full URL; instead, you can use what's called a *relative address*. For example, if the Web site www.zangogroup.com has a page called aboutus.html in a directory called aboutus, you could enter the full address — www.zangogroup.com\aboutus\aboutus.htm — or the relative hyperlink \aboutus\aboutus.htm. The relative hyperlink starts at the current address and adds the relative link to that. A full hyperlink gives the entire address from the very beginning. The pros of relative hyperlinks are that they're shorter and that if a page moves in your directory structure, the links to pages in directories below it won't have to change. Figure 38-11 shows a directory structure in Microsoft's FrontPage Web editor that has been modified. The insertion of the Projects page won't affect any relative hyperlinks from the Private page. But if we had inserted a page between the Private page and, say, the Resources page, the relative hyperlinks would no longer have worked from Private to Resources.

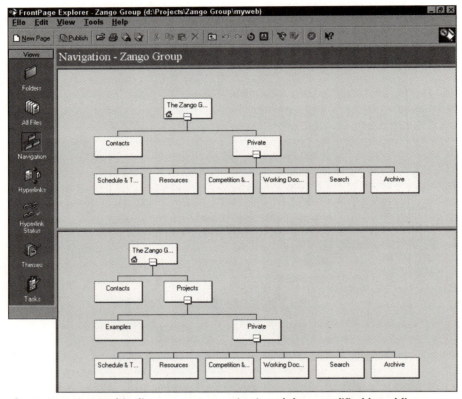

Figure 38-11: A Web's directory structure (top) and then modified by adding a new level (bottom).

Note Unlike the other Web document tools in QuarkXPress, the Hyperlinks palette is available when a print document is open, too, because hyperlinks also work with Portable Document Format (PDF) files — at least they do when the document is being displayed on-screen. So you may want to apply hyperlinks to a print document if you plan on also saving it as a PostScript file or PDF to be opened in Adobe Acrobat. Chapter 40 covers PDF file creation in more detail.

Caution Although QuarkXPress appears to preserve hyperlinks in imported word processor files, all QuarkXPress does is import the formatting (the blue underline), not the underlying hyperlink information. So you'll have to reapply any hyperlinks in QuarkXPress that existed in the word processor document.

There's another type of hyperlink called an *anchor* that QuarkXPress lets you create. An anchor is a spot on a page that a link will jump to. You use it when you want to link from one place on a page to another, rather than to a new page. An example would be if a page has several sections and you provide a list of those sections at the top of the page for quick access. To create an anchor point, you select the text or graphic you want to jump to, then click the anchor icon in the Hyperlinks dialog box, as shown in Figure 38-12, or use Style ⇨ Anchor ⇨ New. Edit the default name given in the resulting dialog box, then click OK to create it. You'll see a pink arrow appear at the anchor location.

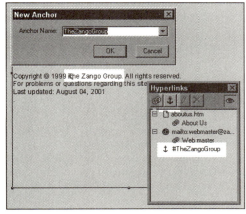

Figure 38-12: Creating an anchor point in QuarkXPress 5.

You can now link to that anchor by creating a hyperlink elsewhere and choosing the anchor point from the URL pop-up menu in the New Hyperlink (or Edit Hyperlink) dialog box. An anchor will be preceded with the # symbol. You can also get the list of available hyperlink destinations, including anchors, from the Style ⇨ Hyperlink submenu, but the easiest way is simply to select the text or graphic you want to link from and then click the anchor link name in the Hyperlinks palette.

You edit hyperlinks and anchors by selecting the anchor or link you want to edit and then clicking the edit icon (the pencil) in the Hyperlinks dialog box, or use Style ⇨ Hyperlink ⇨ Edit or Style ⇨ Anchor ⇨ Edit.

To delete a hyperlink of anchor, you can use the delete icon (an X in Windows and a trash can on the Mac) after selecting the link in the Hyperlinks palette, or use Style ⇨ Hyperlink ⇨ Delete (or Style ⇨ Anchor ⇨ Delete).

Tip   If you Control+click or right-click a hyperlink or anchor point in your Web document, or a hyperlink or anchor name in the Hyperlinks palette, you'll get a context menu that lets you create, edit, or delete a hyperlink or anchor. In the Hyperlinks palette, the context menu also lets you go to a location and remove unused URLs, as Figure 38-13 shows.

Figure 38-13: Context menu options in the Hyperlinks palette.

Creating image maps

Image maps are multiple *hot spots* (hyperlinks) placed on images, where you can click and get to another page, send an e-mail, submit information, and so on. They are, in effect, a hyperlink assigned to an entire area. They're called maps because they resemble a world map where each country has its own shape and outline — in a Web page's image map, specific regions of an image are outlined, each region linking to a different location.

You create these image maps very much like you'd create a text or picture box. First, you bring in the picture (or draw it in QuarkXPress) that has the various elements you want to create links from. Then, using the Image Map tool in the Web Tools palette, select the Image Map tool you want to use from the Image Map pop-up menu — rectangle, oval, and Bézier — then draw the area over the imported picture where you want the image map to appear. After you've created the image map, you'll see a red outline indicating where it is, as Figure 38-14 shows, so that you can assign a hyperlink to it. You'll also notice a visual indicator in the upper-right-hand corner of the picture box to remind you that the box contains image maps in addition to the picture.

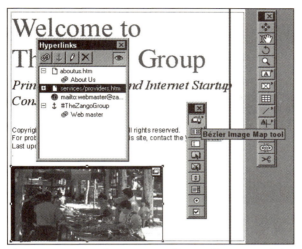

Figure 38-14: An image map (the outline around the two vendors at left) created on a picture box. Note the icon at the picture box's upper-right corner indicating the box has an image map associated with it.

With the image map defined and selected, create or associate an existing hyperlink as described in the previous section.

There are three Image Map tools. They are:

✦ **Rectangle Image Map tool:** This produces a standard rectangle much like the ones created with the Text Box tool and the Picture Box tool, the big difference being of course that these boxes are used as hyperlinks. Hold down the Shift key while drawing the box to get a perfect square.

✦ **Oval Image Map tool:** This tool produces an ellipse. Hold down the Shift key while drawing to get a perfect circle. If all this sounds familiar, it's because this tool works pretty much like the Oval Text and Picture Box tools.

✦ **Bézier Image Map tool:** This tool produces *polygons* (shapes composed of a series of flat sides) and *polycurves* (shapes composed of a series of curves), as well as shapes that combine both sides and curves. To create a Bézier shape, you click and release at each corner (technically known as a node). When you want to complete the box, click back on the origin point. (Notice how the pointer changes to a circle from the normal cross.) If you click and drag for a little bit at each desired node, you see the Bézier control handles appear that let you create a curve. You can have both straight and curved sides based on how you use the mouse at each node — experiment to get the hang of it.

Using rollovers

One of the coolest things about Web pages is that they can be designed to be interactive, and one of the most common of these interactive features is the rollover. A *rollover* is a picture (usually text saved as a JPEG or GIF) that changes when you move the mouse pointer over it in a Web browser. When you roll your mouse over some text on a Web page, it turns a different color, or starts to glow, or turns into a completely different picture. Rollovers are easy to create in QuarkXPress.

Although rollovers are easy to make, they do require some prep work. A rollover is composed of two superimposed graphics, not unlike a cartoon. So to create this little two-picture cartoon, you need to create two pictures of the same size. You create these pictures in an image-editing program like Fireworks or Photoshop. In this case, we've created our pictures in Photoshop — two versions of the Zango Group logo using different color schemes. Figure 38-15 shows these two images.

Figure 38-15: Two images used in a rollover. The one at right will be the one the user sees when he hovers his mouse over the image at left, which displays the rest of the time.

Now you can go back to QuarkXPress and make that rollover happen:

1. First place your default picture — that is, the picture that will usually appear on-screen — in your Web document.

2. Use Item ➪ Rollover ➪ Create Rollover to get the Rollover dialog box. You'll notice that the path to your default picture has already been placed in the Default Picture field in the Rollover dialog box, shown in Figure 38-16. That means QuarkXPress has already done half the work for you.

Figure 38-16: The Rollover dialog box.

3. Click Browse next to the Rollover Image field and locate your other picture—the rollover picture—then select the picture and click OK.

4. In the Hyperlinks field, select the URL to which you'd like to link the rollover. *Remember:* A rollover is really just a fancy hyperlink. When you click on it, it should be set up to take you somewhere. In our example, we've linked our rollover image to the About Us page.

5. Click OK. You'll see two icons appear in the rollover's picture box (see Figure 38-17), indicating the rollover and the hyperlink. If you hover the mouse pointer over an icon, you'll get a pop-up description of what the rollover or hyperlink is to.

Figure 38-17: The rollover and hyperlink icons in a picture box.

When you select an image in a rollover, it will be fit to the box, even if the originating image has been cropped or sized differently. (QuarkXPress doesn't apply the image settings of the picture box to the first image.) So make sure that you do all cropping and sizing in your image editor, for both the originating and the rollover image, to ensure they're both the proper size.

To delete a rollover, use Item ⇨ Rollover ⇨ Delete Rollover or choose the Delete Rollover option in the context menu when you Control+click or right-click the picture box containing the rollover.

Adding meta tags

To make Web sites easier to find in search engines, most Web creators add keywords in a part of the Web page called the *meta tags*. Meta tags are basically internal notes, such as those describing the purpose of a page or site.

In QuarkXPress, meta tags are entered in the Meta Tags dialog box found in the Edit menu. Figure 38-18 shows the dialog box. Give your meta tags list a name, enter the tags you want, then click Save. Then use Page ⇨ Page Properties to open the Page Properties dialog box. In the Meta Tags pop-up menu, select your meta tags list, and click OK.

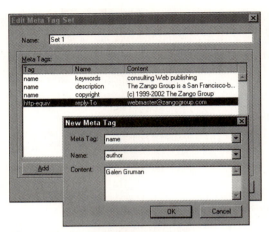

Figure 38-18: Entering meta tags.

Cross-Reference You can include several types of meta tags in your HTML file. Refer to *HTML For Dummies,* 3rd Edition, by Ed Tittel and Stephen N. James (published by Hungry Minds, Inc.) for more information about meta tag types.

Finishing Up

After you've created your page, you should test how it will look in a browser, by selecting the browser preview button (the globe icon) at the bottom of the QuarkXPress window, as described earlier in this chapter. Figure 38-19 shows an example.

You'll likely want to adjust your layout based on how well it renders in the various browsers you use to test it. When you're happy with the results, go to Page ⇨ Properties and make sure you specify an export file name (otherwise, QuarkXPress will call the page Export1). Figure 38-20 shows the dialog box. We recommend you give it a title as well, because some browsers will display that in search results or at the bottom of the browser window.

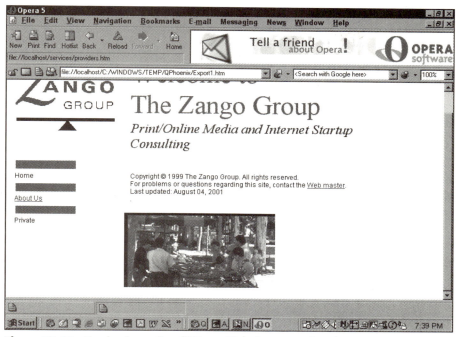

Figure 38-19: Previewing a QuarkXPress Web document in a browser.

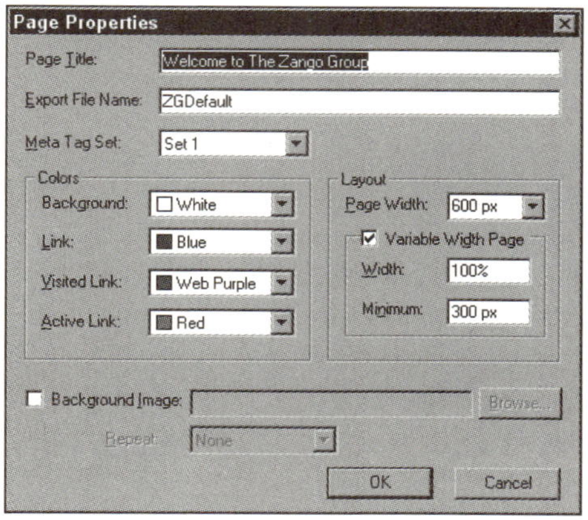

Figure 38-20: The Page Properties dialog box is where you set the Web page's file name and other settings.

Note   Be sure to go to the Page Properties dialog box for each page in your Web document, because the settings are applied only to the current page.

When you're all set, go to File ➪ Export ➪ HTML to save the document's pages as separate HTML files and gather all the images into one folder. You do have a few options, as shown in Figure 38-21:

✦ **You can specify the pages you want to export in the Pages field.** All is the default.

✦ **You can select External CSS File to save the style sheet information in the folder that contains the exported images (that file is called *image*).** CSS means Cascading Style Sheets, which saves font and size information so browsers on computers with the same or similar fonts as you used will display the formatting as close as possible to your display when creating the file.

✦ **You can select whether to have the default browser launch and display the first page after you export.**

✦ **If your Web document is using XML placeholders (as covered in Chapter 39), you can enable their export.**

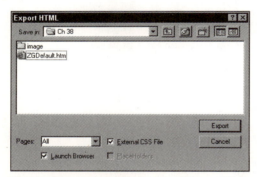

Figure 38-21: Exporting a QuarkXPress Web document to HTML.

After you've exported your pages, you'll need to get them onto your Web server. There are several File Transfer Protocol (FTP) tools to do that if you use a remote server. If you're using a Web server you have direct access to, you can simply copy the files there with a disk or over the network. However you get your files onto the Web, chances are you'll need to copy the various files in specific directories that match the page hierarchy of your site (refer to Figure 38-11 for an example). Often, images are stored within an Images folder inside the folder that contains their Web pages, but they can also all be stored in one master folder. Work with your Webmaster to determine how the pages are saved on the server. In many cases, the Web page designer won't have to worry about this, but in smaller operations, the Web page designer could just as easily be the Webmaster. What's key is that the pages are named and organized clearly so they can be figured out easily when it comes time to put them on the server in the right locations.

Summary

Creating a Web document in QuarkXPress is straightforward, because the program uses many familiar tools and dialog boxes. But it adjusts these tools and interface elements to narrow creation choices to those that make sense for the Web.

Because the Web is page-oriented, you can set up pages differently and have unrelated pages in the same document. But this also means that you must set up defaults for each page, such as the page name, rather than rely on document-wide settings.

QuarkXPress's Web tools focus to a large extent on the Web's key differentiator: the ability to create links from one page to another so readers can quickly jump to relevant material elsewhere, avoiding a linear, predetermined experience. QuarkXPress offers tools to create the basic hyperlinks that allow such navigation, as well as for anchors (links within a Web page) and graphically sophisticated forms of links: image maps and rollovers.

QuarkXPress also lets you annotate your Web document with keywords and other information that helps search engines find your Web pages and that lets others, such as network administrators, know who created a page and how to contact that person.

When you're done creating your Web pages, you can — and should — preview them from several Web browsers, which QuarkXPress lets you do from within the program. After everything is to your liking, you can export the Web document into its separate HTML pages and also have all the images converted into Web-compatible formats and placed with the exported HTML pages.

✦   ✦   ✦

Creating Interactive Documents

◆ ◆ ◆ ◆

In This Chapter

Creating forms and
user controls

Working with XML

◆ ◆ ◆ ◆

Web documents have been transformed since the initial Web wave of the mid-1990s. They've gone from relatively static pages (the dynamism of hyperlinks aside) to software-like entities that run programs, let users fill in forms, and in essence react to user actions.

There are two basic reasons for that: Web programming languages like Java and Perl, and the Extensible Markup Language (XML) database-oriented language. Java runs programs within a Web page. But XML goes further, letting Web-page creators work with databases of information and adjust the content mix and presentation on the fly. For example, a stock chart that lets you select the number of days for which to see data and that lets you choose to compare a stock's performance against various indices is likely produced in XML, which, when you select the stock, period, and indices you want, accesses a database of stock information, pulls out those that were requested, and delivers it to the page in a presentation template.

But there's more to interactivity than XML and Java/Perl. QuarkXPress also has tools to create forms and active elements such as buttons to allow user control and data entry for functions such as online stores and user registration.

Creating Forms and User Controls

Many Web pages contain forms for readers to enter information, such as an e-mail address for a newsletter subscription or name and address for delivery of a product. These pages also contain user controls such as buttons, pop-up menus, and radio buttons to let readers choose from various options (such as which newsletter to subscribe to). QuarkXPress 5 lets you add such forms and controls to Web documents. These features had been available as the separate QuarkImmedia product but are now integrated into QuarkXPress.

New Feature QuarkXPress 5 integrates part of the QuarkImmedia tool to create forms and actions such as buttons.

The various forms and user-control tools are shown in Figure 39-1.

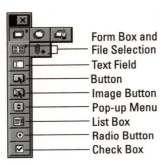

Form Box and File Selection
Text Field
Button
Image Button
Pop-up Menu
List Box
Radio Button
Check Box

Figure 39-1: The forms and user-control tools in the QuarkXPress Web Tools palette. (The top row contains the Image Map tools, covered in Chapter 38.)

Creating a form box

Although the meat of most forms is comprised of a combination of buttons, fields, and entry fields, the form itself is contained in a rectangular box, called a *form box,* that you create using the Form Box tools, located directly below the Image Map tools in the Web Tools palette. The first of these two tools is the Form Box tool. The other tool in the Form Box pop-up menu is the File Select tool.

As you might imagine, creating a form box is pretty much like creating any other kind of box in QuarkXPress. Here are step-by-step instructions:

1. Select the Form Box tool in the Web Tools palette.

2. Move your pointer to the area where you'd like to place the form. (You'll add the fields within the form later.)

3. Click and drag the mouse pointer until you've covered the area where you'd like your form to be. A form box looks exactly like a text box when it's first created, with the exception of the visual indicator in the upper-right-hand corner that looks like the form icon (see Figure 39-2).

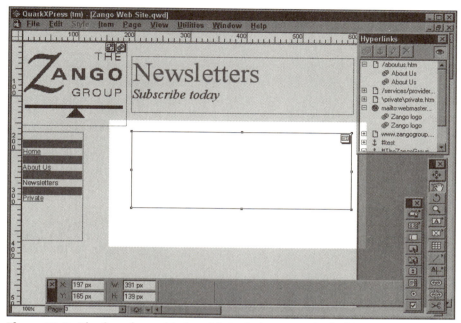

Figure 39-2: The form box added to this Web document looks like a typical text box with the exception of the visual indicator in its upper-right-hand corner.

4. Choose Item ➪ Modify to display the Modify dialog box.

5. Click the Form tab and enter the name of the form box in the Name field. Figure 39-3 shows the Form pane.

Figure 39-3: The Form pane in the Modify dialog box.

6. Now, choose a method for submitting your form's information from the Method pop-up menu. The choices are as follows (your Webmaster will tell you what's best for your environment):

- The Get option tells the Web browser to append the data from your reader's form to the end of the URL of the target script or application.

- The Post Option tells the Web browser to send the data from your reader's form to the target script or applications via a separate transaction. If you choose Post from the Method pop-up, you must specify a Multipurpose Internet Mail Extension (MIME) type for the data in the form in the Encoding pop-up menu. Your choices are urlencoded, form-data, and plain. Check with your Webmaster to see what's appropriate for your environment. (You specify the post location in the StreetPost pane of the Preferences dialog box, accessible via Edit ⇨ Preferences ⇨ Preferences, or Option+Shift+⌘+Y or Ctrl+Alt+Shift+Y.)

- The Action field is where you tell QuarkXPress which script contains the information on how your page should reply when it receives the reader's submitted information (the action). That script is typically written in a language such as Java, Perl, or C and conforms to the Common Gateway Interface (CGI) protocol.

With the exception of perhaps the first couple fields, the rest of the choices in the Form pane are no doubt confusing. Don't worry. Unless you're already a trained Webmaster, this stuff *should* look a bit sketchy. QuarkXPress can build all the pieces of your form for you. It can even provide you with a map of what you need to get it working. The one thing it can't do is tell you what to put in those fields. Why? Because to make a form interact between you and your reader, you must send commands to the server where your Web page will eventually be stored. The server processes the information from your form using the CGI protocol.

So does this mean you'll have to take a class in Java just so you can make your simple, little form work? Not at all. On the contrary, if you poke around on the Web, you may find some good primers about CGI scripting, and these primers usually have some scripts you can copy and paste or download to your computer for use in QuarkXPress. (Two good sources are the Web Resource Centre at `www.wrc-uk.com` and the University of Illinois's National Center for Supercomputing Applications at `http://hoohoo.ncsa.uiuc.edu/cgi`.) Many Internet service providers (ISPs) also provide you with readymade CGI scripts for creating forms. (An ISP is the company that hosts your Web page after it's finished.) If these avenues fail you and you want to find out more about the inner workings of CGI, pick up *HTML For Dummies,* 3rd Edition, by Ed Tittel and Stephen N. James, and *XML For Dummies*, 2nd Edition, by Ed Tittel (both published by Hungry Minds, Inc.).

Tip

You can also create a form box automatically by drawing a form control (button, menu, and so on) in a blank section of a Web document. QuarkXPress automatically renders a form box around your chosen form control according to the specification for the Form Box Tool in the Preferences dialog box (Edit ⇨ Preferences ⇨ Preferences, or Option+Shift+⌘+Y or Ctrl+Alt+Shift+Y). These form controls are covered later in this chapter.

Creating a text field

The Text Field tool lets you create fields in which readers can enter text. On the Web, you often see these text fields in the form of Name, Address, City, and so on. Passwords can also be included; for such purposes, QuarkXPress 5 lets you have readers enter text that appears only as a series of asterisks or bullets, depending on the browser. A hidden field control then translates the text but doesn't display that value to the reader — only to you.

To add a text field to your form:

1. Select the Text Field tool in the Web Tools palette.

2. Move the pointer to a spot *within* your form box, then click and drag until the text field is close to the length you desire. **Remember:** The entire text field must remain in the form box.

3. Open the Modify dialog box (Item ➪ Modify, or ⌘+M or Ctrl+M) and click the Form tab, shown in Figure 39-4.

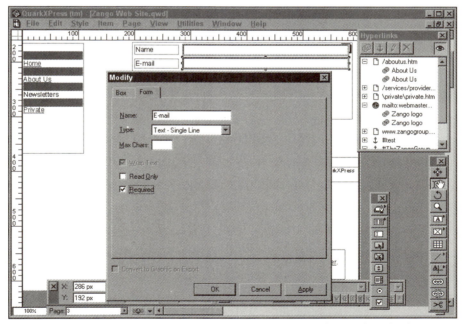

Figure 39-4: The Form pane for a text field, with the field shown directly above.

4. In the Name field, enter an appropriate name of the field. For example, if it's a field for an address, use a logical name like *Address* or *addr.*

5. In the Type pop-menu, choose one of the following:

- **Text – Single Line:** This control lets the reader enter only one line of text, for example a name or address.

- **Text – Multi Line:** This control lets the reader enter more multiple lines of text. These sorts of fields are generally reserved for additional comments or messages in custom greeting cards.

- **Password:** This control displays text in asterisks or bullets as described earlier.

- **Hidden Field:** This control is submitted with a form, but it doesn't display in the reader's Web browser. These fields can be used to calculate information about the visitors submitting the forms, such as what type of browser they're using, without displaying on the users' screen.

6. The Form pane also has the following options, which you can select if you want:

- **Max Chars:** Enter a number in the Max Chars field to specify the maximum number of characters the control will accept. Note that the number you choose doesn't necessarily have anything to do with the length of your field — you can allow 40 characters in a field of 25 characters in length. However, keep in mind the readers might be more inclined to make a mistake if their typing begins to scroll outside the range of the character field where they can't see it.

- **Wrap Text:** Check this box if you want the text entered into a multiple-line text box to break to the next line in a multiple-line text field. We recommend you always keep this checked. Otherwise visitors' typed text will begin to scroll outside the range of the field, and before long they won't be able to see what they're typing.

- **Read Only:** To indicate that the readers shouldn't be able to edit the contents of a field, check Read Only. This may be used to automatically fill in, for example, a URL or the user's browser type gathered by a script.

- **Required:** To indicate that the readers must complete a field, check Required. If the user doesn't enter information in a required field, the browser will display the error message you indicated in the Modify dialog box's Form pane for the form box (refer to Figure 39-3).

7. Click OK.

Tip

As you create fields, keep in mind that they should never overlap. Only hidden fields can overlap other fields, and in all honesty, you'll probably never use a hidden field for anything.

Creating a file-submission form

The File Selection tool creates a form field that lets visitors upload files from their local computer to your remote server. When the readers click the Browse button, the Open File dialog box appears in their Web browser, where they can select the file they want to upload. After they've located the file, they click Submit, and the file is sent to your remote server. Chances are you won't use this feature much — if ever. Still, there may be times when you want to incorporate this feature into a page, such as for contests in which readers submit programs, art and music files, or whatever, or for a private system in which contributors and providers can send you files via a private Web page.

To create a file submission control:

1. Choose the File Selection tool from the Web Tools palette.

2. Move the pointer to someplace within your form box. Click and draw your submission control as you would an ordinary text box.

3. Open the Modify dialog box (Item ➪ Modify, or ⌘+M or Ctrl+M), and click the Form tab.

4. Enter the name (such as /Music_MP3) of the control submission in the Name field.

5. If you've brushed up on your MIME, specify a list of acceptable MIME types in the Accept field. (*Note:* These MIME types must be separated by commas.)

6. Click Required. This ensures that the attached file will upload with the form data.

7. Click OK.

Figure 39-5 shows the result of the File Selection tool.

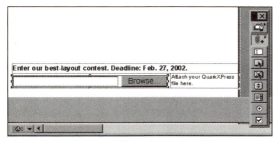

Figure 39-5: A user file-submission form created with the File Selection tool.

A quick guide to MIME types

The Multipurpose Internet Mail Extension (MIME) lets a server or client program know what kind of file is attached, so it knows what kind of program to use to open the file. PCs and Macs use a similar scheme to know what icons to associate with files and programs, and MIME lets files moved from one computer to another over e-mail and via Internet connections retain that key "what am I?" information. Among the most popularly used MIME types are the following:

✦ text/plain, for plain ASCII text

✦ text/richtext, for Rich Text Format files

✦ text/tab-separated-values, for tab-delimited files (often exported from spreadsheet programs)

✦ text/html, for HTML files

✦ text/xml, for XML files

✦ text/css, for Cascading Style Sheet definition files

✦ image/jpeg, for JPEG files

✦ image/gif, for GIF files

✦ image/tiff, for TIFF files

✦ image/bmp, for Microsoft's bitmap format

✦ image/png, for the Portable Network Graphics format

✦ image/x-pict, for the Mac's PICT format

✦ audio/mpeg, for audio MPEG files

✦ audio/w-wav, for Microsoft's audio format

✦ audio/x-aiff, for Apple's audio format

✦ audio/x-midi, for the MIDI audio format

✦ video/mpeg, for video MPEG files

✦ video/quicktime, for QuickTime files

✦ model/iges, for IGES geographic information files

✦ model/vrml, for Virtual Rendering Model Language files

✦ application/msword, for Microsoft Word files

✦ application/excel, for Microsoft Excel files

✦ application/postscript, for PostScript files

✦ application/pdf, for Portable Document Format files

✦ application/acad, for Autodesk AutoCAD files

✦ application/dxf, for AudoCAD Drawing Interchange Format (DXF) files

✦ application/macbinary, for Apple binary program files and compressed files

✦ application/mac-binhex40, for BinHex-compressed Mac files

✦ application/zip, for Zip-compressed files

✦ application/xml, for XML files

✦ application/xml-dtd, for XML data description files

You can get a complete list of MIME types from `ftp://ftp.isi.edu/in-notes/iana/assignments/media-types/media-types`. Another great source for these definitions is `www.ltsw.se/knbase/internet/mime.htp`.

Creating buttons and menus

QuarkXPress lets you create several types of buttons and menus to let users select items on a Web page. The creation process is similar for each.

Text and image buttons

As Figure 39-6 shows, the Button tool lets you create two kinds of buttons: Submit buttons and Reset buttons. Chances are that after you've learned to create a proper form, you'll be using these two buttons more than any other. The Submit button is used to submit the information the visitor has entered in your Web page to your remote Web server. The Reset button is simply a "do over" button: If the visitors make a mistake or change their minds about what they've entered in a form, they can click Reset and everything they've entered in the form is wiped clean. Usually, you'll see these buttons side by side in a form.

Figure 39-6: Text buttons (Submit and Clear) and an image button (Get Acrobat Reader).

To create a Submit or Reset button:

1. Select the Button tool in the Web Tools palette.

2. Move the cursor within your form box, then click and drag to draw the button. You don't get to size the button yourself; instead, the button automatically sizes as you enter its name using the Content tool. (The Button is essentially a special type of text box.)

3. Open the Modify dialog box (Item ⇨ Modify, or ⌘+M or Ctrl+M), and click the Form tab. In the Form pane, enter the name of the button in the name field. The CGI script will use this name to associate commands to the button.

4. In the Type pop-menu, choose either Submit or Reset.

5. Click OK.

Note   The CGI script attached to the form box that holds the buttons will contain the actual script that implements the submit and reset functions. The script will need to access each button by the name you entered in the Form pane for the button.

Buttons need not be limited to text. You can turn pictures into buttons as well. Not to be confused with image maps, image buttons are used to submit forms. They, like the regular text buttons, require some scripting before they'll be of any use on a Web page.

To create an image button:

1. Choose the Image Button tool for the Web Tools palette.

2. Move the cursor to the place in the form box where you'd like to place the image button, then click and drag the cursor until the image is the size you desire.

3. Open the Get Picture dialog box (File ⇨ Get Picture, or ⌘+E or Ctrl+E), and import the picture file you'd like to make into a button. You'll see a picture button icon appear in the box's upper-right corner, so you'll be reminded this is a button.

4. Open the Modify dialog box (Item ⇨ Modify, or ⌘+M or Ctrl+M), and enter the name of the button in the Name field in the Form pane.

5. Click the Export tab in the Modify dialog box.

6. In the Export pane, choose a graphic format from the Export As pop-up menu. The Export pane will then display different options, depending on the graphic format you choose. You can choose from three graphic formats:

   • **JPEG:** When you choose the JPEG format, you're asked to enter a description of the picture in the Alternate Text field. If the picture doesn't show up in someone's browser for some reason (usually lack of memory), the text you enter in this field will show up in its place. Next, select an option from the Image Quality pop-up menu, ranging from Lowest (pure resolution, but quicker download time) to Highest (crispest resolution, but slower download time). Last, check the Progressive check box so that the image displays as a progressive JPEG, which you should use for very large images. A progressive JPEG file appears line by line, so the viewer can tell something is in the space as it fills in; unchecked, a large image could confuse a reader because it wouldn't appear at all for a few seconds to maybe a few minutes.

- **GIF:** When you choose the GIF format, you're again asked to enter a description in the Alternate Text field. You can then check the Use Dithering check box if you want the picture displayed using dithered colors. Likewise, you can check Use Interlacing to display the images as interlaced GIF images. Finish things up by choosing a color palette in the Color Palette pop-up menu. Your best choice is probably Web-safe. This ensures that the picture's color will remain consistent over different platforms. However, you can also choose Windows, Adaptive (the picture is displayed according to what colors are available on a given monitor), and Mac OS. GIF is the best format for most buttons, because it's intended for small graphics that load quickly on-screen.

- **PNG:** The Portable Network Graphics (PNG) format is a new format that only newer browsers can handle. The choices that go along with a PNG are essentially the same as those that go with a GIF — with one added choice. In the PNG export pane, you can tell the Web browser to display the picture as either True Color or Indexed Color. True Color will display the maximum number of colors it can muster from a given computer monitor. Indexed color lets you apply dithering and/or interlacing to the picture via the Use Interlacing and Use Dithering check boxes.

7. Click OK.

With the proper CGI scripts attached to the form box, your picture can now be used as a button to submit information just like any other button.

Radio buttons, check boxes, pop-up menus, and list boxes

There are four kinds of buttons that let readers pick from predefined options: radio buttons, check boxes, pop-up menus, and list boxes. They each have different uses.

A group of radio buttons lets a visitor choose one value from an entire list of values. For example, you can use a group of radio buttons to determine the approximate age of a customer, or, as illustrated in Figure 39-7, a list of options for subscriptions. When a reader selects one radio button, all the other radio buttons in the group are deselected.

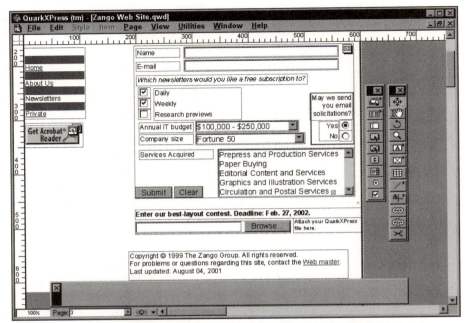

Figure 39-7: Examples of the various button and form tools: text fields (Name and E-mail), check boxes (the newsletter options), radio buttons (the solicitation permission section), pop-up menus (Annual IT budget and Company size), and list boxes (the Services Acquired section).

To add a group of radio buttons to a form:

1. Select the Radio Button tool in the Web Tools palette.

2. Move the cursor to the place in the form where you'd like to position the radio button, then click and draw a selection control for each button you want.

3. Select one of the radio buttons and choose the Modify command in the Item menu, or ⌘+M or Ctrl+M; click the Form tab in the Modify dialog box.

4. Choose Radio Button from the Type pop-up menu (if it isn't already selected).

5. Radio button controls with same name are considered to be part of the same group. So decide on a name for the radio button group and enter the name in the Group field.

6. Enter a value for the selected radio button in the value field. This value is what will be transmitted to the CGI script.

7. Repeat Steps 1 through 6 until you've created all the radio button controls in the group.

8. To select a default radio button, choose the radio button, choose Modify in the item menu, click the Form tab in the Modify dialog box, and check the Use as Default check box.

9. To indicate that one of the buttons must be selected before the form can be entered, check Required in the Modify dialog box. Of course, it isn't necessary to check Required if you checked Use as Default, because at least one of the buttons — the Default button — will always be selected if one of the other buttons isn't.

10. Click OK

Unlike radio buttons, the check box button control can be used for all sorts of things. It can be used to answer yes/no questions, to create a list, or even to activate a function in a form. You create check box buttons basically the same way you create radio buttons, with a few slight differences. Here's how you create check box buttons:

1. Select the Checkbox Button tool in the Web Tools palette.

2. Move the cursor to the place in the form where you want to position the check box, then click and draw a selection control for each check box you want.

3. Select one of the check boxes and choose the Modify command in the Item menu, or ⌘+M or Ctrl+M; click the Form tab in the Modify dialog box.

4. Choose Checkbox from the Type pop-up menu (if it isn't already selected).

5. Enter a name for the check box in the Name field.

6. Enter a value for the check box in the Value field. This value is what will be transmitted to the CGI script.

7. To indicate the check box control should be checked when the Web page first displays, check Initially Checked.

8. To indicate that one of the buttons must be selected before the form can be entered, check Required in the Modify dialog box.

9. Click OK.

You hear us referring to pop-up menus quite a bit in this book. Now you get a chance to build your own pop-up menu using the Pop-up Menu tool in the Web Tools palette. You can also create list boxes in QuarkXPress 5. The difference? In short, a pop-up menu lets you choose only one item from its menu, while a list box — which looks something like a multi-line text field — lets you choose one or more items from its menu.

To add a pop-up menu or list control to a form:

1. Choose the Pop-up Menu tool or List Box tool from the Web Tools palette.

2. Move the cursor to the place (within the form box) where you'd like to place the pop-up menu, then click and drag the cursor to draw the pop-up menu or list box. Make sure the perimeter stays within the form box.

3. Go to the Item menu and open the Modify dialog box; click the Form tab to display the Form pane.

4. Enter a name for the pop-up menu in the Name field. If you'd like to convert your pop-up menu to a list box or vice versa, you can do so in the Type pop-up menu.

5. Pick the menu list that will be displayed in the pop-up menu, or click New to create a new one. Figure 39-8 shows the dialog boxes that appear for creating a pop-up menu's list. In the Edit Menu dialog box, enter a name for the menu, then click Add to create an entry for the pop-up menu or list box; fill in the name (what appears in the menu or box) and the value (what is transmitted via the CGI script). Repeat for each value you want in the pop-up menu or list box. You can check Use as Default for items you want preselected. For list boxes only, note the Navigation Menu check box; selecting this will make the list box into a list of hyperlinks rather than standard list options. When you're done adding menu or list items, click OK to return to the Form pane.

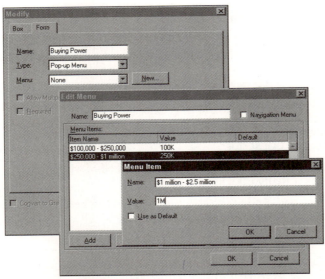

Figure 39-8: The dialog boxes that appear when you create a set of items for a pop-up menu. The dialog boxes are nearly identical for list boxes.

6. If you're working with a list box, check the Allow Multiple Selections check box if you want readers to have the option of selecting more than one item in the list.

7. If you want to make sure the reader clicks at least one item in the list, check the Required check box.

8. Click OK.

You can also create — as well as edit — item lists for pop-up menus and list boxes in the Menus dialog boxed, accessed via Edit ➪ Menus. Menus are created in the Menus dialog box found in the QuarkXPress Edit menu. Figure 39-9 shows the dialog box. (Refer to Figure 39-8 for the dialog boxes brought about by clicking New or Edit.)

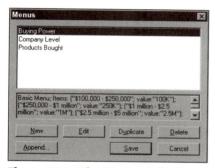

Figure 39-9: The Menus dialog box for creating and editing item lists.

Working with XML

The most complex addition to QuarkXPress is its set of XML features. XML is a structured language that essentially treats document components as data, so you can manage them through a database. The XML tools in QuarkXPress let you treat QuarkXPress documents as sources for XML databases, which are then linked into Web pages, PDF files, CD-ROMs, and so forth. You could use XML to create very different versions in multiple media of information that resides in a QuarkXPress file.

New Feature

QuarkXPress 5 integrates the Avenue.Quark tool to create and manipulate XML documents.

The key to XML is the fact that it's extensible. You create the tags, or labels, for various kinds of content (these are called *data type descriptions,* or DTDs) based on what makes sense for your content. Then you specify what happens to each of the types of labeled content in terms of what's published, how it's presented, and so forth. Compare that to the more rigid HTML and PDF formats, where there are only certain tags available that cannot be changed, and the presentation is fixed based on the label chosen.

XML code is similar to HTML in the sense that there are tags surrounded by angle brackets (< and >) and that commands and labels are turned on and off (such as <standardHeader> at the beginning of a header item and </standardHeader> at the end of it. Comments begin with <!- - and end with >, while custom commands and declarations begin with <? and end with ?>. You don't have to understand this level of detail — just keep in mind that there are different codes to look for in examining XML code, if the need arises.

Note   A DTD may define several types of content that have their own subcontent types and rules. These are called *branches*. For example, there could be an AuthorInformation branch and a CustomerList branch that both contain tags named Name. You'll need to know which branch text tagged Name should go into, because XML won't know the context.

Cross-Reference   The use of XML will likely involve assistance from a Webmaster, content engineer, or other programming-savvy person. To understand XML in the QuarkXPress context, both page designers and XML experts should refer to the PDF documentation that comes with QuarkXPress 5: Guide to avenue.quark.pdf in the XTensions Documents folder in the QuarkXPress folder and the Tutorial.pdf file in the avenue.quark Tutorial folder in the QuarkXPress folder. Page designers might also want to read *XML For Dummies* (Hungry Minds). *QuarkXPress 5 Bible* limits itself to an overview of QuarkXPress XML functions and is no substitute for a thorough understanding of XML.

Creating an XML document

The first step to creating an XML document is to create the data type definitions (DTDs), which will be required by QuarkXPress to create any new XML file. (The exception is for XML templates designed to create Microsoft eBook files; QuarkXPress comes with a template called Modified eBook.xml that contains the necessary DTDs.) When the DTD file (which should have the .dtd file name extension) is ready, use File ⇨ New ⇨ XML, or Shift⌘+X or Ctrl+Shift+X, to get the dialog box shown in Figure 39-10. Click Custom.xmt to create a new template. If you've created templates of your own that you want to use as a basis, select that template instead. Templates are stored in the Templates folder in the QuarkXPress folder. Although you can have DTD files stored anywhere, it's a good idea to put copies of standard ones in this folder as well.

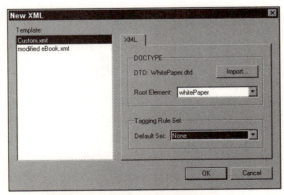

Figure 39-10: The New XML dialog box.

One option is to choose a Root Element, which is the starting point in the XML tree that we'll work on later. This should be the most basic style or tag used in the document. The other option is to choose a tagging rule set, if defined in the DTD, which becomes the default set of labels for elements in your QuarkXPress document. You can create tagging rules via Edit ➪ Tagging Rules, as shown in Figure 39-11. The dialog box shows the XML tags defined in the DTD. The available tags are in black, while tags that don't permit content being added are grayed out. You select a tag and click New Rule to associate specific styles or text formatting with a tag. This lets you tell the XML database that text with the paragraph style Caption, for example, is what should be tagged with the caption XML tag.

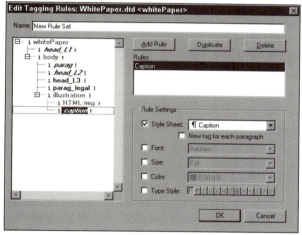

Figure 39-11: The Edit Tagging Rules dialog box.

You can set how tags appear on-screen and how they're treated using the avenue.quark pane in the Preferences dialog box (Edit ➪ Preferences ➪ Preferences, or Option+Shift+⌘+Y or Ctrl+Alt+Shift+Y). Figure 39-12 shows the pane. The Show Tagged Content section contains two buttons to choose the colors of tagged text and untagged text, while the Marker text button lets you choose the color of the on-screen brackets that will surround tagged text.

The pane also has the Enable Dynamic Content Update check box, which ensures that active XML documents are continually updated as the QuarkXPress document they refer to is updated. However, this can slow performance noticeably, so you may want to turn it off.

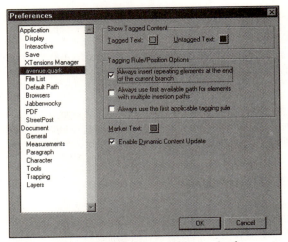

Figure 39-12: The avenue.quark pane in the Preferences dialog box.

Finally, the avenue.quark pane has three options that control how tags are applied in three circumstances:

✦ **Always insert repeating elements at the end of the current branch:** If checked, any DTD elements marked as repeating are added to the end of the active branch. (This is how the preference should usually be set.) Unchecked, you'll be asked to manually determine the position of a new repeating element when you move text with a repeating element (such as a new instance of text set as <Text>) into the XML Workspace palette, described later in this chapter.

✦ **Always use first path for elements with multiple insertion paths:** If checked, QuarkXPress will use the first of multiple rules in the DTD for an element that has multiple rules. For example, if the DTD defines <Paragraph> element to be created at both the end of a current branch and after a new <Sidebar> element, checking this box will use whichever rule is first. Otherwise, you'll be prompted when adding the element to the XML Workspace palette.

✦ **Always use the first applicable tagging rule:** If checked, this uses the first tagging rule if there is a conflict between tagging rules. Otherwise, you'll be prompted when adding the element to the XML Workspace palette.

When you've completed the New XML dialog box's options and clicked OK, you'll get the XML Workspace dialog box, shown in Figure 39-13. Here's where you do most of the XML work in QuarkXPress.

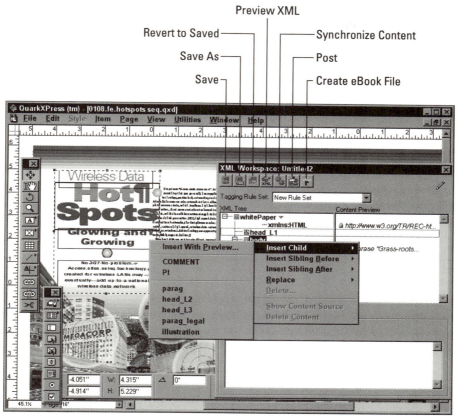

Figure 39-13: The XML Workspace palette and the context menu for an XML item.

The XML Workspace palette shows the tags defined in the DTD as well as the XML tree — the tags used and their relationship to each other in a branch. There are three basic relationships: parent, sibling, and child. When you Control+click or right-click an XML item, you get the pop-up menu shown in Figure 39-13. Here's where you insert a new element for each item you want transferred to the XML document. Therefore, if you have a document with multiple stories, you'll want to create copies of the tags — or entire branches — for each story. You can insert a sibling (at the same level in the branch before or after the selected item) or a child (essentially, a subordinate item). You can also add comments. The context menu will display legal items from the DTD based on your selection. Figure 39-14 shows a revision to the XML tree in Figure 39-13 where we've added a parag item.

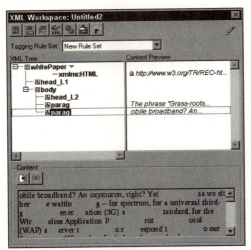

Figure 39-14: A modified XML tree with tagged text added.

To add text content to an XML item, just ⌘+drag or Ctrl+drag the text box, using the Item tool, to the selected XML item. If you want to add a selection of text, highlight it with the Content tool, hold ⌘ or Ctrl, and drag it to the XML item. To add a picture box to an XML item that is specified to handle graphics formats, ⌘+drag or Ctrl+drag the picture box to the XML item.

Text in that box that matches the specifications in the tagging rule set selected in the XML Workspace palette will be added to that XML item. This can lead to issues if you use paragraph styles extensively. For example, paragraphs using a Drop Cap style sheet or a Body No Indent style sheet might not be added to the XML item even though you think of them as part of the story. Why not? Because your tagging rule specified only text using the Body Text style to be added to the parag XML type. So be sure to define tagging rules to cover all the bases. (If you choose None in the Tagging Rule Set pop-up menu, all the text will be added to whatever XML item is selected.)

You'll use this process for all elements you want to bring into the XML document. When you're done, use the Save or Save As button, depending on whether you want to make a new copy. Be sure to first click the Synchronize Content button if Enable Dynamic Content Update is unchecked in the avenue.quark pane of the Preferences dialog box. And be sure to check the Save XML as Standalone option in the Save As dialog box—this copies the DTDs into the XML file so they're available to other programs. This makes it much easier to share the files, because you don't have to worry about also sharing the right DTD files.

You can also view the XML code by clicking the Preview XML button and post the XML content to a Web location (as set up in the StreetPost pane of the Preferences dialog box). Or create a Microsoft eBook file from the XML data by clicking the

Create eBook File button. We recommend that you use the eBook template if you're producing eBook-format files for portable electronic books, since the DTDs that come with it are sure to produce the expected output.

 Windows will not recognize the .xml and .xmt file name extensions that QuarkXPress creates for XML files and templates, respectively. So you can't double-click them to have QuarkXPress launched automatically. Instead, you'll have to open them from within QuarkXPress.

When you've posted the XML data, your Webmaster or other technical expert will take that data into the Web, CD, or other content-creation system used to produce the various documents based on that XML-formatted data.

 If you close the XML Workspace palette, you're actually closing the XML document. To reopen the document, use File ∫ Open, or Ô+O or Ctrl+O, and select the XML file again.

The Placeholder palette

QuarkXPress has a new palette called Placeholder that is used with XML. To be honest, the palette does little more than show you the DTD definitions in an XML file or template and let you toggle the display of XML markers in your QuarkXPress document. Figure 39-15 shows the palette.

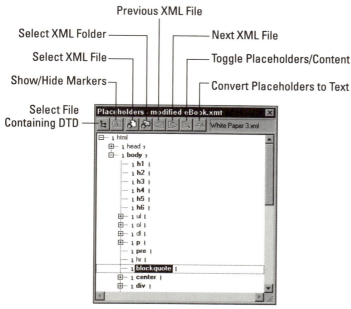

Figure 39-15: The Placeholders palette.

Use the Select File Containing DTD to open a file that contains DTDs, which will then be displayed in the palette. You can also use the Select XML file button to open a QuarkXPress XML file or template.

Creating sequences within documents

QuarkXPress has a feature that lets you create sequences of items in both regular and Web documents — essentially a form of hyperlinking. You create the sequences in the Sequences palette (View ➪ Show Sequences). The palette, shown in Figure 39-16, is fairly straightforward to use:

1. Click the New Sequence button to create a sequence. You can edit the sequence's name with the Edit Name button.

2. Select the first item in the sequence with the Item tool or Content tool, and then click the Add Item button in the Sequences palette.

3. Repeat Step 2 for each item in the sequence.

4. Use the Move Up and Move Down buttons to change the order of an item in a sequence. Use the Delete icon (an X in Windows and a trash can on the Mac) to remove an item.

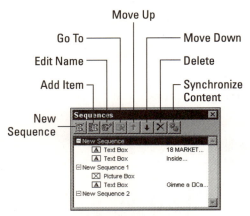

Figure 39-16: The Sequences palette.

QuarkXPress 5 integrates part of the avenue.quark tool to create sequences.

You cannot add a line or a no-content box to a sequence. Any such items in a group will be deleted from the sequence automatically.

If you want to see an item, select it in the palette and click the Go To button. If you hold Option or Alt, you'll get the Go To Next button instead, which is a handy way to jump from one item to the next.

If you change an item that's in a sequence, be sure to click the Synchronize Sequence button so QuarkXPress has the updated information for all elements in the sequence. It's always a good idea to click this button when you're done with a project.

So what do you do with a sequence? You tag them in XML as covered in the previous section — as long as the XML file uses a DTD that supports the elements in the sequence.

Summary

QuarkXPress includes a series of tools that let you add interactivity to Web documents. The forms and button tools are perfectly suited to let you create Web forms such as surveys, product ordering forms, and demographic data input.

In addition to these tools, QuarkXPress also lets you tag content within QuarkXPress documents with XML tags, transferring that content to an XML database from which it can be used in a variety of media, formatted as appropriate for each. But QuarkXPress's XML tools are only the beginning — you'll need an XML database and content-creation and -presentation tools to use the XML data derived from QuarkXPress documents.

✦   ✦   ✦

Exporting Documents as PDF Files

In the age of digital processing, you, as a graphic designer, are producing sophisticated collateral with high-end graphics and complex layout issues. Chances are, your clients often want to publish the same content in print, on CD-ROMs, and on their Web site—all different media, each with unique production characteristics. Even though desktop applications have become exceptionally adept and data can be transferred electronically to anywhere you want, producing a document is still fraught with compatibility issues and graphical incongruities in the final stages.

Although printing is immensely sophisticated, slow workflows involving complex graphics and numerous fonts from original applications make even the simplest of documents a monumental task for prepress production to decipher. And this doesn't even factor in the problem of other issues, such as compatibility importing files from one application to another or between different operating systems and using different output devices. Varying versions of fonts often cause reflow, and layouts may not print as anticipated. File sizes are often enormous, taxing even the fastest pipelines.

Publishing professionals have devised ingenious bandages to resolve these issues, but most cannot solve the biggest issue: creating a complete process that fosters a productive workflow, saving time and helping, rather than hindering, your profitability.

QuarkXPress users herald the arrival of Adobe Acrobat and the Adobe Portable Document Format (PDF) Filter, which comes with QuarkXPress 5 in the form of an XTension. This new XTension makes it easier than ever to reduce production issues by eliminating many common file problems, trimming immense file sizes, and drastically reducing production issues. Producing PDF files through the new PDF Filter provides an effective way to create and deliver reliable, consistent print-ready files for traditional and digital printing, and for Internet output.

Understanding PDF Files

Portable Document Format is a file format based on what Adobe calls its *Adobe imaging model,* the same device-independent representation used in the PostScript page-description language. The PDF file format is growing in popularity because it produces files that are independent of the program, operating system, and equipment used to create and display the files, as shown in Figure 40-1. A file converted into PDF format may contain all the components that were originally used to create it, including the text, graphics, fonts, color specifications, and any other interactive elements. Interactive elements may include hypertext links, rollovers, interactive form fields, file attachments, sounds, and movies.

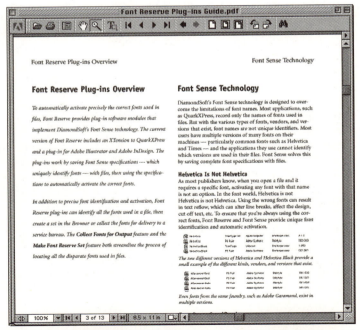

Figure 40-1: This printed booklet, also distributed in PDF form, is easy to read on-screen and prints clearly. Created in QuarkXPress for Mac, it displays the same on any Mac or Windows system.

A document in PDF can also contain information that is used between programs. In addition to specifying appearance, a document's content can include identification and structural information that lets it be searched, edited, or extracted for reuse elsewhere. The PDF structure is exceptionally geared for representing a document as it moves through successive stages of a prepress production workflow.

Users of Adobe PDF files find that they can reduce prepress production issues as well as streamline the production workflow, then easily transfer their files for display on their Web sites. In summary, the most common benefits of using Adobe PDF in your production cycle are:

✦ PDF files provide consistency because documents appear as they were originally created, both online and on paper.

✦ PDF provides security for transmitting digital files, resolves missing fonts, and prevents distorted graphics issues.

✦ PDF ensures that files are replicated in exactly the same way when displayed or printed on different platforms, regardless of the authoring application or output device. At the same time that the appearance is identical, the underlying structural code is included with the file to provide the ability to deal with the document in any number of ways.

✦ For designers, using PDFs offers greater ease in collaboration, proofing, archiving, and digital use. You can use PDF files for high-resolution production requiring separations and composite color files. Documents intended for digital consumption can be fully indexed, searchable, and contain video, audio, and hyperlinks to other PDF documents and Web sites. Interactive PDFs can incorporate forms, buttons, and links to other documents.

Creating PDF Files in QuarkXPress

Now that we've talked about the ease of use and benefits of PDF, we want to examine the actual creation of files as PDF files using the new PDF Filter included in QuarkXPress 5. With Adobe Acrobat Distiller, which you must use to create PDF files, you can export an entire document, a range of pages, or an individual page of a document as a PDF file from QuarkXPress.

Cross-Reference

In addition to exporting PDF files from QuarkXPress, you can also import one PDF page at a time into a QuarkXPress picture box. It's becoming more common for ads to arrive to a publication in PDF form (rather than EPS form), and importing them into a QuarkXPress picture box is an easy way to work the PDFs into your workflow. For more information, see Chapter 20.

Checking system requirements

To produce PDF files from QuarkXPress 5, you need:

✦ Adobe Acrobat Distiller 3.0 or greater, which you can purchase from
www.adobe.com. At the time of this printing, version 5.0 cost $249 from
Adobe.

✦ A PostScript printer driver, which you can download from www.adobe.com/
support/downloads/main.html. You must also select a PostScript printer
from the Mac Chooser or Windows Printers control panel while creating PDFs.

✦ The Acrobat Distiller PPD must be installed in the PPD folder in your
QuarkXPress folder (to confirm, choose Utilities ➪ PPD Manager). If you
can't locate it on your computer, copy it from your Acrobat CD.

✦ The PDF Filter included with QuarkXPress must be enabled through the
XTensions Manager dialog box (Utilities ➪ XTensions Manager).

If you're on a Mac, bump the memory allocation of QuarkXPress up by 2,000K
above the default setting. To do this, select the QuarkXPress program icon, then
press ⌘+I. Choose Memory from the Show menu, then use the Preferred Size field
to change the memory allocation.

Pointing QuarkXPress to Distiller

When you determine you have all the software in place to export PDF files, you
need to tell QuarkXPress where your copy of Distiller is and how you want to
use it. To do this, choose Edit ➪ Preferences ➪ Preferences, or Option+Shift+⌘+Y or
Ctrl+Alt+Shift+Y, and then click the PDF option in the Application list. In the Acrobat
Distiller area, click the Select button (Mac) or the Browse button (Windows) to
select your copy of Adobe Acrobat Distiller. Click OK to save your change.

The export-to-PDF feature works only for QuarkXPress documents, not for
QuarkXPress Web documents.

STEPS: Exporting QuarkXPress pages in PDF format

1. Choose File ➪ Export ➪ Document as PDF to open the Export as PDF dialog
box.

2. In the Name field, enter the name for your PDF file.

3. In the Pages field, enter the number of the page or the range of pages you want
to export. As with other Pages fields, you can enter section page numbers
(such as A.1) or absolute page numbers, which indicate a page's position in the
document (such as +1 for the first page, regardless of its section number). A
quick way to export all the pages in a document — even if you don't know the
page numbers — is to type All in the Pages field.

4. If your document is set up in facing-page spreads or spreads you've created, and you want the PDF to display the same way, check Spreads. In general, Spreads don't make sense on-screen because you can't usually see an entire spread at once.

5. If you want to change any of the standard settings for exporting documents (set through PDF Preferences), click the Options button. Use the PDF Export Options dialog box to change any settings — for example, if you decide not to embed fonts in this particular PDF file. When you're finished changing settings, click OK.

6. Click Save to create the PDF file.

Note   You don't have to use the PDF export option to create PDF files from QuarkXPress. You can still do it the old-fashioned way: Install Adobe Acrobat on your system and include the Adobe Distiller PPD file with your other PPD files, then choose Acrobat Distiller as your printer. But the PDF export built in to QuarkXPress 5 gives you more control over output settings.

Setting the PDF Filter options

The PDF Filter has a variety of options that you can set as Application Preferences, which means they apply to all new documents. You can then override the settings for individual documents in the PDF Export Options dialog box. The controls work the same, whether you access them through the Options button in the Export as PDF dialog box (File ➪ Export ➪ Document as PDF) or through the Options button in the PDF Preferences pane (Edit ➪ Preferences ➪ Preferences ➪ PDF pane). The PDF Export Options dialog box contains four panes, described in the following sections.

The Document Info pane

When Mac users choose Get Info or Windows users open the Properties dialog box for a PDF file, information about who created the document and why displays. You can specify this information in the Document Info pane of the PDF Export Options dialog box, shown in Figure 40-2. The options include Title, Subject, Author, and Keywords.

The Hyperlinks pane

If your QuarkXPress document contains hyperlinks, lists, and indexes, you can convert all these to hyperlinks on the pages in your PDF file. The hyperlinks on the PDF pages will jump you directly to other related text. In addition, you can convert QuarkXPress lists such as tables of contents to bookmarks, which display on the side of a PDF page for easy navigation. This means that any effort you put into creating hyperlinks, generating automatic lists, and indexing in QuarkXPress can result in interactivity in your PDF files. The Hyperlinks pane of the PDF Export Options dialog box, shown in Figure 40-3, controls how this conversion works.

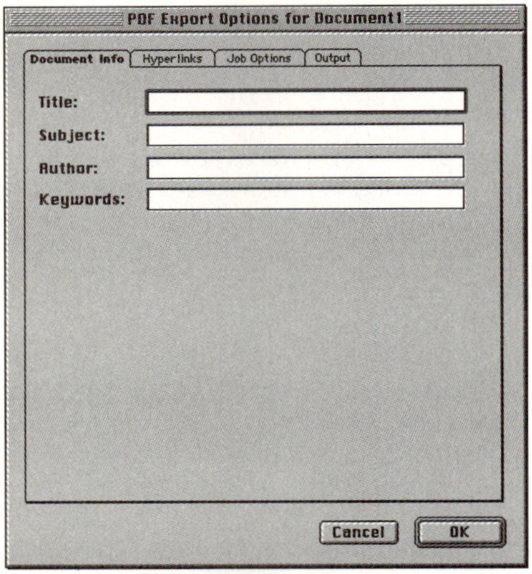

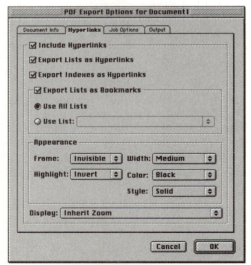

Figure 40-2: The Document Info pane of the PDF Export Options dialog box.

Figure 40-3: The Hyperlinks pane of the PDF Export Options dialog box.

✦ If you want hyperlinks in your PDF file, first check Include Hyperlinks. This not only enables the conversion of lists and indexes to hyperlinks, but it also converts hyperlinks created in QuarkXPress (Style ➪ Hyperlinks) to hyperlinks in the PDF.

✦ If you created lists with the Lists feature (Edit ⇨ Lists, View ⇨ Shows Lists), you can convert these to hyperlinks by checking Export Lists as Hyperlinks.

✦ To convert the lists to bookmarks, as shown in Figure 40-4, check Export Lists as Bookmarks. If you only want to convert one list, click Use List and select it from the menu.

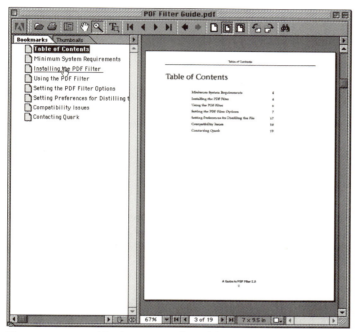

Figure 40-4: In this document, the table of contents list was converted to both bookmarks (shown at left) and to hyperlinks (shown on the main page).

✦ If your document contains an index produced with the Index XTension — and you want to create hyperlinks from the index entries to the text in the PDF — check Export Indexes as Hyperlinks. Note that the Index XTension must be running for this to work.

✦ To identify hyperlinks for users — so they know what they can click on — use the controls in the Frame area. You can choose the Width, Color, and Style of the frame surrounding a hyperlink.

✦ To change the look of a hyperlink while it's being clicked on, use the controls in the Highlight area. Choose None if you don't want the hyperlink to change, or choose Invert, Outline, or Inset.

✦ Use the Display menu to control how bookmarks display when a user is resizing and scaling a PDF document she's viewing. The Inherit Zoom option displays bookmarks at the same view scale as the PDF pages. The remaining three options scale the bookmark area along with the PDF pages: Fit Window scales bookmarks and pages at the same time; Fit Width retains the width of the bookmark area as the pages are scaled; and Fit Length retains the length of the bookmark area as the pages are scaled.

The Job Options pane

The Job Options pane, shown in Figure 40-5, lets you override Acrobat Distiller's settings for font embedding and image compression.

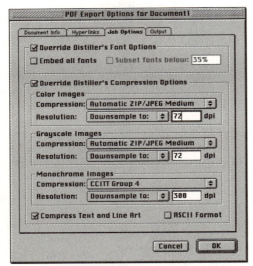

Figure 40-5: The Job Options pane of the PDF Export Options dialog box.

For control over font embedding, first check Override Distiller's Font Option. This enables the two options for embedding fonts:

✦ If you want to distribute the PDF file without sending the font files as well — which is generally the case for online distribution and prepress — check Embed All Fonts.

Caution The Embed All Fonts feature is supposed to embed all TrueType and Type 1 fonts, but in reality it generally doesn't embed TrueType fonts. Most experts recommend that you avoid using TrueType fonts in documents targeted for PDF output.

✦ To keep PDF file sizes smaller when you're embedding fonts, you can prevent Distiller from including each font's entire character set with the PDF file. To do this, check Subset Fonts Below. You can then specify a threshold of character usage below which a subset is created—for example, at the default setting of 35%, a subset is created if less than 35 percent of a font's characters are used in a document. If your workflow involves editing text with the PDF Touchup Text tool in Adobe Acrobat, you will probably not want to check this because, to edit text, Acrobat needs access to all the characters in a font.

On the Mac, when you override Acrobat Distiller's font options on a Mac OS, the result can be a large PostScript file. To alleviate this, you can adjust the image-compression options without altering the font options, because the two options are independent of each other.

To override the way images in the PDF file are compressed, check Override Distiller's Compression Options. This enables the remaining controls in the Job Options pane:

✦ The Compression menus in the Color Images and Grayscale Images areas let you specify how all color and all grayscale images are compressed in the PDF file. If you choose Automatic, Distiller chooses the best option for you. If the images have continuous, smooth tones, you'll get JPEG compression for 8-bit grayscale images and for 8-bit, 16-bit, and 24-bit color images. If the images have sharp color changes, you'll get Zip compression for 2-bit, 4-bit, and 8-bit grayscale images; 8-bit indexed color images; and 4-bit, 16-bit, and 24-bit color changes. If you choose a different option, you can choose the amount of compression (High, Medium High, Medium, Medium Low, or Low). See the sidebar "Understanding compression methods" for more information about compression types.

✦ The Resolution menus and fields in the Color Images and Grayscale Images areas let you resample images for the PDF. In each area, you can choose Average Downsampling To or Bicubic Downsampling To and enter a resolution in dots per inch. For prepress purposes, the resolution should be one and a half to two times the line screen ruling used to print the file. For on-screen purposes, keep in mind that higher resolutions are better when users need to increase the view scale in the PDF (for example, if they need to see detail in a map). In the Acrobat support section of www.adobe.com, you can find more details about specific image resolutions that work well with printer resolutions.

Choose Average Downsampling for faster conversion of documents to PDF. Choose Bicubic Downsampling for better image quality featuring the smoothest gradations in tone.

✦ For Monochrome Images, you can specify the Compression and Resolution as well. The Compression menu lets you choose CCITT Group 4, CCITT Group 3, Zip, or Run Length compression for all monochrome images (see the sidebar "Understanding compression methods"). The Resolution menu lets you resample the images (using Average Downsampling or Bicubic Downsampling) and enter a new dots per inch (dpi). The dpi you enter for monochrome images should be the same as the resolution of the output device. Note that Average Downsampling may cause display problems with monochrome images.

✦ Check Compress Text and Line Art to use Zip compression for all text and line art (such as Bézier items) in the document. This retains all the detail in the PDF file.

✦ To export the PDF file as ASCII instead of binary format, check the ASCII Format option. The advantage to ASCII is that you can open and edit the PDF file in a text editor. However, ASCII files are larger, so only check this if you — or your service bureau — really need to do this.

Preparing Files for Prepress Using PDF

After you have your QuarkXPress document ready for printing, you can create a PDF to move it to production where the production editors can conduct their prepress tasks before sending the file to plates, film, or digital output. A PDF file provides the flexibility to make minor edits to text, specify colors and separations, and provide final graphics without having to return your work to the native application file. A single PDF file can be used for any type of print output. PDF files eliminate the need for multiple versions of a file for different uses. For example, a single PDF file can be used for output on a color laser printer, an offset press, a CD-ROM, and a Web site.

PDF files can handle spot colors, composite color, color separations, bleeds, trapping, and Device N (a color specification, such as the use of two spot colors in a blend). Unlike PostScript files, which must be processed in their entirety, PDF files are page-independent. This means any page or range of pages can be independently processed or replaced. The benefit is you can consolidate multiple PDFs into a single file, making it easier to replace final corrected pages.

Understanding compression methods

The act of choosing a compression method for the color, grayscale, and monochrome images in a PDF is simple — you just pick something from a menu in the Job Options dialog box. The challenge is in knowing what to pick. Take a look at the type of images the compression methods work best for, then choose the one that represents the bulk of the images in your document.

✦ Zip compression is appropriate for black-and-white or color images with repeating patterns (usually screenshots or simple images created in paint programs).

✦ JPEG compression works well for continuous-tone photographs in grayscale or color. JPEG results in smaller files than Zip compression because it throws out some image data, possibly reducing image accuracy.

✦ Use CCITT compression for black-and-white images or 1-bit images. Group 4 works well for most monochrome images, while Group 3 is a good for PDFs that will be faxed electronically.

✦ Run Length yields the best results for images of large areas of solid black or white.

Tip

Print providers generally preflight files upon receipt to find problems inside the file. To prevent any problems, there are a number of third-party XTensions for pre-flighting both native-application and PostScript files to ensure that they contain all the necessary fonts and that all the appropriate graphics are included. Verify that all your elements are present and properly created in your document; this is essential for creating valid PDF files.

Practically all the changes that print production staff encounters can be made using Acrobat, but more important, all changes can be made to the single PDF file instead of using other native applications to make the changes and then reimport the file for printing. This reduces prepress time and reduces the chance of errors.

Specifying Output options for PDF

If you're creating a PDF for prepress rather than online use, you need to pay attention to the settings in the Output pane of the PDF Export Options dialog box (see Figure 40-6). You can do this while exporting a file by clicking the Options button in the Export as PDF dialog box (File ➪ Export ➪ Document as PDF) or through the preferences by clicking the Options button in the PDF pane in the Preferences dialog box (Edit ➪ Preferences ➪ Preferences). The options for selecting a printer description file, setting separation options, using OPI, and specifying registration and bleeds work the same as the controls in the QuarkXPress Print dialog box.

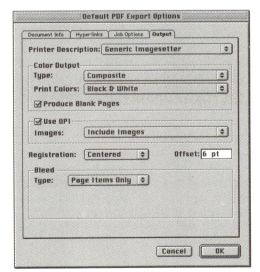

Figure 40-6: The Output pane of the PDF Export Options dialog box.

Cross-Reference

Options in the Output tab correspond to options in the Print dialog box, explained in Chapter 35.

Using PDF for prepress

Although Adobe has been predicting—or promoting—PDF for prepress workflow for several years now, many publishers still send QuarkXPress files along with fonts and graphic files to the printer. But the ultimate goal is to segue to an all-PDF workflow, in which the designer creates a single PDF file and sends it to a service bureau or printer. The workflow would be something like this:

✦ A graphic designer creates a document in QuarkXPress, includes the for-placement-only (FPO) images received from a Web site, and then exports the entire document to a PDF file. Any printing control features specified in QuarkXPress are already embedded in the document.

✦ OPI comments specified in the PostScript file are included in the PDF file so high-resolution images can be added back into the work before going to press.

✦ The PDF file is then transmitted to the print center, reducing the time and effort it takes to transfer the document.

✦ When the PDF file is received at the production shop, preflight tasks are reduced because all the components are in one neat package and viewable on-screen.

✦ Last-minute text edits can be made in PDF files.

✦ The PDF document maintains the print controls originally specified in the authoring application. It is routed through a prepress workflow, high-resolution images that remained at the print shop are replaced in the file, and then it is output to final print.

Slowly but surely, this transition is happening, now that the PDF format has been revised a few times to handle color better and to include the key prepress trapping and output functions. As expensive imagesetters are eventually replaced, new ones are bought that include native PDF support. Ditto for proofing printers. So more service bureaus and commercial printers accept PDF files for output than ever before. They're still a minority—but a growing one.

Summary

With Adobe PostScript language as the standard printing technology for producing high-quality print, it's little wonder that PDF, which is based on PostScript, has had such widespread acceptance as quickly as it has. PDF's device-independent page-description language ensures your documents will always print with the highest quality achievable by almost any output device.

No matter where or how your document will be used, the characteristics of PDF are the basic tenets for print service providers for creating an efficient workflow for high-quality output. Using QuarkXPress to create a document and PDF to usher it through to production is an efficient marriage of creation and production. And now with the new QuarkXPress PDF filter, it's easier than ever to take full advantage of PDF from within your QuarkXPress documents.

✦   ✦   ✦

Going Beyond the Program

One of the biggest pluses that QuarkXPress has had is its use of plug-ins, called XTensions, to add new capabilities to the program. Not only do other companies offer their own XTensions to give QuarkXPress whole new capabilities, but Quark itself has used and continues to use XTensions as a way of adding functions to the program.

The beauty of XTensions is that they intertwine themselves with QuarkXPress's regular features, so the menus and dialog boxes get placed where it makes sense to put them — they're not placed in a plug-in ghetto. QuarkXPress even has a tool to manage them.

XTensions aren't the only way to make QuarkXPress do more. On the Macintosh, you can ***script*** QuarkXPress — create little programs that use QuarkXPress's tools — to automate your work.

This part shows you how to use XTensions and scripts to make your life easier. And it gives you a description of many XTensions that you may want to use yourself.

Using XTensions

If you use QuarkXPress long enough, you'll eventually encounter tasks it simply doesn't offer. Perhaps you'll need to output a printer's spreads or flats, import native Photoshop files, or create a custom palette that contains your favorite commands. You won't find these capabilities in QuarkXPress, but don't get discouraged. *XTensions* (add-on modules) begin where QuarkXPress ends — with literally hundreds of commercial XTensions available and a steady stream of new ones each time a new version of QuarkXPress is released. You'll also find many free XTensions online — some from Quark, others from third-party developers and individuals.

This chapter shows you how to install, set the preferences for, and control QuarkXPress XTensions with the XTensions Manager. There's also a sidebar on XTension information you can find on the Web. Free and demonstration versions of XTensions are included on the CD that comes with this book.

Getting Started

You may not be aware of it, but chances are good you've been running — if not using — several XTensions every time you've used QuarkXPress. If you personally installed your QuarkXPress 5 program, and you performed a Custom Install, you may have noticed that you had the option to install or not install QuarkXPress XTensions. (Actually, this setting simply determines which ones run by default — all the XTensions provided with QuarkXPress will be installed on your computer.)

Installing XTensions with QuarkXPress

Figure 41-1 shows the Custom Install option in the installation dialog box that allows you to install the XTensions that ship with QuarkXPress. If you checked this option, and you checked all the XTensions listed under it, 25 or so XTension files were placed in a folder called XTension inside your QuarkXPress program folder. These XTensions range from features that you may never use (such as Jabberwocky, for

XTensions for QuarkXPress: A brief history

In its early years, QuarkXPress gained a foothold in the publishing industry because it had an impressive feature set and a slick interface. The more people used it, the more they liked it. And as quickly as Quark could add new features, requests for even more features poured in. It soon became apparent to Quark that if all requests for new features were implemented, the program would become prohibitively large. Trying to be everything for everybody would ultimately backfire. On the other hand, if specialized features for vertical publishing markets were not available to QuarkXPress users, the program's usefulness would be severely limited. What to do?

Quark founder Tim Gill came up with a clever plan. He decided to build the QuarkXPress application with an open program architecture that let software developers add specialized features to off-the-shelf QuarkXPress via add-on software modules. Nowadays, nearly every program includes plug-in capabilities, but add-on software was a new, untested concept when Quark began its XTension-development program. In keeping with the X factor, these plug-in software components were called XTensions. By letting software developers create specialty XTensions, Quark could continue to focus on developing broad-based features for the core program. With XTensions, QuarkXPress could be everything for everybody without being a humongous piece of software with a voracious appetite for RAM.

As QuarkXPress sales grew around the world, the demand for XTensions also grew. And as more XTensions became available, QuarkXPress became a viable solution for a growing number of publishers, particularly at high-end publishing sites, where previously — without XTensions — QuarkXPress had made only small inroads. It's not stretching things to say that the worldwide success of QuarkXPress is due in large part to XTensions.

importing dummy text) to filters that allow you to import WordPerfect and Microsoft Word files to significant features (such as indexing and HTML export).

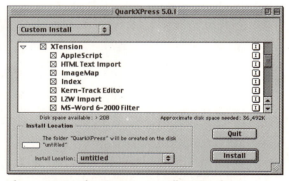

Figure 41-1: The Custom Install option lets you choose which XTensions to install with QuarkXPress. We recommend that you install them all.

Figure 41-2 shows what the XTension folder looks like after installation if you choose to install XTensions. In addition to the XTension folder, another folder called XTension Disabled is created within the program folder during program installation. If XTensions are not installed during installation, they're placed in the XTension Disabled folder.

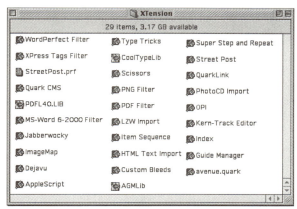

Figure 41-2: After installation, the XTension folder inside your QuarkXPress folder contains all the XTensions you choose to install.

In versions of QuarkXPress prior to version 4, you could store XTensions in either the XTension folder or within the QuarkXPress program folder. But with versions 4 and 5, only XTensions stored in the XTension folder are loaded when you launch the program.

Determining which XTensions are running

When QuarkXPress is running, displaying the QuarkXPress Environment dialog box shown in Figure 41-3 will give you a quick look at which XTensions are running. These are the XTensions that are currently operational and adding features to your copy of QuarkXPress. To open the Environment dialog box from QuarkXPress for Mac OS, hold down the Option key and choose About QuarkXPress from the Apple menu. On Windows, hold down the Alt key when choosing About QuarkXPress from the Help menu.

You can also choose XTensions Manager from the Utilities menu to see which XTensions are running. The XTensions with a check mark next to them in the Enable list are running.

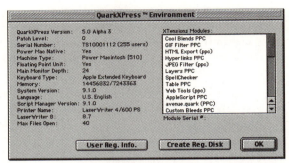

Figure 41-3: The QuarkXPress Environment dialog box displays information about your copy of QuarkXPress, your computer, and currently running XTensions.

Installing additional XTensions

If you download or purchase a new XTension, all you need to do is drag the file into the XTension folder inside your QuarkXPress folder. Some commercial products include installer programs that place the XTension in the XTension folder automatically. (These programs often install other files in your Mac's System folder or the Windows System folder that the XTension needs to do its thing.) Either way, if QuarkXPress is running, you'll need to restart it to load the XTension and make its features available. Figure 41-4 shows the palette the Index XTension adds to QuarkXPress when it's running. You can disable an XTension by moving it to the XTension Disabled folder or using the XTensions Manager (in the Utilities menu).

Figure 41-4: When the Index XTension, which is provided with QuarkXPress, is running, the Index palette lets you tag words and automatically generate a formatted index.

Note   XTensions developers often provide demo versions of their XTensions on CDs (handed out at trade shows or mailed to you) and on their Web sites. Sometimes, these are full-featured versions of the XTension with a time limit. Other times, they shift QuarkXPress itself into demo mode, which doesn't allow you to save or print clean copies. After evaluating such XTensions, disable them to revert QuarkXPress to standard operating mode.

Tip

QuarkXPress 5 cannot run XTensions written for any previous versions of QuarkXPress. The XTensions provided with QuarkXPress are already updated by Quark. For possible updates for any third-party XTensions you own, contact the developer.

Handling XTension-loading errors

If any XTensions are unable to load at startup, an alert lists those XTensions. Click the name of the XTension to display a possible reason, and click About for additional information about the XTension (such as the version and developer). The XTension Loading Error alert displays the following controls:

✦ **Ignore:** Click this if you want to launch QuarkXPress without launching the XTensions listed in the scroll list.

✦ **Manager:** Click this to display the XTension Manager dialog box, in which you can change the current startup set of XTensions or create a new set.

✦ **Don't show this dialog again:** Click this if you don't want to be alerted when QuarkXPress is unable to load an XTension.

Managing XTensions

To help you control which XTensions are running — without forcing you to move files in and out of folders on your desktop — QuarkXPress provides an XTensions Manager. Preferences control how the XTensions Manager works, giving you options such as the ability to review the XTensions that load each time you launch QuarkXPress.

Setting XTensions Manager preferences

The XTensions Manager preferences are Application preferences, which means they are program-level defaults. If you make any changes to XTensions Manager preferences (whether a document is open or not), the changes are implemented the next time you launch QuarkXPress.

To open XTensions Manager preferences, choose Edit ➪ Preferences ➪ Preferences (or press Option+Shift+⌘+Y or Alt+Shift+Ctrl+Y). Then click the XTensions Manager option under Application, as shown in Figure 41-5.

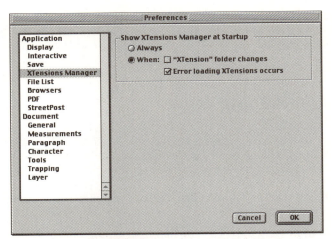

Figure 41-5: The XTensions Manager preferences let you open the XTensions Manager every time you start QuarkXPress; when you add files to or remove files from the XTension folder; or when an XTension-loading error occurs.

Set the XTensions Manager preferences as follows:

✦ **Click the Always option if you want the XTensions Manager dialog box to open each time you start QuarkXPress.** This setting is handy for service bureaus and other organizations that work with many client documents that have many different requirements. When the XTensions Manager opens, you can load a particular set of XTensions, create and modify XTension sets, and enable or disable individual XTensions for the current set.

✦ **Click the When option if you only want the XTensions Manager dialog box to open under certain circumstances dictated by the two check boxes.** Check "XTension" Folder Changes to open it when XTensions have been added to or removed from the XTension folder since the last time you used QuarkXPress. Check Error Loading XTensions Occurs to open it if QuarkXPress encounters a problem trying to load an XTension.

Tip   Any time you want to display the XTensions Manager dialog box at startup, regardless of your XTensions Manager preferences, press the space bar as QuarkXPress starts up.

Using the XTensions Manager

Whether you run only a few XTensions with QuarkXPress or you run lots of them, chances are you don't need all your XTensions every time you use QuarkXPress. In workgroup environments, not every user requires the same kinds of XTensions. Instead of loading unnecessary XTensions, you can use the XTensions Manager feature to create startup sets of XTensions. An individual QuarkXPress user can use the XTensions Manager to create separate startup sets for page design, editorial, and output work. A workgroup site can create startup sets for each class of QuarkXPress user. For example, a page-layout artist may use a set of design and typographic XTensions, while an editor uses a different set of editorial-specific XTensions.

Changing XTensions on the fly

Any time you want to change the XTensions that are running, choose XTensions Manager from the Utilities menu. To run an XTension, click in the Enable column to place a check mark next to it, as shown in Figure 41-6. To disable an XTension, click to remove its check mark. Click OK to close the XTensions Manager dialog box, then restart QuarkXPress to have the changes take effect.

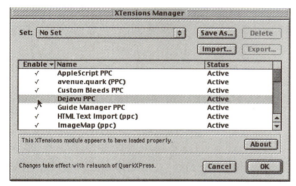

Figure 41-6: The Enable column in the XTensions Manager dialog box lets you control which XTensions load the next time you launch QuarkXPress.

Using XTensions sets

If you have certain projects or clients that require specific XTensions, you can create sets of XTensions for those jobs. You can then select the set you want from the Set menu in the XTensions Manager dialog box, click OK, then restart QuarkXPress to load only those XTensions. QuarkXPress provides the following default sets:

✦ **No Set:** Okay, it's not really a set, but it's an option in the Set menu. Choose this option to enable and disable XTensions on the fly, without using or changing sets.

✦ **All XTensions Enabled:** Choose this to move all XTensions in the XTension Disabled folder to the XTension folder; all XTensions in the scroll list are checked.

✦ **All XTensions Disabled:** Choose this for the opposite results: All XTensions in the XTension folder are moved to the XTension Disabled folder; all XTensions in the scroll list are unchecked.

STEPS: Creating an XTensions Set

1. Choose Utilities ➪ XTensions Manager.

2. Enable the XTensions you want in the set and disable all others.

3. Click Save As.

4. In the Save Set dialog box, name the set according to its contents, the client, or the projects it is intended for (see Figure 41-7).

Figure 41-7: Give your XTensions set a useful name.

5. Click Save to create the set. The set is automatically selected in the Set menu and will load when you restart QuarkXPress.

6. Click OK to close the XTensions Manager dialog box and save the set in your XPress Preferences file.

7. Restart QuarkXPress to load the new set.

Tip

The Import and Export buttons in the XTensions Manager dialog box allow you to share set definitions with other users who own the same XTensions. Exported sets consist of information about XTensions in the set — not copies of XTensions.

A few XTension-related caveats

The ability to set XTension-related preferences and to turn XTensions on and off via the XTensions Manager makes managing XTensions much easier than with previous versions of QuarkXPress, but the following list alerts you to other XTension-related pitfalls you should be aware of:

✦ Some XTensions, often referred to as *required XTensions,* must be present whenever a QuarkXPress user opens a document that was created when these XTensions were running.

✦ If you use a required XTension when you create a document, you must be careful to include the XTension if you send the document to a service provider for output.

✦ Some XTension developers offer freely distributable, viewer-only versions of their required XTensions. A viewer-only XTension lets you open documents created with the full working version of the XTension, but the functionality is disabled.

✦ You may encounter incompatibilities when running certain combinations of XTensions. Theoretically, if all XTensions were created correctly, any XTension would work flawlessly with any other XTension. But in the real world, problems can occur. If you experience odd or unpredictable results while working with QuarkXPress, you may want to start looking for XTension incompatibilities. Unfortunately, there are no tools that check for such problems. Your best bet is to disable suspect XTensions one by one until the problem goes away. It's also a good idea to keep your XTensions as up to date as possible. Many XTension developers offer free updates and fixes on their Web sites. You should check these sites periodically to see if updated versions of XTensions are available.

Acquiring XTensions

The best way to obtain information about XTensions, upgrade XTensions you own, and purchase new XTensions is to get on the Web. The Internet has an abundance of information about desktop publishing, QuarkXPress, and XTensions.

If you're the adventurous type, perform a search for "QuarkXPress" or "XTensions" at your favorite search engine; then start clicking. Or start by heading to www.quark.com. Quark moves things around often, but you can generally find an XTension section on their site that takes you to links for XTension developers and information about Quark's XTension-development program. In addition, Quark may post updates to its XTensions and free XTensions.

Commercial sites for XTensions

Over the last decade or so, many businesses emerged to distribute XTensions and plug-ins for publishing. However, many have combined and joined forces, leaving primarily a single powerhouse for selling XTensions to the U.S. market: The PowerXChange Online (www.thepowerco.com). This easy-to-search site, shown in Figure 41-8, sells stand-alone publishing applications, XTensions, and plug-ins. In addition, the company provides technical support and impartial advice. Although this is probably the biggest clearinghouse for XTensions at the time of this writing, explore the Web for other sites in the future.

For information about XTensions and QuarkXPress in general, a good site is the XPresso Bar (www.xpressobar.com). One of the best sites on the Web for information about QuarkXPress, the XPresso Bar's Make It Faster link and Telalink Archives take you to loads of XTensions information and downloads.

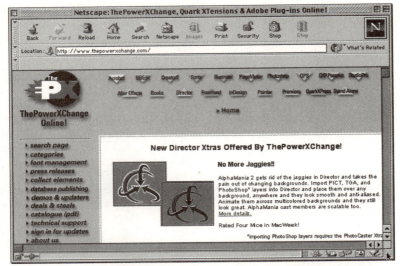

Figure 41-8: The PowerXChange Online serves as a clearinghouse for XTensions.

XTension developer sites

Many XTension developers maintain their own Web sites. Generally, you'll find company information, product information, demo versions of XTensions, and updates. Often, you can purchase XTensions right from the site. Some sites offer tech support; others have electronic versions of manuals.

The following longtime XTensions developers are a good place to start:

✦ A Lowly Apprentice Production (www.alap.com)

✦ Extensis (www.extensis.com)

✦ Gluon (www.gluon.com)

✦ Koyosha (www.koyosha.com)

✦ Markzware (www.markzware.com)

✦ Vision's Edge (www.visionsedge.com)

Tip

With every new version of QuarkXPress, new features make some of the old XTensions obsolete. For example, the tables featured in QuarkXPress 5 may decrease the need for an XTension to create tables. But don't get rid of your old XTensions before researching the new features and checking with the XTension developer for possible upgrades. Unlike Quark, XTensions developers have the luxury of concentrating on, studying, developing, and user-testing a single feature for years.

Summary

XTensions are add-on software modules that integrate features directly into QuarkXPress. Many of QuarkXPress's own features are implemented through XTensions. You can also purchase XTensions from third-party developers, most of which have a strong presence on the World Wide Web.

The XTensions Manager dialog box (Utilities ⇨ XTensions Manager) helps you control which XTensions are running in QuarkXPress. If you create a document with a certain XTension, sometimes that XTension is required to open and print the document in the future — something to consider if you're working in a collaborative environment or with a service bureau. Many demo XTensions are provided on the CD that comes with this book.

✦   ✦   ✦

Scripting QuarkXPress

Introduced in version 3.2 of QuarkXPress for Mac, scripting lets you automate many features in the program by taking advantage of a system-wide Mac capability called *Apple events*. You can take advantage of scripts provided with the program, write your own scripts, and use scripts that others have written specifically for your workflow. Because Mac OS 8.6 is the minimum operating system version required by QuarkXPress 5, you're guaranteed that your Mac system has all the components you need to run scripts and write your own.

Scripting is not available for QuarkXPress for Windows.

As you become comfortable with scriptwriting, you're also likely to discover that virtually everything you do with QuarkXPress is a repetitive task. The more you can free yourself of this kind of work by using AppleScripts, the more time you have to be creative. You can also communicate with and exchange data with other scriptable programs and XTensions. The possibilities are endless.

QuarkXPress 5 includes the Scripts XTension, which adds a Scripts menu to the right of the Utilities menu. When scripts are stored in the Scripts folder within your QuarkXPress program folder, they display in the Scripts menu and you can start them from there just like using any other feature. QuarkXPress 5 includes a variety of scripts you can use both as ready-made features and as a starting place for other scripts.

Using Scripts

Whether you decide to write your own Apple-events scripts or not, you can use the scripts provided with QuarkXPress. When the Scripts XTension included with QuarkXPress 5 is running (Utilities ➪ XTensions Manager), you'll see the Scripts menu shown in Figure 42-1.

Figure 42-1: The Scripts menu in QuarkXPress 5.

Checking system requirements

Unless you purposely altered your system, it's likely that your system is prepared to run scripts. All you need is to have the AppleScriptLib system extension running; if you aren't sure whether it's running, check the Extensions Manager control panel. In addition, the Scripting Additions folder and a Scripts folder should be in your Mac's System Folder.

Reviewing Quark's scripts

Although some of these scripts are useful, they bear only the most rudimentary of interfaces and provide little in the form of error messages and user feedback. It's doubtful they made it through much of a quality-assurance process, much less usability testing. A quick look at the odd capitalization patterns and abbreviations in the names of the scripts illustrates this point. Some of the scripts actually make up for features missing in previous version of QuarkXPress — such as the ability to specify text inset for all four sides of a box — that are now included in version 5. In fact, some of these scripts have been hanging around Quark as far back as version 3.3, which came out in the mid-1990s.

Nonetheless, as we said, some of the scripts are useful, and all can be opened in the Script Editor so you can modify them or copy code into other scripts. The Scripts menu is broken down into submenus, which reflect the contents of folders within the Scripts folder (in your QuarkXPress program folder). The scripts in each sub-menu are described in the following sections.

Box Tools submenu

The scripts in this submenu work on the selected box or group:

✦ **Add Crop Marks:** Places crop marks on all four corners of the selected box.

✦ **Center Box on Page:** Centers the selected box in the middle of the current page.

✦ **Drop Shadows:** Creates a drop shadow behind the selected box; you define the horizontal and vertical offsets.

✦ **Easy Banner:** Creates an odd-shaped polygon text box with a dark background; the text you enter is added in white for a reverse-type effect (see Figure 42-2).

✦ **Make Caption Box:** Places a small text box under the selected picture box; the text you specify is entered automatically.

✦ **Shrink or Grow at Center:** Proportionally enlarges or reduces the size of the current box from the center rather than from a resize handle; the box contents are not resized.

Figure 42-2: The banner created with the Easy Banner script included with QuarkXPress 5.

Grid submenu

The Grid submenu can create a grid of guides on the page or divide a box into many smaller boxes:

✦ **By Cell Size:** Draws vertical and horizontal guides on the page according to your specifications. This script, though, is no rival for the Guide Manager XTension included with QuarkXPress 5, which provides a much more intuitive interface.

✦ **By Dividing a Box:** Creates a series of boxes in a grid pattern that you specify; if you create text boxes, you have the option of linking them automatically.

Images submenu

The scripts in the Images submenu work on the contents of the active picture box:

✦ **Contents to PICT file:** Creates a PICT graphic from the selected image; you specify the name and location of the file.

✦ **Copy to Folder:** Locates the graphic file imported into a picture box and copies it to a folder you specify.

✦ **Fldr to Select Pboxes:** Lets you specify a folder containing picture files that need to be updated in the document; the pictures are then updated automatically.

✦ **Update & Retain Settings:** Reimports picture files while retaining settings in picture boxes such as placement and scale.

Picture Box submenu

The Picture Box scripts work on the selected picture box:

✦ **Crop Marks & Name:** Places crop marks around the selected picture box, and then places a text box under it. The name of the graphic file is centered in the text box, as shown in Figure 42-3.

✦ **Place Name:** Places a text box under the selected picture box, then centers the name of the graphic file in the text box.

✦ **Set All Bkgnd None:** Gives all the picture boxes in the document a background of None (transparent).

✦ **Set All Bkgnd:** Changes the backgrounds of all the picture boxes in the document to the same color and shade that you specify.

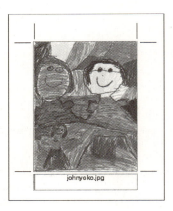

Figure 42-3: The Crop Marks & Name script adds crop marks to a selected picture box, then adds the name of the graphic file in the picture box.

Printing submenu

The scripts in the Printing submenu might be useful for service bureaus or others who incorporate OPI into their workflow. The scripts don't actually change anything in the document — they simply change the ability of the selected picture box to have its image replaced or not. They are:

✦ **OPI Don't Swap Image:** Prevents the image in the selected picture box from being swapped for OPI comments.

✦ **OPI Swap Image:** Lets the image in the selected picture box be replaced by OPI comments.

Saving submenu

The Saving submenu's scripts let you export pages in the document in EPS, PostScript, and PDF format (all of which you can do with other commands in QuarkXPress 5):

✦ **Each Page as EPS:** Lets you select a document and save each page as an EPS file in the location you specify. The current settings in the Save Page as EPS dialog box (File ➪ Save Page as EPS, or Option+Shift+⌘+S or Ctrl+Alt+Shift+S) are used, but you don't get to name each file.

✦ **Each Page as PS or PDF:** Exports each page of the current document as a PostScript file or a PDF file (which requires Adobe Acrobat Distiller to be installed on your Mac).

Special submenu

The Special submenu is useful for managing scripts and XTensions, plus it has one anomalously placed script in it, the Delete Unused script:

✦ **Delete Unused:** Lets you delete all unused style sheets, paragraph style sheets, character style sheets, colors, and/or H&J sets in the active document to streamline the file and make it easier for others to use (see Figure 42-4).

✦ **Move to Scripts folder:** Opens a dialog box that lets you find any AppleScript and move it to the Scripts folder inside your QuarkXPress folder. The script will show up in your Scripts menu the next time you launch QuarkXPress.

✦ **Open Apple Events Scripting PDF:** Opens Quark's Apple-events scripting documentation in Adobe Acrobat Reader.

✦ **Open QuarkXPress Folders:** Displays a list of folders within the QuarkXPress folder that you can open — including Scripts and XTension.

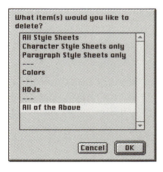

Figure 42-4: The Delete Unused script's dialog box.

Stories submenu

The scripts in the Stories menu are for working with text boxes:

✦ **Link All Text Boxes:** Links all the text boxes in the document from the first page to the last, and from left to right, top to bottom, on each page. This script doesn't work if boxes in the document are already linked.

✦ **Link Selected Text Boxes:** Links multiple-selected text boxes (Shift+click to select multiple items).

✦ **To or From XPress Tags:** Converts text in XPress Tags format in the selected text box into actual formatting. Also lets you convert formatted text back to XPress Tags so you can look at the codes.

Tables submenu

The lone script in the Tables submenu automatically adds color to alternating columns or rows in the selected table:

✦ **Row or Column Color:** Lets you select a color, shade, and which rows or columns to apply background color to.

Typography submenu

The Typography scripts automate common changes in the selected text box or document:

✦ **Baseline Grid +1 pt:** Increases the Increment setting for the baseline grid in the Paragraph pane of the Preferences dialog box (Edit ➪ Preferences ➪ Preferences, or Option+Shift+⌘+Y or Ctrl+Alt+Shift+Y). Paragraphs locked to the baseline grid adjust accordingly.

✦ **Baseline Grid –1 pt:** Decreases the Increment setting for the baseline grid; paragraphs locked to the baseline grid are adjusted accordingly.

✦ **Columns & Gutter Width:** Lets you divide a text box into columns and specify the amount of space between them in one step. This script is not much different from using the Text pane of the Modify dialog box (Item ➪ Modify, or ⌘+M or Ctrl+M).

✦ **Make Fractions • Document:** Converts all the fractions in a document to typesetter's fractions according to the current settings in the Fraction/Price dialog box (Edit ➪ Preferences ➪ Fraction/Price).

✦ **Make Fractions • Story:** Converts all the fractions in a story rather than the entire document.

✦ **Set Textbox Insets:** Lets you specify text inset for the top, bottom, left, and right edges of the selected text box — no matter what its shape. The text inset controls in the Text pane of the Modify dialog box are limited to rectangular text boxes.

Exploring AppleScript

AppleScript is a scripting language developed by Apple and initially released with System 7.0 that can be used to control Macs, networks, and scriptable applications, including QuarkXPress. The AppleScript language was designed to be as close to normal English as possible so that average Mac users — specifically, those who aren't familiar with programming languages — can understand and use it.

Learning the language

Many of the actions specified in AppleScripts read like sentences you might use in everyday conversation, such as:

```
set the color of the current box to "Black"
```

or

```
set the font to "Times"
```

If you're thinking about dabbling with AppleScript, the following words of both caution and encouragement are in order. First the encouragement: You don't necessarily need programming experience, scripting experience, or a pocket protector to begin creating AppleScript scripts. A bit of curiosity and a touch of patience will suffice. Now the caution: Scripting is essentially a euphemism for programming. As user-friendly as the AppleScript language is, writing scripts isn't a matter of choosing commands from menus, clicking and dragging, or entering values into fields; nor is it like writing a limerick. If you're starting from scratch, know in advance that you'll have to learn some new skills.

Although this chapter explains how to create AppleScript scripts, you can also create scripts for the Mac and QuarkXPress using other scripting languages, such as UserTalk and MacPerl. For beginning scripters, AppleScript is a bit easier to grasp than the others. However, UserTalk provides more verbs and is considered to be more powerful than AppleScript. Frontier, now a freeware program, has gained popularity as a tool for building and managing high-performance Web sites and can be used to create Mac scripts in any programming language.

AppleScript: Background and basics

In 1991, Apple introduced an inter-application communication (IAC) technology called Apple events. The next year, a company called UserLand Software began shipping a program called Frontier that let Mac users create Apple-events scripts using a scripting language called UserTalk, which controlled the Mac desktop, networks, and scriptable applications. Shortly thereafter, Apple released AppleScript, a commercial product that included a scripting language and an accompanying set of utilities for creating scripts. AppleScript has been included with the Mac OS software since version 7.5. Basically, here's how AppleScript works within QuarkXPress:

✦ **Using correct grammar:** All languages, including programming languages such as Pascal and C++, and scripting languages such as AppleScript, include grammatical components that are used in standardized sequences. In English, we combine nouns, verbs, adjectives, adverbs, and so on to create sentences. Everybody knows the meaning of "The weather is especially nice today," because it uses common words in a sequence that makes sense. The sentence "Nice is the especially today weather," has the right components, but it's arranged in the wrong sequence, so the meaning is lost.

✦ **Statements and syntax rules:** In AppleScript, verbs, nouns, adjectives, and prepositions are combined to create statements; statements are combined to form scripts. In AppleScript, verbs are also called *commands;* nouns are called *objects;* and adjectives are called *properties.* Syntax rules specify how statements and scripts must be constructed so that they can be understood by a computer.

✦ **The object hierarchy:** AppleScript also uses a structural element called an object hierarchy, or, to be precise, the Apple Events Object Hierarchy. It's a fancy term for a simple concept. The Apple Events Object Hierarchy works like a set of boxes within boxes. A large box contains a smaller box, which contains a smaller box, which contains a smaller box, and so on, until you reach the smallest box, which contains nothing and is the final level in the hierarchy of boxes.

✦ **The QuarkXPress hierarchy:** QuarkXPress contains its own hierarchy, which lends itself nicely to AppleScript. A document contains pages, pages contain boxes, and boxes contain text and pictures. You can create AppleScripts that perform actions at any of these levels. In other words, with scripts you can create documents, add pages, add items to pages, and modify the contents of boxes — right down to a particular character in a text box. You can think of this hierarchy in QuarkXPress as a chain of command. You can't talk directly to an item that's at the bottom of the chain. Rather, you must first address the top level, then the next, and so on, until you've reached the item at the bottom of the chain. This is analogous to the way you use QuarkXPress: You create new documents, add pages, place boxes on the pages, and, finally, modify the contents of the boxes.

Learning to create scripts is like learning to swim: You can read books, documentation, and articles until your head spins, but eventually you have to get a little wet. The best way to learn about AppleScript is to write a script. So put on your swimsuit and dive in.

Getting more information on AppleScript

Before you venture too far into scripting, you should review the AppleScript-related information provided with the Mac OS and with QuarkXPress:

✦ **Mac scripting documentation:** On your hard drive, you should have a folder called Apple Extras, and inside this folder you'll find a folder called AppleScript. This is where the Script Editor program resides, along with an introductory SimpleText file called About AppleScript and the AppleScript Guide help file. To view the help file, launch the Script Editor and choose AppleScript Help from the Help menu. The help file provides information on getting started and writing scripts.

✦ **QuarkXPress scripting documentation:** Inside your QuarkXPress 5 folder you'll find a folder called Documents, which contains a folder called Apple Events Scripting. Here, you'll find the complete scripting documentation, called Apple Events Scripting.pdf along with a sample script that is used in the documentation. This document, although a bit on the technical side, is a valuable resource. It includes an overview of Apple events scripting and the object model, as well as a list of QuarkXPress-specific scripting terms and scripting examples written with both AppleScript and UserTalk.

If you want still more information about AppleScript, several books are available, including *AppleScript in a Nutshell: A Desktop Quick Reference,* by Bruce W. Perry; *Danny Goodman's AppleScript Handbook,* 2nd Edition; and *AppleScript For Dummies,* by Tom Trinko (published by Hungry Minds). Plus, in the Tech•Notes section of Quark's Web site, www.quark.com, you'll find an entire list of publications that cover scripting.

Creating and Running Scripts

At this point, we're assuming that the Apple-events system extensions have been correctly installed and are running. If this is the case, you're ready to begin. For our first trick, we're going to make QuarkXPress roll over — sort of. Actually, we're going to rotate a box. First, we'll prepare QuarkXPress for its role. Launch the program, then create a new document (do not check Automatic Text Box). In the middle of the first page, draw a rectangular box — text or picture. Make sure that it remains active after you create it.

Launching the Script Editor

The Script Editor, provided with the Mac OS, lets you write scripts. You'll find the Script Editor inside the AppleScript folder inside your Apple Extras folder (at the root level of your hard drive), as shown in Figure 42-5. An uncompiled script is essentially a text file, so you can actually write scripts with any word processor. The Script Editor, however, was created for writing AppleScripts and includes several handy features for scriptwriters.

Figure 42-5: The Script Editor icon on your hard drive.

Double-click the Script Editor icon, and you're ready to create your first script. *Be forewarned:* There's something almost narcotic about creating scripts, and it's not uncommon for novice scriptwriters to get hooked. Don't be surprised if what starts out to be a 15-minute look-see turns into a multi-hour, late-night programming episode.

The scripting process

When the Script Editor is running, you'll see the program's menu bar and an empty window. You can enter a description for a script in the scroll field at the top of the window; the scroll list at the bottom of the window is where you enter the statements that make up your script.

Writing simple scripts

Enter the lines that follow this paragraph exactly as they're written, as shown in Figure 42-6. Enter a return character at the end of each line. Make sure to enter the name of your QuarkXPress program exactly as it appears on the desktop. Because you're free to rename your program, the name may not match the name in the first line of the script. Note also the use of straight quotation marks instead of curly typesetter's quotes (the Script Editor does this for you). Be very careful when you enter the text: Typos are script killers.

On the CD-ROM Rather than enter the text for this script, you can simply open the compiled version of the script from the CD that comes with this book. Look for the script called "Simple Script" in the Scripting Tools folder.

```
tell application "QuarkXPress"
activate
tell document 1
set the rotation of the current box to 45
end tell
end tell
```

Figure 42-6: The Script Editor window containing sample script text.

Perhaps you noticed the chain of command used in the script. First, the script addresses QuarkXPress, then the active document, and finally the active box. If you understand this concept, you'll be scripting like a pro in no time. If you're in an adventurous mood, try substituting the statement that begins "set the rotation of the current box to 45" in the preceding script with each of the following statements:

```
set the color of the current box to "Blue"
set the shade of the current box to 50
set the width of the frame of the current box to 10
set the box shape of the current box to ovular
```

All the preceding statements change one of the active box's properties. You know all about a box's properties. They're all the things you can change when you use the panes in the Modify dialog box (Item ⇨ Modify, or ⌘+M or Ctrl+M). If you want to get really fancy, combine all the Set statements into a single script, so you can use the script to make all the changes at once.

Checking for syntax errors

The next step is to determine if the statements are correctly constructed. Click the Check Syntax button. If the Script Editor encounters a syntax error, it alerts you and highlights the cause of the error. If the script's syntax is correct, all statements except the first and last are indented, and a number of words are displayed in bold, as illustrated in Figure 42-7. Your script has been compiled and is ready to test.

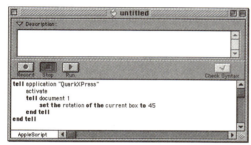

Figure 42-7: When you check the syntax of a script, the Script Editor applies formatting and indents.

Running your script

Click the Run button and then sit back and watch. (While a script runs, you're free to use your hands for other work!) If you've done everything correctly, you'll see QuarkXPress become the active program, and then the actions you put in your script will take place. Voilà — and congratulations! You can now call yourself a scripter without blushing. That's all there is to creating and running a script.

If you have trouble getting a script to run, double-check the name that QuarkXPress uses for itself. It might use QuarkXPress® 5 or simply QuarkXPress® (yes, the name may include the registered trademark symbol). If you run a script from AppleScript (rather than just double-clicking it) and AppleScript can't find QuarkXPress, it will give you a dialog box with which you find the QuarkXPress program. When you've found and selected the QuarkXPress program file, AppleScript will find out what QuarkXPress's file name is and use that in your script.

Saving your script

When you're finished writing and testing a script, choose Save from the Script Editor's File menu. Name your script, choose its storage location, and choose Compiled Script from the Format pop-up menu. Figure 42-8 shows the dialog box that's displayed when you save a script — in this case, we're saving the script in the Scripts folder inside the QuarkXPress folder, so it will show up in the Scripts menu (after you restart QuarkXPress).

Figure 42-8: If you save your Apple-events scripts in the Scripts folder inside your QuarkXPress folder, they display in the Scripts menu.

If you want to edit your script later, you must open it by dragging and dropping it on the Script Editor application. This is because you saved the script in Application format. If you simply double-click the script, the script will run and try to make changes to the active box in QuarkXPress.

Writing more complex scripts

Let's take a look at the following, more complex, script. Created by Kelly Kordes Anton for this book, it replaces trademark (^{TM}) and registered trademark (®) symbols with your choice of superior or superscript versions.

On the CD-ROM

The compiled version of this script is on the CD included with this book. Look for the script called "Format Legal Symbols" in the Scripting Tools folder.

```
tell application "QuarkXPress"
    activate
    if exists (document 1) then
        tell document 1
            set x to display dialog "Select a Type Style for (r) ¬
                and (tm)." buttons {"Superior", "Superscript", ¬
                    "Cancel"} default button 1
            if button returned of x = "Superior" then
                set style of every character of every story ¬
                    where (it is "(tm)") or (it is "(r)") to ¬
                    {on styles:{superior}, off
styles:{superscript}}
            else if button returned of x = "Superscript" then
```

```
                              set style of every character of every story ¬
                                  where (it is "(tm)") or (it is "(r)") to ¬
                                  {on styles:{superscript}, off
styles:{superior}}
                         else
                                  - - no characters present in document
                         end if
             end tell
             display dialog "This script was completed ¬
                      successfully."
       else
             display dialog "You must have a document open to ¬
                      run this script."
       end if
end tell
```

In English, here's what the script says:

✦ Send a command to QuarkXPress.

✦ See if a document is open.

✦ If it is, then send a command to that document to display a dialog box with three buttons — Superior, Superscript, and Cancel — and make the first button (Superior) the default button.

✦ If the user clicks Superior, set the style for every occurrence of the ™ and ® symbols to superior.

✦ If the user clicks Superscript, set the ™ and ® symbols to superscript.

✦ If the user clicks Cancel, do nothing. (The text beginning with two hyphens is a comment, not an instruction.)

✦ After the ™ and ® symbols are modified, put up a dialog box saying the task is completed.

✦ If no document is open, put up a dialog box saying that no document is open.

✦ Tell QuarkXPress that the script is complete.

Play with this script to see if you can add a third button to raise the baseline or boldface the trademark symbols. Then try adding some new features. Here's one possible addition: replacing all double hyphens with an em dash (something QuarkXPress doesn't do as you type). Pretty soon, by extending this script's structure, you could have a pretty complex script that looks for certain attributes and modifies them accordingly.

Looking at scripting conventions

The following are the kinds of things you'll encounter (and want to use) when writing your own useful scripts:

✦ Note the use of the ¬ symbol (Option+Return in Script Editor): It's used when you want to break a statement onto several lines (usually for readability). You can see it in use for the "set style" statement in our complex script example. The scriptwriter could have put the entire "set style" statement on one line, but by breaking the statement into three distinct pieces, you can more easily follow the logic: Set the style of what, then under what conditions, and finally to what new style. Later, if you wanted to alter the statement, you'd easily see what the three factors are in this statement and could quickly change just the factor(s) you wanted to.

✦ Also in this script, notice the use of conditionals — if, else, end if — that let the script make choices based on what it finds.

✦ Note the use of two consecutive hyphens (- -) to indicate a comment (any text following the two hyphens is ignored by AppleScript). You should use comments freely to document what the code does so you or someone else later understands more easily what the script does if it needs to be updated or fixed.

✦ Finally, note the ability to create a simple dialog box with buttons: In our more complex sample script, the user can choose whether to set the trademark symbols to superior or superscript by clicking a button.

Connecting with Other Programs

When you get the hang of it, you can create scripts that make QuarkXPress do anything you want. But automating QuarkXPress is only the beginning of what you can do with scripts. Many other applications are scriptable, and those that are scriptable can talk to one another and exchange data via scripts. For example, a catalog publisher might use a script to automatically import text from a FileMaker Pro database into a QuarkXPress document containing a real estate catalog. Or, a service bureau might write a script to automatically add customer fonts to Font Reserve, and then launch the customer's QuarkXPress document.

Today, almost all Mac applications are scriptable to some extent. Some are even recordable — meaning that you can actually write simple scripts by recording the actions you perform inside a program. Unfortunately, QuarkXPress and most other graphics applications are not recordable. For a complete list of scriptable applications — including a rating of just how scriptable they are — see www.apple.com/applescript/enabled.00.html.

Locating More Scripting Tools

Several software utilities—some free, some commercially distributed—are also available for AppleScripters. Here's the scoop:

✦ **FaceSpan:** From Digital Technology International ($199, 801-853-5000), this utility is an interface development tool that lets you quickly create AppleScript-based applications that have the standard Mac look and feel.

✦ **Scripter2:** From Main Event Software ($189, 202-298-9595), this utility is another full-featured AppleScript development and debugging application.

A pair of XTensions—Script Manager and ScriptMaster—add scripting capabilities to QuarkXPress. Here's the skinny on these:

✦ **Script Manager:** From Vision's Edge (free, 800-983-6337), this XTension provides a palette that displays a list of the scripts you create for QuarkXPress. Clicking on a script's name launches the script. Script Manager also lets you run multiple scripts in sequence.

✦ **ScriptMaster:** From Jintek ($199, 858-836-4455), this XTension lets you create scripts for QuarkXPress by recording actions as you perform them. Some scriptable programs are also recordable, which means that they have the built-in ability to convert a sequence of actions into a script. Without ScriptMaster, QuarkXPress is not a recordable program. However, when ScriptMaster is running you can generate a script without having to do any writing.

Surfing for scripts on the Web

If you enjoy creating AppleScripts for QuarkXPress and want to expand your arsenal of scripting tools, several scripting-related XTensions are available. If you decide to venture beyond QuarkXPress and explore other areas, such as system-level scripting and interapplication scripting, you can find considerable information and tools on the Internet. For example, you can download the AppleScript Software Development Toolkit from the Apple Web site.

Now that virtually every piece of information ever recorded by humanity is readily available on the World Wide Web, it's probably not surprising that you can find gobs of information about scripting, AppleScript, and automating QuarkXPress with scripts. Here are some good places to start:

Continued

Continued

✦ **Quark** (www.quark.com): You have to dig around to find the scripting information, but once you do, it's worthwhile. As of now, you'll find it by clicking "Where can I find more AppleScript information resources" in the Tech•Info section, but because Quark's site continually evolves, don't be surprised if the information moves. When you do find it, you'll discover links to various helpful sites, a list of helpful books, information about AppleScript training from third parties, and more. Registered users can post questions on Quark's AppleScript Support forum or e-mail questions to scriptsupport@quark.com.

✦ **ScriptWeb** (www.scriptweb.com): This is a great place to find all kinds of information about Macintosh scripting. It has general scripting information, as well as specific information about AppleScript, UserLand Frontier, and other Mac scripting languages. The General Scripting Info page has links to pages with information about scripting utilities, articles, books, tech support, and "every known scripting link."

✦ **The AppleScript Sourcebook** (www.AppleScriptSourcebook.com): Much like ScriptWeb, this repository of information about AppleScript has enough information and links to keep scripters of any level occupied for hours. Tips and techniques, news and events, opinions and notes . . . you'll find it all, plus a load of links to other sites.

✦ **Main Event** (www.mainevent.com): This is another good starting point for those in search of AppleScript-specific information. In addition to information about its own commercial scripting utilities, the site has an informative About AppleScript page, links to Apple's AppleScript site, and a number of AppleScript-related mailing lists. Main Event also offers scripting classes that you may want to look into.

Summary

If your workflow goes beyond original designs for each client and reaches into repetitive production, scripting is for you. Apple-events scripts are ideal for automating repetitive tasks — from importing pictures to creating and formatting entire documents. You can even link QuarkXPress to other scriptable applications. A few things to remember about scripting:

✦ Your Mac comes with everything you need, including the Script Editor program.

✦ Although scripting is a form of programming, the AppleScript language is designed to be user-friendly and as close to English as possible.

✦ A great deal of information is available about scripting both from the Quark Web site and from other sites on the Web.

✦ ✦ ✦

Appendixes

Odds and ends. When you're working with a program as complex, capable, and extensible as QuarkXPress, you're going to have odds and ends. The five appendixes to this book collect such odds and ends. Some recap key material — such as Appendix C: "Most Useful Shortcuts," which brings together all the keyboard shortcuts mentioned throughout the book in one handy place. Others, like Appendix B: "Using XPress Tags" and Appendix D: "Cross-Platform Issues and Solutions," delve into supplemental details.

Make no mistake: These appendixes cover key issues about QuarkXPress. But the book is organized around publishing workflow and the discrete segments in that workflow. The topics in the appendixes either transcend that workflow breakdown or live outside it.

Installing or Upgrading QuarkXPress

APPENDIX

◆ ◆ ◆ ◆

In This Appendix

QuarkXPress 5
system requirements

Installing
QuarkXPress 5

Upgrading from
prior versions of
QuarkXPress

◆ ◆ ◆ ◆

Installing QuarkXPress 5 is surprisingly easy, and the new online registration process is a nice change from the old floppy-disk method employed by Quark. Before installing or upgrading, make sure your system meets the QuarkXPress 5 system requirements. Then use the steps in this appendix to make quick work of the installation process. If you're upgrading from an earlier version, you'll actually perform a new installation. But read the section on upgrading at the end of this appendix for information about making the transition to QuarkXPress 5.

QuarkXPress 5 System Requirements

There are Quark's official system requirements for QuarkXPress 5, and then there's reality. Quark's system requirements, listed here, ensure that you can actually install and start up the software, but that's it.

 Cross-Reference See Chapter 5 for our advice on the computer, operating system, and amount of RAM you need to run QuarkXPress.

Mac OS

+ ✦ PowerPC-based Mac OS–compatible computer

+ ✦ Mac OS 8.6, 9.0, 9.04, 9.1, or Classic mode of OS X

+ ✦ LaserWriter printer driver version 7.0 or higher

+ ✦ CD-ROM drive (or access to a CD-ROM over a network for installation)

✦ 14MB free RAM (with virtual memory turned off)

✦ 14MB available hard disk space for full installation

Windows

✦ 486 or faster processor

✦ Microsoft Windows 95, Windows 98, Windows Me, Windows NT 4.0, Windows 2000, or Windows XP

✦ CD-ROM drive (or access to a CD-ROM over a network for installation)

✦ 12MB total RAM

✦ 14MB available hard disk space for full installation

Installing QuarkXPress 5

Both the Mac OS and Windows installers for QuarkXPress 5 provide easy-to-follow on-screen instructions. Before beginning the installation process, make sure you have your Validation Code (serial number) provided by Quark.

Tip

Both installers provide a Custom Install option that lets you decide what to install with QuarkXPress. Even if you're not sure if you want all the QuarkXPress XTensions, the Color Management system, the Tech Support documents, and the other items, you may want to install them anyway. Installing more than you absolutely need is better than not having a feature or information available when you need it. (**Remember:** You can always disable XTensions and filters using the XTensions Manager, covered in Chapter 41.)

STEPS: Installing QuarkXPress for Mac OS

1. Quark always recommends that you disable all non-Apple system extensions and control panels before you begin installing QuarkXPress. Use the Extensions Manager control panel to do this, and then click Restart.

2. Insert the CD in the CD-ROM drive or access the CD over the network. If necessary, double-click the CD icon to open the CD.

3. Double-click the Installer program.

4. Click Continue to bypass the QuarkXPress 5 Installer dialog box.

5. Read the License Agreement, and click Accept to continue. If you want to file this information, click Print to create a hard copy or Save As to file it electronically.

6. Read the information about disabling system extensions and control panels in the Welcome dialog box. Because you've already done this, click Continue.

7. In the next dialog box, type your serial number in the Please Type in the Validation Code field. Click OK.

8. Type your name, address, phone number, e-mail address, and other information in the Enter Registration Information dialog box, shown in Figure A-1. Then click Next.

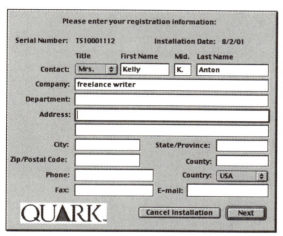

Figure A-1: Quark uses the registration information you provide to contact you about product updates.

9. The Important dialog box shows you how your registration information will look on a mailing label. Proof this, then click Previous to edit it or Next to continue.

10. The dialog box shown in Figure A-2 gives you the opportunity to decide where to install QuarkXPress and whether to perform a custom installation.

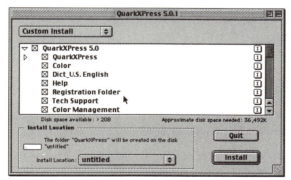

Figure A-2: When you're performing a Custom Install, uncheck the items you don't want to install.

- By default, the installer places QuarkXPress in a folder at the root level of your hard drive. If you want to change the location (for example, to your Applications folder), choose Select Folder from the Install Location menu. Select or create another folder, and click Select.

- If you're short on hard-drive space — or you're very confident that the installation includes items you don't need — choose Custom Install from the menu at the top of the dialog box. Click the arrow next to QuarkXPress 5 to see all the options. Uncheck any items that you don't want to install. If you need more information about an item to make this decision, click the I button next to the item.

11. When you've decided what to install and where to install it, click Install. The installation should only take a few minutes.

12. When the installation is complete, an alert asks if you want to register online. If you have an Internet connection and are ready to register, click Yes. This launches your default browser and takes you through the registration process.

13. After you register online, an alert prompts you to restart your computer.

STEPS: Installing QuarkXPress for Windows

1. Insert the CD in the CD-ROM drive or access the CD over the network. If necessary, double-click the CD icon to open the CD.

2. Double-click the Installer program.

3. Click Next to bypass the Quark Installation Wizard's welcome screen.

4. In the Software Verification screen, type your serial number in the Product Validation Code field. Click Next.

5. Read the License Agreement. Click the I Accept the Terms in the License Agreement option. Click Next.

6. Type your name, company name, and department name in the fields in the Customer Information screen. Click Next.

7. Type your name, address, phone number, e-mail address, and other information in the User Registration Information screen, shown in Figure A-3. Click Next.

8. In the Destination Folder screen, determine if you want to install QuarkXPress in the default directory, c:\Program Files. If you don't, click Change. Use the Change Current Destination Folder dialog box to select a new location, then click OK. Click Next when you've decided on a location.

9. The Setup Type screen allows you to decide between a Complete installation and a Custom installation. If you click Custom, the Custom Setup screen shown in Figure A-4 lets you decide what to install with QuarkXPress. If you don't want to install an item, click its plus sign to uncheck it. When you've decided what to install, click Next.

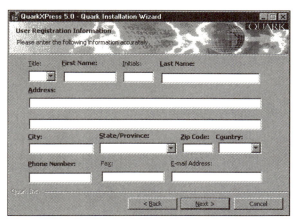

Figure A-3: Quark uses the registration information you provide to contact you about product updates.

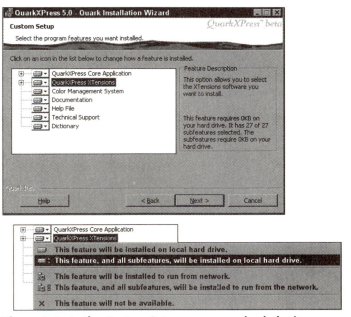

Figure A-4: In the Custom Setup screen, uncheck the items you don't want to install.

10. In the Ready to Install Program screen, check Run Online Registration After Installation if you have an Internet connection and will be ready to register as soon as you install. Then click Install.

11. When the Installation Wizard Complete screen displays, click Finish.

12. If you decided to register online, your default browser launches and takes you through the registration process.

Upgrading from Prior Versions of QuarkXPress

Actually, all installations of QuarkXPress 5 are new installations. The installer creates a new folder and places your new copy of QuarkXPress in it — regardless of whether you were using a 3.x or 4.x version of QuarkXPress. The only difference between purchasing a new product and upgrading is the price you pay for the software.

Installing new software has its good points and bad points. On the plus side, your existing, earlier-version copy of QuarkXPress is available for future use. You never know when you'll need it — for example, for that new client who has no intention of upgrading to QuarkXPress 5 yet — so it's worth keeping on your machine or at least storing on a CD or Zip disk. The drawback is, of course, that you need space in which to store this old software.

A bigger drawback to the fact that QuarkXPress 5 requires a new installation is that QuarkXPress 5 won't have any of the custom settings you've selected in your earlier version of QuarkXPress — you often don't realize how many preferences you've set over time until you switch to a new version of the software.

If you did put some effort into customizing QuarkXPress, when you start using QuarkXPress 5, do the following:

✦ See if any of the QuarkXPress 4 XTensions that you rely on will work with version 5 (if necessary, check with the developer). If you want to keep using the XTensions, copy them to the XTension folder inside your QuarkXPress 5 folder.

✦ Reset your Application Preferences, now found in the Application section of the Preferences dialog box (Edit ➪ Preferences ➪ Preferences, or Option+Shift+⌘+Y or Ctrl+Alt+Shift+Y). Also, with no documents open, reset any Default Document preferences in the same dialog box.

✦ With no documents open, create any colors, style sheets, H&J sets, and so on that you want to include in all new documents. Use the appropriate Edit menu commands — for example, to create default colors, choose Edit ➪ Colors. You can also use the Append dialog box (File ➪ Append) to bring in attributes from existing documents — a handy way of transferring lots of such preferences is to create a new document in your old copy of QuarkXPress (that document will automatically get any default colors, styles, and so on), then use File ➪ Append in the new version of QuarkXPress to bring in those settings.

✦ If you use the Normal paragraph and character style sheets, change them to suit your needs.

✦ Copy any spelling and hyphenation exception dictionaries from the old version of QuarkXPress into the new version's folders.

✦ If you modified the kerning/tracking tables for fonts, we're sorry to say that you'll have to do this again.

Although the customizing process can be tedious, it's definitely preferable to performing repetitive tasks such as creating the same style sheet for each document.

✦   ✦   ✦

Using XPress Tags

APPENDIX

B

◆ ◆ ◆ ◆

In This Appendix

The up side

The down side

Using XPress Tags codes

◆ ◆ ◆ ◆

QuarkXPress offers a file format of its own: XPress Tags. XPress Tags is actually ASCII (text-only) text that contains embedded codes telling QuarkXPress which formatting to apply. You embed these codes, which are similar to macros, either as you create files in your word processor or in text you save out of QuarkXPress.

The use of XPress Tags has an up side—primarily that it supports all QuarkXPress native formatting. And it has a down side—the codes are very complex.

The Up Side

XPress Tags come in very handy because this format is the one format sure to support all the formatting you do in QuarkXPress. Advantages include:

◆ XPress Tags can be useful in transferring text (and only text) files created in QuarkXPress to another QuarkXPress user (including someone using the Windows version) or to a word processor for further work. You can export a QuarkXPress story or piece of selected text in the XPress Tags format and then transfer the exported file to another QuarkXPress user or to a word processor for further editing.

◆ XPress Tags files are small, and therefore much more portable than entire QuarkXPress documents.

◆ Exporting an XPress Tags file into a word processor makes sense if you want to add or delete text without losing special formatting—such as fonts, kerning, or style tags—your word processor doesn't support. After you edit the text, you can save the altered file (making sure it's saved as ASCII text) and reimport it into your QuarkXPress layout.

✦ XPress Tags can also be good for complex search-and-replace operations that QuarkXPress doesn't support. For example, you cannot search and replace a tab setting or horizontal text scale setting in QuarkXPress; however, you can search the codes in an exported XPress Tags file from your word processor.

In an all-QuarkXPress workflow, in which the editors and graphic designers have access to QuarkXPress, the editors can submit completely formatted text files in XPress Tags format. The editors can flow text into columns of the appropriate size; apply paragraph and character style sheets; add nonbreaking spaces, nonbreaking em dashes, discretionary hyphens, and more as necessary. The editor can see how the text fits in the columns, then save out an XPress Tags file using the Save Text command (File ➪ Save Text, or Option+⌘+E or Ctrl+Alt+E), as shown in Figure B-1.

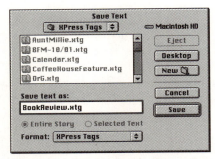

Figure B-1: Saving text in XPress Tags format.

Tip   Adobe InDesign can import XPress Tags files, so if you're working with someone who uses InDesign, you can maintain text formatting done in QuarkXPress. (Granted, you can even open QuarkXPress files themselves in InDesign, but results are mixed. Reflowing imported text may be a better idea.)

The Down Side

Most people do not use XPress Tags because most writers and editors don't have a copy of QuarkXPress, and entering manual codes in a word processor is nothing short of torturous, as you can see in Figure B-2. You cannot use XPress Tags with your word processor's formatting. If you create a file in Microsoft Word, for example, you cannot use XPress Tags to apply a style to a paragraph while using Word's own boldface and italics formatting for text. You either code everything with XPress Tags and save the document as an ASCII file, or you don't use XPress Tags at all.

```
<v3.00><e0>¶
@Normal=<Ps100t0h100z12k0b0cKf"Helvetica">¶
@Intro Dept
Italic=<Ps100t5h100z14k0b0cKf"Minion-Italic">¶
@Body Italic=<Ps100t0h100z10k0b0cKf"Minion-
Italic">¶
@Normal=[S"","Normal","Normal"]<*L*h"Standard"
*kn0*kt0*ra0*rb0*d0*p(0,0,0,0,0,0,g,"U.S.
English")>¶
@Headline Dept=[S"","Headline
Dept"]<*L*h"Standard"*kn0*kt0*ra0*rb0*d0*p(0,0,
0,21,0,0,g,"U.S.
English")Ps100t0h100z17k0b0cKf"HelveticaNeue
-Roman">¶
@Byline=[S"","Byline"]<*J*h"Standard"*kn0*kt0*ra
0*rb0*d0*p(0,0,0,15,0,5.976,g,"U.S.
English")Ps100t10h100z8k0b0cKf"Helvetica-
Light">¶
@Article Intro Dept=[S"","Article Intro
Dept"]<*J*h"Standard"*kn0*kt0*ra0*rb0*d0*p(0,0,
0,18,0,5.976,g,"U.S.
```

Figure B-2: XPress Tags codes that aren't translated into formatting.

This either-or situation is too bad, because the ability to combine a publishing program's formatting codes with a word processor's formatting features adds both power and flexibility — as users of Corel Ventura Publisher and Adobe PageMaker know.

Using XPress Tags Codes

The best way to use XPress Tags is to save formatted text out of QuarkXPress in XPress Tags format. Use the Save Text command (File ➪ Save Text, or Option+⌘+E or Ctrl+Alt+E), choose XPress Tags from the Format menu, and use the file extension .xtg. You then have three options:

✦ Import the formatted text into a QuarkXPress text box with Include Style Sheets checked in the Get Text dialog box (File ➪ Get Text, or ⌘+E or Ctrl+E), as shown in Figure B-3.

✦ Import the text file with untranslated codes into a QuarkXPress text box so you can modify the codes manually or use Find/Change (Edit ➪ Find/Change, or ⌘+F or Ctrl+F) to search and replace codes. In this case, you would uncheck Include Style Sheets to see the codes rather than the formatting. When you're finished modifying the codes, you can then save the text as ASCII and import it with Include Style Sheets checked to translate the codes into formatting.

✦ Open the text file in a word processor and edit the text or modify the codes manually or using search-and-replace. When you're finished, save the text as ASCII, and then import it into QuarkXPress with Include Style Sheets checked.

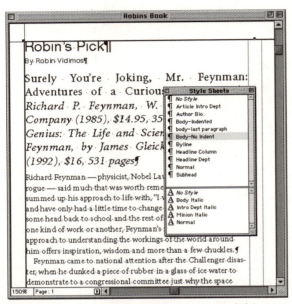

Figure B-3: An editor formatted and saved this article in XPress Tags format in QuarkXPress. The editor is working in a text box with the appropriate size columns and applying style sheets applied by the graphic designer. When the graphic designer imports the story into the actual newsletter template, the formatting is done and the designer only needs to touch it up.

The appendix in the QuarkXPress manual defines the dozens of XPress Tags codes and their variants you embed in your text file. These codes range from the simple, such as < I > for italicized text, to the moderately complex. The following code is for a 2-point, 100-percent red rule that uses line style 1, is indented 18 points to the right and left of the column, is offset 25 percent, and is placed above the current paragraph:

```
<*ra(02,1,"Red",100,18,18,25%>
```

Basically, you can use as many of the XPress Tags codes as needed, and place them between < and > characters. In the preceding example, we are using the *ra code (which stands for right-aligned) and filling in the parameters it expects.

Tip   If you wanted to make a global change to a color, you could search and replace. For example, in an XPress Tags file, you could search for *Red* and replace it with *Blue.*

Some codes are programming-level codes, for which you define the style tags by combining as many of the basic XPress Tags codes as appropriate. The following example defines a style called Lead as black, 9.5-point Cheltenham Book Plain with a four-line drop cap, 12 points of leading, a 10-point first-line indent, no left or right indents, no space above, 100-percent shade and scale, full justification, and locked to the baseline grid:

```
@Lead=[S"","Lead"]<*J*kn0*kt0*ra0*rb0*d(1,4)*p(10,0,0,12,0,0,G,
"U.S. English")Ps100t0h100z9.5k0b0cKf"Cheltenham Book">
```

The = after @Lead in the preceding example signals QuarkXPress to *define* the Lead style with the codes between the angle brackets. To use that style, you type @Lead: at the beginning of the paragraph you want to format; the colon tells QuarkXPress to *use* the style tag. (You can't apply a style tag that you did not define earlier in your text file.)

In practical terms, you may not mind editing XPress Tags slightly in a file exported from QuarkXPress or leaving them in a file when you alter its text. But you're not likely to forgo the friendly formatting available in your word processor and in QuarkXPress to apply XPress Tags coding to everything in your text files as you create them.

✦   ✦   ✦

Most-Useful Shortcuts

The most efficient QuarkXPress users rarely reach for the mouse, preferring to keep their hands firmly planted on the keyboard within easy access of keyboard shortcuts. For starters, you can always use your operating system's standard keyboard shortcuts such as ⌘+S or Ctrl+S for Save and ⌘+P or Ctrl+P for Print (and of course the ubiquitous commands for Cut, Copy, and Paste). Then start looking at the keyboard shortcuts shown next to the menu commands that you find yourself choosing over and over — once you find out that F7 will show and hide guides on-screen, you'll never again reach for the View menu.

Most keyboard shortcuts duplicate commands found in menus, dialog boxes, and palettes — but some offer exclusive access to special characters such as em dashes and nifty power-user capabilities such as the ability to import a grayscale graphic in black-and-white. Skim through the list in Table C-1 to see if you find anything new, something you've always wanted to be able to do. Before you know it, you'll have a host of keyboard shortcuts memorized, and you'll be flying through your text-formatting and document-creation processes.

Table C-1
QuarkXPress 5 Keyboard Shortcuts

Opening/Closing/Saving	Mac	Windows
New document	⌘+N	Ctrl+N
New library	Option+⌘+N	Ctrl+Alt+N
New XML file	Shift+⌘+X	Ctrl+Shift+X
New Web document	Option+Shift+⌘+N	Ctrl+Alt+Shift+N
Open file	⌘+O	Ctrl+O
Save file	⌘+S	Ctrl+S
Save as	Option+⌘+S	Ctrl+Shift+S
Revert to last Auto Save	Option+choose Revert to Saved	Alt+choose Revert to Saved
Get text or picture	⌘+E	Ctrl+E
Save text	Option+⌘+E	Ctrl+Alt+E
Save page as EPS	Option+Shift+⌘+S	Ctrl+Alt+Shift+S
Append	Option+⌘+A	Ctrl+Alt+A
Close current document	⌘+W	Ctrl+F4
Close all documents	Option+⌘+W	not available
Print	⌘+P	Ctrl+P
Quit	⌘+Q	Ctrl+Q or Alt+F4
Miscellaneous	**Mac**	**Windows**
Undo	⌘+Z	Ctrl+Z
Revert dialog box values	Shift+⌘+Z	Ctrl+Shift+Z
Keep Apply button selected	Option+click Apply button	Alt+click Apply button
Display next pane in dialog box	⌘+Tab	Ctrl+Tab
Display previous pane in dialog box	Shift+⌘+Tab	Ctrl+Shift+Tab
Display context menu	Control+click	Right-click
Help	Help	F1

Opening Preferences and Setup	Mac	Windows
Application preferences: Display pane	Option+Shift+⌘+Y	Ctrl+Alt+Shift+Y
Document preferences: General pane	⌘+Y	Ctrl+Y
Document preferences: Paragraph pane	Option+⌘+Y	Ctrl+Alt+Y
Document preferences: Trapping pane	Option+Shift+F12	Ctrl+Shift+F12
Document preferences: Tool pane	Double-click Zoom or any item-creation tool	Double-click Zoom or any item-creation tool
Document setup	Option+Shift+⌘+P	Ctrl+Alt+Shift+P
Page setup	Option+⌘+P	Ctrl+Alt+P

Changing Views	Mac	Windows
Use Zoom tool	Ctrl+Shift (or Ctrl)	Ctrl+spacebar
100%	⌘+1	Ctrl+1
Fit in window	⌘+0	Ctrl+0
Fit largest spread in window	Option+choose Fit in Window	Alt+choose Fit in Window
200%	Option+⌘+click	Ctrl+Alt+click
Thumbnails	Shift+F6	Shift+F6
Change view percentage	Control+V	Ctrl+Alt+V
Force redraw	Option+⌘+period	Shift+Esc
Halt redraw	⌘+period	Esc
Go to page	⌘+J	Ctrl+J
Zoom in	Control+Shift+click*	Ctrl+spacebar+click
Zoom out	Option+Control+Shift+click*	Ctrl+Alt+spacebar+click
Windows submenu (tile, stack)	Shift+click title bar	Alt+W

Working with Rulers and Guides	Mac	Windows
Show/hide rulers	⌘+R	Ctrl+R
Show/hide guides	F7	F7
Delete all horizontal guides	Option+click horizontal ruler	Alt+click horizontal ruler
Delete all vertical guides	Option+click vertical ruler	Alt+click vertical ruler

Continued

Table C-1 *(continued)*

Working with Rulers and Guides	Mac	Windows
Show/hide baseline grid	Option+F7	Ctrl+F7
Snap to guides	Shift+F7	Shift+F7

Using Palettes	Mac	Windows
Show/hide Tools palette	F8	F8
Select next tool	⌘+Tab	Ctrl+Alt+Tab
Select previous tool	Shift+⌘+Tab	Ctrl+Alt+Shift+Tab
Keep tool selected	Option+click tool	Alt+click tool
Show/hide Measurements palette	F9	F9
Show/hide Document Layout palette	F10	F4
Show/hide Style Sheets palette	F11	F11
Show/hide Colors palette	F12	F12
Open Colors dialog box	Shift+F12	Shift+F12
Show/hide Trap Information palette	Option+F12	Ctrl+F12
Show/hide Lists palette	Option+F11	Ctrl+F11
Open Index palette	Option+⌘+I	Ctrl+Alt+I
Show Font Usage	F13	*not available*
Show Picture Usage	Option+F13	*not available*

Navigating Documents	Mac	Windows
Page grabber hand	Option+drag	Alt+drag
Enable/disable live scroll	Option+drag scroll box	Alt+drag scroll box
Display master page	Shift+F10	Shift+F4
Display next master page	Option+F10	Ctrl+Shift+F4
Display previous master page	Option+Shift+F10	Ctrl+Shift+F3
Display document page	Shift+F10	Shift+F4
Next page	Shift+PageUp or Control+Shift+L	Shift+PageDown
Previous page	Shift+PageDown or Control+Shift+K	Shift+PageUp

Navigating Documents	*Mac*	*Windows*
First page	Shift+Home or Control+Shift+A	Ctrl+PageUp
Last page	Shift+End or Control+Shift+D	Ctrl+PageDown
Beginning of document	Home or Control+A	Ctrl+Home
End of document	End or Control+D	Ctrl+End
Selecting Items	*Mac*	*Windows*
Select all	⌘+A	Ctrl+A
Select hidden item	Option+Shift+⌘+click	Ctrl+Alt+Shift+click
Deselect all	Tab (when Item tool is selected)	Tab (when Item tool is selected)
Multiple selection (series)	Shift+click	Shift+click
Multiple selection (noncontiguous)	⌘+click	Ctrl+click
Moving Objects	*Mac*	*Windows*
Nudge selected object 1 point	arrow keys	arrow keys
Nudge selected object 1/10 point	Option+arrow keys	Alt+arrow keys
Constrain movement	Shift+drag	Shift+drag
Cut	⌘+X or F2	Ctrl+X
Delete	⌘+K	Ctrl+K
Copy	⌘+C or F3	Ctrl+C
Paste	⌘+V or F4	Ctrl+V
Modifying Items	*Mac*	*Windows*
Modify	⌘+M	Ctrl+M
Edit shape	Shift+F4	F10
Frame	⌘+B	Ctrl+B
Clipping	Option+⌘+T	Ctrl+Alt+T
Edit clipping path	Option+Shift+F4	Ctrl+Shift+F10
Runaround	⌘+T	Ctrl+T
Edit runaround	Option+F4	Ctrl+F10
Duplicate	⌘+D	Ctrl+D

Continued

Table C-1 *(continued)*

Modifying Items	Mac	Windows
Step and Repeat	Option+⌘+D	Ctrl+Alt+D
Space/align	⌘+comma	Ctrl+comma
Send to back	Shift+F5	Shift+F5
Bring to front	F5	F5
Send backward	Option+Shift+F5	Ctrl+Shift+F5
Bring forward	Option+F5	Ctrl+F5
Lock/unlock	F6	F6
Group	⌘+G	Ctrl+G
Ungroup	⌘+U	Ctrl+U

Selecting Text	Mac	Windows
Word	Double-click	Double-click
Paragraph	Quadruple-click	Quadruple-click
Line	Triple-click	Triple-click
Story	⌘+A or quintuple-click	Ctrl+A or quintuple-click
Character to left	Shift+Left Arrow	Shift+Left Arrow
Character to right	Shift+Right Arrow	Shift+Right Arrow
Word to left	Shift+⌘+Left Arrow	Ctrl+Shift+Left Arrow
Word to right	Shift+⌘+Right Arrow	Ctrl+Shift+Right Arrow
Up one line	Shift+Up Arrow	Shift+Up Arrow
Down one line	Shift+Down Arrow	Shift+Down Arrow
To start of line	Shift+Option+⌘+Left Arrow	Ctrl+Alt+Shift+Left Arrow or Shift+Home
To end of line	Shift+Option+⌘+Right Arrow	Ctrl+Alt+Shift+Right Arrow or Shift+End
Up one paragraph	Shift+⌘+Up Arrow	Ctrl+Shift+Up Arrow
Down one paragraph	Shift+⌘+Down Arrow	Ctrl+Shift+Down Arrow

Selecting Text	Mac	Windows
To top of story	Shift+Option+⌘+ Up Arrow	Ctrl+Alt+Shift+ Up Arrow or Ctrl+ Shift+Home
To bottom of story	Shift+Option+ ⌘+Down Arrow	Ctrl+Alt+Shift+Down Arrow or Ctrl+Shift+ End

Editing Text	Mac	Windows
Show/hide invisibles	⌘+I	Ctrl+I
Next line in Line Check	⌘+comma	Ctrl+comma
Check selection	⌘+L	Ctrl+W
Check story	Option+⌘+L	Ctrl+Alt+W
Check document	Option+Shift+⌘+L	Ctrl+Alt+Shift+W
Lookup spelling	⌘+L	Alt+L
Skip word	⌘+S	Alt+S
Add word to dictionary	⌘+A	Alt+A
Add all suspect words to dictionary	Option+Shift+click Done button	Alt+Shift+click Close button
Suggest hyphenation	⌘+H	Ctrl+H
Open Find/Change	⌘+F	Ctrl+F
Close Find/Change	Option+⌘+F	Ctrl+Alt+F
Change Find Next to Find First	Option+click Find Next	Alt+click Find Next

Special Characters (in Finds)	Mac	Windows
Carriage return	⌘+Return	Ctrl+Enter
Tab	type \t	type \t
Line break	Shift+⌘+Enter	Ctrl+Shift+Enter
Column	⌘+keypad Enter	type \c
Backslash (\)	⌘+\	Ctrl+\
Wildcard	⌘+?	Ctrl+?
Flex space	type \f	type \f
Punctuation space	⌘+period	Ctrl+period

Continued

Table C-1 *(continued)*		
Special Characters (in Finds)	*Mac*	*Windows*
Current box's page number	⌘+3	Ctrl+3
Previous box's page number	⌘+2	Ctrl+2
Next box's page number	⌘+4	Ctrl+4
Opening Text-Formatting Dialog Boxes	*Mac*	*Windows*
Edit style sheets	Shift+F11	Shift+F11
Edit H&Js	Option+Shift+F11 or Option+⌘+H	Ctrl+Shift+F11
Character attributes	Shift+⌘+D	Ctrl+Shift+D
Paragraph attributes	Shift+⌘+F	Ctrl+Shift+F
Change size	Shift+⌘+\	Ctrl+Shift+\
Change leading	Shift+⌘+E	Ctrl+Shift+E
Define tabs	Shift+⌘+T	Ctrl+Shift+T
Define rules	Shift+⌘+N	Ctrl+Shift+N
Text-Formatting Tricks	*Mac*	*Windows*
Copy format to select paragraphs	Option+Shift+click	Alt+Shift+click
Apply No Style, then style sheet	Option+click style sheet name	Alt+click style sheet name
Choose font in Measurements palette	Option+Shift+⌘+M	Ctrl+Alt+Shift+M
Apply previous font	Option+Shift+F9**	Ctrl+Shift+F9
Apply next font	Option+F9**	Ctrl+F9
Symbol font (next character)	Shift+⌘+Q	Ctrl+Shift+Q
Zapg Dingbats font (next character)	Shift+⌘+Z	Ctrl+Shift+Z
Changing Text Size and Scale	*Mac*	*Windows*
Increase to next size on type scale	Shift+⌘+>	Ctrl+Shift+>
Decrease to next size on type scale	Shift+⌘+<	Ctrl+Shift+<
Increase 1 point	Option+Shift+⌘+>	Ctrl+Alt+Shift+>
Decrease 1 point	Option+Shift+⌘+<	Ctrl+Alt+Shift+<

Changing Text Size and Scale	Mac	Windows
Increase scaling 5%	⌘+]	Ctrl+]
Decrease scaling 5%	⌘+[	Ctrl+[
Increase scaling 1%	Option+⌘+]	Ctrl+Alt+]
Decrease scaling 1%	Option+⌘+[	Ctrl+Alt+[
Resize interactively	⌘+drag text box handle	Ctrl+drag text box handle
Resize interactively constrained	Shift+⌘+drag text box handle	Ctrl+Shift+drag text box handle
Resize interactively proportional	Option+Shift+⌘+ drag text box handle	Ctrl+Alt+Shift+drag text box handle

Modifying Text Spacing	Mac	Windows
Increase kerning/tracking 1/20 em	Shift+⌘+]	Ctrl+Shift+]
Decrease kerning/tracking 1/20 em	Shift+⌘+[	Ctrl+Shift+[
Increase kerning/tracking 1/200 em	Option+Shift+⌘+]	Ctrl+Alt+Shift+]
Decrease kerning/tracking 1/200 em	Option+Shift+⌘+[	Ctrl+Alt+Shift+[
Raise baseline shift 1 point	Option+Shift+⌘+plus	Ctrl+Alt+Shift+)
Lower baseline shift 1 point	Option+Shift+⌘+hyphen	Ctrl+Alt+Shift+(
Increase leading 1 point	Shift+⌘+'	Ctrl+Shift+'
Decrease leading 1 point	Shift+⌘+semicolon	Ctrl+Shift+semicolon
Increase leading 1/10 point	Option+Shift+⌘+'	Ctrl+Alt+Shift+'
Decrease leading 1/10 point	Option+Shift+⌘+ semicolon	Ctrl+Alt+Shift+ semicolon

Applying Type Styles	Mac	Windows
Normal	Shift+⌘+P	Ctrl+Shift+P
Bold	Shift+⌘+B	Ctrl+Shift+B
Italic	Shift+⌘+I	Ctrl+Shift+I
Underline	Shift+⌘+U	Ctrl+Shift+U
Word underline	Shift+⌘+W	Ctrl+Shift+W
Strikethrough	Shift+⌘+/	Ctrl+Shift+/
All caps	Shift+⌘+K	Ctrl+Shift+K
Subscript	Shift+⌘+hyphen	Ctrl+Shift+9

Continued

Table C-1 *(continued)*		
Applying Type Styles	*Mac*	*Windows*
Superscript	Shift+⌘+=	Ctrl+Shift+0 (zero)
Superior	Shift+⌘+V	Ctrl+Shift+V
Outline	Shift+⌘+O	Ctrl+Shift+O
Shadow	Shift+⌘+S	Ctrl+Shift+S
Applying Paragraph Alignments	*Mac*	*Windows*
Left justify	Shift+⌘+L	Ctrl+Shift+L
Right justify	Shift+⌘+R	Ctrl+Shift+R
Center	Shift+⌘+C	Ctrl+Shift+C
Justify	Shift+⌘+J	Ctrl+Shift+J
Force justify	Option+Shift+⌘+J	Ctrl+Alt+Shift+J
Entering Dashes, Hyphens, and Spaces	*Mac*	*Windows*
Em dash	Option+Shift+hyphen	Ctrl+Shift+=
Nonbreaking em dash	Option+⌘+equal	Ctrl+Alt+Shift+=
En dash	Option+hyphen	Ctrl+Alt+Shift+ hyphen
Nonbreaking hyphen	⌘+=	Ctrl+=
Discretionary hyphen	⌘+hyphen	Ctrl+hyphen
Nonbreaking space	⌘+spacebar	Ctrl+5
En space	Option+spacebar	Ctrl+Shift+6
Nonbreaking en space	Option+⌘+spacebar	Ctrl+Alt+Shift+6
Punctuation space	Shift+spacebar	Shift+spacebar or Ctrl+6
Nonbreaking punctuation space	Shift+⌘+spacebar	Ctrl+Shift+spacebar or Ctrl+Alt+6
Flex space	Option+Shift+spacebar	Ctrl+Shift+5
Nonbreaking flex space	Option+Shift+⌘+spacebar	Ctrl+Alt+Shift+5
Controlling Text Flow	*Mac*	*Windows*
Indent here	⌘+\	Ctrl+\
Current page number	⌘+3	Ctrl+3

Controlling Text Flow	Mac	Windows
Previous box's page number	⌘+2	Ctrl+2
Next box's page number	⌘+4	Ctrl+4
New line	Shift+Enter	Shift+Enter
Discretionary new line	⌘+Enter	Ctrl+Enter
New column	keypad Enter	keypad Enter
New box	Shift+keypad Enter	Shift+keypad Enter
Right-indent tab	Option+Tab	Shift+Tab

Importing Images	Mac	Windows
Import picture at 36 dpi	Shift+click Open button in Get Picture dialog box	Shift+click Open button in Get Picture dialog box
Import color TIFF as grayscale	⌘+click Open in Get Picture dialog box	Ctrl+click Open in Get Picture dialog box
Import grayscale TIFF as black-and-white	⌘+click Open button in Get Picture dialog box	Ctrl+click Open button in Get Picture dialog box
Import EPS without importing spot colors' definitions	⌘+click Open button in Get Picture dialog box	Ctrl+click Open button in Get Picture dialog box
Reimport all pictures in a document	⌘+click Open button in Open dialog box	Ctrl+click Open button in Open dialog box

Sizing and Placing Images	Mac	Windows
Center image within box	Shift+⌘+M	Ctrl+Shift+M
Fit image to box	Shift+⌘+F	Ctrl+Shift+F
Fit image proportionally to box	Option+Shift+⌘+F	Ctrl+Alt+Shift+F
Resize box constrained	Shift+drag	Shift+drag
Resize box at aspect ratio	Option+Shift+drag	Alt+Shift+drag
Resize box and scale picture	⌘+drag	Ctrl+drag
Resize box constrained and scale picture	Shift+⌘+drag	Ctrl+Shift+drag
Resize box at aspect ratio and scale picture	Option+Shift+⌘+drag	Ctrl+Alt+Shift+drag

Continued

Table C-1 (continued)

Sizing and Placing Images	Mac	Windows
Increase picture scale 5%	Option+Shift+⌘+>	Ctrl+Alt+Shift+>
Decrease picture scale 5%	Option+Shift+⌘+<	Ctrl+Alt+Shift+<
Modifying Images	**Mac**	**Windows**
Negative image	Shift+⌘+hyphen	Ctrl+Shift+hyphen
Picture contrast specifications	Shift+⌘+C	Ctrl+Shift+C
Picture halftone specifications	Shift+⌘+H	Ctrl+Shift+H
Modifying Lines	**Mac**	**Windows**
Increase line width to next size	Shift+⌘+>	Ctrl+Shift+>
Decrease line width to next size	Shift+⌘+<	Ctrl+Shift+<
Increase line width 1 point	Option+Shift+⌘+>	Ctrl+Alt+Shift+>
Decrease line width 1 point	Option+Shift+⌘+<	Ctrl+Alt+Shift+<
Editing Illustrations	**Mac**	**Windows**
Delete Bézier point	Option+click point	Alt+click point
Add Bézier point	Option+click segment	Alt+click segment
Create corner point	Option+F1	Ctrl+F1
Create smooth point	Option+F2	Ctrl+F2
Create symmetrical point	Option+F3	Ctrl+F3
Create straight segment	Shift+Option+F1	Ctrl+Shift+F1
Create curved segment	Shift+Option+F2	Ctrl+Shift+F2

*On the Mac, the default keyboard command for zooming in is Control+Shift+click and zooming out is Option+Control+Shift+click. You can change these commands to Control+click and Option+Control+click, respectively, in the Interactive pane of the Preferences dialog box (Edit ➪ Preferences ➪ Preferences, or Option+Shift+⌘+Y). To make this change, click Zoom in the Control key area. If you do this, you will need to press Control+Shift to display context menus.

**Font-manager programs such as Adobe Type Manager can interfere with this shortcut's ability to operate.

In addition to shortcuts, you'll discover the benefits of using *context menus* — little menus that pop up on palettes, items, pages, and more — offering quick access to commonly used functions. The later versions of both the Mac and Windows operating systems use context menus to save you time. By Control+clicking on the Mac (see Figure C-1) or right-clicking an item in Windows (see Figure C-2), you get a menu of options just for that item. This saves you time going through menus, dialog boxes, and palettes.

Figure C-1: In QuarkXPress for Mac, we Control+clicked a round picture box and got the options shown in the context menu.

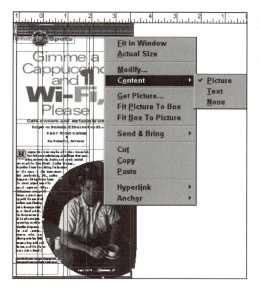

Figure C-2: In QuarkXPress for Windows, we right-clicked a circle picture box and got the options shown in the context menu.

New Feature   QuarkXPress 5 adds a bevy of context menus for working with pages, palettes, and items.

Each context menu contains commands appropriate to the item you're clicking on—for example, if you click on the Style Sheets palette, you can create, edit, and delete style sheets. If you click on a page, you can change its size, and if you click on a graphic, you can replace it or resize it.

Tip

The experienced Mac QuarkXPress user will likely ignore context menus because these menus use the keyboard command — Control+click — previously reserved for access to the Zoom tool. Most longtime users will have a difficult time remembering to press Control+Shift now for the Zoom tool. If you can't get used to it, though, you can change the Control Key preference for your copy of QuarkXPress in the Interactive pane of the Preferences dialog box (Edit ⇨ Preferences ⇨ Preferences, or Option+Shift+⌘+Y). By doing so, you set the Zoom tool to Control+click and context menus to Contol+Shift+click (within QuarkXPress only).

✦   ✦   ✦

Cross-Platform Issues and Solutions

In most publishing environments, writers and editors prepare text in Windows (because the computers are less expensive) and graphic designers work on Macs (because many consider the Mac to have superior available fonts, color handling, and so on—and because they were trained on Macs). But it is increasingly common for people to use both QuarkXPress for Mac and QuarkXPress for Windows in the same environment, even editing the same documents. Because QuarkXPress is nearly identical on both platforms—and its documents are designed to travel smoothly between platforms—it's easy for people to use either.

However, when you're working with QuarkXPress, you're not working in a bubble. You're dealing with operating systems, file transfers, graphics prepared in other applications, fonts in a variety of formats, and more. These outside elements may have fundamental differences that present problems in a cross-platform workflow. And some QuarkXPress files don't behave perfectly either. Take a look.

Operating-System Issues

The icons and names of files affect how well files transfer between platforms. Issues with icons include the following:

✦ Mac and Windows both use icons to show you (and tell programs) what format a file is in. But the way these icons are created differs between the two platforms, so when you move files from one platform to another, you can easily lose file icons.

✦ On the Mac, QuarkXPress doesn't usually need file icons. It displays iconless files with a PC icon for text files in the Get Text dialog box, for graphic files in the Get Picture dialog box, and for QuarkXPress files in the Open dialog box. Even without the icon, you can import or open the files — as long as they're in a supported format.

✦ In Windows, the file icon is important for QuarkXPress, because QuarkXPress often filters out files with unexpected icons. Fortunately, you can force QuarkXPress to display all files by choosing Display All Files (*.*) from the Files of Type menu in the Get Text, Get Picture, and Open dialog boxes.

The difference between how Mac and Windows handles file formats, regardless of icons, affects file transfer between platforms as well:

✦ On the Mac, a hidden piece of the file called an *extent* tells the Mac what kind of format the file has. This extent file has two pieces of key data — the ID for the program that created the file and the ID for the type of format the file is in.

✦ In Windows, the icon is based on the file name extension at the end of the file, such as .doc in the file name How to Import.doc. (***Note:*** Capitalization doesn't matter: .DOC is the same as .Doc is the same as .doc.)

✦ Windows hides the extension from users by default, however, so you may not realize that all file names have these extensions after the name. You can see them in DOS, but in Windows 95 and later, you have to disable the feature that hides them. You can do that by using View ➪ Options (Windows 95), View ➪ Folder Options (Windows 98), or Tools ➪ Folder Options (Windows 2000), and then selecting the View tab. (You need to have a disk or folder open in order to see the View menu.)

✦ The smoothest way to work on both platforms is to use the PC extension on all file names, even those created on the Mac. That way, you're assured that Windows users see the correct icon (at least for formats that exist in both Windows and on the Mac). Some file formats have no PC equivalents and, thus, no PC extension. Mac users need to remember to look at files that have the PC icon.

✦ Some programs automatically map the Mac creator and type IDs to the PC extensions and vice versa, as described in Chapter 5, so files always look like native ones no matter where they were created. If you move files back and forth a lot, these are a wise investment.

File-Transfer Issues

Moving files between Macs and Windows PCs is easier now than ever before, thanks to a selection of products on both platforms that let each machine read the other's disks (floppies, removable disks like Zip disks, and even hard drives). Here is a brief summary of the major products:

✦ **File Exchange:** This control panel included in the Mac OS lets you use Windows disks in a Mac floppy drive or removable drive and lets the Mac recognize files immediately and know which applications are compatible with each type of PC file. File Exchange also can automatically add the right Mac icon and file-type information to a Windows file transferred to the Mac based on the Windows file's extension.

✦ **MacOpener 2000, from DataViz (203-268-0030, www.dataviz.com):** This Windows program lets you open any type of Mac disk in Windows. Double-click any file to launch the appropriate Windows program. The Conversions Plus product includes MacOpener and a file-format translation utility.

✦ **MacDrive 5, from Mediafour Productions (515-225-7409, www.media4.com):** This is similar to DataViz's MacOpener in that it lets Windows 98, Me, NT 4.0, 2000, and XP PCs open, read, write, and format Mac disks.

Another method of transferring files is to use a cross-platform network — if you're using one:

✦ Miramar Systems's PC MacLAN (805-966-2432, www.miramarsys.com) lets a Windows PC be a server to Macs and other PCs via an Ethernet network using AppleTalk or TCP/IP protocols. It also lets a Windows PC be accessed on a Mac network. In both cases, it matches Windows file extensions with Mac icons, so files transferred between the two platforms have the icons expected. Note that there is one version for Windows NT and 2000, and another for Windows 95, 98, and Me.

✦ Thursby Software Systems's Dave (817-478-5070, www.thursby.com) is software for the Mac that makes a Mac appear as a PC to a Windows server using the TCP/IP network protocol on an Ethernet network.

✦ Netopia's Timbuktu Pro (510-814-5000, www.netopia.com) lets both Macs and PCs exchange files via an Ethernet network.

✦ Windows NT and 2000 Server editions include a utility called MacFile that lets you designate specific directories on the server that Macs can access. (Note this utility is not installed by default — you must select it as an option under File Services for Macintosh during installation of network services.) This is fine when you want the NT server to hold shared files, such as images, fonts, QuarkXPress templates, shared QuarkXPress projects, and so on. MacFile does not let the NT system access any Macs on the network.

✦ For larger networks, you'll likely want to use networks based on the TCP/IP protocol and on Ethernet wiring (and/or 802.11b "Wi-Fi" wireless Ethernet transmitters), using a server operating system such as Windows NT/2000/XP, Unix, or Linux; you'll need a consultant or in-house network manager to set up such large networks.

The Macintosh assigns a hidden creator and file type attribute to each file; these hidden attributes tell it which icon to display for the file and which program to launch if you double-click the file. Windows files have no such hidden attributes, so they will appear as either SimpleText or PC binary files when you move them to the Mac. To load these files into QuarkXPress (or other Mac applications), you must first load your application and then use File➪Open, or ⌘+O.

Note that File Exchange, MacLinkPlus, Conversions Plus, MacOpener, MacDrive, Timbuktu Pro, Dave, and PC MacLAN all can be set to create these hidden attributes automatically based on the Windows file's extension, as well as to add the Windows file extension based on the Mac creator and file type, which means that you can double-click the transferred files to open them.

QuarkXPress Issues

A few types of QuarkXPress files are not cross-platform: XPress Preferences (and basically any other program files), auxiliary dictionaries, and libraries.

XPress Preferences and program files

The XPress Preferences file, inside your QuarkXPress program folder, is not cross-platform. This file includes the following information: kerning table changes, tracking table changes, and hyphenation exceptions; default style sheets, colors, dashes and stripes patterns, lists, H&J sets, and print styles; all default Preferences. If you make company-wide changes to these default settings, then distribute the XPress Preferences file to all users, you will need to make the changes twice: once on Mac and once in Windows.

Other program files in QuarkXPress, such as auxiliary dictionaries and XTensions are not cross-platform. Be sure to create the same auxiliary dictionaries for both Mac and Windows. If you have the same XTension needs on both platforms, only purchase XTensions that are available for Mac and Windows. That will limit your use of XTensions because a great deal fewer are available in Windows versions than in Mac versions.

Books and libraries

Books, ostensibly, are cross-platform. However, users from both platforms cannot open a book file at the same time — making books useless for a cross-platform workgroup. To use a book in a mixed environment, you would need to have Mac users work on it at one time and Windows users work on it at another time.

Libraries are not cross-platform at all. Although Quark promised the compatibility for version 4, and then again for version 5, it just hasn't happened. Issues with libraries include that the previews you see in a library may not display on the opposite platform, many items contain fonts that may not be available, and many items contain graphics that may have previews in the wrong format. If you need a specific library on both platforms, you can save the items in a document and create the library twice (but you should still watch out for font and graphic issues).

Font Issues

Two issues arise with fonts: which fonts you use and which special characters you use in those fonts.

Mac and Windows fonts

When it comes to fonts, the bottom line is that Mac and Windows fonts are not the same. Sure, there are tons of fonts with the same name. And TrueType fonts are supposed to be the same between platforms. But most of the fonts used in a professional design environment — PostScript Type 1 fonts — are available in a variety of versions from various foundries. With even small differences, it's hard to guarantee that text will flow the same between platforms, especially in text wraps.

To help with font compatibility, make sure the fonts you use in cross-platform projects are available for both Mac and Windows. Then purchase the font from the same vendor (if possible, with the same version number). You can also convert fonts from Mac to Windows and vice versa using a utility such as FontLab's TransType (509-272-3260, www.fontlab.com). If you do this, check the font's license agreement — you didn't necessarily purchase the right to use the font on any machine you want. Even with the exact same font, or a converted font, issues with spacing and metrics may still cause text reflow. You may need to compare printouts to make sure fonts are flowing the same between platforms.

Special characters in fonts

Even if you're dealing with the exact same fonts on Mac and Windows, the fonts may not include the same set of characters. Often, the Mac font contains more special characters than the Windows fonts. Or the fonts map differently, so the character you enter on Windows is something else on the Mac (or pure gibberish). See Chapter 18 for more information on which characters to avoid in a cross-platform environment.

Graphic-File Issues

A cross-platform environment presents two primary issues when it comes to graphics: displaying previews and file paths.

Graphic previews

When you import a graphic file into a QuarkXPress document through the Get Picture dialog box, QuarkXPress actually displays a preview that is saved with the graphic file. This preview is saved with the QuarkXPress document. These previews do not always behave well when transferred between platforms:

✦ Many times, graphic files created on a Mac have a PICT preview, which may not display or print correctly on Windows. The same goes for imported or pasted PICT graphic files. In both cases, try reimporting the graphic file.

✦ Graphic files created in Windows often have a Windows Metafile preview, which may not display correctly on a Mac. In this case, resave the graphic with the preview in a different format such as TIFF.

✦ For best cross-platform results, stick to TIFF and EPS files (print) and GIF and JPEG (Web).

✦ Save EPS files with TIFF previews for guaranteed display on both platforms.

File paths

When you import a graphic file into a QuarkXPress document, a link is created between the document and the location of the graphic file. The link consists of the file path between the document and the graphic file, and it's used when QuarkXPress needs to find the graphic file to reimport it or to print it.

If you move the graphic file — or the document — the link is considered broken, and so the Pictures pane of the Usage dialog box (Utilities ➪ Usage) will show the pictures as missing. Because moving documents to another platform obviously requires moving the file, the link is not maintained. This applies to graphics imported through the Mac's Publish & Subscribe and Windows' OLE technology as well.

The solution to this dilemma depends on what you're doing with the document. If you're simply opening a file to edit some text, you do not need to be concerned about graphic file links. Basically, it's okay if all graphics are not linked — unless graphic files have changed or you're performing high-resolution output. If you output from both platforms, be sure to keep the graphic files in a central and known location so they're easy to relink.

✦   ✦   ✦

CD Contents

The CD that accompanies this book contains a wealth of software — some freeware, some shareware, and some demo. All are meant to make QuarkXPress or your publishing environment work even better. Some are XTensions that enhance QuarkXPress directly, while others are stand-alone utilities that you will use before or after QuarkXPress. This appendix tells you everything you need to know to install, road-test, and enjoy what's on the CD.

Exploring the Types of Software

There are three types of software on the CD. Some won't cost you a dime, but others are meant to give you a chance to test them out before you decide to buy. The following sections describe how they work.

Freeware

This is exactly that: free. You may use it at no charge. (You may not sell it to others, however. And you must get permission from the software's authors to redistribute it, even if you distribute it at no charge.)

Shareware

This software is meant to be used on a trial basis, so you can see if you like it. If you do like it, you should buy the full version, usually available by sending in a registration fee and getting a code that converts the shareware into a fully functioning version, or getting a fully functioning version on CD or in downloaded form. Shareware can usually be redistributed for no charge so other people can try it out as well. Most shareware does one of three things to ensure that people don't use it instead of purchasing the complete product:

✦ Prevents you from being able to save QuarkXPress documents while the software is loaded

✦ Provides limited functionality until you purchase the full version

✦ Expires after a certain number of days of use

Demo software

Demo software is also meant to be used on a trial basis, so you can see if you like it If you do, you can buy the full version from a catalog, distributor Web site, or developer's Web site. If you purchase a download, often at a discount, you usually receive documentation in PDF format. If you purchase software in a box, you usually get a CD along with printed documentation. Most demo software does one of the following three things to ensure that people don't use demo software instead of purchasing the retail product:

✦ Prevents you from being able to save QuarkXPress documents while the software is loaded (in the case of XTensions).

✦ Provides limited functionality until you purchase the full version.

✦ Expires after a certain number of days of use.

Installing the CD

Installing the CD's software is easy. Insert the CD into your computer. On a Mac, the CD will automatically display on your desktop like a CD or hard disk. On a PC, you may have to open the CD from the Explorer or from the window that appears when you double-click your My Computer icon. After the CD is mounted, install the software as follows:

✦ For most XTensions, just drag the XTension file into the XTension folder in your QuarkXPress program folder. The next time you launch QuarkXPress, the XTension will be launched as well.

✦ Some XTensions require that you run an installation program, as do most of the utilities. Just double-click the installation icon and follow the on-screen instructions.

Play, but please pay

Please pay for and register any demo software or shareware that you use regularly. It's fine to use these programs without paying while you're figuring out if they would really help you. But after you decide they're worthwhile, please support the companies and individuals who created the software so they can afford to create even better software in the future.

Touring What's on the CD

The CD provided with this book is divided into folders for different types of software and information. The ReadMe files included with the products and information included in the products themselves will point you to the appropriate developers and distributors.

Color insert

Because the bulk of this book is printed in black-and-white, we provide color PDF files for Chapters 27, 28, and 30 on the CD. You can print these chapters or refer to them online to see the screen captures in color. We also supply GIF versions of the screenshots in case you'd rather open specific images in your browser. In addition, you can view the book's color insert as a PDF file. Viewing and printing these chapters will help bring the topic of color—and color management—to life for you.

Macintosh software

The CD's offerings are organized by several folders, to help you more easily navigate the contents.

Publishing utilities

Several utilities enhance QuarkXPress even though they are not plug-in XTensions. We include:

✦ **Font Reserve Light (trial version):** From DiamondSoft, www.fontreserve.com, Font Reserve is a full-featured font manager for activating fonts with precision as well as previewing fonts and printing font samples. The unique database architecture records detailed font information and allows it to be used for searching and sorting criteria. The demo's only limitation is that you can only add 100 font files to it. The included Font Reserve XTension for the Mac version of QuarkXPress provides automatic font activation as you open documents.

Using demo XTensions

Most of the demo XTensions on the CD put QuarkXPress itself into demo mode when you run them. You cannot save documents while QuarkXPress is in demo mode. You're alerted of this when you launch QuarkXPress and when you open a new or existing document. Some demo XTensions show a splash screen when they load, implying that QuarkXPress will let you save documents, but this usually is not true. With some demo XTensions, you can save documents, but they cannot be opened later unless the demo XTension is installed.

Most of the demo XTensions included on the CD were developed (or updated from previous versions) before QuarkXPress 5 was released. Therefore, it's possible that you may experience problems with the XTensions. If so, check with the XTension's developer to see if an updated demo is available. Because XTensions are developed by different people and companies, XTensions don't always get along with one another. If you begin to have bizarre problems while working in QuarkXPress, you may want to try turning off all XTensions you're not currently using.

To try an XTension, drag-copy it to the XTension folder in your QuarkXPress program folder, then launch QuarkXPress. If you're impressed to the point that you want to purchase one of the demo XTensions, the CD also includes electronic catalogs from several XTension vendors.

Note: To make sure QuarkXPress for Mac has enough memory to run all the XTensions you've loaded, you may want to increase its memory allocation. To do this, select the QuarkXPress icon in the Finder, choose File ⇨ Get Info or ⌘+I, and increase the value in the Preferred Size field of the Memory pane.

✦ **Suitcase 10 (demo):** From Extensis, www.extensis.com, Suitcase is probably the most widely used font manager on both Mac and Windows. The demo version, which has a 30-day limit, lets you experiment with activating fonts, creating sets, previewing fonts, and more with all your fonts. The included Suitcase XT is for automatic font activation. In this same folder, you'll find information about the most popular XTensions from Extensis: QX-Tools and QX-Effects.

✦ **PopChar Pro (shareware):** From UNI Software Plus, www.unisoftwareplus.com, this system extension adds a little pop-up menu to your menu bar for locating special characters within a font and inserting them into documents.

✦ **Graphic Converter (shareware):** From Lemke Software, www.lemkesoft.com, this Macintosh program lets you translate odd graphics formats into ones that QuarkXPress imports.

✦ **TechTracker Pro (30-day demo):** From TechTracker, www.techtracker.com, this application lets you access software support information and create tracking lists for the software that you care about.

Design tools

Joseph Stubbs Creations, `www.josephstubbscreations.com`, provides free templates and design aids specifically for QuarkXPress users:

- ✦ **Stubbs Designer Strokes and Splatters** is a collection of original black-and-white clip art for use with any program.

- ✦ **Stubbs Designer Palettes** consist of predefined color sets that look good together.

- ✦ **Stubbs Designer Templates** provide predefined templates for common documents such as business cards and brochures.

You can copy these to your computer and use them at will.

XTensions

The following XTensions are included on the CD in their respective developer's folder. Some are demos, some are shareware, and some are free.

- ✦ **Badia Software, `www.badiaxt.com` (demos, except Vistas XT, which is freeware):** LiveKeys XT lets you completely customize keyboard shortcuts, FullColor XT improves color handling; Duplica XT lets you copy selected attributes from any item or contents and also provides many copy and paste options; FaxReady XT outputs documents optimized for clear and legible fax transmission; Vistas XT adds a palette for quick navigation and zooming; PrintTools XT provides live print previews, batch printing, and preflighting; FullMeasure XT adds 80 more controls to the Measurements palette.

- ✦ **Gluon, `www.gluon.com` (demos):** ProScale 6 improves nonproportional scaling and lets you scale multiple pages at the same time; Cropster 5 sets up page markings with matching guides; Slugger 6 lets you add custom job slugs to pages to track operators, fonts, images, and more; iDropper 1 lets you pick up colors from anywhere on-screen and add them to the Colors palette; DocuSlim 2.14 automatically streamlines graphics files and reimports them; QC preflights and collects files for prepress; ColorBreaker 4 performs color markup quickly and accurately; ProGuides 5 enhances QuarkXPress guides, letting you print guides and save sets of guides; SpecTackler 2.0 tags a document with all text, style, and picture information; TableMaker 5.5 provides an alternative to QuarkXPress, offering more control over formatting and allowing for tables across multiple pages; WebXPress 5 converts QuarkXPress documents to HTML in seconds; and XPressImage 4 lets users export selections, pages, spreads, and so on in different file formats, including HTML.

- ✦ **Koyosha Graphics of America, `www.koyosha.com` (15-day trial):** Enhance Preview XT (EPXT) provides dramatically improved high-resolution image previews for on-screen proofing, color proofing, and clipping path creation.

✦ **Vision's Edge, www.visionsedge.com (10-day full-featured demos):** Bookletizer converts reader's spreads to printer's spreads for output. Resize XT adds scaling controls like those found in illustration programs.

Windows software

The CD's offerings are organized by several folders, to help you more easily navigate the contents. Each folder has a different label color as well.

Publishing utilities

Several utilities enhance QuarkXPress even though they are not plug-in XTensions. We include:

✦ **Font Reserve Light (trial version):** From DiamondSoft, www.fontreserve.com, Font Reserve is a full-featured font manager for activating fonts with precision as well as previewing fonts and printing font samples. The unique database architecture records detailed font information and allows it to be used for searching and sorting criteria. The demo's only limitation is that you can only add 100 font files to it.

✦ **TechTracker Desktop (freeware):** From TechTracker, www.techtracker.com, TechTracker Desktop automatically matches the most current software versions and patches from our database to the software on your computer and notifies you when software on your machine needs updating.

✦ **WinZip 8.0 (shareware):** From Nico Mac Computing, www.winzip.com, this is one of the most popular programs for compressing (stuffing) Windows files.

Design tools

Joseph Stubbs Creations, www.josephstubbscreations.com, provides free templates and design aids specifically for QuarkXPress users:

✦ **Stubbs Designer Strokes and Splatters** is a collection of original black-and-white clip art for use with any program.

✦ **Stubbs Designer Palettes** consist of predefined color sets that look good together.

✦ **Stubbs Designer Templates** provide predefined templates for common documents such as business cards and brochures.

You can copy these to your computer and use them at will.

XTensions

The following XTensions are included on the CD in their respective developer's folder. Some are demos, some are shareware, and some are free.

- ✦ **Badia Software, `www.badiaxt.com` (demos, except Vistas XT, which is freeware):** LiveKeys XT lets you completely customize keyboard shortcuts, FullColor XT improves color handling; Vistas XT adds a palette for quick navigation and zooming; PrintTools XT provides live print previews, batch printing, and preflighting.

- ✦ **Gluon, `www.gluon.com` (demos):** ProScale 6 improves nonproportional scaling and lets you scale multiple pages at the same time; Cropster 5 sets up page markings with matching guides; Slugger 6 lets you add custom job slugs to pages to track operators, fonts, images, and more; iDropper 1 lets you pick up colors from anywhere on-screen and add them to the Colors palette; DocuSlim 2.14 automatically streamlines graphics files and reimports them; QC preflights and collects files for prepress; ColorBreaker 4 performs color markup quickly and accurately; ProGuides 5 enhances QuarkXPress guides, letting you print guides and save sets of guides; SpecTackler 2.0 tags a document with all text, style, and picture information; TableMaker 5.5 provides an alternative to QuarkXPress, offering more control over formatting and allowing for tables across multiple pages; WebXPress 5 converts QuarkXPress documents to HTML in seconds; and XPressImage 4 lets users export selections, pages, spreads, and so on in different file formats, including HTML.

- ✦ **Koyosha Graphics of America, Inc., `www.koyosha.com` (15-day trial):** Enhance Preview XT (EPXT) provides dramatically improved high-resolution image previews for on-screen proofing, color proofing, and clipping path creation.

- ✦ **Vision's Edge, `www.visionsedge.com` (10-day full-featured demos):** Resize XT adds scaling controls like those found in illustration programs.

Troubleshooting

If you have difficulty installing or using any of the materials on the companion CD, try the following solutions:

- ✦ **Turn off any antivirus software that you may have running.** Installers sometimes mimic virus activity and can make your computer incorrectly believe that it is being infected by a virus. (Be sure to turn the antivirus software back on later.)

- ✦ **Close all running programs.** The more programs you're running, the less memory is available to other programs. Installers also typically update files and programs; if you keep other programs running, installation may not work properly.

✦ **Reference the ReadMe:** Please refer to the ReadMe file located at the root of the CD-ROM for the latest product information at the time of publication.

If you still have trouble with the CD, please call the Hungry Minds Customer Care phone number: 800-762-2974. Outside the United States, call 317-572-3994. You can also contact Hungry Minds Customer Service by e-mail at `techsupdum@ hungryminds.com`. Hungry Minds will provide technical support only for installation and other general quality-control items; for technical support on the applications themselves, consult the program's vendor or author.

✦ ✦ ✦

Index

Continued

Hungry Minds, Inc.
End-User License Agreement

READ THIS. You should carefully read these terms and conditions before opening the software packet(s) included with this book ("Book"). This is a license agreement ("Agreement") between you and Hungry Minds, Inc. ("HMI"). By opening the accompanying software packet(s), you acknowledge that you have read and accept the following terms and conditions. If you do not agree and do not want to be bound by such terms and conditions, promptly return the Book and the unopened software packet(s) to the place you obtained them for a full refund.

1. **License Grant.** HMI grants to you (either an individual or entity) a nonexclusive license to use one copy of the enclosed software program(s) (collectively, the "Software") solely for your own personal or business purposes on a single computer (whether a standard computer or a workstation component of a multi-user network). The Software is in use on a computer when it is loaded into temporary memory (RAM) or installed into permanent memory (hard disk, CD-ROM, or other storage device). HMI reserves all rights not expressly granted herein.

2. **Ownership.** HMI is the owner of all right, title, and interest, including copyright, in and to the compilation of the Software recorded on the disk(s) or CD-ROM ("Software Media"). Copyright to the individual programs recorded on the Software Media is owned by the author or other authorized copyright owner of each program. Ownership of the Software and all proprietary rights relating thereto remain with HMI and its licensers.

3. **Restrictions on Use and Transfer.**

   (a) You may only (i) make one copy of the Software for backup or archival purposes, or (ii) transfer the Software to a single hard disk, provided that you keep the original for backup or archival purposes. You may not (i) rent or lease the Software, (ii) copy or reproduce the Software through a LAN or other network system or through any computer subscriber system or bulletin-board system, or (iii) modify, adapt, or create derivative works based on the Software.

   (b) You may not reverse engineer, decompile, or disassemble the Software. You may transfer the Software and user documentation on a permanent basis, provided that the transferee agrees to accept the terms and conditions of this Agreement and you retain no copies. If the Software is an update or has been updated, any transfer must include the most recent update and all prior versions.

4. **Restrictions on Use of Individual Programs.** You must follow the individual requirements and restrictions detailed for each individual program in Appendix E of this Book. These limitations are also contained in the individual license agreements recorded on the Software Media. These limitations may include a requirement that after using the program for a specified period of time, the user must pay a registration fee or discontinue use. By opening the Software packet(s), you will be agreeing to abide by the licenses and restrictions for these individual programs that are detailed in Appendix E and on the Software Media. None of the material on this Software Media or listed in this Book may ever be redistributed, in original or modified form, for commercial purposes.

5. Limited Warranty.

(a) HMI warrants that the Software and Software Media are free from defects in materials and workmanship under normal use for a period of sixty (60) days from the date of purchase of this Book. If HMI receives notification within the warranty period of defects in materials or workmanship, HMI will replace the defective Software Media.

(b) **HMI AND THE AUTHOR OF THE BOOK DISCLAIM ALL OTHER WARRANTIES, EXPRESS OR IMPLIED, INCLUDING WITHOUT LIMITATION IMPLIED WARRANTIES OF MERCHANTABILITY AND FITNESS FOR A PARTICULAR PURPOSE, WITH RESPECT TO THE SOFTWARE, THE PROGRAMS, THE SOURCE CODE CONTAINED THEREIN, AND/OR THE TECHNIQUES DESCRIBED IN THIS BOOK. HMI DOES NOT WARRANT THAT THE FUNCTIONS CONTAINED IN THE SOFTWARE WILL MEET YOUR REQUIREMENTS OR THAT THE OPERATION OF THE SOFTWARE WILL BE ERROR FREE.**

(c) This limited warranty gives you specific legal rights, and you may have other rights that vary from jurisdiction to jurisdiction.

6. Remedies.

(a) HMI's entire liability and your exclusive remedy for defects in materials and workmanship shall be limited to replacement of the Software Media, which may be returned to HMI with a copy of your receipt at the following address: Software Media Fulfillment Department, Attn.: *QuarkXPress 5 Bible*, Hungry Minds, Inc., 10475 Crosspoint Blvd., Indianapolis, IN 46256, or call 1-800-762-2974. Please allow four to six weeks for delivery. This Limited Warranty is void if failure of the Software Media has resulted from accident, abuse, or misapplication. Any replacement Software Media will be warranted for the remainder of the original warranty period or thirty (30) days, whichever is longer.

(b) In no event shall HMI or the author be liable for any damages whatsoever (including without limitation damages for loss of business profits, business interruption, loss of business information, or any other pecuniary loss) arising from the use of or inability to use the Book or the Software, even if HMI has been advised of the possibility of such damages.

(c) Because some jurisdictions do not allow the exclusion or limitation of liability for consequential or incidental damages, the above limitation or exclusion may not apply to you.

7. U.S. Government Restricted Rights.
Use, duplication, or disclosure of the Software for or on behalf of the United States of America, its agencies and/or instrumentalities (the "U.S. Government") is subject to restrictions as stated in paragraph (c)(1)(ii) of the Rights in Technical Data and Computer Software clause of DFARS 252.227-7013, or subparagraphs (c) (1) and (2) of the Commercial Computer Software - Restricted Rights clause at FAR 52.227-19, and in similar clauses in the NASA FAR supplement, as applicable.

8. General.
This Agreement constitutes the entire understanding of the parties and revokes and supersedes all prior agreements, oral or written, between them and may not be modified or amended except in a writing signed by both parties hereto that specifically refers to this Agreement. This Agreement shall take precedence over any other documents that may be in conflict herewith. If any one or more provisions contained in this Agreement are held by any court or tribunal to be invalid, illegal, or otherwise unenforceable, each and every other provision shall remain in full force and effect.